D0148245

AMERICAN MULTICULTURAL STUDIES

AMERICAN MULTICULTURAL STUDIES

Diversity of Race, Ethnicity, Gender and Sexuality

SHERROW O. PINDER

California State University, Chico

Los Angeles | London | New Delhi
Singapore | Washington DC

Los Angeles | London | New Delhi
Singapore | Washington DC

FOR INFORMATION:

SAGE Publications, Inc.
2455 Teller Road
Thousand Oaks, California 91320
E-mail: order@sagepub.com

SAGE Publications Ltd.
1 Oliver's Yard
55 City Road
London EC1Y 1SP
United Kingdom

SAGE Publications India Pvt. Ltd.
B 1/I 1 Mohan Cooperative Industrial Area
Mathura Road, New Delhi 110 044
India

SAGE Publications Asia-Pacific Pte. Ltd.
3 Church Street
#10-04 Samsung Hub
Singapore 049483

Copyright © 2013 by SAGE Publications, Inc.

Printed in the United States of America

Library of Congress Cataloging-in-Publication Data

American multicultural studies : diversity of race, ethnicity, gender, and sexuality / Sherrow O. Pinder, editor.

p. cm.
Includes bibliographical references and index.

ISBN 978-1-4129-9802-4 (pbk.)

1. Multiculturalism—United States. 2. Cultural pluralism—United States. 3. Ethnicity—United States. 4. Multicultural education—United States. I. Pinder, Sherrow O.

E184.A1A636644 2013
305.800973—dc23   2012011334

This book is printed on acid-free paper.

Acquisitions Editor: David Repetto
Editorial Assistant: Lydia Balian
Production Editor: Laura Stewart
Copy Editor: Kim Husband
Typesetter: C&M Digitals, Ltd.
Proofreader: Sally M. Scott
Indexer: Judy Hunt
Cover Designer: Bryan Fishman
Marketing Manager: Erica DeLuca
Permissions Editor: Karen Ehrmann

12 13 14 15 16 10 9 8 7 6 5 4 3 2 1

#78048\540

Table of Contents

Introduction: The Concept and Definition of American Multicultural Studies

Sherrow O. Pinder

This book seeks to bring together foundational works of scholars writing within the framework of multicultural studies, a fairly new and exciting area of study that is developing across disciplines. Rather than representing a discipline in itself or a single ideological position, this collection of essays responds to the need to open up a rich avenue for addressing issues of race, gender, ethnicity, cultural diversity, sexuality, and education in their varied forms. Although this grouping reflects a diversity of concerns, substantial thematic overlaps are found between sections and essays, all of which are oriented toward a single broad objective, that is, to develop new ways of addressing how multicultural issues, in their discursive sociocultural contexts, are inextricably linked to operations of power. Power produces certain forms of consequential epistemologies and extends and legitimizes the interests of those served by the effect of such operative power (Butler, 1997). In other words, power is despotic; it fastens marginalized individuals and groups to the image of the "other" that positions and upholds them, especially their social position in the United States. French philosopher Michel Foucault has taught us that power must remain imprecise since this very imprecision is the very state of its existence.[1] His American counterpart, the postcolonial scholar Homi K. Bhabha (1998), understands power as "a tyranny of the transparent" (p. 21) that necessarily and essentially prompts the question of how to relinquish power. Since "there are no relations of power without resistance" (Foucault, 1980, p. 142), power cannot be separated from the complexity of power itself or, in the words of Foucault, "the polymorphous techniques of power" (Foucault, 1980, p. 142).

In thinking about the range and reach of American multicultural studies, the authors in this book address both continuing and key current issues in American multicultural studies. The book is divided into seven sections in order to address each subject separately and emphasize different aspect of the themes and questions that are important. For example, John Tawa, Karen L. Suyemoto, and Jesse J. Tauriac point to the need for race relations in the United States to move beyond the Black–White paradigm because such a paradigm excludes Asian Americans. Their essay is oriented toward understanding "Blacks and Asian relations outside of a Black–White paradigm" while, at the same time, it demonstrates how Black and Asian relations have been influenced by Whiteness as domination and non–Whiteness as subordination. By revisiting race relations in the United States, Kevin Johnson's expressive comments that non–Whiteness "often frames non-dominant cultures outside the American cultural psyche as 'aliens' to American cultural identity" reintroduces into the discussion the tensions between an American cultural identity (majority) and multicultural identities (minority), which is another way of capturing the multifaceted meaning of Black as it should be reconfigured within the Black–White model of race relations in the United States. In a word, Black signifies non–Whiteness. A good illustration of this understanding is when a Chinese laundryman quickly places a sign that reads "Me Colored Too" on his laundry window the night of the Harlem riot, during World War II, to affiliate himself with the Black rioters (Wu, 2002, p. 19). This does not prevent Tawa and his colleagues from pointing out the "complex interactions between minority groups such as the interactions between Blacks and Asians." In considering, for example, the "triangulated threat theory" that they employ, the attempt to aptly capture the interactive dynamics of Blacks and Asians in relations to each other and to the majority group is precocious. When Chinese, Blacks, and other non–White groups identify themselves and each other as colored (non–White), they are appealing to a common political identity. In other words, the term *colored* was invented out of the prevailing codes of racial discourse and reinvented as signs of grouping and unity among non–Whites, supposedly sharing familiar experiences that are historically structured "by the psychic representation and the social, economical, and political reality of America's racism" (Pinder, 2010, p. 64). The signifying system of racism with its conception of "essential differences" remains a fundamental factor for positioning Blacks, Asians, and other racialized ethnic groups as "other." However, more recently, concepts such as "model minority" and "honorary Whites" have surfaced, which only serve to generate incessant conflicts within and among racialized ethnic groups.

The sections in the book are inescapably arbitrary and, to some degree, minimize or overstate the relations between the authors' ideas and recurring themes. However, I think that the structuring of the book will help readers in acquainting themselves with the meticulous concerns and queries that impel the different approaches presented. The first section of the book is explicitly concerned with theorizing and expanding on some of the issues that have helped shape and define American multicultural studies as interdisciplinary as well as multidisciplinary. Babacar M'Baye, for one, in critiquing Afrocentrism, makes clear that it is important not to think of the movement "as irrelevant, out-dated, essentialist, and anachronistic." And if one does, according to M'Baye, it is "an easy way of dismissing Afrocentrism." Furthermore, one would "fail to inscribe the movement in its proper historical and intellectual context." In order to put Afrocentrism in its rightful context, M'Baye uses "the effective approach that Tunde Adeleke employs in his book, *The Case Against Afrocentrism*. By interpreting 'Afrocentric essentialist thought' as 'a comprehensive and dynamic agency in Black history' while 'underscoring the contradictions and limitations' of this ideology,'" Afrocentric thought is not rejected but demystified, interrogated, and brought directly into the sphere of politics.

M'Baye's epigrammatic exposition of Afrocentrist and postmodernist discourses of Blackness and Black culture is underscored by a convincing analysis that focuses on the changeable influence that race and ethnicity have had on such nonmainstream critical approaches to diversity in American society. It is commonplace to speak of diversity. And even though most mainstream Americans would agree that diversity is a defining characteristic of American society, it is quite another thing, to borrow from Will Kymlicka (1995), "to be swamped by it" (p. 104). Whites, for example, in many cases, do feel "swamped" when Blacks, Mexicans, First Nations, Chinese, and other racialized minorities move into "their" neighborhoods. The resulting "White flight" from those neighborhoods is visible.[2] As Joe R. Feagin (2006) notes, around the 1970s, many Whites started to move from large cities with an increasing Black, Asian, and Latino American population "to Whiter suburban and exurban areas or into guarded-gated communities in those cities" (p. 238). This is a good manifestation of how White privilege works to create an unbridgeable social gap between Whites and non–Whites.

One helpful way of understanding Whites' attitudes about racial diversity, for example, is analyzed in Christopher B. Zeichmann and Nathanael P. Romero's essay through "Bourdieu's theory of habitus," which explains how individuals "are socialized into patterns of interaction that combine to form . . . [their] 'habits of thought and practice' constituted and reconstituted by societal dominant norms and values that are racist." Whites, by enthusiastically identifying with these given norms and values that are racist, which is a process of racist "acquired identification," a term used by Paul Ricoeur (1992), allows for Whites to recognize themselves through such a process (p. 121). Here identification, because of its psychoanalytic significance, carries an ontological and an epistemological valence that shapes the dominant "I." According to Kevin Johnson, "The formation of the 'I' in intrapersonal subject formation is homologous to the formation of the 'I' at the cultural level. . . . Once a cultural 'I' is formed, a whole host of rules, rituals, proprieties, customs, and/or norms are established to refine and define culture." Because culture is an important part of who we are as human beings and because it shapes the ways in which we give meaning to our world, it matters.

In fact, the very concept of diversity has its meaning only in terms of a system of oppression that serves to exclude subordinate groups from positions of power. Cultural membership is important, then, for an individual's well-being because it provides him or her with an anchor for self-identification and the security of belonging to a cultural group. However, if a particular cultural group, for whatever reasons, is not generally respected, then the dignity and self-respect of its members will also be in dire danger. It is the task of the liberal state to promote such policies as multiculturalism and cultural pluralism so that nondominant cultural groups can be recognized and celebrated. This is important because it not only propels us to take into consideration a typically liberal defense of certain group-differentiated rights but also "it provides the spectacles through we identify experiences as valuable" (Dworkin, 1989, p. 228).

Even though multiculturalism and cultural pluralism have allowed for the celebration and recognition of nondominant cultures, Kulvinder Arora, in her essay "Multicultural Rhythms: Musical and Racial Harmony," is critical of multiculturalism and its strategy to recognize cultural differences. Arora points out that "[t]he emphasis on cultural essentialism, which advances the celebration and cultural recognition of non-dominant ethnic groups, provides for a type of multiculturalism that celebrates culture at the expense of an understanding of race as structuring American society." Culture is an identity marker that continues to be the determinant of social distinction. Notwithstanding that the very conceptualization of culture has changed, culture is mostly associated with marginalized groups and is given a certain kind of essence. Arora shows how "Funkadesi's music, by offering a dynamic rendering of inter-cultural fusion, challenges the notion of cultural essentialism," and shows that cultures are always in a state of flux and are opened to negotiation and renegotiation. In other words, cultures are totally imbricated with rights and materiality. And given that there is a constant struggle for nondominant groups to re-create themselves outside of the norms of the mainstream culture, their cultures' understood meanings are continuously changing and continue to be challenged and disputed. What we have here is a form of cultural hybridity that makes the mainstream uncomfortable. Hence, cultural borders must be enacted so as to separate the dominant culture from the nondominant cultures. Furthermore, in terms of gender arrangement, because the cultural practices undervalue the position of women in society as a whole, what we have within the rubrics of multiculturalism is the endorsement and continuation of the otherness of the "other." In fact, Cynthia S. Bynoe and Sherrow O. Pinder seem to have seen this sufficiently when they criticize multiculturalism's "quest for cultural recognition and celebration of non-dominant cultures" as ill equipped in addressing the otherness of the "other," in this case women. Hence, Bynoe and Pinder's aim in their essay is to point out that "for women, multiculturalism and the politics of cultural recognition promote a 'double bind.'"

Cindy LaCom is one of the most energetic in theorizing and reframing disability studies within multicultural studies. It is not a secret that ableism operates through an absolute sense of culture so powerful that it works to stigmatize people who are "disabled" and places them into separate spaces that must be understood as mutually impermeable. And since, as LaCom makes clear, "disability informs and is informed by cultural notions of success, of independence, of time, of productivity," when living in an ableist society, which associates disability with "lack," "it is imperative that disability be considered and integrated in multicultural studies, where we work so hard to consider how race, ethnicity, age, gender, sexual orientation, and religion might shape one's place in the world." The exclusion or negation of the voices and concerns of "disabled" people, according to LaCom, do not spare us from participating "in a kind of ableist colonization of people with disabilities." The continuing struggle to uncover and uphold a genuine voice in a culture that normalizes ableism is a theme that runs throughout LaCom's work.

By taking into consideration how racialized otherness, as a site of constitutive impropriety and exclusion, is manifested within the United States to uphold Whiteness, our understanding of multicultural studies is sharpened, extended, and broadened. The section on race, in part, highlights this concern. More specifically, it focuses on how race is constituted and contested through multifaceted hierarchies of power, over the whole social framework of America's culture. The alternation of race as the problem and those who, as the French postcolonial scholar Frantz Fanon (1967) puts it, are marked by race has now become the standard means through which race is pushed outside of America's history and integrated into the realm of accepted, unavoidable actions so that discourses of colorblindness and postracial can become fashionable. The discourse of race, its ontology, and the articulation between them are the interconnected features of a single political and theoretical problem that must be addressed. With all of this in mind, Jennifer Asenas, in her essay, "The Political Efficacy of Nonviolence in *Eyes on the Prize*: Creating Activist, Complicating Tactics," explains that "the history of racial struggle in the United States is a matter of rhetoric as much as of information; stories about what happened, who was responsible, and how racism, for example, should be addressed are elemental political acts." Asenas's move from history to memory in a way that reclaims the marginalized history of African Americans is clearly manifested within the remit of *Eyes on the Prize*. Asenas, especially, pays considerable attention to the many ways in which nonviolence is "useful when protesters can enlist the sympathy of White liberals." Her reading and rereading of nonviolence as "the primary way to carve out political agency by controlling and politicizing the context of violence that African Americans were already enduring and as a method of gaining self-respect" is necessary for locating nonviolence within a system of unrestrained state violence. Asenas significantly provides several accounts of nonviolent actions such as "the lunch-counter sit-ins and the Freedom Rides" that were "met with substantial violence."

The power to abandon any historical dimensions of the lives of racialized ethnic groups remains a fundamental achievement of racist ideology in the United States. Race cannot be sufficiently comprehended if it is unconnected or distracted from other social relations such as gender, class, ethnicity, or sexuality. This does not mean that race should be reduced or substituted for ethnicity as such. Both Nicole Amber Haggard's and Mariangela Orabona's essays call attention to the specific intersection of gender and race. "Sensing Race and Gender in Contemporary Postcolonial Art," as the title of her essay states, Orabona, by using the artworks of African American artist Kara Walker, examines the cultural representation of the raced and gendered body as "a form of resistance to normative cultural representation." By focusing on the "specificity of race-and-gender in interracial relationships," Haggard demonstrates how "Hollywood's representation of interracial relationships truly connects to the changing face of sexism and racism in American culture." In fact, the "new racism," or what Fanon labels "cultural racism" (Fanon, 1964)[3], is coded within a cultural logic so that culture is substituted for race. Now we talk about poor single mother welfare recipients, for example, with an invidious racist subtext.

As is evident in Bynoe and Pinder's essay, gender functions as an act of cultural inscription that is inevitably positioned within our society. Therefore,

Introduction: The Concept and Definition of American Multicultual Studies

how gender expectations and roles are played out in particular cultures is important. In fact, in terms of gender configuration, because the cultural practice devalues the status of women in society as whole, what constitutes gender inequality, in terms of culture, remains fundamental. In the section on gender, whether gender identity is linked to other identities such as race, class, ethnicity, and sexuality is discussed. Yvonne Sims, in her essay, "*J'ai deux amour*: Josephine Baker and the Duality of Identity in the United States and Paris, France," explores the conflicting attitudes of "Blackness" and "womanhood" in the United States and France, more specifically, Paris. The French feminist Simone de Beauvoir (1964) once asked the metaphysical question, "What is a woman?" (p. 13). What we get from Beauvoir's question is that the West's concept of "woman" is erroneously portrayed as having a certain kind of essence. Because women are constructed as White men's "other," "an imperfect man," this essence is perceived as "inessential as opposed to essential" (p. 16). Transcending Beauvoir's conceptualization of the category "woman," Sims, taking her cue from Evelynn Hammonds's understanding of the "West's metaphoric construction of 'woman,'" reasserts that "White is what woman is; not-White is what she had better not be." In the same vein, Thelma Pinto's essay, "Claiming Sarah Baartman: Black Womanhood in the Global Imaginary," is exemplary of the kind of critical reflections on the constructions of Black womanhood. Pinto's discussion describes with precision the construction of Black womanhood as occurring "at the intersection of multiple identities influenced by the legacy of the Sarah Baartman trauma." And given that gender is reproduced through the understood privilege of Whiteness, "Whiteness," as Kalpana Seshadri-Crooks (1998) explains, "often functions as an ontologically neutral category" (p. 353) that renders it unmarked and unraced.

With meticulous examination, Mariam Esseghaier, in her essay, "'Assimilation in a Bikini': The Unveiling, Reveiling, and Disciplining of Rima Fakih," shows that in the United States, even though a seemingly "multicultural mentality" is being promoted and largely accepted, "an East versus West understanding of the world" still prevails. Esseghaier observes how Rima Fakih, the first Muslim-Arab woman to win the Miss USA title, is unveiled, reveiled, and reviled by the American media to maintain her as a racialized "other." Racial otherness is looked on as un–Americanness (Pinder, 2011). Esseghaier draws on the "distinctions between who is an American, who is not, and how the borders between American and un–American are drawn and sustained in ideological formations." In fact, "American = White." And given that American = White, non–Whites are always looked on as different, as foreigners and therefore not American (Pinder, 2010, p. 70). In fact, Esseghaier demonstrates how Fakih, before, during, and after the Miss USA pageant, "was constructed in opposition to the runner-up—a blonde-haired, blue-eyed, all-American, Morgan Elizabeth Woolard, from Oklahoma." Sarah Kanbar's chapter, in contrast to the understanding of foreignness as un–Americanness, analyzes how the Syrian American identity was constructed, "during a time when being a 'hyphenated American,' was frowned upon in the United States." And even though Syrian Americans were able to imagine themselves to be Americans, Johnson, quoting Pinder, writes: "all hyphenated Americans are cultural hybrids, living in two different cultures, one American and White, and the other, a sub-culture and non–White, producing 'a hybrid subject, almost the same but not quite, almost the same but not White,' whose identities are shaped as 'outsiders within.'"

Even though this book presents readers with a clear distinction between race and ethnicity, the racialization of ethnicity, reinscribing rather than confronting the formidable inequalities that accompany racial difference cannot be dismissed. Racialized ethnic groups, including First Nations (Native Americans), Blacks, Chinese, Mexicans, and Japanese have been and, to a large extent, still are subject to the inescapability of American racism. The dominant culture, simply assumed to be unmarked, tries on no account to speak its own name, which is the basis of its power. In the section on ethnicity, Wendy M. K. Peters, in "The Indigenous Soul Wounding: Understanding Culture, Memetics, Complexity, and Emergence," draws upon the lived experiences, both past and present, of First Nations, or what she calls First Peoples. Peters, in sensing the past in the present, issues of poverty, for example, puts forward, "are but symptoms that evidence an interrelated complex of conditions long recognized by indigenous elders as a soul wound." Instrumental in understanding the lives of First Nations, Peters's explanation and definition of soul wound, "as a common thread that weaves across much of the pain and suffering found in most of the Native communities," which, for Peters, has "shaped the lived experience of the First Peoples of North America and Hawaii" is a continuous theme in her work.

Other essays in this section, for example, look at the representation of racialized ethnicities in cinema, the media, and literature. Cynthia Lytle, through the use of Nora Okja Keller's novels *Comfort Woman* and *Fox Girl*, explores the role of language in the construction and representation of multiracial identities of "children who have a Korean mother and a White or African American father." Paola Bohórquez demonstrates "the place of language among the various markers of ethnic and cultural identity" and shows how it "can be further specified by considering that language 'is above all a means of cultural construction in which our very selves and sense are constituted.'" The constituted self or the "twoness," as W. E. B. Du Bois (2003) calls it (p. 5), leads to racial in-betweenness, which still signals non–Whiteness. Non–Whiteness is seen through what Fanon (1967) calls the "corporeal malediction" of one's unavoidable non–Whiteness (p. 111), bearing witness to the existential dilemma that inhabits the very core of one's sense of "self." In Lytle's essay, "The Power of Language in the Construction and Representation of Mixed-Race Identities in Nora Okja Keller's *Comfort Women* and *Fox Girl*," Beccah, a character in the novel *Comfort Woman*, is the daughter of Akiko (whose real name is Soon Hyo), a Korean woman, and Richard, a White American man. According to Lytle, "Beccah continually fights against the foreignness of her mother and her own 'guilt by association' through the embracing of her Caucasian Americanness." Eventually, Beccah comes face to face with Akiko's life as a "comfort woman" after Akiko dies. Lytle demonstrates, "By performing the death ritual of preparing her mother's body, Beccah accepts what she has long denied: the language and culture of her mother." Lytle's essay not only generates room for a good discussion that engages largely with the question of multiracial identities, it also effectively allows us to question whether and to what extent there is room for the hermeneutic self, one's understanding of oneself through self-interpretation.

Given that sexuality is constructed in terms of "difference," it is important to scrutinize the social, political, and personal consequences that stem from this construction. Some of the essays provided in this section focus on the meanings and implications of heterosexism and how it oppresses gays, lesbians, bisexual people, and transgendered and transsexual people. They look, for example, at arguments against Proposition 8. Henry Zomerfeld and Kyeonghi Baek's essay and Sean Robinson's essay, both highlighting that "legislation providing same-sex marriage equality such as the protests against Proposition 8 in California, which would have banned same-sex marriage in that state," are important. However, Zomerfeld and Baek, for good reasons, are more concerned with investigating why African American churches and their ministers were not at the forefront in the debates and struggles for same-sex marriages.

Seeing that heteronormativity can be viewed as hamstringing homosexuality, broader issues of "institutionalized passing" such as marriage, as a way to pass as heterosexual, gesture toward what Elizabeth Renfro's essay, "'I Do,' Therefore I am: Marriage as Institutionalized Passing," offers as an innovative and complex response to the challenges that marriage, the union between a man and a woman, poses, especially for women. Here is how Renfro explains it: "Marriage has historically provided a mechanism for distinguishing 'real,' proper people from improper people," and the "proper body's physicality is tamed, controlled [and] brought into moral status by 'true love.'" Indeed, this is not just any love, but a love that positioned one woman above all other women and silently weighs her down with domestic, reproductive work. Hence, taking from Mara Marin's essay, marriage "needs to be reformed in order to advance gender equality and, [at the same time,] challenge heteronormativity."

Helen Lindberg, in her assessment of "*Mut'ah* as Social Contract," sees women, for example, as "rational subjects with the ability or possibilities of conducting their own lives and own choices, especially, regarding marriage and reproduction." The opposite holds true for women who are positioned within the nuclear family unit. Reproduction, as oppressive for women, has already been well argued in a variety of different ways by many feminists. While there is no need to rehearse these arguments in great detail here, the burden of women's reproductive role, giving men a sure advantage by granting them the opportunity and power to establish and uphold the organization of society that would advance their interests, needs to be emphasized. In fact, heteronormativity, what is in essence cultural when we treat it as nature, is important for sustaining women's reproductive role as, to quote Renfro, "the 'central organizing principle of sexuality' and sexual orientation" in order to perpetuate and uphold a cultural hegemony that is habitually heterosexual.

Marin, in her essay, "Marriage as Commitment: A Revisionary Argument," shows "that if marriage is viewed as 'commitment,'" it can, in part, "promote gender equality and challenge heteronormativity," which is trapped in the matrix of androcentrism. Marin's question, "How should we transform what we take marriage to mean in order to prevent it from supporting gender subordination and heteronormativity?" seems to resonate with Renfro's understanding of Western practice of marriage as functioning as "what Judith Butler terms the powerful yet rarely consciously unpacked 'norms of cultural intelligibility by which [gender roles] are defined.'" Is there, then, an ethical space in which marriage can be reclaimed, refigured, and transformed beyond Western practice of marriage? We can attempt to answer this question, in part, by drawing from Lindberg's examination of *Mut'ah*, a fixed-term marriage and custom practiced within the Islamic community. Lindberg explicates that "the practice of *Mut'ah* demands core rights for each of the contracting parties, the woman as well as the man, entering the temporal marriage." Lindberg's characterization of the *Mut'ah* in terms that it is often misconstrued as women "being evicted from the realm of agency" is expressive of her twin commitments to draw on the aporetic differences that manifest themselves in categories such as gender or race and to argue, with tremendous amount of justification, why it is paramount that we "move away from the narrative of Muslim women as oppressed and voiceless." Even though some constraints might present themselves, Muslim women are capable of "autonomous choices" and, thus, by establishing relations with oneself and with others, they are constituted as ethical subjects (Rabinow, 1991, p. 334). Indeed, Bynoe and Pinder show the complexity of cultural practices, which fall prey to cultural hierarchy, structuring human existence with a string of dialectically related dualities, for example, superior and inferior, civilized and uncivilized, and caution us especially against the problematic conjecture that Western culture is more egalitarian than non–Western cultures. Hence, it is frequently noted in Lindberg's work that *Mut'ah*, for example, cannot simply be analyzed by Western norms and values that immediately deem it "oppressive to women." In fact, we should move away from the dominant and nondominant cultural relations—Western culture (us) against non–Western cultures (them)—that follows a certain kind of Eurocentric logic, determining in advance that Western culture, because of its purported naturalness, is necessarily superior and, hence, must function in such a way so as to marginalize the nondominant cultures. This is one of the main challenges that Bynoe and Pinder set out to meet in "Multiculturalism, Women, and the Need for a Feminist Analysis."

In America, there is a new emphasis on cultural diversity, or "America's cultural manyness." Cultural diversity is a radical break from America's past, in which the focus was on assimilation into the White hegemonic culture, or "America's cultural oneness," which is defined and understood as that of Whiteness. Unlike European Whites, for racialized ethnic groups, including First Nations, Blacks, Chinese, and Mexicans, assimilation is unreachable because they are not White. Hence, promoting cultural diversity in America's public sphere is important because it breaks away from America's past of assimilation to the dominant norms. Given that some scholars have argued that cultural diversity is a threat to "America's cultural oneness," what exactly does cultural diversity mean for "America's cultural manyness"? In the section on cultural diversity, Alan Ashton-Smith, in his essay titled, "*Multi Kontra Culti*: The Gypsy Punk Counterculture," with uncommonly vigorous thinking, shows that gypsy punk, "in its amalgamation of different forms of music and culture, its appropriation of elements from an array of cultures and languages, and its self-conscious awareness of influences such as punk and traditional 'gypsy' music, might be thought of as being postmodern itself," which is important for cultural diversity. Ashton-Smith concludes that *Multi Kontra Culti* "is an alternative set of values for the production of culture and music in a multicultural age." In a different way, Eduardo Barros-Grela's essay,

"Chicano Visualities: A Multicultural Rewriting of California Spatialities," gives a key role to the ways visuals are important in adding to the concepts of multiculturalism and cultural diversity. Barros-Grela Grela uses, "as an example of the confluence of rhizomatic urban development and visual expression of multiculturalism," Asco, a Chicano street performance group whose name means "nausea" or "disgust" in Spanish, to highlight the "recent manifestations of Californian visual expressions to articulate the machineries of both centripetal and centrifugal inertias with rhizome-like tendencies of multicultural identification production."

The underrepresentation of speech and language impairment (SLI) research in multicultural scholarship is apparent. In the section on education, Nicholas D. Hartlep and Antonio L. Ellis's unwavering concern in their essay, "Rethinking Speech and Language Impairments within Fluency-Dominated Cultures," is that "Multicultural education textbooks frequently center on issues of race, gender, ethnicity, sexuality, and/or cultural diversity. Rarely, if ever, do readers of these texts have the opportunity to read research conducted on students who suffer from speech and language impairment." One reason for the lack of such a research, as Teresa L. Cotner explains, "is the result of hegemonic cultural norms that has created and sustained a mere marginal role for integrated and multicultural" SLI issues "in the big curricular picture." As Sean Robinson, in "Multicultural Studies and Sexual Diversity: A Postmodern Queer(y) for All," points out, "A curriculum that is 'mainstream-centric' has negative consequences for all." For this precise reason, we are obliged to find new ways of elaborating our critique of the educational practices in the United States and of rethinking the relationship between education and cultural diversity. In other words, how can we extend and refocus multicultural studies to include issues of such concern as SLI? In searching for an answer, Cotner ponders the fact that we need "to develop a culture of interdisciplinarity and a discipline of interculturality." And even though the educational curriculum tries to include issues that are important for a multicultural education, Robinson suggests that often there are "additive approaches to multicultural education." Seeing that, according to Christine Dobbins and Mark Malisa's discussion of the role that educators do play in shaping "the nature and course of the curriculum," it is necessary then for the curriculum to broaden its focus and to seriously take on issues such as SLI and truly be, to borrow from Cotner, the "powerful pedagogical practices and proponents of social change." A multicultural curriculum is truly multicultural when issues such as SLI are rigorously addressed. It is precisely for this reason that Dobbins and Malisa's suggestions for promoting "a just and multicultural United States, especially in the field of education," cannot be ignored.

While there is no escape from multicultural studies, there is also no limit to the contexts in which grappling with issues that are critical to multicultural studies can be productive. From this standpoint, this book cannot address the whole range of topics that continue to define and shape multicultural studies. Nonetheless, my hope is that people of all backgrounds find in this work useful information and enlightening interpretations of what it means to live in a multicultural society. Most importantly, this book introduces readers to a more critical way of looking at race, gender, ethnicity, sexuality, cultural diversity, education, and other issues that are important to American multicultural studies.

Jürgen Heinrichs, in his essay, "Can We? Visual Rhetoric and Political Reality in American Presidential Campaigns," writes: The "Obama presidential campaign had stirred people to imagine a better world." "Hope" is a theme that is echoed in the Obama snapshot among the images that Heinrichs has selected as illustrations. According to Heinrichs, "how images are utilized, how they draw from historical traditions and how they engage the day's contemporary social and political realities" are "the very arenas in which meaning constitutes itself." Perhaps it is not too much to *hope* for a future in which we are no longer frightened by differences. Stuart Hall (1993), a few years ago, observed that "the capacity to live with difference is . . . the coming question of the twenty-first century" (p. 361). In other words, differences, without seizing them as forces in a struggle for power, are the future of the United States. Precisely for this reason, Whites, for example, cannot proclaim themselves as unresponsive to race politics and pretend that the United States, as Jenny Heijun Wills points out—because Barack Obama, an African American man, holds the highest position of power—is colorblind and postracial. Wills, in her paper "Transnational and Transracial Adoption, Multiculturalism, and Selective Color-Blindness," shows that "transnational and/or transracial adoptees have paradoxical relationships to the notions of color-blindness and post-raciality, thus illustrating further how racial hierarchies are persistent."

In addition, gender issues have to be broadened to include the interlocking nature of race with other identity markers such as class, sexuality, physical and mental abilities and disabilities, and ethnicity. In the name of diversity, multiplicity, and heterogeneity, we cannot ignore, for example, ableism, xenophobia, racism, sexism, and homophobia that are present in our society. We are living in a time of divergence and differences. Needless to say, thinking about the abovementioned invariable systems of oppression and marginalization is not entirely dissipated unless we work individually and as a collective body to resist all forms of oppression and marginalization. American multicultural studies, in its present orientation, provides a

good starting point to reflect on these issues. The essays in the collection open up a plurality of approaches to discuss race, gender, sexuality, ethnicity, cultural diversity, and education, and, most certainly, attest to the continued relevance of theorizing and problematizing issues that inform American multicultural studies.

References

de Beauvoir, S. (1964). *The second sex*. Trans. H. M. Parshley. New York: Alfred Knopf.

Bhabha, H. K. (1998). The White stuff. *Artforum, 36*, 21–24.

Butler, J. (1997). *The psychic life of power: Theories in subjection*. Stanford: Stanford University Press.

Du Bois, W. E. B. (2003). *The souls of Black folk*. New York: Modern Library.

Dworkin, R. (1989). Liberal community. *California Law Review, 77*(3), 479–503.

Fanon, F. (1964). *Towards the African revolution: Political essays*, Trans. Constance Farrington. New York: Grove Press.

Fanon, F. (1967). *Black skin, White masks*, Trans. Charles Lam Markmann. New York: Grove Press.

Feagin, J. R. (2006). *Systemic racism: A theory of oppression*. New York: Routledge.

Foucault, M. (1980/1990). *Power/knowledge: Selected writings and interviews, 1972–1977*. Ed. and trans. Colin Gordon. New York: Pantheon Books.

Hall, S. (1993). Culture, community, nation. *Cultural Studies, 7*(3), 349–363.

Kallen, H. M. (1956). *Cultural pluralism and the American idea: An essay in social philosophy*. Philadelphia: University of Philadelphia Press.

Kymlicka, W. (1995). *Multicultural citizenship: A liberal theory of minority rights*. Oxford, UK: Clarendon Press.

Pinder, S. O. (2010). The politics of race and ethnicity in the United States: Americanization and de-Americanization of racialized ethnic groups. New York: Palgrave Macmillan.

Pinder, S. O. (2011). *Whiteness and racialized ethnic groups in the United States: The politics of remembering*. Lanham, CO: Lexington Books.

Rabinow, P. (1984). *The Foucault reader*. New York: Random House.

Ricoeur, P. (1992). *Oneself as another*. Trans. Kathleen Blamey. Chicago: University of Chicago Press.

Seshadri-Crooks, K. (1998). The comedy of domination: Psychoanalysis and the conceit of Whiteness. In Christopher Lane (Ed.), *The psychoanalysis of race* (pp. 353–79). New York: Columbia University Press.

Wu, F. H. (2002). *Yellow race in America beyond Black and White*. New York: Basic Books.

Notes

1. See Michel Foucault, *Power/Knowledge: Selected Writings and Interviews, 1972–1977* (1990).

2. For a good illustration of "White flight," see the documentary *Why Can't We Live Together*.

3. Also, see Horace M. Kallen, *Cultural Pluralism and the American Idea: An Essay in Social Philosophy* (1956).

Theorizing Issues Concerning American Multicultural Studies

1

What Is Black in the Melting Pot?

A Critique of Afrocentrist and Postmodernist Discourses on Blackness

Babacar M'Baye

Since the late 1980s, the field of Black studies has witnessed intense debates during which schools of thoughts with different orientations have attempted to define the meaning of Black identity in particular or plural terms that suggest unavoidable ideological clashes that demonstrate the richness and vivacity of the discipline. While there are many trajectories in these intellectual conversations about the meaning of Black identity, this chapter will focus on the salient ones that have surfaced among the works of many scholars of Afrocentrist or postmodernist schools of thought who have cogently examined the meaning of Blackness on their own terms. Referring specifically to intellectuals such as Molefi Kete Asante, Kwame Anthony Appiah, Paul Gilroy, Gerald Early, Stuart Hall, Manthia Diawara, and many others who made strong contributions to the debates on multiculturalism within Black studies, this chapter will suggest the varying influences that race and ethnicity have had on such nonmainstream critical approaches to diversity in American society. Moreover, it will suggest how universalist tropes of Blackness have been interpreted by scholars from the Afrocentrist or postmodernist schools of thought.

Defining Postmodernism

Any study of the ideological clashes between Afrocentrist and Black postmodernist theory must begin with a study of the central tenets of the latter school of thought. Understanding Black postmodernism requires analysis of the ways in which it defines the concepts of representation, narrative, meaning, and experience in ways different from how modernism describes such notions. Representation is not emphasized in modernism since the basic premise of this theory is that it is antirepresentational. This antirepresentationality refers to the impossibility of modernism to convey the voices and the vision of marginal culture. High culture and avant-gardist aesthetics of selected intellectuals such as Charles Baudelaire, T. S. Eliot, and Ezra Pound, not those of the supposedly "unenlightened" mob, are the focus of modernist representation. In his interpretation of Clement Greenberg's theory, Hans Bertens points out that Greenberg "defined modernism in terms of a wholly autonomous aesthetic, of a radically anti-representational self-reflexivity" (Bertens, 1995, p. 3). In modernist representation, art and language are, like in French impressionist painting and in the linguistics of Ferdinand de Saussure, antirepresentational because they are autonomous and self-reflexive. In modernism, the value of art can be apprehended only in its form and self-referentiality, not in its relation with social and political context.

In a sense, postmodernism is antirepresentational like modernism. Postmodernism does not seek to represent things that suggest an essential meaning. It rejects the modernist tendency to represent or codify meaning in a singular and rational mode of investigation and understanding. In this sense, as Appiah suggests in his essay "Is the 'Post-' in 'Postcolonial' the 'Post-' in 'Postmodern'?" (1997), "Postmodernism is the rejection of the mainstream consensus from Descartes through Kant to logical positivism or foundationalism" (p. 426). However, postmodernism is still interested, to some degree, in representation. The goal of postmodernism is to discuss the areas of subcultural and subpolitical representations and meaning that modernism denied and repressed. This agenda, according to Bertens, focuses on "the return of representation and narrative, which for obvious reasons is only possible in those art forms—such as painting—where representation and narrative had been repressed" (p. 64).

The modernist definition of representation influenced its views about narrative, meaning, and experience. In modernism, narrative is not dependent on the social context. Like postmodernist representation, modernist narrative is a self-reflexive, self-referential, and autonomous story that can be understood only through a study of the form of the text and the aesthetics of the author. Yet postmodernism attacks modernist reduction of narrative.

Unlike modernism, postmodernism seeks to bring narrative back on the table and deconstruct its relationships with past, present, and future. For example, in the essay "The Virtues, the Unity of a Human Life and the Concept of a Tradition" (1998), Alasdair MacIntyre rereads *Homer*, *Hamlet*, and *Julius Caesar* not as a mere authentication of Greek or Elizabethan tradition but as a game that allows us to discover the theories and actions of the past and to fantasize about the past by reassessing it according to our time and beliefs (p. 538). As MacIntyre suggests when quoting Barbara Hardy, "we dream in narrative, day-dream in narrative, remember, anticipate, hope, despair, believe, doubt, plan, revise, construct, gossip, learn, hate and love in narrative" in arguing the same point (p. 542). MacIntyre's universalist and critical approach to narrative suggests how postmodernism brings back to life the individual memories and experiences that modernism dismissed and viewed as dispensable and non–self-referential.

Moreover, MacIntyre's definition of narrative suggests the meaninglessness and antiessentialist nature of postmodernist study of text. According to Bertens, modernism tended to search for "timeless meaning" (p. 31). Unlike postmodernism, modernism perceives meaning as some sort of a universal truth that only the great mind can apprehend. From this perspective, the illiterate and unsophisticated reader cannot understand the meaning of the literary allusions and imagery of Dante, Henry James, Picasso, and other prominent writers and artists. In such modernist perspective, meaning has a mental, universal, and transcendental quality that dominates personal opinion. Some premises of the Enlightenment such as the Aristotelian perception of stars as the world of gods and heavens or Copernicus's claim that planets are circular were designed to be universal truths of the premodern era. Modernism rejected most of the premodernism cosmology by suggesting that religion is mostly brought about by psychological factors. Man created gods and heavens so that he could project his anguish and desires onto this being and weaken his fear of overthrowing bourgeois capitalism and building himself a paradise on earth. According to Karl Marx's and Friedrich Engels's argument in "Economic and Philosophic Manuscripts of 1844," "The more man puts into God, the less he retains in himself. The worker puts his life into the object; but now his life no longer belongs to him but to the object" (p. 765). In this sense, religion, like the object, prevents human beings from demanding and gaining their full rights on earth since it eliminates the necessity of want.

However, despite its rejection of premodern assumptions about man, modernism came to establish essentialist meanings. Orthodox Marxism and Freudianism established the same limitations that they had sought to destroy. Orthodox Marxism ended up essentializing the class and power basis of social struggle. Likewise, Freudianism established an essentialist dichotomy between "conscious self" and "unconscious self" (Kishlansky, 1991, p. 777), creating an oppositionality within identity that postmodernism seeks to destroy. Essentialism is also apparent in the interpretation of human psychology in Freudian psychoanalysis as a greatly unconscious sphere (therefore, not perfect as Rousseau used to think).

Yet, unlike modernism, postmodernism looks for and finds meaning not in stars or ideology but in texts, textuality, intertextuality, and the death of the author. Most importantly, postmodernism finds meaning in man and his immediate environment. As Bertens argues, postmodernist meaning is "inevitably, local, contingent, and self-sufficient" (p. 31) and does not represent an underlying truth. Certainly, the postmodernist rejection of unanimous and transcendental truth is in great opposition to modernist consensus on the essential quality of meaning. Therefore, one can say that postmodernism is a critique of and a break with modernism. The postmodernist emphasis on representation, multiple meanings, narratives, and experiences indicates a *dépassement* or a step beyond modernism. In this sense, there is a discontinuity between postmodernism and modernism. However, because modernism predates postmodernism and serves as a subject of its investigation and criticisms, one could say that there are continuities between the two theories. Postmodernism cannot exist without modernism.

The Impact of Postmodern Theory on Black Studies

Postmodernism has strong influences on the theorizing of identity in Black studies. For instance, in Black studies, the "Black family" is a concept that scholars have often used to explain the complex nature of Black identity within postmodern and (or) postcolonialist theories. Some Black scholars have used the concept of the "Black family" in order to suggest a therapy for the structural, behavioral problems that confront the Black community. Others have used it to criticize a sense of nationalism and essentialism that reacts against the political, social, and cultural fabrics of Western hegemony.

In many works of contemporary Black scholars, the family is a metaphor that is introduced by the collective possessive pronouns "we," "our," and "us." In "Black Pleasure, Black Joy: An Introduction" (1992), Gina Dent begins her rhetoric by suggesting the sense of double consciousness that the narrative of a "Blackness" filtered through notions of a collective Black experience and community brings into the life of the Black individual (pp. 1–2). The concepts bring the individual to a close relationship with the community while, at the same time, keeping him or her away from its center and fundamental purpose. As Dent points out, "Every gathering has its points of profound collective understanding, never to be fully grasped except in the elusive phrase with which we attempt to reconstruct them. These phrases serve to remind us of our collective goals for the future, and yet point continually to our distance from them" (p. 1). Dent's statement begins a debate among Black scholars on issues about the Black family. As Dent points out, this debate is not an attempt to determine which point of view (essentialist or moderate; liberal or conservative) shall win, but about whether "we, peoples of the African diaspora, any longer have the right to invent an Africa?" (p. 7).

In his essay "What is this 'Black' in Black Popular Culture?" (1992), Stuart Hall offers one of the most liberal and moderate answers to Dent's question. Drawing on the genealogy of Black resistance, Hall recognizes a tradition of postcolonial and civil rights struggle in which various Black scholars (such as Frantz Fanon, Léopold Sédar Senghor, W. E. B. Dubois, and John Blassingame) tried to create what Ngugi Wa Thiong'O calls "the decolonization of the minds of the peoples of the Black diaspora" (p. 22). Yet Hall believes that the postmodern continuation of this Black struggle should be centered on "sexual difference, cultural difference, racial difference, and above all, ethnic difference" (p. 23). Hall foresees the postmodern Black family in terms of what Gilroy considers a postcolonial African traditionalism that cannot be apprehended in essentialist terms only since it is a way to resist the dictates of hegemony and contribute to human struggle (Gilroy, 1993, p. 196). Like Stuart Hall, Gilroy, in his essay "It's a Family Affair" (1992) calls for a redefinition of the study of the Black family in terms of postmodern difference. Gilroy asserts: "We will have to refine the theorizing of the African diaspora if it is to fit our changed transnational and intercultural circumstances . . . we might consider experimenting, at least, with giving up the idea that our culture needs to be centered anywhere except where we are when we launch our inquiries into it" (p. 305). Gilroy's statement is an implicit criticism of the global nationalism of pro-Afrocentric scholars such as Asante whom he considers essentialist. Like Gilroy, Hall proposes a study of the cultural environment that surrounds the Black individual and is most distinguishable in local popular culture. According to Hall, "Popular culture always has its base in the experiences, the pleasures, the memories, the traditions of the peoples. It has connections with local hopes and local aspirations, local tragedies and local scenarios" (p. 25).

Building on Hall's emphasis on local space, Cornell West calls for a serious "holistic" analysis of the problems of the African American family. Witnessing a growing sense of nihilism, cynicism, self-denial, and anger in the Black American family, West proposes a cessation of the conflicts between liberal structuralism/conservative behaviorist scholarship and rhetoric and a serious moral focus on the problems which afflict the local Black family (West, 1992, pp. 43–44). According to West, "The politics of conversion proceed principally on the local level—in those institutions in civil society still vital enough to promote self-worth and self-affirmation" (p. 44).

One wonders why there has been such an urge among contemporary Black scholars to warn against nationalist essentialism. Gilroy (1992) laughs at the etymology of the term *nationalism* when he says, in *It's a Family Affair*, that "the 'ism' in nationalism is often lacking . . . it is no longer constructed as a coherent political ideology" (p. 305). Likewise, West (1992) criticizes the Black nationalist tendencies of Louis Farrakhan and Al Sharpton for their "myopic mode," which is often, "though not always, reeking of immoral xenophobia" (p. 45).

Among other scholars, Diawara and Appiah have suggested how one can easily fall into the trap of essentialism. In his essay, "Reading Africa Through Foucault: V. Y. Mudimbe's Reaffirmation of the Subject" (1997), Diawara shows how, in his 1982 novel *L'Ecart*, V. Y. Mudimbe falls into the trap of nationalism by creating characters who represent an inappropriate antithesis of Negritude intellectuals. According to Diawara, Nara, one of the central characters in the novel, "argues against the anthropologists and historians who project images of their own desires onto the surface of Africa and posits as an imperative for himself the need to be more sensitive to the specificity of local knowledge" (p. 465). Nara's ideology reflects Mudimbe's attempt to suggest a redefinition of Africa outside of European terms. As Diawara suggests, Mudimbe's essentialism is blatant when he says: "We [Africans] must reanalyze for our benefit the contingent supports and the areas of enunciation in order to know what new meaning and what road to propose for our quest so that our discourse can justify us as singular beings engaged in a history that is itself special" (p. 463).

Like Diawara, Appiah suggests that essentialism is a constant risk that faces the postcolonial scholar. Appiah shows that the process of commodification of African art in Western territory often forces the native artist to present his object in essentialist terms. In "Is the 'Post-' in 'Postcolonial' the 'Post-' in 'Postmodern'?" (1997), Appiah gives the example of Lela Kouakou, a Baule artist, who, in 1987, presented his sculptures at the Center for African Art in New York. One of Kouakou's pieces, called *Yoruba Man with a Bicycle*, caught the attention of the audience and was interpreted by James Baldwin as a "contemporary" piece that shows an African man who is going to town (p. 422). For Appiah, Baldwin's judgment is a proof that African art can be interpreted in a personal way outside its original or African context. Appiah salutes the freedom from which Westerners such as Baldwin benefit in having the power to judge other arts according to their own world. Yet Appiah (1997) finds injustice when many Westerners refuse to allow the African artist to present his art according to his own personal terms (outside of any reference to a specific tribal culture, for example; pp. 422–423). Appiah's criticism of the African artist's silence in the assessment of his own art stemmed from a footnote to an essay in which Susan Vogel, the curator of the above art exhibit, wrote: "African informants will criticize sculptures from other ethnic groups in terms of their own traditional criteria, often assuming that such works are simply inept carvings of their own aesthetic tradition" (Vogel, 1997, p. 11). Such a footnote encourages essentialism by giving the impression that African art is superficial when it is not made by an authentic artist and according to his or her traditional values. According to Appiah (1997), this discrimination between what is "authentic" and "inauthentic" is an essentialist dichotomy that European and American-educated African postmodernist intellectuals have promoted (p. 422).

Therefore, nationalism presents an everlasting danger since it can promote essentialism that is apparent in the rhetoric of racial, cultural, and ethnic uniqueness that permeate contemporary Black scholarship. Influenced by the theories of postmodernity and postcoloniality, Black scholars such as Hall, Gilroy, Diawara, Appiah, and others have sought to undermine essentialist nationalism in contemporary writing and political rhetoric. Yet, as the next part of this chapter suggests, similar kinds of essentialism can be promoted when Western-educated Black scholars undervalue the ideas of cross-cultural difference, indeterminacy, and meaninglessness in Afrocentric paradigms.

Afrocentrist Approaches to Race and Ethnicity

Since its popularity in American and world academic circles in the middle of the 20th century, the scholarship that is often described as being part of "Afrocentrism" has been misjudged and often ridiculed by numerous critics who either conflate it with ethnonationalism or reduce its significance to mere romanticization of Black history or Black pride. As a result, the core of the scholarship that ended up endorsing the label "Afrocentrist," which has been unduly imposed upon it, is often misunderstood by critics who cannot perceive its celebration of Black culture as a strategy for achieving political, economic, and social development. In an attempt to give a brief and clear synopsis of the history of Afrocentrism, this chapter will uncover and dismantle the myths that critics have often developed to support or criticize this school of thought.

First, it is important to stress that the terms *Afrocentrism* and *Afrocentricity* mean different things and that the expression *Afrocentrism* itself is a misnomer. A good definition of the notion of Afrocentrism appears in the book *Afrocentric Thought and Praxis: An Intellectual History* (2001), in which, citing James Stewart and Maulena Karenga, Cecil Conteen Gray argues that the concept is used "most frequently in 'ideological discourse between advocates and critics'—especially those engaged primarily in popular media or popular exchanges" (p. 45). As Gray points out, another definition of the term *Afrocentrism* is the way in which "some people understand—or attempt to posit—Afrocentrism as being the African version or opposite of the oppressive, hegemonic European ideology known as 'Eurocentrism'" (p. 45). The bottom line is what Gray (2001) clearly states:

> Whatever Afrocentrism is, it is not Afrocentricity. Afrocentricity is an intellectual concept and category; it has "intellectual value"; and, as Stewart asserts, it adds to and contributes to "systematic intellectual approaches in the field" of Black Studies. (p. 45)

This last point is worth stressing because it alludes to the fact that Afrocentricity is a long and established intellectual discourse about the experiences of African-descended people that modern or contemporary theorizing of Blackness (that its preceded in the arena of critical inquiry) have often miscategorized as "Afrocentrism," a term that so-called "liberal" or "progressive" intellectuals imagine as being a Black form of narrow, Western, or White conservative nationalisms and concepts of culture. In "The Afrocentric Idea in Education" (2003), Asante corrects this misconception about Afrocentricity by saying that:

> Afrocentricity is *not* a Black version of Eurocentricity . . . Eurocentricity is based on White supremacist notions whose purposes are to protect White privilege and advantage in education, economics, politics, and so forth. Unlike Eurocentricity, Afrocentricity does not condone ethnocentric valorization at the expense of degrading other groups' perspectives. Moreover, Eurocentricity presents the particular historical reality of Europeans as the sum total of the human experience . . . It imposes Eurocentric realities as "universal," i.e., that which is White is presented as applying to the human condition in general, while that which is non-White is viewed as group-specific and therefore not "human." (p. 39)

If Afrocentrism is not the universalism that its detractors have etymologically and ideologically associated it with, what is it, then? Asante (2003) provides an answer:

> Afrocentricity is a frame of reference wherein phenomena are viewed from the perspective of the African person. The Afrocentric approach seeks in every

situation the appropriate centrality of the African person . . . in education, this means that teachers provide students the opportunity to study the world and its people, concepts, and history from an African world view. (p. 39)

Asante's point is valid because it goes against the grain of multiculturalist theories of education in which the European worldviews are considered the undisturbed and unshakeable truths, while those of the diverse members of American society are denied and forced to adapt to the universal White concepts of history. In *The Disuniting of America* (1998), Arthur M. Schlesinger, Jr., berates Afrocentricity, and specifically Asante's conception of the ideology, as a laughable attempt "in breaking the White, Eurocentric, racist grip on the [American] curriculum and providing education that responds to colored races, colored histories, colored ways of learning and behaving" (p. 70). Schlesinger (1998) continues: "Europe has reigned long enough; it is the source of most of the evil in the world anyway; and the time is overdue to honor the African contributions to civilization so purposefully suppressed in Eurocentric curricula" (p. 70). While he derides Afrocentricity's representation of Eurocentricity as a dominant and oppressive paradigm, Schlesinger fails to see how he himself agrees that this dominance and potential of oppression are real. While mocking the Afrocentric view of education as an interest in history "not as an intellectual discipline but rather as social and psychological therapy" for minority groups, Schlesinger (1998) warns that such a practice will only make Whites angrier and more prone to abuse Blacks. He writes:

> In seeking to impose Afrocentric curricula on public schools, for example, they go further than their white predecessors. And belated recognition by white America of the wrongs so viciously inflicted on black Americans has created the phenomenon of white guilt—not a bad thing in many respects, but still a vulnerability that invites cynical black exploitation and manipulation. (p. 76)

Schlesinger's message is clear: Blacks should not ask for more than they are given because doing so will only give Whites more reasons to be intolerant toward them. In such a restrained context in which Blacks are confined, where is the fulfillment of American pluralism that Schlesinger dubiously celebrates in his book? Schlesinger (1998) seems to have a general bias toward not just Blacks but also many minority groups, as evident in the passage in which he represents the reconstruction of American history since 1987 in the "long-neglected fields" of "the history of women, of immigrants, of Blacks, Indians, Hispanics, [and] homosexuals," as a scholarship that is "partly on the merits and partly in response to gender and ethnic pressures" (p. 71). In this sense, Schlesinger would perceive Afrocentricity and its contemporaries as subnarratives not worthy of attention, thus denying the significance of Afrocentricity in the theorizing of American pluralism and ignoring the centrality and agency of the ideology in the conceptualization of postmodern American conditions. In *Afrocentricity* (1988), Asante captures the meaning of *Afrocentricity* when he states:

> Afrocentricity is the belief in the centrality of Africans in post modern history. It is our history, our mythology, our creative motif, and our ethos exemplifying our collective will. On basis of our story, we build upon the work of our ancestors who gave signs toward our humanizing function. (p. 6)

This quotation suggests that Afrocentricity is not an ethnocentrist or anti–White intellectual paradigm, since it begins with recognition of the interrelatedness between the African subjectivity and the myriad identities of Blacks in "post modern" American history.

During the past quarter of a century, a number of Black critics have made harsh remarks against Afrocentrism, creating unnecessary gaps between the Afrocentric and the so-called postmodern approaches to Black studies. In his essay "A Blacker Shade of Yale: African-American Studies Take a New Direction," published in the March 2001 issue of *Lingua Franca*, Christopher Shea contrasts what he called "the academic cutting-edge" approach of the African-American Studies Program at Yale University with what he described as—supposedly from the terms of Henry Louis Gates, Jr.—the "voodoo methodology" of Temple University (p. 44). This statement reflects the deep schism that has been going on for the past quarter century or more and that has so far prevented Black scholars from recognizing and translating into action the strong similarities that their schools of thought share despite their differing political and cultural approaches to Black struggle and their variant conceptualizations of this struggle.

Among many Black postmodern critics, Appiah, Gilroy, and Early have expressed concern toward what they interpret as the tendency of the Afrocentrist movement to override the local specificity of Black identity in favor of a transcending Blackness that defines the position of all people of African descent in the modern world. Appiah, in his book *In My Father's House* (1992), refutes a definition of Blackness that overlooks the diversity of African communities and local customs when he says that "the pan–Africanists responded to their experiences of racial discrimination by accepting the racialism it presupposed" (p. 17). Appiah (1992) argues that

> though race is indeed at the heart of the pan–Africanist's nationalism, however, it seems that it is the fact of a shared race, not the fact of a shared racial character, that provides the basis for solidarity. Where racism is implicated in the basis for national solidarity, it is intrinsic, not extrinsic. (p. 17)

Racial essentialism has had practical utilities in the development of resistance in the Black diaspora since, as Schmeisser (2004) argues, "the historical significance of 'race,' racial essentialism and racism and how the cultural significance of 'race' was explained or expressed, were defining elements in the aesthetic debates of the New Negro movement during the interwar years" (p. 117). Schmeisser's quotation opposes the postmodernist representation of pan–Africanists as mere racial essentialism by suggesting how Black intellectuals invoked racial purity to further their cultural and political resistance.

Appiah's theory about pan–Africanists recoups with the postmodernist interpretations of Black identity of Gilroy, which prioritize the weakening significance of race in American society and ideological disassociation of the Black diaspora from Africa. Locating Afrocentricity in the early discourses of Cheikh Anta Diop and George James, Gilroy (1993) claims, in *The Black Atlantic: Modernity and Double Consciousness*, that such Black intellectuals, who once proclaimed the anteriority of Black civilization, misunderstood the currents of modernity and their relationships with slavery and imperialism (p. 190). Furthermore, as Karen J. Winkler (1994) posits, Gilroy criticizes Afrocentrists for tracing contemporary Black culture directly to African roots (p. A8). Such attacks on Afrocentrists are apparent when Gilroy (1994) derides Asante for saying that "Our anteriority is only significant because it re-affirms for us that if we once organized complex civilizations all over the continent of Africa, we can take those traditions and generate more advanced ideas" (p. 190). This is the type of statement that critics of Afrocentrism use to present the movement as irrelevant, outdated, essentialist, and anachronistic. Such an easy way of dismissing Afrocentrism and its proponents fails to inscribe the movement in its proper historical and intellectual context. In order to put Afrocentrism in its right context, I use the effective approach that Tunde Adeleke (2009) employs in his book, *The Case Against Afrocentrism*, by interpreting "Afrocentric essentialist thought" as "a comprehensive and dynamic agency in Black history" while "underscoring the contradictions and limitations" of this ideology (p. 22).

Afrocentrism is not irrelevant in that it is a Black cultural movement that seeks to rewrite the neglected history of Blacks in a modern history that has been marked by slavery, imperialism, and colonization. As Asante (1980) pointed out in *Afrocentricity: The Theory of Social Change*, "Afrocentricity is the belief in the centrality of Africans in post modern history" (p. 6). Asante's Afrocentrism is steeped in the belief that race and class relations in modern United States are characterized by constant shifts in power relations and diversity of cultures. As Asante states, in his essay "Harold Cruse and Afrocentric Theory"(2009),

> The future of the heterogeneous United States is not one giant amalgamation of cultures but rather a multiplicity of cultures without hierarchy resting on certain political and social pillars that support racial and cultural equality and respect. This multiplicity of cultural centers revolving around respect and equality is the future. (p. 4)

Thus, Afrocentric theory is a materialistic interpretation of socioeconomic relations that the continuity of the color line in the United States has complicated. Yet, in spite of its importance, Afrocentric theory is either ignored or vituperated in mainstream Black intellectual discourses on multiculturalism. For instance, Gilroy (1993) denies the democratic nature of Asante's Afrocentric agenda by displacing "Afrocentrists" from their social and political context. For example, he dismisses Cheikh Anta Diop's idea that Egyptian civilization was Black (Gilroy, 1993, p. 190) without putting this theory in the historical context that produced it. Such a dismissal is unfair since, as J. D. Walker (1995) suggests in his essay "The Misrepresentation of Diop's Views," "Diop must be understood in the context of French/Old World intellectual traditions" (p. 78). Within such traditions, Diop's thesis serves as a counterpoint to Europe's cultural hegemony. Gilroy (1993) admits that Asante's idea of the "anteriority" of Black civilization has the virtue of demystifying and rejecting "European particularism" dressed up "as universal" (p. 190).

Yet Gilroy (1993) does not develop Asante's claim and prefers to override the issue by saying that "A discussion of the extent to which these historiographical and linguistic claims can be substantiated would be a distraction" (p. 190). By refusing to explore the historiography and the contexts that shaped Asante's and Diop's views, Gilroy fails to regard them as part of the struggles of modernity. Most importantly, Gilroy's (1993) minimization of Diop and Asante contradicts the well-accepted theory that Greek civilization owes many of its great developments to Egypt. As Martin Bernal (1987) showed in *Black Athena: The Afroasiatic Roots of Classical Civilization*, there is considerable evidence that Egyptian vocabulary influenced the vocabulary of Aischylos's play *The Suppliants* and the writings of Plato (p. 22). Likewise, as Bernal (1987) pointed out, Egyptian divinities, rituals, and religion were earlier than the Greek ones (p. 23). In the preface to *The African Origin of Civilization: Myth or Reality*, Diop (1974) gives the reasons that led him to affirm that ancient Egypt was a Negro civilization. Diop (1974) perceives his thesis as part of a national, scientific, and cultural Third World revolution that sought to resist Europe's intellectual hegemony. Diop (1974) states:

> Have foreign intellectuals, who challenge our intentions and accuse us of all kinds of hidden motives or ridiculous ideas, proceeded any differently? When they explain their own historical past or study their languages, that seems normal. Yet, when an African does likewise to help reconstruct the national personality of his people, distorted by colonialism, that is backward or alarming. We contend that such a study is the point of departure for the cultural revolution properly understood. (p. xiv)

Diop's theory must be understood as part of a discourse in which Third World scholars question the methods and efficiency of the Western scholarly perspectives that tend to write Black people out of the history of great achievements. As Diop (1974) states, "Our investigations have convinced us that the West has not been calm enough and objective enough to teach us our history correctly, without crude falsifications" (p. xiv). In this sense, the highly criticized Afrocentric perspective of history should be viewed not as the antithesis to Western history but as a dialectical response to it. Diop's Afrocentrism must be considered an attempt to decenter history from its Western domination. In his preface to *Moving the Center: The Struggle for Cultural Freedom*, Ngugi Wa Thiong'O (1993) argues for the necessity to move history from its Western location:

> I am convinced with moving the center in two senses at least. One is the need to move the center from its assumed location in the West to a multiplicity of spheres in all the cultures of the world. The assumed location of the center of the universe in the West is what goes by the term Eurocentrism, an assumption which developed with the domination of the world by a handful of western nations. (p. xvi)

By failing to represent Diop as a narrative that resists Western hegemony, Gilroy compromises objectivity and neutrality. Instead of acknowledging and discussing this subaltern quality of Afrocentrist paradigms, Gilroy simply put its major thinkers such as Asante and Diop in the category of outdated traditionalists. Gilroy's (1993) representation of Afrocentrists as "obsessive purist[s]" prevents him from understanding their definition of tradition, time, and modernity as subaltern defense against logocentric and Manichean Western conception of history. Gilroy's (1993) idea that Afrocentrists glorify their past because they want to escape reality is defeated by Diop (1974), who argues, in *The African Origin of Civilization*, that his purpose "is not a matter of looking for the Negro under a magnifying glass as one scans the past" (p. xvi). Diop's intent is not to present the Black individual as a perfect or superior being but rather as a determinate "agent" who has strength as well as weaknesses.

Taking on Appiah's and Gilroy's lead, Gerald Early (1999) argues in his essay "Understanding Afrocentrism: Why Blacks Dream of a World Without Whites" that Afrocentricity "is meant to be an ideological glue to bring Black people together, not just on the basis of color but as the expression of a cultural and spiritual will that crosses class and geographical lines" (p. 621). Early's statement misrepresents Afrocentrism by failing to interpret its conceptions of cultural and spiritual continuities outside the theoretical frame of essentialism. Hidden in Early's assessment is the notion that African American students' identification with Africa is a defense mechanism against White racism which, when pushed to the extreme, might prevent these students from immersing themselves in the mainstream American culture. This notion is apparent when Early (1999) dismisses the position of a Black student who told Angela Davis that "She [the student] was simply an African, wishing to have nothing to do with being an American or with America itself. She wanted Black people to separate themselves entirely from 'Europeans,' as she called White Americans, and wanted to know what Davis could suggest to further that aim" (p. 619). Although this student's position can be considered essentialist, as Early suggests, one cannot simply describe it as such without examining the structural realities and personal experiences that led the student to develop such a radical view of her identity. Finding such information, which requires statistics, studies on social and economic inequalities, and psychoanalytic factors that influence the student's sense of self, can help her benefit from the openness to multiculturalism that Early prescribes to the student. Summarizing Davis's response to the student, Early (1999) writes: "Davis answered that she was not inclined to such stringent race separation. She was proud of being of African but wished to be around a variety of people, not just people like herself" (p. 619). Davis's representation of her African identity as a factor that does not preclude openness to diversity suggests that collective identity must not always be perceived as an orientation that necessarily precludes intimacy within mainstream American culture.

Afrocentrism is, first and foremost, a movement grounded on actual social and political realities such as the exploitation and objectification of Black people across the globe for more than 400 years. Experienced in transatlantic slavery, European colonization, and neocolonization of African lands, this exploitation has led not only to the displacement of millions of Black people from Africa but also to the formation of planter-bourgeois classes across Western Europe, North and South America, and the

Caribbeans, where Black people have been exploited for centuries on the basis of their race. When one accepts that slavery and colonization were historical facts that displaced human and economic resources from Africa to the Western world, one must agree that theories of return to the African past such as Afrocentrism, which stress a continuum between the past and present conditions of people of African descent, are legitimate counterattacks to Western hegemony. This African-centered interpretation of the relationships between the conditions of modern Blacks and slavery is corroborated in the essay "The Ideology of Racial Hierarchy and the Construction of the European Slave Trade," in which Asante (1998) states:

> What some have called a trade, trafico negreiro, comercio negreiro, la traite negriere, and what Walter Rodney called a racial violence, I call a racial war prosecuted against presumed inferiors to establish the idea of white supremacy in economics, culture, religion, education, industry, politics, and culture power, thus the enslavement of Africans must be seen in a larger context of European domination where nothing was to prevent the use of collective violence, enslavement, against Africans in order for Europe to carry out its aims. Yet in the end we must declare victory over racism, racial hierarchy and racialized histories that seek to protect even now the racist project by denying its base in the enslavement of Africans.

This quotation suggests that Afrocentrism is postmodern in its approach since it requires that critics displace the Western narratives of conquest and victory and reinterpret them according to the moral, physical, and psychological violence that they have perpetrated against people of African descent. As Irena R. Makaryk (1993) suggests, like other postmodern theories such as postcolonialism, Marxism, poststructuralism, and feminism, Afrocentrism seeks to denaturalize the Eurocentric historical narrative that accounts for how capitalism, humanism, and patriarchy were formed without acknowledging the price that Africans (men, women, and children) paid for such developments (p. 612). In this sense, Afrocentrism is a theory that calls for racial and social justice through reparations for slavery and its consequences on the Black world. The notion of violence needs to be displaced from its normalized locus that reinforces traditional Western materialism and ethos and be evaluated in the continuity of discrimination, exploitation, and alienation of Black people. Such a relocation of violence in modern contexts requires analysis of the traumatic effects of a brutal past and racism on Black people, which is what Afrocentrist scholars do persistently against all odds.

The field of Black studies reflects strong and important debates among minority scholars whose conversations on identity, race, and culture mirror the changes in an American society that is increasingly becoming multicultural.

Such diversity is apparent in the various approaches of academics who use either an Afrocentrist, a modernist, or a postmodernist lens to study the complex nature of Blackness in American society. Scholars such as Appiah, Gilroy, and Hall, whose views on race somewhat mirror the mainstream American approach to multiculturalism, against more racially conscious scholars such as Asante, Early, and Diawara, provide differing interpretations of identity and culture that have greatly enhanced the prolific field of Black studies in past decades. In a next phase of my research, I will identify the various levels at which the theoretical premises of Afrocentrist and postmodernists scholars converge in ways that transcend the binary opposition between the two schools of thought and point to the need for all Black scholars in the Black diaspora and in Africa to recenter their paradigms in the complex and transnational Black political and cultural struggle for survival and independence.

References

Adeleke, T. (2009). *The case against afrocentrism*. Jackson: University Press of Mississippi.

Appiah, K. A. (1992). *In my father's house: Africa in the philosophy of culture*. New York: Oxford University Press.

Appiah, K. A. (1997). Is the "post-" in "postcolonial" the "post-" in "postmodern"? In Anne McClintock, Aamir Mufti, & Ella Shohat (Eds.), *Dangerous liaisons* (pp. 420–444). Minneapolis: University of Minnesota Press.

Asante, M. K. (2009). *The ideology of racial hierarchy and the construction of the European slave trade*. Retrieved from http://www.asante.net/articles/14/the-ideology-of-racial-hiearchy-and-the-construction-of-the-european-slave-trade/.

Asante, M. K. (1980). *Afrocentricity: The theory for social change*. Buffalo, NY: Amulefi Publishing.

Asante, M. K. (1988). *Afrocentricity*. Trenton, NJ: Africa World Press.

Asante, M. K. (2003). The Afrocentric idea in education. In James L. Conyers (Ed.), *Afrocentricity and the academy: Essays on theory and practice* (pp. 37–49). Jefferson, NC: McFarland & Company.

Asante, M.K. (2009). "Harold Cruse and Afrocentric Theory." Retrieved from http://www.asante.net/articles/18/harold-cruse-and-afrocentric-theory/.

Bernal, M. (1987). *Black Athena: The Afroasiatic roots of classical civilization* (Vol. 1, The fabrication of ancient Greece, 1785–1985). New Brunswick, NJ: Rutgers University Press.

Bertens, H. (1995). *The idea of the postmodern*. New York: Routledge.

Dent, G. (1992). Black pleasure, Black joy: An introduction. In Gina Dent (Ed.), *Black popular culture: A project by Michelle Wallace* (pp. 1–19). Seattle, WA: Bay Press.

Diawara, M. (1997). Reading Africa through Foucault: V. Y. Mudimbe's reaffirmation of the subject. In Anne McClintock, Aamir Mufti, and Ella Shohat (Eds.), *Dangerous liaisons: Gender, nation, & postcolonial perspectives* (pp. 456–467). Minneapolis: University of Minnesota Press.

Diop, C. A. (1974). *The African origin of civilization: Myth or reality.* New York: Lawrence Hill.

Early, G. (1999). Understanding Afrocentrism: Why Blacks dream of a world without Whites. In Randall Bass (Ed.), *Border texts: Cultural readings for contemporary writers* (pp. 618–629). New York: Houghton Mifflin.

Gilroy, P. (1992). It's a family affair. In Gina Dent (Ed.), *Black popular culture: A project by Michelle Wallace* (pp. 303–316). Seattle, WA: Bay Press.

Gilroy, P. (1993). *The Black Atlantic: Modernity and double consciousness.* Cambridge, MA: Harvard University Press.

Gray, C. C. G. (2001). *Afrocentric thought and praxis: An intellectual history.* Trenton, NJ: Africa World Press.

Hall, S. (1992). What is this "Black" in Black popular culture? In Gina Dent (Ed.), *Black popular culture: A project by Michelle Wallace* (pp. 21–33). Seattle, WA: Bay Press.

Kishlansky, M., et al. (Eds.). (1991). *Civilization in the west.* New York: HarperCollins.

MacIntyre, A. (1998). The virtues, the unity of a human life and the concept of a tradition. In L. Cahoone (Ed.), *From modernism to postmodernism: An anthology* (pp. 534–555). Oxford, UK: Blackwell.

Makaryk, I. R. (1993). *Encyclopedia of contemporary literary theory: Approaches, scholars, terms.* Toronto: University of Toronto Press.

Marx, K., & Engels, F. (2001). From *Economic and Philosophic Manuscripts of 1844.* In Vincent B. Leitch (Ed.), *The Norton anthology of theory and criticism* (pp. 759–788). New York: Norton.

Schlesinger, A. M., Jr. (1998). *The disuniting of America.* New York and London: W. W. Norton.

Schmeisser, I. (2004, Automne). "Vive l'union de tous les noirs, et vive l'Afrique": Paris and the Black diaspora in the interwar years. *Sources: Revue d'Études Anglophones, 17,* 114–143.

Shea, C. (2001, March). A Blacker shade of Yale: African-American studies take a new direction. *Lingua Franca, 11*(2), 42–49.

Vogel, Susan, et al. (1997). *Perspectives: Angles on African art.* New York: Center for African Art.

Wa Thiong'O, N. (1993). *Moving the center: The struggle for cultural freedoms.* Portsmouth, NH: Heinemann.

Walker, J. D. (1995, September). The misrepresentation of Diop's views. *Journal of Black Studies, 26*(1), 77–85.

West, C. (1992). Nihilism in Black America. In G. Dent (Ed.), *Black popular culture: A project by Michelle Wallace* (pp. 37–47). Seattle, WA: Bay Press.

Winkler, K. J. (1994, September 28). Flouting convention: A British sociologist makes friends and enemies with theories on how cultures influence each other. *Chronicle of Higher Education, 41*(5), A8–A9, A15.

2

Multicultural Rhythms

Musical and Racial Harmony[1]

Kulvinder Arora

I n *Multicultural Encounters*, Sanjay Sharma's introduction is titled "What's Wrong With Multiculturalism?" (Sharma, 2006, p. 3). The answers he provides reflect a critique of the liberal universalist principles that undergird multiculturalism. For instance, he argues that the advocacy of group-based cultural identity seemingly legitimizes a type of communitarian multicultural educational strategy that encourages the preservation of particular racial and ethnic identities. I would add that this might have the effect of promoting cultural essentialism so that groups may think of racial and ethnic identities as having fixed meanings that are not subject to historical changes. For example, South Asian immigrants to the United States may think of themselves through ethnic differences in terms of regional languages (Punjabi, Bengal, Gujarati, etc.) or religious group affiliations (Hindu, Muslim, Sikh, etc.), which may be important for homeland politics but less salient in the United States. In this way, South Asians may have come to rely more on ethnic identity to define themselves than on a racial identity as South Asian Americans. In the United States, given the racialization of ethnicity, I would argue that a racial consciousness may be more effective for political advocacy but also in creating a sense of community with other South Asians that goes beyond ethnic, regional, and religious differences. However, in a society such as the United States, multiculturalism allows for the celebration and recognition of nondominant cultural groups.

In "Gender, Class and Multiculturalism," Angela Davis has argued that "Multiculturalism can become . . . a way of affirming persisting unequal power relations by representing them as equal differences" (Davis, 1996, p. 44). This is to say that instead of noting that certain minority groups hold more economic power, all minorities are represented as similarly situated through recourse to their particular ethnic culture (dress, food, and cultural festivals) rather than an emphasis on historical material relations between groups. Placing an emphasis on historical conditions that created material differences between groups is important because an emphasis on ethnic culture alone may have the effect of placing blame on minority groups for being disadvantaged due to their "culture." Placing historical material relations at the center of discussions of multiculturalism helps us to understand that ethnic cultural particularity does not contribute to racial hierarchies in our society as much as the histories of colonialism, slavery, and exploitation.

This chapter is premised on the idea that multicultural representations often take the most culturally essentialist versions of nondominant cultures to be recognized and celebrated. The emphasis on cultural essentialism, which advances the celebration and cultural recognition of nondominant ethnic groups, provides for a type of multiculturalism that celebrates culture at the expense of an understanding of race as structuring American society. In other words, while multiculturalism allows for the cultural recognition of nondominant groups, the nondominant groups remain separate from the dominant group. And culture, which may be seen as the specific historical forms of any given society, is, instead, given a certain essence defined as ethnic particularity. I will show how Funkadesi's music, by offering a dynamic rendering of inter-cultural fusion, challenges the notion of cultural essentialism, that is, the idea that cultures have particular fixed meanings. This provides for a new way of thinking about nondominant cultures and how they are positioned within America's multicultural society. Before focusing on the main argument, I want to point, in brief, to some essential characteristics of the Funkadesi band.

Funkadesi Band

Funkadesi is a multiethnic band that prides itself on cultural display of its many different heritages. This is manifested in the clothes the members wear, the musical styles they perform, and the instruments they use. In addition, Funkadesi delights, partly, in being a band that works out disagreements that occur among the members of the band. Rather than denying that they may disagree on a particular song because of class, gender, or race, they try to acknowledge how members of the band are shaped by different identity markers, which, in a group interaction, would manifest themselves in various ways. So when Kwame Steve Cobb, the drummer, who is African American, felt passionate that there was a conspiracy of exploiting people of color in the government's handling of the Hurricane Katrina crisis, some members of the band, even though they disagreed with his assertion, acknowledged and respected his position by including the song "No Leans" on their CD.

The members of Funkadesi include Navraz Basati, a South Asian woman who is the only woman in the band. Valroy Dawkins, a Jamaican man, often sings lead vocals with Basati. Other band members like Inder Paul Singh and Rahul Sharma sing some of the songs solo or with accompaniment. Singh, Sharma, and Maninder Singh, who is the tabla/dhol player, are South Asian. As I have mentioned before, the drummer is Kwame Steve Cobb, who is African American; Carlos Cornier is an Afro-Caribbean percussionist and is Latino; Abdul Hakeem is the guitarist and is African American; Rich Conti is a Brazilian percussionist who is White; and Lloyd King is the saxophone/flute player and identifies as Black and White. Many musicians such as the African American rapper Anacron, who was featured on the song "Galsun" on Funkadesi's CD release called *Yo Baba*, would join the band from time to time.

Not only are the members of the band from different ethnic and racial backgrounds, but the music itself is also a mixture of various funk and desi (South Asian musical styles). When Barack Obama was state senator of Illinois, he said of the Chicago-based musical group that "Funkadesi really knows how to get a crowd going. There's a lot of funk in that desi."[2] Obama's statement reflects that he understands the multicultural fusion of funk and desi that comprises the band. The band is the "dream-child" of Rahul Sharma, a musician of South Asian origin. Sharma grew up grooving on funk music and sought a name for a band that would echo his interest in funk alongside his emerging involvement in South Asian cultural forms of music. South Asians refer to themselves as *desi* to connote their belonging to a South Asian diaspora.

Understanding Cultural Essentialism and Cultural Pluralism

"Funkadesi" meant a lot more to the band's founder, Rahul Sharma, than just a personal reflection of musical styles he was interested in. Sharma states that Funkadesi was his way of countering the label American-Born Confused

Desi (ABCD) that had been tacked onto him by some desis he knew growing up. *ABCD* is a derogatory term used by desis to label other desis who do not conform to their sense of what it means to be an authentic South Asian. Often, it is applied to desis who may or may not be American born per se but identify primarily with American cultural forms. For example, someone who enjoys American popular music may be seen as less authentic than a desi who exclusively enjoys Bollywood music. The label ABCD implies that one does not understand one's roots and is overtly assimilated into American culture. Rahul was born in Kalamazoo, Michigan, 2 years after his parents emigrated there from Kenya. He grew up visiting Kenya in the summers and observing Kenyan culture. Thus, having observed Indians living in Africa and Indians living in the United States, Sharma grew up knowing there was nothing "essential" about Indian culture in the United States. Like many South Asians, Sharma wanted to disavow and deconstruct the label ABCD.[3] Yet unlike the trajectory of desi immigrant children who seek cultural "authenticity" as desis, in contrast to Westernization, Sharma's ideas of desi sprang from a diasporic de-essentialized understanding of desis.

It is interesting that Sharma chose to merge his interest in funk music with desi music. Both musical styles themselves imply a blending or fusion of forms. Many people use the term *desi* to imply a mixing of various South Asian cultural forms. *Desi*, in Hindi, means "belonging to the nation." The way the term is used, however, connotes a belonging to the South Asian diaspora rather than a South Asian nation of origin (India, Pakistan, Bangladesh, etc.). Therefore, *desi*, for some, may connote cultural authenticity, or it may alternatively connote a diasporic consciousness of cultural hybridity. I would argue that this diasporic consciousness is ideally not rooted in any kind of essentialism about what it means to be desi but is open to a blending and mixing of forms of one's strategic choosing. Ananya Chatterjea's discussion of African dance, in *Butting Out*, is useful here. She is critical of choreographers who look to essentialized notions of Africa and set up a hierarchy in which artistic traditions of the originative country are celebrated over the diasporic choreographies of African American people (Chatterjea, 2004, p. 164). Instead, she prefers to think about "Africanism" itself as a range of aesthetic and philosophical approaches rather than a more essentialized notion of Afrocentricity (2004, p. 6).

The idea of selectively constructing identity is important to Funkadesi's ethos, and it impacts how the multiethnic members of the band work together to compose ideas about race and gender in their music. Funkadesi's music is composed of a syncretism of funk, Latino rhythms, reggae, rap, bhangra, and other forms of traditional folk music. The band sings in English, Jamaican patois, Spanish, Punjabi, Telegu, Tamil, and Hindi.

I would describe Funkadesi's music as a form of strategic syncretism. By this, I mean, that as a group, they choose to strategically blend certain musical forms with others just as Sharma describes blending his interests in funk and Indian music as a way of negotiating his identity. Funkadesi also chooses compositions for their music that reflect a progressive political agenda. From singing about the government's failure to respond to the needs of Hurricane Katrina victims in the song "No Leans" and a call for racial unity in the song "Galsun" to a critique of arranged marriage in the song "Saheli," Funkadesi's music reflects an antiracist and feminist agenda. While ethnic cultural display is important to their sound and vision, an emphasis on political agendas defines the type of multiculturalism that Funkadesi is invested in, a multiculturalism that moves away from cultural essentialism that is visible in the way that multiculturalism is understood and defined. As Sherrow O. Pinder, in *The Politics of Race and Ethnicity in the United States*, puts it, multiculturalism in the United States denotes "a plurality of cultures" that are essentialized and static (2010, p. 95).

Funkadesi's multiculturalism is important because it is through recognition of both similarities and differences in the social structure that multicultural identity is defined rather than through merely the playing of Indian instruments or singing the blues. In this way, the choices Funkadesi makes as a band reflect a desire to create multiracial unity through the acknowledgement of similarities and differences between groups rather than through ideas of "cultural essence" of any one particular group. Rather than thinking of ethnic groups through a prism of cultural differences, Funkadesi cares about how groups relate to each other through political interests of community building and antiracist agendas. In this way, Funkadesi is able to foreground the idea that racial groups share cultural similarities but also have historical material differences that may structure their understanding of the world. This is where "strategic syncretism," a concept recently advanced by Christopher Jaffrelot's "Hindu Nationalism: Strategic Syncretism in Ideology Building," becomes important.

The term *strategic syncretism* captures a way to think about the type of multiculturalism that Funkadesi employs because the band strategically chooses selective politicized cultural forms in their project of creating a multiracial unity.[4] By this, I mean that the choice to intermix cultural forms such as funk and desi music is not merely an aesthetic choice based on the sounds of musical styles but also is a way to create an understanding between African American and South Asian Americans. As I listen to Funkadesi's music, I am reminded of the misrecognition and misperceptions that these groups have of each other but also of why solidarity between these groups is important. Rather than allowing capitalism to pit racialized ethnic groups against each other, this band allows for the creation of common interests that do not elide differences. This is what needs to be taken seriously for group harmony (musical and political) to exist.

An example of their critically syncretic approach to culture was seen at their performance at the 2005 Dance Chicago event. At this festival, dance troupes presented examples of tango, tap, kathak, modern western, bharatnatyam, West African, and other styles, all on the same program but not relating to one another. Tamara Roberts reviews this event in her dissertation, *Musicking at the Crossroads*. She notes that Dance Chicago erected multicultural barriers around performance by featuring what were seen as "authentic" versions of dance from various countries (Roberts, 2009, pp. 135–136). Therefore, kathak comes to symbolize all of India when there are multitudes of Indian dance forms. In this way, the type of multiculturalism employed in the festival may be thought of as gesturing toward cultural essentialism in that particular aesthetic forms come to represent all of a nation's culture. Funkadesi's performance at the festival, however, moved beyond isolated aesthetic forms. They integrated musical genres to make a statement about the intermixing and connectedness of cultures and groups. In between dance segments at Dance Chicago, Funkadesi played a primarily improvised piece that built upon a musical tradition associated with the dance form, but then layered on other pieces from various musical traditions. For example, after the tango piece, Cornier began to play the cajon, traditionally used to accompany the dance. The rest of the band then improvised around Cornier's playing of Latin music. For Funkadesi, each cultural form was not seen as a discrete and "authentic" version of national cultures, but they, in fact, disrupted the idea of cultural essence of a group embodied in a musical form by playing various musical forms in a dynamic relation to each other. At Dance Chicago, Funkadesi was countering the very idea of cultural essentialism by recognizing that identity—especially musical identity—is a composite of cultural influences. Barack Obama's statement that "There's a lot of funk in that desi" nicely illustrates that Funkadesi is strategically choosing to highlight multiracial affiliations in a way that does not essentialize identity. By saying that desis have funk, Obama implies that there is a commonality among African American musical forms and South Asian music, thereby implying a shared agenda among these two groups as well.

On the band's website is the following statement:

> Funkadesi proudly hails from Chicago, representing the diverse multi-ethnic communities within the city. What distinguishes Funkadesi as a group is each band member's unique and uncompromised cultural/musical contribution merging to create one unifying sound and vision.

Yet critics may argue with my premise that Funkadesi offers a type of multiculturalism that is any different than the multiculturalism that fails to understand the actual differences between groups. In trying to create unity, does it elide important differences between members? Some of Funkadesi's cultural display could lead one to making this conclusion. However, on Funkadesi's CD *Uncut Roots*, the phrase "One family, many children" appears next to a map in which the geographical imagination is reworked so that India is a part of Africa. How may we think about this as a strategic choice? The phrase evokes the idea of cultural pluralism, which is to say that all cultures are represented as equal members of a community. Critics of cultural pluralism have noted that this type of equality is mythical since our society is structured by important differences in access to resources that are often determined by race, for example.

Nevertheless, I think that embedded within this idea of cultural pluralism are some ideas that need to be unpacked. Why does Funkadesi present a mapping of the world that does not include North America, especially since the band is situated in North America? Contradicting the idea of the family as a hierarchical and patriarchal unit of organization, the geographical mapping attests to power relations in a way that foregrounds reshaping the relationship between non–Western cultures, here Africa and India. These are two locations that have many circuits of cultural exchange and migration. Though Whiteness is not mentioned in Funkadesi's performances, it becomes clear at one of their concerts that it is not their interest to foreground Whiteness but to put non–Western cultural formations in a relation to each other. An example of this is when they routinely speak to each other during the shows about the musical forms they are employing with little translation for the audience. This is because they want to create unity among groups that may be obscured when Whiteness remains the norm. Too often, the focus of multiculturalism remains explaining non–Western cultures to White audiences rather than creating a space for unity among non–White people. In this regard, it is interesting that the band chooses to strategically highlight the syncretic elements of Indian and African racial unity and musical styles without referencing the United States. Ananya Chatterjea (2004) explains this dynamic of nondominant groups and their relation to Whiteness, as dominance, poignantly from her own subject position as a performer and scholar. She writes:

> I am often impatient to work through what I describe as the "great distraction of whiteness" and write from an awareness of differences marked horizontally and internally—across non-white, non-western cultures—in a way that moves us to a more complex theorization of racial and cultural difference. Most of

the time the conversations around these issues are formulated in strictly bichromatic terms: white versus the rest, a tendency that only reifies the picture and prevents vital dialogues across populations of color. It is important not to write about artists of color only reactively, only in terms of an over-arching racism where one dominant culture dictates the terms of dialogue between all cultures. Ultimately, this creates a reductive picture where the only conversation of race relations is one where the struggle is always to assert one's identity against the dominance of whiteness. Instead, I want to write from a complex location where racial and cultural differences are understood not simplistically and only vertically, but a more complex network of relationships where the commitment to a similar politics of resistance does not still demand uniformity of aesthetic or discursive formations. (p. 13)

Chatterjea helps us to see that collective resistance by nondominant groups is at the heart of cooperation between non–White performers. In this way, Funkadesi's project is not just an aesthetic one but also a political one.

Nevertheless, is there a problem with the specific metaphor of family that Funkadesi uses to define relations between the members of the group? Does this embody a cultural pluralism that presents all non–Western groups as marginally equivalent without displacing Whiteness at the center? The idea of cultural pluralism as equality between all groups may obfuscate how one minority group may have dominance over another. Tamara Roberts tends toward this argument in her dissertation when she claims that Funkadesi elides differences and disagreements in the band. Her claim is that the concerns of African American members of the group are ignored in favor of privileging South Asian musical forms and dress. Roberts assumes that unity in diversity would be created if African American cultural forms were more prominent in the band's display.

The band's founder, Rahul Sharma, disagrees with Roberts' assessment that Funkadesi devalues differences. As a band, Funkadesi is nonhierarchical in organization, which means that each band member has a voice in what gets performed or recorded. When there is disagreement, a consensus approach is used to decide what is performed, as mentioned earlier in regard to the "No Leans" song. Sharma claims that through consensus formation, the band is able to negotiate differences, both within the band and in what gets performed. The band acknowledges differences between racial groups and social classes by discussing them. While some of the South Asian members of the band are middle-class professionals in other fields besides music (medicine and education), some of the African American members are full-time musicians and depend upon the band as their sole source of income. Instead of assuming an equivalent status among band members, the group constantly comes together to discuss such differences, especially in regard to the distribution of income among band members. Instead of assuming that all band members have a shared opinion on any matter and that unity exists based on their similarities, unity is created out of an understanding of all kinds of racial, gender, and class differences that form the group. Funkadesi realizes that it is differences in experiences pertaining to discrimination, for example, that define their experiences as a group rather than a perceived equivalence of resources and opinions.

By specifically analyzing Funkadesi's lyrics, which appear on their liner notes on their CD *Yo Baba*, I'd like to further elaborate how they represent a type of multiculturalism that puts minority racial relations at the center and calls for unity based on understanding differences. On the song "Galsun," which means "Listen up" in Punjabi, Funkadesi brought in the rapper Anacron to sing along with the members of the band. The song begins with a female voice (Navraz Basati) singing in Punjabi. I have translated the Punjabi lyrics into English (they appear in italics below), and the English lyrics are taken from Funkadesi's liner notes:

Galsun

If you are going far, don't forget the earth

Where you played day and night, lovely one

Earning fame and respect for your nation,

You will return for your mother's blessings.

After Basati sings in Punjabi, Anacron, a contributor to this song, raps in English:

Everywhere I go, everywhere I been

L.A., that's my native homeland where I planted my soul

And became a grown man

I'm a Californian from the surf to the sand

Inserted when I can no matter what turf I stand

The birth of a man isn't purely physical

See, I was born again when I moved to Cali from the east

Yea, though I walked through the valley of the beast

I stalked late nights dodging mallies and police

And learned so much with my pallies on the streets

And we rallied for beliefs that were burned so deep

Torn between the teachings of my parents and experience

Apparently developed myriads of contradiction

Clearly it was time to embark on a mission

Traverse the globe until my vision came to fruition

No matter how far I branch out I'm a stand out, hand out

Fingers panned out to a dove.

In rap and hip-hop music, the personal is often political, meaning that performers often take a stand against oppressive conditions that are the symptom of American racism. Anacron's phrase "dodging police" alludes to the criminalization of African American men. He foregrounds points of communal resistance to getting in trouble by rallying for "beliefs that were burned so deep." The narrative Anacron constructs is not just a personal reflection but also a critique of American racism in which a disproportionate number of Black men have been criminalized in the United States. In this sense, Anacron's lyrics can be read also as offering a critique of the criminal justice system for disproportionally punishing African American men and curtailing the hopes and dreams of African American families. That this is a form of structural racism is reflected in Bruce Western's book *Punishment and Inequality* (2006). In the book, he cites that Blacks have been more likely than Whites to go to prison, at least since the 1920s. "Southern prisons operated quite transparently as instruments of racial domination, using forced labor to farm cotton and build roads" (p. 3). He argues that there is little evidence to link the post–1970 prison boom in the United States to shifts in crime. Rather, his argument is that prisons mediate race and class relations in a way that unjustly affects African American young men. He writes:

> . . . the prison boom was a political project that arose partly because of rising crime but also in response to an upheaval in American race relations in the 1960's and the collapse of urban labor markets for unskilled men in the 1970's. The social activism of the 1960's fueled the anxieties and resentments of working-class whites. These disaffected whites turned increasingly to the Republican Party through the 1970's and 1980's, drawn by a law and order message that drew veiled connections between civil rights activism and violent crime among blacks in inner cities. Incarceration rates grew most in states that elected Republican governors and adopted punitive regimes of criminal sentencing. (Western, 2006, pp. 5–6)

Although Anacron does not spell out these connections in his lyrics, the situation of disproportionate incarceration is one that is familiar to young

Black men. Anacron offers performance itself as a point of resistance. He notes his musical success as a vehicle to achieve social justice, presumably by educating people about the injustices of the criminal justice system and its criminalization of African American men.

In theorizing the relationship of Asian and African diasporic populations, Paul Gilroy (1993), in *The Black Atlantic*, has shown that these populations have both struggled to make a home in the United States while simultaneously trying to understand their relationship to Asian and African identities. The line "a friend from home and abroad," the English translation from Punjabi, which Inderpaul Singh, another singer in the band, sings to Anacron, signifies the position South Asians, for example, occupy in relation to the United States as both insiders and outsiders. Blacks and Asians, even though they were born in the United States, for the most part, because they are non–Whites, are not allowed to claim their Americanness. In other words, given that "'American = white,' nonwhites are always viewed as different, as aliens and therefore not Americans" (Pinder, 2010, p. 70).

Given that America is considered White, members of the band, because they are racialized, are looked on as foreign and exotic. They are excluded from dominant cultural representations of Americanness. For members of racialized ethnic groups, including Asian Americans and African Americans, America's history of enslaving Blacks and exploiting South Asians as farm laborers has impacted them in important ways. I do not mean to suggest that the enslavement of African Americans was similar to the exploitation of South Asians as farm laborers in the 19th-century United States. We are familiar with the harsh and inhumane treatment of Blacks under slavery. What I am suggesting, however, is that both groups have been and continue to be subjected to America's racism. Therefore, the history of racism bonds these groups into a shared fight for antiracist causes. In this way, the song evokes the idea that a feeling of marginalization in not being able to claim the United States as a home may also be mobilizing in creating a shared sense of identity and purpose for both Asian Americans and African Americans.

Racial politics are present not only in Funkadesi's music but also in the social spaces their performances engender. The relationship between space and sound is important to understanding Funkadesi's music. Although they do sell CDs at their shows, they have primarily remained a performance band. Tamara Roberts, in *Musicking at the Crossroads*, has noted that Funkadesi's audiences defy the segregated logic of the Chicago music scene, constructing an embodiment of multiracial spaces. "In the diverse yet segregated city of Chicago, their shows foster temporarily un-segregated spaces" (2009, p. 139). By foregrounding mostly non–Western styles of music and group members, Whiteness is displaced in these spaces. Being in a space in which different minority groups come together to experience multicultural music highlights the different and yet shared experiences of minority groups in the United States.

Racial politics are also embedded in the types of music Funkadesi plays. Funkadesi draws musical influences from British bhangra music. Bhangra grew specifically out of resistant and antiassimilationist racial formations in Britain where Asian and Afro-Caribbean people identified with each other as former colonized populations and worked together in antiracist causes. Out of this political collaboration, musical forms like bhangra—originally a traditional folk musical and dance form in Punjab, India—evolved in Britain by mixing Caribbean music and hip-hop with traditional Punjabi lyrics. Sanjay Sharma and colleagues (1996) importantly pointed out, in *Dis-Orienting Rhythms*, that British bhangra, or the form that became popular all over the world starting in the 1980s, was a confluence of this shared musical and political identity. South Asians and Afro-Caribbeans referred to themselves as Black to signify their shared histories as formerly colonized populations who are outside the construct of Britishness, which is defined by Whiteness, and work to exclude non–Whites from Britishness (Sharma, p. 38). Like in Britain, Whiteness determines and continues to determine America's cultural identity, having implications for those who are marked by cultural otherness. Funkadesi often falls into a generic category of world music that lumps all global sounds into a marketable category of otherness. Sanjay Sharma argues in *Dis-Orienting Rhythms* that market differentiation between "Black music" such as hip-hop and world music is an attempt to bifurcate the dominant culture from the nondominant cultures (Sharma, p. 38). British bhangra, which is a part of Funkadesi's music, adds to making Funkadesi's music a diverse form of music. Iain Chambers also makes this point well in *Migrancy, Culture, Identity*:

> This would be to propose that the sounds of "World Music" function not as a stereotypical "other" that confirms and closes the circle of ethnocentric iden-tification: exotic embellishments requested for refurbishing the rock track. It would be to suggest that such sounds also offer a space for musical and cul-tural differences to emerge in such a manner that any obvious identification with the hegemonic order, assumed monolithic market logic, is weakened and disrupted by the shifting, contingent contacts of musical and cultural encoun-ters. This represents the instance of a musical and cultural conversation in which the margins are able to reassess the centre while simultaneously exceed-ing its logic. (Chambers, 1994, p. 79)

One is left asking questions of Funkadesi such as "Are you rap? Are you bhangra? Or are you world music?" These questions are indicative of structural issues around how nondominant groups are marketed within strictly defined categories or else generally lumped into popular music. The difficulties that Funkadesi present for market categorization are also what provide them with a radical outlook on music and multiculturalism. By decentering Whiteness and foregrounding racial unity among minorities, their music and ethos provide a template to consider the future of multiculturalism.

Conclusion

In closing, I'd like to mention a few things I have learned in writing this chapter about multicultural music and what this may suggest about the field of multicultural studies. First, I see an important and fruitful link between cultural and political formations. That is to say that aesthetics cannot be divorced from political understandings of culture. Funkadesi as a band has to be understood not just as making aesthetic choices to join various minority musical styles in performance but also as making strategic political choices in the music they perform and the social relations they engender. A mere stylistic fusion of multicultural "otherness" is not what they strive for; rather, by strategically choosing some musical styles and lyrics over others, they create musical and political harmony.

In investigating the categories of cultural essentialism, and pluralism, I have learned that multiculturalism is full of pitfalls in this regard. Some multicultural displays have a tendency to essentialize identity and flatten out differences between groups. The multicultural music of Funkadesi, however, is able to de-essentialize cultural authenticity in promoting more fluid notions of group identity based on historical and political circumstances. Also, the members of the band are able to create a unity in diversity that challenges the equivalence between groups that cultural pluralism gestures toward. By strategically choosing lyrics that promote antiracist agendas, Funkadesi offers a strategic notion of multiculturalism that is instructive for American multicultural studies.

References

Apter, A. (1991, Winter.) Herskovits's heritage: Rethinking syncretism in the African Diaspora. *Diaspora, 1*(3), 235.

Chambers, I. (1994). *Migrancy, culture, identity.* London: Routledge.

Chatterjea, A. (2004). *Butting out: Resistive choreographies through works by Jawole Willa Jo Zollar and Chadralekha.* Middletown: Wesleyan University Press.

Davis, A. (1996). Gender, class and multiculturalism: Rethinking race politics. In Avery Gordon and Christopher Newfield (Eds.), *Mapping multiculturalism* (pp. 40–48). Minneapolis: University of Minnesota Press.

Gilroy, P. (1993). *The Black Atlantic: Modernity and double consciousness.* London: Verso.

Jaffrelot, C. (1993, March). Hindu nationalism: Strategic syncretism in ideology building. *Economic and Political Weekly* 28, no 12/13, 517–524.

Matory, J. L. (2005). *Black Atlantic religion.* Princeton, NJ: Princeton University Press.

Pinder, S. O. (2010). *The politics of race and ethnicity in the United States: Americanization, de-Americanization, and racialized ethnic groups.* New York: Palgrave Macmillan.

Roberts, T. (2009). *Musicking at the crossroads of diaspora: Afro Asian musical politics* (Dissertation). Northwestern University.

Sharma, S. (2006). *Multicultural encounters.* New York: Palgrave-Macmillan.

Sharma, S., Hytynyk, J., & Sharma, A., Eds. (1996). *Dis-orienting rhythms: The politics of new Asian dance music.* London: Zed Books.

Western, B. (2006). *Punishment and inequality.* New York: Russel Sage Foundation.

Notes

1. I'd like to thank several friends and colleagues for providing insights and comments on this essay: Roderick Ferguson, Ananya Chatterjea, Jigna Desai, Catherine Becker, and John D'Emilio. Their own amazing scholarship has inspired me to think through the ideas presented here. I thank Rahul Sharma of Funkadesi, for providing information on the band, and Tamara Roberts, whose work on Funkadesi was influential.

2. This quote appears on Funkadesi's website, http://www.funkadesi.com/. This statement was made by Barack Obama when he was an Illinois state senator in Chicago before he became president of the United States. The band proudly displays Obama's statement on its website and supported him throughout his campaign to become president.

3. Calling someone an ABCD is often meant to be hurtful and is taken as such. In the midst of figuring out which cultural forms young South Asians want to iden-tify with, this critique registers as an indictment with experimentation in the name of cultural "authenticity." This authenticity is, however, a constructed notion itself and based on selective understandings of traditions. I would add that the label ABCD carries gendered expectations that are different for young men and women, as women are more often seen as "bearers of culture" and, therefore, gendered issues of authenticity attach more severely to young girls. Nevertheless, the term is used to police "proper desi" masculine and feminine identities. It is no wonder that many countered with alternative terms of positive valence for the acronym ABCD such as American-Born Cool Desi or American-Born Confident Desi. This is a way

of reclaiming that space that was being made abject by essentialist arguments about what it meant to be desi.

4. I'd like to discuss my understanding of the term *syncretism*'s genealogy in African diaspora studies. Melville Herskovits used the term *syncretism* and defined it as an attempt to reconcile disparate or contrary beliefs while melding practices of various schools of thought. Herskovits understood syncretism as a blending of two distinct traditions into a hybrid form. The term literally means "growing together." Herskovits's research question was "What is 'African' in the African Diaspora?" This question presumed a static and fixed notion of Africa that would be present in the diaspora. Recent scholars of African diasporic studies have reanimated the concept of syncretism, however, differently than the static assumptions about culture that Herskovits held. Andrew Apter reframes Herskovits's question toward thinking about syncretism as a cultural strategy imbued with agency rather than as a static cultural form (Apter, 1991, p. 235). In a similar way, J. Lorand Matory's interest is in considering the transnational processes that have constantly informed the meanings of African diasporic cultural forms. He animates Herskovits's paradigm of syncretism to examine the more encompassing geographical frames, political hierarchies, and networks of long-distance communication that have long made it impossible for cultures to reproduce themselves within the closure of a bounded, self-defining set of meanings (Matory, 2005, pp. 267–294).

3

In-Between Languages

Translingual Living and Writing in the United States

Paola Bohórquez

The question of language affiliation—the identification with and attachment to a particular language independently of expertise and inheritance (Rampton, 1990)—is central to the ways in which translingual individuals and communities define their national, cultural, and ethnic identities. In migrant and multicultural contexts, language becomes invested with complex and often contradictory valences and significations that reveal the arbitrary character of the traditional identification of language with nation and common ethnicity. As deterritorialized languages become inflected with racial, class, and gendered connotations, migrant and diasporic subjects experience language choice as a process fraught with ambivalence. Whether one's mother tongue is reinforced, maintained side by side with a borrowed tongue, or eventually abandoned, the question of language affiliation always involves a redefinition of self, of one's relationship to history and tradition, and to personal memory.

The place of language among the various markers of ethnic and cultural identity can be further specified by considering that language "is above all a means of cultural construction in which our very selves and sense are constituted" (Chambers, 2001, p. 22). In other words, language is not merely a cultural object but the vehicle through which we articulate our own embeddedness in culture. Culture "is an essential part of who we are as human beings because it shapes the ways we give meaning to our world" (Pinder, 2010, p. 4). From this perspective, the question of language affiliation acquires ethical and political significance insofar as the power to define, appropriate, or resist categories of cultural definition depends on one's access to the dominant language and its epistemic authority.

Furthermore, issues of language affiliation cannot be thought of independently of the historicity of the subject's linguistic attachments insofar as they represent the plurality of object relations through which the subject comes into being. From the infant's babble reflected by the mother's voice to the adult's belonging within various "speech communities,"[1] these contexts and relations configure the subject's linguistic identity and provide her with the symbolic resources that sustain her self-intelligibility. For migrants and other minorities who have undergone experiences of linguistic displacement, the term *mother tongue* simultaneously denotes the subject's most contiguous possession and emblem of an imagined community, thus merging one's most private voice with a sense of cultural belonging. This double status of language as "the most intimate and the most shared thing we have" (Derrida & Dufourmantelle, 2000, p. 84) suggests that in order to account for the vicissitudes of linguistic identification, we need to address not only the individual's subject position—that is, the set of positive determinants that defines our location in a particular sociocultural setting—but also the subject's strategies of investment, complicity, and resistance to such totalizing inscriptions. In considering how the subject is *positioned, affected,* and *effected* by the translingual experience, the notion of language affiliation reveals itself as a complex and unstable relation with incommensurable languages that represent different and often conflicting psychic investments, bodily and gendered dispositions, ethical imperatives, and cultural configurations.

Within the larger transitional and translational phenomena characteristic of multicultural and cross-cultural arrangements, the question of linguistic affiliation is further complicated by the fiction of the permanence of language in displacement. In *Of Hospitality*, Jacques Derrida and Anne Dufourmantelle (2000) observe that:

> the mother tongue isn't only the home that resists, the ipseity of the self set up as a force of resistance, as a counter-force against these dislocations. Language resists all mobilities because it moves about with me. It is the least immovable thing, the most mobile of personal bodies, which remains the stable but portable condition of all mobilities. (p. 91)

The designation of the idea of permanence as a "fiction" should not deter us from examining it closely, as it is this and other sedimented fantasies that structure our private and collective relations to language in our increasingly diverse and fluctuating sociocultural landscapes. Rather than deconstructing this fiction, I am interested in interrogating both its function in structuring the experience of linguistic displacement and its implications for our understanding of the status of language in multicultural contexts. If, as Derrida and Dufourmantelle (2000) argue, the experience of displacement renews our imaginary bonds with language by endowing it with the promises of self-continuity and cultural survival, we need to consider the theoretical and ethical implications of acknowledging the constitutive power of such fantasy.

As outlined above, language constitutes a medium of cultural identification, placeholder of historically constituted attachments, and signifier of permanence in displacement. In articulating these dimensions, the experience of linguistic in-betweenness reveals its specificity among the myriad transitional phenomena that characterize the cross-cultural experience of migrant and diasporic subjects. It is in this context, therefore, that I examine the experience of linguistic displacement and propose a conceptual framework to understand the process of translingual subject formation. My use of the term *translingualism*[2] is meant to convey the transitional and translational character of the condition of linguistic in-betweenness. It is a heuristic concept that illuminates the process of *coming to terms in resistance* with "the more than one/no longer one" language (Derrida, 1994, p. xx), that is, with the problem of linguistic multiplicity and the loss of the all-encompassing and auratic quality of the mother tongue. Rather than invoking a merely cognitive process of language appropriation, I am interested in theorizing the translingual condition as an existential inscription within and between languages and the sociocultural universes they embody. In shifting my focus away from questions of linguistic proficiency or expertise, which are embedded in the categories of bilingualism and multilingualism, I am able to consider a wide variety of linguistic choices—abandoned, dormant, reinforced, adversarial, or coexisting languages—that constitute various ways of coming to terms with the predicament of linguistic multiplicity and represent the subject's affective investments in and detachments from her languages.

To reflect on the translingual condition through the medium of multicultural Anglophone literature in the United States implies taking into account the status of English as a national, literary, and global language. Despite the lack of a national language policy in the United States, the English Language Empowerment Act enacted in 1996 allows states to endorse English as the official language. Twenty-six states have already undergone the English-only initiative. Historically, and predicated on the eradication of the ancestral languages of indigenous groups and African slaves, English monolingualism has been the systematic yet covert linguistic policy since the foundation of the American nation. As John Trimbur (2006) argues, current American ambivalence toward multilingualism finds its roots in the myth of a pure Anglo-Saxon heritage and the concomitant disavowal of the multilingual foundation of the nation and its systematic eradication. Multilingualism is perceived as un-American even for Anglo Americans and the shift to English only, which de facto occurs in immigrant families by the third generation (Veltman, 1983), is ideologically coded as a natural process of assimilation into an American way of life. Deeply intertwined in the American history of exclusions of ethnic "others," English monolingualism marks the desired trajectory of citizenship and, less explicitly, class mobility and ethnic disaffiliation. The Mexican American author Richard Rodriguez is a case in point. As his memoir *Hunger of Memory: The Education of Richard Rodriguez* (1983) illustrates, Rodriguez's transformation into a fully assimilated middle-class American man is predicated upon his rejection of Spanish as the language that represents his parents' immigrant identity, his Mexican inheritance, and the dark skin that he equates with poverty and social disadvantage. Framed within the either-or logic characteristic of migrant acculturation, Rodriguez's story of Americanization is the story of his systematic erasure of the cultural markers that are incompatible with the ideal of what it means to be a legitimate member of the American nation.

The gradual opening up of the American literature canon to minority, immigrant, and diasporic voices has meant the restoration of forgotten, repressed, and displaced (hi)stories to the national literary consciousness. In addition, and in the context of the 1980s cultural turn in global studies, multicultural literature has become the privileged site of knowledge production about the vicissitudes and intricacies of postnational, hybrid, and diasporic cultural formations. Nevertheless, it has proven to be much more difficult to problematize the nature of the American canon within which multicultural literature remains conveniently marginalized. Toni Morrison's (1992) *Playing in the Dark: Whiteness and the Literary Imagination* shows how American literature has been oblivious to people of color and carefully safeguarded Whites' viewpoints, especially those of White men (p. 5). It is in this context that Morrison (1989) has proposed "an examination and reinterpretation of the American canon, the founding nineteenth century works, for the 'unspeakable things unspoken'; for the ways in which the presence of African Americans has shaped the choices, the language, the structure—the meaning of so much American literature" (p. 11). Morrison's proposal to unearth the disavowed presence of the racialized "other" within the canon suggests that multicultural literatures must engage critically with the politics of cultural production, reception, and representation that shape their own positionality. In this sense, we need to problematize the prevailing representations of ethnicity that emerge and circulate within multicultural literature and literary criticism, the editorial choices and strategies through which these literatures are positioned vis-à-vis the American canon, and, finally, the political conditions that shape the reception and consumption of these texts within mainstream literary markets.

English monolingualism remains the implicit yet hegemonic grounds of American literary production and critical reception. Marc Shell and Werner Sollors' 2000 publication of *The Multilingual Anthology of American Literature,* which includes multilingual texts ranging from the 17th to the late 20th century, poignantly highlights the lack of circulation of non–Anglophone multicultural writing in mainstream publishing as well as its non-place in the definition of American literature. It is this regime of literary monolingualism that determines the hegemony of English in American translingual writing and the problematic absence of studies on non–Anglophone literature in the field of multicultural literary theory and criticism.

In addressing the status of English as global language, we need to take into consideration that:

> While English as such does not necessarily convey an imperial or colonizing valence, its embeddedness within various pedagogical and disciplinary regimes of subjugation (whether these relate to colonization, imperialism, or migration) and its attachments to a tradition of English studies mean that it cannot function neutrally as a worldwide lingua franca. (Gunew, 2001, p. 730)

The global spread of "American English" as the language of communication technologies, American transnational corporations, and international language of instruction means that the process of English acquisition for migrant and postcolonial subjects is not simply predicated on a vertical relation with the American state but also configured in the horizontal relation of heterogeneous transnational ties and affiliations. These relations impose further burdens but may also allow for certain "degrees of freedom" given the necessarily contingent and conflicting valences of English(es) that emerge in the interstices among institutional, economic, and pedagogical practices, both locally and globally.

Against the backdrop of the national, literary, and global hegemony of English monolingualism, migrant and diasporic English language acquisition reveals itself as an ambivalent process of investment, complicity, and resistance to the demand for cultural and linguistic assimilation. How, then, do the constitutive determinants of linguistic hegemony and standardization shape the process of translingual subject formation? This is the question I address in the next section.

The Experience of Linguistic Exile

Several recent works in the field of American multicultural studies[3] examine the implications of large-scale transformations of our linguistic landscape on the way in which subjects experience the embodiment, imposition, acquisition, and loss of languages. These works have turned to contemporary ethnic American writings, such as Gloria Anzaldúa's (1990) *Borderlands/La Frontera: The New Mestiza*, Maxine Hong Kingston's (1977) *The Woman Warrior: Memoirs of a Girlhood Among Ghosts*, and A. J. Verdelle's (1996) *The Good Negress*, to shed light on the complex relation between dis/placement and identity and to elucidate the ways in which new forms of subjectivity emerge through practices of intercultural translation. Although issues of language and linguistic identity figure prominently in the wide spectrum of ethnic American literature, there exists a distinct genre of autobiographical writing that focuses on the complexities of further language acquisition and its effects on one's sense of identity and cultural belonging. This form of cross-cultural self-writing, which Alice Kaplan (1994) has identified under the rubric of "the language memoir" (p. 59), provides us with a unique view on the complex trajectory of translingual subject formation in migrant and diasporic contexts. In grappling with the questions of who is the "I" that speaks in translingual self-narration and how this "I" testifies to experiences lived in another language, these narratives reveal that both subjectivity and textuality are traversed by the problem of language choice in the representation of the translingual life. As the cleavages between first and second language, monolingual and translingual, narrated and narrating selves are simultaneously thematized and performed, the tacit assumption of the continuity between language and identity is brought to the fore as the unstable ground of self-enunciation. It is this particular imbrication of narrative, language, and subjectivity that positions the language memoir as the *via regia* to the understanding of the translingual condition. Because neither the "self" who writes nor the language that sustains memory and narrative can be taken for granted, the language memoir re-enacts the very crisis of signification that a life between languages entails. Here, the experiential and textual processes of self-rewriting overlap, producing *a self that writes a text that writes a self*.

I would argue that the genre of the language memoir articulates itself around two questions: What is at stake for the self in appropriating a foreign language? And what does it mean to configure a translingual self? The first question directs us toward the experience of linguistic exile, to the fate of the former monolingual self who finds herself outside of language, made powerless by her inability to speak, in short, toward the psychic cost of inarticulateness. The second question addresses the problem of self-translation, that is, the psychic, cultural, and ethical challenges entailed in the constitution of a self positioned between languages.

The concept of "linguistic exile" denotes the experience of "dislocation of one's linguistic identity effected by the process of further language acquisition" (Bohórquez, 2009a, p. 158). Positioned between the language of "there and then," which turns enigmatic in losing its power to denote, name, and signify, and the language of "here and now," which remains indecipherable as long as one fails to grasp its internal coherence, the translingual subject loses her grounding within the socio-symbolic coordinates that secure one's self-intelligibility. As Eva Hoffman, Luc Sante, and Ariel Dorfman illustrate, this crisis of signification is experienced as "a loss of language":

Eva Hoffman (1999) writes:

> For a while, like so many immigrants, I was in effect without language, and from the bleakness of that condition, I understood how much our inner existence, our sense of self depends on having a living speech within us. To lose an internal language is to subside into an inarticulate darkness in which we become alien to ourselves; to lose the ability to describe the world is to render that world a bit less vivid, a bit less lucid. (p. 48)

Luc Sante (1999) points out:

> Instead French festers. It is kept in darkness and fed meagrely by spoonfuls. It isn't purposely neglected, of course, there is nothing intentionally punitive about the way it is sequestered and undernourished. On the contrary: it is cherished, cosseted, rewarded for just being, like an animal in a zoo. But like that animal it can only enact a semblance of its natural existence. Its memory of the native habitat grows sparser all the time, and its attempts at normality become playacting, become parody, become rote. Its growth has been stunted, and it correspondingly retains many infantile characteristics. Even as the boy grows gradually tougher and more worldly in English, he carries around a French internal life whose clock has stopped. (p. 264)

Ariel Dorfman (1998) explains:

> But the stone of my past became smoother and more enigmatic the more I fingered it. The harder I tried to access those children who occupied my body, see through their dual eyes what they saw, the further I drifted from what they

witnessed that day. One of them, the child inside who speaks Spanish, will not respond, because I left him to die in the dark, atrophied the language with which he might have transmitted these memories to me; and the other child, the one who speaks English, he was present of course, but he was swept that moment from the fierce abscess of his mind, preferring to pretend that his start with me was painless and splendid and immaculate, that when he caught me as I fell I had no previous language. (p. 43)

The testimonies of these authors make apparent that the experience of language loss does not necessarily convey a decreased use of a particular language or the attenuation of the ties to one's language of origin. Rather, and despite their different trajectories of displacement,[4] their translingual makeup and relation to English as their adopted language, the trope of loss remains as a powerful narrative organizer even when the mother tongue is not lost in its communicative or representational dimensions. This thematic recurrence suggests that what is at stake in conditions of linguistic displacement is the destiny of the subject's dependence on language as symbolic horizon of signification. As these testimonies powerfully articulate, an unrooted language is simultaneously lost and overly present, a disorienting absence and an impassable presence. Through this paradox, we can discern the particular topology of language as "ex-timate object"[5]: both proper and foreign, both inside and radically outside of the subject.

Articulated around the crisis of signification produced by the encounter with a foreign language, the experience of linguistic exile is governed by an economy of loss and a retrospective temporality that anchors ontological certainty in the "there and then." As I have argued elsewhere[6], the experience of linguistic exile condenses two simultaneous and interrelated processes: the retroactive constitution of the mother tongue as a memorial for a lost way of "being-in-the-world" (Heidegger, 1996, p. 49) and the loss of the monolingual to the translingual self. Having lost the everyday life context that animates one's language, the subject in linguistic transition replaces her sense of cultural and linguistic embeddedness with an attachment to the mother tongue: an auratic object that comes to represent one's lost symbolic grounding, inalienable possession, and medium of authentic self-expression. Here, the mother tongue emerges as a paradoxical object. For if the "language of there and then" functions as an anchoring point that shelters the subject from semiotic disorientation, its very existence is, nonetheless, a reminder of one's estrangement, a surrogate object that can only connote and insinuate without ever replacing the subject's lost dwelling in language. In the inevitably failed gesture of holding on to the mother tongue as the remnant of displacement, the subject encounters the otherness of language, its impossible appropriation.

with "the more than one/no longer one" language (Derrida, 1994, p. xx) is a process fraught with resistance, as the subject in linguistic transition attempts to bypass the impossibility of a translation without remainder.

The process of working through the structural losses that allow for playful dwelling between languages is hindered by regimes of monolingual hegemony that "demand full assimilation and don't allow it" (Sommer, 2004, p. 8). As Homi Bhabha elucidates, the demand for assimilation is typically structured as an ambivalent interpellation that compels the subject to appropriate dominant cultural ideals while retaining a recognizable difference. The injunction to assimilate assumes then the contradictory form of "Be like me," "Don't be like me" that inevitably produces "its slippage, its excess, its difference" (Bhabha, 1994, p. 122). Faced with an impossible interpellation that further exacerbates the conflict between languages, translingual subjects engage in a struggle between consent and rejection that typically takes the form of a melancholic monolingualism in which one language is eventually sacrificed to the other. Under these conditions, the process of further language acquisition produces symptomatic translingual configurations that range from recalcitrant enclavism in one's language of origin to furious conversion into English.

In Hoffman's (1990), Sante's (1999), and Dorfman's (1998) language memoirs, the process of articulating a self between languages configures a wounded self-narration that testifies to the suffering entailed in working through the disjunction between experience and text, substance and speech, and life-story and life-narrative. Hoffman's (1990) nostalgia amidst a too-successful self-translation into English, Sante's (1999) self-translation in complicity with the gendered ideology of self-refashioning, and Dorfman's (1998) portrayal of his agonistic translingualism as a "lone hero's quest" constitute some examples of the symptomatic resolution of the psychic, ethical, and cultural tensions that configure a life between languages. Despite their sustained and nuanced awareness of their translingual trajectory, Hoffman's (1990) and Sante's (1999) unidirectional process of self-translation ultimately reveals the ascendancy of English over the vestiges of primary languages buried under multiple layers of an English life that cannot be "translated backwards" (Hoffman, 1990, p. 184). On the other hand, and although Dorfman's (1998) peculiar trajectory of displacement might appear sufficient to explain his bidirectional self-translation, I would argue that the survival of his Spanish in both life and text suggests that a displaced language can only subsist as *a structure of address,* that is, as a language that contains more than the echo of one's vanishing voice, a language therefore, through which one can address and be addressed by real and imagined communities in transit. What we need, in Bhabha's (1990) words, "is a tribe of interpreters of such metaphors—the translators of the dissemination of texts and discourses across cultures—who can perform what Said describes as the act of secular interpretation" (p. 293). In the face of the assimilatory pressures of American cultural politics and the strict imposition of Anglo monolingualism, it remains to be seen whether playing "bilingual games" (Sommer, 2004, p. xi) can become a viable and visible cultural practice through which to overcome our symbolic and imaginary investment in the homohegemonic dominance of English.

References

Anzaldúa, G. (1990). *Borderland/la frontera: The new mestiza*. San Francisco: Aunt Lute Books.

Bhabha, H. K. (1990). DissemiNation. In Homi Bhabha (Ed.), *Nation and narration* (pp. 291–321). London: Routledge.

Bhabha, H. K. (1994). *The location of culture*. New York: Routledge.

Bohórquez, P. (2009a). Dwelling in the mother tongue: The status of language in displacement. In Matt Hackler and Ari Adipurwawidjana (Eds.), *On and off the page: Mapping place in text and culture* (pp. 243–266). New Castle: Cambridge Scholars Publishing.

Bohórquez, P. (2009b). Psychic and ethical dimensions of language loss. *Journal of Intercultural Studies, 30*(2), 157–172.

Chambers, I. (2001). *Migrancy, culture, identity*. London: Routledge.

Derrida, J. (1994). *Specters of Marx: The state of the debt, the work of mourning and the new international*. Trans. Peggy Kamuf. New York: Routledge, 1994.

Derrida, J., & Dufourmantelle, A. (2000). *Of hospitality*. Trans. Rachel Bowlby. Stanford, CA: Stanford University Press.

Doane, M. A. (1980). The voice in the cinema: The articulation of body and space. *Yale French Studies, 60*, 33–50.

Dorfman, A. (1998). *Heading south, looking north: A bilingual journey*. New York: Farrar, Straus, and Giroux.

Dorfman, A. (2004). Footnotes to a double life. In Wendy Lesser (Ed.), *The genius of language: Fifteen writers reflect on their mother tongues* (pp. 206–217). New York: Pantheon Books.

Gunew, S. (2001). Technologies of the self: Corporeal affects of English. *South Atlantic Quarterly, 100*(3), 729–747.

Heidegger, M. (1996). *Being and time*. Trans. Joan Stambaugh. Albany: State University of New York Press.

Hoffman, E. (1990). *Lost in translation: A life in a new language*. New York: Penguin Books.

Hoffman, E. (1999). The new nomads. In Andre Aciman (Ed.), *Letters of transit: Reflections on exile, identity, language, loss* (pp. 35–63). New York: New Press.

Johnson, B. (2003). *Mother tongues: Sexuality, trials, motherhood, translation*. Cambridge, MA: Harvard University Press.

Kaplan, A. (1994). On language memoir. In Angelika Bammer (Ed.), *Displacements: Cultural identities in question* (pp. 59–70). Indianapolis: Indiana University Press.

Kellman, S. G. (Ed.). (2003). *Switching languages: Translingual writers reflect on their craft.* Lincoln: University of Nebraska Press.

Kingston, M. H. (1977). *The woman warrior: Memoirs of a girlhood among ghosts.* New York: Vintage Books.

Labov, W. (1972). *Sociolinguistic patterns.* Philadelphia: University of Pennsylvania Press.

Lacan, J. (1992). *The seminar of Jacques Lacan, book 7: The ethics of psychoanalysis, 1959–1960.* Trans. Dennis Porter. New York: W. W. Norton.

Molloy, S. (2003). Bilingual scenes. In Doris Sommer (Ed.), *Bilingual games: Some literary investigations* (pp. 289–296). New York: Palgrave Macmillan.

Morrison, T. (1989). Unspeakable things unspoken: The Afro-American presence in American literature. *Michigan Quarterly Review, 28*, 1–34.

Morrison, T. (1992). *Playing the dark: Whiteness and the literary imagination.* Cambridge, MA: Harvard University Press.

Pérez-Firmat, G. (2003). *Tongue ties: Logo-eroticism in Anglo-Hispanic literature.* New York: Palgrave Macmillan.

Pinder, S. (2010). *The politics of race and ethnicity in the United States: Americanization, de-Americanization, and racialized ethnic groups.* New York: Palgrave Macmillan.

Rampton, B. (1990). Displacing the "native speaker": Expertise, affiliation and inheritance. *ELT Journal, 44*(2), 97–101.

Rodriguez, R. (1983). *Hunger of memory: The education of Richard Rodriguez.* New York: Bantam Books.

Sante, L. (1999). *The Factory of facts.* New York: Vintage Departures.

de Saussure, F. (1959). *Course in general linguistics.* New York: Philosophical Library.

Shell, M., & Sollors, W. (2000). *The multilingual anthology of American literature: A reader of original text with English translations.* New York: New York University Press.

Sommer, D. (2004). *Bilingual aesthetics: A new sentimental education.* Durham, NC: Duke University Press.

Todorov, T. (1992). Bilingualism, dialogism and schizophrenia. *New Formations, 17*, 17–25.

Trimbur, J. (2006). Linguistic memory and the politics of U.S. history. *College English, 68*(6), 575–588.

Veltman, C. (1983). *Language shift in the United States.* New York: Mouton.

Verdelle, A. J. (1996). *The good Negress.* New York: Harper.

Notes

1. "The speech community is not defined by any marked agreement in the use of language elements, so much as by participation in a set of shared norms. These norms may be observed in overt types of evaluative behavior, and by the uniformity

of abstract patterns of variation which are invariant in respect to particular levels of usage." (Labov, 1972, p. 120–121).

2. I borrow the term *translingualism* from Steven Kellman's literary study of authors "who write in more than one language, or at least, in a language other than their primary one" (2003, p. ix).

3. Some of these works include Martha J. Cutter's *Lost and Found in Translation: Contemporary Ethnic American Writing and the Politics of Language Diversity*; Azade Seyhan's *Writing Outside the Nation*; Perez-Firmat's *Tongue Ties: Logo-Eroticism in Anglo-Hispanic Literature*; Alfred Arteaga's *An Other Tongue: Nation and Ethnicity in the Linguistic Borderlines*, and Doris Sommer's *Bilingual Aesthetics: A New Sentimental Education*.

4. A child of Holocaust survivors, Eva Hoffman was born in Cracow, Poland, in 1945. In her adolescence, she migrated with her family to Canada, where she resided until moving to Texas to study English Literature at Rice University. In a similar pattern of one-way migration, Luc Sante was born in Belgium and brought by his parents to the United States at 6 years of age. Dorfman, on the other hand, followed a much more complex migratory trajectory. Born in Argentina into a first-generation migrant Eastern European Jewish family, Dorfman was brought to the United States at 3 years of age in the wake of the military government of Ramón Castillo. Nine years later, his family was forced to flee again, this time for Chile, after the communist persecution reached Dorfman's father in the United Nations. Except from 1968 to 1970, when he lived in Berkeley, California, Dorfman resided in Chile until Pinochet's coup in 1973, which forced him and his family into exile in Argentina, a temporary shelter before the threat of Perón dictatorship would return him to the States.

5. My use of the concept of extimacy or "intimate exteriority" (Lacan, 1992, p. 139) borrows from Lacan's problematization of the opposition between inside and outside.

6. For an in-depth discussion of the concept "mother tongue" and its status as retroactive construction effected by the encounter with a foreign language, see "Dwelling in the Mother Tongue: The Status of Language in Displacement" (Bohórquez, 2009a). See also "Psychic and Ethical Dimensions of Language Loss" (Bohórquez, 2009b) for a detailed examination of the structural and contextual dimensions of the experience of linguistic exile.

4

Ableist Colonizations

Reframing Disability Studies in Multicultural Studies

Cindy LaCom

A "Whites Only" sign over a public bathroom door today would elicit outrage and a possible lawsuit, yet everywhere there are signs that read, "Ablebodied People Only." They may not actually be there—if you consider yourself ablebodied, it's quite likely that you do not see them—but that is due to the situational blindness that comes from being temporarily ablebodied.[1] However, if you use a scooter or a wheelchair, if you rely on a service dog to get around, if you are sight impaired and there is no Braille signage outside the restroom door, if you are a little person and want a place to hang your bag, then you have just been segregated as effectively as if that sign were there. Many so-called "handicap accessible" bathrooms are anything but—too cramped for people to transfer out of wheelchairs, too narrow to accommodate scooters, too small to accommodate a human or canine aide, too difficult to use for people with amputations. More than 20 years after the passage of the Americans with Disabilities Act (ADA), accessibility is still largely an ideal for many people with disabilities; there are an overwhelming number of public places in which spatial segregation occurs with disheartening regularity, and this is worth considering, since place has ideological implications.

Rejecting empiricism and rationalism, early 20th-century philosophers like Edmund Husserl and Martin Heidegger gave both place and embodiment a new focus with the development of phenomenology, which considers the intersections of phenomena, perception, intentionality, and an awareness of the body. Three decades later, in *Phenomenology of Perception* (published in French in 1945 and translated into English in 1962), Maurice Merleau-Ponty (1962) more fully and explicitly theorized the role of the body in terms both of perception and intentionality, arguing that "it is the body which 'understands'" (p. 144). In other words, it is only through one's body that one is definitely in contact with reality. Therefore, it is through one's bodily relationship with the world that meaning is, for the most part, established. For Merleau-Ponty, then, embodiment structures our understanding and experience of and in the world in concrete and literal ways; disembodied perception would literally be unthinkable for him.

Building upon earlier phenomenological theories and especially on Merleau-Ponty's focus on how the body structures knowledge and perception, Edward Casey (1993) has developed, in *Getting Back Into Place*, the concept of what he calls "implacement" to emphasize not time or space but *place* in our capacity to perceive the world around us and, further, the ways in which place contributes to the development of community and to patterns for inclusion (and, by extension, though he does not develop this in his work, patterns for exclusion). Implacement means "being concretely placed" in a particular place, and this particularity "determines not only *where* I am . . . but *how* I am together with others . . . and even *who* we shall become together" (Casey, 1993, p. 23). Casey (1993) argues that "There is no knowing or sensing a place except by being in that place" (p. 18) and, further, that "built places return us, immeasurably enriched, to the same implacement. . . . All of these [homes, gardens, cities] are distinctive world places that offer ways into a continually enriched implacement" (pp. 78–81). Though his work has faced various critiques,[2] his arguments are nonetheless compelling and, I believe, persuasive, and if place in fact has such far-reaching psychological, phenomenological, and cultural consequences, then it means that exclusion from place(s) can diminish our lives in profound ways.[3]

This is true for all of us and not just for people with disabilities. Referencing Eve Kofosky Sedgwick's work in queer theory, Rosemary Garland Thomson (1997) argues that we need to use a universalizing rather than minoritizing view of difference in understanding disability, one in which disability "would then be recognized as structuring a wide range of thought, language, and perception that might not be explicitly articulated as 'disability'" (p. 22) instead of seeing disability primarily as affecting only a minority of people. Disability informs and is informed by cultural notions of success, of independence, of time, of productivity—and of place. In her essay "Out of Line: The Sexy Femmegimp Politics of Flaunting It," Loree Erickson (2010) recalls a situation when a fellow bus rider grumbles about her "taking up too much space" while they're waiting for a bus, shooting angry looks at her wheelchair. As she observes, "the idea that people take up 'too much space' underscores the notion that some people are worthy of occupying space and others are not—and is reminiscent of other sociohistorical practices of isolation and segregation" (p. 136).

In multicultural studies, where we work so hard to consider how race, ethnicity, age, gender, sexual orientation, and religion might shape one's place in the world—one's opportunities to speak and be heard, to be present in communities, to be respected and be equal—it is imperative that disability be considered and integrated into our work. Otherwise, we arguably participate in a kind of ableist colonization of people with disabilities by excluding or negating their voices, concerns, and contributions. Clearly, we cannot truly be inclusive if our built environment excludes a critical part of our population. Yet, as Michael Davidson (2006) points out, though universal design offers one means by which to make buildings more accessible, the very concept of universal design itself "remains largely a first world concept rather than a global reality" (p. 126); if in the United States the ADA has failed to create the kind of access we once dreamed of, that is even more true in developing countries, in poor regions in the United States, and for certain underserved populations facing different kinds of discrimination.[4] That's one reason why multicultural studies needs to take an interest in built environment issues, in place and access or lack of access to places. Place is imbued with cultural values about who matters and who does not, about how we do and don't value voices, about how we define diversity and accept or reject perceived differences.

Clearly, then, one objective in multicultural studies might be to foster awareness of the ways in which built environments create, reinforce, and potentially challenge broader cultural values. But we also need to consider the curricular *position* of disability studies in multicultural studies. Though most current multicultural studies textbooks address intersectional identities, considering class, race, religion, ethnicity, age, sexual orientation—and though more are beginning to include disability as one such identity category—disability is still too often the poor cousin consigned to the curricular corner. One or two essays that reference disability studies or one short stand-alone chapter in a textbook are not enough. We need to try to consider disability in every aspect in all of our discussions about embodiment, colonization, sexuality, and access to power.

A foundational argument in disability studies is that disability is a cultural construct and that "knowledge about disability is socially produced" (Linton, 1998, p. 4). In the early 1990s, when the field was beginning to take shape, many scholars (the majority of whom were at that point in the humanities) began with analyses of disability in literature and film to better understand how depictions of disability frame a wide variety of cultural concerns while inscribing disability itself in particular, often negatively stigmatized ways so that having a disability was (and still unfortunately often is) colored by shame and an experience of self as deficient. Joan Tollifson (1997) tells the story of reclaiming selfhood by embracing her disability and rejecting the internalized prejudices that encouraged her to equate disability with lack, but she also concedes that "Being disabled is a deep wound, a source of pain. . . . Life is the way it is, not the way we wish it was, and disability is a constant embodiment of this basic truth" (p. 110). Coming at this from a different perspective, Virginia Blum (2003), in *Flesh Wounds: The Culture of Cosmetic Surgery*, analyzes how a cultural imperative of physical beauty has been fostered by the cosmetic surgery industry and cites one craniofacial surgeon who says of a "disfigured" infant that surgery may not make a "bizarre" or "hideous" child cute but may make it "more normal in appearance" (p. 121). Another surgeon she interviews is more brutal: "You turn monsters into very ugly. Is it worth it? Sometimes I think a bump on the head at birth may be the answer." This surgeon's comment reminds us that a eugenics based on ableism has deep historical roots in the United States, where even today, so-called selective abortion based on the perceived disabilities of fetuses is accepted by many—often even those who identify as "pro-life."[5]

Though all identity categories carry ideological meanings, "disability bears the onus of a permanent biological condition such as race and gender from which the individual cannot extricate him- or herself. . . . This equation of . . . disability with social identity creates a tautological link between biology and self (imagined or real) that cannot be unmoored" (Mitchell & Snyder, 1997, p. 3). Analyzing and, in some cases, revising or rejecting that tautological link and deconstructing an ablebodied/disabled binary became the focus for many in disability studies as we began to rethink the dichotomous nature of that binary in terms of an array of issues: autonomy, competence, wholeness, dependence, health, physical appearance, and notions of progress and perfection. Seeking to complicate the intersections of identity politics and embodiment, we have borrowed from feminist, queer, postcolonial, and race theories. At the center of the field is a belief that the cultural and ideological work of disability is pervasive; though it may seem marginal, even invisible as in the example of public restrooms with which I open this essay, disability has historically done the important cultural work of defining a "norm," situating and stigmatizing disabled bodies metaphorically and literally as markers of sin, criminality, and moral deviance.[6] More recently, in the 20th and 21st centuries, disability has been understood within a medical paradigm—seen as a "problem" to be fixed or cured through medical, surgical, or pharmaceutical intervention. Disability has been and continues to be equated with social identity and is used as a mechanism to organize *both* personal and public experience. As Tobin Siebers (2008) notes, "The politics of identity . . . are not about narrow personal claims, resentment, or narcissistic feelings. Rather, they are based on insights about how communities are organized" (p. 83). Disability studies demands that we take into account the truths behind the idea that "the personal is the political" while not simply individuating experiences of disabilities. In sum, disability has a cultural, discursive, sociopolitical, and literary context, and in failing to consider that context in multicultural studies, we fall short in our important work of understanding ourselves and others.

I want to turn from the general to the more particular here by way of something that occurred on my campus. Many of us working in disability studies realize that on university campuses (and perhaps in society more generally), "disability" is still strongly linked in the collective imagination to special education, physical therapy, medicine, and nursing. On my campus, we added a President's Commission on Disability Issues to a trinity of other commissions (on the status of women; on race and ethnicity; on LGBTQI issues) 2 years ago; its mission is to "create a campus environment and climate that is free of barriers and discrimination to empower people with disabilities to be full participants in all facets of university life [and to work] toward an understanding and appreciation of disability within and among our administration, faculty, staff and students" (President's Commission on Disability Issues, 2009). During the fall 2010 semester, the President's Commission on Disability Issues[7] considered showing *Sound and Fury—Six Years Later* (Aronson, 2000), a documentary about a Deaf girl in a Deaf family[8] whose parents succumb to familial pressure to get their daughter a cochlear implant, as the inaugural event that would introduce the campus community to the newly organized commission and begin educating people on disability issues by asking them to recognize and begin "unpacking" their own potential ableist biases. However, the film uncomplicatedly celebrates cochlear implants without at all considering how a medical paradigm for "fixing" deafness reinforces ableist biases (an example of understanding disability within a medical paradigm). Yet this was one of the films the commission considered showing. Discussions among commission members about the movie's ableist biases were evocative and interesting, and we ultimately made a different choice, but that those biases were largely invisible, even for members of a commission dedicated to education and advocacy on disability issues, speaks volumes about how difficult it can be to even discern, much less deconstruct, the functions and "invisibility" of ableism.

One way to understand how cultural values can be so widely held yet still somehow invisible is to turn to the theories of Marxist theorist Louis Althusser (1971). Althusser complicates Marx's concept of false consciousness (though Marx himself never used this phrase), in which the bourgeoisie misrepresent the reality that the workers are exploited, a theory Marx used to explain how and why oppressed populations do not rebel against their oppressors.[9] Essentially rejecting the idea that we are incapable of recognizing our own exploitation and disempowerment, Althusser argued instead that ideology is not "voluntary but the result of structural factors in society" (Leitch, 2001), structural factors he calls ideological state apparatuses (ISAs). These include education (for Althusser, the central ISA in the 20th century), the church, the family, and other informal structures that typically reinforce dominant cultural values and make those values feel "obvious," "natural," and "true," both because we are raised with them and because they are pervasive. (Consider current North American notions that define "success" in monetary, material terms. There is nothing "natural" about this definition outside of a capitalist, materialist, and competitive culture; in a Buddhist or Amish community, such a definition of success might be alien and unnatural.) An array of ISAs construct cultural notions of both normalcy and disability, and they so saturate our society that asking a person on the street about how she or he might react to having paralysis or blindness or a developmental disability would typically evoke a response along the lines of, "Oh my god—I can't imagine" or "I'd rather be dead." That is how easy and how "natural" it feels to stigmatize disability. One powerful ISA (alluded to in my reference to Blum's (2003) book on cosmetic surgery) is the appearance industry, which makes millions annually by marketing exaggerated ideals of physical beauty and handsomeness and cultural norms for fitness, youth, and Whiteness.[10]

But another, equally powerful ISA is the ADA. More than any other legislation, the ADA articulated and "normalized" a particular understanding of disability in terms that then shaped public discussions of place, access, and, more broadly speaking, of how and why we define disability as we do. The ADA website (www.ada.gov) defines it as "a physical or mental impairment that substantially limits one or more of the major life activities"; as an individual who has a "record of such impairment or someone being regarded as having such an impairment" (http://www.ada.gov/pubs/adastatute08 .htm#12102.). The EEOC Compliance Manual Section 902: Definition of the Term "Disability" includes these further qualifications:

These parts of the definition reflect a recognition by Congress that stereotyped assumptions about what constitutes a disability and unfounded concerns about the limitations of individuals with disabilities form major discriminatory barriers, not only to those persons permanently disabled, but also to those persons either previously disabled, misclassified as previously disabled, or mistakenly perceived to be disabled. (http://www.eeoc.gov/policy/docs/902cm .html 902.1 Introduction and Summary)

The federal power of the ADA, like the federal power of *Roe V. Wade*, has largely been gutted by state challenges and by losses in Supreme Court cases. As Eli Clare (1999) notes, "The movement has made headway— disabled children are more likely to go to integrated schools alongside their nondisabled peers, the ADA . . . is providing a certain level of civil rights protection, and barrier-free access is a growing reality—but not enough" (p. 121). Despite the diminishment of its powers, I am still grateful for its existence. Discrimination is extensive and damaging, and the ADA offers some recourse, but it has unfortunately done little to challenge the stigma of disability. So one very basic question to consider is, "What are some of the ways we might challenge ableist biases?"

Both theories of abjection and theories of the carnivalesque body provide useful touchstones here. In *Purity and Danger: An Analysis of Concepts of Pollution and Taboo*, an anthropological analysis of how pollution and purity are both culturally determined concepts, Mary Douglas begins with the dictum that "dirt is matter out of place" and suggests that "matter" which cannot be neatly categorized and arranged "is conceived as threatening to the social order and hence as dangerous and polluting" (Douglas, 2003). She considers various ways in which communities deal with dirt (expulsion, segregation, annihilation, acceptance), and her argument that transitional moments in society are dangerous *because* of their liminality has echoes in Julia Kristeva's theories of bodily abjection, in which transitions between the inside and outside of bodies—vomit, feces, urine, menstrual blood, and semen—are traumatic because they mark the body as unstable and remind us that the notion of a cohesive body is illusory. In an interview, Kristeva described abjection as

an extremely strong feeling . . . which is above all a revolt of the person against an external menace from which one wants to keep oneself at a distance, but of which one has the impression that it is not only an external menace but that it may menace from the inside. So it is a desire for separation. (Weiss, 1999, p. 93)

For Kristeva, abjection constitutes an inability to maintain even a pretense of regulated and clear-cut boundaries between inside and outside, and this failure, by extension, undermines a host of other binaries we use to try to create order in our lives. One such binary in an ableist world, as I've suggested, is that which contrasts ablebodiedness and disability. A person with a "disability" is seen as a "shocking, terrifying, horrific abject," to borrow from Sigmund Freud's "Fetishism" (Freud, 1981, p. 354), which threatens the ableist world and, therefore, such a person must be radically excluded from such a world and deposited on the other side of the border that separates the ableist world from that which threatens such a world.

Scholars like Francette Pacteau (1994) in *The Symptom of Beauty* and Le'a Kent (2003) in "Fighting Abjection: Representing Fat Women," among others, have argued that deviant bodies "function as the abject" (p. 135), that we displace anxieties about abjection onto people with disabilities as a means of coping with our own corporeal fears and anxieties, however ineffectively. An us/them distinction between ablebodied people and people with disabilities is tenuous—a fall down the stairs, an illness, an automobile accident could collapse that distinction in seconds. In fact, if we live long enough, we will all become disabled. Sensing the vulnerability and artificiality of this division, temporarily ablebodied people arguably endow it with excessive meaning, even in the face of the realization that that distinction is fluid, variable, sometimes even imperceptible (and that imperceptibility can make it even more frightening. I believe that many resist hearing aids because they do not want to claim "deafness" as an identity category, for example, yet the line between hearing and hearing impaired is often difficult to discern, which may be why so many furiously insist that "there's nothing wrong with my hearing"—what they are really saying is, "I do not have a disability"—when clearly, there is an impairment). To cope with the anxiety that this produces, ablebodied people displace it onto people with disabilities. Their bodies become the (ideological and culturally constructed) markers that define in opposition our own "normalcy," theirs the abject bodies with messy boundaries from which we recoil in pity, discomfort, hatred.[11]

However, we could well ask why *other* bodies might not serve the same function for the displacement of our embodied disquietude. Why not babies' bodies? After all, babies' bodies—leaky, poopy, barfy, tearful—remind us forcefully of our own abjection. And yet the typical reaction to a baby is not horror or recoil but instead a softly intoned "ahhh!" Or—to go to a different extreme—why not the hypermuscular, gladiatorial bodies of NFL athletes? Any fans of professional football are reminded all the time that their bodies are liminal and leaky: they bleed, they break, they develop tears and strains. Bones splinter and muscles bend. Faces sweat, noses are broken, and bodies violently collide, often resulting in a tangled heap in which it is difficult to tell where one body begins and another ends. These are truly often bodies out of control. Yet these bodies are heralded and socially celebrated while disabled bodies are scorned, stigmatized, segregated. Why? I'm suggesting that there *is* no inherent or intuitive reason why we might displace abject anxieties onto *disabled* bodies rather than onto infant or hyperathletic bodies. Rather, there are cultural and ideological processes behind such a move that we need to interrogate in multicultural studies.

Along that line, Mikhail Bakhtin (1984) offers us one way to reconfigure ableist attitudes toward disability that merits attention. I'm not the first and will not be the last disability studies scholar to turn to Bakhtin in an effort to revise cultural stereotypes about deviant bodies.[12] In the context of the carnival, the grotesque body—transgressive, disruptive, excessive—has all sorts of political potential to subvert structures of power. It's why so many of our students (and many of us) sport tattoos, facial and body piercings, funky haircuts, and weird clothes. These aren't just means of dissing parents or thumbing our noses at the administration: They are often political statements, means by which we challenge dominant ISAs that inform us about what a professor is "supposed" to act like or what a business major is "supposed" to wear. But for many, these acts typically constitute relatively minor challenges to the status quo. We can hide tattoos, take out nose rings, cover the purple hair that we dyed in a moment of wild resistance to a culture of blandness in our academic hallways. Nonetheless, we perform such acts of rebellion because of a deep understanding that embodiment can pose a potent challenge to the status quo. If this is the case, consider the potential of deviant bodies that challenge cultural notions of what "sexy" looks like, that reject the equation of dependence with weakness, that revise ideological assumptions about power, success, autonomy, mobility, and human worth and dignity. Loree Erickson (2010) (the woman whose wheelchair took up "too much" space at the bus stop), depressed by the absence of women with disabilities in lesbian pornography, decided to write, produce, and star in her own film, titled *want*. In it, she is sexy, desirable, and hot. Rejecting ableist values that asexualize or fetishize disability, Erickson simultaneously reclaims her sexuality and reconfigures disability, and in doing so she arguably challenges the sexism and ableism of the porn industry as well. There is something subversive and carnivalesque about doing so. If the challenges and changes wrought in and by the carnivalesque are often minimal and temporary, I would argue that they are nonetheless important and can do critical cultural work.

To that end, I want to close with a small and admittedly limited linguistic and ideological act of carnival. I am still discussing disability within a very specific paradigm that understands "disability" in physical or cognitive/mental terms, terms legitimated by the ADA. But it's worth considering why we delimit understandings of "disability" to physical and cognitive difference and how refusing to do so might constitute an act of resistance.

I'm going to ask that we think about this by way of an example that is, in my opinion, both ridiculously simple and amazingly profound. Years ago, in a college writing I class, I taught Nancy Mairs's wonderful essay, "On Being a Cripple" (2005). Mairs, who has multiple sclerosis, writes in thoughtful and provocative ways not only about living in an abelist society that equates her and her disease with "lack" but also with the power of language in conceiving of and appropriating power. It's a great introduction for undergraduates to disability studies. But in this particular classroom, I had a student with cerebral palsy, and I worried that he might feel self-conscious during class discussions, so we talked before class, and contrary to my expectations, he was jazzed about reading and discussing it. However, during discussion, it became clear that other students were anxious about offending James,[13] hypercareful not to say anything derogatory, terrified to voice their belief that having MS or any other disability might just be worse than death.

Finally, James spoke up. He said, "I know that most of you look at me and don't know how to react. You see my limp and my spasms and probably feel sorry for me, probably feel like I'm a 'trooper' for being so upbeat and funny. But here's something to think about. I am a really good artist and a really nice person. I'm in a fraternity and have a job and a girlfriend. Back home, I live next to a man who is a racist asshole and who treats his wife and kids like crap. And you know what? When people look at me, they see a disability. But when people look at my neighbor, they see Mr. Jones. So here's my question to you: why aren't racism or mean-spiritedness considered disabilities?"

I thought then and continue to think that this is a superb question, one that compels us to contemplate the historical, economic, legal, and political implications of our shared understandings of "disability." Scholars like Michael Oliver (1990) and Deborah Stone (1984) have argued that 19th-century notions of work and productivity, fed by the industrial revolution, the political and population theories of men like Adam Smith and Thomas Malthus, and the development of public policies that included the workhouse and questions about the responsibilities of the state, shaped public concepts of disability in myriad ways, many of which continue to inform public policies. Such policies ultimately encouraged 19th-century America to link pauperism with laziness, and given that many paupers were people with disabilities, this led many to equate disability with welfare, dependency, and poverty.[14]

In an analysis of *current* notions of care and dependency, Carol Thomas (2007) considers how a successful businessman might rely on his secretary to schedule his meetings, his travel agent to schedule his flights and hotel reservations, and his wife to prepare his dinner and host business parties in their home. Yet we do not see that as "need"; rather, we see that as power. As she notes, despite this businessman's dependence on others,

> our culture attributes "neediness" and "dependency"—devalued, sometimes stigmatized, states of being—to the person with impairment, and celebrates the businessman's "self-sufficiency" and "independence." . . . Underlying both evaluations, of course, is the question of pecuniary give and take—credit and debit. In an economic and social system governed by commodity exchange values, judgements [sic] of individuals' social worth rest fundamentally on their waged or non-waged status. (p. 88)

This is indeed a problem when only 20.6% of people with disabilities are in the labor force, while, "By comparison, the percentage of persons with no disability in the labor force was 69.6" in 2010 (Office of Disability Employment Policy, 2011). Rates of unemployment for people with disabilities in the United States remain almost unchanged in the last 20 years, and prejudices continue to stack the odds against the job seeker with a disability. Clearly, ableism has measurable, often profound consequences for people with disabilities.

There is thus abundant evidence that we are not ready to reject the ADA definition of "disability." It is too deeply ingrained in our cultural and collective psyche by myriad ISAs. For the same reasons that we do not live in a postfeminist or postracial world, we cannot simply discard cultural understandings of disability, because to do so would be to allow discrimination to thrive. But I will conclude by asking that we at least begin to contemplate a world in which "disability" is unmoored from embodiment and cognition, in which "normalcy" exists along a continuum that includes character traits like generosity and bigotry and aesthetics, a continuum we understand as liminal and in which we work to become comfortable with that liminality, perhaps even to celebrate it rather than attempting to regulate and "manage" difference.

References

Althusser, L. (2001). From *Ideology and ideological state apparatuses*. In Vincent Leitch, et. al. (Eds.), *The Norton anthology of theory and criticism* (pp. 1476–1509). New York: W. W. Norton and Company.

Americans with Disabilities Act. (n.d.). http://www.ada.gov/pubs/adastatute08 .htm#12102.

Aronson, J. (Producer & Director). (2000). *Sound and fury—six years later* (Motion picture). United States: Aronson Film Associates.

Bakhtin, M. (1984). *Rabelais and his world.* Trans. Helene Iswolsky. Bloomington: Indiana University Press.

Blum, V. L. (2003). *Flesh wounds: The culture of cosmetic surgery.* Berkeley and Los Angeles: University of California Press.

Brockelman, T. (1996). Getting back into no place: On Casey, deconstruction and the architecture of modernity. *Human Studies, 19*(4), 441–458.

Brockelman, T. (2003). Lost in place? On the virtues and vices of Edward Casey's anti-modernism. *Humanitas, 16*(1), 36–55.

Casey, E. (1993). *Getting back into place: Toward a renewed understanding of the place-world.* Bloomington: Indiana University Press.

Clare, E. (1999). *Exile and pride: Disability, queerness, and liberation.* Cambridge, MA: South End Press.

Davidson, M. (2006). Universal design: The work of disability in an age of globalization. In Lennard Davis (Ed.), *The disability studies reader* (pp. 117–128). New York & London: Routledge.

Davis, L. (2006). Constructing normalcy: The bell curve, the novel, and the invention of the disabled body in the nineteenth century. In Lennard Davis (Ed.), *The disability studies reader* (pp. 3–16). New York: Routledge.

Dines, G. (2010). *Pornland: How porn has hijacked our sexuality.* Boston: Beacon Press.

Douglas, M. (2003). *Purity and danger: An analysis of the concepts of pollution and taboo.* London and New York: Routledge Classics Edition.

EEOC Compliance Manual Section 902: Definition of the Term "Disability." (n.d.). http://www.eeoc.gov/policy/docs/902cm.html902.1.

Erickson, L. (2010). Out of line: The sexy femmegimp politics of flaunting it. In Mindy Stombler et. al. (Eds.), *Sex matters: The sexuality and society reader* (pp. 135–140). New York: Pearson.

Fanon, F. (1963). *The wretched of the earth.* Trans. Constance Farrington. New York: Grove.

Foucault, M. (1995). *Discipline and punish: The birth of the prison.* New York: Random House.

Freire, P. (2000). *Pedagogy of the oppressed.* Trans. Myra Bergman Ramos. New York: Continuum.

Freud, S. (1981). *On sexuality.* Harmondsworth, London: Pelican Freud Library.

Frueh, J. (1999). Monster/beauty: Building the body of love. In K. Woodward (Ed.), *Figuring age: Women, bodies, generations* (pp. 212–226). Bloomington: Indiana University Press.

Garland Thomson, R. (1997). *Extraordinary bodies: Figuring physical disability in American culture and literature.* New York: Columbia University Press.

Hubbard, R. (2006). Abortion and disability: Who should and who should not inhabit the world. In Lennard J. Davis (Ed.), *The disability studies reader* (pp. 93–103). New York: Routledge.

Kent, L. (2001). Fighting abjection: Representing fat women. In Jana Evans Braziel & Kathleen LeBresco (Eds.), *Bodies out of bounds: Fatness and transgression* (pp. 130–150). Berkeley and Los Angeles: University of California Press.

Leitch, V. (2001). Louis Althusser (1918–1990). In Vincent B. Leitch (Ed.), *The Norton anthology of theory and criticism* (pp. 1476–1479). New York & London: W. W. Norton & Company.

Linton, S. (1998). *Claiming disability: Knowledge and identity*. New York and London: New York University Press.

Longmore, P., & Umansky, L. (2001). *The new disability history: American perspectives*. New York: New York University Press.

Mairs, N. (2005). "On being a cripple." In Gail F. Henderson et. al. (Eds.), *The social medicine reader, Vol. II: Social and cultural contributions to health, difference, and inequality* (pp. 70–81). Durham, NC: Duke University Press.

Merleau-Ponty, M. (1962). *Phenomenology of perception*. Trans. Colin Smith. London: Routledge & Kegan Ltd.

Mitchell, D., & Snyder, S. (1997). Introduction: Disability studies and the double bind of representation. In David T. Mitchell & Sharon Snyder (Eds.), *The body and physical difference: Discourses of disability* (pp. 1–31). Ann Arbor: University of Michigan Press.

Office of Disability Employment Policy. (2011) U.S. Department of Labor – Office of Disability Employment Policy. Retrieved from www.dol/gov/odep.

Oliver, M. (1990). *The politics of disablement: A sociological approach*. London: Macmillan Press, Ltc.

Ordover, N. (2003). *American eugenics: Race, queer anatomy, and the science of nationalism*. Minneapolis: University of Minnesota Press.

Ostrander, R. N. (2008). Meditations on a bullet: Violently injured young men discuss masculinity, disability and blame. *Child and Adolescent Social Work Journal, 21*(1), 71–84.

Pacteau, F. (1994). *The symptom of beauty*. Cambridge, MA: Harvard University Press.

Pfeiffer, D. (1999). Eugenics and disability discrimination. In R. P. Marinelli & A. E. Dell Orto (Eds.), *The psychological and social impact of disability* (pp. 12–31). New York: Springer Publishing Company.

President's Commission on Disability Issues. Slippery Rock University. (2009). http:/www.sru.edu/president/commissions/pages/disabilityhome/aspx.

Russo, M. (1994). *The female grotesque: risk, excess and modernity*. New York: Routledge.

Saxton, M. (2006). Disability rights and selective abortion. In Lennard J. Davis (Ed.), *The disability studies reader* (pp. 105–116). New York: Routledge.

Shakespeare, T. (2006). *Disability rights and wrongs*. New York: Routledge.

Siebers, T. (2008). *Disability theory*. Ann Arbor: University of Michigan Press.

Snyder, S. L., & Mitchell, D. (2001, Fall). Re-engaging the body: Disability studies and the resistance to embodiment. *Public Culture 13*(3), 367–389.

Stone, D. (1984). *The disabled state*. Philadelphia: Temple University Press.

Thomas, C. (2007). *Sociologies of disability and illness: Contested ideas in disability studies and medical sociology*. London: Palgrave.

Thomas, M. (2010). Disability, psychiatry, and eugenics. In A. Bashford & P. Levine (Eds.), *The Oxford handbook of the history of eugenics* (pp. 116–133). New York: Oxford University Press.

Tollifson, J. (1997). Imperfection is a beautiful thing: On disability and meditation. In Kenny Fries (Ed.), *Staring back: The disability experience from the inside out* (pp. 105–112). New York: Plume.

Weiss, G. (1999). *Body images: Embodiment as intercorporeality*. New York: Routledge.

Notes

1. I will use the terms *ablebodied* and *temporarily ablebodied* throughout this chapter, though many in disability studies prefer the term *nondisabled* to draw attention to the cultural and linguistic construction of the categories. My preference is *temporarily ablebodied* because it reminds us both that ablebodiedness is temporary and that many might label themselves *ablebodied* despite wearing glasses, using hearing aids, or taking medications for obsessive compulsive disorder. In other words, we configure "ability" and "disability" in ways that are arguably arbitrary, particular, and transient.

2. Casey's work has been critiqued for being antimodernist and, in places, contradictory; see especially Thomas Brockelman's "Getting Back Into No Place: On Casey, Deconstruction and the Architecture of Modernity" (1996) and "Lost in Place? On the Virtues and Vices of Edward Casey's Anti-Modernism" (2003).

3. Sharon Snyder and David Mitchell (2001), leading scholars in disability studies, turn their attention to the problem of an emphasis in the field on disability primarily or solely as a social construct when they question what is lost when we negate too entirely "the embodied experience of disabled people" (p. 374). Though it was initially useful (in theoretical, political, and pedagogical terms) to concentrate on the cultural constructs of disability in our efforts to argue that disability is not an essential or fixed category but is cultural, historical, geographically bound, and therefore liminal, such a focus too often negated or minimized lived experiences. Thus, like many in the field, Snyder and Mitchell (2001) conclude that it is important that disability studies "reinvest the disabled body with a phenomenology predicated upon more than the rejection of stigmatizing assumptions" (p. 386). This explains, in part, a measurable increase in the field of autobiography and memoir in the last 10 years.

4. In "Meditations on a Bullet: Violently Injured Men Discuss Masculinity, Disability and Blame," Noel Ostrander (2008) uses ethnographic research to

understand how living in an inner-city environment affects young African-American men after they have paralysis resulting from violence; one man, compelled to live in public housing without an elevator because he can't afford accessible housing, relies upon his friends to carry him up and down the stairs and is stuck outside the housing development if they leave him there. Sharply cognizant of his increased vulnerability on the streets due to his inability to return to the relative safety of his home if a rival gang member were to show up, he experiences access issues differently than an individual living in a wealthy community and residing in a fully accessible home. Race, class, education, and gender inform disability and the experience of disability in many ways.

5. For a fuller discussion of abortion within disability studies, see Ruth Hubbard's (2006) "Abortion and Disability: Who Should and Who Should Not Inhabit the World?" and Marsha Saxton's (2006) "Disability Rights and Selective Abortions," both published in the second edition of *The Disability Studies Reader* (Ed. Lennard Davis). On eugenics and disability, see Chapter III in Nancy Ordover's *American Eugenics: Race, Queer Anatomy, and the Science of Nationalism* (2003); Matthew Thomas's "Disability, Psychiatry, and Eugenics" in *The Oxford Handbook of The History of Eugenics* (2010); Tom Shakespeare's *Disability Rights and Wrongs* (2006); and David Pfeiffer's "Eugenics and Disability Discrimination" in *The Psychological and Social Impact of Disability* (1999).

6. In "Enforcing Normalcy: The Bell Curve, the Novel, and the Invention of the Disabled Body in the Nineteenth Century," Lennard Davis (2006) argues that statistics and the bell curve shaped cultural notions of "normalcy" and "norms" in the 19th century. In fact, he points out that "The word 'normal' as 'constituting, conforming to, not deviating or different from, the common type or standard, regular, usual' only enters the English language around 1840" (p. 3). Referencing Francis Galton (often referred to as the father of eugenics) and Alexander Graham Bell's dystopic view of deaf people and the need to eliminate them, Davis suggests that in the place of a bodily ideal comes the "imperative of the norm," one which punishes those whose bodies or psyches via a politics of elimination.

7. As a member of this commission, I served on the committee to organize an inaugural event that might begin to challenge ableist perceptions.

8. The use of capital (D) Deaf indicates cultural Deafness and is associated with a shared language, history, and literary traditions; the use of lower-case (d) deaf indicates biological deafness and is associated with a pathological understanding of deafness as a medical/audiological condition.

9. Also, see Fanon, F. (1963). *The wretched of the earth*. Trans. Constance Farrington, New York: Grove; and Freire, P. (2000). *Pedagogy of the oppressed*. Trans. Myra Bergman Ramos. New York: Continuum.

10. As Gail Dines, antiporn scholar and activist and author of *Pornland: How Porn Has Hijacked Our Sexuality*, points out in her campus presentations, the cosmetic industry would disappear if it didn't induce self-hatred in its customers. It is difficult to imagine a world in which we might be encouraged to love ourselves and to accept our embodiments—though it is lovely to try.

11. I am including myself in the *we* and *ours* not because I consider myself able-bodied but because I want to position myself as one of the many in our society who might be uncomfortable with or frightened by the thought of acquiring or having a disability.

12. See specifically Mary Russo's *The Female Grotesque: Risk, Excess and Modernity* (1994) and Joanna Frueh's "Monster/Beauty: Building the Body of Love" (1999) for examples of applications of Bakhtin's theories of the carnivalesque to embodiment and deviance. By using the term *deviant bodies*, I am intentionally referencing the terminology of Michel Foucault. Disability studies scholars have turned to Foucault's theories about the production of docile bodies, developed in *Discipline and Punish: The Birth of the Prison* (1995), in thoughtful and often provocative ways to explore how "deviance" is pathologized, staged, and managed.

13. I am using a pseudonym here.

14. Historically, by attributing "disability" to women and Blacks, "disability" was used to justify discrimination against these groups. Please see Paul Longmore and Lauri Umansky, *The New Disability History: American Perspectives* (2001).

5

Ontological Violence and American Cultural Psyche

A Psychoanalytic Inquiry of an American Cultural Identity

Kevin A. Johnson

From Freud's couch to the mental institution, psychoanalysis has traditionally been deployed in the service of the analysis, diagnosis, and treatment of intrapersonal psyches. With the establishment of psychoanalytic institutions, there have been a number of problematic consequences experienced by people who have been unjustly subject to inhumane treatment. As a result, scholars such as Michel Foucault have expressed skepticism and resistance to psychoanalytic inquiry.[1] For the most part, critiques of psychoanalytic inquiry have centered on the power of the analyst over the patient, as well as the labeling of behaviors as disorders.

In order to move beyond these problems, there is an emergent field of psychoanalysis pertaining to the study of culture. Barbara Biesecker (1998) suggested that

> contemporary rhetorical theorists and critics will be considerably enriched by risking contact with the best and brightest of the "new" psychoanalysts of culture and society whose primary aim is to move Lacanian psychoanalysis out

of the rarefied space of the analytic situation and press its insights into the service of ideological critique.[2] (p. 228)

To risk contact with "new" psychoanalytic approaches to the critique of American cultural psyche, which, in part, has shaped an American cultural identity, frames the discussion in this chapter. Namely, this chapter analyzes American cultural identity as a product of distinctions between who is an American, who is not, and how the borders between American and un–American are drawn and sustained in ideological formations.

One of the aims of cultural psychoanalysis is to posit the formation and analysis of cultural subjectivity in the social field. If there is one thing we have learned from the psychoanalysis of intrapersonal psyches, it is that intrapersonal psyches are formed out of the biologically forced confrontation between the self and the world. In other words, at the intrapersonal level, we are biologically born into the world of images and language that "infect" intrapersonal psyches and help to constitute our intrapersonal subjective experience. Images and language precede the intrapersonal psyche, influence the intrapersonal psyche, and will exist so long as they are implanted in future generations of people.

Moving from the analysis of an intrapersonal psyche to the analysis of a cultural psyche requires the construction of a cultural psyche in the first place. This chapter argues that an American cultural psyche is marked by an ontological violence that conditions the possibility for tensions between an American cultural identity (dominant) and multicultural identities (nondominant). In order to defend this argument, this chapter is divided into four sections. The first section explains the philosophy of cultural psychoanalysis as it pertains to the construction of cultural subjectivity. The second section analyzes the formation of the American cultural subject and its subsequent development. Section three offers a contemporary look at American cultural subjectivity through the lens of illegal immigration rhetoric. The final section explores some of the dimensions of anti–illegal immigrant rhetoric that maintain and sustain an American cultural psyche so that there can be an American cultural identity.

Psychoanalysis and Cultural Subject Formation

The psychoanalysis of culture requires an accurate account of the nature and scope of cultural subject formation. Unsurprisingly, a cultural psyche is formed in a homologous way as the intrapersonal psyche—both are products of the dimensions of consciousness (experience and language), the Unconscious (structured like a language), and the Real (in between consciousness and the Unconscious). Since this chapter relies on the psycho-analytic theories of Jacques Lacan, it is worth noting the Lacanian formulation of the intrapersonal psyche (conscious, Unconscious, and Real) as the basis of the homology for cultural subject formation.

Lacan's (1981) subject is fundamentally different than the preceding humanist or Cartesian foundational, rational, unified, self-certain human subject. Instead of positing a self-certain subject who is more or less in control of its own actions, Lacan insists that there is a "barred" subject that is constituted by an irreparable or irreducible split between the ego and the unconscious. Bruce Fink (1995) explained that

> [t]he subject is nothing but this very split. Lacan's variously termed "split subject," "divided subject," or "barred subject"—all written with the same symbol, $ —consists entirely in the fact that a speaking being's two "parts or avatars share not common ground: they are radically separated. (p. 53)

Within the makeup of the divided subject, consciousness is displaced by an unconscious, which is understood as "another scene" about which con-sciousness or the ego can have no knowledge and within which it cannot intervene or exert any control (Biesecker, 1998, 223).

This does not mean that the Lacanian subject is *entirely* different from the rational unified subject of humanism or Cartesianism. To the contrary, both share the initial infinite possibilities before they are, in Heidegger's (1971) terminology, "thrown" into Being. That is, for Lacan, there is no subject that exists prior to its entrance into language, speech, or the symbolic since it is precisely this movement that marks the advent of the necessarily self-alienated "I."[3] As Biesecker (1998) explains,

> Given that any human being becomes a subject only by adopting or incorporating a language or symbolic order which is not its own but which constitutes its "I," any value or power it "has" comes to it from the outside, from the system of language or the symbolic order. In and of itself, the subject is nothing, radically empty, powerless. (p. 223)

The formation of the "I" in intrapersonal subject formation is homolo-gous to the formation of the "I" at the cultural level. Namely, for culture to establish itself as such, the formation of the cultural subject begins with the establishment of an "I" function in language in order to differentiate it from "other" cultures. By extension, the "I" function of cultural differentiation is, in part, the basis for differentiating the dominant and nondominant cultures. Once a cultural "I" is formed, a whole host of rules, rituals, proprieties, customs, and/or norms are established to refine and define culture. The refinement and definition of culture is predominantly found in what Lacanian psychoanalysis (1971) refers to as the symbolic law. Lacanian cultural psychoanalysis is not predominantly concerned with only those cultures with a symbolic law, with a judge and jury as found in legal thought (though it certainly is concerned with legal thought). Rather, the psychoanalysis of culture shares a more general concern by focusing on the way(s) a cultural "I" attaches itself to a symbolic law (as the culmination of rules, rituals, proprieties, customs, and/or norms).

Understanding the symbolic law of culture begs the question of the ontological conditions of a cultural "I" in the first place. Importantly, from a Lacanian psychoanalytic perspective, the establishment of a cultural "I" is most often the result of a primordial ontological violence. Slavoj Žižek (2002) described the establishment of symbolic law:

> "At the beginning" of the law, there is a certain "outlaw," a certain Real of violence which coincides with the act itself of the establishment of the reign of law: the ultimate truth about the reign of law is that of an usurpation, and all classical politico-philosophical thought rests on the disavowal of this violent act of foundation. (p. 204)

He continued by noting that the concealment of founding "illegitimate" violence "is the positive condition of the functioning of law" (p. 204). Ontological violence, as a condition for cultural identity's existence, may be demonstrated in the case of the formation of an American cultural identity.

Ontological Violence and the Development of an American Cultural Psyche

In order for an American cultural psyche to be established, there must be a cultural "I" to begin the process of differentiation between "self" and "other." There are at least two ways to view the ontological violence in the establishment of an American cultural "I." One way is to focus on the origins of Western expansion to North America prior to the establishment of American colonies. If one begins with Christopher Columbus, one begins with the violence against people already on the North American continent. When Columbus arrived on the shores of the Bahamas Islands, Arawak men and women greeted him with food, water, and gifts[4] (Zinn, 1980, p. 1). Referring to the Arawak people, Columbus wrote in his log,

> They were well-built, with good bodies and handsome features. . . . They do not bear arms and do not know of them, for I showed them a sword, they took

it by the edge and cut themselves out of ignorance. . . . They would make fine servants. . . . With fifty men we could subjugate them all and make them do whatever we want. (Zinn, 1980, p. 1)

Columbus continued, "As soon as I arrived in the Indies, . . . I took some of the natives by force in order that they might learn and might give me information of whatever there is in these parts" (Zinn, 1980, p. 1). Viewed from the perspective of Columbus's violence against the Arawaks, the ontological violence served as the way of clearing the space for the creation of an "American" cultural psyche. The violence against the Arawaks is the precursor for establishing colonial dominance that led to the establishment of colonies. And, by extension, the colonies were pivotal in establishing the United States.

Another (and not incongruous) way of viewing the ontological violence in the establishment of an American cultural "I" is to focus on the violence of the Revolutionary War. "America," as the necessary prerequisite to an American cultural psyche, was founded in the violence that led to the Declaration of Independence and the American Revolution. For instance, by violent means, the Empire Loyalists—that was what they were nicknamed because of their loyalty to the British throne—were driven out of the United States and ended up in Canada. Without the violence to clear the space for America's creation, an American cultural psyche would not exist. More importantly, the American Revolution was necessary for America's Founding Fathers to produce the Declaration of Independence, the Constitution, and the Bill of Rights as the founding laws, constructing, shaping, and maintaining the American cultural psyche. As an extension of the founding ontological violence that created the conditions for the "I" function of the American cultural psyche, the birth of an American cultural identity was made possible.

For example, in her detailed work on the politics of race in America, Sherrow O. Pinder (2010) documented the category of Whiteness as a category of definitive conceptualization of an American cultural identity (in psychoanalytic thought, to have an identity is to have a psyche capable of formulating identity as such). Pinder traced the evolution of this identity through American history and into the 20th century. According to Pinder (2010), "nothing offered a more powerful description of who was an American than the first Naturalization Act of 1790, which provided citizenship only to white men" (p. 39). Furthermore, the many cultures in America that are hyphenated in terms of their identity (e.g., African-Americans) exist outside the construction of an American identity. Pinder (2010) wrote,

all hyphenated Americans are cultural hybrids, living in two different cultures, one American and white, and the other, a sub-culture and nonwhite, producing "a hybrid subject, almost the same but not quite, almost the same but not white," whose identities are shaped as "outsiders within." (p. 81)

With the establishment of the "I" of an American cultural psyche came the construction of "outsiders without," to also include illegal immigrants. With the foundational definition of "Americans" also came the mostly implicit identification of who were not "Americans"—the conditions were set forth for illegal immigrants to be defined as "outsiders" within the domain of America and without the rights of Americans. Thus, we can turn to an analysis of anti–illegal immigration rhetoric to provide glimpses into an American cultural psyche because American cultural identity may be understand by the instances whereby the line is drawn between American and un–American.

Anti–Illegal Immigration Rhetoric and Americanness

Lately, there are a few groups of people such as terrorists who are also looked on as un–American as much as illegal immigrants. And since in America terrorists are translated to mean Muslim Americans, their rights and liberties must be severely curtailed. Given that in the United States there is a long history in which rights are tied to Whiteness, Whiteness determines who is an American; in the case of Timothy McVeigh, McVeigh was given his American right to a fair trial. Like Muslim Americans, illegal immigrants are constructed as cultural "others" that defy assimilation into American culture. Cultural otherness threatens the American way of life. Hence, the "other" must be radically rejected from the dominant culture. One of the clearest manifestations of the American cultural psyche's rejection of illegal immigrants is found in the nostalgic rhetoric about the formative stages of American culture "I"'s function. Namely, there are at least two ways illegal immigration is rhetorically associated with the formative stages of the American cultural psyche: the Puritans and Thanksgiving, and the Founding Fathers. Both of these areas may be evidenced by writers in America who are concerned about illegal immigration.

For example, one anonymous letter to the editor of the *New York Sun* wrote "America has nothing to fear from legal immigration, even at significantly higher levels. Immigration has historically been a source of American strength" ("The Immigration Fight," 2005). Then the writer made a note based on the Thanksgiving holiday, "That's a point that even the most xenophobic policymakers may find themselves reminded of this week as they gather to feast on the bounty of our land and to give thanks to God in a tradition that was started by the religious Pilgrims who took the first steps toward the creation of America" ("The Immigration Fight," 2005). Notably, the idea of "legal" immigration tied to the Pilgrims' role in "creating" America paints a picture free from the violence of its creation.

However, violence was a central feature of America's foundation, even though the violence of the religious Pilgrims is disavowed in the rhetorical rejection of illegal immigration. In other words, the cultural psyche attempts to disavow the founding violence of the Pilgrims in order to paint a nostalgic picture of the formative stages of America's psychic formation. Here, "legal" immigration serves to conceal the ontological violence of the Pilgrims as the condition for paving the way for the establishment of the American cultural psyche's "I" function.

When the Pilgrims are mentioned in opposition to illegal immigration, there is no mention of the horrific acts of the Pilgrims. For example, there is no justification endorsing Pilgrim Governor William Bradford's orders to his militia to conduct a night attack on the sleeping people of a Pequot Indian village in a land-grabbing act. To Bradford, a devout Christian, the massacre was imbued with religious meaning: "It was a fearful sight to see them frying in the fire and the streams of blood quenching the same and horrible was the stink and stench thereof. But the victory seemed a sweet sacrifice and [the Massachusetts militiamen] gave praise thereof to God" (Katz, 2003). Reverend Increase Mather, Pilgrim spiritual father and still a hero in most U.S. textbooks, asked his congregation to give thanks to God "that on this day we have sent 600 heathen souls to hell" (Katz, 2003). The American cultural psyche's distantiation from these violent episodes against Native Americans functions to purify and/or trivialize the terrible acts of the Pilgrim militia in the American cultural psyche. At the same time, the way the violence is covered up through the celebration of the creation of America serves as a predicate to the notion of a "legal citizen" and, by extension, a predicate to the formation of an American cultural identity in the first place.

Anti–illegal immigration rhetoric is also ripe with the rhetoric concerning the intent of the "Founding Fathers." For instance, according to the Americans for Immigrant Control (2007), "Our Founding Fathers did not encourage unlimited immigration. George Washington felt that immigration should be limited to 'useful mechanisms and some particular descriptions of men or professions.'" The group also noted that Thomas Jefferson "was concerned that unrestricted immigration of peoples from lands unacquainted with the principle of representative government might undo the careful work of our Founding Fathers." This glorification of the work of the "Founding Fathers" serves to stress the "careful work" as opposed to the horrific work that was without mercy to the subject of ontological violence that cleared the way for the creation of an American cultural psyche. For example, there is a clear distantiation from the violence documented by Friedenburg (1996), which described, in detail, the horrific tactics of land grabbing by "the founders," including Benjamin Franklin, Patrick Henry, George Rogers Clark, Ethan Allan, Robert Morris, George Washington, and Thomas Jefferson. In one instance in 1780, General George Rogers Clark burned more than "500 acres of corn as well as every species of edible vegetable" that the Shawnee (a Native American tribe) relied on for food. In addition, after 1780, he scalped Native and White captives in order to expand his colonization campaigns into what are now the states of Ohio, Indiana, and Illinois (Churchill, 1997, p. 149).

Furthermore, the American cultural psyche draws lines between the self and "aliens." Anti–illegal immigration rhetoric often frames nondominant cultures outside the American cultural psyche as "aliens" to American cultural identity. For instance, the Missourians Against Illegal Immigration (2007), an anti-immigration group, made a plea that read, "Help Stop the Invasion of Illegal Aliens into Missouri and into the U.S.A.!" The Americans for Legal Immigration (2007) created a flyer that featured the words "Help STOP Illegal Aliens" in big bold words at the top to draw attention. Fox News published a story titled "Illegal Alien Influx May Threaten Security" (2005) in order to warn of the threat that "aliens" pose to American cultural identity. Dwyer (2006, n.p.) even used the term "Mexican invader" to describe "the illegal immigrant" as hedging a "desert invasion." The alienization of illegal immigrants is a mechanism by which the American cultural psyche is able to maintain a safe distance in establishing a boundary between cultural inclusion and cultural exclusion. In quite simple terms, if the alien where not alien, American culture would not know itself as culture—there would not be the "other" to distinguish the culture from anything else. As such, there would be no defining elements of culture.

In addition to alienization, the American cultural psyche is also constituted in part by what constitutes a "crime" in the culture—a crime is that which violates the rules of a culture. For example, it is part of American driving culture to drive on the right side of the road. If a person drives on the left side of the road, he or she is usually violating the rules of the culture (unless, of course, it is in a passing area). Unsurprisingly, illegal immigrants are cast as criminals not only in their agent status (i.e., who they are is defined by their illegal criminal identity), but also with the focus on the criminal acts (i.e., what they do) of members of illegal immigrant culture. For example, the Immigration's Human Cost (2007) organization took up the task of compiling a list of numerous crime victims of "criminal illegal aliens." On their website, they collect a host of news stories to construct illegal immigrants as drug dealers, murderers, thieves, drunk drivers, kidnappers, cop killers, child molesters, bank robbers, terrorists, rapists, drug addicts, illegal firearms distributors, horse killers, hate criminals, and uninsured drivers. The Federation for American Immigration Reform (2007) made a keen observation by pointing out the tautological claim that "illegal immigration is a crime" (because it is illegal). Newswriter Bruce (2007) blames illegal immigration for crimes in the United States that are committed by "citizens" because "police departments in virtually every major city (and not-so-major ones) spend their time responding to crime by illegal aliens, looking for the illegal alien culprits, arresting illegal aliens (when their local laws allow them to), processing them through the system" which means that "more officers, more departments, are stretched to the limit, by people who shouldn't be here in the first place."

One of the problematic dimensions of the American cultural psyche is its selfishness. Perhaps nowhere is the selfish dimension of the American cultural psyche more apparent than in its formulation of illegal immigrants as criminals. This is made apparent in the complexities of illegal immigrant criminality. If, on the one hand, the illegal immigrant was not a criminal by nature but turned into a criminal once he or she entered America by going on shooting sprees, driving drunk, molesting children, and the like, then there is a unique role that America has played in fostering the criminal behavior of illegal immigrants. And, if the American treatment of the illegal immigrant fostered the criminality, then blocking off the border is a form of denial to come to terms with those cultural elements that foster criminality in the first place. If, on the other hand, the illegal immigrant is a criminal by nature, then American culture tacitly confirms its selfishness through the recognition that the illegal immigrant criminal is someone else's problem. The troubling dimension of the American cultural psyche, therefore, is that the psyche becomes an externalizing machine—often working to allow for someone else to deal with problems facing civilization and keeping a safe distance from coming into contact with other cultural psyches in a consubstantial manner to address criminality in the United States.

Undoubtedly, there are many rhetorical characterizations of illegal immigrants that are left to be explored. In fact, scholars elsewhere have discussed many of these areas. D. Robert Dechaine (2009) focused on the rhetoric of "the border" as a way of arguing about the "alienization" of illegal immigrants as a "reactionary rhetoric goaded by a profound anxiety of incompleteness" (p. 45). Anne Demo (2005) analyzed rhetoric concerned by examining "the erosion of U.S. sovereignty as the defining warrant of immigration restriction and border enforcement arguments" (p. 292). In a different essay, "The Afterimage: Immigration Policy after Elian," Demo

(2007) advanced the idea of "afterimages" and found that "the relative lack of afterimage stories on immigration enforcement tactics underscores a tacit acceptance of a paramilitary approach to illegal immigration" (p. 43). Moreover, Demo has correctly noted the contribution of studies concerning how "Discourses of criminality, immorality, and disease, which form secondary themes in the literature, further animate economic arguments by scapegoating undocumented immigrants as sites of contagion, prone to criminal behavior." J. David Cisneros (2008) analyzed the metaphor of the immigrant as "pollutant" by arguing that such a metaphor in popular discourse "is significant for the ways in which it constructs immigrants, through racial and xenophobic stereotypes, as objects, aberrations, and dangers" (p. 591). There is not enough space in this chapter to detail each of the characterizations.

Implications

This chapter is able to scratch the surface for understanding how psycho-analysis may be a productive method for studying American cultural identity by formulating the idea of an American cultural psyche. This chapter advanced the argument that an American cultural psyche is marked by an ontological violence that conditions the possibility for tensions between American identity (dominant culture) and multicultural identities (nondom-inant cultures). In defending this argument, this chapter has laid out the theoretical features of the ontological violence that clears the way for the "I" function of a cultural psyche. It then traced the role of ontological violence in the creation of the "I" function of the American cultural psyche. Then the chapter explored some of the dimensions of anti–illegal immigrant rhetoric that maintain and sustain an American cultural psyche so that there can be an American cultural identity in the first place—without clearing the space for the establishment of an American cultural psyche, there could be no "American" in "American" cultural identity. There are at least a few impli-cations that stem from this chapter.

First, illegal immigration rhetoric is implicated in a rhetoric of American exceptionalism. Specifically, the American cultural psyche is the exception for rights that the "other" is unprivileged to deserve. Carving out an American cultural psyche in defense against the cultural other is symptomatic of a paranoia that fuels anti–illegal immigration rhetoric. At its core, anti–illegal immigration is about keeping the "other" (them) at a safe distance from the us—on the *other* side of the border that separates the *us* and *them*, the dominant culture from the nondominant cultures. As such, the American cultural psyche concerning illegal immigration is consistent with Žižek's

(2004) observation concerning the obsessive fear of harassment directed at the American cultural psyche from the cultural other (i.e., the illegal immigrant). Žižek (2004) wrote that this paranoid attitude is characterized by welcoming the "other"

> insofar as its presence is not intrusive, insofar as it is not really other. . . . [T]olerance thus coincides with its opposite: my duty to be tolerant towards the other effectively means that I should not get too close to her, not intrude into her space—in short that I should respect her *intolerance* towards my over-proximity. (p. 152)

For Žižek, this is becoming the central human right in an advanced global multicultural capitalist society. Thus, the critical analysis of anti-illegal immigration rhetoric forces us to reconsider the global multiculturalist project so that we are able to move toward "the Christian love of one's neighbor" rather that the "pagan privileging of our tribe versus the barbarian Other" (Žižek , 2010). Žižek's (2010) criticism of the multiculturalist project is important. He draws our attention to the fact that

> for the multiculturalist, white Anglo-Saxon Protestants are prohibited, Italians and Irish get a little respect, blacks are good, native Americans are even better. The further we go, the more they deserve respect. This is a kind of inverted, patronizing respect that puts everyone at a distance.

Second, the critical analysis of anti–illegal immigration rhetoric in the American cultural psyche suggests that "postmulticulturalism" might be worth further consideration. According to Pinder (2010), postmulticulturalism "is not a leaving behind of the past, or erasing the past and present aesthetic practices that maintain America's cultural identity as white" (p. 35). To the contrary, postmulticulturalism promises to "fully capture the vexed history of whiteness in the United States of America that self-evidently works incongruent to nonwhiteness . . . postmulticulturalism would dislocate the association of 'otherness' as un-Americanness" (Pinder, 2010, p. 35). Moving to postmulticulturalism would allow for a sense of vulnerability to harassment and an opening for an authentic encounter. In other words, postmulticulturalism embraces a move toward the deconstruction of the establishment of the American cultural psyche in a way that confronts the illegal immigration without the predetermined ideology of keeping "them" at a safe distance. Doing so risks cracking the very defining characteristics of what it means to be an American—or, at the very least, requires a type of nationalism that embraces otherness in way that invites illegal immigrants rather than perpetually trying to "keep them away."

In the end, psychoanalysis informs the study of American cultural identity by forcing us to question the constitutive dimensions of a complex set of cultural conditions that make up a cultural psyche. If there are any defining characteristics that delineate one culture from another, they exist in much the same way as intrapersonal psyches differ from other intrapersonal psyches. Intrapersonal psyches are constituted in part by the rules, rituals, proprieties, and/or customs that a person engages in and that make up her or his identity. Similarly, cultures have a host of rules, rituals, proprieties, and/or customs that come to be symbolic of the culture itself. Intrapersonal psyches are constituted in part by repressed material that does not fit within the rational processes of consciousness. Similarly, cultural psyches repress material that does not fit within the rational processes of collective consciousness. While the idea of a cultural psyche is not perfect, neither is the psyche itself. Taken together, psychoanalytic theories of cultural subjectivity and postmulticulturalism may offer the ability to question the ontological conditions of an American culture in the first place.

References

Americans for Immigrant Control. (2007). *A brief history of immigration*. Retrieved May 1, 2010, from http://www.immigrationcontrol.com/index.php?option=com_content&view=article&id=85&Itemid=55.

Americans for Legal Immigration. (2007). Official website. Retrieved May 1, 2010, from http://firecoalition.com/docs/employer2.pdf.

Biesecker, B. A. (1998). Rhetorical studies and the "new" psychoanalysis: What's the real problem? or Framing the problem of the real. *Quarterly Journal of Speech*, *84*, 222–259.

Bruce, T. (2007). Illegals: The crime rampage. *Front Page Magazine*. Retrieved May 1, 2010, from http://www.frontpagemag.com/Articles/ReadArticle.asp?ID=19749.

Churchill, W. (1997). *A little manner of genocide: Holocaust and denial in the Americas 1492 to present*. San Francisco: City Lights Books.

Cisneros, J. D. (2008). Contaminated communities: The metaphor of "immigrant as pollutant" in media representations of immigration. *Rhetoric & Public Affairs*, *11*, 569–601.

DeChaine, D. R. (2009). Bordering the civic imaginary: Alienization, fence logic, and the Minuteman Civil Defense Corps. *Quarterly Journal of Speech, 95*(1), 43–65.

Demo, A. (2005). Sovereignty discourse and contemporary immigration politics. *Quarterly Journal of Speech, 91*(3), 291–311.

Demo, A. (2007). The afterimage: Immigration policy after Elian. *Rhetoric & Public Affairs, 10*, 27–50.

Dwyer, M. A. (2006, August 17). U.S. Attorney General protects Mexican invaders. *Conservative Voice*. Retrieved May 1, 2010, from http://www.theconservativevoice.com/article/17215.html.

Federation for American Immigration Reform. (2007). Official website. Retrieved May 1, 2010, from http://www.fairus.org/site/PageServer.

Fink, B. (1995). *The Lacanian subject: Between language and jouissance*. Princeton, NJ: Princeton University Press.

Foucault, M. (1988). *Madness and civilization: A history of insanity in the Age of Reason*. New York: Vintage Books.

Friedenberg, D. M. (1996). *Life, liberty, and the pursuit of land: The plunder of early America*. Amherst, NY: Prometheus Books.

Harkin, J. (2005, October 8). Joker apart: James Harkin hears the cultural critic Slavoj Žižek's serious message. *The Guardian*. Retrieved May 1, 2010, from http://www.guardian.co.uk/books/2005/oct/08/internationaleducationnews .highereducation.

Heidegger, M. (1971). *On the way to language*. San Francisco: Harper.

Illegal Alien Influx May Compromise Security. (2005, March 16). FOX News. Retrieved May 1, 2010, from http://www.foxnews.com/story/0,2933,150520,00.html.

The Immigration Fight. (2005, November 21). *New York Sun*. Retrieved May 1, 2010, from http://www.nysun.com/article/23339.

Immigration's Human Cost. (2007). Official website. Retrieved May 1, 2010, from http://www.immigrationshumancost.org/.

Missourians Against Illegal Immigration. (2007). Official website. Retrieved May 1, 2010, from http://www.missouriansagainstillegalimmigration.org/missourian sagainstillegalimmigration/index.html.

Katz, W. L. (2003, November 27). Rethinking the Thanksgiving holiday. *New York Amsterdam News*, n.p.

Lacan, J. (1981). *The four fundamental concepts of psychoanalysis*. Ed. Jacques Alain Miller, Trans. Alan Sheridan. New York: W. W. Norton.

Pinder, S. O. (2010). *The politics of race and ethnicity in the United States: Americanization, de-Americanization, and racialized ethnic groups*. New York: Palgrave MacMillan.

Zinn, H. (1980). *A people's history of the United States*. New York: HarperCollins.

Žižek, S. (2002). *For they know not what they do: Enjoyment as a political factor* (2nd ed.). New York: Verso.

Žižek, S. (2004). *Iraq: The borrowed kettle*. New York: Verso.

Žižek, S. (2010, October 3). Liberal multiculturalism masks an old barbarism with a human face. *The Guardian*. Retrieved May 1, 2010, from http://www.guardian .co.uk/commentisfree/2010/oct/03/immigration-policy-roma-rightwing-europe.

Notes

1. For example, see Foucault, M. (1988). *Madness and civilization: A history of insanity in the Age of Reason*. New York: Vintage Books.

2. Biesecker refers specifically to Slavoj Žižek, Renata Salecl, Joan Copjec, and Peggy Phelan. Biesecker, B. A. (1998), Rhetorical studies and the "new"

psychoanalysis: What's the real problem? or Framing the problem of the real. *Quarterly Journal of Speech*, 222.

3. The Heideggerian "throwness" may appear as a contradiction to the Lacanian subject since there is nothing to be thrown. However, the radical nothingness is that which exists prior to being. If there is primordial nothingness, then there is infinite possibility since there is no constraint by "some-things."

4. There is not enough space to detail the ontological violence that created Arawak culture, though it is important to note that ontological violence is not always created by people. Often times, ontological violence may be the result of natural forces. For example, Arawak culture may be defined by the shared values necessary to combat such ontological violences brought by hunger, famine, storms, drought, and so forth.

Race

6

The Political Efficacy of Nonviolence in *Eyes on the Prize*

Creating Activist, Complicating Tactics

Jennifer J. Asenas

Heritage tours, museums, history classes, memorials, television, films, and the Internet are some of the ways particular memories of a shared past become public memories that dominate the way in which a society comes to understand its past. Collective memories that become dominant or popular do so through the circulation of cultural texts and public ceremony. Dominant memories are not simply the "true" or preferred interpretations of the past. They are the product of and are indicative of power relations within a society. Jacquelyn Dowd Hall (2005) argues that the dominant version of the Black freedom struggle rehearsed in United States popular culture "chronicles a short civil rights movement that begins with the 1954 *Brown v. Board of Education* decision, proceeds through public protests, culminates with the passage of the Civil Rights Act of 1964 and the Voting Rights Act of 1965," and ended with the assassination of Dr. Martin Luther King, Jr. (p. 1234). This version of the Black freedom struggle is conveniently packaged, decidedly uncontroversial, and disconnected from the present. Thus, the history of racial struggle in the United States is a matter of rhetoric as much as of information; stories about what happened, who was responsible, and how racism, for example, should be addressed are elemental political acts.

Viewing the past rhetorically recognizes the ability of ordinary people to work with the discursive resources around them to produce new ways of seeing and to move communities to action. To use the past in this way is not to claim that the past is purely invented by some figurative sleight of hand. Rather, the past becomes a *topos*, or a place a rhetor "turns to" for "ideas, terms, formulas, phrases, propositions, argument-forms and so on . . . in order to discover what to say on a given matter" (Jost, 1991, p. 3). So even though "there exists today . . . a consensus memory, a dominant memory of the movement's goals, practices, victories, and, of course, its most lasting legacies," the past remains a powerful resource for social change (Raiford & Romano, 2006, p. xiv–xv). It is only when we examine the past can we "make sense of the suffering of the present" (Pinder, 2010, p. 88).

Documentary film is a powerful way to re-present the past and offers an interesting opportunity for people of color, for example, to represent their communities on their own terms. Many African American documentary filmmakers see documentary films as "the most compelling mode with which to present an alternative, more authentic narrative of Black experience and an effective critique of mainstream discourse, [as well as] a welcome site for challenging the authority of mainstream American history and culture" (Klotman & Cutler, 1999, p. xvii).

The purpose of this chapter is to analyze the memories of nonviolence in the documentary *Eyes on the Prize*. My analysis of the documentary's presentation of nonviolence reveals that the documentary's portrayal of the tactic differs from popular memory. In contrast to the unqualified support that nonviolence enjoys in the popular memory of the civil rights movement, *Eyes on the Prize* presents the complexity of nonviolence as it was used during the civil rights movement. I argue that *Eyes on the Prize* portrays nonviolence as a powerful tool to politicize people but is an instrumentally inconsistent method of social change. To demonstrate my argument, I begin by describing the popular memory of the use of nonviolence. I then analyze how the documentary *Eyes on the Prize* portrays the politicizing effects of nonviolence and then turn to an analysis of the documentary's portrayal of the political efficacy of nonviolence. Before I begin my discussion, I want to, in brief, point to some essential elements of *Eyes on the Prize*.

Eyes on the Prize

One of the most extensive and vivid portrayals of the Black freedom struggle is the 14-part documentary series, *Eyes on the Prize I: The Civil Rights Years* and *Eyes on the Prize II: America at the Racial Crossroads*. In combination, these films "are without a doubt the definitive documentaries on the Civil Rights Movement" (Harris, 2005, p. 43). The documentary takes up the issues of the movement including integration, Black nationalism, and the use of violence as well as the utility of nonviolence, the subject of this chapter.

Eyes on the Prize does not challenge the morality of nonviolent direct action, but it does complicate its utility. Groups like the Southern Christian Leadership Conference (SCLC), the Congress of Racial Equality (CORE), and the Student Nonviolent Coordinating Committee (SNCC) went to great lengths and suffered tremendously to publicize the violence of racism. However, it was not a simple case of presentation and reformation. Fred Shuttlesworth explains,

> We thought that you could just shame America. Say, "Now, America, look at your promises. Look at how you treated your poor, Negro citizens. You ought to be ashamed of yourself." But you . . . can't shame segregation. Rattlesnakes don't commit suicide. Ball teams don't strike themselves out. You got to put them out. (Hampton, 1986, "Awakenings")

Eyes on the Prize presents a political rather than a moral calculus to the effectiveness of nonviolence. The documentary presents both political victories and losses that it attributes to nonviolence. *Eyes on the Prize* uses live footage, still images, oral history interviews, and narration by Julian Bond, a civil rights leader, in its presentation of nonviolence. Through these images and voices, the documentary presents valuable insight about the effect of nonviolence on activists' self-image and political capability. Importantly, both of these portrayals of nonviolence eschew the morality of tactic that is often highlighted in popular memory, which I will now describe.

Popular Memory of Nonviolence in the United States

Popular memory of nonviolence in the United States focuses primarily on Dr. Martin Luther King, Jr. and celebrates nonviolence as *the* method citizens should use to change society. Dr. King's philosophical commitment to nonviolence was based on his belief that it allowed people to "struggle without hating; you can fight war without violence" (King, 1962, p. 9). As a means of change that offers the hope of unity among people, politicians often endorse the use of nonviolence. For example, Bill Clinton observed, during a speech on the anniversary of the March on Washington, that "even if you're not a pacifist, whenever possible peace and nonviolence is always the right thing to do" (1998, para. 14). In addition, speaking about the Martin Luther King, Jr. memorial on the National Mall, Senator Paul Sarbanes (2003, pp. 10–11) declares that he hopes people who visit the memorial will remember that "change, even very fundamental change, is to be achieved through nonviolent means.

Citizens and politicians who endorse nonviolence as the only tactic of social change often neglect the context of violence in which nonviolence operates. African Americans, living in the United States and particularly in the South, were subject to all manner of terrorism to maintain their subordination. A report from the Southern Poverty Law Center (Turner, 1988, p. 23) documents more than 1,000 incidents of violence between 1956 and 1966 including bombing, burning, flogging, abduction, castration, and murder to impede the progress of civil rights groups. The ever-present possibility of violence led some groups like the Deacons for Self Defense to believe that nonviolence "reproduced the same degrading rituals of domination and submission that suffused the master/slave relationship" (Hill, 2004, p. 3). Thus, the actual use of nonviolence in the civil rights movement was contested. According to James H. Cone (2001), "No issue has been more hotly debated in the African-American community than violence and nonviolence" (p. 173). Yet these internal struggles over tactics are not included in the dominant memory of the civil rights movement, nor are they part of grade school curricula.

The reality and purpose of violence in nonviolent movements such as the civil rights movement are also discouraged in many schools in the United States. In an ethnographic analysis of two second-grade classrooms in the Rochester, New York, area, David S. Wills (2005) found that the teachers focused on nonviolence and deflected or redirected children from discussing, for example, violence and the civil rights movement. In a telling example, a student declares that during the civil rights movement "some people died." The teacher affirmed the comment, but ultimately the teacher used the moment to talk about Dr. King's belief in nonviolence and its origins in Mahatma Gandhi's struggle against the British (p. 115).

Although the children's knowledge of violence points to the fact that culture is not monolithic and that the memory of the Black freedom struggle is contested, it is also true that those who would neglect the role of violence in the Black freedom struggle often have more access and power to shape popular memory. Hence, analyzing texts that contribute to the public's repertoire of narratives about the civil rights movement is important because these narratives not only inform the public about the past but also offer lessons and guidelines about future action. Narratives about the civil rights movement instruct students and citizens about the nature of social change and their role as civic actors, which is why narratives about the civil rights movement remain "powerful, dangerous, and hotly contested" (Hall, 2005, p. 1233). Neglecting the role that actual and threatened violence played in the exigence and response of activists during the civil rights movement ill equips the public for possible future action.

Enlisting Activists: The Practice and Discipline of Nonviolence

When educators and politicians offer nonviolence as the only acceptable form of civil protest, the implication is that if the cause is just, then nonviolence will work. *Eyes on the Prize* portrays nonviolence as useful when protesters can enlist the sympathy of White liberals. It also gives meaning to the violence Blacks were already facing and the political will to agitate for their dignity and overall well-being.

One of the most powerful ways that the documentary supports popular memories of nonviolence is through the subjective experience of the participants of the civil rights movement. Through word and image, the documentary links the use of nonviolence as a motivating activity that politicized groups of African Americans willing to challenge rather than endure racism. The narratives and images associated with the practice of nonviolence are chronologically arranged in a "before and after" structure. The movement's participants recall their experiences of racism and then detail how nonviolence changed their perspective about individual and collective Black agency.

To show how participation in nonviolence changed individuals who withstood racism into activists who challenged it, *Eyes on the Prize* begins by describing Jim Crow racism, a racial caste system that justified the subordination of Blacks politically, socially, and economically through laws and customs primarily—but not exclusively—in the American South and bordering states. This system relegated African Americans to second-class citizens and justified both legal and extralegal means to maintain that system. In the first episode, titled "Awakenings," *Eyes on the Prize* demonstrates the brutality and strength of Jim Crow racism in its opening segment with the story of Emmitt Till, a boy who was tortured and then murdered for talking to a White woman. The images, testimony, and voiceovers that convey Till's story establish the economic, psychological, and physical terrorism African Americans endured under Jim Crow. The documentary shows the shanty from which Roy Bryant and his half-brother J. W. Mylam abducted Till and the infamous image of Till's mutilated body as well as his school picture for a point of comparison. The episode "Awakenings" also includes details about the fateful night and the callousness of defense attorney John C. Whitten, who told the jurors, in his closing statement, "I'm sure that every last Anglo-Saxon one of you has the courage to free these men," to establish the power of the White establishment. These "facts" are juxtaposed with the bravery of Till's uncle Mose Wright, who risked his life to testify against Bryant and Mylam. Narrator Julian Bond tells viewers that the jury deliberated only an hour before returning with a "not guilty" verdict. After their acquittal, Bryant and Mylam sold their story about how they murdered Till to reporter William Bradford Huie for $4,000. The function of Till's story in the documentary is to familiarize viewers with the context of racism that civil rights activists challenged. The tragedy of the Emmitt Till story succinctly establishes the breadth and scope of racism as well as Blacks' inability to challenge a system from which they had been barred.

Following the Emmitt Till story are the stories of African Americans and their White comrades who challenge the racial caste system in the United States during the 20th century. Nonviolence becomes the primary way to carve out political agency by controlling and politicizing the context of violence that African Americans were already enduring and as a method of gaining self-respect.

The Emmitt Till story establishes the constant threat of violence against African Americans. Nonviolent direct action did not lessen the threat of violence but allowed Blacks the ability to use the violence against them for political gain. Although there are many examples of violence against protesters throughout *Eyes on the Prize*, the lunch-counter sit-ins and the Freedom Rides are telling. Both are examples of nonviolent direct action, and both are met with substantial violence; however, the violence against protesters, according to *Eyes on the Prize*, results in the policy changes that the students desired.

The segment in *Eyes on the Prize* detailing the lunch-counter sit-ins begins with the nonviolence training students received from James Lawson, who was a nonviolent philosopher and tactician. Lawson came to Memphis, Tennessee, and trained college students at Fisk, an all-Black university, in the discipline and practice of nonviolence. Their first target was the segregated lunch counters downtown. The documentary shows footage and images of the students sitting down at the lunch counters. At first, they are ignored, but after 2 weeks, Julian Bond, a leader in the civil rights movement and the documentary's narrator, explains in a voiceover that "on February 27th, [activists received] a warning. Gangs of toughs were gathering downtown. . . . The police did nothing to protect them . . . [and then arrested] more than 80 demonstrators [who] were charged with disorderly conduct (Hampton, 1986, "Ain't Scared"). During Bond's explanation is footage of

White males throwing sit-inners to the ground and then punching and kicking them. The next footage is of police escorting sit-inners into police vehicles. The issue took a few months to resolve, but, ultimately, the lunch counters were desegregated.

Following the sit-in movement that spread across the South, the 1961 Freedom Rides were also meant to address segregation, but on interstate travel. Like the lunch counter sit-in story, *Eyes on the Prize* juxtaposes images, footage, and narratives of nonviolent activists with the inaction of law enforcement and violence of White racists. For example, while riding through Alabama, Freedom Rider Frederick Leonard recalls, in an oral history interview, looking out the bus window and seeing "White people" with "sticks and bricks" yelling "Kill the niggers." The angry men outside wanted the African American riders to exit from the back of the bus. But Leonard and others decided "no, no, we'll go off the front and take what's coming to us. We went out the front of the bus." The Freedom Riders were beaten; in particular, a White man named Jim Zwerg exited first and took the brunt of the attack. But the violence meant to stop the riders strengthened their resolve. In an oral history interview, founding member of the Student Nonviolent Coordinating Committee Diane Nash explains the necessity of continuing to ride:

> I strongly felt that the future of the movement was going to be just cut short because the impression would have been given that whenever a movement starts, that all that has to be done is that you attack it with massive violence and the blacks would stop. (Hampton, 1986, "Ain't Scared")

The documentary does not include information about the successful outcome of the Freedom Rides. Instead, it ends with Frederick Leonard's recollection about his time in jail for his participation in the Freedom Rides. Leonard recalls, in an oral history interview, that a Black inmate named Peewee was ordered to beat him for refusing to give up his mattress: "Peewee came down on my head. . . . He was crying. Peewee was crying. I still had my mattress. And that's when I—You remember when your parents used to whip you and say, 'It's going to hurt me more than it hurt you'? Hurt Peewee more than it hurt me" (Hampton, 1986, "Ain't Scared"). What is clear from this vignette is that the violence that once politically crippled African Americans was now a means of political agency when framed in the context of nonviolent direct action that highlighted the problem of American racism.

In addition to political agency, nonviolence was also a means of gaining self-respect. In oral history interviews, civil rights movement activists attest to the indignities of racism. For example, in "Awakenings," Jo Ann

Robinson, activist, educator, and member of the Women's Political Council, explains why she thinks African Americans were willing to sacrifice their convenience and safety to boycott the buses in Montgomery in 1955. She recalls that so many "Blacks had been touched by the persecution, the humiliation that many of them had endured on buses" (Hampton, 1986, "Awakenings"). In the third episode of *Eyes on the Prize*, "Ain't Scared of Your Jails," Diane Nash explains the injustice she experienced in Nashville, Tennessee. She had looked forward to college as an opportunity to expand herself and grow, and she "keenly resented segregation and not being allowed to do basic kinds of things like eating at restaurants in the ten cent stores, even. So, you know, I really felt stifled and shut in very unfairly" (Hampton, 1986, "Ain't Scared"). Member of the Montgomery Improvement Association Georgia Gilmore recalls, in an interview, that at the church meetings, people "would tell you how they was being mistreated, and they were glad that they were able to come up and not have to take the same treatments that they was—had taken and was afraid to admit" (Hampton, 1886, "Awakenings"). These examples demonstrate that activists wanted to address more than issues of access; they wanted respect.

In contrast to the descriptions of the indignity of racism, *Eyes on the Prize* includes oral history stories from civil rights activists who describe nonviolence as a way to regain their self-respect. In the episode "Awakenings," it is clear in the documentary that the bus boycott was not just about Blacks securing a place to sit but about their rights of democratic citizenship—which, even though problematic because of its emphasis on the rights of citizens of the United States to vote and hold office, did not extend themselves to include socioeconomic equality. These were some of the basic rights of citizenship. Nevertheless, images of church meetings packed to the rafters and the enthusiasm with which boycotters sang attests to the feeling of empowerment of acting together through nonviolence. Joe Azbel, a White reporter, recalls, in on oral history interview, that he arrived at one of the Montgomery bus boycott meetings a few minutes late to find the audience "on fire. The preacher would get up and say, 'Do you want your freedom?' And they would say, 'Yeah. Yeah, I want my freedom'" (Hampton, 1986, "Awakenings"). Head of the Montgomery branch of the Pullman Porters union and president of the local NAACP branch E. D. Nixon recalls, in an interview, that after the first day of the boycott, he told the audience that he first began fighting for civil rights so that the "children who came behind me wouldn't suffer the same thing I suffered. . . . And I said, 'Tonight I changed my mind.' I said, 'Hell, I want to enjoy some of this stuff myself.' And you ought to heard people holler" (Hampton, 1986, "Awakenings"). At the segment's end, Jo Ann Robinson explains that the experience of "forc[ing] the

White man to give what we knew was a part of our own citizenship . . . is a hilarious feeling that just goes all over you, that makes you feel that America is a great country and we're going to do more to make it greater" (Hampton, 1986, "Awakenings"). The sense of empowerment continues even when violence against civil rights activists is expected.

Activists who learned to respond to violence with nonviolence made themselves agents of change rather than subjects of violence. Civil rights activist Reverend C. T. Vivian's oral history interviews and news footage from actual protests demonstrate the self-empowerment activists experienced when engaging in nonviolence. Vivian recalls that Jim Lawson's nonviolent workshops were integral to the success of nonviolent direct action in the United States because activists in training "began to understand the philosophy behind [nonviolence], the tactics, the techniques, to in fact begin to take the blows and still respond with a sense of dignity" (Hampton, 1986, "Ain't Scared"). In a later segment of the documentary that focused on voting rights, Vivian recalls a clash with Selma, Alabama, sheriff Jim Clark. The documentary portrays Vivian defiantly standing on the courthouse steps chastising Clark and his men, yelling, "It's a matter of you facing your judge. We're willing to be beaten for democracy, and you misuse democracy in this street" (Hampton, 1986, "Bridge"). Other still images, like the one of Diane Nash, during the lunch counter sit-ins, capture the spirit of people who were emboldened through their activism and steadfast despite threats to their personal safety. The willingness to respond nonviolently in the most precarious of situations transforms violence against Blacks from moments of shame into honor and political power.

The portrayal of nonviolence in *Eyes on the Prize*, in terms of the effect it has on the practitioners of nonviolence, is overwhelmingly positive. Clips of interviews during the time of the civil rights movement, as well as oral history interviews with members of groups like SNCC and SCLC, and still images all attest to a newfound personal and political power derived from the practice of nonviolence. However, the documentary does not portray nonviolence as a foolproof plan for addressing American racism.

Complicating the Political Efficacy of Nonviolence

Eyes on the Prize presents nonviolence as a useful tool for social change, but it is a qualified affirmation. As the documentary progresses, images of violence against protesters accumulate and switch from the stills that are featured toward the beginning of the documentary and that highlight the resolution of the protesters to the moving images that highlight the agency of the antagonists. These moving images undermine public memories of a bloodless revolution. For example, *Eyes on the Prize* features a story about Project C for Confrontation in Birmingham, Alabama. During the Project C campaign is the infamous clash between civil rights protesters and Bull Connor, the commissioner of public safety for the city of Birmingham. Connor, having already filled his jails with protesters, allowed police officers to use dogs and firefighters to use water hoses to stop demonstrators from marching. Pictures of dogs attacking protesters and images of people falling over from the force of the water as well as pictures of the damage the water cannons did to trees are accompanied by screams and yells. Bull Connor repeated this treatment a second time, which sparked anger and rioting among some Birmingham African Americans. The police responded with more violence. In live-action footage, police are seen beating African Americans with nightsticks. These depictions that include nonviolent protest are in contrast to the still images and video highlighting the resolve of protesters. Instead, these inclusions in the documentary highlight the strength and willingness of racists to use city resources to squash protests against segregation.

The episode "Bridge to Freedom" highlights the massive violence used against nonviolent protesters and the difficulties of maintaining a nonviolent movement in those conditions. A telling example is the march from Selma to Montgomery. The clash between local and state law enforcement agencies at the Edmund Pettus Bridge, referred to as Bloody Sunday, was during a march inspired by the murder of Jimmie Lee Jackson. Jackson was shot at point-blank range during a nighttime march in Marion, Alabama. Jackson's murder made even committed nonviolent activists question nonviolence. SNCC's John Lewis has confessed in an oral history interview that he

> just felt during the period, it was too much, too much, too many, too many funerals and some of us will say, "How many more?" . . . [W]e had determined or decided that we were going to get killed or we was going to be free and be frank about it. And all of us just about felt that way. (Hampton, 1986, "Bridge")

Weary from the violence, SCLC proposed a march from Selma to Montgomery, which was met with more violence.

The documentary shows footage of marchers lined up two by two as they approach the bridge. They are stopped from crossing the Edmund Pettus Bridge by state troopers and are told to turn back. Remaining still, troopers move toward the marchers and begin to push the marchers and knock them to the ground with their nightsticks. Troopers then chase marchers attempting to retreat. Jim Clark's men, who have been watching on the sidelines, move in on horseback to join the fray. State troopers then fire tear gas into the crowd and white plumes fill the frame. Through the smoke, however, the nightsticks of the troopers are clearly seen thrusting toward the ground, presumably landing on fallen protesters. An older woman emerges from the smoke and tries to gain her balance as two law enforcement agents swat at her with their nightsticks. The last images of the bridge include some marchers running away while others lie on the ground. Some marchers are able to retreat to the Brown Church, which is turned into a first aid center for the wounded. In the area where the Brown Church is located, police on horseback patrol the streets as wounded marchers are carried away on stretchers. The images of the bridge are repeated on a television screen as Julian Bond explains that the scene on the Pettus Bridge interrupted ABC's showing of *Judgment at Nuremburg*.

The images of the beating at the Pettus Bridge are not interpreted by Julian Bond or accompanying commentary as a moment of productive suffering. The march was supposed to address "great violation of the people," and then they were "violated yet again" (Hampton, 1986, "Bridge"). Indeed, the documentary includes a comment by SCLC member Andrew Young that attests to the anger and frustration of marchers. He recalls people returning to Brown Church "talking about going to get their guns," and the only way he could deter them was to make then consider the "specifics of violence," like the fact that the ".32, [or] .38" caliber guns they would wield would not stand up against the "automatic rifles and 10 gauge shotguns that [local and state law enforcement] got" (Hampton, 1986, "Bridge"). Young helped keep the peace only by reasoning that angry protesters were outnumbered and underequipped to violently challenge local and state law enforcement.

The moving images of the violence on the Edmund Pettus Bridge and absence of civil rights activists reinterpreting the events as personally or politically empowering impact the interpretation of the event. Instead of demonstrating resolute marchers, it shows marchers as victims of violence who were growing increasingly frustrated and angry. In a voiceover, Bond explains that Lyndon Johnson responded to Bloody Sunday by asking for a comprehensive voting rights bill and then cuts to the end of Johnson's speech, in which he uses the language of the movement by ending with the phrase, "and we shall overcome." Vivian recalls that he looked over at Dr. King and saw him "quietly sitting in the chair and a tear ran down his cheek. It was a victory like none other. It was an affirmation of the movement" (Hampton, 1986, Bridge). But the documentary, through Julian Bond's voiceovers, frames the political victories as insufficient responses to the violence activists had to endure to secure them.

Questioning the Efficacy of Nonviolence: Bond's Voiceovers

Julian Bond's voiceovers also complicate unqualified praise of nonviolence through narrative framing. As the "voice of God," in the documentary, Bond's interpretation and evaluation of events are uncontested. With the exception of the Montgomery bus boycott in "Awakenings," each episode that features nonviolence as the primary tactic of the civil rights movement ends with a monologue by Bond that mitigates the political effectiveness of nonviolence or highlights the continuation of violence endured by those who were a part of the movement. Endings of documentaries are important because the "overarching function of the ending is epistemological" (Platinga 1997, p. 131). Endings "fill in gaps, sum up main points, or suggest a 'correct' frame by which the previous data can be interpreted" (Platinga 1997, p. 131). In this way, the documentary influences possible readings of the preceding images, interviews, and footage.

In most cases, Bond presents information in contrast to the gains that the movement achieved through nonviolence. In "Ain't Scared of Your Jails," Bond says of the Freedom Riders, "The students had won their victory, and they had become a major force in America's civil rights movement, experienced in direct action and its consequences" (Hampton, 1986). The episode "No Easy Walk" ends with positive reflections of the March on Washington by participants. However, Bond's last words in the episode attest to the violence elsewhere.

> Eighteen days after the March on Washington, Birmingham, Alabama, a bomb exploded in the 16th Street Baptist Church just before a Sunday morning service. Fifteen people were injured, four children were killed. The murder of these children shook the nonviolent movement to its core. As the people buried their dead, they sang "We Shall Overcome," but in anger and in rage, many wondered how. (Hampton, 1986, "No Easy")

Commenting on the aftermath of the struggle in Selma, Bond says:

> That night, Viola Liuzzo, a white housewife from Michigan, was murdered by Klansmen as she transported marchers back to Selma. . . . August 11, five days after the Voting Rights bill was signed, the Watts area of Los Angeles, California, exploded in racial violence. More than 1,000 people were injured, 34 died. It signaled a new direction for the movement, the next phase of America's civil rights years. (Hampton, 1986, "Bridge")

Through his commentary, Bond negates simplistic interpretations of the use of nonviolence. Although nonviolence was successful in some areas, his commentary suggests that the scope of nonviolent "wins" is incommensurate to the problem of racism in the United States. Thus, the voiceovers mitigate the extent to which legal remedies, like the Voting Rights Act of 1965, or symbolic wins, like the president using the language of the movement, could address inequality and question whether nonviolence could produce the kind of social change necessary to end racism.

These conclusions by Bond are even more significant when the rest of his comments throughout the documentary are considered. Although many of Bond's comments are a means to connect historical footage, interviews, and oral history narratives to create a coherent story, he also highlights the paradox of nonviolence. The episode "Awakenings" is perhaps the most positive portrayal of nonviolence and its effectiveness. However, even in "Awakenings," Bond questions the efficacy of nonviolence. He states, "It was clear the boycotts hurt the bus companies, businesses, and the cities. It was not clear if they could end segregation" (Hampton, 1986, "Awakenings"). More poignant criticisms are levied against the effectiveness of nonviolence in later episodes.

The episode "No Easy Walk" begins with the Albany, Georgia, campaign to desegregate the city. Albany's chief of police, Laurie Pritchett, studied the tactics of nonviolence and negotiated with surrounding jailhouses in order to keep his own empty. If protesters could not overflow the jails, he reasoned, they would lack the social leverage they would need to win their demands. Bond explains, near the beginning of the episode, "Segregation had learned to beat the civil rights movement at its own game. The [Civil Rights] movement leaders had to find new ways to fight back" (Hampton, 1986, "No"). But movement leaders were unable to find a way to use nonviolence to challenge segregation in Albany. Bond concludes the segment, stating, "Albany remained as segregated as it was the previous December when [Martin Luther King, Jr.] first arrived" (Hampton, 1986, "No"). Finally, in "Bridge to Freedom," Bond frames the episode in terms of national turmoil: "Race riots in northern cities during the summer of 1964. The civil rights movement was ten years old, nonviolence had been the strategy. But could nonviolence work in a society which grew angrier each day?" (Hampton, 1986, "Bridge"). Later in the same segment, interviews with SCLC members argue that Lyndon Johnson's speech, which ended with the lyrics to a popular civil rights movement song, "And we shall overcome," was a victory for the civil rights movement. However, Bond points out the symbolic nature of the victory. While Johnson may have taken up the language of the civil rights movement, SNCC members "were being beaten by Alabama police as they tried to confront Governor Wallace" (Hampton, 1986, "Bridge"). Thus, through his commentary, Bond complicates the political capability of nonviolence as a political tactic by framing the civil rights movement within the larger context of U.S. race relationships and highlighting the weaknesses of nonviolence.

Conclusion

I have argued that the documentary's position on the use of nonviolence is ambivalent. The documentary does not unequivocally support or wholly condemn its use. Instead, it allows the experiences of activists to attest to both its strengths and weaknesses and frames those experiences with Julian Bond's voiceovers that remind viewers of the scope of nonviolent victories and the limits of nonviolence as a movement tactic.

The strength of nonviolence was its ability to change individuals stifled by oppression. The members of the movement "found" themselves through activism and by standing up for their rights. Nonviolence gave their suffering meaning and made violence against them a tool for social change rather than a means to keep them in their place. Thus, nonviolence was an incredibly effective tool for social change because it had an effect on the mentality of thousands of African Americans.

The weakness of nonviolence was the federal government's ability to ignore violence that was not public. In public, Laurie Pritchett appeared nonviolent, and the federal government did nothing to help desegregate Albany. Pritchett was unchanged by the methods of nonviolence. He told SNCC's Charles Sherrod one day, "You know Sherrod, it's just a matter of mind over matter. I don't mind and you don't matter" (Hampton, 1986, "No"). As long as the violence was not public, it was not a problem. SCLC's Wyatt Tee Walker explains the impossibility of responding nonviolently to a nonviolent movement: "It's almost bizarre to say that a segregationist system or a law enforcement official of a segregationist system could be nonviolent because first of all, nonviolence works in a moral climate, and segregation is not a moral climate" (Hampton, 1986, "No"). However, Laurie Pritchett's tactics worked for quite a while to maintain segregation in Albany. The inability to fill the jails and to create a nonviolent spectacle to shame segregationists in Albany into changing their policies required activists to be bolder and take more risks to achieve their goals, whether those goals were desegregating public institutions or voting. For nonviolence to work, the civil rights movement required media attention to shame politicians and the public into supporting desegregation and full citizenship for Blacks. For example, during Project C, it took the images of children being knocked over by water cannons and dogs biting at protesters to rouse the conscience of White Americans.

By complicating the memory of the use of nonviolence, *Eyes on the Prize* provides crucial information to potential activists and movements about the kinds of situations and historical moments in which nonviolence is effective. It also implicitly argues that a successful movement cannot depend on nonviolence alone because nonviolence depends on public sympathy—which is not always forthcoming—for social change. The documentary seems to suggest that nonviolence is a powerful tool to constitute political actors, but its instrumental effectiveness is dependent on the historical and political context.

References

Clinton, W. J. (1998, August 28). Remarks on 35th anniversary of Martin Luther King's "I Have A Dream" speech [transcript]. Union Chapel in Oak Bluffs, MA Retrieved from http://www.washingtonpost.com/wp-srv/politics/special/clinton/stories/clintontext082898.htm.

Cone, J. H. (2001). Martin and Malcolm on nonviolence and violence. *Phylon, 49*, 173–183.

Hall, J. D. (2005). The long civil rights movement and the political uses of the past. *Journal of American History, 91*, 1233–1263.

Hampton, H. (Creator/Executive Producer), Vecchione, J. (Director/Producer), & Smith, L. M. (Producer). (1986). *Eyes on the prize I: America's civil rights years*. Alexandria, VA: Blackside, Inc.

Harris, H. R. (2005, March/April). Documentary filmmakers face rising copyright costs. *The Crisis*, 43–44.

Hill, L. (2004). *The deacons for defense: Armed resistance and the civil rights movement*. Chapel Hill: University of North Carolina Press.

Jost, W. (1991). Teaching the topics: Character, rhetoric, and liberal education. *Rhetoric Society Quarterly, 21*, 1–16.

King, M. L. (1962). Hate is always tragic. In Robert F. Williams & Marc Schleifer (Eds.), *Negroes with guns* (pp. 9–10). New York: Marzani & Munsell, Inc.

Klotman, P. R., & Cutler, J. K. (1999). *Struggles for representation: African American documentary film and video*. Bloomington: Indiana University Press.

Pinder, S. O. (2010). *The politics of race and ethnicity in the United States: Americanization, de-Americanization, and racialized ethnic groups*. New York: Palgrave Macmillan.

Platinga, C. R. (1997). *Rhetoric and representation in nonfiction film*. New York: Cambridge University Press.

Raiford, L., & Romano, R. C. (2006). Introduction: The struggle over memory. In Renee C. Romano, and Leigh Raiford (Eds.), *Civil rights movement in American memory* (pp. xi–xxiv). Athens: University of Georgia Press.

Sarbanes, P. S. (2003, June). Prepared statement. *Senate hearing before Subcommittee of National Parks: Memorial to honor Armed Forces; requirements for name on*

Vietnam Veterans Memorial; memorial to Martin Luther King Jr., and Center for Vietnam Veterans. S68, S470, S296, S1076 3, 10–11.

Turner, John. (1988). *Ku Klux Klan: A history of racism and violence.* Montgomery, AL: Southern Poverty Law Center.

Wills, J. S. (2005). "Some people even died": Martin Luther King, Jr., the civil rights movement and the politics of remembrance in elementary classrooms. *International Journal of Qualitative Studies in Education, 18,* 109–131.

7

Transnational and Transracial Adoption

Multiculturalism and Selective Color-Blindness

Jenny Heijun Wills

In the introduction to his recent book *Claiming Others: Transracial Adoption and National Belonging*, Mark Jerng (2010) charts the histories of transnational and transracial adoption in the United States. He begins with events that occurred during the height of American frontierism, discusses the "entanglements of kinship, slavery, and dependence" in the pre-emancipation era, and ends with a discussion of our contemporary understanding of transracial adoption as it offers an "increased public visibility of adoptees and the proliferation of public debates on the rights and needs of transracial and transnational adoptees" (pp. xl–xli). Jerng's purpose is to challenge the notion that transracial adoption began in the 20th century and to reveal that different formations of kinship and nationality have shaped the way adoption is thought about today. However, it was not until the early 1950s that documented instances of transracial adoption occurred within the United States; an American host family adopted its African American foster child after the child had lived with them since 1944. Also, in the 1950s, the first examples of institutionalized transnational transracial adoption (to nonmilitary families) occurred, as South Korean multiracial "war babies" were able to migrate to the United States under the auspices of orphan visas. Over the next 60 years, an estimated 200,000 Korean children would be adopted by families from countries such as France, Australia, Norway, Denmark, Canada, and Switzerland. The popularity of adoption from Korea paved the road for "sending nations" in Africa, South America, Eastern Europe, and other parts of Asia (including South and South East Asia) to participate in transnational adoption. According to sociologist Peter Selman (2007), in 2004, China, Russia, Guatemala, Korea, the Ukraine, Colombia, and Ethiopia were among the top sending nations of transnational transracial adoptees[1] (p. 58). In the same year, families in the United States alone adopted 22,884 foreign children (Selman, 2007, p. 56). The majority of the children were adopted by Caucasian parents. Reflecting this trend, in the 21st century, images of transnational and/ or transracial adoptees are becoming increasingly commonplace.

Certainly, the racial climate in the United States has changed significantly since the early days of transnational and/or transracial adoption; the fall of immigration exclusion acts, antimiscegenation laws, and Jim Crow have altered the ways that different races interact and live together. This chapter focuses on the ways the current context of racial politics in the United States influences and informs experiences of transnational and/or transracial adoption. Since Obama's election, the media problematically proclaimed the United States to be "postracial." In fact, lately in the United States, notions of color-blindness and "postracial" have been surfacing. How do we read the circumstances of transnational and/or transracial adoption, circumstances that speak both for and against color-blind and "postracial" claims? For instance, do latent hierarchies continue to exist because "adoptable" Asian children are considered "model minorities" and there-fore "more assimilable" into white American families and communities? And at a moment when racist and xenophobic state-level policies are only thinly veiled as efforts to "identify, prosecute and deport illegal immigrants" (Archibold, 2010), how do we consider the thousands of adoptees from Latin American nations?

In this chapter, I argue that transnational and/or transracial adoptees have paradoxical relationships to the notions of color-blindness and postraciality, thus illustrating further how racial hierarchies persistent. Transnational and/ or transracial adoption force us to reconsider the possibility that multiculturalism and color-blindness are not stable concepts and that some circumstances are predicated upon the paradoxes that can occur when actions are made on their behalves. In the end, I believe that circumstances of transnational and/or transracial adoption offer an opening into thinking about what I call "selective color-blindness." I define and explain "selective color-blindness" as the fluctuation between admitting to seeing racial difference and not to seeing racial difference in an effort to achieve what one desires. This is particularly intriguing here, since transnational and/or transracial adoption is encouraged by and perpetuates through its continued existence of the belief that the United States is a multicultural, color-blind, and now "postracial" space.

20th-Century Adoption and Race in the United States

The ongoing and unavoidable significance of race (and racial difference) in American society is ironically reiterated by the institution of transnational and/or transracial adoption.[2] In her book *Adoption in a Color-Blind Society*, Pamela Anne Quiroz (2007) relies on Michael Omi and Howard Winant's description of the "racial projects" that include the "sociohistorical processes involved in explaining, organizing, and distributing resources according to racial categories" (pp. 6–7) as a way of understanding the circumstances of transracial adoptions of African American children. From its outset, race and adoption have been inextricably linked, especially given the fact that transnational and/or transracial adoption gained popularity as "fewer, healthy, White infants became available for adoption due to lowered voluntary relinquishment rates [. . .] more infertile White couples sought children" (Javier, 2007, p. 125).[3] As adoption wait times and costs for Caucasian children became increasingly elevated, prospective adoptive parents were made aware of the thousands of adoptable nonwhite children in orphanages and foster care facilities across the United States. Barbara Katz Rothman (2004) offers an explanation when she claims that, in the 1960s,

> [t]he "sexual revolution," which, with the availability of contraception and greater acceptability of women without husbands keeping their babies, made for a "shortage" of adoptable babies. White infertile families were encouraged to look farther afield: to other countries, and to the African- and Native-descent children of this country. (p. 194)

Several factors made adopting Asian children from abroad more appealing than adopting other minority children domestically. First, given the obvious hardships faced by African American and Native American people in America, where they continued to be segregated from other racial groups (on account of Jim Crow and reservation sovereignty), prospective adoptive parents believed that Asians in the United States faced less discrimination and had higher rates of assimilation. Second, due to historical mistreatments of Natives and blacks in the United States, activist groups protested the adoption of these children by Caucasian parents, seeing transracial adoption as an act of forced assimilation and even cultural genocide. Third, strong rhetoric promoting transnational transracial adoption from Asia appeared, claiming that Americans' exceptional moralism and democratic philosophies made them ideal parents for orphaned children from Korea, Japan, India, and Vietnam. Coupled with the messages of American multicultural idealism that encouraged prospective adoptive parents to turn their attention to war babies overseas, a rise in transnational and/or transracial adoption became a desirable option for parents who were unwilling or unable to afford the time or price of domestic adoption of white children. Importantly, transracial adoption almost exclusively meant adoption from Asia.

Because of immigration restrictions in the 1950s and 1960s, it was difficult to adopt an Asian child who resided outside of the United States. Thus, when couples began the process of adoption, their choice of adopting domestically or from a foreign country was already invested in the politics of race and desirability. At this time, foreign adoption almost always meant adoption from Asia and, thus, of a child of a different race, whereas domestic adoption could mean transracial adoption, but it could also refer to the adoption of a Caucasian child. Thus, when adoptive parents opted for transnational adoption, it was likely that they were also opting for transracial adoption. Furthermore, to choose transnational adoption from Asia was also to choose a child from a space that held significant symbolic meaning to the United States and American citizens. In the mid-20th century, Asia was still an exotic but socially, morally, and economically inferior place that few Americans had directly seen in person. In the American imagination even today, the Orient, to borrow from Edward Said (2003), is envisioned as such a distant and unapproachable space (*Orientalism*) that adoption from Asia gives adoptive parents an illusion of permanence: Adoptees' biological families will never reclaim their children. Following Said's argument that people with Occidental perspectives often view the uncivilized and underdeveloped Orient as inferior, there is no doubt in adoptive parents' minds that transnational transracial adoption is justified in the "best interests of the child."[4] Furthermore, as Monica Dalen and Barbaro Saetersdal (1987) explain, vast geographic distance and nonrelatable cultural backgrounds represent very "few threats to the family unit when it is distant enough," whereas "the cultural background is more threatening with a geographically present minority group of your own, especially if such a group has a marginal and low-status affiliation to society" (p. 44). In other words, adoptive parents might be discouraged from adopting African

American and Native American children because their geographic proximity allows them to see the socioeconomic causes for their hardship: institutionalized and systematized racism and colonialism that undermine the idea of liberal equality that Americans cherish today. By pointing out the cultural and socioeconomic flaws of countries in Asia, prospective parents can rationalize adopting children from these countries as serving the best interests of the children.

In their article "Shared Fates in Asian Transracial Adoption," authors Jiannbin Lee Shiao and Mia H. Tuan (2009) explain how adoption in both transnational and domestic forms, "raise provocative issues about racial hierarchy that add fuel to the ongoing debate over the relative importance of race in America" (p. 179). These issues include the belief that some minority groups are considered desirable because they uphold the liberal narrative of American success and democracy, whereas other minority groups are seen as undesirable because they have achieved fewer successes (in the eyes of the dominant American hegemony) and because they protest the incongruences of rights and treatments of their communities. Shiao and Tuan (2009), arguing that when one juxtapositions "'desirable' Asian adoptees and 'less desirable' African and African American adoptees" (p. 179), the juxtapositioning reveals one of the many holes in the color-blind philosophy that transnational and/or transracial adoption are predicated upon. In other words, if transnational and/or transracial adoption disavows the idea that racial difference can be seen or holds any social significance, as many of its proponents suggest it does, then why are there considerably different numbers of adoptees of different racial backgrounds?

Despite the recent rises in adoption from some African and Caribbean countries, as well as the increasing popularity of adopting black children domestically, Asians continue to be the most sought-after visible minority adoptees even today. In 2010, approximately 30% of transnational adoptions were of China-born children, but almost 20% were from Ethiopia, making it the second most popular "sending nation" ("Annual Report on Intercountry Adoptions"). This pattern partly reflects that in the United States, Asian Americans are viewed as the "model minority." Beginning in the 1960s, the stereotyping (and dangerous) myth of the "model minority" that illustrated Asian Americans as successful, obedient, and easy to assimilate was used as a strategy to disavow discontent and protest from other minority groups. In *Minority Invisibility*, Wei Sun (2007) elaborates,

> The model minority stereotype emerged during the 1960s in the midst of the civil rights era. Critics of the stereotype argue that the press began to popularize the stereotype of Asians as model minorities in order to silence the

charges of racial injustice being made by African Americans and other minorities. Prior to the period, Asian Americans had often been stereotyped as devious, inscrutable, unassimilable, and in other overtly negative ways. (p. 20)

In other words, by demonstrating that one minority group is able to achieve success in America, this ideology implies that other minority groups are given equal footing in the United States and yet are unable to rise to the same level. In the end, the model minority myth has created animosity between Asians and other minority groups.[5] Pamela Anne Quiroz (2007) points out that "[s]ome sociologists suggest that over the decades, Chinese Americans have moved from being "almost black" to "almost white" and are the next immigrant group in line to become white" (p. 78). Quiroz (2007) follows this observation with the thought, "[t]his may explain the significant interest in Chinese adoptions, with these children viewed as the model minority and assigned honorary white status" (p. 78). Notably, the idea of "honorary whiteness" undermines the beliefs of color-blind ideology, since "whiteness" is rarely acknowledged as a race outside of critical race discussions, and because the term *honorary white* reiterates the hegemonic dominance and power of said whiteness within American society. To be deemed an "honorary white person" is to be seen has having been elevated, implying that other races are inferior. Ironically, this term undermines the color-blind claim, since it draws on the social significance of racial difference through its very framework.

Transnational and/or Transracial Adoption and Color-Blindness

In its earliest incarnations, transnational and/or transracial adoption has always depended on the liberal rhetoric of color-blindness. First, activists for transnational and/or transracial adoption vocalized their discontent with what they deemed adoption agencies' discriminatory practices of "matching" orphans with like-race parents, since it resulted in thousands of "unadoptable" war babies who had been "alienate(d) [by] neglect or desertion" both by biological parents and the racist system that overlooked them[6] (Buck, 1955). Twenty years later, when the National Association of Black Social Workers (NABSW) protested that transracial adoption of black children by nonblack parents was "racial genocide" (Schmidt, 1997, p. 134), protransracial adoption supporters reiterated the beliefs that love could overcome racial differences. As a result, proponents of transnational and/or transracial adoption declare that adopting across racial lines is within the best interest of the child, who would otherwise suffer through the foster system or remain without the stability of a family for his or her entire childhood. In the words of Pamela Anne Quiroz (2007), "color-blind individualists look to transracial and minority adoption as the solutions" whereby "[a]bsorbing African American children into a white hegemonic system is promoted as race-neutral, altruistic, and advantageous to children of color" (p. 19).

It is important to consider color-blindness as it pertains to transnational and/or transracial adoption. Color-blindness is about *not* seeing difference. Color-blindness is not about *not* seeing racial differences as important aspects of a person's identity; it is about overlooking them. The idea about color-blindness directly influences the practices and policies related to transnational and/or transracial adoption. Referring to the period when transnational adoption was at its most popular moment, Pamela Anne Quiroz (2007) explains, not only have notions of color-blindness affected policy making whereby new laws passed in the 1990s "prohibit denying or delaying adoption placement based on race"[7] (p. 3), but people have also argued that, in the names of multiculturalism and cultural diversification, "racism could be eradicated by absorbing minority children into families who may or may not be of similar racial background" (p. 3). In other words, transnational and/or transracial adoption is legalized through notions of color-blindness. Eleana Kim (2010) perfectly summarizes the work requested of the transnational and/or transracial adoptee in *Adopted Territories*, when she critiques the "dominant story of transnational adoption as the realization of multiculturalism's promises of a truly pluralist society" and the "discourses of pluralism and color-blindness that may have encouraged and celebrated [adoptive] parents' choices" (p. 118). Transnational and/or transracial adoption signifies some of the key elements of American identity: open-mindedness, multiculturalism, acceptance, and opportunity.

But as Kim (2010) explains, often these color-blind idealisms would unintentionally leave adoptees feeling alienated, since being raised as "a non-white child hampered their own identity formation because they were left isolated when faced with the realities of racial difference and discrimination" (p. 118). What Kim is pointing to is the disconnection between the multiculturalist and color-blind beliefs reflected in transnational and/or transracial adoption and the social realities of living in the United States. As Foggs-Davis (2002) explains in her book *The Ethics of Transracial Adoption*, "No serious analysis of U.S. color-blindness can sidestep the issues of racism and racial difference because the idea of race is so central to what it means to be an American" (p. 64). Race influences social, economic, educational, and judicial aspects (to name a few) of our existences. It also influences our relationships, kinships, and understandings of community as well as history.

Given the fact that the United States was founded and built upon different racial conflicts, oppressions, and interactions, it is impossible to divorce our current social climate from an acknowledgement of the ongoing significance of race and racial difference. Indeed, despite the aims or personal beliefs of well-intentioned adoptive parents, transnational and/or transracial adoptees raised under the pretense that "people no longer 'see' or 'notice' race" (Quiroz, 2007, p. 1) will inevitably be confronted by the social experiences that demonstrate that this is not actually the case. As Edmund D. Jones (1972) puts it, "I question the ability of white parents—no matter how deeply imbued with good will—to grasp the totality of the problem of being black, for example, in this society. I question their ability to create what I believe is crucial in these youngsters—black identity" (p. 157).

These concerns exist even if we do not consider the problematically dangerous implications of color-blindness, which presuppose that racial difference *should* be disregarded. For instance, as Sandra Lee Patton (2000) argues in *BirthMarks,* "[w]hile color blindness" has frequently been embraced as antiracist, it has also been shown to be an *evasion* of race that situates Whiteness as the 'norm' and denies the salience of racial difference" (p. 49). This problematic contradiction is literalized through transnational and/or transracial adoption, as racially "different" children are raised in domestic environments in which whiteness, even if unintentionally, is the norm. As Eleana Kim (2010) explains, by ignoring the ways that racial difference can affect transnational and/or transracial adoptees, parents may leave the children "hampered" in "their own identity formation because they [are] left isolated when faced with the realities of racial difference and discrimination" (p. 118). In other words, by discounting the importance of racial difference, adoptive parents leave their children unprepared for circumstances of discrimination outside of the home.

Patton's observation is not the only contradiction that can be used to challenge color-blind ideologies. As Michael K. Brown argues in *Whitewashing Race* (2003), "[t]he proponents of color-blind policies and their critics have very different understandings of race and of the causes of racial inequality" (p. 4), whereby proponents of color-blind ideologies (those whom he calls "racial realists") assume that individual choice is responsible for racism and, alternatively, also is what will eliminate that racism. He elaborates, "[b]ecause the realist analysis of racial inequality assumes that racism is produced exclusively by the intentions and voices of individuals, intermediate institutions that play a crucial part in generating and maintaining racial inequality are rarely analyzed" (p. 19). Brown (2003) is referring to the practices of corporations, the medical industry, banks, and educational institutions; but we can also extend his list to adoption agencies, not just because transnational and/or transracial children are often raised in ways that do not properly prepare them for instances of discrimination outside of the family unit. This could include instances of adoptive parents who cannot help their children face the trauma of racism because they have not experienced those feelings themselves.

In her book *Figurations: Child, Bodies, Worlds*, Claudia Castañeda (2002) suggests we must not forget the "relation between race, histories of racial inequality, and their manifestation in terms of how children are made 'available' for transracial and transnational adoption. [. . .] These inequalities make transnational adoption desirable as well as possible" (p. 108). Indeed, transnational and transracial adoption presupposes that removing a child from his or her socioeconomic destitution is the key to the child's salvation. Instead of offering financial and social support for biological families or prospective domestic adoptive families within the adoptees' country or community of origin, transnational and/or transracial adoption practices opt for the complete removal of the child from hopeless circumstances.

Advocates of transnational and/or transracial adoption use color-blindness to justify adoptive parents' (and adoptive nations') desire for a child of a different racial background but conveniently do not translate that same color-blind mentality to those nations, communities, and families from which they take the children. In other words, advocates of transnational and transracial adoption practice a kind of "selective color-blindness" that allows them to identify what they perceive to be the inferiorities of certain different people's circumstances while simultaneously claiming that, when they remove children from those inferior environments and raise them in their own, those differences do not matter. It is on this contradictory and selective usage of color-blindness that transnational and transracial adoption precariously exists.

Adoption, Postracial, and Colorblindness

On November 4, 2008, the United States of America elected its first African American president, Barack H. Obama. Enthusiastic community reactions ranged from impromptu jubilation on the streets of Cambridge, Massachusetts, and mass celebration in Chicago, Illinois, to singing in the Kogelo village of Kenya as well as knowing and hopeful reverence in Basra, Iraq. In the afterglow of this momentous event, journalists, celebrities, and media voices across the United States proclaimed the nation to be "postracial." In the words of Dina Gavrilos (2010), "America was redeemed" for its past crimes (p. 4), institutionalized and ideological racisms that included indentured servitude, slavery, Jim Crow, head taxes, and lynching. To pundits and journalists, by electing an African American leader for the nation, Americans had challenged racial inequality and had won.

It seems to me that "postracial" America is a way of broadening the individualistic notion of color-blindness into the collective, even national, sphere. Whereas color-blindness is a personal and individual belief (as is evidenced by the corporeal terminology used), postraciality is a social belief, a marker that points to a collective of people, a community, society, or nation. The same idealistic and problematic thoughts are present. For example, proponents of "postracial" America believe that because an African American man is democratically elected as the leader of the nation, minorities have equal opportunities, and the idea that we can go beyond race implies that racial difference is undesirable, something that we must overcome and overlook. On the one hand, "postracial" America is a myth that Obama used in 2004 to describe the unification of people from different backgrounds when he proclaimed, "[t]here's not a black America and white America and Latino America and Asian America; there's the United States of America" (Obama, 2004). These are the notions that supporters were eager to repeat when he was elected as president a few years later, and these are the ideals that are promoted. On the other hand, since the 2008 election, through various examples of discrimination, race and racism are just as existent as they were before Obama's election. For instance, the 2010 Arizona Senate Bill 1070 that worried many, in its likelihood for promoting racial profiling directed toward Latino Americans, reinforces what Bernadette Marie Calafell (2007) terms the "pervasiveness of dominant discourses that continue to position Latina/os as Others" (p. 39) as "forever foreign" (p. 33). Also, anti–Arab discrimination persists in the United States, in the name of which Americans with Middle Eastern and South Asian origins are the victims of vigilante violence. In 2010, a Florida-based nondenominational church promoted an Islamophobic protest that was termed the "International Burn a Koran Day." In 2011, a UCLA undergraduate student's online rant, protesting the "hordes of Asians" admitted to the public university despite their refusal to assimilate to "American manners," went viral, and that student was compelled to resign from school on account of death threats (Lovett, 2011, p. A21). Today, neoconservative pundits are quick to undermine discourses about minority rights, claiming that they are direct, racist attacks against white people; in 2011, the journal *Perspectives on Psychological Science* published an important and necessary article titled "Whites See Racism as a Zero-Sum Game That They Are Now Losing" (Norton & Sommers, 2011). However, just 6 months after Obama's historical inauguration in 2009, the president publically voiced his disappointment over hearing that a well-known African American professor at Harvard, Henry Louis Gates Jr., had been arrested in his home under suspicions of burglary. In response to this event, Lawrence Bobo (2009) quipped, "[a]in't nothing post-racial about the United States of

America" (n.p.) shortly thereafter. Bobo's comments unquestionably resonate not only with the situation that he is directly discussing but also with these other clearly racialized (and racist) practices and policies listed above.

But what do these examples of racialized (and racist) actions mean for transnational and/or transracial adoption in the United States? How does a parent, for example, raise an adopted child who is Latino American when state-level policy makers contradict this message with laws that promote racial profiling? Latino Americans, Asian Americans, and Arab Americans often are deemed "forever foreigners" because they are not white. And how can an adoptive parent explain racial profiling and institutional discrimination to a transracially adopted African American child, for example, without admitting that racial inequality exists? There seems to be a striking paradox between the ways that racialized people are treated in the United States and the fact that transnational and/or transracial adoptions of black, Asian, Latino, and Native American children are based on the *desire* for those children to become "American," when we think about how often racially Other citizens are discriminated against and treated as though they are *unwanted*.

This means that we have to problematize color-blindness and "postracial" America. Race and racism need to be critically investigated so that we can point to the dangers of increasing inequality. Transnationally and/or transracially adopted people's struggles will go unheard and, worse, unarticulated. This chapter is not intended as an ethical vouching for or against transnational and/or transracial adoption; those arguments are usually reductive and conversation halting. What I hope to accomplish is to expose the ways the notions of color-blindness and "postracial" America have been selectively manipulated to allow for Americans to adopt from overseas and across racial lines. Transnational and/or transracial adoption reveals the shortcomings (and contradictions) of these narratives as well as their potentially dangerous legacies. This chapter exposes the fact that we are most definitely not "postracial," despite what our politicians and media pundits tell us. Even seemingly color-blind acts, like adopting transnationally and/or transracially, are inevitably imbued with selective color-blindness and acknowledgement of racial difference.

References

Annual Report on Intercountry Adoptions. (2010). *US Department of State*. Retrieved from http://adoption.state.gov/content/pdf/fy2010_annual_report.pdf.

Archibold, R. C. (2010, April 23). Arizona enacts stringent law on immigration. *New York Times*. Retrieved from http://www.nytimes.com/2010/04/24/us/politics/24immig.html.

Bobo, L. (2009, July 22). Post-racial America looks pretty racial to me. *Atlanta Journal Constitution*. Retrieved from http://www.ajc.com/opinion/post-racial-america-looks-98280.html.

Brown, M. (2003). *Whitewashing race: The myth of a color-blind society*. Berkeley: University of California Press.

Buck, P. (1955). The children waiting: The shocking scandal of adoption. *Women's Home Companion, 33*, 129–132.

Calafell, B. M. (2007). *Latina communication studies*. New York: Peter Lang.

Castañeda, C. (2002). *Figurations: Child, bodies, worlds*. Durham, NC: Duke University Press.

Dalen, M., & Saetersdal, B. (1987). Transracial adoption in Norway. *Adoption and Fostering, 11*(4), 41–46.

Doss, H. (1954). *The family nobody wanted*. Boston: Northwestern University Press.

Foggs-Davis, H. G. (2002). *The ethics of transracial adoption*. Ithaca, NY: Cornell University Press.

Gavrilos, D. (2010). White males lost presidency for first time: Exposing the power of whiteness through Obama's victory. In H. Harris, K. Moffitt, & K. Squires (Eds.), *The Obama effect: Multidisciplinary renderings of the 2008 Campaign* (pp. 3–15). Albany: State University of New York Press.

Holt, B., & Wisner, D. (1956). *The seeds from the east*. Los Angeles: Oxford University Press.

Javier, R. A. (2007). *Handbook of adoption: Implications for researchers, practitioners, and families*. Thousand Oaks, CA: Sage.

Jerng, M. (2010). *Claiming others: Transracial adoption and national belonging*. Minneapolis: University of Minnesota Press.

Jones, E. D. (1972). On transracial adoption of black children. *Child Welfare, 51*(3), 156–164.

Katz Rothman, B. (2004). Transracial adoption: Refocusing upstream. In H. Dalmage (Ed.), *The politics of multiculturalism: Challenging racial thinking* (pp. 193–202). Albany: State University of New York Press.

Kim, E. (2010). Adopted territory: Transnational Korean adoptees and the politics of belonging. Durham, NC: Duke University Press.

Lovett, I. (2011, March 15). UCLA student's video rant against Asians fuels firestorm. *New York Times*. Retrieved from http://www.nytimes.com/2011/03/20/us/20rant.html.

Norton, M. I., & Sommers, S. R. (2011, May). Whites see racism as a zero-sum game that they are now losing. *Perspectives on Psychological Science, 6*(3), 215–218.

Obama, B. (2004, July 27). Address at the Democratic National Convention. Retrieved from http://obamaspeeches.com/002-Keynote-Address-at-the-2004-Democratic-National-Convention-Obama-Speech.htm.

Patton, S. L. (2000). *BirthMarks: Transracial adoption in contemporary America*. New York: New York University Press.

Quiroz, P. A. (2007). *Adoption in a color-blind society*. Lanham, MD: Rowman and Littlefield.

Said, E. (2003). *Orientalism*. Toronto: Random House of Canada.

Schmidt, A. J. (1997). *The menace of multiculturalism: The Trojan horse in America.* Westport, CT: Greenwood Publishing Group.

Selman, P. (2007). Intercountry adoption in the twenty-first century: The rise and fall of countries of origin. *Proceedings of the First International Korean Adoption Studies Research Symposium* (pp. 55–76). Seoul: International Korean Adoptee Association.

Shiao, J. L. & Tuan, M. H. (2009). Shared fates in Asian transracial adoption: Korean adoptee experiences of difference in their families. In A. Grant-Thomas & G. Orfield (Ed.), *Twenty-first century color lines: Multiracial change in contemporary America* (pp. 178–98). Philadelphia: Sage University Press.

Sun, W. (2007). *Minority invisibility: An Asian American experience.* Lanham, MD: University Press of America.

Notes

1. Selman's findings show the statistics of both sending nations and receiving nations. For instance, the largest number of adoptees brought to the United States was from China, to France was from Haiti, and to Italy was from Russia. An obvious distinction between what are considered "have" and "have not" countries separates receiving and sending nations.

2. It is ironic because, as I mention above, adoption supposes a degree of non-essentialism, and transnational and/or transracial adoption appears as evidence that we live in a time and space in which racial difference can be overcome even in the intimate realm of kinship.

3. The rise in white women's civil rights in the 20th century explains the trends of there being fewer adoptable Caucasian babies and more prospective adoptive parents. As social structures were put in place to support single mothers, fewer children were relinquished; as more women sought higher levels of education and employment, motherhood tended to be something that was pursued later in life, arguably resulting in elevated numbers of childless couples looking to adopt.

4. The "best interest of the child" is a phrase that is deployed in most adoption guidebooks and policy laws. It is also a phrase that is reiterated by adoption agency workers, social workers, and adoptive parents alike. Notably, the "best interest of the child" is not a fixed notion, since this could refer to transracial adoption so that the child can evade the foster system, but this could also mean staying with biological family members and being raised by kin.

5. Feeding into this model minority myth are the extremely gendered ways that Asian people, and especially females, are exoticized in Western notions of the Orient as obedient and desirable objects. Since a large majority of transnational and/or transracially adopted Asian children are female (for instance, as an outcome of China's One-Child Policy from the 1980s), this connection opens many doors for considering other outlets between racial preference, gender, ideology, and adoption.

6. Racial matching is the systematic placement of racially like children and adoptive parents together. Pearl Buck's article here, alongside books by Bertha Holt and David Wisner (1956) and Helen Doss (1954), all expose adoption "matching,"

what Hawley Grace Fogg-Davis (2002) calls the systematic placement of racially like children with adoptive parents in a way that keeps "race in mind as we deliberate about adoption" (p. 10), to be debilitating to the multiracial war orphans that were the initial subjects that made transnational and/or transracial adoption necessary in the 1950s.

7. Quiroz (2007) explains that the Multi-Ethnic Placement and Inter-Ethnic Placement Acts from the 1990s are responsible for "reversing the traditional stance taken by adoption professionals in the context of a historically color-conscious society, with its political and legal sanctions against race mixing" (p. 3).

8

Race, Sex, and Hollywood

Black Men and White Women Censored

Nicole Amber Haggard

Negro and White Love Scenes That Shock-It-To-You!

Negro boy gets White girl in torrid love scenes that break the last of Hollywood's great taboos! Hollywood is now asking Guess Who's Coming to Bed?

Coronet magazine, April 1969

The question of interracial sexual relations remains virtually untouched.

Jane Gaines (Williams, 2004, p. 271)

From 1927 to 1956, the Motion Picture Producers and Distributors of America (MPPDA) officially mandated that "Miscegenation (sex relationship between the White and Black races) is forbidden."[1] Although the miscegenation clause speaks directly to White-Black relationships, the MPPDA also used the clause to censor scripts that portrayed interracial relationships beyond Black-White pairs. A range of censorship ensued, from forbidden to acceptable interracial screen couples, leading film scholars to summarize the genre as such: "No nonWhite man can have sanctioned sexual relations with a White woman" in contrast to the "frequently actualized relation between a nonWhite female and a White male" (Browne, 1992, p. 8). This work, however, questions the vague term *nonWhite* and calls attention to the specific intersection of gender and race in interracial relations.[2]

By focusing on the gender and race of couples censored by the MPPDA, it becomes clear that the only "sex relationship" they consistently forbade was *Black men* and *White women*; they repeatedly banned these films and permitted scripts that featured other interracial combinations such as White men and Chinese women or Mexican men and White women.[3] In fact, William Hayes, the renowned first president of the MPPDA, declared that it was "inadvisable always to show White women in scenes with Negroes where miscegenation is implied."[4] This explicit censorship of Black men and White women is at the core of interracial relationships in film and history. One would therefore assume that the exact cinematic frame we literally see as a "sex relationship" between a Black man and a White woman would be documented and analyzed in various studies of interracial romance, sex in cinema, or "Hollywood firsts." However, there is no such scholarly agreement on this precise visual moment.[5] This chapter will identify the landmark scene and use it to develop an interdisciplinary reading that will intervene into existing analyses of cinematic interracial relationships.

bell hooks (1992) adamantly reminds us that "from slavery on, White supremacists have recognized that control over images is central to the maintenance of any system of racial domination." As an explicit statement of image control and a literal mediator between the screen and reality, the MPPDA reinforced and maintained racism by determining which race-and-gender interracial pairs could and could not be visually represented and how that representation looked when it was actually screened. This censorship mirrored America's antimiscegenation laws, which Peggy Pascoe (2009) shows were *also* a multiracial project in White supremacy that have much to tell us about bans against "illicit" interracial sex. The judicial obsession with interracial sex and the MPPDA's specific forbiddance of sex relationships clue us in to the crucial role that *sex* plays in America's conception of interracial relationships. As renowned American author and activist James Weldon Johnson stated, "in the core of the heart of the American race problem the sex factor is rooted" (Hernton, 1988, p. xx).

Yet when discussing interracial relationships in film, we seem uncomfortable talking about sex; we discuss interracial romance, marriage, and the complexities of their children, but what about the "in between"? As Jane Gaines has noted (2001), we seem to skip over the important step of interracial *sexual* relations. Linda Williams (2008) has taken up the task of looking directly at sex in film and reminds us that "To dismiss these 'dirty parts' as gratuitous—as not part of the cultural story of the history of movies—is to fail to write the formal and cultural history of those moving pictures" (p. 7). As the title of her work *Screening Sex* reveals, we need to understand the dialectic between both what is revealed to us and what is concealed during any historical moment and, as I would add, between any specific race-and-gender pair. Taking a cue from Williams, what happens when the "ob/scene" of interracial sex comes "on/scene"?

Although film scholars may overlook the topic, the presence of Black man–White woman sex in the movies was a rousing theme in popular culture. In 1969, the cover of *Coronet* magazine titled "Negro and White Love Scenes That Shock-It-To-You!" announced that "Negro boy gets White girl in torrid love scenes that break the last of Hollywood's great taboos." The magazine is filled with steamy still images of James Brown and Raquel Welch embracing in *100 Rifles*; Sidney Poitier kissing Joanna Shimkus in *The Lost Man*; and the pantless White Joanna being held by her Black shirtless lover in the UK import *Joanna*. Playing on the overtly purposeful lack of sex in *Guess Who's Coming to Dinner?*, the article claims that Hollywood is *now* asking *Guess Who's Coming to Bed?* as Black men–White women love scenes are filling the screen. *Coronet* announces what we have avoided: It is the "torrid love scenes" that are taboo, the "sex relationships," *specifically* between Black men and White women that caught the attention of American audiences. Considered with the Production Code's ban on "sex relationships between the White and Black races," *Coronet's* announcement made me wonder in what film exactly was "the last of Hollywood's great taboos" broken, and how did we get there?[6]

In order to trace this visual development, I began chronologically watching every American film that includes a Black man–White woman interaction in which a sexual relationship occurs or is implied.[7] I discovered that the first film to depict a Black man–White woman marriage is *The View From Pompey's Head* (1955).[8] We are shown the first Black man–White woman kiss and the couple half-clad in bed together in *The Black Klansman* (1966). The first time sex is implied through elliptical editing is in Sidney Poitier's *The Lost Man* (1968)[9]; and the first time the couple appears completely naked together in a sexually suggestive position is in *Last of the Mobile Hot Shots* (1970), based on a Tennessee Williams play. Finally, the first visualized sex scene occurs in Melvin Van Peebles' *Sweet Sweetback's Baadasssss Song* (1971).

Fifty minutes into *Sweet Sweetback's Baadasssss Song*, the Black male fugitive Sweetback is caught trespassing by a White male motorcycle gang.

As punishment, they challenge him to a duel with their leader, Pres. Pres rides a motorcycle onto the screen and begins showing off various feats of weightlifting and knife throwing, while the gang chants to Sweetback, "Come on man, your choice! What's it gonna be?" Pres then removes the motorcycle helmet, and long red hair flows out from beneath it, revealing that she is a White woman. Sweetback coolly pronounces "fucking" as the challenge. The White male crowd cheers and Pres assertively yells, "Shut up!" while motioning them to "round up." The men create a circle of motor-cycles and throw their jackets on the pavement as a surface for the duel to occur on. Pres enters the circle, fully naked, with fists clasped in the air as a victorious champion. She lies on her back as Sweetback enters the circle and gets on top of her. Although we have previously seen Sweetback in sex acts, this is the first time we see his naked backside in motion between a woman's legs, as he circles his pelvis around, rhythmically penetrates and even moves Pres's legs into different positions. The crowd claps and cheers "Get him, Pres," creating the soundtrack for the fucking duel. The scene lasts for about 2 minutes, and toward the end she tightly wraps her legs around his torso and then spreads them out as she screams, "Whoa, Sweetback, oooooooh, Sweetback." The image freezes on her smiling face. Sweetback then gets off her and we are shown, for the first time, rather than just his sweet back, a full frontal naked shot of his body, including his flaccid penis. Sweetback has won. The crowd quietly disperses. Pres remains lying on the floor.

This explicit sex scene introduces cinema to visualized sexual relations between a Black man and a White woman. From the film's opening sequence, we are cued in to the primacy of the theme of interracial sexual relationships when a White woman is told she cannot have sex with a Black man at a sex club. As Linda Williams (2008) notes, our landmark scene "finally delivers the interracial sex so anxiously diverted in the sex club (not to mention . . . in countless other Hollywood flirtations with miscegenation)" (p. 98). So why have we overlooked this landmark moment specifically as the first Black man-White woman visualized sex scene in American film? And how does *Sweet Sweetback's Baadasssss Song* fit into the trajectory of interracial films? It is not a film about a relationship or love or marriage; it is a film about institutionalized racism and the role that sex plays within that system. How then do we read *Sweetback*? And what does it have to teach us about inter-racial sexual relationships on film in general? In order to answer these ques-tions and understand the significance of *Sweetback*, we first need to parcel out the analytical framework we currently employ.

Regardless of the thesis of their work, interracial film scholars begin from the tenet that a gendered dichotomy exists in the narrative construction of these films in which White *men* freely have sexual relationships with all races of women, while White *women* rarely have sexual access to nonWhite men. Nick Browne (1992) introduced this semiotic theory based on the matrix of sexual relations that regulates Hollywood's system of racial representation. His description of the White gender dichotomy compiled with a binary notion of race (White v. nonWhite) has become the logical starting point for the field. Although this framework has helped us to identify and read the distinct themes that separate White men from White women in interracial relationships, it has also promoted a lumping together of all nonWhite races and has limited our understanding of the representation and repression of specific race-and-gender pairings. It also implicates us in a colonialist signifying system, which Abdul JanMohamed (1992) explains "reduc[es] the colonized or racial subject to a generic being that can be exchanged for any other 'native' or racialized subject" (p. 106). Rather than continue with this framework, I suggest we look to Peggy Pascoe's work on the intricacies of antimiscegenation laws for a solution. She states, "it is essential to examine the distinctive historical trajectories of each of the various communities affected by the laws, to examine which groups were and were not named in miscegenation law (and where and when)" (Pascoe, 2009, p. 8). Applying this to the prohibitions of the Production Code, we can look to the representation and repression of specific race-and-gender pairs and give an analysis that heeds these distinctions.

For example, when Carlos Cortés (2002) argues, "Code or no Code, taboos make titillating screen material. So filmmakers skirted the borders of the Code-hardened convention, teasing audiences with touches or hints of interracial love" (p. 134), he defends his claim by pointing to various interracial films made during the Code era: *The Bitter Tea of General Yen* (1933, White woman–Chinese man), *Bordertown* (1935, White woman–Mexican man), and *Bird of Paradise* (1932, White man–Polynesian woman). Note, however, that none of his examples involve a Black man-White woman pair. This is because it was not until almost 20 years later, in the 1957 film *Island in the Sun*, that audiences were "teased" with even a hint of a sexual relationship between a Black man and a White woman on Hollywood screens. By this time, miscegenation was not forbidden by the Production Code but rather moved to "special subjects" to be treated with care. So, although filmmakers "teased audiences" with other interracial race-and-gender combinations during the Production Code era, they did not do so with Black men and White women. Unlike other interracial pairs, films were continually rejected during this period if they merely implied a sexual relationship between a Black man and a White woman. Inattention to the specific race and gender of the interracial pair misses this crucial distinction. Like Pascoe, if we pay attention to the race and gender of the interracial pairs named and not named, represented and repressed, we are able to make conclusions based on the historical context of their specific pairing.

We also must be careful when discussing Black–White love when scholars do not call attention to the specific genders of the interracial couple discussed, such as when Susan Courtney (2005) argues that *Island in the Sun* "was partly responsible for the cycle of Black–White 'miscegenation films,' as some called them, that followed it . . . the sheer volume of such films attests to the popularity of the trend" (p. 193). However, out of the seven "miscegenation films" she lists made between 1957 and 1959, only one of them, *The World, The Flesh, and the Devil*, has even the possibility of a Black man–White woman relationship in it, and that relationship never actualizes on screen. The other six films depict a White man–Black woman relationship. So, although the topic of White man–Black woman "miscegenation" may have become a popular trend, this has quite different historical and cultural implications than Black man–White woman "miscegenation" becoming popular, and generalizing Black–White relationships overlooks this important distinction. We need a framework that sees the continued silence of Black men–White women on the screen in direct contrast to the newfound popularity of White men–Black women. Doing so would allow us to read the history and significance of these films differently.

This is not to say that interracial scholars never utilize this method of parsing the race and gender of interracial pairs; in fact, when they do so, they notice the specific patterns and tropes that fully depend upon both the gender and race of the characters. For example, Cortés (2002) announces the genre's racial hierarchy: "[There was] a screen pecking order for interracial love, with Latinos requiring the most careful internal differentiation, Asians, Indians, and Arabs enjoying some flexibility, and African Americans becoming the least likely to cross interracial barriers" (p. 133). Here, Cortés announces the range of censored male characters paired with White women and is able to make a specific argument about their censorship. He acknowledges that the Production Code Administration did not treat all "nonWhite" men equally but, rather, on a gradated scale. This acute attention to race-and-gender differentiation begins the work of outlining the distinct qualities of varied interracial pairs, and it is from this framework that we should engage the field.

This framework would allow us to see the implications of Black men and White women or any other race-and-gender interracial pairing as unique, with its own history and culturally constructed narrative attached to it. Reading the couple in this way allows us to draw across disciplines in order to understand how the filmic representation of the couple relates to the historical lived experience of the interracial pair and the narrative tropes that have defined their union in various cultural outlets. It will also allow us to compile a canon of films based specifically on their pairing, as opposed to interracial relationships generally, which will reveal the cinematic patterns and tropes associated with their particular union. We can then begin to reread these films and intervene into previous analyses.

With this framework in hand, we shall turn to the representation of Black men and White women specifically. Susan Courtney (2005) shows us that *"The Birth of a Nation* holds pride of place in cultural memory, and in film studies, as American cinema's primal fantasy of miscegenation" (p. 44). She describes this originating fantasy as the story of the idealized White woman under assault by a Black male rapist, and nearly every work on "miscegenation" in film, or the history of Black masculinity in film, includes a discussion of the intersection of these archetypal characters. Donald Bogle (2004) explains that *"The Birth of a Nation* was the motion picture to introduce the mythic type the brutal Black buck" through the characters of the "renegade Black Gus [who] sets out to rape the younger Cameron daughter . . . [and] the mulatto Sylas Lynch [who] attempts to force the White Elsie Stoneman to marry him" (pp. 10–12). Bogle describes the brutal Black buck as "big, baaaaad niggers, oversexed and savage, violent and frenzied as they lust for White flesh" (p. 13). This claim falls within a plethora of scholarship that analyzes and refers to the scene in which Gus proposes marriage to Little Sister, which leads to her committing suicide, as the "Gus rape scene." [10] Gus becomes the synecdoche for the image of the Black male as rapist, the Black male beast–versus–idolized White woman rape scene that haunts representations of Black men and White women on screen. And yet, as Gerald R. Butters Jr. reminds us in his work *Black Manhood on the Silver Screen* (2002), "Gus never implies anything provocative, he never makes any sexual advances. He indirectly proposed marriage so his intentions appear honorable" (p. 79). Although what the audience may have been "trained" to see at this time remains debated, ultimately no rape has to occur on screen for Gus to be interpreted as a rapist.[11] By looking at the scene directly and paying attention to what we are shown instead of how we have been culturally constructed to interpret it, Gus transforms from a brutal, flesh-hungry rapist to a man whose marriage proposal to a White woman is so degrading and appalling that she would rather kill herself than face this offer. We must focus on what we actually see versus what is imagined; for as Gaines (2001) shows us, "The censorial gaze does not look . . . [it] is a very particular point of view putting the interpretation before the image in such a way that the interpretation stands on its own quite apart from the scenes themselves" (p. 240).

Richard Wright spotlights this cultural act of "putting the interpretation before the image" in his work *Native Son*. As Ishmael Reed (1997) explains,

"Though sexual contact may have been in Bigger's thoughts, there is *no* sexual contact between Bigger [, a Black man,] and Mary Dalton [, a White woman,] when he 'accidently' murders her. Yet, from the very beginning of the case, the newspapers charged Bigger with rape" (p. 190). Like Bigger, Gus may or may not have had sexual thoughts while chasing Little Sister. However, merely having sexual thoughts and chasing a woman does not make him a rapist. Seeing Gus and Bigger as rapists rather than the scorned suitor and baffled murderer that appear on screen, we perpetuate the fallacious interpretation that a Black man in pursuit of/presence of a White woman must always/already be a rapist.[12] Gus is our first cinematic example of this phenomenon.

What then happens when we are actually given a sex scene? We can see the effect of this misreading in a review of James Baldwin's 1962 novel *Another Country*. While describing the characters in the novel, the critic Bill Ott (1994) claims: "He's Black, bisexual, and a jazz drummer; she's White, timid, and newly arrived in New York from the Deep South. Their relationship begins with an encounter that, by modern standards, would certainly qualify as date rape." Similar to descriptions of the scene with Gus and Little Sister, when I read this I was confused, for the description I read was anything but a date rape. Rufus and Leona have been engaging in flirtatious banter with sexual undertones all night long. When Rufus finally asks her, "You seen anything you want since you been in New York?" Leona replies, "Oh, I want it all!" Later they replay this conversation and he whispers to her, "Well then, come and get it" (Baldwin, p. 20). They then aggressively, passionately, and playfully roll around on the balcony, finally having sex while sobbing and cursing during their interaction. Baldwin does not sugar coat the moment with soft sweet nothings, but he is also not giving us a scene of date rape. He allows two people, a Black man and a White woman, who know nothing about one another except a mutual attraction, to collide on a balcony; they consume one another and, being fully, poetically, in the moment, feel each tide of emotion that falls from their bodies. How then does this moment that ends with Leona looking up at Rufus with "a shy, triumphant smile" kissing him and exclaiming, "It was so wonderful" (p. 22) get critically interpreted as date rape by the reviewer? Sure, Leona cries and screams out, but it comes from that erotic intersection of pleasure and pain that sex produces, not fear or rejection of Rufus. Perhaps Baldwin has better insight into the joyful pain that penetration produces for Leona, which Ott can dismiss as rape. Or perhaps Bill Ott's comment should be dismissed as mere misinterpretation, but that would disconnect it from all the historical precedents that have called rape at the mere sight of a Black man and White woman together.

And this "myth of the Black rapist" has not existed merely in our films and literature; it has explicit consequences on the lives of *real* Black men. The historical legacy of lynching Black men falsely, accusing them of raping White women, has been well documented and, as Patricia Hall (1983) notes, Black men "have received disproportionate punishment for sexual assault . . . of the 455 men executed for rape since 1930, 405 were Black, and almost all of the complainants were White" (p. 343). Perhaps to the culturally constructed eye, Gus, Bigger, and Rufus may all look like rapists. However, when we call attention to the narrative tropes that historically plague not just interracial couples but specifically the sexual relationship of Black men and White women, we find a completely different story.

These misreadings are not reserved for the alleged Black rapist; they also latch on to images of White women involved in sexual relationships with Black men. In a demeaning and misleading summary, Henry Louis Gates Jr. claims that in the film *Shaft,* "the eponymous hero makes love to a prostitute in his shower" (p. 163). However, if we once again focus on what we are shown versus what we imagine, the woman, Linda, is not by any means a prostitute. She is a White woman who picks up a Black man, Gates's hero Shaft, in a bar. She comes back to his house. We see them passionately kissing in his shower, and then he kicks her out of his bed the next morning with promises that they will do it again. This does not make her a prostitute. Gates's assumption makes sense, however, if we consider feminist scholar Ruth Frankenberg's (1993) observation that, "Like the negative stereotypes of African American men, images of White women in relationships with men of color frequently reduce them to sexual beings" (p. 87). We must not allow these historical negative stereotypes to further impede and misdirect our analysis of interracial couples.

Film scholar Robin Wood also notes this typical misreading of a sexual White woman in his critique on Leonard Maltin's summary of the film *Mandingo*. Maltin assigns the film a bomb and describes it thus: "Trashy potboiler will appeal only to the s&m crowd. [James] Mason is a bigoted plantation patriarch. [Susan] George his oversexed daughter, [Ken] Norton—what else?—a fighter. Stinko!" (Wood, 1998, p. 266). Wood notes, "one may reasonably begin questioning whether the writer has even *seen Mandingo!*" (p. 266). As I was, Wood is rightfully astounded at Maltin's misdescription of Susan George's character Blanche:

> That "oversexed" is wonderful, a sociological testament in itself: rejected by her husband after their wedding night when he discovers she isn't a virgin . . . Blanche is forced into a life of total abstinence, and experiences what one would assume to be the perfectly natural need of an adult woman

for sexual satisfaction. This, in the writer's eyes, makes her "oversexed"—apparently the Victorian belief that women should merely "lie on their backs and think of England" still thrives. (p. 266)

What Wood fails to mention here is that Blanche fulfills this "need for sexual satisfaction" by having sex with her husband's *Black male* slave Mede. Although Wood aptly notes the sexism involved in Maltin's misreading, he avoids stating the obvious intersection of gender *and* race that signals Blanche not as the sympathetically forlorn woman driven into an affair (of which Hollywood historically loves), but as the "strange *White* lady" (as her husband calls her), the sex-crazed maniac, or, as the DVD summary describes her, a nympho. It is the presence of a *Black* man in her arms that brands her "oversexed," a Victorian belief in the purity of *White* women, conjured up at the sight of a Black man and a White woman together, that fully defines Maltin's mislabeling of Blanche as "oversexed."

In her work *Racism, Misogyny, and the Othello Myth*, Celia R. Daileader argues, "Miscegeny from a racist point of view is always at some level rape. And if it isn't rape, if she 'wanted it,' it is not miscegenation, but rather proof that the woman is not truly White" (p. 22). For Gates, Maltin, and many other scholars and critics, the sight of a White woman openly and willingly engaging in sexual activity with a Black man signals them as "not-quite-White" sexual deviants—what Ann duCille has termed the Mandingo Syndrome.[13] By paying attention to the race and gender of the pairs represented, the fact that these are scenes portraying specifically a Black man and a White woman engaged in a sexual relationship allows us to recognize these misreadings.

Like the myth of the Black rapist, White women have also been historically persecuted for sexual relationships with Black men. Paul Lombardo (1987) revealed that the state of Virginia deemed White women who engaged in sexual relations with Black men "feebleminded" and "depraved;" therefore, they were liable to both the state's 1924 Racial Integrity Act and Eugenic Sterilization Act. This ultimately produced a state-mandated sterilization of White women who produced children with Black men.[14] By continuing to blatantly misread the representation of White women in relationships with Black men as sexual deviants, we perpetuate the stereotypes that have historically discriminated against the specific sexual union of Black men and White women. We must first highlight these blatant misreadings, understand where and why they appear, and then analyze the images that actually appear on screen, not the ones that live in ingrained stereotypes.

Abdul JanMohamed (1992) argues that "racialized sexuality is driven by a will to conceal its mechanisms and a reliance on unempirical stereotypes"

(p. 106). When interracial sexuality is then represented, these two concepts go hand in hand. As Calvin Hernton explains, in his work *Sex and Racism in America*, we are plagued by "a superstitious imagining of the pornographic nature of interracial sex" (p. xvi). Through this imagining, we conjure up symbolic stereotypical images, quite distant from the bodies on screen or the lived experience of interracial couples. By concealing the mechanisms of interracial sex, we can continue to "imagine" the stereotypes that plague them. But what happens when a Black man-White woman sexual relationship actually comes on screen? Do we view Gus differently once we literally see Black Rafe rape White Miss Wyckoff in *Secret Yearnings*? Does Linda continue to be a prostitute when White Angie openly and willingly gives herself to Black Flipper in *Jungle Fever*?[15] It is specifically the sexual in these explicit relationships that we have generally misread and avoided. Perhaps it is because as with *Sweetback*, these unmistakable sex scenes prove much more difficult to read than the ambiguous or implied sex scenes we can "imagine" in multiple ways.

Sweet Sweetback's Baadasssss Song is fully complicated and challenging. Typical of the Blaxploitation genre, it complicates the "normal" character tropes for Black men and White women and challenges the very taboo it transgresses. The character of Sweetback does not fit the brutal Black buck or Uncle Tom character type associated with Black men in the presence of White women, and as the leader of the White male motorcycle gang Pres is not bound by the system of White patriarchal power, dictating her Whiteness or sexuality. Ironically and brilliantly, Sweetback must "fuck" the White woman in order to escape punishment by the White male mob as opposed to the historical legacy of Black men receiving punishment from a White mob for the mere allegation of sex with a White woman. It also denies the trappings of Hollywood romance and gives instead the performance of sex as a public competition, placing Black man-White woman sex literally in the public sphere. These are just a few elements of the film that allow *Sweetback* to open up a space for a new cinematic story to be told, one that escapes and transgresses the confines of imagined sexual stereotypes between Black men and White women. It also opens a space for other race-and-gender pairs; it helps us understand the significance of being attuned to the cultural constructs that define specific interracial unions. If we acknowledge this scene as the first, *Sweetback* can pave a new path and allow us to go back and reread other films with fresh eyes.

In referring to the Black man's alleged desire for White women, Franz Fanon (1967) pleads, "this sexual myth . . . must no longer be allowed to impede active understanding" (p. 81). Literally seeing Sweetback and Pres have sex makes the misreading of other Black man-White woman characters even more apparent, for when their union is visualized, we discover that the

Black man is no brutal Black buck thirsting for White flesh, and the White woman is not a sexual deviant suffering from Mandingo Syndrome. In describing Jean Tommer's sexually provocative work *Cane*, Jonathan Smith argues that one must be "less concerned with making large moral judgments about behavior than with simply mapping and charting the territory."[16] We have far too often allowed our interpretations (judgments) to obliterate the images on the screen, and must now simply map and chart each couple's specific story as it appears.

By focusing on race and gender, I suggest we can utilize an interdisciplinary reading specified to the cultural history of specific race-and-gender pairs, not merely a generalization of interracial romance in Hollywood cinema. When race specificity enters the conversation, we can develop specified canons and begin to trace the patterns that define the representation and/or repression of specific interracial pairs. We also must pay attention to what we see on the screen, as opposed to the patterned misinterpretations of imagined stereotypes. Through this two-fold method, we can begin the work of intervening into existing analyses of interracial cinema. Acknowledging the specificity of race-and-gender in interracial relationships will help us begin the work of analyzing how Hollywood's representation of interracial relationships truly connects to the changing face of racism and sexism in American culture.

References

Baldwin, J. (1962/1993). *Another country*. New York: Vintage Books.

Bogle, D. (2004). *Toms, coons, mulattoes, mammies, and bucks: An interpretive history of Blacks in American films* (4th ed.). New York: Continuum.

Browne, N. (1992). Race: The political unconscious of American film. *East-West Film Journal*, 6(1), 5–16.

Butters, G. R. (2002). *Black manhood on the silent screen*. Lawrence: University Press of Kansas.

Cortés, C. E. (2002). Hollywood interracial love: Social taboo as screen titillation. In P. Loukides & L. K. Fuller, *The making and remaking of a multiculturalist* (pp. 21–35). New York: Teachers College Press.

Courtney, S. (2005). *Hollywood fantasies of miscegenation: Spectacular narratives of gender and race, 1903–1967*. Princeton, NJ: Princeton University Press.

Daileader, C. R. (2005). *Racism, misogyny, and the Othello myth: Inter-racial couples from Shakespeare to Spike Lee*. Cambridge, MA: Cambridge University Press.

Davis, A. (1983). Rape, racism, and the myth of the Black rapist. In A. Davis, *Women, race and class* (pp. 172–201). New York: Vintage.

duCille, A. (1997). The unbearable darkness of being: "Fresh" thoughts on race, sex, and the Simpsons. In Toni Morrison (Ed.), *Birth of a nation'hood: Gaze, script, and spectacle in the O.J. Simpson case* (pp. 293–338). New York: Pantheon Books.

Fanon, F. (1967). *Black skin, white masks.* New York: Grove Press.

Frankenberg, R. (1993). *White women, race matters: The social construction of Whiteness.* Minneapolis: University of Minnesota Press.

Gaines, J. (2001). *Fire and desire: Mixed-race movies in the silent era.* Chicago: University of Chicago Press.

Gates, H. L. (1991). Jungle fever; or, guess who's not coming to dinner? In Spike Lee (Ed.), *Five for five: The films of Spike Lee* (pp. 163–169). New York: Stewart, Tabori & Chang.

Hall, J. D. (1983). "The mind that burns in each body": Women, rape, and racial violence. In Ann Snitow, Christine Stansell, & Sharon Thompson (Eds.), *Powers of desire: The politics of sexuality* (pp. 328–349). New York: Monthly Review Press.

Hernton, C. C. (1988). *Sex and racism in America* (1st Evergreen ed.). New York: Grove Press.

hooks, bell. (1992). *Black looks: Race and representation.* Boston: South End Press.

JanMohamed, A. (1992). Sexuality on/of the racial border: Foucault, Wright, and the articulation of racialized sexuality. In Domna C. Stanton (Ed.), *Discourses of sexuality: From Aristotle to AIDS* (p. 415). Ann Arbor: University of Michigan Press.

Lombardo, P. A. (1987–1988). Miscegenation, eugenics, and racism: Historical footnotes to *Loving v. Virginia. U.C. Davis Law Review, 21,* 421–52.

MPPDA. (1982). The Motion Picture Production Code of 1930. In Gerald Mast (Ed.), *The movies in our midst: Documents in the cultural history of film in America* (pp. 321–332). Chicago: University of Chicago Press.

Ott, B. (1994, February). Unlikely love stories. *American Liberties,* 208–213.

Pascoe, P. (2009). *What comes naturally: Miscegenation law and the making of race in America.* New York: Oxford University Press.

Reed, I. (1997). Bigger and O. J. In Toni Morrison (Ed.), *Birth of a nation'hood: Gaze, script, and spectacle in the O. J. Simpson case* (pp. 169–196). New York: Pantheon Books.

Williams, L. (2004). Skin flicks on the racial border: Pornography, exploitation, and interracial lust. In Linda Williams (Ed.), *Porn studies* (p. 516). Durham, NC: Duke University Press.

Williams, L. (2008). *Screening sex.* Durham, NC: Duke University Press.

Wood, R. (1998). "Mandingo": The vindication of an abused masterpiece. In R. Wood, *Sexual politics and narrative film: Hollywood and beyond* (pp. 265–282). New York: Columbia University Press.

Notes

1. Note that the organization changed its name to the Motion Picture Association of America in 1946.

2. Referring to the White person's partner as simply "nonWhite" rather than delineating that character's particular race dismisses the significance that the intersection of both race and gender hold in the identity of an interracial couple. Similar to the work of Peggy Pascoe (2009), I will be reading a Black man–White woman interracial couple differently than a White man–Chinese woman couple or any other pairing. I will use her terminology, *race-and-gender pair*, to emphasize this distinction.

3. Including White women with other *nonWhite* men besides Black. See, for example, films *Son of India* (1931, Indian man and White woman), *The Bitter Tea of General Yen* (1933, Chinese man and White woman), *The Last of the Mohicans* (1936, Native American man and White woman), and *Right Cross* (1950, Mexican man and White woman).

4. Cited in Auster memo, March 13, 1934, *Imitation of Life* file, Production Code Administration Collection, Margaret Herrick Library, Academy of Motion Picture Arts and Sciences, Beverly Hills, California. Susan Courtney's (2005) work directed me to this memo, as well as other informative holdings of the Production Code Administration

5. Susan Courtney (2005) claims that "*Mandingo* (1975), [is] the first Hollywood film to . . . actually show interracial sex between a White woman and a Black man" (p. 361–339) specifically emphasizing the race-and-gender of the pair. However, Linda Williams (2004) reveals the debate in a footnote of her work, "[*Mandingo*] is not the first extended representation of interracial lust in Hollywood. A case could be made for the shower sex scene in *Shaft*, and even for the sex scene between Jim Brown and Raquel Welch in *100 Rifles*, both mentioned by Henry Louis Gates as rare moments of interracial sex" (p. 306). In *Screening Sex*, Williams also states that the scene in *Sweet Sweetback's Baadasssss Song* (1971) "finally delivers the interracial sex so anxiously diverted in the sex club (not to mention in *Vixen* and in countless other Hollywood flirtations with miscegenation)" (p. 98).

6. Linda Williams (2004, 2008) has argued repeatedly that to merely transgress a taboo does not defeat it, but rather it must also contain the combination of fear and desire that established it as taboo in the first place. In other words, merely showing a Black man and White woman having sex would not break this taboo; there must be within the scene reference to the fear and desire that make Black man–White women sex taboo. It is beyond the scope of this work to take up this aspect of her argument; however, her insight sheds light on many of the issues we can explore by looking directly at interracial sex. For my purposes, any representation of Black men–White women always/already conjures our preconceived notions of the taboo that dictates their pairing.

7. I compiled a list of films beginning with *Birth of a Nation* to the present that include a Black man–White woman interaction in which a sexual relationship

occurs or is implied between the characters. I ordered the films chronologically based upon the date of their USA release according to the American Film Institute. I define the first visualized Black man–White woman sex scene as consisting of nude or partially nude bodies engaged in sexual relations in which we are shown from some angle and motion the physical act of sex, not simply implied sex through kissing and rubbing or elliptical editing.

8. Note that we previously granted this distinction to *One Potato Two Potato* (1964), which traces the couple's courtship to marriage. Some may disagree with granting this moment to *View From Pompey's Head* due to the fact that the husband has been "passing" and we and his wife do not discover that he is Black until the end of the film. However, I find it fascinating and significant that a "passing" film is the first representation of a Black man-White woman marriage on Hollywood screens.

9. Also note Van Peebles's film *The Story of a Three Day Pass* (1968) previously had implied Black man–White woman sex through elliptical editing. However, technically, this would be considered a French film made during the time that Van Peebles expatriated to France. Al Johnson submitted it to the San Francisco Film Festival as a French entry.

10. See, for example, Jane Gaines (2001); she explains that the scene has been read in countless ways, and her intentional use of quotation marks signifies the debate: "Gus chase" scene and "Gus rape" scene. She also argues that Little Sister "dies both instead of and because of the rape" (p. 238).

11. There is also debate over whether the "rape" scene was cut from the original version. As Gaines (2001) notes, many arguments ride on the uncovering of this missing footage. She states we should not focus on whether the rape occurred but rather "the use of imagery that stands for 'rape,'"—and, as I am arguing, what this imagery does for future interpretations of "rape" (p. 340).

12. See Davis, 1983.

13. Ann duCille (1997) somewhat cynically coined the phrase in response to the alleged Othello Syndrome. She describes the Mandingo Syndrome as "White women's penchant for and willing submission to Black men and the national anxiety that even the possibility of such coupling has traditionally evoked" (p. 303).

14. Virginia's Racial Integrity Act of 1924 outlawed miscegenation for being scientifically unsound and polluting America with mixed-blood offspring. The Eugenic Sterilization Act required the sterilization of the insane and socially inadequate. Lombardo (1987) uncovered a report in which John Plecker, head of Virginia's Statistic Bureau, wrote, "Not a few White women are giving birth to mulatto children. These women are usually feebleminded, but in some cases they are simply depraved" (p. 438).

15. Linda Williams (2004) has used interracial pornography to explore these questions, concluding that stereotypes refunction throughout history and are not always held with the same negative connotation (p. 285–288).

16. J. C. Smith, *A Thin Line to Stand On: Mapping Poetics in Contemporary African American Poets*, 264.

Gender

9

Multiculturalism, Women, and the Need for a Feminist Analysis

Cynthia S. Bynoe and Sherrow O. Pinder

The diversification of American society is reflected and reinforced by the shift from assimilation (the melting pot) to multiculturalism (the mosaic).[1] Multiculturalism is about culture, "a microcosm of the social" (Goldberg, 1994, p. 24), which restricts cultural homogeneity and promotes cultural heterogeneity. To speak of multiculturalism, then, is to speak of a plurality of cultures that are unique and distinct from each other. Against this background, multiculturalism, as a way of nurturing America's cultural diversification by encouraging racialized ethnic groups to maintain their distinctive cultures, seems especially appealing. Culture, an essential part of who we are as human beings, matters because it shapes the ways in which we give meaning to our world (Pinder, 2010). While multiculturalism allows for the recognition and celebration of nondominant cultures, it sets apart the dominant culture from the nondominant cultures and promotes a form of cultural hierarchy based on the ideology of white supremacy, which is maintained and nurtured by an essentialist view of culture.

Given that cultures, for the most part, are submerged with practices and ideologies concerning gender conscription, it is critical to examine how women are positioned within nondominant cultures. In other words, how are cultural differences to be recognized while at the same time securing the rights of women? In fact, identification of cultural difference is associated with deviance, stigma, and inequality; and a stereotypical view of the "other" is promoted, which inevitably lends credence to a false dichotomy between oppressive nondominant cultures and the egalitarian dominant culture. Taking our cue from Susan Moller Okin's *Is Multiculturalism Bad for Women?*, in this chapter we want to show that multiculturalism is "bad for women" because gender functions as an act of cultural inscription. In other words, gender hierarchy allows for the rights of men to take precedence over the rights of women. And because the "culture card" is used to uphold and maintain violence perpetrated by men against women, we want to show, then, that multiculturalism, in its quest for cultural recognition and celebration of nondominant cultures, it is the otherness of the "other" or, to borrow from Anne Phillips (2007), "minorities within minorities,"[2] in this case women, that multiculturalism cannot account for. Hence, for women, multiculturalism and the politics of cultural recognition promote a "double bind."

How are we to conjure a multiculturalism that treats women as equal to men when multiculturalism itself promotes and sanctions cultural hierarchy in which the dominant culture is separated from the nondominant cultures?[3] The dominant culture provides the content for how the nondominant cultures are to "shape some of their beliefs and practices, and remains their point of reference" (Song, 2007, p. 35). All members of nondominant cultures have to adhere to a public culture, or "a meaningful way of life across the full range of human activities, including social, educational, religious, recreational, and economic life, encompassing both public and private spheres" (Kymlicka, 1995, p. 76), which is infused with patriarchal norms and values.[4] Hence, we want to show that this oppression, for the most part, stems from the fact that patriarchal prescriptions allow for men to have a disproportionate amount of power, which works to subordinate women. In fact, the patriarchal norms and practices of the dominant culture pose tremendous obstacles for women who are situated within nondominant cultures. Hence, cultural practices such as polygamy, arranged marriages, or female circumcision, which appear to be intraculturally influenced, conflict with multiculturalists' analyses and, therefore, should be problematized and located within a broader patriarchal culture upheld by the dominant institutions and structures that work in the interest of men. However, it is important not to treat these practices as one and the same phenomenon, that is, oppressive to women. In fact, we are aware that cultural practices are very complicated and cannot simply be juxtaposed and analyzed by Western norms and values that automatically chastise these practices as oppressive to women. And given that cultural practices have meaning in relation to other realities shaping practices such as female economic dependence on men, for example, they do exist independently of the entire cultural way of life in which they are practiced. It is important, therefore, to forego ethnocentric impulses and be attentive to the patriarchal norms and practices of the dominant culture if we are to truly evaluate women's position within the nondominant cultures. For us, then, a feminist analysis that focuses on the problems of gender inequities that are imbedded within the nondominant cultures, which are upheld by the patriarchal norms of the dominant cultures, is more relevant and informative. We will locate this kind of a feminist analysis within a broader framework, which we will call multicultural feminism.[5] Rather than conceptualizing nondominant cultures as separate and unaffected by the dominant cultural norms, multicultural feminism offers an alternative analytic tool to problematize the ways in which cultural practice, with the help of the state, works in the interest of men. Thus, we argue against cultural claims unless these claims work to embrace intracultural recognition among marginalized groups or subalterns, especially women.[6]

Multicultural feminism calls into question the very notion of culture itself and how women are, for the most part, positioned as subordinates within nondominant culture. Culture, in itself, is coded with gender meanings, and stereotypes of women located in nondominant culture are conformed, leading to a desperate need for multicultural feminism to challenge the dominant culture and nondominant cultures' dichotomy in which women in the latter are viewed as more oppressed than in the former. In fact, multicultural feminism takes into consideration the dialogical relations between the dominant and nondominant cultures and shows how patriarchal underpinnings, as the source of cultural values and meanings, have managed to generate a multifaceted critique of how women are positioned within nondominant cultures as a gender subaltern population and are excluded from the circuits and possible benefits of cultural recognition. In fact, to borrow from the postcolonial theorist Gayatri C. Spivak (1988), women, as the subaltern, a subordinated social group that is located within a nondominant cultural group, "cannot speak." In other words, they cannot be heard by the male privilege of either the dominant culture or nondominant cultures. Hence, it is indispensable for women to be positioned within a counterculture in which they can be heard and cease to be a subaltern who "cannot speak." We will call this the gender subaltern counterculture. And even though the scope of our chapter does not allow for a comprehensive discussion of the gender subaltern counterculture, as a start, this form of counterculture, in part, would work to dislodge the "culture card," especially when it works to strengthen patriarchal predisposition such as rape, murder, and other forms of violence that are directed toward women.

Defining and Explaining Multiculturalism

In the United States, multiculturalism starts from the premise that there is a dominant and various nondominant cultures. The need for the recognition and celebration of the nondominant cultures is important. And even though multiculturalism has been defended by many liberal thinkers such as Will Kymlicka, Charles Taylor, and Bhikhu Parekh, it remains a concept that is hard to define and explain. Okin (1999), for one, captures, at best, the ephemeral nature of multiculturalism and the difficulty of defining it when she admits that she finds it hard "to pin down" multiculturalism (p. 10). Also, Paul Gilroy (2005) points to the fact that "there is no consensus on how the term 'multiculturalism' should be defined or employed" (p. 432). Before we address our main concern that multiculturalism "is bad for women," it is important to define multiculturalism as the acknowledgement and support of cultural pluralism but at the same time focus on the unequal relationship of nondominant and dominant cultures in which cultural hierarchy is upheld. Cultural hierarchy in itself is fractured by gender hierarchy. Cultural pride is expected to make members of nondominant cultures feel good. However, for women, their gender positions them as subordinates within nondominant cultures, which is even more extreme in how they are positioned as subordinates in every aspect of the larger society. In other words, nonwhite women's subordination is defined and shaped by the intersectionality of their race, ethnicity, class, and gender.[7]

Even in cases in which the claims for recognition and accommodation by a nondominant culture are denied—the case of arranged marriages, for example, which for Okin is a problem of "multiculturalism v. [Western] feminism"—the focus on the patriarchal practice of the nondominant culture can serve to direct our attention from gender hierarchy within the nondominant culture to the gender hierarchy as it is embedded within the dominant culture. In other words, the dominant culture has shaped some of the gender practices of the nondominant cultures and has remained a point of location. For example, in the United States, the 1887 Dawes Act undermined the position of First Nations[8] women in agricultural work by making First Nations men the landowners, the head of the household, and farmers. Sexist practices in nondominant cultures are approved and sanctioned by the state. For example, in the case *Santa Clara Pueblo v. Martinez*, even though Pueblo membership rules discriminated against women and go against the federal Indian Civil Rights Act, the court upheld the rule.[9]

The tensions between cultural recognition and gender impartiality are the kinds of dilemmas that multiculturalism is not prepared to deal with. In this sense, nondominant cultural practice, even though it subordinates women, exempts the nondominant groups from laws that interfere with such a practice. And, given that multiculturalism frames cultures as distinct and fixed sets of fairly stagnant traditions and practices that differentiate the nondominant cultures as backward and traditional from the civilized and enlightened dominant culture, it treats cultural identities as fixed and as a "natural" part of our social life as human beings. Hence, identities become essentialized and conceived as social constructions. It is our contention, then, that culture needs to be problematized in any of the debates about multiculturalism. Instead, as multiculturalism does, viewing culture as a practice in which language, ethnicity, dress, and food become the most important signifiers; culture, for us, is a dynamic practice of making and remaking cultural meanings that are conditional, changing, and incomplete so that individuals positioned within groups that may be shifting and transforming, such as the disabled, lesbians and gays, bisexual, and transgendered who have recently made claims for recognition must be granted such recognitions. As human beings, we partake in cultural acts and unending cultural contestation and negotiation that encompass multifaceted and developing identities that allow differences within groups to blossom and flourish. However, identity here is not conceptualized through singular, one-dimensional, and distinct categories such as culture-based rights that shape cultural practices. And given that all practices that have meaning involve power relations, culture, in this sense, situates power as the core of identity struggles and resistance over meaning making and what a meaning symbolizes (Jordon & Weedon, 1995, p. 11). In terms of gender relations, as black feminists have argued, gender cannot be extracted from culture-based rights and processes of meaning making that include ethnicity, nationality, language, and, in some cases, certain non–Western religious practices. The liminal positioning of women, or what Homi Bhabha (1994) refers to "in-between the designations of identity" (p. 5), is what signifies their positions as "other other."

Multiculturalism is supposed to recognize cultural differences and not make them liabilities. Cultural differences, which can never occupy a privileged status, include experience of "language, speaking style or dialect, body comportment, gesture, social practices, values, group-specific socialization and so on" (Young, 1987, p. 547). And since the recognition of nondominant culture "is bad for women," for Okin, a meaningful way of dealing with the harm that multiculturalism poses for women is for the nondominant cultures to be enculturated into the dominant liberal culture either by regulating gender norms within nondominant cultures so that they promote gender equality or, alternatively, by incorporating members from the nondominant cultures into the dominant culture until the former becomes extinct (Okin, 1999, pp. 22–23).

While Okin's formulation revives the colonial dynamics of civilized (dominant) and uncivilized (nondominant) cultures as well as conceptualizing women as the "inessential other," what Okin fails to come to terms with is that multiculturalism, in its quest for the promotion of cultural recognition of nondominant cultures, aims to promote a politics of cultural exclusion—that is, members of the nondominant cultures continue to be defined by their cultural identity and recognized as belonging to the nondominant cultures. So inessential is the "other" that Joanne Harumi Sechi (1980), a Japanese American author, confesses, "I was made to feel that cultural pride would justify and make good my difference in skin color while it was a constant reminder that I was [culturally] different" (p. 444). Sechi's acknowledgment is a reminder of the racialist ontology from which multiculturalism has evolved and its legacy of cultural hierarchization. The marginal position of the nondominant culture as the natural order of cultural positioning is celebrated by multiculturalism. If nondominant cultures disappear, the need for multiculturalism and the politics of recognition will be obsolete.

Multiculturalism and Gender

A primary focus of multiculturalism is to augment cultural diversity and encourage public protest against the suppression of cultural differences. Culture is a fundamental part of who we are as human beings because it shapes the way we give meaning to our world. However, membership in these nondominant cultural groups depends, for the most part, on individuals possessing the attributes associated with a particular group and how these individuals identify with and participate in the collective life of the group. While cultures, as are viewed from a constructivist perspective,[10] are internally varied and change eventually because of their interaction with each other (interculturalism) and with the dominant (multiculturalism),[11] they are nevertheless taken to be basic, disconnected wholes characterized by a set of attributes that distinguish each from the rest (Taylor, 1994, p. 31). Based on women's social positions within nondominant cultures, women are defined in various and conflicting ways. More importantly, while male members of the group might value a particular practice and desire its preservation, other female members might find this practice at fault. Hence, the recognition and celebration of cultures, as is the aim of multiculturalism, may risk reinforcing intragroup gender hierarchy. And as institutions and systems take on and normalize cultural claims to the exclusion of women, these claims are then advanced as common and worthy of the groups' compliance. In recognizing and celebrating nondominant cultures, multiculturalism poses a serious problem for ensuring gender equity within nondominant cultures. While multiculturalism became the scapegoat for the violence perpetrated again women in the name of "culture," it becomes one of the mechanisms through which gender hierarchy is maintained (Phillips, 2007, 15).[12] And, as Joseph Raz (1999) points out, "It is a mistake to think that multicultural measures can counteract this fact" (p. 90), which is the otherness of the "other," working, in important ways, to disadvantage women who are situated within nondominant cultures.

The emphasis on gender and culture, to a large extent, cannot be avoided when one analyzes the discourse of multiculturalism. Okin (1998), for one, is concerned with the tension that arises between multiculturalism and feminism because, in her mind, nondominant cultures "are highly patriarchal" (p. 679) and hostile to women, and these cultures have no local customs of dissent, no indigenous feminist movement, and no basis of political contention (Bhabha, 1999, p. 83). She writes:

> While virtually all of the world's cultures have distinctively patriarchal pasts, some—mostly, though by no means exclusively, Western liberal cultures—have departed far further from them than others. Western cultures, of course, still practice many forms of sex discrimination. . . . But women in more liberal cultures are, at the same time, legally guaranteed many of the same freedoms and opportunities as men. In addition, most families in such cultures, with the exception of some religious fundamentalists, do not communicate to their daughters that they are of less value than boys, that their lives are to be confined to domesticity and service to men and children, and that the only positive value of their sexuality is that it be strictly confined to marriage, the service of men, and for reproductive ends. This, as we have seen, is quite different from women's situation in many of the world's other cultures, including many of those from which immigrants to Europe and Northern American come. (Okin, 1999, p. 16–17)

Some of her examples of the patriarchal nature of nondominant cultures are drawn from cultural practice such as female circumcision, veiling, arranged marriages, and polygamy—not that polygamy, described as an extremely patriarchal practice, is more or less oppressive to women than monogamy. In fact, these kinds of critiques of nondominant cultural norms and practices, for the most part, divert attention from the dominant cultural practice of enabling women's inequality and mask the reality of women's oppression; this weapon of mass distraction only serves to shield the latter from criticism that points to the many ways in which women's rights of citizenship are curtailed under the masculine symbolic, shaping and upholding gender roles and expectations. The reinforcement of these distinctive categories is grounded in notions of oppositional binaries such as superior (dominant culture) and inferior (nondominant cultures). This model remains crucial for maintaining the hegemony of the values and norms of the dominant culture as the standards against which the nondominant cultures are measured and reduced to cultural otherness. While, in the spirit of multiculturalism, cultural otherness is recognized and celebrated, the otherness of the "other" operates as a metonymic form of the "new sexism" clothed in its old ways that multiculturalism cannot account for. **It is in this instance of gender differentiation that domination, in the form of sexism, is fashioned and disseminated.**

Okin, in her focus on the more patriarchal nature of nondominant cultures, ignores the fact that the protection of one patriarchal culture (nondominant) is being made by another patriarchal culture, the American culture in this case, and how the liberal state upholds "culture" in the interest of men. For example, in 1984, Kong Pheng Mousa, a 23-year-old Hmong man living in the United States for the past 6 years, abducted 19-year-old Xeng Xiong, a Laotian woman, from the Fresno City College campus in California and raped her. Xiong reported the incident of rape to the police. In his defense, Mousa claimed that he was performing the customary Hmong practice of matrimony, "marriage by capture," in which the man would determine his power and virility by snatching the woman and she would ritually protest his sexual advances in order to establish her virtue. Mousa maintained that he had not comprehended Xiong's resistance as conveying nonconsent. The court agreed that the man had to be judged according to his culture. Accordingly, the charges of kidnapping and rape were dismissed, and Mousa was charged with false imprisonment and was fined $1,000 and sentenced to 120 days in jail.[13] While the defense of rape, in this case, has explicitly appealed to cultural traditions, there is a remarkable intercultural similarity between the gender norms of the dominant culture and those of the nondominant cultures. Rape, in this case, reverberates with and has found support in the gender norms that permeate the legal dogmas of the dominant culture (Song, 2007, p. 102). When "culture" and a reliance on assumed "cultural traditions" as ways to legitimize crimes against women take precedence over the rights of women, it leaves unchallenged the patriarchal norms of the dominant culture, which is extended to the nondominant cultures. To put it differently, when women's subordinate position is defended in the name of "culture," the "culture card" is even more effective because it resonates with the mainstream patriarchal practice of rape. Hence, when men put forward such a claim as "my culture made me do it," these men are claiming the kind of male privilege that, according to Bonnie Honig (1999), "must be resisted for the sake of both [women's rights] and 'culture': neither is well served by it" (p. 36). In this sense, the justice system is not a reflexive receptor that is detached from the practice of patriarchal norms and values that manipulate cultural meanings to the exclusion and oppression of women as internal members of the nondominant cultures. It is important, then, to think of the justice system as a partaker in making meanings and, further, as a fundamental locus for the organization and propagation of those signifying forms with which gender differences are fashioned and refashioned into normality.

In addition to rape, women are murdered in the name of "culture." A well-known case is that of the murder of a Chinese woman by her husband, Dong Lu Chen, both immigrants living in New York, after he discovered that she was having an affair. The Brooklyn district attorney, Elizabeth Holtzman, charged him with second-degree murder. Cultural evidence from an expert witness, showing that "in traditional Chinese culture, a wife's adultery is considered proof that a husband has a weak character, making him undesirable even after a divorce, and because of this stigma a Chinese man could reasonably be expected to be enraged," was used to explain the state of Chen's mind. Chen's lawyer, employing the "culture card," got the charges reduced from murder to involuntary manslaughter or second-degree murder. After further considering the evidence, the court granted Chen a reduced charge and sentence on the basis of the cultural evidence. Chen was convicted of second-degree manslaughter and was sentenced to 5 years of probation with no jail time (Song, 2007, pp. 94–95). And even though Chen's reduced sentence was severely criticized by many Asian American groups and women's organizations, including the National Organization for Women, justice prevailed in the name of patriarchal manhood, which is predominantly injurious to women. Hence, discrimination that is aimed at nonwhite men is not because of their gender. Their race, ethnicity, class, sexual orientation, religious background, and so on put them at risk. The court's logic seems to indicate that when women are being unfaithful to men, it is not surprising that men are outraged to the point of perpetrating violence against women.[14] For this precise reason, it is important to render the multifaceted interconnections between dominant and nondominant gender norms. Only then can we be able to oppose monolithic views about nondominant cultures as more oppressive to women, which have proliferated, for example, into an irrational Islamophobia. The argument that is uncritically articulated is that the Muslim culture is oppressive to women.

Marrianne Yen (1989), in an article written for the *Washington Post*, explained and highlighted that Chen's behavior "has nothing to do with being Chinese or having a Chinese background. In modern China, under socialist law and culture, it is not acceptable conduct" (p. A3). In fact, as Sarah Song (2007) noted:

> There are many contemporary Chinese cases in which husbands killed their wives after discovering their wives committed adultery. If you run a search of *"tonjian shaqi"* (adultery killing wife) on Google or Baidu.com, you will find plenty of such cases. In some of these cases the husbands were sentenced to life in prison or death with two years suspension of execution. (p. 108)

In this sense, if we should juxtapose courts in China and courts in the United States and how respective courts treat "crimes of passion," it seems that Chinese courts are much more severe than American courts. And given that Chinese culture has nothing to do with men killing women, we have to locate such atrocity against women within a larger framework of patriarchy and how women's subordination is linked to a cultural devaluing of femaleness. As a matter of fact, no woman is unaffected from cultural devaluing and the ongoing threat of sexual and intimate partner violence. However, violence perpetrated toward women is not culturally specific but, for the most part, universally accepted. In the end, this kind of "culturology" approach toward violence against women only serves to reinforce and uphold sexism.

In the following section, we examine how upholding women's subordination in the name of the "culture card" serves to show that groups' cultural recognition is blind to internal group differences, in this case women as a social group. We are not implying here that women, as a group, are not also internally differentiated by identity markers such as social class, religion, sexuality, ablebodiedness, and age. However, we want to situate the "culture card" strategy within the framework of multiculturalism and cultural recognition and highlight the many problems that such a strategy poses for women and society as a whole.

The Problematics of the "Culture Card" Strategy

Feminists have drawn our attention to the inherent tension between nondominant groups' rights and the rights of women that are positioned within these groups. From the preceding examples, in which a defendant invokes his cultural background to defend and justify violence that is perpetrated toward women, this kind of practice is referred to as pulling the "culture card," or the cultural defense strategy. The "culture card" strategy "maintains that persons socialized in a minority or foreign culture, who regularly conducted themselves in accordance with their own cultural norms should not be held fully accountable for conduct that violates official law, if that conduct confirms to the prescriptions of their own culture" (Phillips, 2003, p. 512). Robert LeVine's (1984) definition of culture as "a shared organization of ideas that includes the intellectual, moral, and aesthetic standards prevalent in a community and the meanings of communicative actions" is important here for three interrelated reasons: one, the emphasis on community standards, determining what are acceptable attitudes and behavior for its members; two, how these cultural norms are to be communicated to the members; and, three, how the members, in turn, are expected to display culturally suitable responses (p. 67). These cultural standards are shared, and through socialization, the members of the cultural group have come to internalize these standards. And since culture affects and determines our behavior and attitudes, for the most part, one's behaviors and attitudes that correspond with group's norms are interpreted as culturally grounded. In this sense, "culture" is used as an explanatory framework for behavior employed by men to violate, degrade, exploit, subordinate, and keep women in a subservient position. For instance, even though Mousa's action degraded, violated, and humiliated Xiong, he consciously, with help of the patriarchal state, employed the "culture card" to legitimize his action. In fact, it is important to consider that Chinese Americans' knowledge of Chinese culture is shaped and determined by the Dubosian double consciousness. Because of their hyphenation, Chinese and American, their cultural knowledge is, for the most part, fractional, unfinished, wide ranging, and predisposed by the dominant cultural norms.

The legal accommodation of sexist practice within nondominant cultures, as in the cultural defense cases that we have highlighted, further threatens women's fight for the rights of equal citizenship within a democratic society. Furthermore, when behavior of a member of the nondominant culture is explained and determined exclusively by culture, nondominant cultures are conceptualized as transporters of traditions that are incapable of any meaningful transformation. What is even more disconcerting is that although cultural defense jeopardizes equal respect for nondominant cultures, the courts, taking seriously these cultural defense arguments, only serve to reinforce and uphold stereotypes about nondominant cultures as traditional, backward, and uncivilized. A good illustration of this perception is in the case *People v. Hundal,* in which the prosecutor, in defending why an Indian woman did not leave her abusive relationship and brought rape charges against her husband, characterized Indian culture as traditional; "'men control women' and 'have a higher status than women'" (Song, 2007, p. 112).

The use of the "culture card" strategy for actions and behavior that harm women only serves to show that the problem is not only about how patriarchal predispositions manifest themselves within nondominant cultural practices but also the norms and values of the dominant cultures that, for the most part, uphold androcentric structures. The problem cannot be addressed by delegitimizing cultural practices and putting a ban on multiculturalism's call for cultural recognition. So long as the legal systems and institutions work in the interest of men located in the nondominant cultures and in society as a whole, their adversarial attitudes and behavior projected against women will continue to find support for patriarchal practices within the legal system. In America, because of patriarchal cultural inscriptions in which gender inequality is endemic to its heritage, epistemologies, and everyday customs, the gender norms of the nondominant cultures are inextricably linked and even determined by the dominant cultural norms, values, and expectations. And given that multiculturalism and the politics of cultural recognition make invisible women's position and location within cultures, it is more urgent than ever for a multicultural feminism analysis. Thus, relying loosely on Drucilla Cornell's (1991) definition of "ethical feminism"—which would attend to hierarchies of differences so that gender differences, for example, would be recognized within nondominant cultures, to focus more attention on how the cultural practices of nondominant cultures that subordinate women are not in isolation, but are shaped by the dominant patriarchal culture—is here fundamental. While at the same affirming differentiated identities, multicultural feminism would also take into consideration Gayatri C. Spivak's (1987) conceptualization of "strategic essentialism," which would work to promote "a scrupulously visible political interest" (p. 205). It would aim at conceptualizing both essentialized and fluid significations of identity (Spivak, 1987) as a form of subaltern consciousness that works to challenge dominant cultural scripts or hegemonic cultural narratives to make way for new cultural expression that recognizes women as bearers of culture.

Conclusion

Multiculturalism's quest for promoting cultural pluralism is at the forefront of America's race and ethnic relations. However, nondominant groups, in this sense, have homogenizing effects that are imposed by cultural recognition. And while multiculturalism's focus on culture takes attention away from the real issues of gender inequality, women, the "inessential other," are, for the most part, omitted from the debate for cultural recognition and celebration. For this precise reason, any discussion of multiculturalism and gender politics must acknowledge the need for a subaltern counterculture that places women at the center and, simultaneously, allows for intracultural knowledge that, in terms of gender, recognizes hybridity as points of difference. In this sense, a gender subaltern counterculture would point to the unequal gender differences within the nondominant cultures, without proposing that women is either a homogenized or resolute group. It will continue to question the privileging of the dominant culture as well as to highlight and interrogate the dialogical relations between the dominant culture and nondominant cultures, in terms of women's subordinate positioning. A gender subaltern counterculture, as an emancipatory site for women, would allow them to reinvent and express counter discourses that formulate oppositional interpretation of their identities, interests, and needs. Only then can we redress the imbalances of power between the genders and the cultures, and provide women, for instance, with arenas for reflection external to cultural inscriptions.

References

Bhabha, H. K. (1994). *The location of culture.* New York: Routledge.

Bhabha, H. K. (1999). Liberalism's sacred cow. In J. Cohen, M. Howard, & M. C. Nussbaum (Eds.), *Is multiculturalism bad for women? Susan Moller Okin with respondents* (pp. 79–84). Princeton, NJ: Princeton University Press.

Crenshaw, K. (1989). Demarginalizing the intersection of race and sex: A black feminist critique of antidiscrimination doctrine, feminist theory and antiracist politics. *University of Chicago Legal Forum,* 139–167.

Cornell, D. (1991). *Beyond accommodation: Ethnical feminism, deconstruction, and the law.* New York: Routledge.

D'Souza, D. (1991). *Illiberal education: The politics of race and sex on campus.* New York: Free Press.

Du Bois, W. E. B. (2003). *The souls of black folk.* Introduction by David Levering Lewis. New York: Modern Library.

Gilroy, P. (2005). Multiculture, double consciousness and the "war on terror." *Patterns of Prejudice 39*(4), 431–443.

Goldberg, D. T. (1994). *Multiculturalism: A reader.* Oxford, UK: Blackwell.

Honig, B. (1999). My culture made me do It. In Joshua Cohen, Matthew Howard, and Martha C. Nussbaum (Eds.), *Is multiculturalism bad for women? Susan Moller Okin with respondents* (pp. 35–40). Princeton, NJ: Princeton University Press.

Huntington, S. P. (2004). *Who are we? The challenges to America's national identity.* New York: Simon and Schuster.

Jordon, G., & Weedon, C. (1995). *Cultural politics: Class, gender, and race and the postmodern world*. Cambridge, MA: Backwell.

Kallen, H. M. (1915, February 26). Democracy versus the melting pot. *The Nations*, 217–220.

Kallen, H. M. (1924). *Culture and democracy in America*. New York: Boni and Liveright.

Kymlicka, W. (1995). *Multicultural citizenship: A liberal theory of minority-rights*. Oxford, UK: Clarendon Press.

LeVine, R. A. (1984). Property of culture: An ethnographic view. In Richard A. Shweder and Robert A. LeVine (Eds.), *Culture theory: Essays on mind, self, and emotions* (pp. 67–87). Cambridge, NY: Cambridge University Press.

Okin, S. M. (1998, July). Feminism and multiculturalism: Some tension. *Ethics 108*, 661–684.

Okin, S. M. (1999). *Is multiculturalism bad for women?* Princeton, NJ: Princeton University Press.

Phillips, A. (2003, July). When culture means gender: Issues of cultural defense in the English court. *Modern Law Review 66*(4), 510–531.

Phillips, A. (2007). *Multiculturalism without culture*. Princeton, NJ: Princeton University Press.

Pinder, S. O. (2010). *The politics of race and ethnicity: Americanization and de-Americanization of racialized ethnic groups*. New York: Palgrave Macmillan.

Raz, J. (1999). How perfect should one be? And whose culture is?" In Joshua Cohen, Matthew Howard, & Martha C. Nussbaum (Eds.), *Is multiculturalism bad for women? Susan Moller Okin with respondents* (pp. 95–98). Princeton, NJ: Princeton University Press.

Schlesinger, A. M. (1998). *The disuniting of America: Reflections on a multicultural society*. New York: W. W. Norton.

Sechi, J. H. (1980). Being Japanese-American doesn't mean "made in Japan." In Dexter Fisher (Ed.), *The third woman: Minority women writers of the United States* (pp. 442–449). Boston: Houghton Mifflin.

Shohat, E. (2001). *Talking visions: Multicultural feminism in a transnational age*. Boston: MIT Press.

Song, S. (2007). *Justice, gender, and the politics of multiculturalism*. Cambridge: Cambridge University Press.

Spencer, M. E. (1994). Multiculturalism, "political correctness," and the politics of identity. *Sociological Forum 9*(4), 547–567.

Spivak, G. C. (1987). *In other worlds: Essays in cultural politics*. New York: Methuen.

Spivak, G. C. (1988). Can the subaltern speak? In Cary Nelson and Lawrence Grossberg (Eds.), *Marxism and interpretation of culture* (pp. 271–313). Urbana: University of Illinois Press.

Taylor, C. (1994). *Multiculturalism: Examining the politics of recognition*, with commentaries by K. Anthony Appiah, Jürgen Habermas, Steven C. Rockefeller, Michael Walzer, & Susan Wolf. Ed. Amy Gutmann. Princeton, NJ: Princeton University Press.

Yen, M. (1989, April 10). Refusal to jail immigrant who killed wife stirs outrage; judge ordered probation for Chinese man, citing his "cultural background." *Washington Post*, A3.

Young, I. M. (1987). Differences and policy: Some reflections in the context of new social movements. *University of Connecticut Law Review 56*, 535–550.

Notes

1. Horace M. Kallen rejected the notion of the melting pot and replaced it with cultural pluralism. See "Democracy versus the melting pot" (1915) and *Culture and Democracy in America* (1924).

2. The "minorities within minorities" point to the many ways in which internal oppression is practiced within groups in which not only women are oppressed but other groups as well, such as homosexuals and the poor. For a more thorough reading, see Anne Phillips (2007), *Multiculturalism without Culture.*

3. In fact, the dominant culture is intolerant of members who are homosexuals or mentally or physically challenged. Not that tolerance is a good thing. One who is tolerant of differences stemming from identity markers such as gender, ethnicity, race, sexuality, and class is equally intolerant of such differences.

4. Also, the public culture interacts with other norms and identities including race, ethnicity, sexuality, class, nationality, and physical and mental abilities.

5. For a comprehensive reading on multicultural feminism, see Ella Shohat (2001), *Taking Vision: Multicultural Feminism in a Transnational Age.*

6. Cultural claims by First Nations to protect their resources from the dominant group are important.

7. Black feminists and other feminists of color have focused on the intersectionality framework for analyzing the oppression of black and other nonwhite women. The intersectionality framework was developed by Kimberlé Crenshaw in her 1989 article titled "Demarginalizing the Intersection of Race and Sex: A Black Feminist Critique of Antidiscrimination Doctrine, Feminist Theory and Antiracist Politics."

8. In this essay, we employ the term *First Nations* to mean *Native Americans.* The latter, for us, is embedded with colonial implications. *First Nations* is one of the existing terms referring to persons registered as Indians in Canada. In Canada's Constitutional Act of 1982, *Aboriginal* is used to refer to indigenous people of Canada. This term is still used by some First Nations in certain geographical locations in Canada. Also, it refers to the communities of Indians in Canada. In the United States, First Nations have continued to identify themselves in terms of Mohawks, Cree, Oneida, Kiowa, Navajo, Comanche, Apache, and Wichita, for example. For a more comprehensive reading, see Martin E. Spencer (1994), "Multiculturalism, 'Political Correctness,' and the Politics of Identity" (557–558).

9. The children of First Nations women who are not married to men belonging to Santa Carlo Pueblo are not recognized as First Nations. The state, in this sense,

is complicit in upholding gender inequity. More important, we see how the state, by its actions, determines who has the right to claim First Nationness, and thus First Nations' identity is intimately connected with the state's recognition. For a more comprehensive discussion on the Santa Cara Pueblo case, see Sarah Song (2007, pp. 114–141).

10. For a more comprehensive reading on the constructive view of culture, see Sara Song (2007), *Justice, Gender, and the Politics of Multiculturalism* (pp. 31–40).

11. We do not mean to de-emphasize the importance of cultural borders for multiculturalism—that is, nondominant cultures are separated from dominant culture.

12. Multiculturalism, in the United States, had become associated with a change in curriculum and university admission to reflect the experiences of America's diverse population, which has, nonetheless, provoked reactions from scholars including Samuel Huntington (2004), Arthur M. Schlesinger (1998), and Dinesh D'Souza (1991).

13. For a more comprehensive reading of this case, see *People v. Moua*. Also, see Pinder (2010), *The Politics of Race and Ethnicity* (p. 194–232).

14. See *Regina v. Mawgridge*.

10

Claiming Sarah Baartman

Black Womanhood in the Global Imaginary

Thelma Pinto

Truth, far from being ready-made, takes time to be born, slowly takes shape in the very act of repetition, telling again and again.

Wicomb, 2000, p. 103

Sarah Baartman, also known as "The Hottentot Venus," was a Khoisan woman from the Cape employed by Peter Cezar in 1810 (Samuelson, 2007, p. 86). Samuelson sees the reclaiming of her body from her imperial captors as an act of nationalism. She constructs the return of the body of Sarah Baartman at the birth of this new South African nation only as a symbol of the nationalist pursuit. Meg Samuelson sees this use of women's bodies to construct nations as a form of appropriation that is not liberating.

Sarah Baartman's name and identity were constructed by her captors mesmerized by her body. She was taken to London for purposes of exhibition. Her steatopygous buttocks and *sinus* pudonis "Hottentot Apron" were seen as deviant. This, according to Gilman (1985), was seen as the proof of Black female sexuality. Key here is the fact that her body form, the size and shape of her buttocks, were regarded as sexually erotic, exotic, and provocative. Baartman was displayed in Piccadilly, London, on a stage 2 feet high on which she had to walk, sit, and stand like a wild beast while prurient spectators stared at her.

Her phenomenon attracted so much attention that the Africa Association took up her case and a hearing was held in London. Although they lost the case, the exhibition closed down because of adverse publicity. She was baptized in Manchester in 1811. Three years later, she was contracted by a Parisian showman and animal tamer who paraded her at society balls in Paris. Leading French scientists became involved in her phenomenon. Georges Cuvier, Etiennne Saint-Hiliare, and Henri de Blainville were mesmerized by her pudendum. She died soon after this from disputed causes.

The fascination with Sarah Baartman's anatomy did not end with her unfortunate premature demise. Cuvier gained access to her remains and dissected and preserved her sexual organs and her skeleton and made a plaster cast of her body, which remained on display at Musee de L'Homme until 1974. It was only after the independence of South Africa in 1994 that serious negotiations could be started for the return of Sarah Baartman's remains. In May 2002, they finally repatriated her body to South Africa.

All of the above is history, but Sarah Baartman still represents the historical memory of the ultimate other. Even in today's world, she is the blueprint for the humiliation of Black womanhood on a global level. In postcolonial studies, the issue of Western representation of others is central. How does Sarah Baartman become the prime example of the "sexualized savage" as Samuelson (2007) posits (p. 98)? This is because Black womanhood is seen as the ultimate "other." In the examination of portrayals of Black female characters in recent South African literature, I will try to show how their agency and womanhood are undermined by the Sarah Baartman syndrome.

This chapter will examine contemporary texts, novels, and other prose texts to examine current representations of women in South African and diasporan literature. Issues that need to be highlighted relate to societal imposition of a White aesthetic, especially on Black females. This can be described as the White gaze, which I define as the cumulative effect of centuries of racism, which have created institutional forms far more ingrained and pernicious than simple racial prejudice. Constructions of Black South African womanhood occur at the intersection of multiple identities influenced by the legacy of the Sarah Baartman trauma. As we celebrate our diversity and our multiple histories, the voyeuristic Western gaze still constructs ours as a deviant sexuality. Avtar Brah (1996) posits that "looks mattered a great deal within the colonial regimes of power" (p. 3).

South African literature has truly taken off in a variety of directions since independence. For those of us who have been following the many directions and reading the pre- and postapartheid predictions, it is interesting to note how the lifting of the veil of apartheid exposes a reality and variety none could predict. The artificiality of the imposition of pigmentologist divisions did affect the creativity of the writers. Those who were unjustly privileged are the ones who now have to learn to swim against the stream. The rest of us live in exciting times. South African literature shows the intricate ways in which history and literature are intertwined. The end of apartheid brought in a new era that unlocked what had been hidden, distorted, and suppressed. Even though Meg Samuelson (2007) sees this as a time when "the nation was actively re-invented and re-imagined" (p. 2), I would plead for an understanding of the impact of disruptive forces. There is a veritable explosion of creative endeavors emerging from the new formation. Writers like Gordimer, Antjie Krog, and Coetzee who were long-term beneficiaries of apartheid seem to be having the hardest times. The collection of short stories by Gordimer (2007), *Beethoven Was One Sixteenth Black,* shows in the very title how hard it is to transcend "ethnicized" perceptions so that what has to be dismembered in South Africa, to borrow a term from Samuelson, will take a long time.

When we juxtapose Gordimer's writing with that of Zoe Wicomb, the reader sees how the Baartman syndrome persists in Gordimer's work. In the novels *The Pick Up* of Gordimer (2001) and *David's Story* of Wicomb (2000), different aspects of the illusive concept of ethnicity will be examined and discussed as they are embedded in these women's narratives. Wicomb's novel is a good starting point, as she situates *David's Story* in the social and cultural history of the Khoisan and later the Griqua people of the Cape. We can assume that these are some of the cultural groups from which Sarah Baartman originated. The novel contains frequent references to her, although she is peripheralized, and her ethnicity is problematized. The way in which David reluctantly tells the story of Sarah Baartman at the very end of his text makes this story pivotal to the text. When confronted, he exclaims in exasperation that "Baartman belongs to all of us" (Wicomb, 2000, p. 135).

The Pick Up is located within the White middle class in Johannesburg into which an unspecified Arab intrudes. Whereas *David's Story* is a self-conscious and confrontational discourse with the past, questioning concepts of storytelling, history, and truth, *The Pick Up* has a more conventional and, in a sense, essentialist approach to ethnicity. It portrays Whites as not having it and Arabs as a defining category.

Wicomb's novel is about rewriting, retelling histories, and reinscribing the discourse of the past. Sarah Baartman's location in this retelling of the story, though illusive, is present and central in a nonessentialist way.

The search for roots and sexual gratification of an aging male are recurring themes in Coetzee's later works. That in itself is related to the Baartman narrative. The rights of White middle-class and middle-aged males to sexual pleasures are central. The trend set by Coetzee to infuse his fiction with nonliterary subjects or the combination of biographical, geographical, and political ideological works contains all the elements Black writers were accused of in preindependence South Africa. The novels *Disgrace* (1999), *Elizabeth Costello* (2003), and *Diary of a Bad Year* (2007) show a Coetzee, a product of systemic minority entitlement, struggling to come to terms with the challenges that political freedom brought to literature. Contrary to appearances, the portrayal of Blacks, especially Black women, locates Baartman in the Coetzee discourse.

Representations of male sexuality and violence and the White male gaze are already present in *Disgrace*. We would assume that the literary expertise of a Coetzee should make it more possible to hide the racist perceptions of the character, David Lurie, a White, middle-aged, twice-divorced professor of foreign languages at the University of Cape Town. The novel plunges us into his sex life immediately, holding aging male sexuality up to ridicule. We are told of his weekly encounter with Soraya in a 90-minute session for R400.00, arranged by Discreet Escort. His peaceful sex life comes to an abrupt end when he sees Soraya in the street with her two sons. Unable to come to terms with his life without the 90 minutes per week, he pounces on the first attractive student he sees and invites her to drinks at his house. Melanie Isaacs is a Black student who is a drama major and attends his Romantic poetry class. It is at this stage that we first become aware of the role of the authorial narrator, who focalizes on Lurie and does not give any interiority to Melanie. We are presented only the thoughts and desires of Lurie, while Melanie is filtered through his not-unbiased envisioning. It is especially in the description of the sexual encounter that our sense of discomfort and unease is aroused:

> The girl is lying beneath him, her eyes closed, her hands slack above her head, slight frown on her face. (Coetzee, 1999, p. 19)

What is he trying to communicate to the reader? It is not difficult to link this text to Sarah Baartman, for here as well, the Black female character is mute and experienced as a desirable body that should be available for the taking. The reader's perceptions are undermined by the authorial voice, which claims that young people are not attracted to aging male bodies. Although Melanie misses some classes after the above encounter and seems to be avoiding him, he seeks her out and finds her through the student records and insists on having sex with her again:

> All she does is averting herself: avert her lips avert her eyes. She lets him lay her out on the bed and undress her: she even helps him, raising her arms and then her hips. Little shivers of cold run through her; as soon as she is bare, she slips under the quilted counterpane like a mole burrowing, and turns her back on him.
>
> Not rape, not quite that, but undesired nevertheless, undesired to the core. As though she had decided to go slack, die within herself for the duration, like a rabbit when the jaws of the fox close on its neck. (Coetzee, 1999, p. 25)

What is the authorial narrator position here? It is clear that the narrator does not describe a scene of consenting sexual bliss, but we could hardly speak of an affair between a student and her professor as the blurb on the cover of *Disgrace* suggests. This sexual encounter has overtones of housemaster and servant/slave owner and enslaved woman. Lurie is definitely exhibiting predatory behavior, and we are subjected to the White male gaze. The silenced Melanie must have informed her boyfriend about the liaison, because Lurie's car is vandalized. If Lurie still needed convincing, the boyfriend comes to one of his classes and insults and embarrasses him in front of his students. Yet Lurie continues to pursue his sexual desires. To his surprise, Melanie turns up at his house one evening at midnight, obviously in trouble of some sort, and he takes her in. She had missed several of his classes, including the midterm, for which he gave her a grade.

We are not in any position to judge how Melanie looked at the "affair," as we have several contradictory bits of information. Why did Melanie seek shelter at his house? Why did she have sex with him if she resented it? During the stay at his house, she asks Lurie whether he often does "this kind of thing" (Coetzee, 1999, p. 29) with his students. At this point, we understand that she did not think this was a relationship. Yet it is only when Lurie is summoned to a Committee of Inquiry that he realizes that he is in trouble. Even though he is told that Melanie "lodged a complaint" (Coetzee, 1999, p. 39) accusing him of sexual harassment, he is convinced that she must have been manipulated, as in his perception, she is "too innocent for that, too ignorant of her power" (Coetzee, 1999, p. 39). He has constructed her as a colonized female without any agency of her own. Melanie is envisioned in a fixed reality of her "coloured" background. However, his own racialization does not appear apparent to him because "White" is a signifier of dominance.

Lurie's passive-aggressive response to his loss of agency and his apparent affront at having to appear before a university committee have strong overtones with the Truth and Reconciliation Commission (TRC) discourse. Melanie, objectified and represented without any complexity in his discourse, makes her an enigma to the reader. Lurie's experience of her cannot be construed as an unmediated guide to the truth, and the reader has to struggle with narrative constructions that influence the understanding. These have *raakvlakken* (overlaps) with the Sarah Baartman narrative. It is essential to ask which ideological matrices are at play in the creation of certain characters in *Disgrace* and what economic, political, and cultural processes they inscribe. Melanie is not only denied subject position and deprived of interiority but also objectified and subsequently peripheralized.

Thus, her filing of a complaint against her professor appears unjust and even ungrateful. His summons to appear before the university committee has strong overtones with the TRC not only in terms of the discourse but also in the "representative construction." Lurie, the White professor, arrogantly refuses to even read the charges made against him. He disdainfully pleads guilty to all the charges and wants them to proceed with the sentence. The recently democratic South Africa, in which all sexualities are still inscribed by matrices of power, makes encounters as described by the authorial narrator fraught with deep ambivalence. His dismissal from the university is not because of what he is alleged to have done but because of his refusal to answer any questions and his disdainful behavior to the committee members.

This "incident" of what the committee called "human rights abuse" between a White male professor and a Black female student could hardly be described as violent, coated in the Lurie presentation. The reader cannot but wonder about the Baartman discourse at this juncture. Both Melanie and Sarah are objectified without subjecthood, interiority, or agency. However, when this is juxtaposed to the rape of Lurie's White daughter by three Black men on a small farm in the Eastern Province, the male violence euphemized in the first section is seen in a different dimension.

Lurie visits his daughter, Lucy, to escape the disgrace at the university and the comments of his friends and colleagues. He approves of neither Lucy's appearance or her lifestyle. She had lived in a commune before and later lived with a female partner, Helen, unflatteringly described as "a sad-looking woman with a deep voice and a bad skin" (Coetzee, 1999, p. 60). Lucy now shares her farm with Petrus, who used to work on the farm but, since independence, has been able to get a loan to buy part of the farm. They form a sort of partnership, sharing facilities and equipment.

The only other significant characters are Bev Shaw and her husband, who run a dog clinic. The role of dogs in the novel is symbolic and pivotal. Although my focus will not be on them, I cannot pass over their significance at the intersection of various discourses. As a South African, I realize the importance of the dog metaphor. Dogs were used as one of the main instruments of terror used against Blacks. Dogs, especially the breeds mentioned in *Disgrace*, were trained to attack Blacks. Thus, the fact that violence and dogs are closely linked in the subconscious of Black South Africans is exploited. However, even in terms of male sexuality, Lurie seems to identify with the desire of dogs, which he describes at length. Lurie, in his portrayal of his disinterested and fading sexuality, reflects not only his own loss of zest and agency but also that of the entire farming community. Previously, the farmers were all Whites, and they formed one of the most repressive sectors of the South African society. These farmers invented the tot system as a way of creating and maintaining the alcohol dependency of the workers. The angst in this farming community can thus be related to the different roles Blacks assumed since independence.

The attack on Lucy's farm happens during a period when Petrus and his family are away. Three men enter Lucy's house, steal all the electronic equipment, the rifle, and Lurie's car, and, as we later find out, rape Lucy (undescribed) while Lurie is locked up in the toilet. They attempt to set him alight by pouring paraffin over him. They don't kill the humans, but the dogs are shot even though they are in kennels and form no threat to the intruders. The reader is only witness to what happens to Lurie, as the focalization restricts the reader to his experience and envisioning of the event. In his interpretation, he relates the reason for Petrus's absence at this crucial period to the attack, too. And the fact that one of the intruders is later present at a party given at Petrus's house convinces Lurie of his collaboration.

Lurie's injuries are all superficial, but the impact of the attack on his psyche is profound. He is brought face to face with his loss of agency in the new South Africa at this crucial time. His inability as a White man to even force the Black Petrus to "confess" to collaboration keeps him in a constant state of exasperation. It is during this period of high tension that it becomes obvious how racially programmed this man is, which is a huge part of his inability to come to terms with democratic processes.

Lucy, like Melanie, is given no interiority; thus, her motives remain unspoken. She just manages to verbalize what *Disgrace* wants the reader to be aware of:

> It was so personal, she says. It was done with such personal hatred. That was what stunned me more than anything. The rest was . . . expected. But why do they hate me so? I had never set eyes on them. (Coetzee, 1999, p. 156)

Ideologically, this is the most reactionary comment in terms of both racist and sexist statements. This suggests that the violent attacks on women are all politically motivated. What about the rape of Black women?

Violence in South Africa is by no means a Black-on-White phenomenon as *Disgrace* suggests. What about the sexual abuse of Melanie? Framed in the context of *Disgrace,* the portrayal focuses on the limited recognition of White abuse. Whites in South Africa think that they can refer to the violent society from a very comfortable position because they are not perpetrating very much of it. In the juxtaposition of Melanie and Lucy as victims of sexual abuse, it is obvious that Lucy has so much more to deal with. This is what makes the portrayals in *Disgrace* not as open-ended as we are led to believe. In the final analysis, this is what makes *Disgrace* norm affirmative. Would it be discomforting and disconcerting to Whites to think that they could be any worse as perpetrators than a David Lurie? Does this remind us of what happened to Sarah Baartman's body when she died? Her genitals were excised and preserved in bottles with a plaster cast of her body, exhibited in Museé de l'homme: made available and accessible to the voyeuristic White gaze.

Inside South African literature, several women writers have opened new areas—Zoe Wicomb (2000, 2006, 2008), Rayda Jacobs (2008), Lisa Fugard (2006), Sindiwe Magona (2008), and Kopano Matlwa (2007), among others. They focus on the difficulty for women characters to come to terms with a new social construction. Constructing Black womanhood in the new decade of the 21st century is still fraught with problems of representation. How do we wrest Black womanhood from the frame of the spectacle and invest her with self-aware agency? How do the different discourses intersect? Zoe Wicomb endeavors in *David's Story* (2000), *Playing in the Light* (2006), and *The One That Got Away* (2008) to construct counter-discourses. The portrayal of Black women will be examined in a cross-section of recent South African literature. We would like to see whether/how this relates to the return of Sarah Baartman. Is Meg Samuelson (2007) right in her claim that women's bodies are being dismembered in the process of nation building?

As we examine recent South African literature, we will focus on the gaze. It is time for us to take charge of the discourse. A random sample of contemporary South African prose will be examined to see whether any tenaciousness of stereotypes is present. The works to be examined are *Beauty's Gift* by Sindiwe Magona (2008); *Country of My Skull* (1998) and *Begging to be Black* by Antjie Krog (2009); *Coconut* by Kopano Matlwa (2007); *Summertime* by Coetzee (2009); *When She Was White* by Judith Stone (2007); *Black Diamond* by Zakes Mda (2009); and some other texts.

Sindiwe Magona addresses the problem of representation in her latest novel, *Beauty's Gift*, in which her Five Firm Friends are real beauties unfettered by the White gaze. She has little problem with the vulnerability, which Toni Morrison (1992) calls "romanticizing Blackness rather than demonizing it" (p. xi). Her portrayal of the five beauties, trying to survive the onslaught of the HIV/AIDS epidemic in urban South Africa, puts our obsession with White representations in context. It is time that African writers transcend certain forms of Western discourses and concentrate on what is crucial to their survival, as a nation and as women. Texts like the above make the return of Sarah Baartman essential for the regaining of the dignity of Black womanhood destroyed by the White gaze and by other societal structures. This is not as easy as it sounds. The globalized world comes with hegemonic discourses solidly in place. Writers, like Antjie Krog in *Country of My Skull*, have to be moved from the center of the discourse to make place for other portrayals. Black women have to reclaim a voice that is not only the scream on the South African airwaves. The scream to be heard on the radio during the TRC hearings represented the emotional Black woman not in charge of her own fate. The way in which our subjectivity is materially embedded is obvious from these Truth Commission hearings. What is transmitted has to pass through the White Afrikaner mind of Antjie Krog. Here follows a description of one such hearing of the Truth Commission:

> While Dirk Coetzee tells of how Griffiths Mxenge was stabbed, how the knife was twisted in behind his ribs and couldn't be pulled out, how his throat was cut and his intestines jerked out, his security men sit behind him, half-concealed by a curtain. One of them is Klein Dirk. His blonde girlfriend is with him today. She is wearing a little Black foliage of a dress with thin straps. As Coetzee is relating the details to gasps of horror from the audience, she is busy lacquering her nails. Her left hand is splayed on Klein Dirk's thigh—he holds the bottle while she applies neat layers of dark cutex to her nails. (Krog, 1998, p. 62)

The ambiguity of this passage is obvious. This is a Baartman-like exhibit of the Mxenge family trauma. We are hard put to understand Afrikaners' sensibility. The words that come to mind are unkind. But unfortunately, this is only the beginning of a downward trend.

> I refused to have sex with them. Then they tortured me between two chairs. I fell on the ground. They were kicking me across the face, they treated me like a donkey. . . . They pushed a pipe with a condom in and out of my vagina. While they did it they asked how it felt. When I did not respond it was put deeper and deeper—to satisfy me they said. . . . (Krog, 1998, p. 183)

The final quote either shows the level of racialized complicity or criticism of a culture that stigmatizes in this way:

> If I see a Black woman crying, then I remember two Afrikaans expressions from my youth: "to cry like a meid" and "to be scared as a meid." What do I do with this? The most despicable behaviour, cowardice and loss of control, we have equated with the actions of a Black woman. (Krog, 1998, p. 190)

As a final comment on Antjie Krog's observation, we should remember the title of her latest book, *Begging to Be Black,* in which she ventures out of Afrikanerdom and tries to relate a more inclusive narrative of South Africa. Her explanation of why she chooses a nonfiction genre is enlightening in itself:

> Whereas I can imagine myself poor, ill, scared, beautiful, strange, powerful, I can't even begin to imagine myself Black. . . . Somewhere, somehow, the residues of as yet unrecognized reflexes of racism are still smouldering. That I cannot imagine myself Black because I actually despise Black. (Krog, 2009, p. 122)

This is a startling comment in a book in which Krog struggles with the realization that she has to listen to and talk to Blacks instead of objectifying them. She has come full circle and probably welcomed the return of the Baartman remains.

The Western gaze referred to in the Coetzee texts is further parodied and decentered by Jackey Kay (1985), in the poem "So You Think I'm a Mule" in *Black British Feminism* (p. 53–54). The poem parodies the way in which Whiteness is central in Northern discourse. The idea that only some people are mixed becomes progressively more offensive, for, as Avtar Brah (1996) points out, "identities are inscribed through experiences culturally constructed in social relations" (p. 123). The rejection of the focus on geographical dislocation of the Black female body on the hegemonic "mainland" is something all of us share. Sarah Baartmann, Krotoa Eva, and Nongqawuse and others are discussed by Meg Samuelson (2007) in her work, *Remembering the Nation, Dismembering Women?* In our attempt to rewrite our fractured histories, our literature is a good place to start the process. Several writers have taken on the challenge to rewrite the South African history in their literary texts. Two good examples are Zakes Mda in *The Heart of Redness* (2000) and Zoe Wicomb in *David's Story* (2000). They address issues of history and memory, introducing new modes of social cartography.

The American author Judith Stone (2007) relates the Sandra Laing story in *When She Was White* in a disturbing way for South Africans. Her understanding of the problem of Blackness in the South African context is flawed. It is not about her Blackness but about Sandra's childlike innocence of the significance of color just like Janie in *Their Eyes Were Watching God* by Zora Neale Hurston (1978). She assumes like Janie that if everybody else is White, then so is she. She has not been given words by her primary caregivers. She has loving White Afrikaner parents who are confronted with Blackness in their progeny. How are they supposed to handle this? Again, Antjie Krog's discourse in *Begging to Be Black* (2009) could explain Sandra's father's position.

He responds legally to her exclusion from a White school because he is unable to talk to his daughter about her Blackness. Antjie Krog struggles with the concept of Blackness in *Begging to Be Black* and attempts to explain the phenomenon of a White South African in the following way:

> I don't think I know how to talk about social imaginings. I think I am experiencing a racial awareness crisis. Whereas I can imagine myself poor, ill, scared, beautiful, strange, powerful, I can't imagine myself Black. Why is that? . . . I think I can imagine the indignity and hurt and empathize with that, I can't imagine the being-Blackness. . . . (Krog, 2009, p. 122)

Sandra Laing understands the meaning of Blackness only in terms of absence of love and caring. *When She Was White* by Judith Stone (2007) is a biography of Sandra Laing. Problematic in this version is the American interpretation of the events. This biography situates the Baartman narrative in the 20th and 21st centuries. For most of us, we can assume that Baartman's premature death was brought on by the absence of love. This shows again the inability of Whiteness to deal with Blackness. The only possible way, as has been shown in the Baartman narrative, is to gaze. Paradigmatically, we could interrogate the understanding of the biographer of the complexity of the links between Blackness and Afrikaners. Does she ask Sandra the right questions? Sandra is too young and/or too naïve to understand the impact of her Black body on either the White community or the Black Swazi man, Petrus, she runs off with. Stone's dilemma as an American journalist to write Sandra's story is understandable. She operates from the centrality of the body. Sandra, like Sarah Baartman, did not understand the impact of her Black body.

The irony and tragedy of this case is the fact that nobody talked to Sandra Laing about her body. Her father took her case to the Supreme Court without explaining to his daughter why they had a court case: "My father and I were close during the time I was at home. . . . I knew he was making a case, but I still thought it was about hitting the children at school" (Stone, 2007, p. 100). In July 1967, the 11-year-old Sandra was reclassified White. This meant that she could attend a White school again. The tragedy of Sandra's story is not to be compared to Sarah Baartman's because she was not on display as Sarah was in a hostile Europe with a voyeuristic audience. In Swaziland, she lived with Petrus, with whom she had several children. Her tragedy is one of racist bureaucracy, which did not recognize her children as being part of the same group she was. This is a racist trauma that goes on and on. She has the same innocence also exhibited by Sarah Baartman about her own body. Sarah Baartman could not have understood the reason for the staring Europeans, because she looked no different from other Khoisan women.

It remains a struggle for Black women to claim space within the feminist discourse while remaining mindful of inclusivity and while recognizing national, religious, and class differences.

The threat of unbounded Black female sexuality is only paralleled by the voyeuristic White male gaze as is portrayed in a variety of novels by many different authors. J. M. Coetzee's (1999) portrayal of Melanie Isaacs, the young Black student, in *Disgrace* is only one of many examples I can cite. The reader does not suspect rape of her (the Black female) in this context of the novel, as only the White woman is seen as being raped. The very fact of this kind of portrayal by a "respectable" writer like J. M. Coetzee points to the perception of the availability of the Black female body. The ironic gaze of Zakes Mda (2000) in *Black Diamond* shows how difficult it is to operate outside the stereotypes. Although his girlfriend Tumi wants to participate in postapartheid society, her portrayal as a money grabber obscures her full portrayal, including her responsibility toward the community. Her portrayal is juxtaposed to the Afrikaner magistrate. How to avoid the male gaze and the suggestion of political bias toward former exiles? Is there a new form of xenophobia surfacing that wants to lay claim to the liberation struggle?

Beauty's Gift by Sindiwe Magona (2008) portrays an intracultural problem in a South Africa plagued by the HIV/AIDS epidemic. Do women have a responsibility? Even those adhering to Africana Womenism (Hudson-Weems, 2007, p. 289) among us we are aware of the problem. Do we address this problem within the Black community and within the Black marriage? This courageous portrayal of female protagonists is situated in what still is a cultural taboo. What are the choices Black wives have? How to police a husband in a patriarchal setting is a real challenge. The threat of HIV/AIDS still is a cultural taboo.

What is it we want to assert as we reclaim the heritage of Sarah Baartman? We would like to remove Black women from the category "spectacle" as in the spectacular background in movies (*Avatar*, for example) or in music videos, where we perpetuate the myth of the Black female body as spectacle. This is as much a male as a female responsibility. Does the exhibitionism of the Black female body in hip-hop music make the abuse of Black women much more acceptable? As Sindiwe Magona (2008) helps to empower female characters in *Beauty's Gift* we, as scholars, should interrogate the process that empowers White and male portrayals of easy distortions.

South African Black women, while honoring this foremother, wish to distance themselves from the discriminating concepts of Black female sexuality. For, as others have stated, physical bodies are always social bodies in the West (Oyewumi, 2005, p. 14). How do we negotiate the assertion that there is a centrality of sight in Western thought? We should revisit the aesthetics of Black women in their body types. Wicomb's (2000) *David's Story* seems a good starting point for rewriting, retelling histories, and reinscribing herstories. It is about alternative truth commissions, justice, and the land issue also present and focused on in *Begging to Be Black* by Antjie Krog (2009). Wicomb's novel problematizes history, fiction, and related categories of autobiography and biography. This is also evidenced in the Coetzee's (2009) *Summertime*.

The essentialist construction of Black South African womanhood in the 21st century should be interrogated. We are at the intersection of multiple histories and identities. Essentialist perceptions of our multiple histories and geographic origins should be confronted. We should foreground our first-nation rights, transnationality, and migration politics. The 21st century is also a period of biography and autobiography and can be matched with the period of the 1960s and 1970s, when many writers went into exile. The titles—*Tell Freedom* (1954); *Home and Exile* (1965); *Let My People Go* (1963); *Blame Me on History* (1963)—tell their own stories. The next phase consists of survivor narratives in works of Biko (1978), Walter Sisulu and Albertina Sisulu (2002), Ramphele Mamphele (1995), Ahmed Kathrada (2004), Emma Mashinini (1991), and Gcina Mhlope (2002). These stories and the many works of fiction are important for the reclaiming of the discourse that had been distorted by racist hegemonic ideologies. The new literary historical paradigm will not have a single notion of origin and development but a multidimensional notion of breaks, ambiguities, and contradictions. Some of our narratives are by definition fractured, lacerated by a legacy of racism and colonial exploitation and oppression. In the words of the South African singer and civil rights activist Miriam Makeba (Mama Africa), "the struggle continues."

References

Abrahams, P. (1954). *Tell freedom*. London: Faber and Faber.

Biko, S. (1978). *I write what I like*. London: Bowerdean Press.

Brah, A. (1996). *Cartographies of diaspora: Contesting identities*. London: Routledge.

Coetzee, J. M. (1999). *Disgrace*. Harmondsworth, NY: Penguin Books.

Coetzee, J. M. (2003). *Elizabeth Costello*. London: Secker & Warburg.

Coetzee, J. M. (2007). *Diary of a bad year*. New York: Viking.

Coetzee, J. M. (2009). *Summertime*. London: Harvill Secker.

Fugard, L. (2006). *Skinner's drift*. New York: Scribner.

Gilman, S. L. (1985). Black bodies, white bodies: Toward an iconography of female sexuality in late nineteenth-century art, medicine and literature. *Critical Inquiry 12*, 204–42.

Gordimer, N. (2001). *The pick up*. London: Bloomsbury.

Gordimer, N. (2007). *Beethoven was one sixteenth Black*. New York: Farrar, Strauss, and Giroux.

Hudson-Weems, C. (2007). *Contemporary Africana theory, thought and action*. Trenton, NJ: Africa World Press.

Hurston, Z. N. (1978). *Their eyes were watching God*. Chicago: University of Illinois Press.

Jacobs, R. (2008). *Masquerade*. Roggebaai, Cape Town, South Africa: Umuzi.

Kathrada, A. (2004). *Memoirs*. Cape Town, South Africa: Zebra Press.

Kay, J. (1985). So you think I'm a mule. In B. Burford, G. Pearce, G. Nichols, & J. Kay (Eds.), *A dangerous knowing: Four Black women poets* (pp. 53–54). London: Sheba Press.

Krog, A. (1998). *Country of my skull: Guilt, sorrow, and the limits of forgiveness in the new South Africa*. New York: Random House.

Krog, A. (2009). *Begging to be Black*. Johannesburg, South Africa: Random House Struik.

Luthuli, A. (1962). *Let my people go*. London: Collins.

Magona, S. (2008). *Beauty's gift*. Cape Town, South Africa: Kwela Books.

Mashinini, E. (1991). *Strikes have followed me all my life*. New York: Routledge.

Matlwa, K. (2007). *Coconut*. Sunnyside, South Africa: Jacana Media.

Mda, Z. (2000). *The heart of redness*. Oxford: Oxford University Press.

Mda, Z. (2009). *Black diamond*. Johannesburg, South Africa: Penguin Books.

Mhlope, G. (2002). *Love child*. Pietermaritzburg, South Africa: University of Natal Press.

Modisane, B. (1963). *Blame me on history*. London: Thames and Hudson.

Morrison, T. (1992). *Playing in the dark: Whiteness and the literary imagination*. Cambridge, MA: Harvard University Press.

Nkosi, L. (1965). *Home and exile*. London: Longmans.

Oyewumi, O. (Ed.). (2005). *African gender studies*. New York: Palgrave Macmillan.

Ramphele, M. (1995). *Across boundaries*. New York: Feminist Press.

Samuelson, M. (2007). *Remembering the nation, dismembering women?* Pietermaritzburg, South Africa: University of KwaZulu-Natal Press.

Sisulu, W., & A. Sisulu, A. (2002). *In our lifetime.* Claremont, Cape Town, South Africa: David Philip Publishers.

Stone, J. (2007). *When she was white.* New York: Miramax Books.

Wicomb, Z. (2000). *David's story.* New York: Feminist Press.

Wicomb, Z. (2006). *Playing in the light.* Johannesburg, South Africa: Umuzi.

Wicomb, Z. (2008). *The one that got away.* Johannesburg, South Africa: Umuzi.

11

"Assimilation in a Bikini"

The Unveiling, Reveiling, and Disciplining of Rima Fakih

Mariam Esseghaier

In 2010, Rima Fakih became the first Muslim-Arab woman to win the Miss USA title.[1] Following her win, Fakih, a seemingly assimilated, unveiled Muslim woman, became the site of controversy. News coverage from various media outlets, both conservative and liberal, categorized her win through four dominant narratives. These narratives labelled Fakih as an example of successful assimilation, a member of Hezbollah, a stripper, and an Other, in which Fakih's image was constructed in opposition to the runner-up—blonde-haired, blue-eyed, all-American, Morgan Elizabeth Woolard, from Oklahoma. When categorized as "assimilated," Fakih was commended for unveiling her body—however, when defined as a "stripper," Fakih was condemned for unveiling her body. The contradictory classifications of Fakih's body place her in a liminal space between two universes. While these two opposing discourses label Fakih in contradictory ways, they demonstrate the malleability and construction of the Other to satisfy the needs of the dominant culture.

In this chapter, I argue that the narratives that materialized from the news coverage of Fakih's win were used as a means to "re-veil" and "discipline"

Fakih. The traditional manner of Othering a Muslim woman is through the headscarf. However, in this case, these narratives function as veiling through discourse. Fakih's disciplining allows American society to maintain a stable and fixed identity of Otherness while American society, seemingly open to a multicultural mentality, is ultimately reinforcing an East versus West understanding of the world.

My analysis employs Foucault's *Discipline and Punish* (1995), in which Michel Foucault argues that "[a]t the heart of all disciplinary systems functions a small penal mechanism" (p. 17). Foucault outlines how this mechanism identifies what is considered normal behavior and functions to punish and correct when bodies do not conform to that norm (p. 178). I will demonstrate the way the news coverage of Fakih's win function to discipline Fakih into a position of Other rather than into a position of norm. This functions in conjunction with Edward Said's (1994) concept of "Orientalism" in which the East is created in the image of the West (p. 1–2). In his work, Said outlines the manner in which the East serves to function as the complete opposite to the West. The West relies on this distinction as it maintains a dichotomous image of the West as liberated, while the East remains oppressed. This dichotomy operates to create the East as the Other in contrast to the norm of the West and rarely allows bodies to inhabit both worlds. However, because Fakih alters a way of being a Muslim woman, the Orientalist dichotomy must be re-created and reinforced in another manner in order to stabilize her position away from an American identity, which is based on Whiteness. As Sherrow Pinder (2010) argues in *The Politics of Race and Ethnicity in the United States,* beginning with the Naturalization Act in the 1790s, it allowed for only White men to be citizens of the United States. By doing so, "the United States successfully managed to forge a single American cultural identity among its diverse multicultural and multiracial population" (p. 151). This was successful in constructing Whiteness as associated with American identity and as "an unmarked and implicit norm" (p. 153). Furthermore, in employing Meyda Yeğenoğlu's (1999) analysis of the veil, in which she argues that "[t]hey [as in the Orient] *should* remain different, because I should remain the *same*: they are not/ should not be a possibility within my own world, which will thus be different" (p. 57), I demonstrate how the veil functions as a way to visibly embody that dichotomy, but with Fakih as an unveiled Muslim woman, this dichotomy becomes more difficult to reinforce. Therefore, I argue that these narratives function as a means of "re-veiling" Fakih so that she may remain the Other.

Beauty Pageants

Studies on pageantry provide a basis for the manner in which certain gender and race identities combine to create the ideal American citizen. Sarah Banet-Weiser (1999) argues that the title Miss America suggests that there exists an equation in which "'woman = nation,'" implying that notions of nation and gender are inseparable (p. 6). The "relationship between gender and nation has, in the US, always been a crucial one to maintain, and that maintenance requires a glossing over of contradiction and conflict" (Banet-Weiser & Portwood-Stacer, 2006, p. 259). These studies demonstrate the manner in which beauty pageants named after the nation—Miss America, Miss USA—place women as the bearers of the identity of the nation. However, this equation no longer functions as easily with the inclusion of bodies of color (Banet-Weiser, 1999, p. 8). In her analysis of Black bodies in beauty pageants, Valerie Felita Kinloch (2004) asks the question of "what happens with the female bodies that are premarked and nonnational and nonrepresentational beauty?" (pp. 93–94). The question of "marked" bodies demonstrates how race alters the connection between gender and nation. Vanessa Williams, however, was the first African American woman to win Miss America, but her win is often attributed to her light skin and Caucasian features (Watson & Martin, 2000, pp. 112, 115). Her win was categorized in several ways, "[b]lacks claimed her and a few whites threatened her, but more whites looked to her victory as proof that America's racial problem was solved" (Craig, 2002, p. 76). The woman of color's body, then, functions as a political tool that attempts to demonstrate that there is an acceptance of difference in beauty pageants and, subsequently, in the world outside of pageants; however, this is inconsistent with women of color's actual lived experiences. Fakih's coverage employed these concepts of acceptance of difference and multiculturalism by highlighting Fakih's otherness, her Arab American identity, in her Miss USA win. Fakih's win also reinvigorated the unveiling strategy of the Muslim woman, which makes Fakih acceptable in a multicultural society through her unveiling. In this respect, although Fakih does not represent the norm, her unveiling allows her an acceptance through her assimilation.

Unveiling of Fakih

The contemporary academic scholarship on unveiling demonstrates the manner in which wearing the veil, in resistance to the unveiling strategy of colonial forces, served as a symbol of opposition. Frantz Fanon (1965) discusses the trajectory of the veiling and unveiling of the Algerian woman during the French colonial period. Fanon highlights how the veil represented what the European man could not possess. The veil, then, as Fanon has pointed out, "[became] the bone of contention in a grandiose battle" (p. 36). The veil served as the symbol for the colonized community, and unveiling the Muslim women served as a means to destabilize the community (El Guindi, 2000, p. 170). The veiled Algerian woman became part of the "modernizing" of Algeria by the French occupier. Fanon states that when Algerian women did unveil,

> every face that offered itself to the bold and impatient glance of the occupier, was a negative expression of the face that Algeria was beginning to deny herself and was accepting the rape of the colonizer. Algerian society with every abandoned veil seemed to express its willingness to attend the master's school and decide to change its habits under the occupier's direction and patronage. (pp. 42–43)

Additionally, Fadwa El Guindi (2000) argues that in colonial Algeria, "The veil became a target of the colonial strategy to control and uproot—to persuade the Muslim woman to unveil" (p. 170). As El Guindi describes it, the Muslim woman was a target; her unveiling became the objective of colonial forces. These scholars demonstrate how the unveiling strategy was a political manoeuvre designed to destroy Algerian culture from within, resulting in a battle that was firmly fought on women's bodies.

In Fakih's case, her Muslim body is already unveiled to the colonizer/oppressor. As Fakih already appears on the pageant stage unveiled down to a bikini, Fakih has already assimilated herself into the American society. Her unveiled body, then, serves as a means toward her colonization and assimilation, and her Othered identity is less threatening. As will be discussed further, by placing Fakih at the center of the debate about American identity due to her unveiling, Fakih reinscribes the colonialist strategy of situating the battleground on the Muslim woman. Fakih's unveiling, then, becomes synonymous with assimilation.

Assimilation

The narrative that Fakih serves as an example of successful assimilation originates from the common discourses of unveiling the Muslim woman in order to "modernize" her. Two major threads materialized from this narrative. The first was that Fakih's assimilation was contingent on her willingness to wear a bikini and take part in a beauty pageant, which was applauded for assimilating to the concept of liberated sexuality associated with the West. Fakih differentiates herself from the stereotypical representation of Muslim women, who are often depicted in media as oppressed, silenced, and wearing burqas. The second was the manner in which Fakih rejected her Muslim identity. Fakih distances herself from Muslims as a religious group by claiming to be "not religious." In this narrative, Fakih must literally unveil her body and unveil herself of an Islamic identity as her means of her acceptance.

On his HBO program, Bill Maher enthusiastically supported Rima Fakih's Miss USA win and highlighted her sexual attractiveness in comparison to the stereotypical representation of Muslim women. While displaying a photograph of Fakih, a photograph that came to be known as the "stripper" photograph as Fakih was pictured dancing on a pole in a tank top and shorts, Bill Maher said the following: "She's the first Arab-American Miss USA. I just want to say, 'Terrorists Lose!' She puts the 'ass' in 'assimilate'" (Maher et al., 2010). Later on in the program during Maher's "New Rules" segment, he addresses Fakih's win a second time, saying "New Rule: Conservatives have to stop freaking out that an Arab American woman won Miss USA. What are you wing nuts so worried about? We took this [displays a picture of a Muslim woman in an abaya and a niqab, only showing her eyes] and turned it into this [displays a picture of Fakih taken from her participation in the swimsuit competition during the Miss USA contest]. I say 'God Bless, America'" (Maher et al., 2010). Fakih's willingness to be unveiled to the colonizer/oppressor, in this case Bill Maher, so that she may be possessed by the colonizer/oppressor serves as her means toward acceptability.

This same understanding of Fakih as unveiled and sexual is discussed on the late-night FOX show *Redeye*. Host Greg Gutfeld and his guest, conservative political pundit S. E. Cupp, discussed Fakih's willingness to be unveiled. Like Maher, they also display the photograph of Fakih dancing on a pole, as well as one of the official Miss USA photographs from the pageant. In the official photograph, Fakih is sitting in black lingerie, with fishnet stockings and a bra. Upon revealing this photograph, Gutfeld says: "That is an American girl," to which Cupp responds: "That's what we want." Gutfeld continues, "This girl, who is Muslim, would be killed in some Muslim countries doing what she's doing. I don't think they're going to be particularly proud of her is what I'm saying" (Stickney, 2010). These comments characterize Fakih as successfully assimilated based on her bikini, pole dancing, and lingerie photographs. These comments demonstrate that Fakih's embodiment of American identity is contingent on her unveiling her body in a manner that is acceptable to the West. Her unveiling of anything considered "foreign" and "un-American," including clothing and her religion, allows Fakih to embody American identity not as a symbol of diversity but as a symbol of an acceptable diversity, assimilating to the dominant culture.

This notion of sexuality as an integral part of secularism, as Joan Wallach Scott (2009) argues, suggests that "[t]he most frequent assumption is that secularism encourages the free expression of sexuality and that it thereby ends the oppression of women" (p. 1). Scott terms this fusion of sexuality and secularism "sexularism." For Fakih, her seemingly "liberated" sexuality, as evidenced in her photographs, suggests that she accepts secular society and that such a society liberates her from oppressive Muslim regimes. Fakih, as an already unveiled Muslim woman, becomes an ideal that counters the stereotypical and often highlighted representation of Muslim women wearing burqas. Fakih represents an ideal American Muslim: unveiled, beautiful, and sexual.[2]

Fakih's assimilated appearance also functions as a site of containment in which her normalized body serves to appear multicultural, as Fakih is still an ethnic and religious Other being included and celebrated through the beauty pageant. In this case, Fakih's Muslim and Arab identities are deemed acceptable through her appearance. Yasmin Jiwani (2005) argues that many television shows contain difference by making racial differences "palatable for the consuming audience" (p. 189). Jiwani further argues that "Asian women [, for example,] can have strength only if they are shaped by the prevailing dominant Western influences" (p. 189). In this case, Fakih becomes "palatable" for the American public through the way she appeals and conforms to American beauty ideals. While Fakih is an Arab, her bikini body, pageant clothing, and lack of headscarf allow her to be different but attractive in the traditional, American sense. In this sense, Fakih's objectification and sexularization function to make her an acceptable Other, a difference to American society that has been successfully assimilated. Through her beautiful, unveiled, "American-like" characteristics, Fakih is made palatable and acceptable for the American public, while if she were the stereotypical Muslim woman, she would be less acceptable into American society.

The second stream of categorization within the "assimilation" narrative deals with how Fakih minimized her Muslim identity. Fakih often identified herself as an Arab rather than as a Muslim. Since she cannot change her ethnic identity, Fakih must maintain that she is an Arab; but with her religion, which is a choice, Fakih is able to distance herself from unpopular beliefs about Muslims in the United States. When asked by Cody Willard on *FOX Business Happy Hour* (Baker, 2010), "What does your win as the first

Muslim American do for relations between Muslims and Christians, and all the tensions that we've got underlying everything?" (Baker, 2010), Fakih responded by setting her Muslimness aside, stating

> Well, they did confirm that I'm the first Arab-American to win. It hasn't been completely confirmed that I'm the first Muslim, however, I am very honored to be honest with you because I think there's been so much stereotype, so much fear implanted in Arab Americans, that maybe this can be the way to show them that America is still the land of the free and they could just take that pride of being proud of who they are. (Baker, 2010)

Fakih focuses on herself as an Arab American while disassociating herself as the first Muslim to win. In doing so, Fakih safely distances herself from Islamic fundamentalism, which has become a popular stereotype in the United States about Muslims. Since her religion is a choice but her ethnicity is not, Fakih demonstrates that she is choosing against her Muslim identity in favor of the United States.

Fakih made this same point when interviewed on *The Joy Behar Show* (Cliff, 2010), but when directly asked about her Muslim identity Fakih qualifies how she identifies as Muslim. In this interview, Behar asked Fakih if she was a Muslim. Fakih responded, "My family comes from a Muslim background, and we are more not defined by religion, I'd like to say we're a spiritual, liberal family." Behar pursued the questioning by asking, "So, you're not a devout Muslim?" Fakih responded "We do celebrate Christmas, we're very liberal in many ways, I have Christian and Muslim faith in my family, but we are Muslim" (Cliff, 2010). In this response, Fakih refuses to conflate "Muslim" and "liberal" since she finds it necessary, in the interview with Behar, to separate the two terms to set herself apart from the typical, religious Muslim. This nonreligious criterion was the same that followed Zinedine Zidane's infamous head-butt of an opponent during a soccer match. One of the ways Zidane was redeemed was through his categorization as a "good Muslim," which included being classified as "non-practicing" (Jiwani, 2008, p. 26).[3] Both Fakih and Zidane needed to shed their Muslim identity without fully rejecting that identity. In doing so, supporters of Fakih and Zidane appear as though they are accepting the religious Other into Western society when, in fact, Fakih and Zidane are accepted based on their identifying and being identified as not religious.

The preceding coverage of Fakih's win demonstrates the criteria for Muslims to be considered acceptable in the West. However, regardless of the manner in which Fakih's win was categorized as a case of successful assimilation into the United States, soon the image of an Othered body began to surface in the same media outlets that initially supported her. The crisis of the assimilation narrative was that Fakih was altering the Orientalist East versus West dichotomy. Fakih was an Other but was assimilating into the West and was shifting a well-established understanding of the world and how to be American. While Fakih was a controlled difference, as she was a palatable Other, her assimilation still shifted the established cultural norm of being a White American. To rectify this impasse, Fakih's alleged assimilation was soon overshadowed by the three subsequent narratives that functioned to complicate her assimilation.

The Reveiling of Rima Fakih

These "reveiling" narratives were a means to do to Fakih what the veil normally does to Muslims in Western eyes: It creates a distinct opposition to the Western identity. Meyda Yeğenoğlu argues, in *Colonial Fantasies* (1999), that the veil is important to the West because "the European [or Western] subject is able to secure his identity through this supposition or through, to use Teresa Brennan's phrase, this *imaginary anchor*" (p. 49). Muslim women in burqas and niqabs embody the position of the imaginary anchor that Yeğenoğlu discusses. These women, which are often the images of Muslim women present in Western media, are simply representations that the Western world can use as a way to secure its own identity. The Muslim women in burqas and niqabs are the perfect unchanging anchor, so the West may feel progressive, liberated, and modern. By replacing their image with Fakih, the West has a more difficult time with their identity. If a Muslim woman can look like a Westerner, how can Westerners know themselves as Westerners? This image destabilizes the strict dichotomy. Yeğenoğlu (1999) further argues that "[t]hey [as in the Orient] *should* remain different, because I should remain the *same*: they are not/should not be a possibility within my own world, which will thus be different" (p. 57). As a normalized Muslim, as a winner of a beauty pageant, as bikini-clad, and as Miss USA, Fakih disallows the Westerner to remain the same because she has not remained an anchor. Therefore, the narratives work to anchor her within the place she is meant to embody, away from the norm, so the norm may exist unaltered.

On her website, Debbie Schlussel (2011), a "Conservative political commentator, radio talk show host, columnist and attorney" focused on Fakih's participation in the Miss USA pageant even before her win.[4] Schlussel's warnings were in regard to the danger Fakih poses because of her ability to blend into American society. Schlussel contends: "Don't let

[Fakih's] lack of headscarf and her donning a bikini in public fool you. Miss Michigan USA, Rimah [sic] Fakih, is a Muslim activist and propagandist extraordinaire" (Schlussel, 2011). The image of a spy-like woman who is unveiled and dressed like an American begins to undercut the assimilation narrative. Her probable danger is highlighted and reinforced by the assimilation narrative, suggesting that her behavior and dress allow her the possibility of destroying American society from within. By assimilating successfully, Fakih's danger lies not in being visible but through her invisibility. By disappearing into the American landscape, she goes unnoticed and unsuspected of danger, unlike the visible Other who is easily surveilled.

Prior to Fakih's interview on *Fox and Friends* (Petterson, 2010a), the cohosts, Steve Doocy, Gretchen Carlson, and Brian Kilmeade, mention a possible connection to Hezbollah, and even mention it in the teaser to her interview. Brian Kilmeade introduces Fakih in the following manner: "From pole dancing to accusations of Hezbollah connections, scrutiny over racy photos of Miss USA, stirring up a lot of controversy lately, where right now, she's here to set the record straight is Miss USA" (Petterson, 2010b). This teaser for an interview occurred with Fakih sitting on the couch next to the three cohosts. However, during the course of the entire interview, Fakih is never once asked about her alleged Hezbollah connections. This technique prohibits Fakih from being able to disprove the comments and allows the suggestion to remain suspended for the viewer to recognize a possible link between Fakih and Hezbollah.

Fakih's danger stems from an Orientalist perspective in which the Orient "exude[s] dangerous sex" (Said, 1994, p. 167). From this perspective, Fakih herself embodies a dangerous sexuality. This narrative demonstrates a shift from Fakih as a "normal," assimilated, pageant winner toward Fakih as an exotic, different, and possibly dangerous Muslim woman. This narrative only serves as effectual in relation to the assimilation narrative. Without her apparently seamless blend into American society, such a narrative would not exist. In this narrative, Fakih's outwardly "American identity" proved too close for comfort for the American media and was used as a means to classify assimilable Muslim Arab Americans as enemies among real American citizens. However, without appearing as a stereotypical Muslim, the connection to danger must be made.

Fakih's "stripping scandal" emerged when photographs of Fakih dancing on a pole in a tank top and a pair of shorts surfaced.[5] The pole dancing was part of a promotional event for a radio station. Fakih remained clothed, and no pictures surfaced of her without her clothing. Regardless, the "stripping scandal" was addressed in almost every television interview Fakih made following her win. On *Fox and Friends* (Petterson, 2010a), the FOX cohosts,

Steve Doocy, Gretchen Carlson, and Brian Kilmeade, asked the runner-up, Miss Oklahoma, Morgan Elizabeth Woolard, about Fakih's scandal. Brian Kilmeade asked, "Do you think it's going to be a problem with these new pictures emerging from a 2007 stripper contest which she evidently won?" (Petterson, 2010b). On *The View* (Geddie & Walters, 2010), Elisabeth Hasselbeck, the conservative cohost on the panel, suggested that simply because the photos do not portray an unclothed Fakih does not mean that Fakih remained clothed. Hasselbeck stated, "Is it that she won that stripping contest? Is that what they're saying? Because if then she had to, if it is in the contest to then 'strip' and she won the contest, so even though the photo doesn't show it, if she did win it and she had to strip, it depends on what the morals clause is in the contest" (Geddie & Walters, 2010). The "morals clause" Hasselbeck referred to is in the contract that all contestants must sign before competing in the pageant. Such a suggestion from Hasselbeck— that because the evidence does not show Fakih without her clothing does not mean conclusively that she did not take her clothing off—makes an insinuation about what occurs after the photograph was taken. However, Hasselbeck has no evidence for the events following the photograph, and her statement creates an unfounded understanding of the image as a "stripping" photograph. Regardless of the manner in which Fakih defended herself against these claims, the suggestion that Fakih indecently took her clothing off was projected onto her as a sexual deviant.

The sexualized nature of the discussion of Fakih's "stripping" scandal embeds Fakih firmly within an Orientalist discourse on the hypersexuality of Eastern women, which is a component of the Orientalist dichotomy. Such hypersexual language is often attributed to the Oriental woman. Such a theme, conceived by European travelers into the Orient, defined women in the Orient as "the creatures of a male power-fantasy" (Said, 1994, p. 207). These women were depicted as "express[ing] unlimited sensuality, they are more or less stupid, and above all they are willing" (Said, 1994, p. 207). The Oriental women were portrayed as associated with many stereotypical sexual images, including being present in harems (Said, 1994, p. 190). In this context, Fakih does not simply become a sexually deviant woman; she becomes the stereotypical image of the Oriental woman in the harem.

The harem serves as a dominant feature of Orientalist imagination, but specifically in reference to the Muslim woman. The harem serves as a Western culturally constructed idea of sex, the Oriental woman, and the East. The imagery of the harem came out of European versions of *A Thousand and One Nights,* and these were translations that often privileged violent and passionate interpretations of the story (Shohat & Stam, 1994, p. 163). The imagery of the harem "allowed the colonial imaginary to play out its own fantasies of sexual domination" (Shohat & Stam, 1994, p. 41). The harem allowed a site in which women were submissive, sexual, and eager. Furthermore, the image of the harem plays a large role as a part of a "cultural antholog[y] through which mainstream U.S. audiences grapple with sometimes disorienting social processes, such as consumerism, expansionism, and globalization" (Jarmakani, 2008, p. 4). The harem theme is deeply embedded within the Western imagination about the East.

The Orientalist discourse surrounding Fakih's sexuality works more than to Other Fakih: It works to situate Fakih deep within the description of the imagined Orient that Said describes. Fakih's photographs are no more sexual than her official Miss USA lingerie photograph and the bikini she wore in the bathing suit competition, but her sexuality in the "stripping" photographs needs to be problematized to separate them from the endorsed sexuality of the American pageant. Since the assimilation narrative encourages Fakih's wearing a bikini, the stripper narrative needs to find fault with that sexuality. Through this narrative, Fakih's sexuality is removed from American-sanctioned sexuality. As American sexuality is considered liberated, as demonstrated through the pageant in which the women are encouraged to wear bathing suits and evening dresses that reveal the female body, the disgust with the sexuality of the "stripper" photographs serves to differentiate between American, liberated sexuality and hypersexual, foreign, Orientalist sexuality. A problematic sexuality is not associated with being American.

Rima Fakih as the Other

The media focused on comparing Fakih with the runner-up, Miss Oklahoma, Morgan Elizabeth Woolard, in Miss USA.[6] Woolard is White, blonde, speaks with a Southern accent, and portrays the stereotypical image of how beauty is defined in the United States. Woolard's body serves as the norm, and Fakih's body is portrayed as different and inferior in comparison to the White norm (DeFrancisco & Palczewski, 2007, p. 15). Woolard's Whiteness is more than just a beauty norm. "Whiteness is closely tied to power or status, Whiteness is the norm, Whiteness is natural, Whiteness is indicative of nationality and citizenship, Whiteness is beyond the necessity of racial identity labels, and Whites are descendents [sic] of White European ancestry" (DeFrancisco & Palczewski, 2007, p. 15). Woolard's Whiteness is the embodiment of a socially acceptable and natural norm and the standard on which other bodies are compared and highlighted as different, unnatural, and unacceptable for the title of Miss USA.

Fakih and Woolard are further compared through the manner in which they answer their final question at the pageant. Fakih's final question was asked by former Miss USA Tara Conner in regard to the 50th anniversary of the birth control pill and whether the pill should be covered by health insurance. Fakih replied:

> Absolutely. Hi mom. I believe that birth control is just like every other medication even though it's a controlled substance, and it's provided for free by your OBGYN or any close by family clinic. It should be something women should be allowed to get through their insurance because it is costly. Thank you. (Gurin, 2010)

Woolard, on the other hand, was asked a question by Hispanic actor Oscar Nuñez about the Arizona immigration law. His question asked if such a law, which may lead to racial profiling, should be mandated by the state or by the federal government. Morgan replied, "I'm a huge believer in states' rights, I think that's what's so wonderful about America. So, I think it's perfectly fine for Arizona to create that law, and I am against illegal immigration, but I'm also against racial profiling, so I see both sides of this issue" (Gurin, 2010). These responses illustrate Fakih supporting a medication that allows for, possibly, promiscuous sex, while Woolard is supporting states' rights. Fakih appears as a sexual immigrant in her support of birth control, and Woolard appears as a constitutional American in her support for state rights.

Woolard was also made to embody the norm with her comparison to Oscar Nunez, the judge who asked Woolard her final question. Nunez's body does not fit the position of a pageant judge, since the contestants are meant to embody the nation, "the judges must adequately mirror that nation" (Banet-Weiser, 1999, p. 56). The image of a Hispanic man asking a White, young beauty queen a question demonstrates an uneasy shift of power. On Megyn Kelly's FOX news show, *America Live* (Brown, 2010), Kelly interviewed Woolard about this question, asking, "Some saying the first runner-up, Miss Oklahoma, was wrongly denied the title because she answered a question about Arizona's immigration law this way," and she proceeds to air the exchange between Woolard and Nunez. After airing the clip, Kelly asks Woolard, "Do you believe that answer cost you the crown?" Woolard replies "No, I don't believe that answer cost me the crown." Kelly continues to encourage her by asking, "Do you feel like it was an unfair question to you? Do you feel like there was some judgment from that particular judge about that immigration law?" Woolard again replies, "I can see why people think that, but I don't think that was the case, no" (Brown,

2010). Kelly's characterization of the exchange implies that such a question from a Hispanic man who clearly does not embody the nation was unfair. Nunez should not be judging Woolard on how to be an American since he does not embody Americanness, which is based on Whiteness.[7]

Woolard, the norm against which Fakih is compared, embodies the place of the familiar and the norm, and in comparison to Woolard, Fakih is incapable of embodying the norm. This final reveiling demonstrates and highlights to the viewer, through a strict comparison between the two women, who is American and who is an outsider. In this final reveiling, the correct identity of "American" is resituated on Woolard, and Fakih no longer embodies that title. Fakih is returned to the position of Other, no longer a threat to redefine what it is to be "American."

The Disciplining of Rima Fakih

The unveiling and reveiling of Fakih work as a means of disciplining Fakih. In *Discipline and Punish*, Michel Foucault (1995) argues that "[a]t the heart of all disciplinary systems functions a small penal mechanism" (p. 17). Foucault outlines how this mechanism identifies anyone or anything straying from the norm and that deviation must be corrected or punished (p. 178). The narratives created by the news outlets were used as the penal mechanism within the disciplinary system of the media. This is furthered by the ways in which Foucault discusses how "disciplinary punishment has the function of reducing gaps. It must therefore be essentially *corrective*" (p. 179). Fakih inhabits this gap: She exists in a liminal space between the norm and the Other. In Homi K. Bhabha's work *The Location of Culture,* he explores this concept of liminality and hybridity and argues that there is an "interstitial passage between fixed identifications [which] opens up the possibility of a cultural hybridity that entertains difference without an assumed or imposed hierarchy" (Bhabha, 2004, p. 5). In this sense, Bhabha recognizes a place "in-between" that ultimately destabilizes the strict opposing dichotomy. However, as Foucault argues, such a space cannot exist because the disciplinary system does not allow for individuals to exist between "norm" and "deviation;" they must be disciplined into either position. The gap ultimately functions to throw into question an understanding of "norm" and "deviation," self and Other, which allows for overlap and, as Bhabha states, "initiate new signs of identity, and innovative sites of collaboration, and contestation, in the act of defining the idea of society itself" (Bhabha, 2004, p. 2). This in-between space allows for new types of identities, but doing so shifts a comfortable, dichotomous understanding of East and West. While some of the assimilation narratives seemingly allow Fakih to inhabit this space and applaud her for the manner in which she assimilates, the three subsequent narratives are used as a means of correcting the "gap" Fakih creates.

Conclusion

Rima Fakih's 2010 Miss USA win represents a new national identity for the United States. By unveiling and, subsequently, reveiling Fakih through discourse, the American media outlets stabilized Fakih's shifting position between norm and Other and placed her firmly in the position of Other. While the assimilation narrative applauded Fakih on an assimilation based almost entirely on objectification, the three following narratives demonstrate the need for a strict East versus West dichotomy. Fakih's embodiment of a liminal space almost erases such a contrast. These four narratives work as a means of situating Fakih within the Orient, away from the norm, as a means to discipline her within her corrective position. By doing so, Fakih's applauded liberated sexuality becomes an indecent "harem-like" sexuality, her American-like features must be starkly contrasted with Woolard's ideal White, American beauty, and her denial that she is a practicing Muslim suggests that she really is a Muslim-fundamentalist-terrorist-spy. Without a visible appearance of a Muslim identity, Fakih's Otherness is less evident. These narratives distinguish Fakih from American women and allow her to subsist within American culture, as long as she maintains that disciplined and "reveiled" position.

References

Baker, T. (Executive Producer). (2010, May 21). *Fox Business Happy Hour* (Television broadcast). New York City, NY: FOX Business Network.

Banet-Weiser, S. (1999). *The most beautiful girl in the world: Beauty pageants and national identity*. Berkeley: University of California Press.

Banet-Weiser, S., & Portwood-Stacer, L. (2006). "I just want to be me again!": Beauty pageants, reality television and post-feminism. *Feminist Theory, 7*(2), 255–72.

Bhabha, H. K. (2004). *The location of culture*. London: Routledge.

Brown, M. (Producer). (2010, May 18). *America Live with Megyn Kelly* (Television broadcast). New York City, NY: FOX News Channel.

Cliff, C. (Executive Producer). (2010, May 19). *The Joy Behar Show* (Television broadcast). New York City, NY: HLN.

Craig, M. L. (2002). *Ain't I a beauty queen?: Black women, beauty, and the politics of race*. New York: Oxford University Press.

DeFrancisco, V. P., & Palczewski, C. H. (2007). *Communicating gender diversity: A critical approach*. Thousand Oaks, CA: Sage Publications.

El Guindi, F. (2000). *Veil: Modesty, privacy and resistance (dress, body, culture)*. New York: Berg.

Fanon, F. (1965). *A dying colonialism*. Trans. Haakon Chevalier. New York: Grove.

Foucault, M. (1995). *Discipline and punish: The birth of the prison*. Trans. Alan Sheridan. New York: Vintage.

Geddie, B., & Walters, B. (Executive Producers). (2010, May 18). *The View* (Television broadcast). New York City, NY: ABC.

Gurin, P. (Executive Producer). (2010, May 16). *The 2010 Miss USA Pageant* (Television broadcast). Las Vegas, NV.

Jarmakani, A. (2008). *Imagining Arab womanhood: The cultural mythology of veils, harems, and belly dancers in the U.S.* New York: Palgrave Macmillan.

Jiwani, Y. (2005). The Eurasian female Hero(ine): Sydney Fox as relic hunter. *Journal of Popular Film and Television, 32*(4), 182–191.

Jiwani, Y. (2008). Sport as a civilizing mission: Zinedine Zidane and the infamous head-butt. *Topia: Canadian Journal of Cultural Studies, 19*, 11–33.

Kinloch, V. F. (2004). The rhetoric of Black bodies: Race, beauty, and representation. In Elwood Watson & Darcy Matin (Eds.), *There she is, Miss America: The politics of sex, beauty, and race in America's most famous pageant* (pp. 93–109). New York: Palgrave Macmillan .

Maher, B., Martin, B., Griffiths, S., Carter, S., Grey, B., & Gurvitz, M. (Executive Producers). (2010, May 21). *Real Time with Bill Maher* [Television broadcast]. Los Angeles, California: HBO.

Petterson, L. (Executive Producer). (2010a, May 18). *Fox and Friends* (Television broadcast). New York City, NY: FOX News Channel.

Petterson, L. (Segment Producer). (2010b, May 20). *Fox and Friends* (Television broadcast). New York City, NY: FOX News Channel.

Pinder, S. O. (2010). *The politics of race and ethnicity in the United States: Americanization, de-Americanization, and racialized ethnic groups*. New York: Palgrave Macmillan.

Said, E. W. (1994). *Orientalism*. New York: Vintage.

Schlussel, D. (2011, June 12). EXCLUSIVE: Miss USA contestant is Shi'ite Muslim Hezbollah supporter, used pageant name to promote Muslim female subjugation; Hezbo Taqiyyah allows bikinis? *Debbie Schlussel*. http://www.debbieschlussel.com/21757/exclusive-miss-usa-contestant-is-shiite-muslim-who-supports-hezbollah-hezbo-taqiyyah-allows-bikinis/.

Scott, J. W. (2009, April 23). *Sexularism*. Lecture. Robert Schuman Centre for Advanced Studies: Ursula Hirschmann Annual Lecture on Gender and Europe. European University Institute, Florence.

Shohat, E., & Stam, R. (1994). *Unthinking Eurocentrism: Towards a multi-cultural film theory*. London: Routledge.

Stickney, B. (Senior Producer). (2010, May 18). *Redeye with Greg Gutfeld* (Television broadcast). New York City, NY: FOX News.

Watson, E., & Martin, D. (2000). The Miss America pageant: Pluralism, femininity, and Cinderella all in one. *Journal of Popular Culture, 34*(1), 105–126.

Yeğenoğlu, M. (1999). *Colonial fantasies: Towards a feminist reading of Orientalism.* Cambridge: Cambridge University Press.

Notes

1. I first heard about Fakih's Miss USA win from the feminist blog jezebel.com. This blog covers topics ranging from popular culture to politics. They posted many of the videos I used for the research for this paper. A post by Irin Carmon titled "Miss USA Likes Pizza, Believes in Insurance-Subsidized Birth Control," served as a summary of the events at the Miss USA beauty pageant.

2. I also discuss this concept of assimilated/beautiful Muslim versus the unassimilated Muslim in my forthcoming chapter "'The Big Conceal': Representations of the Hijab in CBC's *Little Mosque on the Prairie.*"

3. Yasmin Jiwani's article cites Mahmoud Mamdani, who also discusses this dynamic in his work *Good Muslim, Bad Muslim: America, the Cold War, and the Roots of Terror.*

4. Jezebel posted this discussion in Irin Carmon's post "Today in Ridiculous Responses to Miss USA Rima Fakih."

5. Jezebel posted about this scandal in Irin Carmon's post "Miss USA's Bigot Backlash and Stripping Scandal Begins Now!"

6. Jezbel discussed the runner up's loss in Irin Carmon's post "Miss USA's Bigot Backlash and Stripping Scandal Begins Now!," Irin Carmon's post "FOX News: 'Miss Oklahoma Was Robbed,'" and Irin Carmon's post "Today in Ridiculous Responses to Miss USA Rima Fakih."

7. See Pinder, *The Politics of Race and Ethnicity*, 2010.

12

Sensing Race and Gender in Contemporary Postcolonial Art

Mariangela Orabona

In the United States, at the political and cultural level, the new controversial neoliberal concept of "postracial" has created an anxiety among the masses. "Postracial" seems to acclaim enthusiastically that America has moved beyond race and this movement has signaled an end to racism. In this discourse, culture is being substituted for race, and what has manifested itself is a new form of racism, which is labeled "cultural racism."[1] Taking my cue from Sherrow O. Pinder's *Politics of Race and Ethnicity in the United States*, "cultural racism is a racism of culture." And given that the dominant culture is conceived as superior to the nondominant cultures, cultural racism "shows its connections with racist thinking" that, for one, constructs nondominant cultures as inferior to the dominant culture (Pinder, 2010, p. 113). However, multiculturalism allows for the recognition and celebration of the nondominant cultures. In this sense, multiculturalism is in relation to culture,[2] or as David T. Goldberg (1994), in *Multiculturalism: A Critical Reader*, puts it, "a microcosm of the social" (p. 24), which partly determines the politics of cultural representation. While reflecting on the politics of the representation of the female Black body, which has been both a prolific and an attractive topic in both the United States and the UK, artists such as Coco Fusco, Sonia Boyce, Renée Cow, Lorna Simpson, Kara Walker, and Carrie Mae Weems, among others, through their provocative and irreverent art, have questioned the perception of the female Black body. In this chapter, I want to explore the cultural representation of the racialized and gendered body and the ontological implications of time and memory in contemporary visual art and to show how, in African American contemporary art, the body becomes a form of resistance to normative cultural representation, where cultural representation is essentialized. I draw on a concept of art as a *new aesthetic paradigm* with ethical and political implications, spotlighting the "crisis" of multiculturalism. When we speak of multiculturalism, we are speaking of "a plurality of cultures" (Pinder, 2010, p. 95), where culture becomes essentialized and static. More specifically, I try to understand how race and gender can be considered as two important ethical and aesthetic features to deal with new forms of culturally oriented racism in light of a postcolonial and migration presence.[3] What are the mechanisms of resistance to cultural racism in contemporary postcolonial art? And even though *culture* here is substituted for *race*, I aim to build a new theoretical framework that links the female body to the perception of race. I will insist that race and gender depend on far more than an account of shifts in representational practices. Reasserting the important link between a body's materiality and its temporal transformations, the perception of race and gender and its biopolitical implications occur as a way to deal with discursive practices of subjectification as a visual domain of control. In particular, I will concentrate on the visual reappropriation of the female Black body as a *fetish sign* and the Deleuzian concept of *cutting* by focusing on the artworks of African American artist Kara Walker. One of the chosen artistic modalities of sensing race and gender could be the *silhouette*, as can be found in her artwork, which represents an attempt to deal with racial and gender implications, focusing on the failure of containment and interrogating the limits and boundaries of the cultural representation of the female Black body. Which kind of sensation does the *silhouette* evoke? How is it possible to consider the *silhouette* as a way of sensing race and gender? Dealing with *silhouette* as a matter out of control and as a creative modality to reflect on how race and gender are felt and sensed, it is a way of thinking about the Black body as an aporetic and intensive trace on the surface. Following Elisabeth Grosz, especially where she argues that it is important to reconfigure matter as culturally productive and time as a force of proliferation (in order to) to embrace a politics affirmative of difference (Grosz, 2005), and through Kara Walker's cut-and-paste silhouettes, I will thus aim to produce a different kind of "vision" *over* and *of* the body, which renews the concept of racial and cultural difference as aesthetic.

Some Essential Features of Multiculturalism

In the United States, assimilation into the dominant culture seems to be of absolute importance. The dominant culture as white allows only for those who are white to gain membership, and it nurtures a particular kind of practice that deems whites superior and nonwhites inferior, which Frantz Fanon (1964) labels as "cultural hierarchy."[4] And given that cultural hierarchy protects and privileges members of the dominant culture, this is fundamental in the development of the material conditions of Blacks and other racialized ethnic groups who are members of the nondominant cultures. A politics of assimilation into a culture that is institutionally discriminatory led movements to embrace a politics of difference as their main effort to counterbalance an overrepresentation of Western history and the complete neglect of African Americans', Native Americans', Latinas'/os', and Asian Americans' histories. The shift from assimilation to cultural pluralism, with its emphasis on multiculturalism, is fairly a recent phenomenon. Multiculturalism is supposed to advance the notion that cultural differences are important, so each nondominant group is to be recognized and celebrated. Stuart Hall (1995) defines and explains this new emphasis on cultural pluralism as:

> the extraordinary diversity of subjective positions, social experiences and cultural identities which compose the category "black"; that is, the recognition that "black" is essentially a politically and culturally constructed category, which cannot be grounded in a set of fixed trans-cultural or transcendental racial categories, and which therefore has no guarantees in Nature. What this brings into play is the recognition of the immense diversity and differentiation of the historical and cultural experience of black subjects. This inevitably entails a weakening or fading of the notion that "race" or some composite notion of race around the term black will either guarantee the effectivity of any cultural practice or determine in any final sense its aesthetic value. (p. 200)

What Hall problematizes here is both the constructed category of the term *Black* and the determination of its aesthetic value through a notion of race. While, during the 1980s, Black British artist Isaac Julien, among others, explored creatively the value of those *racialized ethnicities*, creating a strong political engagement in the contemporary art milieu, in the United States, the fixation of African American art into a culturally predetermined art tradition has brought nowadays the formulation of a new concept of African American artistic production: "post–Black" art. On the one hand, the term seems to avoid a notion of race as a still problematic topic, and on the other, it doesn't dismantle the entire constructed category of the term *Black*, if this is strategically the intention. While there is still a "rhetorical triumph" in the interpretation of Black art by some critics, which tends to reduce it to a homogenizing reflection on African American art, an interesting formulation about Black American art sees, in the metaphor *total darkness*, a strategy of resistance of the perpetuation of static icons of Black American culture and a contemplation of Blackness as the expression of the universality of African American culture (English, 2007). We could try to understand this latter concept as a new way to deal with racial implications in the light of new forms of *cultural racism* due to the emergence of migration and racial multiplicity as a way to orchestrate differences in a system of control (Hardt & Negri, 2000, p. 195). Michel Foucault understood the term *governmentality* as the strategic power over the life of the population, which follows the capacity to decide who may live and who must die, which has intensified and affected our lives in terms of bioracism. Foucault declared that forms of biopower are the basis for the inscription of racism within the mechanism of the power of modern states (Terranova, 2007). In the light of the important role of the biological type of relation in the formation of modern states, postcolonial theorist Achille Mbembe also analyzes the ambiguous role of biology in the formation of modern states. In addition, Mbembe points to how the very concept of postcolony, which is considered "a timespace characterized by proliferation and multiplicity [...] an era of dispersed entanglements, the unity of which is produced out of differences," as important in modern state formation. Multiplicity and proliferation as well, to recall again Hall, "the immense diversity and differentiation of the historical and cultural experience of black subjects" (Hall, 1995, p. 200), are modes of strategic resistance in helping our understanding of political and cultural transformations and can be considered aesthetically and ethically as new modalities in reframing postcolonial interrogations in the light of migration movements and against contemporary forms of differential bioracism and sovereign control over life (Höller, 2002). In the end, *cultural racism*, which is directed at a "particular racially defined group," in this case Blacks, "is an acute form of racial essentialism, which is largely true of multiculturalism" (Pinder, 2010, p. 96) and a part of the "crisis" of multiculturalism that I have already, in the preceding paragraph, alluded to.

The Unpredictable Body and the Postcolonial *In-Between Space*

In African American contemporary art, the body, recalling the cruel and uncomfortable colonial past, becomes the pretext of ethical and cultural resistance to cultural representation by reaffirming its renewed biological dimension. As a shared, heterogeneous dimension, a modular and transcultural process, which takes into account the differences between cultures and avoids an essentialist vision of gender and racial differences, African American artists such as Kara Walker, Renée Green, Carrie Mae Weems, and Lorna Simpson, among others, have moved toward what Foucault calls "phenomena of rupture, phenomena of discontinuity," which is considered as interruptions and modalities of creative reappropriation of cultural values prior to colonization (Foucault, 2002, p. 4). Reflecting over the *phenomena of rupture* in order to highlight a fluid passage from an aesthetic to an ethical event is a way for these visual artists to participate in *transcultural* processes as creative reappropriations and translations of cultural roots, posing a critical look over some traumatic historical events and questioning Western epistemological presumption of truth.[5] Though contemporary visual culture is still mediated by the Western gaze, a planetary extension of postcolonial art carries a rich feature that shows artistic creation as a unique moment of *reinvention* of "Black art" and a reworking of the concept of Blackness as a way to problematize the hegemony of Western historical frame where Blackness constructs a body that is defiant of the dominant cultural norms. Given that the construction of Blackness has ironically relied on an absolute contempt for the lived complexities of Blackness in America, Blackness is always reduced to authentic otherness.

In cultural and postcolonial studies, a critical dimension over such a discourse has found its way through Stuart Hall's reflections in the wake of Michael Foucault's thought and thanks to the insights of Homi Bhabha. Recalling Fanon's racial epidermal schema, Bhabha confronts the power/knowledge ambivalence with the concept of the stereotyping body in terms of the fetish sign of colonial discourse. In fact, Foucault's phenomena of rupture have the qualities to bear unpredictable *zones of contact* between two or more cultures; "the capacity to generate something new which is not part of one culture or the other one" is precisely the process of invention.[6] Stuart Hall makes an interesting reflection on what he calls the vectors of *rupture* and the vectors of *continuity,* referring to all the phenomena related to the reappropriation and translation of the "roots" and the cultural syncretism between different cultures and discussing the specifics of Black identity as conveyed by these two operating axes (Hall, 1990, p. 96). The rigidity of the historical frame for Hall has not allowed many identities between two or more cultures to emerge, and America, as the hegemonic *presence* in the new world, has became the *empty earth,* the place where creolization, assimilation, and syncretism are negotiated and where foreigners from everywhere meet (pp. 31–31). According to Hall, it is also important to stress that the beginning of hybridity is the *presence* of

America itself. Furthermore, continuity and rupture seem to bind in totally unexpected insights with the philosophical concepts of similarity and difference, as is expressed by Henri Bergson, who speaks of *similarity* as a deterministic sign, able to articulate a continuity of the human species's adaptation according to the empirical laws of adaptation. This continuity is supported by a concept of difference that Bergson sees as a fundamental part of the unexpected nature of the contact, the uncertainty of the matter. The aporetic terms *similarity* and *difference* go hand in hand with adaptation and uncertainty. If *similarity* means adaptation, preservation, or linearity, on the other hand, *difference* means unpredictability, indeterminacy, intuition, or contamination and becomes the result of the actions and passions of bodies over other bodies.[7] In the act of creation between different cultures as a phenomenon that cuts the similarity of history and appears as overbearing is the unpredictable moment of the contact; and yet it is also the most creative one of invention.

The phenomena of rupture and discontinuity can be considered critical nodes able to highlight the dark side of cultural discriminations, a political strategy that is reflected in the visual arts as a form of reinvention and *rememory* of history in order to open a free and transformative space in the visual representation in which bodies emerge and change and are not confined in continuous transit between past, present, and future. I'm thinking about a reconfiguration of the past that can be actualized in the present, the *ambiguous space* that interrupts the course of the events, an *empty territory* to fill a critical space which, as stated by the postcolonial theorist Iain Chambers (2006), is always a border thought: "Critical thinking as a discourse of the border has been consistently appealed to and obsessed by the invisible, by what can't enter into the arena of representation, or simply drop off the rigid screens of a solid consensus" (p. 47). Chambers's critical reflection clarifies the contemporary sense of being on the border between two or more cultures and draws on the explicit task of culture.[8] In this respect, the border thought recalls what Bhabha (1994) defines as the contingent *in-between space*, which renews the performance of the present.[9]

Cutting the Fetish: The Black Body on Corporeal Surface

In this critical challenge, the postcolonial approach tries to face the trauma of American slavery by announcing the visual reappropriation of the female Black body as a *fetish sign,* as is stated by Bhabha in *The Location of Culture.* By taking into account the Black female body as a fetish *object,* which is considered an entity meanwhile attractive on the one hand and repulsive on the other, creating this twoness—fear *of* as well desire *for* the racialized body—he underlines how problematic it is to calculate the traumatic impact of slavery. Identification, alienation, fear, and desire are the ambivalent results of the fetish body, an inscriptive surface, which Fanon, in *Black Skin, White Masks*, defined as a *racial epidermal schema* that signals pleasure and fear. According to Bhabha (1994), the recognition of difference implies always its representation as a fixation of the fetish object (p. 116). Kara Walker's artwork plays with this form of fixation, which is presented through her use of dark silhouettes to show the Black body as an impossible object to be fixed in cultural representation. Her oeuvre moves forward the impossibility of the representation of a fixed and stable subject/object, which can be understood as a modality of transformation of the condition of being on the border, as an act of the reinvention of Blackness by denouncing the repression of traumatic events such as colonization and slavery.

In fact, Walker was born in California in 1969 and grew up in Atlanta, a city that is continuously relived in her work. Also, in her work, the period of slavery is depicted as an imaginative, real, and creative scenario. She creates volatile visual narratives, staging a variety of stereotypes that are part of Black American popular culture as well as part of her personal imagery. As a form of the recollection of the history of slavery, through the most representative characters of popular culture, including pickaninnies and mammies as well as minstrelsy, Walker creates Black silhouettes as fetish bodies. By drawing, cutting, and pasting Black papers on white walls, she explores the limits of the cultural representation of the racialized body in the ambivalent encounter between asymmetrical powers. This encounter is often a traumatic collision in which the explicit carnality of the experience of trauma shows up. Stuart Hall defines this encounter as a "matter out of place" and insists on the ambivalent concept of differences as destabilizing at cultural level of the integrity of subject identity: "What unsettles culture is 'matter out of place'—the breaking of our unwritten rules and codes. Dirt in the garden is fine but dirt in one's bedroom is 'matter out of place'—a sign of pollution, of symbolic boundaries being transgressed, of taboos broken" (Hall, 1997, p. 236). How is it possible to deal with *silhouettes* as a sensitive matter out of place? Why is Walker's work so controversial? Is it for the provocative and shocking way silhouettes speak? The stereotype, as a fetish sign, is an entity at once attractive and repulsive, evoking together pleasure and fear. It is, as stated by Bhabha, an impossible object of desire, the expression of a meaning that can never be settled in the representation. Following the theoretical articulation of Bhabha, the fetish for Walker, as a tangible sign of difference, is represented through a process of *mimicry*, what

Bhabha calls the partial or virtual absence of the subject marked by race. The concept of *mimicry*, beyond the representation of the body as an ambivalent sign between desire and repulsion can also illuminate its dark features.

Through her *silhouettes*, as dark sensitive matter formed by a multiplicity of stereotypes, attractive and repulsive fetish bodies—which travel inside the exhibition space of the most important museums, including MOMA, Whitney, and the Metropolitan and which should not be regarded purely as the domain of the visible—Walker frays the status of the image. Her dark silhouettes are in the unspeakable and unseen region of the invisible, sensitive matters *out of place* and evanescent forms of the domain of absence rather than of presence. The artist deconstructs and exposes a form of mimicry following an alternative path to the traditional representation of the encounter between asymmetrical powers. Through traumatic encounters between bodies, Walker creates a territory of affection, deploying an indefinite number of memories, changing the roles of her characters and transmitting to the audience a sense of instability. *The Emancipation Approximation*, for example, is a group of large-scale lithographs, measuring 44 × 34 inches, executed in solid fields of black, grey, and white, which alludes to the approximate nature of the promise of freedom proclaimed by Abraham Lincoln in 1863. The whole sequence is accompanied by a contamination of bodies between human and animal spheres and scenes of gruesome decapitation. In particular, in *Scene #26* (one of the lithographs of the artwork), which is illustrated in the image below, we witness the representation of carnage through the cutting off of heads. The one who is responsible for this cruel act is presumably a white woman, leaning against the stump of an oak tree crying. Next to her is an axe leaning against the tree, and all around it are heads of women, men, and children, some in the act of exchanging a kiss. The entire scene describes a cut, definitive and coherent, with the tool used to cut off all the heads left on the ground as is portrayed in the image.

Those outlines are drawn, cut out, and pasted on the white walls of the museum as creative modalities of recollection of the history of slavery: "an approach to slavery as constituting demands upon slavery, not as a fact but as an aspect of lived history" (English, 2007, p. 77). Walker's cut-and-paste silhouettes take inspiration from the artistic technique that was popular in Europe in the late 18th century. Recalling Frantz Fanon, her disruptive historical romances connect *desire* and *difference* as two forms of political intervention. Through a play of absence/presence, of a void that allows a movement, the African American artist Kara Walker works with archival material to undermine the heritage of an American culture that vulgarizes Blackness. She doesn't seek an imaginary reconstruction of the past or an

Kara Walker, Scene #26 from the *Emancipation Approximation* series, 1999–2000. Sikkema Jenkins & Co., New York.

ideal construction of the future. She interrogates the construction of the real and the ruling regime of contemporary visuality. The translation of visual material stored in reservoirs of collective memory can been metaphorically, considered as a *dismembered* body that moves through time, an expanded rather than progressive time, to be reread from a Proustian perspective of involuntary memory. Thus, the aesthetic power of sensing art through the memories (images) is the main core of her visual narratives. Therefore, the artistic act becomes an active territory in which a disembodied process of dislocation, displacement, resistance, infection, and contamination is actualized.[10] It is the *new aesthetic paradigm* discussed by Felix Guattari (1995), which is

a paradigm that has ethico-political implications because to speak of creation is to speak of the responsibility of the creative instance with regard to the thing created, inflection of the state of things, bifurcation beyond pre-established schemas, once again taking into account the fate of alterity in its extreme modalities. (p. 107)

Combining the concept of cutting and that of fetish, it seems to me that Walker's silhouettes can be considered as incorporeal events on the surface of representation. It is an exceeding modality that, from the representation of the fetish as a sign, leads to an affective modality of contamination between bodies, a contagious biological process between bodies, and a passage from the rememored fetish to the dismembered one. Walker transforms into flesh the history of slavery; she dismembers and reassembles it in a game in which the bodies are contaminated with each other, and from their contamination emerges an irrepressible desire to reconfigure the fetish as a disembodied effect on the surface of visual representation. More than a fetish sign, the body becomes an *event*, an immaterial event that inhabits the perceptual imaginary of American popular culture, changing the univocal vision of the Black body and the perception of race. The artist begins to draw her characters on black papers, drawing the outline of the incorporeal. Then she cuts and pastes them as if they were decorations on the museum's walls. Her creative process touches three essential moments: tracing, cutting, and pasting. In the trace, there is already the act of tracing and being traced; and in the cut, there is already the act of cutting and being cut. The act of cutting is the expression of a rupture as well as a manifestation of a way of being, as is recalled by Gilles Deleuze (2001, p. 8). In other words, the act of cutting follows the will of the body to trace and to work on matter, which, as Deleuze (2001) explains, is the act of cutting of a body on another body, from which comes out the attribute rather than the quality of being cut (p. 8). His philosophical reflection draws on a concept of art as a movement, touching both the corporeal body than its incorporeal effect. Through the incorporeal effects of the body, Deleuze (2001) reflects on relation between the bodies and the event of senses. For him, there is a reciprocal interaction going from the power of cutting to the power of being cut. In highlighting the segnic power of cutting, what emerges is the strong link between the figure and the head. Deleuze says, "The body is the Figure, or rather the material of the Figure. [...] the Figure, being a body, is not the face, and does not even have a face. It does have a head, because the head is an integral part of the body" (p. 15). The artistic task is, for Deleuze, "to dismantle the face, to rediscover the head or make it emerge from beneath the face" (p. 16). In this challenge, the artist is called upon to bring out the head from the face as an animal trait of the human. Yet the meat is itself the head, which becomes the *nonlocalized power* of the meat, a *nonlocalized* zone of contact that the becoming human of the animal and the becoming animal of the human encounter, transforming the affective sense of that contamination in the in/corporeal dimension of the body (p. 19). In *Scene #26*, what remains of the body after the cutting off of the heads? The only body, the only figure is the presumably female butcher close by the trunk of the tree, the trunk as the origin of all matter. But the trunk is also the support to beat the meat (the body as butchered meat). All the other bodies, the other figures, violently mortified by the cruel act of being cut, are elsewhere, outside the main scene. What remains of the bodies are just their heads, the animal traits of the human, thrown on the ground in a disorganized way as *"nonlocalized power,"* dismembered fetishes at the edge between human and animal. I think about silhouettes as a decomposition of the form even if represented by the containment of the trace. It's the traced power as a rhapsodic narrative, the power of the limit of the containment to express the ambiguity between the body and the incorporeal, between material and immaterial, and human and animal. Dramatizing the trace as an artistic modality that is able to reveal the passage of Black bodies in the textures of the time is a way to consider the stereotype of the Black body as an impossible object of desire and expression of the impossibility of calculating the impact of slavery's trauma. The material art, constantly researching for the immateriality of the form, exposes this stereotype, carrying it to the extreme, on the threshold of the corporeal through the actions of bodies on bodies. The material art exposes a sensorial dimension of the stereotype as the boundary between the representation of the fetish, which re-presents an excessive memory, and the dismantling of the sign itself, the body, as an incorporeal event that weaves the memory of the trauma with other stories, other bodies, other events.

Here memory and fetish overlap, as Kara Walker's artworks run the fluidity of the *in-between space* to be the *territory* in which the normative hegemonic culture, the racial and gender belonging, is questioned and challenged by the creative transformations of the phenomena of rupture to feed a politics of difference rather than a politics of inequality. Therefore, Walker's artworks are far from a concept of a fixed categorization of African American identity narrating a nomadic sense of being that diverts attention from the cliché of the stereotypical representation of the body of the Other as an exotic object to be observed. The fetishes become the incorporeal event that trace and is traced on the surface from which a sensitive matter appears. The black empty spaces and the dismembered silhouettes enclosed by the margins are the effects of the passions and actions of bodies on other bodies or, as Deleuze (2001) defines it, incorporeal effects on surface. The black silhouettes, inspired by a volatile form that makes them unique, become a series of black shadows that slowly appear as bodies and of body parts, which are multiplying and blending with the spectators' shadows walking through Walker's artworks in the circularity of time. Walker renders problematic the materiality of race and gender through sensation and affection. A multiple *body* of history, in its fragmentation and senses, is dispersed in the same image of its representation through affected dynamics in which the *silhouette* reappears as a faceless construction, as a material trace that anticipates and negates definitions and categorizations: *an impossible trace.*

References

Anzaldúa G. E. (1987). *Borderlands/la frontera: The new mestiza.* San Francisco: Aunt Lute Book Co.

Bhabha, H. (1994). *The location of culture.* London and New York: Routledge.

Chambers, I. (1985). *Urban rhythms, pop music and popular culture.* London: Macmillan.

Chambers, I. (2006, Summer). Borders and the boundaries of democracy. *New Formations, a Journal of Culture/Theory/Politics, 58,* 47–52.

Deleuze, G. (1988). *Bergsonism.* New York: Zone Books.

Deleuze, G. (2001). *The logic of sense.* London: Continuum.

English, D. (2007). *How to see a work of art in total Blackness.* Cambridge, MA: MIT Press.

Fanon, F. (1964). *Towards the African revolution: Political essays.* Trans. Haakon Chevalier. New York: Grove Press.

Fanon, F. (1967). *Black skin, white masks.* New York: Grove.

Foucault, M. (2002). *Archaeology of knowledge.* London and New York: Routledge.

Glissant, E. (1996). *Introduction à une poétique du divers.* Paris: Gallimard.

Goldberg, D. T. (1994). *Multiculturalism: A critical reader.* Oxford, UK: Blackwell.

Grosz, E. (1994). *Volatile bodies: Toward a corporeal feminism (theories of representation and difference).* Bloomington and Sydney: Indiana University Press, Allen and Unwin.

Grosz, E. (2005). *The nick of time: Politics, evolution, and the untimely.* Durham, NC: Duke University Press.

Gruzinski, S. (1999). *La pensée métisse.* Paris: Fayard.

Guattari, F. (1995). *Chaosmosis: An ethico-aesthetic paradigm.* Bloomington: Indiana University Press.

Hall, S. (1990). Cultural identity and diaspora. In Jonathan Rutherford (Ed.), *Identity: Community, culture, difference* (pp. 223–237). London: Lawrence and Wishart.

Hall, S. (1995). New ethnicities. In Bill Ashcroft, Gareth Griffiths, & Helen Tiffin (Eds.), *The post-colonial studies reader* (pp. 223–227). London: Routledge.

Hall, S. (Ed.). (1997). *Representation, cultural representations and signifying practices.* London: Sage Publications.

Hardt, G., & Negri, A. (2000). *Empire*. Cambridge, MA: Harvard University Press.

Höller, C. (2002, Spring). Africa in motion: An interview with the post-colonialism theoretician Achille Mbembe. *Cosmopolitics, 3/02*, Wien: Hefte für Gegenwartskunst.

Kallen, H. M. (1956). *Cultural pluralism and the American idea: An essay on social philosophy*. Philadelphia: University of Pennsylvania Press.

Kymlicka, W. (2007). *Multicultural odysseys: Navigating the new international politics of diversity*. New York: Oxford University Press.

Morley, D., & Chen, K. (Eds.). (1996). *Stuart Hall. Critical dialogues in cultural studies*. London: Routledge.

Pinder, S. O. (2010). *Politics of race and ethnicity in the United States*. New York: Palgrave Macmillan.

Terranova, T. (2007, May). Futurepublic, on information warfare, bio-racism and hegemony as neopolitics. *Theory, Culture & Society, 24*(3), 125–145.

Notes

1. For a more comprehensive reading on "cultural racism," see Horace M. Kallen (1956), *Cultural Pluralism and the American Idea: An Essay on Social Philosophy*, and Frantz Fanon (1964), "Racism and Culture" in *Toward the African Revolution: Political Essays*.

2. See Will Kymlicka (2007), *Multicultural Odysseys: Navigating the New International Politics of Diversity* (p. 98).

3. The prefix *post* has been considered by Homi Bhabha a "controversial shiftiness" of meaning to deliniate new inscriptions and affections of culture in our planetary experience; see Homi Bhabha (1994), *The Location of Culture* (p. 1).

4. See Frantz Fanon (1967).

5. I borrow the term *transcultural* from Fernando Ortiz's reflections over the modern creation of new phenomena generated by the loss of a previous culture in favor of a new one. See also Edouard Glissant (1996), *Introduction à une poétique du divers*.

6. See Serge Gruzinski (1999), *La pensée métisse*.

7. See Gilles Deleuze (1988). *Bergsonism*.

8. Also, see Gloria E. Anzaldúa (1987), *Borderlands/La Frontera: The New Mestiza*.

9. "The borderline work of culture demands an encounter with 'newness' that is not part of the continuum of past and present. It creates a sense of the new as an insurgent act of cultural translation. Such art does not merely recall the past as social cause or aesthetic precedent; it renews the past, reconfiguring it as a contingent 'in between' space, that innovates and interrupts the performance of the present. The past-present becomes part of the necessity, not the nostalgia, of living." (Homi Bhabha, 1994, p. 7)

10. See David Morley and Kuan Chen (1996), *Stuart Hall. Critical dialogues in cultural studies*; and Iain Chambers (1985), *Urban Rhythms, Pop Music and Popular Culture*.

13

J'ai deux amours

Josephine Baker and the Duality of Identity in the United States and Paris, France

Yvonne D. Sims

Introduction

In the 1920s, culture was defined by the transformative works of artists, writers, and performers of the Jazz Age. The Jazz Age and the Harlem Renaissance coalesced to produce an atmosphere conducive to the rise of African Americans' position within the arts. Tyler Stovall (1996) writes in his book, *Paris Noir: African Americans in the City of Light*, "Paris became the creative center of the planet in those years, and artists, writers, and thinkers flocked to it like moths to a flame" (p. 26). In the midst of this artistic revolution, Paris afforded an environment that fostered much creativity, as evidenced in famous writers such as Ernest Hemingway and Gertude Stein, artists such as Pablo Picasso, and many others who came to the city for varied reasons and stayed either permanently, or long enough to write about their experiences or paint artwork that reminded them of a truly vibrant place where intellectuals, artists, musicians, and many others gathered. This most certainly is understandable, as Paris offered respite to

African Americans weary of a homeland where they were not truly free. Thus, many African Americans found Paris far more hospitable to their skin color than urban cities in America (Stovall, 1996, p. 25).

Two common experiences united African Americans in Paris during the 1920s. First, the city offered them a life free from the debilitating limitations imposed by American racism. Second, Black Americans in Paris established an expatriate community that allowed them to enjoy the freedom associated with living abroad while maintaining their distinct Americanness (Regester, 2000, p. 31). While much has been written on African American expatriates living in Paris at the height of the Roaring Twenties, Langston Hughes, Claude McKay, and later writers such as Richard Wright and James Baldwin would include their experiences as Black Americans in their novels. Indeed, with so many writers who were already well established as literati or who would later become so, the intersectionality that occurred among writers, artists, intellegenstias, musicians, and other performers, the Parisian atmosphere served as the perfect background for a young African American female performer seeking fame and fortune. This fertile environment empowered her to cross the barriers of race and gender and become a cultural mediator between her two loves: the United States and Paris. This woman was Josephine Baker.

This chapter explores the conflicting attitudes of "Blackness" and "womanhood." Drawing from Evelynn Hammonds's understanding of the "West's metaphoric construction of 'woman,' white is what woman is; not-white (and the stereotypes not-white gathers in) is what she had better not be" (2004, p. 310). Using Josephine Baker as a case study, I want to show how attitudes toward race and gender are geographically defined by focusing on the United States and Paris. Race, gender, and class are not mutually exclusive categories of oppression. In fact, these identity markers intersect to oppress Black women in important ways. For the most part, it has been the multilayering of race, gender, and class that has kept African American women in the lower social strata in the United States. Black feminist scholar Frances Beale labeled race and gender as double jeopardy, suggesting that both served as significant barriers in terms of Black women's lack of visibility in American culture. Black women's oppression has been, for a long time, located within an intersectionality framework of race, gender, and class constructions. This is to say that in order to understand Black women's invisibility in society, it is necessary to investigate how the intersection of race, gender, and class serves as an impediment to full integration into the privileged institutions controlled by White males.[1] Thus, this chapter critiques Josephine Baker's position as an African American woman in Paris who, though not a woman, in Hammond's sense, "white is what woman is"—invisible/nothing was what a Black woman was, where her Blackness signified her as the "inessential other." However, Baker, in Paris, capitalized on the construction of Blackness as "other" and became famous and a respected artist, partly because Parisian attitudes were more tolerant, as Petrine Archer-Straw has noted in *Negrophilia: Avant-Garde and Black Culture in the 1920s*; Europeans were interested in Black culture because it was "fashionable and a sign of being modern" (Archer Straw, 2000, p. 9).

France versus United States

It is important here to note the significance of location: Being an African American in Paris was different from being an African American performer in the two cultural capitals in the United States: Harlem, New York, and Hollywood, California. In the first half of the 20th century, a succession of "opportunities" for African American performers mushroomed (seemingly overnight), catering largely to those who had gained a foothold in dance, voice, and musical instruments in communities in which scouts found them—for example, in Harlem, and then later as the film industry moved from New York to Hollywood. Of course, many African American artists achieved high visibility and accolades during the Harlem Renaissance; nevertheless, there were still racial boundaries that even the Harlem Renaissance could not overcome. Such was the case with the Cotton Club, where many African American performers entertained audiences but never participated as patrons.

In contrast, as Charlene Regester (2000) writes of Europe, "the pre– and post–World War I Era offered golden opportunities" for African American performers who were "achieving fame and fortune abroad, cultivated the Black aesthetic and transported it to foreign shores" (p. 31). When jazz took root in the United States, particularly in Harlem, it was only natural that the genre would reach Europe as musicians traveled back and forth and found they could earn far more lucrative sessions playing in nightclubs in Paris than in the United States.

It is crucial to note, however, that Europe was not free of racism. In Europe, racism manifested itself differently in that audiences craved and were receptive to African American performances at home, "yet halfway across the world, many European countries were stripping away the natural resources and culture of their colonial subjects or people. Literary figures, musicians, dancers, and singers, as long as they were African American and talented, appealed to the European" (Regester, 2000, p. 31). African Americans were embraced by Europeans, but only within the context of how

Europeans viewed Blackness. Africa was the dark continent, lacking in cultural sophistication and peopled by individuals who, in many European perceptions, were so different that they were uncivilized. Here, a point of comparison might be linked to the 19th-century American love affair with Native Americans as "noble savages" who were portrayed in art and literature as stoic and in harmony with nature, which accounted for a closeness to God that Europeans would never experience.

Karen Dalton and Henry Louis Gates are among those who postulated that "Parisians found in African American music and dance a degree of mirth and hedonistic and voyeuristic pleasure they had not known for some time" (Regester, 2000, p. 31). Jim Crow, the legal system of racial segregation instituted after Reconstruction, reminded African Americans that they were not free to express themselves artistically or otherwise in the same forums as whites were. This form of legal racial segregation did not exist in Paris. The Parisian climate, on the contrary, was more "accommodating" and allowed a young Josephine Baker, determined and more enterprising, an opportunity for artistic expression. It was that determination and an intuition that empowered her to cross the barriers of race and gender.

In the United States, on the other hand, her birthright—nationality—deprived her of any opportunity to become the star that she was destined to be in Paris. What could an ambitious African American woman who wanted to be famous accomplish in the United States? In the 1920s, Baker would have never gotten the opportunity to headline a Broadway show, let alone had a show focused solely on her performing; and when film moved to Hollywood, the only roles available for African American women centered on the mammy or the jezebel. In France, she was allowed much freedom as an African American woman performer in the theater. In Europe, theater was pervasive enough so that those who did not come from a wealthy background could still afford to go to her performances. This is one of many differences between theater in Paris and in the United States during this period.

Though Europe scarcely welcomed her with open arms, it was clearly the better fit for Josephine Baker to pursue her vocation during the 1920s and 1930s. To appear in Hollywood, Baker needed to fit into either the mammy role or the role of the tragic mulatta. With no formal training as a performer, which was not uncommon during that era, Baker had an uncanny sense of comedic timing along with the ability to move her body in such a way that when she performed, audiences would get lost in her rhythmic movements and not focus on her singing. This worked to great effect in her initial trademark Banana Dance. She controlled all aspects of her dance routines and, because she was self-taught and did not learn the technique of dance, she incorporated into her shows in Paris many aspects of what she had learned from her earlier time in all–African American revues that would travel around the country. In this way, she was not replicated onstage.

In *Two Loves: Josephine Baker as Icon and Art*, Bennetta Rosette-Jules (2000) writes,

> Josephine Baker fashioned herself as an icon. Baker's iconicity refers to an exotic performative image that uses a wild, non-Western "other" as a point of reference and a source of fantasy. . . . More broadly, Baker came to be seen as a pop icon whose achievements and celebrity are self-referential, standing as signifiers of her historical importance. (p. 59).

Well before the technological advances of today, those who traveled to Africa traveled, in some cases, with no understanding of cultures that differed from their own. Consequently, when some returned to Europe, they recounted what they had seen while building images that later became stereotypes of a culture and people who were very different from what they were used to seeing in Europe. Baker incorporated the very stereotypes that African Americans were attempting to eradicate in the United States as part of her act in France and other countries; this was an intentional part of her act, giving European audiences their expected version of "Blackness," manifesting her intuition for succeeding in her quest.

In order to understand the demonization of Black people, we might examine the large corpus of literature written on the agency involved in the enterprise. Suffice it to add that missionary agents in Africa and the United States with seemingly benign demeanor accomplished that mission of demonizing Black people emboldened. As Petrine Archer-Straw (2000) writes, "Christianity influenced Europe's perception of blacks more than any other contributing factor, for it was Biblical tradition that originally cast the [black] race into a subordinate role as the children of Ham, the unfortunate soul who had been cursed by his father Noah for failing to cover the older man's naked body while he slept" (p. 24).

"Europe's conquering of Africa and the 'new world,' and its exploration and discovery of different cultures, created 'primitive' types and functioned as a kind of collective therapy to maintain European esteem and belief in its various nationalisms" (Straw, 2000, p. 24). In essence, Paris, like many European cities, and France, like many European countries, used caricatures of Blacks in Africa—the very continent being colonized—to "act our roles and reinforce notions of control (Straw, 2000, p. 24). Many images of Blacks that appeared in advertisements in 19th-century Europe that proliferated into the 20th century presented Blacks as "othered" and "exotic." Hence, the fascination by Europe with Africa as the "dark" continent created frenzy among European audiences for all things exotic. Archer-Straw (and others quoted above) notes the word "primitive was the bottom line in a hierarchy of categories that placed European civilization at its pinnacle" (Straw, 2000, p. 12). In "Embodied Fictions, Melancholy Migrations: Josephine Baker's Cinematic Celebrity," scholar Terri Francis (2005) relates that

> Paris was in no way an uncomplicated freedom zone for African American visitors. Americans, traveling to European cities, found themselves in a hall of mirrors, in which they negotiated their self-perceptions and ideas about America and blacks in the diaspora that were projected on to them. (p. 842)

In playing the primitive, Baker gave the audiences what they wished to see: a female Black body on display (unlike Baartman[2]) who was partially nude, but sexual in a nonderogatory way. Baker was proud of her body and often took liberties to display it for artists and in her own shows. She subverted her performances in such a way that audiences were unaware of the subversion. Her dances played to fantasies about Black female sexuality, enticing European audiences to forget that she was American (which arguably may have been of more importance to that audience than her ethnicity). Too often, Baker's critics overlooked her savvy and rarely saw the chameleon quality of her dances, which were always slippery and unfixed (Francis, 2005, p. 834).

Like other audiences everywhere, Europeans enjoyed entertainment, and Baker's performance in Europe, in contrast to the United States, was as accepted as a fish in water. This was due to the fact that they enjoyed the validation of their supremacy, as a diet of "mission civilisatrice" had developed, and thus any media/entertainment that paraded their own conceptions and racial stereotypes of Africa and other Blacks were a tonic for their appetites. Josephine Baker became an international star in France because she played the role of the "Other" who could only be part of European culture as entertainment. In short, Baker would never be fully welcomed into the upper echelons of aristocratic French society on account of her race and where she had been born. Also, she did not come from wealth, and these three components—race, gender, and class—played an integral role in French aristocratic society, as they did elsewhere. Pedigree mattered. It is paradoxical that, while Baker would not gain admittance as a full participant in that society, she was warmly embraced in the same society as an entertainer. Additionally, Baker received her share of criticism by French reviewers, who praised and exoticized her performances. Ironically, in the 1930s, she was "not French enough" to some critics, who charged "that

Josephine was from Harlem, which is not a French possession; that she wasn't able to speak French; and that her hair was not like that of the French Africans since she has had it straightened" (Regester, 2000, p. 52). For the most part, racial attitudes, at times, for African American performers, were more nuanced, and these critics, while vocal, were not representative of all of the reviewers. She could have coexisted within the upper echelons of French society as long as she understood she was a performer: Though the French loved Baker as a *performer*, her race, economic background, and gender limited her ability to enter the world of French aristocracy. In short, she was a music hall performer who qualified as an object for dalliances (or so they thought), but never for respectability as a French woman.

Another point of contrast is that unlike Europe, slavery had been part of the American cultural fabric for centuries; though the attitudes concerning Blackness between the two continents were not different, in the United States audiences were not fascinated with Blackness in the way they were in Paris. The exception is the Harlem Renaissance, in which African Americans flourished with the backing of wealthy white patrons who were connoisseurs of their arts and literature. Likewise, the Cotton Club in the 1920s was another exception, where African American performers did well performing for wealthy white audiences, but they could not sit in the same club with the very people they performed for. Obviously, this signifies that white American audiences loved African Americans performing for them, but unlike Paris, where they could comingle with patrons, this was not an option for Black performers in the United States. In addition, another similar contradiction exists: Whereas Black performers were given opportunities in Paris, even if it meant entertaining audiences with a stereotypical rendition of sub–Saharan Africa, whites performed in blackface mocking the continent, the people, and the culture.

Life Before Paris

From the beginning, it was clear that Baker's destiny lay beyond her very humble origins as Josephine Freda McDonald in St. Louis, Missouri, and her early career as a chorus girl in Eubie Blake's *Shuffle Along* (1921) and Noble Sissle's *Chocolate Dandies* (1924). Remarkably, Baker was not part of the main revue at this time in New York, but instead toured around the country and became so popular that they brought her in as part of the main chorus girl lineup in New York City. After Baker's meeting with Caroline Dudley, who had ideas for successful African American shows on Broadway that she then transplanted to Paris, she was persuaded to move to Paris. For Dudley, "it was not easy to persuade people to go to Paris such as Ethel Waters," but Baker, after negotiating [$]200 a week instead of the [$]125 Dudley offered, "agreed to go, for at some level she was aware that the glamour she wanted was not possible for her in New York" (Rose, 1989, p. 57) or anywhere in the United States. Even with the deliberate uniqueness of her performance, Baker disregarded boundaries of traditional types of female performances and even those of her peers' expectations. Unable to fit the studios' conception of what an African American actress should be, Baker found her voice and ultimately her persona outside of the industry and of the United States. She positively embraced her race, gender, class, sexuality, and nationality, which, in part, contributed to her success. In this way, Baker defied the racial impediments in her own country by playing to Parisians.

Unlike African American actresses in Hollywood, like Ethel Waters, Freddie Washington, and Hattie McDaniel, Baker, in Paris, managed to overcome the familiar struggle with her penchant for being ostentatious and attracting publicity unparalleled for African American actresses in Hollywood. Baker achieved this on many levels. She also became a fashion icon. In the United States, Baker would never have the same kind of attention lavished on her because African American women in the entertainment industry did not enjoy the luxury of acting out their idiosyncrasies for fear of a public backlash. In fact, actresses in general did not enjoy this degree of freedom. Her behavior would be seen by many as unacceptable for a woman, let alone an African American woman, but the French saw it as an extension of Baker's personality. Her screen presence, in the films *La Sirene des Tropiques* (1927), *Zou Zou* (1934), and *Princesse Tam Tam* (1935), were not compelling, and in these films her roles were stereotypical, but in a different manner from Hattie McDaniel and Louise Beavers, the two most famous African American actresses who portrayed mammy and/or, in the latter's case, a variation of the mammy character in many films throughout the 1930s and 1940s. Although she never enjoyed the celluloid success that her African American counterparts such as Beavers and McDaniel did, it was clear that Baker's career was remarkable in light of the severe limitations her contemporaries (Beavers and McDaniel) encountered.

Her openness and frankness in talking about American racism did not endear Baker to American audiences because she often criticized the government when visiting other countries, and many fellow Americans did not respond kindly to her blunt critique of racism in the United States. In the United States, if Hattie McDaniel had spoken out in the way Josephine Baker did concerning racism, she would have been blacklisted and unable to work in Hollywood again. This, within the milieu of the government-sponsored racism, marked the differences between a successful African American woman performer living, at that time, outside of the United States and one living in the United State. Yet, remarkably, Baker's expatriate status gave her the ability to shun the restrictions and negotiations that bound mainstream stars in Hollywood.

Life in France

In just 3 years, the 22-year-old from St. Louis had become a wealthy, soignée woman whose flamboyant costumes, on stage and off, reflected her intense and uninhibited personality (Rose, 1989, p. 57). She was proud of her body and performed her most famous dance wearing a banana skirt. Also, she posed in the nude for famous artists such as Picasso. Baker was not in the least modest, which, perhaps, was one of the reasons that she was loved and admired. Perhaps most important was her adoption of and endearment of all things French. She became a French citizen and was welcomed into the intellectual circles of Colette and Cocteau, the two most famous French entertainers of the day (Braudy, 1974. p. 39). This amazing accomplishment was a total triumph, especially for a 22-year-old who came from a very impoverished background. Furthermore, it became more remarkable when she single-handedly played to their stereotypical preconceptions of the racialized "other." Also, she was completely uninhibited about her sexuality at a time when most women were not. Compounding all, although she learned to speak French well, she often mispronounced words. Whatever else the French may have thought about notions of Blackness and Baker's lack of sophistication, Baker had won their hearts if not their minds.

Just how much freedom Baker really enjoyed might be questioned, particularly if the height of her success in Paris was performing the "Exotic Other" from Africa during the 1920s. However, the more leverage she gained performing these stereotypical dances, the easier it became to transition from the "wild uncivilized" to wearing haute couture gowns by the 1950s, in which she portrayed a very glamorous diva. Many established designers often created gowns specifically for Baker as they competed for her to wear their designs. Baker started many fashion trends in Paris. In an interview conducted by Susan Braudy for *Viva* in June 1974, Baker stated:

I started lots of things. I was the first person to cut my hair very short. And I started the horse's tail that became the ponytail. All those nice plump Parisian ladies saw me and had to become string beans—*haricots verts*. Before me it was terrible for a woman to be tan. All of a sudden they wanted to be tan at the beach. And I started all that dark makeup and lipstick. (Braudy, 1974, p. 38)

Chasing a Rainbow: The Life of Josephine Baker credits Baker as a strong influence in liberating many French women from corsets and Victorian ideals of femininity. This influence also ushered in the flapper image of the roaring '20s as evidenced in bobbed hair, shorter skirts, and an air of independence (Ehrlich, 1986). Owning a ménage of pets from leopards to pigs and many birds, Baker would walk her pet leopard Chiquita—with a diamond-encrusted collar around his neck—on the street. This was eccentric to many elsewhere, and even in Paris people took note, but Baker thought nothing of the attention she garnered by walking her animals to the theater where she performed. Yet this part of her personality, which would have remained private in the United States, became almost a public spectacle in France and gave her an aura of mystique.

As African Americans increasingly made their way to European shores in a veritable cultural explosion, Josephine Baker emerged as one of the most popular and highest-paid entertainers in theatrical history. In doing so, she overcame not only the dual stigma of being African American and female but also her impoverished background in St. Louis. In 1947, Baker purchased a château. In the United States, where African Americans in general grappled with overt racism in the South while confronting the covert efforts in the North and the rest of the country, few African Americans in general, let alone performers, had that kind of purchasing power. Though many African Americans, such as the writers McKay, Hughes, Richard Wright, and later James Baldwin, left the United States temporarily or permanently, they never achieved the level of wealth Baker did. Her success illustrates the possibilities for a woman from an impoverished background to gain international fame and the wealth that accompanies it. In many ways, her story is a Cinderella fairytale: That an African American woman could become wealthy as an entertainer outside of America and own the theaters where she performed, wear haute couture, and have artists such as Picasso draw her image during a period when African Americans did not have any measure of equality within their own country was remarkable. This wealth allowed her to eventually purchase a chateau and realize her dream of a Rainbow Tribe. A Rainbow Tribe is not an illusion.

In the 1960s, through her involvement in the civil rights movement, Baker firmly believed in a rainbow world in which different colors coexisted in harmony with each other. To her, this was not just theory or rhetoric; she realized a personal dream by adopting children from different continents, calling them the Rainbow Tribe, through which she attempted to demonstrate that racial equality could exist if society began with children. Her dream of this utopia, in uniting people of different racial and cultural backgrounds, coupled with the increasing expenses of the chateau, ultimately cost her financially and emotionally; these were strains that culminated in her being evicted from Les Milandes in the late 1960s and forced to continue touring to support her large family. Once her star status was cemented in France, Baker was the first and only Black actor invited to take part in the *Ziegfeld Follies* in New York, one of the premier Broadway shows starring Fanny Brice and Bob Hope. However, any performer who shone in *Ziegfield Follies* hoped to create film roles alongside more Broadway opportunities. For Baker, a successful performance would mean attention and possibly the opportunity to gain star presence in the United States.

Reviewers in the United States referred to Baker as the "Negro performer," suggesting that in Paris she *was* Josephine Baker and in the United States she was a "performer of color." If her performances had been more positive, she could have resurrected a film career that extended beyond Paris. Perhaps then, Baker might have finally achieved the elusive stardom in her home country that she longed for, but it was not to be. The liberation that Baker had in Paris did not come in New York City, where she was often reminded that she was an African American woman first and Josephine Baker second. The reception, while polite, was not warm, and this she found difficult to endure; in Paris, Baker ruled the theater.

Iconic Status

Baker became so outspoken about American racism that she was a target of the FBI, who kept an extensive file on her. She was banned from entering the United States in 1957. Her unceasing criticism of the government for the second-class treatment of African Americans was voiced in Argentina and Cuba, which did not help her relations with the United States; both countries were communist, and visiting these countries and speaking out against the racial problems in the United States made life very difficult for Baker. She became, like Paul Robeson, a "subversive" in the eyes of the United States government for speaking out against the ills inflicted on people of color, and doing this on foreign soil created many problems for her. It was not surprising that Baker became a vocal opponent of the racially motivated, unfair legal practices of the United States, even when that stance would make her a target of the U.S. government. Subsequently, Baker's passport and privileges were revoked as she became increasingly openly critical of segregation and the separate and unequal injustices inflicted on African Americans.

Baker's international fame allowed her to critique America without harming her career internationally, but in the United States the price she paid was having her passport revoked, and she was unable to visit the United States for many years. Further, she never gained the fame here that she had in France. Phyllis Rose, Bennetta Jules-Rosette, Terri Francis, and other scholars have argued persuasively that modern-day divas owe a debt of gratitude to Baker, who was one of the first divas to reinvent herself with each generation. Josephine Baker of the 1960s was far from the Josephine Baker of 1920s; nonetheless, she garnered new admiration among the young and continued interest from those who remembered her shows in the 1920s and 1930s. In the 1960s, through her involvement in the civil rights movement, Baker became known to and respected by the Baby Boom generation. They were able to see Josephine Baker as the civil rights advocate, while their parents remembered her as the risqué performer of the 1920s.

Ironically, for all of her accomplishments in Europe, South America, and portions of Africa, she never achieved the same level of recognition in the United States—partly because of her renunciation of her U.S. citizenship and the fact that her U.S. citizenship was revoked—and her fame came from live performances at a time when movie stars held more sway among American audiences. While American audiences loved Broadway, they loved films equally because of the mobility of having movie theaters all across the country, whereas one would have to travel to New York to see Broadway plays or live in a big city if such plays went on tour. In this way, audiences came to identify more with movie stars because they could see them on screen more readily.

That Baker was able to create an international following on such a grand scale without the influence of the silver screen further magnifies her accomplishments. Theater was limited in that it was not as readily accessible to the masses; many cities had movie houses, but people who wanted to see theatrical stars like Fanny Brice, Maud Adams, and Florence Mills had to go to New York or other big cities to watch their performances. This excluded a great many who could not afford to travel. In Europe, however, theater was very well orchestrated, and high society and common folk alike flocked to see her performances.

Paris proved to be the place where she could continue to hone the image she was creating and make a name for herself. Baker's growing reputation resulted in her launching international tours; she performed in Austria, Denmark, Germany, Holland, Hungary, Norway, Romania, Spain, Sweden, and South America (Rosette-Jules, 2007, p. 277), and she became famous in all of these places, as well as controversial at times for her remarks and for her support of Juan and Eva Peron, the president and first lady of Argentina.

Conclusion

When Baker died on April 12, 1975, her funeral was akin to that of a great dignitary. The streets were lined with mourners; among them was Princess Grace of Monaco, with whom Baker became friends in the 1960s (Rosette-Jules, 2007, p. 277). In the style of one of her music-hall reviews, Baker was surrounded by supportive players and a large and enthusiastic audience for her final curtain call. The event was a popular celebration for a media icon, one that proved to be the harbinger for later performers and celebrities in the 20th century (Rosette-Jules, 2007, p. 277).

In the 1920s, Baker arrived in Paris, France, chasing dreams of stardom that she never found in the United States; and at her funeral, thousands of people stood by to show their respect at the passing of a legend. Initially she was seen as an African American woman who happened to be living in Paris and who became a successful legend, which she could not have envisioned in her dreams, and yet after achieving star status, Baker's race mattered less as she became more "French" in her performances. This transition began to occur in the 1930s when she retired the banana skirt for a different kind of look that caught the attention and admiration of her audiences. With each passing decade, Baker stayed attuned to the cultural, social, and political climate in Paris and adjusted her performances accordingly.

One of the many examples to point to as evidence of Baker becoming more French and less African American is the way she came to view the world. It was never really clear whether Baker knew about the colonization the French government undertook in sub–Saharan Africa and other places. When she returned to the United States, particularly during her short stay for the *Ziegfield Follies* (1936) and in subsequent years, she made it clear that she would not tolerate racism and refused to perform in theaters where African American patrons were forced to sit in the back.

Some 37 years later, the many books on Josephine Baker indicate the aura and grip she still holds and will continue to have on subsequent generations as they discover her performances. Though she was never fully appreciated in the United States in the way she was abroad, she was larger than theater, the films she starred in, and her recordings. Baker cultivated an international star persona, finding phenomenal success in Europe and South America and, to a lesser extent, in the United States. In America, Baker was constrained by the twin issues of race and gender; outside her homeland, she found the freedom to shine. It was in Paris that Baker was most loved. There, she gained fame through performances filled with the primitive images that Europeans admired about Blackness. They assumed that these images were African inspired, but they were a combination of what she had learned early on as a performer, and many of her dances were improvised. Baker neither hesitated nor apologized for using her sexuality to compliment her talent. However, as already mentioned, she made topless nudity and Victorian-era standards of dress dispensable—she was a woman before her time. Her appearance always elicited a response, thus cementing her own importance in French haute couture and furthering her fame. She had far more agency in ways that eluded many African American actresses in the United States in negotiating her contracts, in opening her own nightclub, Chez Josephine, in buying a chateau, and in dating (though never marrying) a duke. In this way, Baker provided a role model to French women, allowing them to reclaim their voices by discarding the Victorian ideals of womanhood that persisted into the 20th century. Enchanted by Josephine Baker, French critics called her "La Baker" and "the Black Venus." Both labels became synonymous with Baker as she became an iconic presence in France.

During her lifetime, and certainly since, she achieved legendary status by subverting the predetermined roles imposed by Hollywood in embracing her status as a cultural outsider who ultimately became iconic. In essence, she began her long career in France by taking her partial nudity in her performances and turning it into a thing of beauty. In doing so, she was making the statement unconsciously that "Black is beautiful," and though audiences thought she was reinforcing primitive stereotypes, she was also reclaiming that which had been a struggle for African American women, which is their femininity. Baker came to symbolize in France, at least, that Black was beautiful long before "Black is beautiful" became an iconic statement in the 1960s. For all of her accomplishments and even though one of her two loves, the United States, was not always receptive to Baker, and not as welcoming as she should have been, Baker never gave up hope that one day the United States would embrace her the way France had. *J'ai deux amours* is about her love for the United States and France. Her birth country never fully embraced Baker and demonstrates the duality that Baker lived—as an expatriate African American woman in Paris and as an African American woman in the United States who was refused entrance into the famous Stork Club, home to many Hollywood royalty, in the 1950s. Charlene Regester (2000) notes that near the "end of her career, the U.S. again transformed her into a bona fide star and singer" (p. 34). Indeed, this was contradictory for Baker, who wanted, above all else, to achieve the kind of success in the United States that she had in Paris.

In speaking out against racial injustices in the United States, she became the target of inflammatory and scathing criticism by white and African American newspapers during her long career.[3] Throughout her years as a performer, Baker was never able to reconcile the racial attitudes of the United States with her status as "La Baker" in Paris. She became not only a modern diva but also an iconic presence in popular culture who transgressed stage, film, and music, becoming part of the social, political, and cultural fabric across continents. Baker became the precursor to others like Adele Addison, Bridget A. Bazile, Grace Bumbry, Jessye Norman, Shirley Verrett, Beverly Johnson, and a host of others who achieved and cemented an iconic presence in American popular culture and abroad; but her status remained ingrained in France rather than the United States. Baker was one of the first 20th-century entertainers who traveled the world and left a mark wherever she went. She broke racial and gender barriers in Europe, South America, and other parts of the world in a way that she never was able to in the United States because of the intersection of her race, gender, and class, which informed, for the most part, the basis of America's racism. In Paris, she became one of the first truly admired stars with an almost religious following and perpetual impact that resonates very heavily internationally.

References

Braudy, S. (1974, June). Josephine Baker. *Viva*, 38–39.

Collins, P. H. (1990). *Black feminist thought: Knowledge, consciousness, and the politics of empowerment*. London, UK: HarperCollins.

Davis, A.Y. (1983). *Women, Race & Class*. New York: Vintage Books.

Ehrlich, K. (Producer) & Ralling, C. (Director). (1986). *Chasing rainbows. The life of Josephine Baker*. [Motion Picture]. United Kingdom: Channel Four Films.

Francis, T. (2005, Winter). Embodied fictions, melancholy migrations: Josephine Baker's cinematic celebrity. *Modern Fiction Studies, 51*(4), 824–845.

Hammonds, E. (2004). Black (w)holes and the geometry of Black female sexuality. In Jacqueline Bobo, Cynthia Hudley, & Claudine Michel (Eds.), *The Black studies reader* (pp. 301–315). New York: Routledge.

Habel, Y. (2005). To Stockholm, with love: The critical reception of Josephine Baker, 1927–35. *Film History, 17*, 125–138.

hooks, b. (1981). *Ain't I a woman: Black woman and feminism*. Boston, MA: South End Press. 1981).

Regester, C. (2000). The construction of an image and the desconstruction of a star—Josephine Baker, racialized, sexualized, and politicized in the African-American press, the mainstream press and FBI Files. *Popular Music and Society, 23*(1), 31–84.

Rosette, B. J. (2000). Two loves: Josephine Baker as icon and image. *Emergences, 10*(1), 55–77.

——— (2007). *Josephine Baker in art and life: The icon and the image*. Urbana, Champagne, and Chicago: University of Illinois Press.

Stovall, T. (1996). *Paris noir. African Americans in the City of Light*. New York: Houghton Mifflin.

Straw, P. A. (2000). *Negrophilia. Avant-garde Paris and Black culture in the 1920s*. London: Thames and Hudson.

Notes

1. A deeper analyses of these interconnections can be found in several works, including bell hooks's seminal work *Ain't I a Woman: Black Women and Feminism* (1981); Angela Y. Davis's *Women, Race and Class* (1983); and Patricia Hill Collins's *Black Feminist Thought: Knowledge, Consciousness, and the Politics of Empowerment* (1990).

2. For instance, Saartjie Baartman, better known as "the Hottentot Venus," was paraded around Europe and put on display, an examination that focused mainly on her buttocks and breasts, and this particular fact makes the case of otherness poignantly clear. At the same time, the Exposition Universalle held in 1889 had an exhibit of Blacks that European audiences could view in an effort to get a closer inspection of their characteristics, along with specimens of monkeys and other animals—which the French duly plundered from Africa—paralleled by freak shows in the United States. Thus it was that French ingenuity kicked in to disguise their wanton cruelty in Africa while an unusual industry was flourishing in Paris. Comparing Baartman to Baker is not fair. However, what I am trying to say here is that while Baartman was not given a choice, Baker was. Critics demonstrated a marked fascination with Baker's body and skin color, comparing the agility of her body to animals while likening her skin color to chocolate (Habel, 2005, p. 128).

3. Baker had an extensive FBI file for speaking out against discrimination in many places where she performed, as noted in Charlene Regester's "The construction of an image and the desconstruction of a star—Josephine Baker, racialized, sexualized, and politicized in the African-American press, the mainstream press and FBI Files," 2000.

Ethnicity

14

The Indigenous Soul Wounding

Understanding Culture, Memetics, Complexity, and Emergence

Wendy M. K. Peters

Introduction

The assimilation and colonization of First Nation Peoples—hereafter referred to as First Peoples[1]—throughout North America and in Hawaii permitted history to chronicle an alien interpretation and worldview of indigenous cultures and lived experience that would be disseminated and accepted as fact throughout the modern world. Replete with innumerable misinterpretations, erroneous philosophies, and misinformation, the newcomers' history also served to supplant the authentic knowledge, values, and beliefs of First Peoples. Debate over the innocence or intention of the newcomers may never be resolved. However, it is certain that the clash of cultures that occurred with Western expansionism was a major impetus in the cascade of events that has since shaped the current life conditions that exist within the communities of most First Peoples.

Today, norms of poverty and other social maladies are commonplace throughout the communities of most First Peoples. Taking a broader view, these issues are but symptoms that evidence an interrelated complexity of conditions long recognized by indigenous elders as a *soul wound*. Defined by Eduardo Duran (1995, 2006) as a common thread that weaves across much of the pain and suffering found in most of the Native communities in North America and Hawaii, the *soul wound* is a phenomenon so pervasive that it has impacted entire societies and has now been perpetuated over several generations. It is equally important, however, to clarify at the outset that the existential pain and suffering of First Peoples is not exclusively due to soul wounding but may also be attributed to past and present life conditions as well as the ongoing embedded structural barriers that prevail within their communities.

Current literature and research have supported the existence of soul wounding, while a plethora of circumstances such as devaluation, marginalization, disenfranchisement, and massive group trauma have all been implicated as antecedents to the phenomenon. To date, much has been explicated regarding the outward manifestations, or the symptoms and outcome, of the indigenous soul wound. However, despite the many types of interventions that have been instated over the years, the symptoms of the soul wound persist and the issues associated with it have become ever more prevalent.

The impoverished conditions that prevail within the enclaves that are the communities of assimilated indigenous and colonized First Peoples are widely known. Among the manifestations of poverty associated with First Peoples are conditions of deteriorating health and well-being among the populace, economic inequity with the dominant society, and marginalization in matters pertaining to civil, social, and political affairs. Issues relating to decline such as huge inequities in the health of indigenous peoples compared to general populations and the destruction of their ancestral habitats, as well as the devastation of the source of their spiritual and material sustenance, have become all but untenable. What follows is a discussion regarding the origin of the indigenous soul wound and, subsequently, the dynamics present within the nature of the indigenous soul wound that have informed and shaped the lived experience of the First Peoples of North America and Hawaii.

The first section of this chapter briefly discusses the literature and other research that substantiate the basis for the phenomenon that is the indigenous soul wound and also highlights some of the historical events and traumatic incidents that have been implicated in its origins. The second section of this chapter expounds on the theoretical views by which the soul wound might be interpreted. Finally, the last section of this chapter offers an assertion regarding the current state of the indigenous soul wound and its implications for indigenous peoples.

Background and History

Long before Captain James Cook landed on the shores of the most remote archipelago in the world, the Hawaiian people thrived within the confines of their tiny island. It was said that upon initial Western contact, the Hawaiians were found to be one of the most sophisticated, accomplished, enterprising, and self-sufficient people ever known to have existed (Harden, 1999). The Hawaiian people were at one time far advanced and highly knowledgeable. Although their learning was perhaps conceptualized somewhat differently than in Western civilizations, Hawaiians possessed a profound knowledge of science, philosophy, medicine, healing, and agronomy and regarded the oceanic expanse more intimately than could Western scientists or explorers. According to Hawaiian elders and historians, before the time of Western contact, the Hawaiian people were described as living a highly metaphysical existence. It has been told that they possessed superhuman physical and sensory characteristics, were extraordinarily psychic and intuitive, and embodied their ontological beliefs in a very literal way. As with most indigenous cultures, the Hawaiians understood themselves as being part of, and connected to, all things within their known universe (Becker, 1998; Ii, 1995; Kamakau, 1964; Kupihea, 2001, 2005; Long, 1953; Malo, 1971; Pukui & Elbert, 1986).

For the Hawaiians, like many other indigenous peoples of the era, history, after the first Western contact, would witness an ancient people become subsumed by a cataclysmic culture clash and a tumultuous transformation that persists even today. For example, in the span of less than 100 years, indigenous Hawaiians would succumb to a population loss of more than 90% to foreign diseases to which they had no prior immunities. They would also encounter the systematic loss of their land to foreigners and newcomers. As a communitarian society, the Hawaiians believed and practiced stewardship of their ecological habitat versus ownership of land or other types of property. Consequently, they were readily exploited by foreigners and newcomers who did not share the same values (Noyes, 2003; Rezentes, 2006). For Hawaiians, Western integration eventually culminated in the total dispossession of Hawaii's sovereign status and cultural identity.

The considerable differences between the Hawaiians' and the newcomers' cultures, values, and agendas created a scenario that the Hawaiians had not anticipated. Under the auspices of shared communitarian values, the Hawaiians welcomed the newcomers as members into their society. However, having different values and priorities, the newcomers surreptitiously took part in Hawaiian society and, before long, gained a political stronghold representative of their own interests and agendas. Shortly thereafter, the native Hawaiian monarchy was overthrown in favor of American annexation and, as many Hawaiians would later argue, the annexation of Hawaii was illegal (Osorio, 2002).

The U.S. vision of *Manifest Destiny* (Gura, 1999), a guise for imperialism originating in the 1800s, was the primary impetus underlying the annexation of many western lands and territories, including Hawaii. The ideals ascribed to Manifest Destiny resulted in a plethora of hegemonic practices such as the relocation of entire populations onto reservations, which created areas of isolation and segregation, or the forced attendance of native children to Residential Indian (boarding) Schools that supposedly aided in acculturation. Western imposed *civilization* amounted to a change in life conditions that devastated the longstanding social structures of First Peoples and disrupted their ability to continue living in the ways that had previously sustained their societies for millennia (Lyons & Mohawk, 1998; Niezen, 2000; Poupart, 2002; Wells, 1994).

The Americans, however, were not unique in their domination and subsequent treatment of indigenous populations. European expansionists also subjugated First Peoples in their various quests to colonize the new world. Consequently, colonialism, noted as the control and governing influence of a dominant body over a dependent territory or people, also brought with it actions of cultural imperialism perpetrated by the newcomers and the imposition of their foreign viewpoint on the indigenous peoples. Despite some difference in government policy, such was also the case for the indigenous peoples in Canada and elsewhere who were under the rule of the British Crown (Fish Kashay, 2002; Freeman, 2004; Furniss, 1997; Gump, 1998; Wells, 1994).

In Canada and the United States, governmental policy has always been to negotiate *voluntary* treaties and agreements with the indigenous tribes as a measure of good faith and peaceful intent. Despite official declarations of good will toward the indigenous peoples, however, the underlying intent of treaty making on the part of both governments was merely political manipulation to force the aboriginals to move off their lands in order to make them available for settlement by non–Indians (Lyons & Mohawk, 1998; Wells, 1994). Consequently, treaty making for most First Peoples in North America can be most often summarized as Robert Wells described:

> In practice, treaties and other cessions were seldom concluded with willing Indian tribes. The tribes usually knew they must either cede their lands or put their welfare and survival at the mercy of the dominant government, or be pushed aside without even a small reservation to call home. (1994, p. 553)

Since the time when Westerners first made contact with the native peoples in North America and Hawaii, a concurrent process of acculturation has taken place. Acculturation, however, has many forms. Primary among these forms are: *integration*, when individuals maintain an identity with their culture of origin but also opt to take on some characteristics of the new culture; *assimilation*, when people do not keep the identity of their culture of origin but instead adopt all of the characteristics of the new culture; *separation* or *segregation*, when people elect or are forced to be separate from the dominant culture; and *marginalization*, when people are relegated to a lower social standing or to the outer limits of society (Berry, 1992, 2001; Kazarian & Evans 1998; Lyons & Mohawk, 1998; Matsumoto, 2001; Sam & Berry, 2006; Streltzer, Rezentes, & Arakaki, 1996; Wells, 1994). For those of Western or European origin, acculturation might accurately have been described as a process of integration. However, when seen through the lens of First Peoples, acculturation, during the era of Western integration as a process of assimilation, segregation, and marginalization, the aftermath of which would be profound.

For the First Peoples of North America and Hawaii, the result of acculturation brought about the disenfranchisement of indigenous sovereignty. Viewed by the dominant governments as dependent and helpless, "Indians were wards of the government and were to be treated as minors without the full privileges of citizenship" (Kunnie & Goduka, 2006, p. 56). As a consequence, the sovereign rights of indigenous peoples were no longer honored, nor were they afforded equal rights as citizens under the laws of the land. Furthermore, attitudes and declarations upholding those very laws continue to be ratified within the treaties and existing case law in the United States and Canada.

The practice of acculturation also gave rise to well-documented massive group traumas, a phenomenon associated with cataclysmic events impacting a large group or a substantial number of people (Brave Heart, 2003; Brave Heart & DeBruyn, 1998; Brave Heart-Jordan, 1995). The assassination of Sitting Bull, the Wounded Knee Massacre, and the forced removal of Native children to boarding schools were but a few examples of events that resulted in massive group trauma. However, not until centuries and generations later would it be understood that when massive group traumas go unacknowledged, or worse, unresolved, a great potential exists for harmful consequences to emerge in their wake (Brave Heart, 2003; Brave Heart & DeBruyn, 1998; Brave Heart-Jordan, 1995; Duran, 1995, 2006). Today, almost three centuries after Western integration began in North America, social scientists are finally coming to appreciate how far the impact of acculturation has permeated into the cultural psyche of First Peoples.

Currently, there are still troublesome remnants of acculturation and historical trauma that abound in the lives and stories of First Peoples. Tales of residential boarding schools and relocation, outlawed cultural and spiritual practices (including even the speaking of native languages), broken treaties, illegal annexation, and the supplanting of First People's most deeply held beliefs and values have yet to be fully reconciled. Statistically, the prevalence of substance abuse, suicide, infant mortality, incarceration, school dropouts, low median family incomes, and many other issues have become endemic among First Peoples. In addition, widespread stereotypes, misconceptions of inferiority, and assumptions of cultural deficit would imply cultural devolution. However, looking beneath the surface of the existential struggles and challenges and deeper than issues of race, religion, and politics, it can be seen that opposing values between the dominant and subordinate cultures are what lie at the core of the indigenous soul wound (Peters, 2011).

Besides considering the indigenous soul wound, we must also look at the First Peoples' cultures. A society's culture emulates its people's cosmological worldview and conveys their concept of self-identity, beliefs, lifestyle, etiquette, history, language, and place or geography (Abrams & Primack, 2001; Campbell, 2001; Goertzen, 2001; Hay, 1998). For First Peoples, the concept of monism, an ontological philosophy that all things emanate from a single source and are thereby connected, is central to their culture. Their concepts of the spiritual are also monistic and both acknowledge and respect the relationships that they believe exist among all things, seen or unseen, animate or inanimate, past, present, and future. In this regard, the issue of respect, as it relates to monism, is a primary driver of the values, beliefs, behaviors, and actions of indigenous peoples' cultures (Abrams & Primack, 2001; Allen, 1992; Hay, 1998). Monism, then, sits at the root of indigenous wisdom, and all things that emanate from within that worldview are, as a consequence, colored by it. The belief that all things are connected also suggests the reverence with which First Peoples view, value, and honor relationships, especially those with family, ancestors, community, and the natural environment (Abrams & Primack, 2001; Allen, 1992; Hay, 1998).

Theoretical Views

Many theories of human development expound on particular concepts such as *culture*, *memetics*, *complexity*, and *emergence*. In this chapter, Spiral Dynamics integral (SDi), a developmental theory of human value systems, is cited and used to explicate all four concepts in an integral way. Originally uncovered by Clare W. Graves, SDi is best summed as the following:

> The psychology of the adult human being is an unfolding, ever-emergent process marked by subordination of older behavior systems to newer, higher order systems. The mature person tends to change his psychology continuously as the conditions of his existence change. Each successive stage or level of existence is a state through which people may pass on the way to other states of equilibrium. When a person is centralized in one of the states of equilibrium, he has a psychology which is particular to that state. His emotions, ethics and values, biochemistry, state of neurological activation, learning systems, preference for education, management, and psychotherapy are all appropriate to that state. (2005, p. 29)

A meme is a cultural item transmitted by repetition in a manner analogous to the biological transmission of genes (Dawkins, 1982). Memetics, therefore, explain how cultural elements are passed on from generation to generation. A vMEME, specific to SDi, is a term that refers to a particular set of values or an entire belief system that is passed on through biological transmission. This corollary is significant because it explains how an entire society could be impacted by events and circumstances that occurred in its past (Beck & Cowan, 1996).

Currently, SDi recognizes eight distinct phases of human development that are each representative of different *value systems* or *worldviews*.[2] Each phase is a product of interaction between external conditions of existence and internal complex adaptive systems. Don E. Beck and Christopher Cowan (1996) describe the construct of SDi as:

> The forces inside the human spirals that wind through individual minds, drive organizations to new plateaus, and push societies to evolve through layers of complexity. . . . New Times demand New Thinking. . . . Each time we experience the New Times, New Thinking sequence, a controversial if not altogether revolutionary view of human nature evolves. The resulting synthesis of ideas, perspectives, and theories yields a compelling restatement of what it means to be human. (p. 27)

This dynamic between external conditions of existence and internal complex adaptive systems activates the self-organizing creativity of humans as organisms and their inherent capacity to emerge, adapt, and evolve. The open-ended, evolutionary tenor and constituents of polarity, emergence, and transcendence make SDi a suitable, if not superb, tool for explicating the indigenous soul wound because it elucidates the phenomenon in an objective and integral way and excludes the bias or judgments often associated with aspects of race, ethnicity, religion, or nationality. Having been deployed and applied successfully in areas of potential transformation worldwide (Beck, 2006), SDi has been shown to be an effective tool for assessing the vital signs present in large-group dynamics and for understanding the behaviors that emerge in response to changes in life conditions.

Where people and culture are concerned, an example of a system would be an individual person, an ethnic group, or an entire society. Likewise, if referring to the life conditions of humans, be they individuals or groups, as systems, we should also consider the various aspects of their habitats as systems and incorporate how those habitats impact or affect the human systems that are a part of those larger systems. Gene Bellinger defined a system as "an entity which maintains its existence through the mutual interaction of its parts" (2004, p. 1). A system may be a single organism, such as a person, or any organization, group, or society. Accordingly, "systems thinking" is a new scientific understanding that, at all levels, living systems are currently evolving, and the associated systems theory is based on the awareness that everything is interconnected and interrelated. The concepts of systems theory are well suited for explaining processes of renewal, adaptability, and sustainability (Bellinger, 2004; Capra, 1991, 1997; Wheatley, 2006). Moreover, it is the role of systems, how they interact, emerge, and adapt intelligently according to changes in life conditions, that hold meaning and significance in relation to the current conditions, culture, and lived experiences of First Peoples in North America and Hawaii.

Margaret Wheatley (2006) noted that life's first imperative is self-determination, the freedom to create itself. In living systems, boundaries are the place where relationships take form and "individual organisms shape themselves in response to their neighbors and their environments" (Wheatley, 2007, p. 25). Life's second imperative is the search for community (Capra, 1991, 1997; Wheatley, 2006, 2007). As nothing exists for very long in isolation, evolution progresses from the existence of relationships. Cooperation between systems increases the potential for system sustainability, while species that foster greed will tend to die off (Capra, 1991, 1997; Wheatley, 2006, 2007). In a final note on systems, it should be recognized that recurring disorder, instability, and nonlinearity are inherent to their adaptive intelligence because these characteristics are what create the conditions of disequilibrium necessary for emergence to a different state of being. Emergence, then, is what begets adaptation, which in turn contributes to the overall health and stability of the system. The complex process of evolution can be best summed up by Wheatley, who claims that "life seeks organization, but uses messes to get there" (2007, p. 27).

What relevance, then, can systems thinking and change theory offer in relation to the indigenous soul wound? Manuel De Landa (1997) claimed that the value of history is in our learning to distinguish patterns that might lend understanding to the dynamics of cause and effect. De Landa further stated that "all structures that surround us and form our reality (mountains, animals and plants, human languages, social institutions) are the products of specific historical processes" (1997, p. 11). Following that line of reasoning, from an evolutionary standpoint, what appears as devolution in First Peoples societies might also be understood by exploring the patterns and processes that have occurred throughout history as well as those present in our natural surroundings.

This chapter has explicated the evolutionary development of the First Peoples in North America and Hawaii in a manner not unlike De Landa had noted. By looking deeper into the lived experience of indigenous peoples, at what underlies the surface phenomena and symptoms of societal decline, we are better able to integrate the value of history, be informed by the patterns present within it, and can more clearly understand the evolutionary dynamics of both cause and effect as they pertain to the indigenous soul wound. For First Peoples, the implications are that these processes have taken place since the time of Western integration and, as such, are those that have not only shaped the current life conditions of many First Peoples but are also those that will determine their fate.

Humans are always consciously and unconsciously adapting to the changes that happen around them. Nevertheless, individuals seldom take notice of their adaptive process because the changes are usually subtle and typically minute. On occasion, the change that happens is so momentous that people adapt, as they must, in very dramatic and conspicuous ways. People must also adapt according to their existential nature. In other words, people can only adapt according to the *tools* they have to work with at that time. Robert Kegan (1982) asserted that individual emotional and social development is, in fact, an evolutionary process. This idea both supports and explains soul wounding in its multitude of individual manifestations.

Current and Future Implications

In conclusion, it would seem that the indigenous soul wound has become an integral part of the worldview held by First Peoples in North America and Hawaii. It could also be concluded that the indigenous soul wound was caused by the clash of cultures that occurred with Western expansionism and integration. In this regard, the indigenous soul wound has since informed and shaped the current life conditions that exist within most First Peoples communities. However, based on the theoretical concepts put forth in this chapter, it could also be argued that soul wounding does *not* indicate conditions of indigenous devolution. Instead, it would appear that the opposite is true. The societal symptoms that give an impression of decline are really the chaos, or the micro elements that comprise the macro changes we understand as evolution.

By looking deeper than mere surface manifestations and appearances, the indigenous soul wound could be interpreted as an adaptive intelligence for coping with changes in life conditions. Furthermore, as a mechanism, this adaptive intelligence was subject to the *tools*, or alternately, the worldview that was held by the First Peoples in North America and Hawaii during the time that the changes in life conditions were occurring. Additionally, given the cultural beliefs of First Peoples, their fundamental cosmologies, their monistic ontological conceptions, and the high value they placed on relationships, is it any wonder that the wounds created by assimilative and colonial processes manifested in ways that wounded their spirits or their souls?

Currently, the endeavors most successful at inciting social change for First Peoples communities have been those focused around the revival and revitalization of indigenous cultures. *Retraditionalization* is about the return to traditional cultural forms (Arndt, 2004; Edwards, 2002; Hermes, 2001; Menzies, 2005; White, 2004). Unlike efforts of activism, used as a means of political protest, retraditionalization is about healing and directly relates to the indigenous soul wound because it is an intervention that attempts to fill the void created by acts of colonization and assimilation. Retraditionalization is a form of healing that endeavors to replace, reconstruct, and reacculturate things long ago lost or harmed at the time of the original trauma.

Another consequence of colonial naiveté was in the way that Western methods of education have imposed vastly different epistemologies—ways of learning and knowing, language, or ways of speaking, or ways of expression and interaction, and even reading and writing—as compared to the oral transmission of information characteristic of many First Peoples cultures (Kahakalau, 2002, 2004; Kanaiaupuni, 2005; Kossack, 2005; Lambe, 2003; Lightning, 1997; Ole-Henrik, 2005). As a result, efforts in education reform have promoted strategies that seek to move cultural considerations from the periphery to the center of the educational arena by placing an emphasis on culturally based approaches to education. This concept of strategic reform serves not only to reinforce the integrity of the indigenous culture but will also bring the essential knowledge of indigenous wisdom to bear in an integrated and comparative fashion that moves both indigenous and nonindigenous peoples beyond the binary oppositional discourse that currently prevails.

In the enclaves of First Peoples throughout North America and Hawaii, trends have shifted toward more culturally informed alternatives. Additionally, the implementation of community-based education, founded upon traditional values, orientations, and principles while also utilizing the technologies of modern education, has also begun to yield some positive results (Bell & Lim, 2005; Brave Heart Society, 2006; Cole, 2006; Edwards, 2002; Ole-Henrik, 2005; Ridenour-Wildman, 2004; Short, 1999; Smylie, Williams, & Cooper, 2006).

Finally, this chapter proposes that current interventions and remediation, although certainly necessary, are not sufficient to address the core issues of the indigenous soul wound overall. Additionally, it could be argued that solutions that work for some cultures should not arbitrarily be ascribed to another because cultures each hold a particular worldview that is composed of the established patterns, protocols, and values that make them unique to a society. To effectively address the issues relevant to the indigenous soul wound, the entirety of social complexity must be taken into account to arrive at any sustainable remedy.

As a last word, speaking from my own perspective as an indigenous scholar, I have come to learn that contrary to much of what I had previously been taught, the patterns and structures of complexity that were modeled by my ancestors are still present within me. Likewise, I assert that the same holds true for all First Peoples. Propagated and transmitted across the ecologies of the mind, the memes and vMEMEs of our ancestors are still within us. Although our faces may look different today and our ways of finding subsistence may have changed, the greatness of the First Peoples that once was magnified in far greater numbers still flows through our veins. We need only remember our greatness by coming to find and know our authentic selves once again.

References

Abrams, N. E., & Primack, J. R. (2001, September 7). Cosmology and 21st-century culture. *Science, 293*(5536), 1769–1770. Retrieved from http://physics.ucsc.edu/cosmo/primack_abrams/1769.pdf.

Allen, P. (1992). *The sacred hoop: Recovering the feminine in American Indian traditions: With a new preface.* Boston: Beacon Press.

Arndt, L. M. R. (2004). *Soul wound, warrior spirit: Exploring the vocational choice of American Indian law enforcement officers working for non-tribal agencies* (Doctoral dissertation, University of Wisconsin, Madison, Wisconsin). Retrieved from ProQuest database.

Beck, D. E. (Speaker). (2006). *Spiral dynamics integral: Learn to master the memetic codes of human behavior* [CD]. Louisville, CO: Sounds True.

Beck, D. E., & Cowan, C. C. (1996). *Spiral dynamics: Mastering values, leadership, and change*. Malden, MA: Blackwell.

Becker, C. K. (1998). *Mana Cards: The power of Hawaiian wisdom*. Hilo, HI: Radiance Network.

Bell, J., & Lim, N. (2005, Summer). Young once, Indian forever: Youth gangs in Indian country. *American Indian Quarterly, 29*(3/4), 626–650, 744–745. Retrieved from http://proquest.umi.com/?did=986382131&sid=2&Fmt=3&clientId=45836&RQT=309&VName=PQD.

Bellinger, G. (2004). *Systems: A journey along the way* [Article]. Retrieved May 26, 2009, from http://www.systems-thinking.org/systems/systems.htm.

Berry, J. W. (1992). *Cross-cultural psychology: Research and applications*. Cambridge, UK; New York: Cambridge University Press.

Berry, J. W. (2001). A psychology of immigration. *Journal of Social Issues, 57*(3), 165 (17). doi:10.1111/0022-4537.00231.

Brave Heart, M. Y. H. (2003, January). The historical trauma response among natives and its relationship with substance abuse: A Lakota illustration. *Journal of Psychoactive Drugs 35*(1), 7–13. Retrieved from http://proquest.umi.com/?did=338232111&Fmt=3&clientId=45836&RQT=309&VName=PQD.

Brave Heart, M. Y. H., & DeBruyn, L. M. (1998). The American Indian holocaust: Healing historical unresolved grief. *American Indian and Alaska Native Mental Health Research 8*(2), 56-80. Retrieved from http://proquest.umi.com/?did=36164473&Fmt=3&clientId=45836&RQT=309&VName=PQD.

Brave Heart-Jordan, M. Y. H. (1995). *The return to the sacred path: Healing from historical trauma and historical unresolved grief among the Lakota* (Doctoral dissertation). Retrieved from http://proquest.umi.com/?did=741209551&Fmt=2&clientId=45836&RQT=309&VName=PQD.

Brave Heart Society. (2006). *Cante ohitika okodakiciye* [Brave Heart Society winter count]. Lake Andes, SD: Author.

Campbell, G. R. (2001, Fall). The Lemhi Shoshoni: Ethnogenesis, sociological transformations, and the construction of a tribal nation. *American Indian Quarterly, 25*(4), 539–580. Retrieved from http://proquest.umi.com/?did=204359091&Fmt=4&clientId=45836&RQT=309&VName=PQD.

Capra, F. (Writer), & Toms, M. (Director). (1991). Mindwalk: The new paradigm [Radio series episode]. In *New dimensions media*. San Francisco: New Dimensions Foundation.

Capra, F. (Writer), & Toms, M. (Director). (1997). Living systems [Radio series episode]. In *New dimensions media*. San Francisco: New Dimensions Foundation.

Cole, W. M. (2006). *Education for self-determination: The worldwide emergence and institutionalization of "indigenous colleges"* (Doctoral dissertation). Retrieved from http://proquest.umi.com/?did=1158524401&Fmt=6&clientId=45836&RQT=309&VName=PQD.

Dawkins, R. (1982). *The extended phenotype*. New York: Oxford University Press.

De Landa, M. (1997). *A thousand years of nonlinear history*. Brooklyn, NY: Zone Books.

Duran, E. (2006). *Healing the soul wound: Counseling with American Indians and other native peoples*. New York: Teachers College Press.

Duran, E., & Duran, B. (1995). *Native American postcolonial psychology*. Albany: State University of New York Press.

Edwards, Y. (2002). *Healing the soul wound: The retraditionalization of Native Americans in substance abuse treatment* (Doctoral dissertation). Retrieved from http://proquest.umi.com/?did=726390871&sid=2&Fmt=2&clientId=45836&R QT=309&VName=PQD.

Fish Kashay, J. L. (2002). *Savages, sinners, and saints: The Hawaiian kingdom and the imperial contest, 1778–1839*. (Ph.D., the University of Arizona), 372.

Freeman, S. (2004). *The land systems of colonial America: European and Native American land tenure issues in the colonial eras of the Americas*. (M.A., West Virginia University), 88.

Furniss, E. M. (1997). *In the spirit of the pioneers: Historical consciousness, cultural colonialism and Indian/White relations in rural British Columbia*. (Ph.D., the University of British Columbia (Canada)), 337.

Goertzen, C. (2001, Winter). Powwows and identity on the Piedmont and costal plains of North Carolina. *Ethnomusicology, 45*(1), 58-90. Retrieved from http://proquest.umi.com/?did=65956167&Fmt=4&clientId=45836&RQT=309&VNa me=PQD.

Graves, C. W. (2005). *The never ending quest: Dr. Clare W. Graves explores human nature* (C. C. Cowan & N. Todorovic, Eds.). Santa Barbara, CA: ECLET.

Gump, J. (1998, Spring). The imperialism of cultural assimilation: Sir George Grey's encounter with the Maori and the Xhosa, 1845–1868. *Journal of World History, 9*(1), 89–106. Retrieved from http://proquest.umi.com/?did=33705475&sid=2& Fmt=3&clientId=45836&RQT=309&VName=PQD.

Gura, P. F. (1999). Making America's destiny manifest. *Reviews in American History, 27*(4), 554–559.

Harden, M. J. (1999). Introduction. In *Voices of wisdom Hawaiian elders speak* (pp. 9–10). Kula, HI: Aka Press.

Hay, R. (1998, Fall). A rooted sense of place in cross-cultural perspective. *Canadian Geographer, 42*(3), 245–266. Retrieved from http://proquest.umi.com/?did=386 77956&sid=1&Fmt=4&clientId=45836&RQT=309&VName=PQD.

Hermes, S. S. (2001). *A cosmological and psychological portrayal: An integration of psyche, culture, and creativity* (Doctoral dissertation, Pacifica Graduate Institute, California). Retrieved from ProQuest database.

Ii, J. P. (1995). *Fragments of Hawaiian history* (D. B. Barrere, Ed., M. K. Pukui, Trans.). Honolulu, HI: Bishop Museum Press. (Original work published 1959)

Kahakalau, K. H. (2002). *Kanu o ka Aina: Natives of the land from generations back. A pedagogy of Hawaiian liberation* (Doctoral dissertation). Retrieved from http://proquest.umi.com/?did=765250631&Fmt=6&clientId=45836&RQT=30 9&VName=PQD.

Kahakalau, K. (2004). Indigenous heuristic action research: Bridging Western and indigenous methodologies. *Hulili: Multidisciplinary Journal on Hawaiian Well-being, 1*(1), 19–33.

Kamakau, S. M. (1991). *Ka poe kahiko: The people of god*. Honolulu, HI: Bishop Museum Press. (Original work published 1964)

Kanaiaupuni, S. M. (2005, June). Kaakalai ku kanaka: A call for strengths-based approaches from a native Hawaiian perspective. *Educational Researcher, 34*(5), 32–39. Retrieved from http://proquest.umi.com/?did=868764661&sid=1&Fmt=3&clientId=45836&RQT=309&VName=PQD.

Kazarian, S. S., & Evans, D. R. (Eds.). (1998). *Cultural clinical psychology: Theory, research, and practice*. New York: Oxford University Press.

Kegan, R. (1982). *The evolving self: Problem and process in human development*. Cambridge, MA: Harvard University Press.

Kossack, S. N. (2005, April). Exploring the elements of culturally relevant service delivery. *Families in Society, 86*(2), 189–195. Retrieved from http://proquest.umi.com/?did=846327241&sid=3&Fmt=3&clientId=45836&RQT=309&VName=PQD.

Kunnie, J., & Goduka, N. I. (2006). *Indigenous peoples' wisdom and power: Affirming our knowledge through narratives*. Aldershot, Hants, England; Burlington, VT: Ashgate.

Kupihea, M. (2001). *Kahuna of light: The world of Hawaiian spirituality*. Rochester, VT: Inner Traditions.

Lambe, J. (2003, Winter). Indigenous education, mainstream education, and native studies: Some considerations when incorporating indigenous pedagogy into native studies. *American Indian Quarterly, 27*(1/2), 308–326. Retrieved from http://proquest.umi.com/?did=707694851&Fmt=3&clientId=45836&RQT=309&VName=PQD.

Lightning, E. (1997). *First Nations control of First Nations education: An issue of power and knowledge* (Doctoral dissertation). Retrieved from http://proquest.umi.com/?did=738152981&Fmt=6&clientId=45836&RQT=309&VName=PQD.

Long, M. F. (1953). *Secret science at work: The huna method as a way of life*. Marina del Rey, CA: DeVorss.

Lyons, O., & Mohawk, J. (Eds.). (1998). *Exiled in the land of the free: Democracy, Indian nations & the U.S. constitution*. Santa Fe, NM: Clear Light Pub.

Malo, D. (1971). *Hawaiian antiquities* (2nd ed.). Honolulu, HI: Bishop Museum Press. (Original work published 1951)

Matsumoto, D. (2001). *The handbook of culture & psychology*. New York: Oxford University Press.

Menzies, P. M. (2005). *Orphans within our family: Intergenerational trauma and homeless aboriginal men* (Doctoral dissertation, University of Toronto, Canada). Retrieved from ProQuest database.

Niezen, R. (2000). *Spirit wars: Native North American religions in the age of nation building*. Berkeley: University of California Press.

Noyes, M. H. (2003). *Then there were none.* Honolulu, HI: Bess Press.

Ole-Henrik, M. (2005). Indigenous education. *Childhood Education, 81*(6), 319–320. Retrieved from http://proquest.umi.com/?did=885976151&Fmt=3&clientId=45 836&RQT=309&VName=PQD.

Osorio, J. (2002). *Dismembering lahui: A history of the Hawaiian nation to 1887.* Honolulu: University of Hawaii Press.

Peters, W. M. K. (2011). *The indigenous soul wound: Exploring culture, memetics, complexity, and emergence* (Doctoral dissertation, Institute of Transpersonal Psychology, California).

Poupart, L. M. (2002). Crime and justice in American Indian communities. *Social Justice, 29*(1/2), 144–159. Retrieved from http://proquest.umi.com/?did=208056 261&sid=1&Fmt=3&clientId=45836&RQT=309&VName=PQD.

Pukui, M. K., & Elbert, S. H. (1986). *Hawaiian dictionary: Hawaiian-English, English-Hawaiian.* Honolulu: University of Hawaii Press.

Rezentes, W. C. I. (2006). Hawaiian psychology. In L. T. Hosmand (Ed.), *Culture, psychotherapy, and counseling: Critical and integrative perspectives* (pp. 113–133). Thousand Oaks, CA: Sage Publications.

Ridenour-Wildman, S. L. (2004). *A comparative study of indigenous content of multicultural teacher education textbooks in Canada and the United States* (Doctoral dissertation). Retrieved from http://proquest.umi.com/?did=79593839 1&Fmt=6&clientId=45836&RQT=309&VName=PQD.

Sam, D. L., & Berry, J. W. (Eds.). (2006). *The Cambridge handbook of acculturation psychology.* New York: Cambridge University Press.

Short, C. W. (1999). *The cultural metamorphosis of Cree education* (Master's thesis). Retrieved from http://proquest.umi.com/?did=734718821&Fmt=6&clientId=45 836&RQT=309&VName=PQD.

Smylie, J., Williams, L., & Cooper, N. (2006). Culture-based literacy and aboriginal health. *Canadian Journal of Public Health, 97,* S21–S25. Retrieved from http://proquest.umi.com/?did=1074629311&Fmt=4&clientId=45836&RQT=309&VName=PQD.

Streltzer, J., Rezentes, W. C., & Arakaki, M. (1996). Does acculturation influence psychosocial adaptation and well-being in native Hawaiians? *International Journal of Social Psychiatry, 42*(1), 28–37.

Wells, R. N., Jr. (1994). *Native American resurgence and renewal: A reader and bibliography.* Metuchen, NJ: Scarecrow Press.

Wheatley, M. J. (2006). *Leadership and the new science.* San Francisco: Berrett-Koehler.

Wheatley, M. J. (2007). *Finding our way: Leadership for an uncertain time.* San Francisco: Berrett-Koehler. (Original work published 2005)

White, C. (2004, September). Culture, influence, and the "I-ness" of me: Commentary on papers by Susan Bodnar, Gary B. Walls, and Steven Botticelli [Editorial]. *Psychoanalytic Dialogues, 14*(5), 653–691. Retrieved from ProQuest database. (Document ID: 778535741)

Notes

1. The term *First [Nations] People* is used to denote the first, original, or earliest known inhabitants of a geographical region or place. Additionally, terms such as *native, indigenous,* or *aboriginal* have similar meaning and are also used to refer to those descended from the first inhabitants of a place or geographic region. While all terminologies are utilized interchangeably, in this chapter, the term *First Peoples* is used to describe the native North Americans and indigenous Hawaiians.

2. Based on the original research of Clare W. Graves, SDi worldview phases are not simply behavioral patterns or types of people. Rather, value systems are indicative of thinking patterns, or *how* people think, and the level of complexity to which an individual has developed (Beck, 2006). Currently, there are eight confirmed worldview phases, each of which represents a given set of life conditions and the coping patterns human adults have developed to solve the problems associated with those life conditions. Being of an evolutionary nature, the phases are described characteristically as follows, ranging from fundamental to complex: (a) instinctive and survivalistic; (b) magical and animistic; (c) impulsive and egocentric; (d) purposeful and authoritarian; (e) achievist and strategic; (f) communitarian and egalitarian; (g) integrative and intuitive; and last, (h) holistic, experiential, and interconnected.

15

Triangulated Threat

A Model of Black and Asian Race Relations in a Context of White Dominance

John Tawa, Karen L. Suyemoto, and Jesse J. Tauriac

In July 2004, members of the Unity Clothing Association, an alliance of Black-owned clothing businesses, stood outside of the Korean-owned Visionz Clothing Store in the Iverson Mall, located in Washington, D.C. They passed out fliers reading: "There is already a carryout and liquor store in every Black community run by Asians," and "How long will we let them RAPE the Urban community? Wake Up! Don't be Bamboozled or Hoodwinked!" (Hopkinson, 2004). These protests seem to reflect a long-standing sentiment held by some members of the Black community that Asian Americans are taking over economic resources (e.g., corner stores and urban clothing) that more rightfully belong to Black Americans based on their more extended histories and nativity in urban America.

In 2006, Yale undergraduate and second-generation Chinese American Jian Li sued Princeton University on the grounds of race-based favoritism (i.e., preferential acceptance of underrepresented minority applicants). Li claimed that, despite his near-perfect SAT scores, he was overlooked for admission to Princeton in favor of less qualified Black and Latino minority applicants. Li's decision to file the complaint was based on studies by Princeton researchers, which reported that about 80% of the seats at top universities that were currently being given to Blacks and Latinos would be given to Asian Americans if affirmative action policies were not applied (Carroll, 2006). Li's sentiment seems to reflect the belief, shared by some members of the Asian community, that he is the rightful proprietor of educational resources based on his personal merit (e.g., his strong SAT scores).

The racial landscape of the United States has become increasingly diverse since the reform of immigration laws in 1965, which removed previously stringent quotas limiting the numbers of nonWhite/ nonEuropean immigrants to the United States (Bobo & Hutchings, 1996). By 2050, social scientists predict that racial minorities collectively will constitute more than half of the entire U.S. population (Bobo & Hutchings, 1996; Yancy, 2003). Complex interactions between minority groups, such as the interactions between Blacks and Asians[1] in the examples above, are inevitable and raise questions about the relations between groups and groups' members. Is Jian Li enacting antiBlack racism? Do Asian Americans oppress Blacks? Does the Unity Clothing Association's protest of a Korean-owned urban clothing store reflect anti–Asian racism? Do Black Americans oppress Asians? Psychological theory and research that could help answer these questions continues to be framed in relation to minority–majority group interactions and continues to rely heavily on a Black–White paradigm of race relations (Alcoff, 2003; J. Y. Kim, 2006; Perea, 1997), where one group is framed as the absolute oppressor and one group is framed as the absolute oppressed.

In this chapter, we (a) integrate theory from political science and psychology to develop a model of "triangulated threat" for understanding Black and Asian relations outside of a Black–White paradigm, (b) review research on Blacks' and Asians' intergroup perceptions to support triangulated threat, (c) consider the implications of triangulated threat for social distance between Blacks and Asians, and (d) position triangulated threat within a context of White/European American dominance. Our chapter responds to recent calls in the literature for a paradigm shift in the ways in which we understand race relations (Alcoff, 2003; Perea, 1997). We offer "triangulated threat" as one model for community activists, theorists and researchers, and educators to move "beyond Black and White" in the ways in which they think, talk, teach, and write about race relations. Moreover, we position this model within a broader context of White/European American dominance, recognizing the ways in which the dominant White group's constructions of racialized minority groups (i.e., the social constructions of the meanings of "Black" and "Asian") promotes a "divide and conquer" strategy that maintains White power and privilege. First, however, we examine more closely the central tenets of the Black–White paradigm and problematize the application of a binary oppressor/oppressed model of race relations to an interminority context.

The Black–White Paradigm of Race Relations

A paradigm is a conceptual foundation that structures and guides the development of knowledge, including the development of theories and research (Kuhn, 1962). While paradigms facilitate theory and research by providing an organizational structure and shared basis of thought, a dominant paradigm can be so widely accepted as fact that it can hinder theorists' and researchers' abilities to see beyond its basic tenets, particularly if the paradigm is pervasive and unquestioned (Kuhn, 1962; Perea, 1997). "As a paradigm becomes the widely accepted way of thinking and of producing knowledge on a subject, it tends to exclude or ignore alternative facts or theories that do not fit the expectations produced by the paradigm" (Perea, 1997 p. 1216).

The Black–White paradigm is the predominant way of conceptualizing race relations within the United States. Developed within a pre-1965 historical context in which Black and White race relations were most salient, the Black–White paradigm emphasizes a binary positioning of one group (White) as the oppressor and the other group (Black) as the oppressed. The use of the phrase *Black–White paradigm* refers not only to the specific relationship between Black and White people and their communities but also to a particular *way of thinking* about race relations. In exploring the relations between the White dominant group and minority groups—whether Blacks, Asians, Latinos, or Native Americans—the Black–White paradigm is useful in considering the ways that the dominant White group's power affects minority groups' experiences and relations with the dominant group.

However, interminority relations are frequently also framed within the oppressor-and-oppressed paradigm. For example, relations between Blacks and Asians are often discussed with one group being framed as the absolute oppressor and one group being framed as the absolute oppressed. In the example above, Jian Li might be seen as a representative of the oppressor group (Asians) supporting educational policy changes that would be harmful to the oppressed group (Blacks). Or the protestors might be seen as representatives of the oppressor group (Blacks) supporting a boycott that would be harmful to the oppressed group (Asians). In these instances, however, a binary analysis is problematic because neither group has absolute power. Instead, both groups have relative power and both are oppressed by the dominant White group. However, when minority groups or people accept the binary framing, the result is often dissention between and among minority communities, internalization of stereotypes about the other group, and engaging in "oppression olympics"[2] that inevitably leads to invalidating the different types of oppression experienced by different racial minority groups. Thus, it is the White group that benefits most from the divisions resulting from framing minority group relations as binary and absolute (Lipsitz, 2001)[3].

Race-relations theories that developed using the binary Black–White paradigm miss the complexities of interminority relational dynamics in the context of dominant White societies. For example, group threat theory (GTT), as discussed by Herbert Blumer in his 1958 book *Race Prejudice as a Sense of Group Position*, suggests that prejudice results when a minority group threatens to consume resources that are perceived to more rightfully belong to the group in power. It is difficult to apply GTT to minority–minority group interactions because neither group is in a position of *absolute* power. However, different minority groups can be in positions of *relative* power in relation to other minority groups' particular experiences or social statuses. For example, within the mythic U.S. meritocracy, Asians, who are perceived as the "model minorities," may have certain power afforded to them related to Blacks. Blacks, on the one hand, may have certain power afforded to them in relation to being perceived as having longer and more extended histories in the United States; Whites, however, may have a more absolute power in relation to both Blacks and Asians because they are a part of the dominant culture. To address the complexity of relative power, we integrate classic GTT with racial triangulation theory (C. J. Kim, 1999), which offers multiple dimensions on how Blacks and Asians may be afforded certain power in relation to one another. An integration of these theories offers a framework to conceptualize complex power dynamics between multiple minority groups existing within a White power structure and can be applied to understand how Blacks and Asians often perceive one another.

Group Threat and Racial Triangulation Theories

Group Threat Theory

Group threat theory (GTT) emphasizes the role of collective social agreements informed by historical and political developments that determine a presumed social order among racialized groups. Consequently, groups that are privileged in the social order develop a sense of proprietary rights to various resources perceived as limited. GTT posits that groups in positions of power (Whites) develop negative attitudes and larger social distance toward outgroups (Asians and Blacks) with a relative lack of power based on the threat that outgroups will consume limited resources, including political, economic, and educational resources that are perceived to more rightfully belong to the ingroup in power (Blumer, 1958). Blumer outlines four basic feelings that the GTT posits as related to racially prejudiced and socially distancing views for the more powerful group, in this case Whites:

> 1) a feeling of superiority, 2) a feeling that the subordinate race is intrinsically different and alien, 3) a feeling of proprietary claim to certain areas of privilege and advantage, and 4) fear and suspicion that the subordinate race harbors designs on the prerogatives of the dominant race. (p. 4)

Because the GTT explains negative attitudes and perceived social distance from the perspective of a group in a position of power/privilege, it has most frequently been applied to exploring relations between the dominant group and a nondominant group. In terms of interminority relations such as those between Blacks and Asians, it is not clear how GTT can be applied given that neither group has absolute power over the other. Again, although different racial minority groups are not in positions of absolute power and privilege and may not, themselves, have primary control of resources, they may have relative power and privilege in specific areas, conferred upon them from the dominant group. Racial triangulation theory proposes two areas of relative power and privilege between Blacks and Asians.

Racial Triangulation Theory

Claire Jean Kim's (1999) theory of "racial triangulation" considers Blacks' and Asians' relative privilege and oppression in relation to one another and both groups in relation to Whites. To illustrate her theory, Kim suggests that Blacks and Asians are differentially ascribed relative privilege/oppression on two dimensions: inferiority/superiority and insider/ outsider. We use the more specific terms *merit-based power* and *nativity-based power* to describe these dimensions.

Asians (relative to Blacks) may have *merit-based power* afforded to them related to being perceived as "model minorities" within the mythic U.S. meritocracy. Indeed, the dominant group has constructed a notion of Asians as the "model minority." That is, White Americans have touted Asians as successful minorities who have achieved increasing wealth, upward social mobility, and avoidance of the psychosocial difficulties that adversely affect members of other minority groups (Wong & Halgin, 2006). This is a mythical construction, acknowledged by scholars as the model minority *myth* (Delucchi & Do, 1996; Kim, 1999; Wong & Halgin, 2006). For example, Asian Americans' achievements in wealth and education are bimodal, with some Asians having achieved wealth and education at rates similar to those of Whites, while others experience poverty and education levels lower even than those of Blacks or Latinos (Waters & Eschbach, 1995).

In spite of the research that challenges the minority myth, this construction continues to affect colloquial understandings of Asians in the United States. Asians are cast as the model *minority,* while Whites remain the model overall. Within this construction, Asians are compared to other nonWhite minority groups (particularly Blacks) and are regarded as a group that has "made it" and is therefore more worthy than Blacks and other minority groups as recipients of economic, educational, and social resources within the mythic meritocratic system that rewards hard work and intelligence (Cheryan & Bodenhausen, 2000; Delucchi & Do, 1996; Taylor & Stern, 1997; Wong & Halgin, 2006). Many Asians who have internalized the notion of the model minority may also perceive *themselves* to be the more rightful proprietors of resources, such as educational capital, related to "merit," as compared to Blacks (Kim, 1999.) In contrast, Blacks in the United States continue to be constructed as "unintelligent" and "lazy" and are frequently perceived as an example of group that didn't "make it" within the meritocracy (Waters, 1999).

Blacks (relative to Asians) may have *nativity-based power* afforded to them related to being perceived as having longer and more extended histories in the United States. While this dimension of relative privilege may be less explicitly acknowledged than the "model minority myth," research does suggest that Blacks are perceived as being more "American" or native to the United States when compared to Asians, but less so compared to Whites. Devos and Banaji (2005), for example, report on a study testing the extent to which African Americans, Asian Americans, and White Americans were associated with the category "American." Among a predominantly White sample of Yale undergraduates (n = 135), African Americans were significantly more likely to be associated with the national category of "American" compared to Asian Americans, but both were less likely than Whites (Devos & Banaji, 2005). Research has also established that Asian Americans in particular are constructed as "perpetual foreigners" (Devos & Banaji, 2005; Sue et al., 2007; Wong & Halgin, 2005). For example, within a focus group that addressed racial microaggressions among ethnically diverse Asian Americans, Derald Wing Sue and colleagues (2007) found that every participant had the experience of being perceived as foreigners or foreign born.

While Blacks are constructed relative to Asians as having greater privilege in relation to nativity, this construction is also mythical. The foreign-born Black population in the United States is growing rapidly as people from African (e.g., Liberia, Sudan, Kenya, Nigeria) and Caribbean countries (e.g., Haiti and Jamaica) are increasingly seeking greater economic, educational, and occupational opportunities in the United States. Compared to 1980, the immigrant portion of the Black population in 2005 has tripled (Kent, 2007). Despite these facts, the meaning of "Black" in the United States continues to be associated with higher nativity status when compared to the meaning of "Asian." Blacks themselves may also internalize racialized notions of nativity status and, as a result, may perceive themselves to be the more rightful proprietors of socioeconomic resources, such as urban American economic capital. Indeed, in the previously discussed research, the African American subsample (n = 30) placed a significantly stronger association between being American and native born with African Americans than they did with Asian Americans (Devos & Banaji, 2005).

The constructions of Blacks and Asians as "meritorious" and as "native" are problematic on multiple levels. First, they reflect an overaggregation of ethnically and socioeconomically diverse communities into monolithic groups. For example, in regard to educational merit, although all Asians are assigned the mythic "model minority" status, the educational performance of many Southeast Asian immigrant communities lags behind those of their White, East and South Asian, and African immigrant counterparts (Wong & Halgin, 2005). In fact, African immigrants have the highest level of education among all immigrant groups in the United States (Logan & Deane, 2003). To assume that all Asians are academically successful ignores the need for educational intervention among these relatively underperforming communities. Additionally, these constructions often shape perceptions of self and other among Black and Asian communities and impact the social relations and attitudes between these groups. Identifying areas of privilege, as we explained above, may enable us to understand the ways that GTT can be applicable to relations between minority groups.

Integrating Group Threat and Racial Triangulation Theories

By integrating classic GTT and racial triangulation theory, we develop a model of the ways that Blacks' and Asians' internalization of the dominant group's constructions of them may affect intergroup attitudes and social distance. Unlike GTT alone, this model considers multiple dimensions of threat and positions this within a context of White dominance. *Triangulated threat*, as depicted in Figure 15.1, expands on Kim's visual representation of racial triangulation while also accounting for GTT's emphasis on the ways relatively privileged groups perceive marginalized groups as threats. In our model, "domains of racialized privilege" are depicted in dark gray and light gray ovals. The arrows indicate the direction of threat; for example, Asians are depicted as a threat to Blacks' and Whites' sense of proprietary right to resources based on perceived nativity-based privilege. Conversely, Blacks are depicted as a threat to Asians' and Whites' sense of proprietary right to resources based on perceived merit-based privilege.

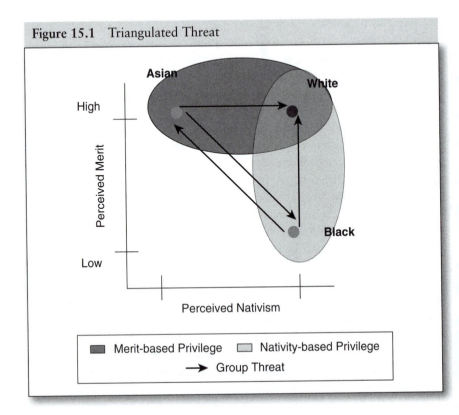

Figure 15.1   Triangulated Threat

Integrating GTT and Blumer's requisite attitudes with RTT suggests that if Blacks have internalized the dominant group's construction of Asians as perpetual foreigner and have internalized their own relative privilege based on the notion of mythical nativity, they may believe that they do have a greater right to resources associated with this nativity (e.g., positions in political offices, land/home ownership). To illustrate, consider the example of the alliance of Black store owners protesting the opening of a Korean-owned urban clothing store. The protestors' sentiment against a Korean-owned urbanwear store may be considered indicative of Blacks' anti–Asian sentiment. However, according to triangulated threat, it is more likely a function of Blacks' perceived "right" to economic opportunities based on their perception of greater nativity as compared to Asian Americans. Although Blacks may recognize that they do not have real privilege (i.e., that they will always be second-class citizens in comparison with Whites), they may simultaneously accept the relative and ascribed privilege, in terms of assumed nativity, afforded to them by the dominant group in relation to Asians. Without considering the relative privilege and oppression between these two groups, we can question the validity of these protestors' perception of "right" while ignoring important contextual factors. Yet conceptualizing the Black storeowners' sentiments in relation to their extended history, endurance of slavery and racism, and fight for full citizenship rights in a White-dominant U.S. context paints a much more informed and contextualized understanding of Black–Asian intergroup psychology. In the absence of such theory, we are reduced to a simplistic analysis of the Black storeowners' sentiment such as the perception that Blacks are inherently prejudiced toward Asians.

Similarly, if Asians have internalized the dominant group's construction of Blacks as lazy, unintelligent, and underserving and have internalized their own relative and ascribed privilege based on the model minority myth, they may believe that Asians do have a right to resources associated with merit (e.g., income, educational seats). Jian Li's decision to sue Princeton University for presumably favoring Black and Latino applicants may be considered indicative of Asians' antiBlack sentiment. However, according to triangulated threat, it is perhaps more likely a function of Li's own perception of right to educational opportunity based on his internalized understanding of himself and his group as meritorious within the White dominant U.S. meritocracy.

Thus, the assumed proprietary right ascribed to specific racial groups affects negative group attitudes and increased social distances between racial groups. Although we are not aware of empirical research directly testing and supporting the tenets of triangulated threat, research examining Blacks' perceptions of Asians and Asians' perceptions of Blacks can assist us in evaluating the merit of the theory. We turn now to this research, asking whether each group does indeed see the other as possessing various traits or attributes that make them unworthy of a right to resources based on each groups' assumption of proprietary right.

Blacks' Perceptions of Asians

Research indicates that many Blacks do commonly endorse the notion that Asians are "perpetual" foreigners (Devos & Banaji, 2005; Guthrie & Hutchinson, 1995). Furthermore, these perceptions of Asians are equated with the belief that Asians are not the rightful proprietors of resources and are perceived as threatening Blacks' access or right to resources. Patricia Guthrie and Janice Hutchinson (1995) observed cross-racial interactions and conducted open-ended qualitative interviews with African American and Asian American residents of a San Francisco housing project. Some African American residents offered that they viewed *all* Asian American individuals and families as "unfamiliar with American lifestyles" (p. 309) and categorically as "immigrant," despite the fact that almost a quarter of the Asian American tenants were native U.S. citizens. Similarly, Lawrence Bobo and Vincent Hutchings (1996) surveyed 4,025 participants in a random-digit-dialing telephone survey in the Los Angeles area in 1994 and found that approximately half of the Black respondents agreed with the statement that "all Asians speak English poorly," presumably reflecting the belief that all Asian Americans are recent immigrants to the United States.

Research on Blacks' perceptions of Asians has also equated perceptions of Asian "foreigner" status as reflecting undeserved resource allocation (Bobo & Hutchings, 1996; Guthrie & Hutchinson, 1995). African American interviewees, in the San Francisco housing project study, described Asian American families as crowding into small apartment spaces and as taking economic, occupational, and governmental resources that more rightfully belonged to African Americans (Guthrie & Hutchinson, 1995). Blacks have also been found to be significantly more likely than Whites to hold anti–Asian immigrant sentiments and to feel that Asian immigration was creating greater competition for resources (Bobo & Hutchings, 1996). As stated by an African American resident in the San Francisco housing project study: "They [Asian Americans] come here and have immediate access to jobs, housing, and money from the government" (Guthrie & Hutchinson, 1995, p. 310). Furthermore, of the 1,800 Black participants in a random-digit-dialing telephone survey also conducted in Los Angeles in 1992, 68.8% of them agreed (rather than disagreed) with the statement that "more good jobs for Asians meant fewer good jobs for Blacks," compared to only 32.9% of White participants who agreed (Bobo & Hutchings, 1996). Fifty-four percent of Blacks (n = 97) surveyed over the telephone in New York City in 1992 agreed that "Korean merchants drain Black economic resources" (Min & Kolodny, 1999, p. 149).

Asians' Perceptions of Blacks

Research indicates that many Asians do accept the negative stereotypes of Blacks as unintelligent and lazy. Furthermore, these perceptions are related to Asians' acceptance of their own model minority status. In one study, 34 Chinese American college students rated Blacks significantly more negatively than their own group on perceived laziness, inconsiderateness, and aggressiveness (Y. T. Lee, 2001). Similar findings have been found within community samples. The 1992 Los Angeles telephone survey described above shows that 63% of Asian participants endorsed that Blacks were less intelligent than themselves (Bobo & Hutchings, 1996). In the larger 1996 survey, approximately half of the Japanese and Korean respondents in Los Angeles agreed with the statement "almost *all* Blacks and almost *all* Hispanics are unintelligent" (Bobo & Hutchings, 1996, p. 9).

Asians also seem to perceive Blacks stereotypically as "lazy" and as "welfare dependents," in some cases relating these perceptions to rationales for why Asians are more deserving of resources than Blacks. In a participant observation and interview study with Korean merchants in New York City during the civil unrest in the mid–1990s, a number of Korean shopkeepers believed that their entrepreneurial success was not shared by Blacks because Blacks were less capable. One of the participants stated, "Blacks cannot own and manage this kind of business. They are lazy . . . they don't have business skills and stamina." Another suggested ". . . for the low-class Blacks especially, they are so much accustomed to enjoying their lives without working" (H. C. Lee, 1999, p. 116). These views appear to be prevalent not only among merchants but within the more general Asian community as well. In the smaller 1992 Los Angeles survey described above, 76.8% of Asian participants believed Blacks were "more likely to prefer to live on welfare" (Bobo & Hutchings, 1996, p. 8). And in the larger sample, approximately 75% of Korean and 66% of Chinese and Japanese respondents felt that Blacks preferred to live on welfare (Bobo & Hutchings, 1996).

This body of research has not directly established that Asians feel that Blacks are consuming resources that more rightfully belong to Asians (as our model would predict); however, it does suggest that Asians view themselves as more meritorious (intelligent and hardworking) than Blacks and as more deserving of resources. Yet given incidents such as the example from Princeton, increasing public discourses around quota-based admission systems in educational settings may encourage researchers to examine Asians' perceptions of resource proprietary right.

In sum, triangulated threat does offer a sociological and psychological explanation for Blacks' and Asians' negative perceptions of one another as rooted in perceived proprietary rights to resources based on dominant social constructions of Asians (e.g., as perpetually foreign) and Blacks (e.g., as lazy, unmeritorious).

Implications of Triangulated Threat for Black–Asian Interactions

Author George Lipsitz has frequently referred to the "divide and conquer" strategy (Lipsitz, 2001), exploring how minority groups are pitted against each other, encouraged to endorse negative stereotypes of each other, and divided from creating alliances that would help racialized minorities resist White supremacy. Triangulated threat is one approach to considering the psychological and sociological processes through which this strategy is developed and successfully enacted in relation to Blacks and Asians. A question, then, is whether the divide-and-conquer strategy actually works to create behavioral distance.

Research on "social distance" between Blacks and Asians suggests that there is, indeed, larger distance between Blacks and Asians than between Blacks and Whites or between Asians and Whites. Social distance is defined as the collective degree of closeness, comfort, and acceptance that members of one group feel toward another (Yancy, 2003) and is measured by feeling, intentions, and experiences. Although research from the early 1970s suggested a closer social distance between Blacks and Asians (Thornton & Taylor, 1988), within the last 30 years Blacks have consistently indicated feeling less close to Asians, interacting with fewer Asians, and having less preference for or experience with Asians as friends or romantic partners, as compared to their feelings and relationships with Whites or Latinos (Chang, 1999; Fiebert, Karamol, & Kasdan, 2000; Haualani, Chitgopekar, Morrison, & Dodge, 2004; Thornton & Taylor, 1998; Wang & Kao, 2007; Wilson, McIntosh, & Insan, 2007).

As Asians' social distance from Blacks has only recently been considered, comparative data over time is not available, but recent research indicates that Asians feel a high degree of social distance from Blacks. Asians report having less comfort, fewer interactions, and lower preference for Blacks as romantic partners as compared to their feelings or relationships with Whites (Fiebert et al., 2000; Halualani et al., 2004; Mack et al., 1997).

The social distance research with Blacks and Asians has not directly explored whether stereotyped perceptions related to triangulated threat specifically contributed to social distance. However, the observation that Blacks' social distance from Asians has increased since the rise of the model minority stereotype in the late 1960s to early 1970s lends some support to the hypothesis that triangulated threat as described here does affect Black–Asian relations.

Research has also examined the specific circumstances under which Blacks and Asians are less likely to endorse negative stereotypes or more likely to have closer social distance. Some of this research suggests that those who internalize negative views of their own group are more likely to endorse negative views of the other group. Scott Cummings and Thomas Lambert (1997) found that African American participants endorsing anti–Asian sentiments were more likely to endorse anti*Black* sentiments as well. Ying-yi Hong and colleagues (2004) found that Asian Americans who were primed to think of themselves as American (versus Asian American, presumably countering the application of the forever foreigner stereotype to themselves) and to think of behavior as malleable were least likely to endorse antiBlack sentiments. Shared experiences of oppression that challenge the view of the self as privileged also seem to relate to more positive Black–Asian relations, such as those described in studies on segmented assimilation (Bankston & Zhou, 1997) or research demonstrating closer social distance when there is shared lower socioeconomic status (Wang & Kao, 2007).

Positioning Black–Asian Interactions and Triangulated Threat in a Context of White Dominance

The research on intergroup perceptions between Blacks and Asians reviewed above suggests the importance of moving beyond a Black–White paradigm and more carefully considering the particular dynamics of relative privilege when considering interminority interactions such as between Blacks and Asians. However, we must also situate these findings and the theory of triangulated threat itself clearly in the context of White dominance. Without this context, it would be possible (and perhaps even justifiable) to view each group's endorsement of stereotypes about the other as simple discrimination from a position of power, as in basic GTT applied specifically to different domains (nativity and merit). The findings that Blacks and Asians both indicate closer social relations with Whites than with each other and that endorsing one's own group stereotypes relates to discrimination against the other minority group further emphasizes the context of White dominance.

It is therefore imperative that we understand that the dynamics within triangulated threat depend upon domains of privilege (e.g., nativity, merit) that are not only relative but also *ascribed* within a sociohistorical context of White dominance. The lack of privilege or the oppression related to being perceived as unworthy of merit or as forever foreign is not primarily created by the other minority group. Blacks, as a group, did not and do not control the media or the educational, political, or legal institutions that created and maintain the myth of the perpetual foreigner or the immigrant as burden/ threat. Asians, as a group, did not and do not have the power to create a dominant discourse of Blacks as lazy, less intelligent, or undeserving. Neither group has the power to create or maintain a negative stereotype of the other without the support or instigation of the dominant group.

It is not only the discrimination but also the relative privilege that is imposed or ascribed. Ascribed privilege is privilege that is afforded to a minority group by the dominant group. Historically, Asians were not seen as the model minority of high merit. They were seen as coolies—unskilled laborers incapable or undeserving of better positions—deviants, opium addicts, prostitutes, or "the yellow peril"—undesirable, sneaky, untrustworthy, evil, enemy (Takaki, 1989). And historically, Blacks were not seen as African *Americans* with full rights, but were instead seen as subhumans or as an inferior race unworthy of citizenship or even human rights (Marable, 2007). While both groups have engaged in various actions to resist these stereotypes, change public perception, and obtain equal rights, the shifts to privilege in relation to merit or nativity have been either created or condoned by the dominant group. And these shifts have been created as relative, placing Blacks in relation to Asians and Asians in relation to Blacks. What we mean by this is that neither Blacks nor Asians are first-class citizens, and neither Blacks nor Asians are seen as the best and the brightest for major leadership positions of power. But they are positioned by the dominant discourse as being better than the other, obscuring the absolute dominance of Whites. Thus, both groups are endorsing and reacting to constructions of the other in relation to the self that are neither self-created nor created by the other minority group.

We must then ask the question "who benefits from the creation and maintenance of triangulated threat?" It is primarily the dominant group that benefits from each group's acceptance of the negative stereotypes of the other in relation to their own ascribed privilege. Why do both Blacks and Asians feel more positively toward Whites than toward each other?

Triangulated threat theory emphasizes how shifts toward seemingly more positive constructions of minority groups (model minorities, Blacks as more American than Asians) are constructed and maintained *in relation to* the negative stereotypes that maintain the subordination of both groups. The *relative* nature of privilege is also ascribed by the dominant group and functions to maintain racial dominance.

A closer examination of the examples with which we began this chapter illustrates this process further. First, we want to acknowledge that there are many complex issues involved in both stories that we recognize we are not fully addressing, such as the complexities of university admissions that were not addressed in the study (Espenshade & Chung, 2005) or in Jian Li's suit, and the historical or economic pressures related to why Asian Americans open stores or businesses in Black areas rather than White areas. However, it is not our goal here to fully deconstruct the reasons or the validity of the actions but to consider these examples in relation to what they can tell us about Black–Asian relations and triangulated threat in a White-dominant context. In this light, it is most telling that although the aspect of Jian Li's suit that made headlines was minority against minority, the study that Jian Li used as part of his suit (Espenshade & Chung, 2005) indicated that Princeton University's admissions policies place Asians at a disadvantage *in relation to White applicants* as well as in relation to Black and Latino applicants. This means the increase in Asian acceptance under a race-blind approach is due not only to not advantaging Blacks and Latinos in relation to Whites and Asians but also to not *disadvantaging* Asians in relation to Whites. However, there was little outcry to stop White advantage in relation to Asian applicants. Similarly, it is rare that it is Asian Americans who benefit from the commodification of Black urban culture. And yet there is little outcry against the primarily White-owned clothing and sneaker manufacturers and retailers that are the usual profiteers of commodifying Black urban culture, frequently through the exploitation of Asian laborers.

Understanding that the divide-and-conquer strategy is working at least partially through the process of triangulated threat emphasizes reasons for overcoming these divides and resisting the allure of relative and ascribed privilege. For example, considering the domains of nativity and merit in relation to each other illuminates the ways that the constructions of Black or Asian in relation to these domains are monolithic and problematic, contributing not only to divisions between Blacks and Asians but also to divisions within each group. For example, tensions between Caribbean and African immigrants and African Americans and among Asian (pan)ethnic groups (e.g., southeast Asians and east Asians) relate to ways in which subgroups do or do not fit the constructions of and interactions between nativity and/or merit and do or do not accept the ascribed oppression and privilege of their "own" group.

Triangulated threat theory, as described here, attempts to capture the interactive dynamics of one moment in time by defining the domains of relative and ascribed privilege for Blacks and Asians and considering how these are constructed as entitlements and threats for one group in relation to another. It provides some exploration of the process by which the divide-and-conquer strategy not only keeps minorities in conflict with each other but also encourages minorities to focus on agendas that encourage gains that come at the expense of another minority group, as illustrated by the two examples that begin this chapter. Although the domains (nativity and merit) may change over time, the dynamic may continue. In presenting this theoretical integration, we agree with George Lipsitz that:

> We will always misread our situatedness in the world unless we are able to view power from more than one perspective, unless we are able to look through multiple, overlapping, and even conflicting standpoints on social relations. In order to challenge the differentiated deployment of power in the contemporary world, we need to create places where our differences and our common interests remain in plain sight. (Lipsitz, 2001, p. 126)

We believe that triangulated threat is an approach to actively engaging multiple perspectives on privilege for Blacks and Asians, and we offer these ideas as a step toward the mutual understanding that is the foundation of cross-racial coalitions for social justice.

References

Alcoff, L. M. (2003). Latino/as, Asian Americans and the Black–White binary. *Journal of Ethics, 7*, 5–27.

Bankston III, C. L., & Zhou, M. (1997). The social adjustment of Vietnamese American adolescents: Evidence for a segmented-assimilation approach. *Social Science Quarterly, 78*(2), 508–523.

Blumer, H. (1958). Race prejudice as a sense of group position. *Pacific Sociological Review, 1*(1), 3–7.

Bobo, L., & Hutchings, V. L. (1996). Perceptions of racial group competition: Extending Blumer's theory of group position to a multiracial social context. *American Sociological Review, 61*(6), 951–972.

Carroll, K. (2006). *Rejected applicant alleges bias against Asians.* Retrieved May 23, 2011, from http://www.dailyprincetonian.com/2006/11/13/16544.

Chang, E. (1999). New urban crisis: Korean-African American relations. In K. C. Kim (Ed.), *Koreans in the Hood: Conflict with African Americans* (pp. 39–59). Baltimore: Johns Hopkins University Press.

Cheryan, S., & Bodenhausen, G. V. (2000). When positive stereotypes threaten intellectual performance: The psychological hazards of "model minority" status. *Psychological Science, 11*(5), 399–402.

Cummings, S., & Lambert, T. (1997). Anti-Hispanic and Anti-Asian sentiments among African Americans. *Social Science Quarterly, 78*(2), 338–353.

Delucchi, M., & Do, H. D. (1996). The model minority myth and perceptions of Asian-Americans as victims of racial harassment. *College Student Journal, 30*(3), 411–414.

Devos, T., & Banaji, M. R. (2005). American = White? *Journal of Personality and Social Psychology, 88,* 447–466.

Espenshade, T. J., & Chung, C. Y. (2005). The opportunity cost of admission preferences at elite universities. *Social Science Quarterly, 86,* 293–305.

Fanon, F. (1963). *The wretched of the earth.* New York: Grove Press.

Fiebert, M. S., Karamol, H., & Kasdan, M. (2000). Interracial dating: Attitudes and experience among American college students in California. *Psychological Reports, 87,* 1059–1064.

Freire, P. (2000). *Pedagogy of the oppressed: 30th anniversary edition.* New York: Continuum.

Guthrie, P., & Hutchinson, J. (1995). The impact of perceptions on interpersonal interactions in an African American/Asian American housing project. *Journal of Black Studies, 25*(3), 377–395.

Halualani, R. T., Chitgopekar, A., Morrison, J. H. T. A., & Dodge, P. S.-W. (2004). Who's interacting? And what are they talking about?—Intercultural contact and interaction among multicultural university students. *International Journal of Intercultural Relations, 28,* 353–372.

Hong, Y.-y., Coleman, J., Chan, G., Wong, R. Y. M., Chiu, C.-y., Hansen, I. G., et al. (2004). Predicting intergroup bias: The interactive effects of implicit theory and social identity. *Personality and Social Psychology Bulletin, 30*(8), 1035–1047.

Hopkinson, N. (2004). Tempest in a t-shirt: The Visionz line of urbanwear sews discontent and activism among rivals. Retrieved May 31, 2011, from http://www.washingtonpost.com/ac2/wp-dyn/A53033-2004Aug9?language=printer.

Kent, M. M. (2007). Immigration and America's Black population. *Population Bulletin, 62*(4), 1–16.

Kim, C. J. (1999). The racial triangulation of Asian Americans. *Politics and Society, 27*(1), 105–138.

Kim, J. Y. (2006). Are Asians Black?: The Asian American civil rights agenda and the contemporary significance of the Black/White paradigm. In H. M. McFerson (Ed.), *Blacks and Asians: Crossings, conflicts, and commonality* (pp. 171–201). Durham, NC: Carolina Academic Press.

Kuhn, T. (1962). *The structure of scientific revolutions.* Chicago: University of Chicago Press.

Lee, H. C. (1999). Conflict between Korean merchants and Black customers. In K. C. Kim (Ed.), *Koreans in the hood: Conflict with African Americans* (pp. 113–130). Baltimore: Johns Hopkins University Press.

Lee, Y. T. (2001). Ingroup preference and homogeneity among African American and Chinese American students. *Journal of Social Psychology, 133*(2), 225–235.

Lipsitz, G. (2001). *American studies in a moment of danger.* Minneapolis: University of Minnesota Press.

Logan, J., & Deane, G. (2003). *Black diversity in metropolitan America.* Accessed July 14, 2010, at http://mumford1.dyndns.org/cen2000/report.html.

Mack, D. E., Tucker, T. W., Archuleta, R., DeGroot, G., Hernandez, A. A., & Oh Cha, S. (1997). Interethnic relations on campus: Can't we all get along? *Journal of Multicultural Counseling and Development, 25*(4), 256–268.

Marable, M. (2007). *Race, reform, and rebellion: The second reconstruction and beyond in Black America, 1945–2006* (3rd ed.). Jackson: University Press of Mississippi.

Martinez, E. (2003, September 9). An open letter to African Americans from Latinos. Retrieved August 15, 2011, from aapo.tamu.edu/files/Open%20Letter.pdf.

Min, P. G., & Kolodny, A. (1999). The middleman minority characteristics of Korean immigrants in the United States. In K. C. Kim (Ed.), *Koreans in the hood: Conflict with African Americans.* Baltimore: Johns Hopkins University Press.

Perea, J. F. (1997). The Black/White paradigm of race: The "normal science" of American racial thought. *California Law Review, 85*(5), 1213–1258.

Sue, D. W., Bucceri, J., Lin, A. I., Nadal, K. L., & Torino, G. C. (2007). Racial microaggressions and the Asian American experience. *Cultural Diversity and Ethnic Minority Psychology, 13*(1), 72–81.

Takaki, R. (1989). *Strangers from a different shore: A history of Asian Americans.* New York: Penguin Books.

Taylor, C. R., & Stern, B. B. (1997). Asian Americans: Television advertising and the "model minority" stereotype. *Journal of Advertising, 26*(2), 47–69.

Thornton, M. C., & Taylor, R. J. (1988). Intergroup attitudes: Black American perceptions of Asian Americans. *Ethnic and Racial Studies, 11*(4), 475–488.

Wang, H., & Kao, G. (2007). Does higher socioeconomic status increase contact between minorities and Whites? An examination of interracial romantic relationships among adolescents. *Social Science Quarterly, 88*(1), 146–164.

Waters, M. (1999). *Black identities: West Indian immigrant dreams and American realities.* Cambridge, MA: Harvard University Press.

Waters, M. C., & Eschbach, K. (1995). Immigration and ethnic and racial inequality in the United States. *Annual Review of Sociology, 21*, 419–446.

Wilson, S. B., McIntosh, W. D., & Insan, S. P. (2007). Dating across race: An examination of African American internet personal advertisements. *Journal of Black Studies, 37*, 964–982.

Wong, F., & Halgin, R. (2006). The "model minority": Bane or blessing for Asian Americans? *Journal of Multicultural Counseling and Development, 34*(1), 38–49.

Yancy, G. (2003). *Who is White?: Latinos, Asians, and the new Black/nonblack divide.* Boulder, London: Lynne Rienner Publishers.

Notes

1. Throughout this chapter, the terms *Black* and *Asian* are used by the authors. Although it is recognized by the authors that both Black and Asian racial groups are composed of a tremendous diversity of ethnic groups and cultures, the authors use this language to emphasize the social constructions of racialization, which considers precisely the ways in which these groups are overaggregated into monolithic groups within dominant discourses. This language also emphasizes the primacy of racialization in the issues that we are discussing.

2. *Oppression olympics* refers to framing oppression as a competition, attempting to demonstrate that you or your group is the *most* oppressed. This term was coined by Elizabeth Martínez (1993), longtime author, activist, and teacher.

3. For a more comprehensive discussion on the oppressor and oppressed model, please see, *The Pedagogy of the Oppressed* and *The Wretched of the Earth*.

16

Rooted in Our Homeland

The Construction of
Syrian American Identity

Sarah Kanbar

We Syrians in America are proud of our race because we are the inheritors of the finest blood of the ages. We are the custodians of preeminent cultures of mankind. We are bequeathing to posterity the glorious urges of humanity.

Reverend W. A. Mansur,
The Syrian World (1931, p. 31)

In the heart of New York City's Financial District at 103 Washington Street is a four-story building bearing the sign "Morans." Behind the sign is a more peculiar carving on top of a red door that reads "St. George's Chapel." For the passerby, it appears as a church renovated into a restaurant, nestled quietly a few blocks away from the site of the World Trade Center. A century ago, however, Washington Street was the center of New York's Syrian Quarter, or, as it was commonly known, Little Syria, one of the first established Arab American (then referred to as Syrian American) communities. It was there that discussions and debates arose concerning the role of Syrian Americans in the United States, Syrian national identity, racial greatness, and passing values on to the next generation. These exchanges were documented in Syrian American publications like *The Syrian World* and caused Syrian American leaders to call for the creation and preservation of Syrian American identity. By using a connection to the histories of the Phoenicians and ancient Syrians and rhetoric implying the greatness of the "Syrian race," Syrian American leaders asserted the importance of establishing a new generation of Syrian Americans.

This chapter examines a small immigrant population in New York City during the early part of the 20th century and shows how this group thrived through literary culture, imported traditions, and claimed legacy. By using those platforms, Syrian immigrants were able to construct a Syrian American identity based on the successes and contributions of Syrian ancestry. This chapter also analyzes the creation of Syrian American identity during a time when being a "hyphenated American" was frowned upon in the United States as a result of immigration reform in the early 20th century and the growth of scientific racism. This chapter therefore explores how Syrians viewed themselves as Americans and the role they played in their new homeland, the United Sates.

Little Syria and Its Perceptions

> *In the shadow of New York's financial district and hemmed in by the skyreaching structures that have all but squeezed out of existence the venerable street that bears the name of Washington, is "Little Syria," a neighborhood fragrant of the East, and a perpetual mystery of the few New Yorkers who know of its existence.*
>
> J. Ray Johnson, "Syrians in America" (1928, p. 21)

Located in the area bounded by Battery Place, West Street, Cedar Street, and Trinity Place, Little Syria was a vibrant community that attracted significant attention from other New Yorkers (Miller, 1904). Situated in the present-day Financial District of New York City, Little Syria was well known for its places of business and cultural landmarks including grocery stores and restaurants (WPA Federal Writers Project, 1936), kimono factories (WPA Federal Writers Project, 1937), news publishers (WPA Federal Writers Project, 1938), and importing stores (WPA Federal Writers Project, 1936). By 1940, Little Syria ceased to exist, and the strong presence of Syrian immigrants shifted from lower Manhattan to Brooklyn Heights. While some observers were fascinated with this new "colony," others had a less-than-favorable attitude toward Little Syria. Some commentators hailed Syrian immigrants for their intelligence and the low crime rates in their community (WPA Federal Writers Project, 1937), and others ostracized Syrians for their "Oriental" traits such as deceit and trickery (Miller, 1904, p. 41).

One of the first instances of Little Syria being mentioned in local press is a *New York Times* article dated May 25, 1890, titled "'Sanctified' Arab Tramps: Wretched Maronite Beggars Infesting This Country," written in response to the growing number of "the Arabic-speaking element from the Lebanon in Syria" ("Sanctified Arab Tramps," 1890). The reporter interchangeably uses the words *Syrian, Maronite, Arab, mendicant,* and *tramp* to describe Syrian immigrants and claims that they are "inferior to the Chinese and Italians, who do possess a certain amount of self-respect, and are willing to work honestly and work hard for a living" ("Sanctified Arab Tramps," 1890). The reporter continues to vilify Syrian immigrants by declaring "at the end of his first day in America the whining Maronite would have added at least $5 to his hoard, while the Irish or German immigrant would be hustling around trying to find work to enable him to earn a dollar" ("Sanctified Arab Tramps," 1890). Through malicious rhetoric, the reporter questioned Maronite beliefs and work ethic and made several inferences that it was within Syrians' nature and religious tradition that they are sly, cunning people to be wary of.

As a response to the growing curiosity that Little Syria was receiving, notably through a previous article, "Red-Fezzed Heads; Languorous Eyes," the *New York Times* published "New York's Syrian Quarter," a two-page article with images, written by Cromwell Childe (1899). Little Syria, or the Syrian Quarter, as both names were used in the article, is depicted as a foreign area filled with "Orientals of many stations of life" (Childe, 1899). As Childe describes his surroundings, he notes that one part of Little Syria has a presence of filth and is not refined. However, a block away, Syrians "of a very diverse social order" were present, mostly composed of "the very prosperous peddlers" (Childe, 1899). In his foreword to the article, Childe claims, "there is nothing gorgeously romantic about this tousled, unwashed section of New York" (Childe, 1899). The area was not as fanciful or mystifying as other reports described it, observing that Little Syria "has no 'languorous eyes' and few 'red fezzes'" (Childe, 1899). Little Syria was filled with people who still maintained their old customs, which gave the colony "spice and a touch of novelty" (Childe, 1899). In the article, Childe describes his tour of Little Syria and comments on the various social classes, businesses, and places of worship that were present. His observations attest to both the growing success of Syrian businesses and the influx of new immigrants.

Childe (1899) expressed admiration and respect for businesses like Sahadi's, a store where *arak* (Syrian wine), lamps, swords, and groceries were sold. While Childe acknowledged that there were prosperous Syrians, he made it clear that Little Syria still carried filth and poverty. Regardless, he noted, "Let it not be thought, however, that this quarter is devoid of charm, that it is not worth a visit, and more than one" (Childe, 1899).

In 1903, another *New York Times* article, "Sights and Characters of New York's 'Little Syria'" was published, describing Little Syria as "A Quarter of City Where Uniform Politeness Goes Hand in Hand with a Determination Not to Allow Total Conquest by the Spirit of Rush and Bustle" ("Sights and Characteristics of New York's 'Little Syria,'" 1903). Life in Little Syria was seen as a relaxing parallel to the hectic pace of life in New York City by making note of how Syrians conducted themselves with "Chesterfieldian politeness" and treated their patrons, both male and female, with the utmost courtesy. The traditions and customs they had brought from the "Orient," mainly the cafés, are cited as the "best advantage" of being in Little Syria ("Sights and Characteristics of New York's 'Little Syria,'" 1903). Restaurants were filled with foreign scents of food and coffee and "[a]round the tables will be found dark-eyed, olive-skinned men, who in face and figure might well serve as models for an artist's masterpiece" ("Sights and Characteristics of New York's 'Little Syria,'" 1903).

Image of a Syrian man selling drinks in Little Syria. Taken from the Library of Congress. Image dated between 1910 and 1915.

The romantic and poetic language that is used to describe Little Syria portrays it as a spectacular sight from a completely different world. For the reporter, the imported culture that was present in Lower Manhattan was a very thrilling and attractive experience, from the restaurants and cuisine, such as sweetmeats, nuts, and pastries, to the board games being played, and the *nargilas* (Syrian water pipe) being smoked by the men. Interestingly, parallels between Americans and Syrians are made, as the author links Syrian liking for *arak* with the "same relish that a good Kentuckian imbibes rye ("Sights and Characteristics of New York's 'Little Syria,'" 1903). By drawing this comparison, the reporter portrays a favorable and meaningful image of Syrian immigrants by connecting a thread of similarity between Syrian immigrants and Americans. The reporter also notes the diversity of occupations to show that many Syrians were well educated and held respectable occupations, such as bankers and court interpreters. While more prosperous Syrian Americans were moving to Brooklyn, there were still "many interesting, cultured men" in Little Syria ("Sights and Characteristics of New York's 'Little Syria,'" 1903). Some of those men included "an ex-teacher of Arabic in Oxford University" who was famed for being a learned man and was sought after if there were disputes, and an Egyptian guide who was known for being a traveler and adventurer ("Sights and Characteristics of New York's 'Little Syria,'" 1903). Yet the article closes with a peculiar line:

> There are many other leading lights in the Syrian quarter, but the types mentioned here represent the most cultured element, and the one possessing the greatest interest for students of Oriental character. ("Sights and Characteristics of New York's 'Little Syria.'" (1903)

Despite how much charm or unique qualities it might have contained, Little Syria was an immigrant neighborhood and an alien area in which one must proceed with caution. Hence, the reporter's admiration of Little Syria and Syrian immigrants was limited to the more prosperous—or "cultured," as the reporter refers to them—immigrants in Little Syria, who were few in number.

Still, some observers noted that the Syrian immigrants had a bright future ahead of them in the United States. In 1904, Lucius Hopkins Miller, a former missionary to Syria, published *A Study of the Syrian Population of Greater New York*, which discussed in great depth the Syrian community in New York City. His study focused on all aspects of the Syrian immigrant experience including arrival to the United States, statistics on how large the population was and where it was primarily located, the type of occupations

Syrians held, and general information on social and economic conditions (Miller, 1904).

Miller's (1904) study was aimed at the New York City Protestant community to increase the number of Protestant Syrians by bringing a preacher from Syria to New York, holding a service in English, and having a Bible class for young men in English (pp. 42–43). Miller's (1904) study also made an appeal to the Board of Education of Greater New York to create more accessible programs for immigrant children "whose ignorance of English naturally shuts them out from the grades in which their age would place them" (pp. 43–44). He noted that the lack of English was not due to a high level of ineptitude, but rather a lack of resources available, and even states that Syrians "are unusually clever linguists" (pp. 43–44). Lastly, Miller (1904) pleaded to philanthropic Syrians and Americans by noting that "worthy but needy Syrian immigrants" required assistance upon their arrival to Ellis Island, that a Syrian employment agency was necessary, and that there would be benefit from the creation of a night school to teach English (p. 44). In making these pleas, Miller (1904) attested that Little Syria, and the Syrian immigrants residing there, could be transformed into a thriving community. Furthermore, Little Syria had destitute conditions and was filled with poverty because of the absence of humanitarian and aid efforts from the city and other citizens. With their assistance, this area could have become one of the most successful immigrant communities in New York City.

James Myers (1929), the Industrial Secretary for the Commission on the Church and Social Service of the Federal Council of the Churches of Christ in America, remarked with great admiration that Syrians began in the United States as peddlers selling religious emblems and they have now evolved into successful businessmen, each having their own store and line of goods (p. 31). This Little Syria was not the same one that the *New York Times* reporters criticized. The Syrian immigrants were the "most law-abiding element in the population and are seldom found in the courts or jails" (Myers, 1929, p. 31). Syrians were much more evolved and civilized than other immigrant groups who had high crime rates, rendering them more suitable for citizenship. Myers (1929) commented on the kind hospitality he received in Little Syria and that this was a place where "one felt a strong inclination to return" (p. 36).

The Syrians were a unique set of immigrants, respected by some Americans and denounced by others. Regardless of how meager their living conditions were, Syrians had the ability, talent, and skill to become better citizens and to prosper in the United States, as some spectators noted (Miller, 1904, pp. 41–42). Observers pointed out that some of the Syrian immigrants

Images of Washington Street taken from Lucius Hopkins Miller's *A Study of the Syrian Population of Greater New York*, 1904.

Birdseye View of the Manhattan Syrian District.   In the Heart of the Manhattan Community.

began finding work in the United States by peddling products and became successful entrepreneurs and business owners through hard labor. When compared to other immigrant groups, like the Italians and the Irish, they were seen as having a special quality that made them model citizens. Syrian immigrants were cleaner (Miller, 1904, p. 8), patriotic, and loyal to not only Syria but also to the United States, and Syrian immigrants were not privy to socialism or anarchism (Miller, 1904, p. 41). Syrian immigrants were also praised for their connections to the Holy Lands and to the Phoenician civilization. The criticism and commendation that Syrian Americans were given would be a strong factor in the shaping of a Syrian American identity.

Constructing Syrian Identity

Communities are to be distinguished, not by their falsity/ genuineness, but by the style they are imagined.

Benedict Anderson,
Imagined Communities (2006, p. 6)

Syrian immigration and the construction of Syrian American identity took place within and was part of a much broader context of social and political movements. The late 19th and early 20th centuries saw the growth of immigration to the United States, with more than 18.2 million immigrants arriving between 1890 and 1920 (Archdeacon, 1984, p. 113). As Syrian immigrants were only a minor part of the massive influx of new arrivals to American shores, they were generally subsumed within the racial and immigrant politics of the late 19th and early 20th centuries. Growing fears of communism, radicalism, socialism, and anarchism, especially among Italian and Jewish immigrants, reached new heights in the 1920s, and immigration restrictions were used as a platform to project national fears (Gerstle, 2001, p. 95). As a result, immigration was reduced by 85% with the passing of the immigration acts in 1917, 1918, 1921, and 1924 (Gerstle, 2001, p. 94).

The use of scientific racism became the framework and justification in creating the Immigration Act of 1924 (Gerstle, 2001, p. 104). While passing the act, Calvin Coolidge's Secretary of Labor, James J. Davis, commented that immigration policy needed a "biological definition" to set the standards of immigration and naturalization (Foner, 2006, p. 744). In the post–Civil War period, as the United States spread westward, the combination of racial and religious supremacy that was embodied in notions of "manifest destiny" found voice in the theory and belief in social Darwinism. Social Darwinism emerged as a predominant trend in American intellectual thought and claimed to provide scientific evidence that the majority of new immigrants, blacks, and Indians were "truly inferior" (Archdeacon, 1984, p. 160). Thus, by 1920, the House Committee on Immigration and Naturalization appointed well-known eugenicist Harry H. Laughlin as its "expert eugenics agent" and asked him to study "degeneracy" and "social inadequacy" of immigrant groups, resulting in the passage of immigration restrictions and banning of "degenerate" groups (Gerstle, 2001, p. 105).

In February 1928, *The Syrian World* featured an article by Joseph W. Ferris (1928) titled "The Syrian Naturalization Question in the United States." Provisions within the Naturalization Act declared that naturalization "shall apply to aliens being free white persons, and to aliens of African nativity, and to persons of African descent" (p. 3). Where Syrians fit into these provisions had to be judicially determined. And, as further explained below, there were various legal proceedings held throughout the United States that determined Syrians' eligibility to naturalization.

In 1913, *Ex-Parte Shahid* was heard in the District Court of South Carolina and was the first case in which the issue of Syrian eligibility for naturalization was adversely discussed. Faras Shahid was a Christian immigrant from Zahle (currently in present-day Lebanon) who, as Joseph W. Ferris (1928) noted in his article, "The Syrian Naturalization Question in the United States," "spoke and understood English very imperfectly." Judge Henry A. M. Smith was presented the petition for naturalization. *The Syrian*

World emphasized Smith's observation that Shahid's skin color was "about that of walnut or somewhat darker than is the usual mulatto of one half-mixed blood between the white and the mixed races" (p. 4). Phillip Hitti, who authored the article's footnotes, noted that "consideration of the color of the face does not in itself constitute a scientific basis for race classification" (Ferris, 1928, p. 4, footnotes). Hindus, as he noted, belonged to the "White Race" but, as a result of living in a semitropical climate, were "darker than North Europeans" (Ferris, 1928, p. 4, footnotes). There was also the question of being a Syrian of Asiatic birth and how this would apply to a "free white person." Judge Smith's interpretation would entitle those who belong to the "European" races to be "free white persons," as was mentioned in America's first Naturalization Act of 1790, and would not incorporate the "Caucasian" or the "Aryan" races (Ferris, 1928, p. 5).

Prior to *Shahid*, *In Re Najour* on December 1, 1909, in the Northern District of Georgia; *In Re Mudarri* on January 8, 1910, in the Circuit Court of Massachusetts; and *In Re Ellis* on July 11, 1910, in the District Court of Oregon, addressed the issue of how to classify Syrians. In these three hearings, respectively, it was concluded that Syrians were "free white persons," that Syrians were of the "Caucasian" or "White" race, and that the Semitic stock was a "markedly white type of race" (Ferris, 1928, pp. 5–6). All three, as concluded from each case, were entitled to admission to citizenship (Ferris, 1928, pp. 5–6).

In Re Dow was held a year after *Shahid*, also in the District Court of South Carolina and before Judge Smith. George Dow was born in Syria and performed "all the necessary formalities" in order to obtain naturalization (Ferris, 1928, p. 6). According to Judge Smith, Dow's intelligence proved his ability to be "a general character entitled to naturalization" (Ferris, 1928, p. 6). His skin color was "darker than the usual person of White European descent and of that tinge of sallow appearance which usually accompanies persons of descent other than purely European" (Ferris, 1928, p. 6). In his footnotes to Ferris' article, Hitti indicated that this conclusion and its reasoning were both unscientific. He stated that the "hair, facial angle, and cephalic index are very important anthropological considerations—in addition to the color" (Ferris, 1928, p. 6). Judge Smith again held Syrians as not being "free white people," and that this term was limited to those who were of European descent or birth. Dow was of Asiatic birth, and the modern Syrian was from Asia (Ferris, 1928, p. 7). The case was reheard 2 months later, and it was argued that Semites were "Caucasian" and Dow was of Semitic heritage. It was also argued that the history of the Syrians is connected with that of the Jewish and Christian peoples, making it "inconceivable that the Statute could be intended to exclude them" (Ferris,

1928, p. 8). Editor of *al-Hoda* magazine Naoum Mokarzel even bravely noted, "If Christ Himself were to apply for citizenship [Judge Smith] would deny it to Him" (Mokarzel, 1929B, p. 40).

The March 1928 issue of *The Syrian World* further discussed the shortcomings of Judge Smith's rulings. Aside from legal arguments, books like *Natural History of Man* by James C. Prichard and *The Human Race* by Louis Figuier also claimed that Syrians fell under the classification of being part of the Caucasian race (Ferris, 1928, pp. 18–19). Joseph W. Ferris (1928) argued that the geographic limits set by the Immigration Act of 1917[1] (p. 22) proved that Syrian immigrants are not part of the excluded class of immigrants, otherwise known as the "Asiatic Barred Zone" (Gerstle, 2001, p. 96). A map with the Asiatic Barred Zone outlined was printed, showing that Persia, Arabia (excluding parts of modern-day Yemen and Oman), and Syria were not part of the "excluded territories" (Ferris, 1928, pp. 22–24). Dow was granted his petition for naturalization after appealing to a higher court (Ferris, 1928, p. 19).

As the founder and editor of *The Syrian World*, Salloum Mokarzel (1928A) (brother of Naoum Mokarzel), observed in the February 1928 issue:

> It is futile to comment on the benefits of united action in the face of a national crisis. But Syrians may well ponder the advisability of experimenting in a united effort every once in a while. They can well realize that it is not so much to their credit to work together with a semblance of harmony under the driving urge or common danger, when the shadow of catastrophe stalks threateningly in their midst. (p. 41)

The origins of the Syrian race and its "greatness" had been challenged on a legal level and, in some instances, served as a reason to deny some Syrian immigrants naturalization. Salloum Mokarzel (1928A) points out that Syrian history could be reframed or forgotten if the community did not stay united, make concrete efforts to preserve racial greatness, or pass Syrian tradition on to the second generation. Regardless of where Syrians hailed from or the milestones that their ancestors had contributed to modern civilization, their legacy had been ignored with the issue of naturalization.

Syrian American leaders like the Mokarzel brothers, Gibran Khalil Gibran, Reverend W. A. Mansur, Phillip Hitti, and Ameen Rihani began to call for formations of Syrian American societies and federations and made appeals to the Syrian youths to preserve their racial legacy. By using Darwinian rhetoric, ethnological evidence, and substantiation based on the teachings of eugenics, such as the ability of the Syrian "race" to overcome difficulty because of their inherited ancestry, Syrian Americans considered themselves to be valuable assets to American society. As Talcott Williams (1924) noted, "Syria and Syrians constitute the first land and the first people in Southwestern Asia who have entered into modern civilization. They stand alone in this" (p. v).

The 1920s marked a period in which politicians in the United States embraced the ideas of scientific racism as justification to reduce immigration (Gerstle, 2001, p. 104). Unlike other Southern and Eastern European and Asian immigrants, who were considered degenerate, Syrians purported themselves as the descendants of the ancient civilization of the Phoenicians (Hitti, 1924, p. 21). The Phoenicians were pioneers in sailing and navigation, improved the alphabet and gave it to Europe, claimed a Greek philosopher known as Thales the Phoenician, and were seen as more influential to Europe than any other civilization (Mansur, 1928, pp. 13–15). For Syrian Americans, this connection between the Phoenicians and the modern Syrians validated their racial superiority in contrast to other immigrant groups and proved that Syrian immigrants were potential valuable assets to the United States.

Racial Greatness and Legacy

> *Syrian race greatness is based on the achievements of our Phoenician ancestors, the contributions of our fathers of the Christian era, and the rise of modern Syrian race and nation.*
>
> Reverend W. A. Mansur,
> *The Syrian World* (1928, p. 3)

The study of immigrant relations plays a key role in understanding the creation of Syrian American identity as a reaction to the Immigration Act of 1924 and to the issues concerning naturalization. Published in the same year, Philip Hitti's (1924) pivotal work, *Syrians in America*, was clearly influenced by and a response to broader political, legal, and social issues in the United States. He opened his work with the statement that "The Syrians are neither Turks, as the United States census would make them, nor Arabs as some of them would take themselves to be" (p. 19). Instead, he defined Syrians as "the remnant of the ancient Phoenician-Canaanite tribes who entered Syria about 2500 B.C., the Aramean Israelite hordes who arrived about 1500 B.C., and the Arabs who have drifted, and still drift in, from the desert and gradually pass from a nomadic to an agricultural state" (Hitti, 1924, p. 19). Hitti used pseudoscientific evidence, typically favored by the eugenics movement at the time, to showcase the evolution of the Phoenician into the modern Syrian and prove them to be more capable of other immigrant groups (Archdeacon, 1984, p. 160).

Building on the legal cases cited in *The Syrian World* and influenced by Hitti's writing, Reverend W. A. Mansur (1928) posed a set of questions as a response to the realization of the greatness of the Syrian race through the doctrines of self-determination and self-realization that were preached during World War I:

> How shall the modern Syrian race meet the struggle between the races? How shall the modern Syrian face those who slander his race? How shall the modern Syrian answer those who have libeled his race? How shall the energetic modern Syrian reply to those who would discriminate against him because of his race? (p. 10)

Mansur argued that it was essential for Syrians to understand and know their origins, history, and ability to survive. This awareness was fundamental for all Syrians, as was knowledge of Syrian race virtues, which in turn prepared Syrians for the "struggles of life" (Mansur, 1928, p. 11). He also claimed that racial greatness was not determined by racial stock, skin color, or population but, instead, was determined by the importance of the civilization, character, and service of the Syrian race and how "superior individuals" within the group affirm this (Mansur, 1928, p. 12). Drawing on Hitti, Mansur linked Syrian greatness to the achievements of the Phoenicians and contributions to Christianity, such as Syrian writers who documented the history of early Christianity (Mansur, 1928, p. 15). Syrians needed to be aware of who they were as a collective and what achievements their claimed ancestry had made.

Two months later, Salloum Mokarzel (1928C) published "Can We Retain Our Heritage?" in *The Syrian World* and called for a "Federation of Syrian Societies." Syrians, according to Mokarzel (1928C), wanted to prove that they were "a valuable element in the composition of the American nation" (p. 36). Creating Syrian American societies would not only validate Mokarzel's claim that Syrians were "a valuable element," but it would also unite Syrian groups across the United States in order to preserve Syrian heritage. Like Mansur (1928), Mokarzel (1928D) emphasized the importance for Syrian Americans, especially the younger generation, to understand where they came from and be able to dispel rumors or assumptions that had been made with regard to the Syrian American community (p. 37).

Image of Syrian American leader and scholar Philip K. Hitti taken from *The Syrian* World, October 1930.

Stereotypes of Syrians as being filthy, ignorant beggars could be eradicated by the Syrian youths. Mokarzel (1928D) stated that "ignorance fosters fear and mistrust," and it was imperative to spread knowledge of the value of the Syrian immigrants. This unity was essential for naturalization and the new immigration quotas that were being passed.[2] Mokarzel's call for the creation of a national federation of Syrian societies would help protect the interests of Syrians in the United States and promote favorable policies toward Syrian Americans (p. 38).

Some readers did take heed of Mokarzel's call and in the following month, A. M. Malouf, former president of the Syrian American Club and vice president of the United Syrian Society, laid out a plan to organize a Syrian federation in the Readers' Forum section of *The Syrian World*. From his personal experience of heading Syrian American societies, Malouf (1928) noted that the current Syrian American societies were weak, lacked support, and had insufficient leadership (p. 41). As a result, these societies and clubs did not achieve the purposes for which they were created. Malouf (1928) stated that communities that had five or more Syrian American citizens should organize their own Syrian American clubs so that they can protect their interests while becoming more active with local politics. Syrian Americans would also have to be ready to pay a small amount of money in order to keep these societies running (Malouf, 1928, p. 41). Some of the readers welcomed the idea of creating societies. Groups like the Syrian Young Men's Society in Los Angeles, California; The Phoenicians in Jacksonville, Florida; the American-Syrian Federation in Brooklyn, New York; the Syrian Young Men's Society and the Good Citizenship Club in Birmingham, Alabama; The Goodfellows Club in Tyler, Texas; and the Syrian-American Club in Detroit, Michigan, responded to Salloum Mokarzel's (1929) call to form Syrian-American clubs and societies (p. 9).

Reverend W. A. Mansur (1929A) made clear that the "Syrian-American fellowship is the result of an awakened race consciousness, race solidarity, and race vision" (p. 18). Syrian American fellowship was "not political in spirit, economic in purpose, or religious in motive" (Mansur, 1929A, p. 16). Rather, the purposes for establishing a Syrian American fellowship were "based on pure Americanism, spiritual heritage, pioneering life, and future well-being" (Mansur, 1929A, p. 16). Syrian American fellowships would foster appreciation and create cooperation among other Americans, reducing any misunderstandings toward Syrians (Mansur, 1929A, p. 16). Through fellowships, Syrian Americans could emulate the accomplishments and contributions that their ancestors had done before, be it the Phoenicians or the early Syrians of the Christian era (Mansur, 1929A, p. 18). While Mansur does not provide specific examples, he states "[t]he modern Syrian has caught the pioneering spirit of his famous Phoenician ancestors" (Mansur, 1929A, p. 19). Syrian immigrants came to the United States and endured the difficulties of not only the journey from across the sea but also the pains of departing from their homeland. Instead of faltering and giving up, Syrian immigrants overcame their struggle through "pioneering," like their Phoenician ancestors (Mansur, 1929A, p. 19). Syrian immigrants were industrious and were loyal to their new homeland, the United States (Mansur, 1929A, p. 19). However, Syrians' loyalty to the United States did not entail that Syria needed to become a faded memory, and Mansur (1929A) claimed that Syria must be seen as a spiritual motherland (p. 17). Syrian ancestry was to be the backbone of any fellowship as a result of how unique it was. The experiences and issues that Syrian Americans were facing, from stereotyping to misconceptions regarding their racial history, would unite Syrian Americans and make the bond of fellowship stronger (p. 20).

"Loyal Americanism" was a key aspect for the Syrian American fellowship, and loyalty to the United States, the country that Syrian

Americans claimed gave them the freedom they longed for, was vital and needed to be maintained among Syrian Americans (Mansur, 1929A, p. 19). While it is not stated, Mansur's assertion of "loyal Americanism" connects with other claims that Syrians sought to immigrate to the United States and seek refuge from the Ottoman Empire (Ferris, 1929, p. 5). It can also be deduced that Mansur (1929A) would reiterate the importance of "loyal Americanism" as a response to the growing hostilities and claims that immigrant groups were not patriotic or loyal to the United States.

Mansur (1929B) further emphasizes the necessity of loyalty to the United States in the April 1929 issue of *The Syrian World*, with his article "Syrians' Loyalty to America," as he repeats his claim that Syrians chose America for its greatness. He uses quotes from Theodore Roosevelt and Calvin Coolidge to explain that Syrians' loyalty to America is because of the "birth of the American spirit in their hearth, and the realization of progress that Syrian Americans chose America as a permanent homeland" (p. 4). America was not given to Syrians, but they migrated to America out of their "love of political liberty, religious freedom, and material prosperity" (Mansur, 1929B, pp. 3–4). Aside from such an "intelligent choice" (1929B, p. 3), Mansur claims that Syrian American loyalty to America is based on the Constitution, the theoretical equality given to all citizens, the ability of the majority to vote, the religious freedom that can be pursued, the law-abiding citizenship that Syrians practice, and Syrians' preparedness and history of defending the nation, notably during the First World War (pp. 3–9). Syrians had a bright and prosperous future ahead of them in the United States. The fact that they came from the land that bore Christianity, Judaism, and, to a lesser extent, Islam and endured wars and conquests was a testament to their tenacious character (Ferris, 1929, p. 4). George Ferris (1929) even deduced that the abilities of the Syrian ancestry to withstand such hardships and adapt to changing political and economic conditions served as justification that Syrians were naturally disposed to withstand such difficulties (pp. 4–5).

As Reverend W. A. Mansur (1928) noted, passing the legacy of Syrian ancestry to the next generation would ensure survival of the greatness of the Syrian race (p. 16). The role of Syrian American youth had been heavily discussed from early on. One of the strongest issues for the Syrian American community was whether the next generation should continue to learn Arabic or focus more on mastering English and studying in public schools. Naoum Mokarzel (1929) argued that knowledge of Arabic was necessary and the next generation needed to retain the language, after noticing the increasing number of young Syrians in the United States having no understanding of Arabic and being apathetic toward learning it (p. 17). Mokarzel's (1929) controversial article, "Arabic as an Asset," blamed parents for neglecting to teach their children the Arabic language, which Mokarzel sees as a vital aspect of Syrian culture (p. 18).

A debate claiming that the lack of knowledge and appreciation for the Arabic language is indicative of shame towards Syrian identity (Mokarzel, 1929, p. 17) was sparked in the pages of *The Syrian World* among the younger Syrian American generation. Salloum Mokarzel, the editor of *The Syrian World*, invited Syrian Americans to share their opinions on how they felt about learning Arabic (Mokarzel, 1928B, p. 36). One reader, E. K. Saloomey (1928), agreed with Naoum Mokarzel's claim that knowledge of Arabic is a vital asset but argued that the resources to study Arabic were not as easily available (p. 38). Many Syrian Americans were born to parents who came to the United States at a young age; therefore, their parents lacked the ability to teach the language. Saloomey (1928) acknowledged that there were youth who deny their Syrian ancestry as a means to get ahead financially or socially, but the acts of a few did not reflect the general sentiment of racial pride held by many Syrian youth (p. 39).

As is noted by Mansur, Lila M. Mandour (1928) agreed that there was minimal effort by these youths to learn and retain the Arabic language but disagreed that young Syrians were ashamed of their native tongue. Mandour (1928) noted that Arabic in the United States would eventually die off in the upcoming decades; however, that did not entail that Syrian legacy would be forgotten. She claimed that Syrians will always be proud of their ancestors and their legacy will always be reflected in the good deeds, such as loyalty to both the United States and Syria, that Syrian Americans do (Mansur, 1928, pp. 40–41).

Little Syria Lives On

We and the mighty and thunderous army of those who come after shall follow your spirit along the corridors of time. Forward and onward, down through the ages until there shall have been written the apocalypse of young Americans of Syrian origin.

Cecil J. Badway, *The Syrian World* (1931)[3]

On April 10, 1931, Gibran Khalil Gibran (best known as Khalil Gibran or Kahlil Gibran) passed away in New York City ("Kahlil [sic] Gibran

Dead; Noted Syrian Poet, 1931). Gibran was not only considered to be one of the century's greatest poets but was also seen as a national hero within the Syrian community. Reverend Mansur (1930) called Gibran the "singer of the Syrian-American soul" (p. 11). In the month of his death, *The Syrian World* reprinted a poem by Gibran, which appeared in the first issue of *The Syrian World*, titled "Gibran's Message to Young Americans of Syrian Origin." Gibran's (1931) poem was a beautiful reminder of his legacy and how his spirit would live on through the younger generation of Syrian Americans (pp. 44–45). Gibran (1931) claims that his faith in the Syrian youths lay in the prospects of good citizenship and the displaying of patriotism toward the United States, along with loyalty and respect toward Syria (pp. 44–45). As Gibran (1931) noted, "It is to be proud of being an American, but it is also to be proud that your fathers and mothers came from a land upon which God laid His gracious hand and raised His messengers. Young Americans of Syrian origin, I believe in you" (p. 45).

A year after Gibran's death, on April 6, 1932, Naoum Mokarzel passed away in Paris (Mokarzel, 1932, p. 14). Mokarzel was seen as the "leader and protagonist" of the movement to establish Syrian American identity (Mokarzel, 1932, p. 14). Reverend Mansur (1932) wisely noted that the passing of Mokarzel meant that the "Syrian Lebanese race pioneer period" had now ended, and the "development period" had begun (p. 24). Mokarzel, along with other Syrian American leaders, laid the foundation of a Syrian American identity by educating Syrian Americans and establishing Syrian integrity, reputation, leadership, and welfare (Mansur, 1930, p. 6). It was now up to the next generation to preserve Syrian American identity. Without the extensive effort, time, and thought Mokarzel gave to the Syrian Americans, namely the youths, the Syrian American movement would be obsolete.

What is left of the original Little Syria in Manhattan are two tenement buildings and a church that is now a bar in the midst of Manhattan's Financial District. The exact date that the community ended is unknown; however, many scholars agree that the creation of the Brooklyn Battery Tunnel was the official end to the community, as some of the area was demolished (Triborough Bridge Authority, 1939).[4] The three buildings that remain are a tribute to the decades of identity formation, community building, and the passing of heritage. The legacy and greatness of the Syrian people, which leaders like Gibran and Naoum Mokarzel spoke of, was evidenced through their lives and love for both their Syrian and American identities.

Image of Washington Street on January 10, 2009, taken by author.

Image of Washington Street drawn by W. Bengough, taken from *Harper's Weekly*, 1895.

References

Anderson, B. R. O. G. (2006). *Imagined communities: Reflections on the origin and spread of nationalism*. London: Verso.

Archdeacon, T. J. (1984). *Becoming American: An ethnic history*. New York: Free Press.

Badway, C. (1931). A pledge (A young American of Syrian origin). *Syrian World, V*(8), 45.

Childe, C. (1899, August 20). New York's Syrian quarter. *New York Times*. Retrieved from http://www.mearo.org/lesson4/New_Yorks_Syrian_Quarter_1899.pdf.

Ferris, G. A. (1929). Syrians' future in America. *Syrian World, III*(11), 3–8.

Ferris, J. W. (1928). Syrian naturalization question in the United States, Part II. *The Syrian World, vol. II* (9), 18–24.

Ferris, J. W., & Hitti, P. K. (1928). Syrian naturalization question in the United States, Part 1. *Syrian World, II*(8), 3–11.

Foner, E. (2006). *Give me liberty!: An American history. Vol 2*. New York: W. W. Norton.

Gerstle, G. (2001). *American crucible: Race and nation in the twentieth century*. Princeton: Princeton University Press.

Gibran, G. K. (1931). Gibran's message to young Americans of Syrian origin (reprinted from the first issue of The Syrian World, July 1926). *The Syrian World, V*(8), 44–45.

Hitti, P. K. (1924). *The Syrians in America*. New York: George H. Doran.

Johnson, J. R. (1928). Syrians in America. *Syrian World, II*(12), 19–24.

Kahlil [sic] Gibran dead; noted Syrian poet. (1931, April 11). *New York Times*. Retrieved from http://www.nytimes.com/books/98/12/13/specials/gibran-obit.html.

Malouf, A. M. (1928). Readers' forum. *Syrian World, III*(6), 41–47.

Mandour, L. M. (1928). Arabic as an issue: To speak or not to speak Arabic. *Syrian World, III*(1), 40–41.

Mansur, W. A. (1928). The greatness of the Syrian race. *Syrian World, III*(3), 10–17.

Mansur, W. A. (1929A). Our Syrian-American fellowship. *Syrian World, III*(8), 16–22.

Mansur, W. A. (1929B). Syrians' loyalty to America. *Syrian World, III*(10), 3–9.

Mansur, W.A. (1930). Great Syrian-Americans of our times. *Syrian World, V*(2), 5–15.

Mansur, W. A. (1931). Our pride in our Syrian race. *Syrian World, V*(9), 29–35.

Mansur, W.A. (1932). Pioneer and seer. *Syrian World, VI*(7), 24–25.

Miller, L. H. (1904). A study of the Syrian population of Greater New York. Available at: http://pds.lib.harvard.edu/pds/view/4151226.

Mokarzel, N. A. (1929B). Arabic as an asset. *Syrian World, II*(12), 17–18.

Mokarzel, S. (1928A). Notes and comments. *Syrian World, II*(8), February 1928, 41–44.

Mokarzel, S. (1928B). Notes and comments. *Syrian World, II*(9), 39–41.

Mokarzel, S. (1928C). Arabic as an issue: A challenge to Syrian-American youth. *Syrian World, III*(1), 35–36.

Mokarzel, S. (1928D). Can we retain our heritage? *Syrian World, III*(5), 36–40.

Mokarzel, S. (1929). Progress of the federation movement. *Syrian World, III*(7), 9–10.

Mokarzel, S. (1932). A great Syrian leader passes. *Syrian World, VI*(7), 14–17.

Myers, J. (1929). Discovering the Syrians. *Syrian World, III*(9), 30–32.

Saloomey, E. K. (1928). Arabic as an issue: An open letter to Mr. N. A. Mokarzel. *Syrian World, III*(1), 37–39.

"Sanctified Arab tramps." (1890, May 25). *New York Times.* Retrieved from http://www.mearo.org/lesson4/Sights_and_Characters_of_Little_Syria_1903.pdf.

"Sights and characters of New York's 'Little Syria.'" (1903, March 29). *New York Times.* Retrieved from http://www.mearo.org/lesson4/Sights_and_Characters_of_Little_Syria_1903.pdf.

Williams, T. (1924). Introduction. In P. K. Hitti, *The Syrians in America.* New York: George H. Doran.

WPA Federal Writers Project. (1936). *Syrians in New York; The Syrian colony in Manhattan.* New York: Author.

WPA Federal Writers Project. (1937). *Economic and political causes of immigration from Syria to the United States.* New York: Author.

WPA Federal Writers Project. (1938). *Syrians in New York; Immigration.* New York: Author.

Triborough Bridge Authority. (1939). *Clearing of slum area in Manhattan for Brooklyn Battery Bridge.* New York: Author.

Notes

1. The article referred to the Immigration Act of 1917 as the "1917 Act of Congress" or the "Restrictive Immigration Act."

2. In the March 1928 issue of *The Syrian World*, it was noted that President Coolidge submitted "revised figures for the 'national origin' basis, and quotas would be founded, beginning with July, 1928." Prior to this, quotas were fixed, but the Syrian quota changed from 100 to 125, Turkey was raised from 100 to 233, and Palestine received a separate quota of 100. Lebanon did not receive its own quota.

3. This poem was written by a Syrian American youth in response to Gibran Khalil Gibran's death.

4. At the time, Robert Moses had intended upon creating a bridge, but through persuasion of then president Franklin D. Roosevelt, it became a tunnel.

17

Redescribing the Redskin Controversy

Multiculturalism, Working-Class Habitus,
and the Mascot's Enduring Popularity

Christopher B. Zeichmann and Nathanael P. Romero

Introduction

Political theorist Andrew Heywood (2009) encourages us to think of multiculturalism as a broad constellation of ideological comportments centered on "a positive endorsement, even celebration, of cultural difference" (p. 25). Within this frame, Heywood identifies as common to the various strands of multiculturalism the notion of "'diversity within unity,' the idea that the public recognition of cultural difference can and should be contained within a single political society" (p. 26). Because multiculturalism involves an acknowledgement of racial and ethnic difference within a single society, it begins with the assumption that such diversity exists and is a politically salient social reality. In other words, if we follow Charles Taylor (1994) and understand multiculturalism as a "politics of recognition," then one precondition for any such politics is a racially and ethnically varied society wherein the question of granting recognition to nondominant groups emerges as a matter of political importance.

But what about those communities in which this question has, historically, come to receive little attention? This chapter will consider one such community: the village of Clinton, Michigan (population 3,753), a farmtown marked by its working-class demographic.[1] Clinton's athletic teams have been nicknamed the Redskins since the 1940s, but a recent campaign to retire the mascot has driven questions of race to the fore, despite the fact that the overwhelmingly White racial makeup of this rural community has generated little perceived need to address such questions in the past. But this lack of attention to matters of race should not thereby suggest that Clintonians who support the mascot have formed no opinion on such matters. Rather, the shape of Clintonian resistance to changing the mascot is marked by a conspicuous antimulticulturalist sentiment, visible both in frequent characterizations of the anti–Redskin campaign as an instance of "political correctness" gone too far and in number of comments made by community members in favor of a "colorblindness" that claims to reject the social import of racial difference altogether.

Despite nearly 2 years of protests and heated school board meetings concerning the Redskins, the Clinton school district is today no closer to retiring the mascot than it was in the fall of 2008, when sisters Elspeth and Kylista Geiger initiated the campaign to change the mascot.[2] From the beginning, the Geigers (then recent alumni) focused on the derogatory nature of the Redskin nickname and logo, claiming that use of the word *redskin* "is akin to celebrating the marginalization of American Indians," and thus contributes to the perception that indigenous Americans "are not real people but characters for our amusement" (Geiger & Geiger, 2008, p. 2). Referring to the Redskin logo, which depicts a man in a feathered headdress, they expressed their view that Clinton should cease to "allow this negative and racist image to represent our children and the community at large" (p. 2). Shortly after the Geigers began their campaign, the question of whether to keep the mascot was put to a nonbinding community poll. With 699 votes tallied, 93.6% were in support of retaining the mascot. Despite the Geigers' previous agreement with the superintendent to abandon the issue if less than 40% of the votes favored the mascot's retirement, the family continued to attend school board meetings, along with representatives from regional minority advocacy organizations. These efforts led to further controversy, since many Redskin supporters understood the matter to be a fundamentally local issue and interpreted this additional presence as an intrusion. The dispute culminated in a school board meeting held on April 29, 2010, with more than 400 attendees—11% of Clinton's population. When the board announced its final, unanimous decision to retain the mascot, the room erupted in cheers. The weekly village newspaper, the

Clinton Local, featured numerous and impassioned letters and opinion-editorials throughout this period. Approximately 85% of letters and op-eds published in the *Clinton Local* defended the mascot.

Why, then, have Clinton residents stood behind the Redskin so overwhelmingly? It would be easy to suppose that supporters of the mascot hold stubbornly to tradition due to ignorance or racism, ignoring repeated claims by Native Americans that the mascot is insensitive and damaging. But if we take seriously Sara Ahmed's (2004) call to "contest the classism of the assumption that racism is caused by ignorance"(n.p.), then we should be suspicious of such explanations, even if (as we contend) Clinton's working-class makeup is a salient factor in explaining mascot support. Following Ahmed (2004, n.p.), we question the classism that allows "racism to be seen as what the working classes do." Indeed, the tendency to locate racism among working-class, rural Whites allows supposedly more "enlightened" Whites to avoid interrogating their own participation in norms and institutions that systematically privilege their own Whiteness. This, in turn, primes working-class, rural Whites to be suspicious of antiracist projects insofar as such projects often display hostility toward working-class Whites. As Slavoj Žižek (2006) observes, White liberals' fight for multicultural tolerance has a tendency to situate itself as "the counterposition to the alleged intolerance, fundamentalism, and patriarchal sexism of the 'lower classes'" (p. 361).

One might naturally turn to academic publications for a better explanation of mascot support, but few works address the widespread resistance to changing such nicknames in its own right, leaving the controversies severely underexplained and completely untheorized. When the topic does arise, scholars tend to link mascot support to "hatred" (Browning, 2010), "uncritical" racism, lack of respect (Pewewardy, 1999), residual colonialism, and willful neglect of Native Americans (Davis & Rau, 2001). In doing so, such publications overlook the role of socialization in the formation of attitudes about racial and ethnic diversity and the significance of racially charged mascots. In the case of Clinton, arguments for retaining the mascot should be seen in view of the interests of the town's population, which largely sees itself as occupying a position of social distance from mascot opponents.

This social distance will be central to our analysis of the Redskin controversy. That is, we understand to be explanatorily significant a number of differences between supporters and opponents vis-à-vis differences in socialization and group affiliation. Many pro–Redskin Clintonians have expressed the sentiment that they are viewed as unsophisticated rednecks by outsiders who have taken it upon themselves to "educate" Clinton's populace, suggesting that backlash against the anti–Redskin campaign can be explained in terms of antagonism toward those viewed as smugly occupying an elevated position of social distance from Redskin supporters. As we have suggested, such perceptions on the part of supporters are not without some justification, given widespread, classist assumptions about socioeconomic status and racism; the aforementioned scholarly literature itself distinguishes implicitly between enlightened activists and the insensitive masses. In terms of Clinton, much of the controversy's discourse operates within the parameters of an oppositional framework wherein affiliation with and internality to the village of Clinton have come to represent both support of Redskin retention and a rural, White, working-class *habitus*—a concept borrowed from social theorist Pierre Bourdieu—and externality to Clinton has come to represent both mascot opposition and a more "enlightened," multiculturalist *habitus*. This oppositional framework takes shape in schemes of internality and externality to Clinton that mark both geographical and social divisions. We will therefore seek to redescribe mascot support in terms of socially situated, class-based interests instead of ignorance or racist sentiment. Such attributions of mascot support to moral shortcoming risk committing a number of individualistic fallacies that we challenge below via Bourdieu's theory of *habitus*. This proposed explanation will avoid the dubious emphasis on individual attitudinal forms of racism in order to take seriously the contexts in which understandings of race, multiculturalism, and recognition are formed, attending closely to the role of socialization into environments in which normalized Whiteness and class antagonism intersect.

Multiculturalism and Class *Habitus*

Given its ideological-normative character, multiculturalism contrasts with other comportments that are more congenial to Clinton's racial homogeneity. Popular among these alternatives is a "colorblindness" that attempts to realize equality through the elimination of all race-based preferences. Proponents of colorblindness position themselves as "committed to a merit-based society . . . that looks beyond mere appearances and does not take into account race, gender and sexuality" (Pinder, 2010, p. 31). One Redskin supporter vocalizes such ideological commitment, writing, "I really haven't paid much attention to any 'race' issues. I believe a person is based upon their own personal worth, not who they claim to be or where they came from" (Letter, 2010c, p. 4A). But unlike multiculturalism, which aims to respect diversity without seeking assimilation, a colorblind ideology of postracial equality claims to ignore difference: "it views difference as 'the problem' because it leads to discriminatory or unfair treatment" (Heywood, 2009, p. 25). Thus, due to activist promotion of Native American interests *qua* specific ethnoracial interests, it is easy to understand how the emergence of Native Americans as a politically mobilized group has been less than positively received among pro–Redskin adherents to colorblindness.

It is worth viewing this colorblind ideology in view of Clinton's homogeneity, a social condition that has tended to generate a misleading feeling of racial egalitarianism. Consider the following pro–Redskin letter to the *Clinton Local*:

> These days everyone seems to have a label: Irish-Americans, Native-Americans, African-Americans, Italian-Americans, Arab-Americans, etc. We are *all* Americans, no matter what our heritage is. We can take pride in our ancestors and the culture they experienced, but this is now, and the great melting pot that is our country seems sometimes to be pouring itself into separate jars. (Letter 2008a, p. 1)

These comments are readily explicable in the context of Clinton's nearly uniform racial makeup. Questions of assimilation, for instance, are not pressing for Clinton's residents, since the metaphor of the melting pot is reflective of their ancestors' Anglo-Germanic cultural experience in America, an experience marked by relatively rapid assimilation. The shift, then, from the melting pot to multiculturalism, where nondominant cultures are recognized and celebrated, has provided a kind of an anxiety for communities that have a small non–White population. In fact, because of Clinton's overwhelming Whiteness, its residents rarely encounter racial others and seldom practice race relations proper. This homogeneity precludes the discursive salience of race in Clinton, thereby creating the impression that its residents are unraced and that they have already accomplished egalitarian colorblindness.

One helpful way for understanding Clintonian attitudes about racial diversity comes through Bourdieu's theory of *habitus*.[3] Insofar as prevailing explanations of mascot support are prone make recourse to personal morality and so rely on individualistic, psychological assumptions, they risk overlooking the socioideological conditions that give meaning to mascot support. Individualistic explanations are not only difficult to verify but also inimical to explanatory nuance. By contrast, the concept of *habitus* situates the individual within society in such a way that problematizes distinctions between individual and society, challenging the notion of an isolated or monadic subject independent from its social world. For Bourdieu, people are socialized into patterns of interaction that combine to form an individual's habits of thought and practice. These habits and dispositions—what he calls *habitus*—vary depending on one's social world and allow one to act in accordance with social norms without necessitating intentional behavior. *Habitus* is most significant for our purposes in that it functions in everyday settings as a means of distinguishing between social formations, insofar as the dispositions that comprise it stand in contrast to other sets of dispositions (e.g., working-class vs. bourgeois, urban vs. rural). One's ability to operate in accordance with a given *habitus*—via political assumptions, points of reference, etiquette, speech patterns, and so forth—tacitly signals one's social background. *Habitus* is not entirely benign, however, as it manifests an unconscious self-interest, conditioning one into practices that preserve or enhance one's social position.

While antimulticulturalist sentiment among mascot supporters is predicated on a problematic colorblindness that ignores the fact that non–Whites continue to be marginalized by White institutions and norms, multiculturalism is itself not without problems. For Sherrow O. Pinder (2010), who is particularly critical of multiculturalism, the "emphasis on tolerance of racial and ethnic differences" allows multiculturalism to propel itself by "masquerading as an antiracist project" (p. 100). Moreover, as Ahmed (2004) notes, "the discourse of tolerance involves a presumption that racism is caused by ignorance, and that anti-racism will come about through more knowledge" (n.p.). This emphasis on tolerance has produced definitions of racism within classist ideological confines, privileging reflexivity and self-consciousness as antidotes to racism and favoring those whose *habitus* is structured in accordance with the norms of bourgeois subjectivity. Targeted for exclusion are working-class Whites whose habitus is seen as lacking in terms of reflexive acumen. As Ahmed (2004) observes, professed self-consciousness is one of the defining features of dominant-class habitus: "Such a self-conscious subject is classically a bourgeois subject, one who has the time and resources to be a self" (n.p.). Elites are thus able to reify the distinction between intellectual and manual laborers by highlighting the moral superiority of the former concomitant with their professional intellectual prowess.

The aforementioned apprehensions regarding multiculturalism among Clintonians can therefore be explained within Bourdieu's theory as manifestations of White, working-class self-preservation in the face of classist notions about racists, reflecting a desire for Clintonians to distinguish themselves from those who proclaim their tolerance in ways that are ultimately hostile to working-class, rural Whites in Clinton. Now, because pro–Redskin Clintonians have expressed a common belief that racism—whatever the word means—is a bad thing, we see that Clinton's homogeneous conditions have reconfigured the meaning of the word *racism* so as not to denigrate its nearly all-White demographic, thus allowing Clintonians to deny charges of racism categorically: "I never connected a racist current to Clinton's mascot"[4] (Letter, 2008a, p. 2). Such denials make sense when one reads Redskin supporters as understanding racism, not as a symptom of inadequate reflexivity or as rooted in imbalances of power between Whites and non–Whites, but primarily as a matter of personal attitudes of contempt for racial others. For example, principal Tim Wilson (2008) writes (in a manner typical among Redskin advocates), "It's a matter of respect, not disrespect. In the five years that I have been principal of Clinton High School, I have never witnessed our students purposely being disrespectful to Native Americans or their culture. I have only seen them act out of pride and respect for what Native Americans represent" (p. 1). Remarks such as these suggest that relations of respect and disrespect are central in pro–Redskin understandings of racism, which is largely limited to locating racism in intentional actions stemming from personal contempt.

Thus, when racism is mentioned in pro–Redskin material from the *Clinton Local*, one rarely finds reference to power positions, suggesting unfamiliarity with scholarly/activist understandings of racism, which have routinely emphasized the institutional character of racism in "direct critique of the idea that racism is psychological" or "simply about bad individuals" (Ahmed, 2004, n.p.). But even on those occasions when academics locate racism in psychological states, there is still a tendency to tie racist views back to uneven relations of power between Whites and non–Whites. Typical here is sociologist David Wellman (1993), who treats racism as a set of "culturally sanctioned beliefs, which, regardless of intentions involved, defend the advantages Whites have because of the subordinated position of racial minorities" (p. x). Unlike Redskin supporters, who defend the mascot by stating that use of the Redskin is not predicated on intentional actions of disrespect, Wellman astutely disregards personal intent in giving consideration to relative power positions. Likewise, Redskin opponents typically speak of racism as operating institutionally: "These two young ladies [Elspeth and Kylista Geiger] have seen fit to stand up and sound their voices to stop institutional racism in your Clinton Public School System" (Letter, 2008c, p. 4A). By contrast, institutional racism appears to be a matter of the past in pro–Redskin perspectives; America no longer operates under segregationist policies, ergo racism is a problem that only exists sporadically among people of all races (e.g., Klansmen, Black Nationalists).

In addition, due to pro–Redskin tendencies to ignore relations of power in their discussions of racism, many Redskin supporters depict minorities as beneficiaries of a pervasive *reverse* racism at (White) Clinton's expense. One such supporter writes, "When Native American groups talk about how 'white people don't understand this' or 'the white man is interpreting that wrong,' I could take that as racism" (Letter, 2010, p. 2). Instead of seeing Native American criticism of White injustice as rooted in Native exclusion from hegemonic White norms and institutions, mascot supporters tend to operate under notions of colorblindness that lead them to see *any* type of ill will or preferential treatment with respect to race as racism.[5] But in view of Wellman's definition of racism, one notes that because Native Americans are not beneficiaries of racist social hierarchies, any prejudices they might hold against Whites cannot be deemed "racism," lest one do violence to the meaning of the word. Such delimitations of racism are not accidental; definitions such as Wellman's act as correctives to the continuance of White privilege and assert the moral necessity of ending racial inequality.

More important for our discussion, however, is the social embeddedness of these varied definitions of racism. Like those in the dominant class who understand racism in terms of deficiencies in reflexivity, Clintonians employ a self-interested definition of the word that distances bigotry from the formulator by locating it among social others. In Clinton, the particular social others in question are those who are seen as advocating reverse-racist policies. Thus, insofar as pro–Redskin understandings of racism are predicated on a *habitus* of White, working-class homogeneity, definitions of racism that derive from elsewhere are easily detectable as such.[6] Accordingly, one's credentials as a Clintonian—and thus authority to discuss the Redskin's legitimacy—correspond to the conspicuousness of Clintonians' working-class habitus. This permits definitions of racism resembling that of Wellman's to be dismissed as alien to Clinton and therefore a priori invalid, allowing mascot supporters to lump those whose habitus differs into a single broad category of outsiders. These parameters of authentic Clinton serve to minimize the effect of opposition by attributing it to an illegitimate fringe.

"Life in the Slow Lane"

Though this delegitmating portrayal of mascot opponents as "outsiders" plainly serves a partisan function, it nonetheless reflects genuine social divisions. As we contend, support for the Redskin should be seen in view of the interests of the town's population, which largely sees itself as occupying a position of social distance from mascot opponents. To situate this distance in terms of broader societal divisions, one can—as Žižek (2009) does—draw lines between "intellectual laborers" and "the old manual working class," attending to the various ways in which antagonisms between the two groups link up with habitus and materialize in the form of liberal, multiculturalist "prejudice against 'redneck' workers," on the one hand, and "populist hatred of intellectuals," on the other (p. 147). As this section will illustrate, pro–Redskin discourse often brings the antagonisms noted by Žižek to the fore.

Take, for example, Maryann Habrick, the editor of the *Clinton Local*, who, in supporting the mascot, casts a critical eye on "outsiders" who have become involved in the controversy. Responding in early 2010 to the entry of the Lenawee County chapter of the National Association for the Advancement of Colored People into the controversy, Habrick (2010) writes, "Now, it appears, more outsiders have become involved, for whatever purpose. Bringing in the NAACP and other groups located a great distance from the community of Clinton only does one thing—brings sadness to a wonderful community" (p. 2). One finds similar complaints, early on in the controversy, in Habrick's weekly column, in which she criticizes neighboring "Tecumseh people" for weighing in on the Redskin debate.

> Honestly, I didn't want to get into this "Redskin" business. I thought we could just watch it play out with petitions being signed and then the issue would fade off into the sunset—Ha! Next thing I know, others became involved, others who really shouldn't make a judgment about issues going on that aren't any of their business. All of a sudden, those people *made* it their business and tried to make us look like hicks, ne'er do wells, lesser beings, or something I cannot fathom. We don't tell Tecumseh people what to do here in our little town—at least not governmentally or through editorials. (Habrick, 2008, p. 1)

There are a number of things worth noting: one, the complaint about Clinton's autonomy not being respected by non–Clintonians who have "made it their business" to get involved; two, the presentation of the village as "our little town," which suggests a self-image of Clinton as a small community that knows its place; and three, the defensive posture taken toward "those people" who have purportedly endeavored to make Clintonians "look like hicks [or] ne'er do wells." Here Habrick expresses solidarity with her Clintonian audience (which is assumed to be sympathetic to her views) and antipathy toward smug others who have allegedly encroached on the autonomy of the town.

While pro–Redskin Clintonians have objected to the classism behind purported characterizations of them as "backwater, uneducated hicks," they have taken up, in a self-affirming manner, their status as working-class, rural Whites. One sees this self-affirmation in the very title of Habrick's column, "Life in the Slow Lane," a column that regularly presents Clinton life as self-willingly "slow," in contrast to urban, fast-track lifestyles.[7] While the column has been the primary medium through which Habrick has aired her views on the mascot, she typically uses the column to relate various features of Clinton life, express patriotic sentiments, profess her Christian faith, and bestow praise on family and community members. While outsiders might deem this way of life provincial, the editor herself presents it as a chosen lifestyle, one that she relishes.[8] Habrick's picture of "life in the slow lane" accords with Bourdieu's theorization on *habitus* insofar as it reflects socially situated habits of thought and perception and presents Habrick's conditions not as a matter of resignation to material necessity but, instead, as a way of life that is attractive to others with similar values.

Now, a sense of social distance between pro– and anti–Redskin camps is visible in anti–Redskin discourse as well, particularly in the Geigers' own depiction of Clinton more as the town in which they grew up than as a place of current habitation. In Elspeth and Kylista Geiger's letter to the *Clinton Local* in October 2008, they take great pains to emphasize their affiliation with the community and its schools. The letter states, "We grew up in Clinton and whenever we are asked where we come from, we have always responded with pride, 'Clinton, Michigan'" (p. 2). Embedded in these declarations of pride, however, are suggestions that the letter was written at a distance from Clinton, presumably from within the undergraduate academic world that the authors have inhabited since graduating from Clinton schools.

Moreover, the social exteriority of antimascot sentiments to Clinton is also visible when the Geigers express worry about the reactions—both potential and actual—of non–Clintonians to the mascot. On multiple occasions, the Geigers depict those outside of Clinton as consistently disapproving of the Redskin. The suggestion is that, for a great many in the world beyond this marginal village, the mascot is clearly unacceptable, even if most Clintonians fail to see why. Of particular note is a passage in the Geigers' letter in which they provide examples of how the mascot makes the school "appear less than it is" to non–Clintonians:

> Our school is one of those listed as having an offensive mascot on the website for American Indian Cultural Support. There have also been instances with our classmates and us where the admission of our mascot has brought reactions of shock and disgust. We have even heard the phrase, "You still think that's okay?" (p. 2)

The narrative suggests that these outsiders, having not been socialized (in Clinton) to "think that it's okay," easily grasp the problematic nature of the mascot. Thus, the Geigers' own discussion of outsider reactions to the nickname corroborates what one finds in pro–Redskin discourse, namely, a discernable sense of social distance between those who embrace the mascot and those who oppose it.

The Geigers and many of their allies come from working-class backgrounds; their material conditions differ little from those typical of Clinton-based families. Nevertheless, important differences in *habitus* exist between the two camps. One notes this, for example, in the Geigers' use of a quasi-academic vocabulary that is absent from pro–Redskin letters and could easily be perceived as smug by working-class individuals. In their letter to the *Local*, the Geigers state that the "racist imagery" associated with the Redskin is "not a correct representation of the village or school system," that the term *redskin* cannot be "casually interchanged with 'Native American' or 'American Indian'," and that the term evokes "derogatory images that are dehumanizing to entire nations of people" (p. 2). These remarks evince a proximity to academic discourse, particularly in how the Geigers express their concerns about the marginalization of ethnic minorities, convey their attunement to the representational force of words and imagery, and state the noninterchangeability of ostensibly synonymous terms for indigenous Americans. In relation to *habitus*, such proximity goes hand in hand with the development of certain habits of thought that crucially structure how one perceives symbols such as the Redskin. It is therefore not surprising that the academic language employed in the letter has neither resonated with nor been used by Redskin advocates.

Many pro–Redskin Clintonians have been quick to label the substitution of *Native American* for *Indian* as merely politically correct nitpicking.[9] While such dismissals are unfairly reductive, it is important to see that—because *habitus* informs one's stance toward antagonistically positioned outgroups—the features that distinguish others from "us" (e.g., linguistic practices) come to be taken as vices from the perspective of one's *habitus*-bound ingroup norms: Mascot supporters do not want to adopt "politically correct" practices because doing so would require taking up the very features that mark certain outgroups as different.

Conclusion

As Ahmed (2004) cogently argues, White declarations of antiracism that locate racism among "unlearned Whites" fail to put into place the conditions whereby those making such declarations are able to transcend their participation in institutions that structurally favor Whites. More importantly, classist assumptions about working-class ignorance do nothing to generate goodwill toward antiracist projects, instead contributing to the sense that such projects are inherently antagonistic toward the working class. This in turn damages the prospects of potential alliances that would be mutually beneficial in projects combating inequality.

References

Ahmed, S. (2004). Declarations of Whiteness: The non-performativity of anti-racism. *borderlands 3* (2), n.p.

Bourdieu, P. (1984). *Distinction: A social critique of the judgment of taste.* (Trans. Richard Nice). Cambridge, MA: Harvard University Press.

Browning, C. C. (2010). Staging an intervention in a virtual dystopia: The online fallout of the race, power and privilege forum and the removal of "Chief Illiniwek." *Studies in Symbolic Interaction, 34,* 137–149.

Davis, L. R., & Rau, M. T. (2001). Escaping the tyranny of the majority: A case study of mascot change. In C. Richard King & Charles Fruehling (Eds.), *Team spirits: The Native American mascots controversy* (pp. 221–238). Lincoln: University of Nebraska Press.

Geiger, E. & Geiger, K. (2008). Letter to the editor. *Clinton Local, 124* (41b), 2.

Habrick, M. (2008). Life in the slow lane. *Clinton Local, 124* (47), 1, 12.

Habrick, M. (2010). In our opinion. *Clinton Local, 126* (11), 2.

Letter to the editor (2008a). *Clinton Local, 124,* (44), 1.

Letter to the editor (2008b). *Clinton Local, 124* (44), 1.

Letter to the editor (2008c). *The Tecumseh Herald, 155* (21), 4A.

Letter to the editor (2008d). *Clinton Local, 124* (45), 2.

Letter to the editor (2008e). *Clinton Local, 124* (47), 2.

Letter to the editor (2009). *Clinton Local, 125* (44), 2.

Letter to the editor (2010a). *Clinton Local, 126* (17), 2.

Letter to the editor (2010b). *Clinton Local, 126* (19), 2.

Letter to the editor (2010c). *The Tecumseh Herald, 156* (45), 4A.

Heywood, A. (2009). Multiculturalism, identity and diversity. *Politics Review, 19*(1), 24–27.

Pewewardy, C. (1999). From enemy to mascot: The deculturation of Indian mascots in sports culture. *Canadian Journal of Native Education, 23,* 176–189.

Pinder, S. (2010). *The politics of race and ethnicity in the United States: Americanization, de-Americanization, and racialized ethnic groups.* New York: Palgrave.

Swartz, D. (1997). *Culture and power: The sociology of Pierre Bourdieu.* Chicago: University of Chicago Press.

Taylor, C. (1994). The politics of recognition. In Amy Gutmann (Ed.), *Multiculturalism: Examining the politics of recognition* (pp. 25–74). Princeton: Princeton University Press.

Wellman, D. T. (1993). *Portraits of White racism.* New York: Cambridge University Press.

Wilson, T. (2008) Letter to the editor. *Clinton Local, 124* (45), 2.

Žižek, S. (2006). *The parallax view.* Cambridge, MA: MIT Press.

Žižek, S. (2009). *First as tragedy, then as farce.* New York: Verso.

Notes

1. Clinton is also 97.7% Caucasian. All data regarding Clinton is from the 2005–2009 U.S. census estimates and includes the village's charter township.

2. We preserve the anonymity of Redskin supporters who are not public figures. Despite the fact that many have published comments in local newspapers (e.g., *Clinton Local, Tecumseh Herald, Daily Telegram*), there is nonetheless a widespread perception among Redskin advocates that these media are closed off, precluding nonlocals from reading them. Text from the *Clinton Local* is edited for clarity. As a matter of disclosure, the authors of this chapter are Clinton High School graduates. Insofar as both have lived in but spent ample time away from the village and oppose the mascot, this analysis reflects personal proximity to the controversy.

3. For an extensive introduction to the concept, see Swartz, 1997, p. 95–116.

4. Also: "We are *not* disparaging an entire tribe of people by using the name or mascot; that has been established so the issue should die" (Habrick, 2008a, p. 1).

5. Also, "I am offended when one race of people is given free land, free fishing, free hunting, casinos, etc. Isn't that racism—for the government to only benefit one race?" (Letter, 2008e, p. 2). "Names such as the 'Vikings' were not mentioned [as racist mascots]. Why was this? Was it because Vikings are white?" (Letter 2010b, p. 2).

6. E.g., "Why am I not getting my sensibilities offended in this controversy over the mascot nickname [even though I am 1/32nd Blackfoot]? As a high school student it never occurred to me to feel offended to be a 'Redskin'" (Letter, 2008b, p. 1). "My family has graduated three generations of *Redskins*, with a fourth generation to join us in 2017. We were *Redskins* then and we are *Redskins* now! And I'm positive the majority of our town feels the same way" (Letter, 2008d, p. 2).

7. Bourdieu (1984) is particularly instructive in addressing this self-interested affirmation of "slowness." He argues that those occupying subordinate positions in the social strata tend to define themselves "as the established order defines them, reproducing in their verdict on themselves the verdict the economy pronounces on them, . . . consenting to be what they have to be" (p. 471), e.g., "modest," "humble," or in this case "slow."

8. That the editor should depict life in Clinton in such a manner is unsurprising. Bourdieu (1984) notes that *habitus* makes "necessity into virtue by inducing 'choices' which correspond to the condition of which it is a product" (p. 175).

9. A group of Clinton women representing the family that owns the local flower shop writes, "In response to the news of the ongoing battle of the Redskin mascot, please accept the views of a proud Indian family. Yes, that's right—we are Ojibwa Indians. We've never accepted the politically correct term, 'Native Americans'"

(Letter, 2009, p. 2). In a pair of even more "politically incorrect" moves, the authors mention a family matriarch "who refers to herself as an 'Old Squaw'" and sign their letter "All of us Redskin Squaws at Floral Fantasy." Note that while many pro–Redskin Clintonians have been quick to claim Native American ancestry, there is little evidence that this ancestry figures prominently in their identity, standing in contrast to those closely allied with the Geigers, who actively participate in tribal culture.

Sexuality

18

"I Do," Therefore I Am

Marriage as Institutionalized Passing

Elizabeth Renfro

What Does Love Have To Do With It?

No matter which polls you look at, a majority of Americans think of marriage as, in Robert Knight's (1996) words, an "independently quantifiable good for society," and almost that many affirm that marriage as "the union of two of opposite sex" is "in accord with natural law." As these results indicate, "marriage" appears to be understood by Americans as something more than merely a civil/legal contract granting economic and other rights, as well as more than simply a sacred religious ritual. What most do not, however, recognize is that marriage functions as one of what Judith Butler (1990) terms the powerful yet rarely consciously unpacked "norms of cultural intelligibility by which persons are defined" (p. 17).

Similarly, most Americans see the tendentious issue of "defending" the definition of marriage hinging upon homosexuality. However, as Anne Bolin (1993) states (referencing Levi-Strauss), "In the Western paradigm, gender operates as the 'central organizing principle of sexuality' and sexual orientation exists only in relationship to gender and physiology" (p. 484). Heteronormativity—and hetero-only marriage—is grounded in the assumption that there are two complementary biological sexes, with their equally complementary prescribed and proscribed behavioral genders and sexual desires, naturally (if not divinely) designed to fit together as matching puzzle pieces. These are the perceived material and "proper" human forms, distinctly dimorphic, polar opposites in desires and characters. Thus, everything from biological to social and sexual gendering comprises one tidy, congruent package. Marriage provides the shiniest, most visible ribbon to secure the package, simultaneously naturalizing the binary and polarized distinctions on which male/female sex, masculine/feminine gender, and normative opposite-sex desire are based.

Further, the reward/punishment capacity of legalized marriage restrictions and conventions serves to reify something far more complex than merely regulating the sex/gender/sexuality package—although that regulatory effect is achieved. As Judith Butler (1993) states, "[T]he order of sexual difference is not prior to that of race or class in the constitution of the subject; indeed, . . . the symbolic is also and at once a racializing set of norms, and . . . norms of realness by which the subject is produced are racially informed conceptions of 'sex'" (p. 130). Located as it is in the intersection of the sex, gender, and sexuality matrix with the constructed identity components of race/ethnicity and class, marriage has historically provided a mechanism for distinguishing "real," proper people from improper people, for assigning physical and behavioral normalcy, as well as morality to those individuals and groups in America who pass, and relegating all nonpassing Others to the category of deviants.

Passing

In exhaustively parsed photo ops during the 2008 U.S. presidential campaign, candidate Barack Obama quaffed a beer with blue-collar workers and went bowling in Altoona, Pennsylvania (scoring a dismal 37). Why? Because voters are considered more likely to vote for someone with whom they can "identify," someone "like us." Called the "likeability" or "identity" factor in political polling, a high rating reflects voter perceptions that the person in question appears to be—*passes as*—a "regular guy." However, then-Senator Obama was visibly awkward in both settings, clearly neither a bowling nor beer aficionado, nor one of the working-class clientele to whom the bowling alley and bars catered. In fact, in his performances of beer drinking and bowling, the future president did not pass at all. He was seen as unnatural in those actions and contexts, and in fact he was mocked in the media as "prissy," childlike, and, in some cases, not a "real man" (Media Matters for America, 2008).

In its most basic definition, *passing* refers to meeting the requirements of an exam or test. In social and cultural frameworks, the concept of *passing* is generally understood to mean being accepted by others as belonging to a certain identity group (e.g., White, heterosexual, middle class) and/or having certain characteristics (e.g., morality, authority, manhood) to which specific culturally granted and/or situational advantages—concrete as well as perceptual—accrue. In popular usage, this social form of passing also tends to carry with it the connotation that the person who is attempting to pass may not actually have those characteristics, cannot legitimately claim membership in that identity group, and therefore is not entitled to those advantages when her/his performance is read as false by the observer(s). Thus, *passing* also tends to be viewed as something that those who are "real," those who eschew artifice, don't do. Those who are dishonest—or disadvantaged, in some "liberal" constructions of the concept—engage in such passing activities in order to feign belonging, even if only temporarily, to the contextually more desirable identity group.

Interactions among the social actors and within the psyche of the individuals themselves involve assessing physical and behavioral markers— heavily freighted signs—to determine the acceptability of each individual's identity credentials, thereby determining whether the individual is admitted into membership (passes) in the identity categories of choice: sex/gender, racial/ethnic, sexual, and socioeconomic class. The "actual" members of an identity group themselves, to varying degrees and in various contexts, also labor both consciously and unconsciously to achieve conforming and confirming performances, measuring their own success against and through the successes and failures of others.

However, passing must be critically unpacked not merely as a performance whereby a person attempts to take on and is assessed according to an identity that in and of itself is an independent reality, that is, a material, stable, natural, "real" entity. Repeated passing performances by everyone, as part and parcel of everyday life, are an integral part of the ongoing construction and reification of normative—and quite powerful—social identities that would not otherwise exist.[1] Yet, as Suzanne Kessler and Wendy McKenna (1978) stress, although "[e]veryone is engaged in passing . . . [i]n order to be perceived as natural . . . [it] must not be seen as passing" (p. 126). Rather, the behaviors and appearances must seem "natural," just who/what people are/do. The repeated acts create an illusion of a material reality. Individuals' repeated exhibitions of the culturally codified (yet unstable) appearances, actions, and behaviors *pre*scribed to certain identities (e.g., "man," "woman," "Black," "White"), as well as individuals' avoidance of those behaviors and actions that are culturally *pro*scribed for certain identities, serve to reify that culture's "tacit collective agreement" (Butler, 1990, p. 140) of what comprises a "normal," "real" individual of a particular identity.

Credentials or norms for belonging and thus successfully passing as particular identities do, of course, vary temporally and contextually, as well as from subgroup to subgroup within America (and any society). To be perceived as a "real man" does not necessarily evoke the same script at different socioeconomic levels; to be accepted as a "real American" may involve different characteristics and performances when perceived from different geographical, educational, or political groups' perspectives. Nor do the expectations and scripts foreclose alternative identity creation. The norms themselves provide sites and opportunities for transgressive and creative rebellion, in the borderlands (Anzaldúa, 1999), the outlawed margins that Judith Butler (1993) terms the "constitutive outside" (p. 188). In fact, transgressive performances—*non*passing appearances and behaviors—serve to simultaneously confirm and destabilize those social identities that are accepted and acceptable. "Attempts at passing" by nonmembers of a privileged identity may result from any of a number of temporal or contextual prompts, ranging, for example, from internalized racism to performances that may be *read* as attempts at passing but that are actually intentional acts of transgressive parody, similar to Judith Butler's (1997) discussions of drag as gender disruption.

There is, nonetheless, a powerful set of normative characteristics that, while not by any means monolithic or static, dominates American ideology and discourse in defining "normalcy" and, concurrently, "real" Americans. This is not to say that these characteristics are necessarily attributes of the basic, "average" American (whatever that may be, if, indeed, the creature exists outside of various statistical calculations). But, as Audre Lorde (1984) once asserted, the qualifications integral to meeting the identity of the American "mythical norm" are nonetheless relatively clear and rooted in the dynamic of cultural privilege:

> In america [sic], this norm is usually defined as White, thin, male, young, heterosexual, Christian, and financially secure. It is within this mythical norm that the trappings of power reside within this society. (p. 116)

That the full set of qualifications of the mythically normative American are actually nonrepresentative of most Americans is reflective of what Sherrow O. Pinder (2010) describes as the "de-Americanization of racialized ethnic groups." I would modify this to the "de-Americanization of stigmatized racialized ethnic, socioeconomic, sexual, and gender identity groups"(p. 1).

Identity-constitutive performances are modeled, disseminated, and confirmed—and the individual actors and identity groups are themselves rewarded or punished—not only by individual people and interactions, but also through powerful institutions such as the legal system, science and medicine, economics, and organized religion. One cultural practice that circumscribes all these institutions that is itself an institution is marriage. Through this legally, religiously, and economically mediated practice, the identity characteristics dominating this country's conceptualization of the normative (and, simultaneously, the morally ideal) American are reified and institutionalized as material realities. In the process, the marriage practice and institution itself is granted authenticity as an accurate signifier of mature, civilized, responsible, normal, and proper humanness.

Proper Bodies

Although what is deemed "proper" in the individual body is temporal and contextual, locating certain physical markers along paired binaries of normal/abnormal and moral/immoral has been a consistent feature in human cultural history. Until very recently, biological gender/sex has been based upon (depending upon the level of scientific sophistication and the social agenda operating at the time) genitals, reproductive organs (uterus, testes, ovaries), hormones, or chromosomes. But no matter which piece of the body has been in vogue as the determining factor, two things have undergirded bio-gender descriptions and have functioned as what sociologist Harold Garfinkel (1967) calls culturally constructed "objective, institutionalized facts" (p. 122)—that is, unquestionable givens that are given the status of "moral facts": First, humans are clearly dimorphic, and second, that that dimorphism is based upon/ serves reproductive complementarity. That is, the human species is physiologically designed to have two interlocking gendered bodies to facilitate sexual activity to reproduce the species. In this sense, "sexuality as a natural fact of life means sexuality as a natural and *moral* fact of life" (Garfinkel, 1967, p. 124).

In order for human reproduction to occur, penetrative heterosexual intercourse is, of course, inferred (though obviously no longer necessary given current reproductive technologies). This act of penetrative sex, according to John Stoltenberg (1989), is the very definition of maleness, "the impersonation of male . . . identity" (p. 16), or what one must do in order to pass as male. And, of course, that identity demands an "opposite" body and identity to penetrate in order not to compromise its own gender integrity as it repeatedly performs its gender reality, "constructing a self-definition round [one's] . . . reproductive capacities" (Stoltenberg, 1989, p. 27). Penetrative acts that do not involve penis in vagina are by contrast read as perversions of this "natural" and proper sexual performance and are thus constitutive of immoral identity.

Sensuality and passion do enter the proper body's morality equation, too. Nineteenth-century America's middle-class "cult of domesticity" (also called the "cult of true womanhood") centered morality on the "purifying" form of love ascribed to married women and men. Jonathon Ned Katz (1986) describes it this way:

> Holding strictly to true love was an important way in which the middle class distinguished itself from the allegedly promiscuous upper class and the animalistic lower class. Those lust-ridden lower classes included a supposedly vicious foreign element (often Irish, Italian, and Asian) and a supposedly sensual dark-skinned racial group shipped to America from Africa as slaves. True love was a hierarchical system, topped by an intense spiritual feeling powerful enough to justify marriage, reproduction, and an otherwise unhallowed sensuality. (p. 44)

The proper body's physicality is tamed, controlled, brought into moral status by "true love," itself signified through the regulatory practice of marriage and reproduction. In contemporary America, we can hear echoes of this in purity and "reclaimed virginity" rituals and pledges.

The actual physical propriety of bodies is itself such a salient constitutive feature of marriage and morality that merely being able to pass under lay scrutiny has not always been deemed sufficient. Western science has taken the authoritative role here, with law and popular opinion generally following suit. Biologists, anthropologists, and sexologists have viewed the human body as intelligible text from which can be accurately read—by those who are proper authorities—the categorical physical, mental, emotional, sexual, and moral strengths and weaknesses of clearly distinguishable human groups: sexes, races, classes, and so forth.[2] Scientifically mediated "natural bodies," constructed through the lens of the mythical norm, have worked in concert with marriage mores and legal conventions. Both visible, material body parts and assumed, unseen body parts, particularly those parts sexualized and those associated with reproduction, have been read as markers predicting and inscribing identity groups' behaviors. That the scrutinized bodies can be passed or failed as signifying proper, moral persons has provided justification for inequitable treatment based upon binarized status markers (free/enslaved, Anglo-European/person of color, male/female, monied/poor).

Nineteenth- to early 20th-century scientists' and sexologists' fascination with the sexual(ized) bodies of African and African American men and women, particularly the latter, provide a telling example. As Suzanne Somerville (1996) has documented, "One of the most consistent medical characteristics of the anatomy of both the African American woman and lesbians was the myth of the unusually large clitoris" (p. 41). Through this and similar analyses, "the discourse of scientific racism . . . constructed both the non–White body and the nonheterosexual body as pathological" (Somerville, 1996, p. 38–39). Indeed, "[t]he racial difference of the African [woman's] body . . . was located in its literal excess, specifically sexual excess that placed her body outside the boundaries of the 'normal' female" (Somerville, 1996, p. 41). This does more than just site the morally sanctioned role of the "pure" woman who is activated by her "true love" outside the realm of possibility for Black women. In the system of binaries by which identities are constituted, the "devalued jezebel [made] pure White womanhood possible" (Collins, 2000, p. 132). The images of the heterosexual Black woman as rapacious jezebel was also paralleled with the "softer" images of Black men and women as childlike and happy-go-lucky but irresponsibly sexual and lazy, justifying the paternalism of both slavery and federal governmental control, especially over marriage and procreation, which continues today in welfare stereotypes, regulations, and reproductive control mechanisms.

These 19th- and early 20th-century theorists' work took shape in the context of America's waves of impoverished immigrants, battles over slavery and subjugation of indigenous peoples, the rise of evolutionary theory and social Darwinism, and a rabid fear of "racial suicide." The middle-class White family was seen as under threat by the rampant immorality of both overly reproductive heterosexual and sexually nonproductive racialized deviants. Though trousers and full skirts might hide African American bodies from public inspection, the outsized and predatory sexual organs (and corollary underdeveloped moral and familial sensitivity) science assigned to people of the "less evolved, lower races" and classes were part of White "common knowledge" and fear (a construct, one might add, still prevalent today).

Those not allowed to legally marry in the pre–Civil War South (nor in some Northern states, e.g., Pennsylvania) not coincidentally were those whose bodies did not allow them to pass as—according to scientific authority—fully evolved humans. African Americans' legible nonpassing status gave Whites comforting confirmation of their own fully evolved state, the physical and moral superiority that reached its celebratory height in legally sanctioned marriage, which was included in many states' (North as well as South) antimiscegenation laws (not abolished at the federal level until 1967). Similarly, eugenic initiatives like the nationwide "Fitter Families" program in the earlier decades of the 20th century codified the conflation of full humanity, morality—or lack thereof—with race/ethnicity- and class-based readings of human bodies. The various contests and the awards given out to selected married people and their children, displayed alongside examples of families exhibiting human degeneracy at county fairs and lecture halls, very literally promoted popular surveillance and assessment of those bodies proper for marriage (and the assumed subsequent reproduction; "Image Archive").

More advanced science and medical technology of the second half of the 20th century have inserted themselves in additional ways into literal construction of proper bodies in response to the existence of individuals with disorders of sexual development (DSD). The bodies of those intersex babies whose genitalia do not clearly, properly proclaim "penis"/"boy" or "clitoris"/"girl" evoke what physicians have termed a "neonatal psychosexual emergency." Again, the too-large clitoris is viewed as "an aesthetic and moral violation" and "an affront to nature" (Kessler, 1998, p. 36–38), while the "undersized" penis deeply threatens the child's future identity as a real man since "he cannot be a boy with this insignificant organ" (Kessler, 1998, p. 37). Medical practitioners' evaluations of intersex individuals' genitalia reveals authorities' deep concerns that genitals not only be clearly dimorphic (i.e., dainty clitoris, assertive penis) but also be of potential size and capability for future (assumed) heterosexual intercourse. The historical legal and religious concept of marriage "consummation" reinforces the point that no other form of sexuality—no other performed gender—can legally sanctify a marriage, and thus no intimate life partnership that does not include heterosexual penetrative intercourse (or spouses equipped to perform it) can pass as real marriage. Sexual organs must therefore fall within certain iconographic bounds in order to constitute a proper, marriageable body. Thus girls born with improper genitals have been routinely subjected to surgical reconstruction to create genitals that pass both visually, for example, cropped clitorises, and (supposedly) performatively, for example, vaginoplasty to create a sheath sufficient to "accept a normal size penis" (Morris, 2001, p. 3).

We might ask at this point whether legal battles regarding official sex designation for transsexuals are not a reflection of society's disbelief in transpeople's ability to reiteratively and constitutively perform this particular heterosex act to prove they are "opposite" to their (future and presumed) spouses. Indeed, current laws and court cases involving transsexual people's "real" sex/gender identity show that intercourse-ready genitals are vital. A successful legal brief filed for a male-to-female transperson petitioning for an amended birth certificate in 1970, for example, noted that the plaintiff's "male organs had been removed and . . . the petitioner [can] no longer have sex as a male" (cited in Kansas State Supreme Court Case 85,030). Forty years later, though revised birth certificate requirements vary from state to state, most include mandatory genital reconstruction ("Transgender People and Birth Certificates"). These requirements are currently being fought in several states, including New York and Illinois, as discriminatory on economic and health bases, since the surgeries are exceedingly expensive and can involve severe side effects and residual health problems. Note, again, how achieving passing documentation, in this case sex/gender documentation in a corrected birth certificate, requires that the individual also display putative membership in the proper socioeconomic class.

Once we move into the legal realm of marriage for transpeople, penetrating genitals are only part of the whole gender package congruency being certified in marriage to an "opposite." Note in the following excerpts from court case documents the incredible slippage and confusion among the gender package components—biological, social, and sexual. In 1970, a British court ruled against the legitimacy of marriage between an MTF transwoman and a chromosomal male, explaining that "[m]arriage is a relationship which depends on sex and not on gender . . . for even [in] the most extreme degree of transsexualism in a male . . . [,] a person with male chromosomes, male gonads, and male genitalia cannot reproduce a person who is naturally capable of *performing* the essential *role* of a woman in marriage" (*Corbett v. Corbett*, cited in Gardiner). More recently (2001), an MTF plaintiff was noted as having a "fully *functional vagina*" and thus, her attorneys and medical experts argued, "should be considered a *functioning* anatomical female," in part because she and her husband Marshall Gardiner "*enjoyed a consummated marriage* relationship." The court ruled against her marriage's legitimacy, however, because her birth certificate change (from Wisconsin) was not recognized in Kansas, where the case was tried. (All cases qtd in J'Noel Gardiner case, 2001, Supreme Court of the State of Kansas, No. 85,030; my emphasis.)

Proper Families

When the PEW Research Center released its 2010 report on marriage and family trends, alarm bells rang in the popular press. "Nearly 40% say marriage is becoming obsolete," cried the headline in *USA Today* (Jayson,

2010). The PEW report itself, based in part on U.S. Census Bureau data, states that at the same time, 69% of respondents decry "single women having children [as] bad for society," and 61% believe that "a child needs both a mother and a father to grow up happy" (PEW Research Center, 2010).

One of the pivotal definitional and morality functions associated with marriage is family, in particular, childbearing and raising. Although Michel Foucault (1990/1976), Jonathon Katz (1996), and Thomas Laqueur (1990), and others have persuasively documented the late 19th- and early 20th-century classification shift from sexual normalcy and morality based on procreative/ nonprocreative to classification based on forms of pleasure and desire, the "family values" linkage of sexuality and morality has still remained strong in legal, religious, and popular middle-class morality discussions. This view has been supported by religion[3] and in carefully selected science, including in the widely disseminated contemporary studies that challenge research ascribing some degree of biological determinism to homosexuality (NARTH). This discourse, of course, is part of the reasoning to justify marriage remaining a heterosexual-only preserve. Marriage, the argument goes, "is not just a private affair. Every marriage is a public virtue in that it responsibly regulates human sexuality, brings the two parts of humanity together in a cooperative and mutually beneficial relationship, and it delivers mothers and fathers to children" (Stanton, 2004). Similar claims are advanced to justify and preserve adoption remaining permissible only to heterosexuals (preferably married).

Our social institutions of religion, economics, law, and science have all served to reinforce this construction of family and marriage as an inextricably linked "delivery system" also pivotal to human identity. Early Hebrew and Christian theologians cited the scriptural creation stories to explain the divine mandate (Genesis 1:28; 2:24). Responding to the huge societal changes resulting from the Age of Enlightenment, as well as the Scientific and Industrial Revolutions and women's movements, 18th- and 19th-century Euro-American Christianity contributed further justification for hetero-gendered marriage by reconstituting male and female sexuality. Instead of the nobler male being victimized by female carnality and seductiveness à la Adam and Eve, "true" female identity and sexuality were now viewed in "purity" terms. Marriage, 19th-century public moralists argued, provided woman a natural site in which she might (if a "True Woman" herself) satisfy, tame, and channel the male heterosex drive, in part through bearing and raising children, whom the moral man would naturally strive to support. Sentimental images of the middle-class domestic hearth, complete with strong father and sweet mother, a cluster of bright-eyed children at her knee, filled novels and magazines of the era, providing clear guidebooks for those who would pass as moral men and women (Katz, 1996; Welter, 1976).

Under slavery, however, as property themselves, African American people were not eligible for legal marriage in any of the Southern states, nor even in certain Northern states. Some plantation owners disallowed marriage as a means of underlining their total control of enslaved people under their jurisdiction, while others encouraged nonlegal forms (e.g., jumping the broom), for religious and/or ostensibly moral reasons, though it also functioned as a measure of domestication to bind slaves to the plantation. After Emancipation, some former slave owners opposed legalizing marriage among freedmen and women since without legal marriage, "there were no legally recognized fathers, and without fathers there were no legally recognized parents, since mothers had no formal rights to their children" (Edwards, 1996, p. 86). Since "illegitimate children became wards of the state," control of freedpeople's children could be readily transferred to plantation owners or to other masters through "apprenticeships" that were remarkably similar to slavery (Ibid.).

Most monied Southern Whites, however, supported legalizing freedpeople's marriages as a regulatory and surveillance mechanism. With the "assumption . . . that irresponsibility, indolence, and sexual promiscuity . . . characterized freedpeople's lives," the belief was that "[i]f marriage couldn't completely resolve these problems, it was the only way to contain them" (Edwards, 1996, p. 93), by placing legal economic responsibility on the shoulders of the parents (particularly the fathers/ husbands). The new legal right thereby instituted family status while simultaneously retaining that racialized character of "irresponsibility, indolence, and sexual promiscuity" (Ibid.) that Blackness signified. Thus, even as legally married couples, Black freedwomen and men did not fully pass as moral Americans heading proper families.

In both pre- and postslavery conditions, enslaved women and men nonetheless formed, maintained, and fought for their identities as moral and real families. That constructive process was certainly affected by the dominant/ dominating ideology and practices around them. Many, however, constituted familial practice and morality through African cultural histories and through active resistance to their oppressive material realities. In the post–Emancipation period, the daily struggle to keep families intact and maintain control over the destinies of their children was claimed as both a symbolic human right and a practical signifier of independence. Within the context of marriage itself, this became particularly weighted with the competing desires of economic and other forms of advancement, development and retention of a counter-racialized identity, and the drive to be respected members of American society.[4]

Proper Consumption and Productivity

There is a substantial history of linking marriage with economics, from the days of dowries and bride price to marriages arranged to secure property, up through today's increasingly extravagant weddings, receptions, and the like. This aspect of marriage is particularly relevant to capitalist societies as it ties this naturalized human ritual to production and consumption. In his writings during the mid-1800s, Frederick Engels (2001/1884) described the rise of the single-pair monogamous family as an evolution-prompted occurrence that was, ultimately, economics based. The effects of the Industrial Revolution among bourgeois classes culminated in that century's middle-class glorification of the nuclear (heterosexual) family supported by the wage-earning father.

The "living wage" campaigns of the late 19th and early 20th centuries illustrate this, as labor unions and religious figures focused their efforts on the "family man's" right and "natural" desire to support "his" family. Pope Leo XIII's 1891 encyclical *Rerum Novarum* makes explicit the link between morality and successful breadwinning (and drive to attain wealth) for men:

> If a worker receives a wage sufficiently large to enable him to provide comfortably for himself, his wife and his children, he will, if prudent, gladly strive to practice thrift; and the result will be, as nature itself seems to counsel, that after expenditures are deducted there will remain something over and above through which he can come into the possession of a little wealth. (n.p.)

Even with strong support in many quarters for legally ensuring this form of capitalistic moral uprightness, however, the dominant American ethos of meritocracy consigned men who did not manage to earn living wages—disproportionately men of color—to failure and deviancy status. Their wives, who often worked outside the home for wages, were similarly deviant from proper or "true" womanhood, confirming the construction of poor, working-class, and racialized ethnic women's innate animalistic sexuality, lack of moral tone, and domineering ways, as well as the corresponding racialized ethnic men's innate sexual and economic irresponsibility toward women and children. Researchers in Europe and America wrote study after study documenting "the equation of the criminal, pauper, and work-shy at home with the savage abroad" (Moscucci, 1991, p. 185).

So firmly is the dominant American ideology of the family rooted in this naturalized construction of gendered, reproductive, and economic-based marriage that the passing performance of moral (and real) manhood remains being the (male) breadwinner even today. While there is some evidence of acceptance of "changed"[5] gender roles in the modern family, the 2010 PEW Research Center reports that "67% [of Americans surveyed] . . . say that in order to be ready for marriage it's very important for a man to be able to support his family financially; just 33% say the same about a woman." This plays into modern stereotypes of working women—especially those with children—as being so greedy for fancy clothes, big houses, and so forth that they are unnatural wives and mothers, putting their own self-indulgences above the good of their husbands and children. The differential employment and income opportunities available to individuals based on race/ethnicity, class, and sex/gender is easily subsumed under the sway of the intersecting dominant constructions of racialized identities and "natural" male and female desires and capabilities.

Trumpeting also "a sharp decline in marriage and a rise in new family forms [that has] been shaped by attitudes and that differ by class, age, and race," the 2010 PEW study notes that the "'new marriage gap' in the United States is increasingly aligned with a growing income gap," and further, that "blacks are more accepting than whites" regarding changes to marriage and family structures. The report does note that while poorer people "are as likely as others to *want* to marry, . . . they place a higher premium on economic security as a condition for marriage" [my emphasis]. A Brookings Institute study, released in 2011, noted that for the first time in American history, fewer than 50% of 2010 American households were married couples. And "[w]hat is more, just a fifth of households were traditional families—married couples with children . . . as the iconic image of the American family continues to break apart" (Tavernise, 2011). While more highly educated people continue to marry (and stay married) at high rates, "women with only a high school diploma are increasingly opting not to marry the fathers of their children, whose fortunes have declined along with the country's economic opportunities. . . . [The] reasoning[:] 'I can support myself and the kid, but not myself, the kid, and him.'" Sabrina Tavernise (2011) does go on to reassure readers: "Married couples may be half of all households, but that does not mean that only half of Americans will ever be married. The overwhelming majority of Americans—with some exceptions—do eventually marry (though increasingly, working-class people do not stay married)."

One can imagine how these data may be spun. Just a sample: The National Marriage Project (2011) issued the following warning (on, the site notes, National Marriage Week, February 7–14, 2011):

New data indicate that trends in non-marital childbearing, divorce and marital quality in Middle America increasingly resemble those of the poor, many of whose marriages are fragile. However, among the highly educated and affluent, marriage is stable and appears to be getting even stronger—yet more evidence of America's "marriage gap."

Though beyond the scope of this chapter, a review of later 20th-century (and 21st, thus far) paternalistic legal policies such as involuntary sterilization and draconian welfare-to-work programs demonstrate the staying power of the constructions of the poor and people of color as lax parents, not "family-oriented," and too economically irresponsible to make marriage work the way it should. Thus does marriage remain a powerful signifier of one's passing status as a moral, "real" woman or man.

Pass It On

Scholars such as Sherrow O. Pinder (2010) have argued that American history is rife with examples of the nation's efforts to construct a template for "a homogenous cultural identity" (p. 1). A key component of the template is the moral superiority of those so identified and identifiable. To maintain the authority of the template, individual vigilance in surveillance, analysis, and categorization of all persons becomes a necessary act of identity/self-preservation in opposition to the (also necessary) Others. That those who do not pass be readily identifiable is also vital to justifying control of their rights, ostensibly for their own good. Because deviants are devious and all too often successfully pass, however, cultural practices and legal mechanisms to separate the proper persons from the improper must be institutionalized. The most effective of these, like marriage, have been grounded in—and obfuscated by—cherished beliefs ("family values," love) and authoritative institutions (religion, science, medicine, free market capitalism). This scaffolding has been sturdy enough to leave marriage relatively unshaken by legal and ideological challenges, until very recently.[6]

References

Anzaldúa, G. (1999). *Borderlands/La frontera: The new mestiza* (2nd ed.). San Francisco: Aunt Lute Books.

Bolin, A. (1993). Transcending and transgendering: Male-to-female transsexuals, dichotomy and diversity. In Gilbert Herdt (Ed.), *Third sex, third gender: Beyond sexual dimorphism in culture and history* (pp. 447–485). New York: Zone.

Beyond Marriage. (n.d.). www.beyondmarriage.org.

Butler, J. (1990). Gender trouble: Feminism and the subversion of identity. New York: Routledge.

Butler, J. (1993). *Bodies that matter: On the discursive limits of "sex."* New York: Routledge.

Butler, J. (1997). *Excitable speech: A politics of the performative.* New York: Routledge.

Collins, P. H. (2000). The sexual politics of Black womanhood. In P. H. Collins, *Black feminist thought: Knowledge, consciousness, and the politics of empowerment* (2nd ed., pp. 123–148). New York: Routledge.

Davis, A. (1994). Black women and the academy. *Callaloo, 17*(2), 422–431.

Edwards, L. F. (1996, Spring). "The marriage covenant is at the foundation of all our rights": The politics of slave marriages in North Carolina after emancipation. *Law and History Review, 14*(1), 81–124.

Engels, F. (2001/1884). *The origin of the family private property and the state.* (Ernest Untermann, Trans.). Honolulu, HI: University Press of the Pacific.

Foucault, M. (1990/1976). *History of sexuality. Volume 1: An introduction.* (Robert Hurley, Trans.). New York: Vintage Books.

Garfinkel, H. (1967). *Studies in ethnomethodology.* Englewood Cliffs, NJ: Prentice-Hall.

Human Rights Campaign. (2011). *Transgender people and birth certificates.* http://2fwww.hrc.org/issues/1531.htm.

Jayson, S. (2010, November 20). Nearly 40% say marriage is becoming obsolete. USAToday.com. http://www.usatoday.com/yourlife/sex-relationships/marriage/2010- 11-18-1Amarriage18_ST_N.htm.

J'Noel Gardiner Case. (2001). In the Supreme Court of the State of Kansas, No. 85,030, In the Matter of The Estate of Marshall G. Gardiner, Deceased. Syllabus by the Court. Kansas Judicial Center. http://www.kscourts.org/cases-and-opinions/opinions/supct/2002/20020315/85030.htm.

Katz, J. N. (1996). *The invention of heterosexuality.* New York: Penguin Groups.

Kessler, S. (1998). *Lessons from the intersexed.* New Brunswick, NJ: Rutgers University Press.

Kessler, S., & McKenna, W. (1978). *Gender: An ethnomethodological approach.* Hoboken, NJ: John Wiley & Sons.

Knight, R. (1996). *Insight, answers to questions about the defense of marriage.* Family Research Council. http://www.eskimo.com/~bpentium/articles/defense.html.

Laqueur, T. (1990). *Making sex: Body and gender from the Greeks to Freud.* Cambridge, MA: Harvard University Press.

Lorde, A. (1984). Age, race, class, and sex: Women redefining difference. In A. Lorde, *Sister, outsider: Essays and speeches* (pp. 114–123). Berkeley, CA: Crossing Press.

Media Matters for America. (2008, March 31). Scarborough on Obama's "dainty" bowling performance: "Americans want their president, if it's a man, to be a real man." http://mediamatters.org/research/200803310007.

Morris, E. (2001). The missing vagina monologue. *Sojourner, 26*(7), n.p. http://mrkhorg.homestead.com/files/ORG/AdditionalMonologue.htm.

Moscucci, O. (1991). Hermaphroditism and sex difference: The construction of gender in Victorian England. In Marina Benjamin (Ed.), *Science and sensibility: Gender and scientific enquiry 1780–1945* (pp. 174–199). Cambridge, MA: Basil Blackwell.

National Marriage Project, University of Virginia. (2011). *The great recession and marriage.* http://www.virginia.edu/marriageproject/.

PEW Research Center. (2010, November 18). *The decline of marriage and rise of new families.* http://pewresearch.org/pubs/1802/decline-marriage-rise-new-families.

Pinder, S. O. (2010). *The politics of race and ethnicity in the United States.* New York: Palgrave Macmillan.

Pope Leo XIII. *Rerum novarum: Encyclical of Pope Leo XIII on capital and labor.* Vatican City: Libreria Editrice Vaticana. http://www.vatican.va/holy_father/leo_xiii/encyclicals/documents/hf_l-xiii_enc_15051891_rerum-novarum_en.html.

Schiebinger, L. (1993). *Nature's body: Gender in the making of modern science.* Boston, MA: Beacon Press.

Somerville, S. (1996). Scientific racism and the invention of the homosexual body. In Brett Beemyn and Mickey Eliason (Eds.), *Queer studies: A lesbian, gay, bisexual, and transgender anthology* (pp. 241–261). New York: New York University Press.

Stanton, G. T. (2004). Is marriage in jeopardy? *The John Ankerberg Show.* http://www.ankerberg.com/wiki/index.php/Is_Marriage_In_Jeopardy%3F.

Stoltenberg, J. (1989). How men have (a) sex. In J. Stoltenberg, *Refusing to be a man: Essays on sex and justice* (pp. 25–39). New York: Meridian Penguin.

Tavernise, S. (2011, May 26). Married couples are no longer a majority, census finds. *New York Times Online.* http://www.nytimes.com/2011/05/26/us/26marry.html?src=rechp.

Tuana, N. (1993). *The less noble sex: Scientific, religious, and philosophical conceptions of woman's nature.* Bloomington: Indiana University Press.

Welter, B. (1976). *American woman in the nineteenth century.* Athens: Ohio University Press.

Whitehead, J. C. (2011, May 6). Wrong reasons for same-sex marriage. *New York Times 5,* A21.

Notes

1. This is not to say that economic situations, sexual orientations, skin tones, chromosomes and genitalia, and so forth do not exist. They do. However, the meanings, significances, and valuations attributed to them are the product of complex social interactions and factors.

2. See, for example, Nancy Tuana, *The Less Noble Sex* (1993); Siobhan Somerville, "Scientific Racism" (1996); and Londa Schiebinger, *Nature's Body* (1993).

3. The Vatican, for example, addressed the issue of sexuality in 2003, again tying sex, gender, and sexuality together through the family/reproduction model, though noting that whether conception occurs or not during hubby and wife's heterosex isn't the point: "[A] man and a woman . . . by mutual personal gift, proper and exclusive to themselves, tend toward the communion of their persons. In this way, they mutually perfect each other in order to cooperate with God in the procreation and upbringing of new lives. . . . Men and women are complementary . . . as male and female. . . . Therefore, in the Creator's plan, sexual complementary and fruitfulness belong to the very nature of marriage. . . . Homosexual acts 'close the sexual act to the gift of life. They do not proceed from . . . sexual complementarity'" (*Libreria Editrice Vaticana*. Quoted in *Catechism of the Catholic Church* online at http://www.vatican.va/archive/ENG0015/_P85.HTM). See also Pope John Paul II's assertion that gay marriage is part of a new ideology of evil . . . which attempts to pit human rights against the family and against man" (*Memory and Identity: Conversations at the Dawn of a Millennium*, Waterville, Maine: Walker Large Print, 2006, page 32 [original NY: Rizzoli, 2005]).

4. Angela Davis (1994) speaks of this in reference to the Black women's club movement of the 19th century in "Black Women and the Academy" in *Callaloo*, *17*(2), p. 422–431.

5. That females/wives working outside the home for wages is viewed as a "change" from the "traditional" family does, of course, reflect Americans' racialized and class-biased popular definition of family, another mark of "colorblind" and "classblind" historicism.

6. See Beyondmarriage.com and Jaye Cee Whitehead's "Wrong Reasons for Same-Sex Marriage" (*New York Times* 5/6/2011, p. A21) for discussions of this issue in regard to gay marriage activism.

19

Marriage as Commitment

A Revisionary Argument[1]

Mara Marin

Introduction

Two debates have dominated recent discussions of marriage. In this chapter, I will leave aside the first debate, between traditionalists, who reject any changes to the legal definition of marriage, and their critics, who defend an enlarged definition of marriage to include at least same-sex couples.[2]

What concerns me here, an issue already discussed by feminist scholars, is that marriage contributes to gender oppression and subordination (Cudd, 2006, p. 146–152; Okin, 1989; Pateman, 1988) and that it supports heteronormativity by making invisible and devaluing ways of intimate living that do not conform to the norm of the heterosexual couple (Butler, 2002; Fineman, 1995; Warner, 2002). Hence, gender equality and diversity of family forms are legitimate normative concerns for the transformation of marriage. But while feminist critics of marriage agree on these normative concerns, they disagree about the legal status that marriage should be granted. Some argue that the legal category of marriage should be abolished, while others think that the legal status of marriage should be reformed but not completely abandoned.[3]

I think that marriage will continue to undermine gender equality and diversity whether marriage as a legal status is abolished or not. Therefore, the focus of the discussion among critics of marriage—the legal status of marriage—is too narrow. In addition to legal reform, the transformation of marriage requires changes in the *informal* processes that contribute to gender subordination and heteronormativity. And changes in these informal processes require a reform of the public meaning of marriage, which guides and provides their structure of justification.

These informal processes will continue to operate even in the absence of the legal category of marriage. Even if the state were no longer involved in granting marriage licenses, other institutions (such as churches) would continue to perform marriages, individuals would continue to get married and to think of themselves and others as married or not, and their actions would be guided by their understanding of what marriage is and what it requires of them. This, in turn, will reinforce or weaken hierarchical and exclusionary practices.

Thus, marriage as a practice and a social institution would not disappear but would continue to have effects on individuals' freedom and equality.[4] Crucial to these effects is the public meaning of marriage. Its public meaning provides a structure of justification for both public and private action, both of which are responsible for the contribution marriage makes to gender subordination and heteronormativity.

For example, if marriage is thought of as an indissoluble union, divorce is not an available option. The model on which we think of marriage (whether, say, we think of it as a friendship rather than as a business association) will make a difference to our arguments about which actions inside married relationships are expected, required, or justified (a concern for the emotional well-being of one's spouse will be required on the friendship model, but not on the business association model). This, in turn, will strengthen or weaken the contribution marriage makes to gender hierarchy and heteronormativity. If, for example, marriage is understood as a relationship between a man (the husband) and a woman (the wife), men and women will have asymmetrical obligations in their marriages.

This means that what we take marriage to mean, not only its legal status, needs to be reformed in order to advance gender equality and challenge heteronormativity. What we then need to ask is: "How should we transform what we take marriage to mean in order to prevent it from supporting gender subordination and heteronormativity?"

To ask this question is to engage in a revisionary approach, which is aptly defended by the feminist philosopher Sally Haslanger. The revisionary approach is the approach in which the aim is to find the concepts that best serve our purposes. Following feminist and queer critics of marriage, I argue that challenging heteronormativity and gender subordination should be our aims in the transformation of marriage. As long as marriage has effects on individuals, we need to define it in a way that undermines gender subordination and heteronormativity. I want to show that if marriage is viewed as "commitment," it can, in part, promote gender equality and challenge heteronormativity. In this sense, I employ a "revisionary approach" in defining marriage, because my definition of marriage is meant to indicate a concept of marriage that would achieve these two purposes.

Before I address my argument, I draw on what I mean by *commitment*. I want to show that commitment is malleable enough to include a wide variety of lived intimate relationships, not only the traditional heterosexual union. Same-sex, romantic and nonromantic, sexual and nonsexual relationships, and relationships between two persons or more can be understood as commitments.

My notion of commitment refers to a relationship created over time through open-ended actions of those involved in it. What is peculiar about commitments is that the partners do not know at the outset the full content of the obligations they incur. They may be called on to attend to the needs of their partners in ways that are not fully transparent and that can turn out to be significantly different from what they could have assumed at the outset. If one of the partners experiences a debilitating accident, for example, we expect the other partner(s) to continue the relationship and respond to that partner's needs. To abandon the relationship and justify it by saying "I never agreed to taking care of someone disabled" strikes us as wrong.

This notion of commitment is different from the idea used by traditionalist defenders of marriage for whom commitment has become synonymous to the idea of marital unity created by marriage under covertures. I view commitment as a relationship between individuals, not an entity distinct from the individuals involved in it. Only individuals can have claims, and only their needs can create obligations. There is no unit created by commitment, and so the rights and obligations of commitment are not rights and obligations of such a unit.[5]

I articulate the structure of commitments by using the idea of open-ended responsive action, which I contrast to tit-for-tat action. To pay immediately (in cash or kind) for the movie ticket you got for me is to respond in a tit-for-tat way. While tit-for-tat-action returns us to a position in which we have no obligations to each other, an open-ended action is one that allows the unpredictability of future circumstances to make claims on its actor. If, instead of paying you back for the movie ticket you bought for me, I say, "next time is on me," I open myself up to claims that will only be specified later, depending on future circumstances. Next time might be another movie, or you might ask me to help you find a present for your sister. One responds in an open-ended way when one welcomes such claims unpredictable at the time of the initial response.

Commitments are relationships of obligations. They are created by open-ended actions and responses over a period of time. Over that time, the repeated open-ended responses constitute endorsement of the relationship. As a result, one incurs *obligations* to respond in an open-ended way to one's partners' actions and needs. To take care of a person is a practice of open-ended responsive action, because caring requires being open to whatever the future may bring, as the cared-for may get sick or may need a special diet or special treatment; and to take care of him or her requires accepting claims created by these changing conditions. Intimate relationships are relationships of care and mutual support, and for this reason, they can be understood as commitments. A reformed understanding of marriage as commitment, one that would inform actions currently guided by the idea of marriage as a monogamous life-long sexual relationship between a man and a woman, would promote gender equality and challenge heteronormativity.

Undermining Gender Subordination

As relationships of open-ended reciprocal obligations, commitments do not rigidify gender norms. They define expectations and obligations; in fact, rights and obligations of commitment are not distributed along gender lines. Thus, on the commitment model of marriage, claims placed on individuals by their intimate relationships are distinct from gender considerations.

This model of marriage undermines the justificatory force of the gendered model of marriage in which the dichotomous positions of the breadwinner (husband) and the homemaker (wife) justify obligations corresponding to rigid gender roles. In contrast, obligations in commitments are determined by considerations about the needs of the partners, changes in those needs, and patterns of action established in the relationships, all of which can diverge from gender roles. Partly, for this reason, I argue that adopting an understanding of marriage as commitment would undermine processes by which marriage contributes to women's inequality.

Okin has argued that gender-structured marriage itself makes women vulnerable by involving them in "a cycle of socially caused and distinctly asymmetric vulnerability" (Okin, 1989, p. 138), which starts before getting married and also affects women who never marry. Because for women, getting married means becoming primary caretakers, girls expecting to get married pursue work, education, or career options that will allow them to combine their work in the private and public spheres. In fact, the sexual division of labor or the family ethic is, for the most part, instrumental in positioning most women in the public sphere of paid work. Marriage limits their options for work early on, confining them to jobs with more flexible hours, low pay, low prestige, and little prospect of advancement. Boys never face this choice between work and domestic life. As a result, women are already in an unequal position when they enter marriage, and the sexual division of labor is embedded with gender inequality. Women continue to be positioned as subordinate to men in both the private and public sphere.

If Okin's account is right, it suggests that a public understanding of marriage plays an essential role in enforcing the gender structure of marriage. What marriage is taken to mean (the fact that it is taken to imply different obligations for men and women) is relied on by parents and educators who guide girls and boys in their decisions about their best educational options (Okin, 1989, p. 142–143). Reforming this meaning of marriage is necessary for grappling with the effects of marriage on gender equality and heteronormativity. Do I overestimate the degree to which marriage has a shared meaning? Different people, one could say, give different meanings to marriage and live their marriages in different ways. There is no such thing as a common understanding of marriage.

However, the fact that individuals invest their relationships with personal meaning does not show that the personal meaning exhausts everything about their marriage; personal meaning need not replace the public one; it may only supplement or elaborate it. Moreover, individuals do not control how their relationships are interpreted publicly—whether they are understood as marriages or marriage-like or not.[6] This shows that there is something like a public meaning of marriage independent of the personal meaning marriage acquires with each relationship.

Finally, women feel the effects of the sexual division of labor before they pursue any relationship they can invest with a less hierarchical meaning. A woman who has prepared to become a wife by training for a job that allows her to combine her work in the private and public spheres is already in a disadvantaged position in the paid labor market. This fact is not changed even if she rebels against the expectation to get married and pursues a less traditional relationship. That women bear the disproportionate burden of domestic work—which is strongly correlated to women's low power inside marriage—is well documented (Coltrane, 2000; Pyke, 1994 cited in Tichenor, 2005, p. 191). What are the mechanisms responsible for this fact is, however, a more controversial issue.

One long-standing line of argument has linked it to men being the breadwinners (Bernard, 1981; Ferree, 1990 cited in Tichenor, 2005, p. 191) or, as married women entered the labor force, to men's larger incomes (Raley et al., 2003; Tichenor, 2005, p. 192). But recent studies have raised doubts about this explanation and have given a stronger independent role to the gender structure of heterosexual couples.

If the unbalanced burden of domestic work were correlated to different earnings, we would expect men whose wives earn more than them to do more housework. Instead, data show the opposite: In those few cases in which women earn more than their husbands, the division of work along traditional lines is reinforced and women's power in the marriage diminishes compared to couples with equal earnings (Bittman et al., 2003).

While different mechanisms may be at work in explaining this finding, all of them show the salience of gender in explaining patterns of domestic labor, an index of women's subordination in marriage. Moreover, as the data in these studies refer to "households containing a couple" and the gendered assumptions explaining the findings refer to the gendered roles of "husband" and "wife," they show the salience of gendered marriage, not only gender roles in general, in the mechanisms that explain women's subordination.

By countering this gendered understanding of marriage, commitment would undermine the two mechanisms of subordination. It would establish a competing view of marital norms and marital obligations to the norms and obligation of the gendered marriage. On a commitment understanding of marriage, decisions about how domestic and paid work should be divided, for example, would be guided by considerations about what each partner needs to develop as an individual, not about his or her gender. Men, not only women, would incur obligations to respond to the needs of their partners, thus extending the caregiver role to men. Importantly, their commitments would require men to respond to women's needs even when women want to change their role as caregivers. By emphasizing open-ended obligations to one's partner, marriage as commitment would distribute more fairly the burden of care and emotional support that intimate relationships provide because care is a practice of open-ended response to the needs of the cared for, and committed obligations go in both directions.

This would transform the choice between family life and work. In heterosexual relationships, it would place some of the burden of that choice on men. For women, the choice between family life and work outside the home would no longer have an "either/or" form. Understood as commitment, marriage would provide support for women, not only make demands on them. Rather than assuming that they would be taking the role of supporting their husband's work when they get married, girls and women could imagine that their husbands will support their work. As a result, their desire to get married will not motivate them to limit their work choices to those compatible with primary responsibility for housework. Marriage would continue to be a source of obligations, which would have to be balanced with other obligations (including those of work in the private sphere), but their structure would not have an asymmetrical impact on women.

Someone could disagree that marriage as commitment is a competing view of marriage, because it does not rule out the traditional couple, the breadwinner (husband) and the homemaker (wife). The husband's work for pay would, on the commitment model, be his response to his wife's domestic work. It is true that the traditional couple is not ruled out. But this is a virtue rather than a problem for my argument. By not ruling it out, commitment can justify strong property claims for the wife if the marriage ends. However, while not ruled out, the traditional couple is not the only arrangement of intimate living rendered legitimate by marriage as commitment, and this, I will argue shortly, has important consequences.

It is true that a couple in which work for pay and domestic work are divided along traditional gender lines can be understood as a commitment. On the commitment view of the relationship, each partner's work is the action by which he or she responds to the other person's action; each new day of work is the response to the other's work. It is open ended because it takes into account the other's work and needs (presumably because both types of work are necessary according to individual needs) and could change to answer new needs (or new understandings of these needs). On this account, the justificatory structure of the traditional work roles is not rigidly gendered. Which type of work and even which particular tasks become one person's response rather than his or her partner's is justified on grounds other than the gender roles of the partners, so they could diverge from traditional gender lines.

Moreover, a certain obligation to respond to one's partner's need or desire for change is implied by the idea of "open-endedness." In commitments, actions are patterned in expectations, but the expectation of open-endedness—to respond to change—trumps any expectation of responding with the same action. This justifies the possibility of change, initiated by individual action. It must be at least possible for the couple to entertain the possibility of changing the gendered roles for it to qualify as commitment. This possibility could have far-reaching transformative effects when individuals in their relationships actually take up these opportunities and do not act the gender roles. If theorists of oppression are right that the choices (or actions) of the oppressed reinforce their oppression (Allen, 2008, p. 51; Cudd, 2006, p. 146), then it must matter what options are open to them and what actions they actually take.

But it is perfectly possible that a couple has responded to each other in the open-ended way I suggested and has divided work along strictly gender lines. In this case, the virtue of understanding marriage as commitment is that it justifies strong claims for the wife when the relationship ends and that makes marriage exit as a viable option for her. If the husband's paid work is a response to her work of care, differences of income that can be traced to differences in their activities are difficult to justify, even if the income differentials occur after the relationship ends. That his work is a response to her personally, not to a union created by their marriage (and dissolved at divorce), lends force to her claims. It undermines his claim that his obligations—which he has fulfilled—were owed to an entity to which both of them belonged, and therefore that he has no further obligation to his wife. This should entitle the wife not only to half the property acquired during the marriage but also to half of the future earnings made with skills acquired during the time supported by her work.

But could we not achieve the same result by abolishing marriage as a legal status and allowing couples complete freedom in drafting their marriage contracts?[7] I think not, for three reasons. First, if the contracting parties have unequal bargaining power before marriage—as men and women do—the weaker party would agree to unfair terms and thus the terms of the contract would reproduce that inequality. Women could agree to terms that, unlike marriage as commitment, would not make exit a viable option. Second, the details of the division of domestic work and paid work is likely to be negotiated and renegotiated throughout a relationship and therefore cannot be easily predicted at the outset. This change, which must be taken into account when dividing property at the end of the relationship, cannot be incorporated by contracts, which are designed at a particular moment of the relationship; and finally, a significant part of the work of care is the effort and energy expended in being attentive and flexible to someone else's needs. That effort is made invisible and undervalued by ideological construction of care as repetitive, mindless, boring activity, producing only what is necessary to maintain life. On this view of care, activities involved in carework are not creative, do not involve thought, and are of limited value.[8] Given the force of this ideological construction of care, the value of its contribution to the needs of the couple would likely not be recognized in a contract. The paid work is likely to be constructed as producing more value than the unpaid domestic work. Even if a contract recognized the necessity of domestic work, it would likely undervalue it, giving the homemaker wife less than her fair share in case of divorce. As an alternative ideological construction of intimate relationships, commitment, in contrast, would make the flexibility of care central and thus much more visible. That in a commitment what we owe to each other are obligations to be open to each other's needs brings into the open the burden of flexibility at the same time as it divides that burden fairly.[9]

Challenging Heteronormativity

Marriage as commitment would challenge heteronormativity by decentralizing the traditional couple as the paradigm on which to think of married relationship. If marriage were understood as commitment, a whole range of relationships—including same-sex, romantic and nonromantic, sexual and nonsexual relationships, relationships between more than two persons, living arrangements between disabled persons, and so forth—would acquire as much legitimacy as heterosexual couples as long as the relationship would be mutually supportive and caring. It would also challenge the exclusivist thinking that associates marriage with a *single* form of relationship.

If the public meaning of marriage would extend equally to all these relationships, it would enlarge the public imagination about relationships and it would enable individuals (some of which will be the children raised in such relationships) to pursue relationships that better support their needs. There is no reason this enlarged imagination about relationships would not affect heterosexual partners. If options other than the heterosexual couple were available and equally legitimate, then we should expect at least some of those who would otherwise pursue traditional relationships to pursue other, more egalitarian, and less gender-structured relationships.

Decentering heterosexual coupling as the only legitimate marital relationship allows more diversity in our conception of legitimate relationships that, in turn, contributes to more egalitarian relationships. Disconnecting marriage from the grip of the traditional heterosexual, romantic, monogamous couple means both a less rigidly gendered understanding of heterosexuality and heterosexual relationships and a more diverse image of what counts as legitimate relationship.

In addition, a public understanding of relationships relied on by different actors is needed for the changes I discussed above to operate in the ways that I have suggested—that is, through influences from relationships of one sort to very different relationships. The public meaning could be thin; it need not exhaust the meaning that different actors would give to their own relationships. It would be a virtue for it to be malleable enough to admit of such personal investment and redefinition.

Marriage, especially in the American context, seems to have such a public meaning, one that different actors are strongly attached to and that has a connotation of legitimacy. This, I think, explains why claims of gay rights have been made to such a large degree (and with such passion) as claims for gay marriage. Rather than trying to erase this connection between marriage and legitimacy, we should extend its reach to a wide variety of relationships and family forms.

It is true that some of the reasons for this (especially but nor exclusively) attachment to marriage should make us suspicious of endorsing marriage even in its more pluralistic form. If we think that health care should be recognized as a universal right, not as a privilege of those lucky to be in long-term relationships, we should be suspicious of efforts to bolster marriage, as they could mean undermining the political possibility for a universal right to health care.

But not all the reasons for the grip of marriage on the public imagination are questionable from an egalitarian perspective. Some of these reasons are embedded in the American history of exclusion and of struggles for equal citizenship. One of the rights that plantation slaves were denied was the right to marry and to have their children recognized as legitimate.[10] We cannot hope for these reasons to disappear if we hope for an egalitarian political community.

Revisionary Approach

In employing a revisionary approach to marriage, the point is to identify an understanding of marriage as a tool for particular purposes. In defining a revisionary concept of marriage, I borrow Haslanger's (2000) model, which she defines in contrast to conceptual and descriptive approaches. In a *conceptual* approach, the aim is to articulate the meaning of marriage as generally used. In a *descriptive* approach, one would focus instead on the extension of the concepts, trying to give better accounts of the practices called "marriage" (p. 33).

In contrast with both of these approaches, in a *revisionary* approach, the task is to identify the concepts that best serve as tools for our (cognitive or practical legitimate) purposes. If our ordinary concepts are not effective tools for achieving our legitimate purposes, then we need to construct concepts that would serve these purposes better (Haslanger, 2000, p. 33).

In constructing a revised concept, one draws on everyday meanings and modifies them to offer an understanding of concepts that achieves our purposes better than everyday meanings. While drawing on everyday meanings, the priority on such an account "is not to capture what we do mean, but how we might usefully revise what we mean for certain theoretical and political purposes" (Haslanger, 2000, p. 34).

In this sense, I contend that marriage should be understood as commitment. By emphasizing the features of commitment in our current understanding of marriage, I argue, we would be closer to achieving gender equality and challenge heteronormativity. This is not to say that "marriage" *means* "commitment." Rather, it means that if we modified and revised the current understanding of marriage to emphasize its commitment features, we would be better able to undermine its contribution to gender subordination and heteronormativity. But, one could say, marriage is a life-long relationship between a man and a woman and the commitment elements do not exhaust its meaning. It is a mistake to think that the elements of commitment are central to what marriage means. If you use *marriage*, you invoke the everyday concept, and then you should respect its meaning.

However, "marriage" is a contested concept. Which elements of the everyday concept are essential to it—and should be respected—and which are accidental—and could be discarded—is a matter of disagreement. For example, there is disagreement whether two persons of the same sex can be married. There is also disagreement whether marriage is essentially hierarchical or can be rescued from its history of the subordination of women and children. Arguably, the commitment elements are also a matter of disagreement. So even in discussions that use everyday language, there is room for reconfiguring the meaning of our concepts, which may mean revising some of these meanings. But if we want an accurate *explication* of "our" concept of marriage, this reply is only partly satisfactory. All it can establish is that contestation is essential to marriage, not that marriage *means* commitment. That is why I emphasize the revisionary character of my argument. What I am after is a *reformed* meaning of marriage because only a reformed meaning would counter marriage's support for gender oppression and heteronormativity. I argue that "commitment" is this meaning.

Conclusion

Is marriage of any use in a world in which care, companionship, and intimacy come in many forms? Should we continue to inhabit this institution that has been the target of much criticism from feminist and queer theorists? If so, is there a way of understanding marriage that would avoid these criticisms? I argued that, in order to challenge heteronormativity and gender subordination, the public meaning of marriage should be reformed to be understood as commitment.

Understood as commitment, marriage would counter current understandings of marriage as creating a union between the breadwinner husband and his homemaker wife that are responsible not only for marriage's implication in gender oppression and subordination but also for its support for heteronormativity. By putting open-ended obligations at the center of understandings of marriage, commitment would open up marriage to a wide variety of relationships and undermine the association between marriage and women's role as primary caretaker.

References

Allen, A. (2008). Rationalizing oppression. *Journal of Power, 1*(1), 51–65.

Bernard, J. (1981). The good provider role: Its rise and fall. *American Psychologist, 36*(1), 1–12.

Beyond same-sex marriage: A new strategic vision for all our families and relationships. (2006, July 26). http://www.beyondmarriage.org/full_statement.html.

Bittman, M., England, P., Folbre, N., Sayer, L., & Matheson, G. (2003). When does gender trump money? Bargaining and time in household work. *American Journal of Sociology, 109*(1), 186–214.

Brake, E. (2010, January). Minimal marriage: What political liberalism implies for marriage law. *Ethics, 120*(2), 203–337.

Brown, W. (2004). After marriage. In Mary Lyndon Shanley, Joshua Cohen, & Deborah Chasman (Eds.), *Just marriage* (p. 87–92). New York: Oxford University Press.

Butler, J. (2002). Is kinship always already heterosexual? In Wendy Brown & Janet Halley (Eds.), *Left legalism/left critique* (p. 229–258). Durham, NC: Duke University Press.

Card, C. (1996). Against marriage and motherhood. *Hypatia, 11*(3), 1–23.

Coltrane, S. (2000). Research on household labor: Modeling and measuring the social embededness of routine family work. *Journal of Marriage and the Family, 62*, 1208–1233.

Cossman, B., & Ryder, B. (2001). What is marriage-like like? The irrelevance of conjugality. *Canadian Journal of Family Law, 18*(2), 269–326.

Cudd, A. (2006). *Analyzing oppression.* New York: Oxford University Press.

Ferree, M. M. (1990). Beyond separate spheres: Feminism, family, and research. *Journal of Marriage and the Family, 52*(4), 866–884.

Fineman, M. A. (1995). *The neutered mother, the sexual family, and other twentieth century tragedies.* New York: Routledge.

Fineman, M. A. (2004). *The autonomy myth: A theory of dependency.* New York: New Press.

Finnis, J. M. (1994). Law, morality, and "sexual orientation." *Notre Dame Law Review, 69*(5), 1049–1076.

Haslanger, S. (2000). Gender and race: (What) are they? (What) do we want them to be? *Nous, 34*(1), 31–55.

Macedo, S. (1995). Homosexuality and the conservative mind. *Georgetown Law Journal, 84*(2), 261–300.

Macedo, S. (1996). Against the old sexual morality of the new natural law. In Robert P. George (Ed.), *Natural law, liberalism and morality: Contemporary essays* (p. 27–48). New York, Oxford University Press.

Macedo, S. (1997). Sexuality and liberty: Making room for nature and tradition? In David M. Estlund and Martha C. Nussbaum (Eds.), *Sex, preference, and family. Essays on law and nature* (p. 86–101). New York: Oxford University Press.

Metz, T. (2004). Why we should disestablish marriage. In Mary Lyndon Shanley, Joshua Cohen, & Deborah Chasman (Eds.), *Just marriage* (p. 99–105). New York: Oxford University Press.

Metz, T. (2010a). *Untying the knot: Marriage, the state, and the case for their divorce.* Princeton, NJ: Princeton University Press.

Metz, T. (2010b). Demands of care and dilemmas of freedom: What we really ought be worried about. *Politics and Gender, 6*(1), 120–128.

Okin, S. M. (1989). *Justice, gender, and the family.* New York: Basic Books.

Pateman, C. (1988). *The sexual contract.* Stanford, CA: Stanford University Press.

Polikoff, N. D. (1990). This child does have two mothers: Redefining parenthood to meet the needs of children in lesbian-mother and other non-contractual families. *Georgetown Law Journal, 78*(3), 459–575.

Polikoff, N. D. (2008). *Beyond straight and gay marriage: Valuing all families under the law.* Boston: Beacon.

Pyke, K. (1994). Women's employment as a gift or burden? Marital power across marriage, divorce, and remarriage. *Gender & Society, 8*(1), 73–91.

Raley, S., Mattingly, M., Bianchi, S., & Ikramullah, E. (2003, August). *How dual are dual-income couples? Documenting change from 1970–2001.* Paper presented at the annual meeting of the American Sociological Association, Atlanta, GA.

Shanley, M. L. (2004). *Just marriage.* New York: Oxford University Press.

Stanley, A. D. (1998). *From bondage to contract: Wage labor, marriage, and the market in the age of slave emancipation.* Cambridge, UK: Cambridge University Press.

Sunstein, C. (1997). Homosexuality and the Constitution. In David M. Estlund & Martha C. Nussbaum (Eds.), *Sex, preference, and family: Essays on law and nature* (p. 208–226). New York: Oxford University Press.

Tichenor, V. (2005). Maintaining men's dominance: Negotiating identity and power when she earns more. *Sex Roles, 53*(3/4), 191–205.

Warner, M. (2002). Beyond gay marriage. In Wendy Brown & Janet Halley (Eds.), *Left legalism/left critique* (p. 259–289). Durham, NC: Duke University Press.

Young, I. M. (1997). House and home: Feminist variations on a theme. In Iris Young, *Intersecting voices. Dilemmas of gender, political philosophy, and policy* (p. 134–164). Princeton, NJ: Princeton University Press.

Notes

1. Thanks to Anita Chari, Andrew Dilts, Dorit Geva, Robert Gooding-Williams, Bernard Harcourt, Jacob Levy, Patchen Markell, Claire McKinney, Jennifer Pitts, Shalini Satkunanandan, Molly Shanley, Anna Marie Smith, Elizabeth

Wingrove, and Iris Young for helpful discussions related to this chapter and comments on earlier drafts.

2. Cass Sunstein (1997) defends same-sex marriage on constitutional grounds. Laws forbidding same-sex marriage, he argues, are a form of sex discrimination and therefore constitutionally unacceptable. See also Macedo's criticism of Finnis's version of natural law arguments against homosexual sex (Finnis, 1994; Macedo, 1995, 1996, 1997).

3. Marriage abolitionists include Fineman (2004); Metz (2004, 2010a, 2010b); Cossman and Ryder (2001); "Beyond Same-Sex Marriage" (2006); Brown (2004); Polikoff (1990, 2008); Warner (2002); and Card (1996). Their most important critic is Shanley (2004). Brake (2010, p. 308–309) also argues for maintaining marriage as a legal category.

4. Some of these effects are mediated by other institutions, such as hospitals and schools. Hospital visitation policies would arguably be influenced by some understanding of who counts as married (or in a particular sort of intimate relationship) even in the absence of a legal status of marriage. The same can be said about employers' determination of eligibility for job benefits like health insurance. As long as in political communities benefits, like health insurance, are not considered universal entitlements, these determinations will have significant effects on individuals' equality and freedom. Other effects are more directed related to the form of each relationship. Patterns of housework and care work in relationships and how they get divided and negotiated influence life prospects of those who marry and those who do not.

5. The desire to continue the relationship, for example, can be understood as a desire of one (or more) individual(s) involved in a relationship, not as a claim independent of the individuals. For a discussion of this idea and related difficulties for the idea of "marital entity," see the exchange between Shanley and Cruz in Shanley (2004, p. 53, p. 113).

6. This public need does not overlap with the political community. It can be the small community of one's family, church, and so forth. My point here is that one does not have control over norms of what counts as "married" in one's community.

7. See Fineman (2004, p. 133–134) for this position.

8. According to Iris Young (1997), philosophical justifications of these ideas can be found in the work of Hannah Arendt and Simone de Beauvoir. Young argues that the activity of preservation in domestic work is creative activity as it involves creation and preservation of meaning. But the peculiarly creative aspect of domestic work, Young (1997, pp. 151–152) argues, is collapsed in De Beauvoir's distinction between immanence and transcendence and Arendt's distinction between labor and work.

9. I develop this argument in a different paper, "Care, Oppression, and Marriage."

10. See Stanley (1998, p. 44–52) for an account of how the right of former male slaves to be married was connected to their right of subjection over their wives.

20

Mut'ah as Social Contract

Helen Lindberg

Introduction

One of the many challenges to a multicultural civil society stems from the tension between affirming the collective dimension of cultural rights without negating or neglecting the indispensible rights of the individual. We know of the contingent character of cultures and traditions and how increased mobility on a global scale, migration, and technical and economic globalization challenge not only the nation-state but also different cultural and political identities, of which some are clearly patriarchal and oppressive of women. Also, we know, there are structural limitations to changing such cultures and traditions because of naturalized male domination, which, in some cultures, is maintained and reinforced by patriarchal religious practices. Women belonging to a minority religious community attempting to actively practice their religion risk undermining their basic individual rights that are safeguarded by the majority culture through legislation and strong collective norms.

Pippa Norris and Ronald Inglehart (2002) argued that it was, most importantly, the differences in sexual politics and sexual morale that separated the Western Christian world from the Muslim world. They construed a normative interpretative schema called the *gender-equality-and-sexual-freedoms frame*. This schema of interpretation frames Muslim culture as inherently sexist and oppressive. Hence, Muslim women are depicted as not only oppressed but also, because of this oppression, devoid of agency and the ability to make use of their rationality as moral subjects (Bhimji, 2009; and Bilge, 2005). Other feminist researchers, including Mary Daly (1973) and Susan Moller Okin (1999), have instead refuted religion and religious practices altogether, claiming them to be androcentric and overly oppressive. These scholars have shown how religious practices are oppressive because they are appropriated by men and, as such, are male practices. Islam has mostly become equated with patriarchal traditions and pre-modernity, leaving little or no room at all for women as rational subjects with the ability or possibilities of conducting their own lives and own choices, especially regarding marriage and reproduction. In sum, Muslim women are mostly viewed as oppressed and also devoid of agency and abilities. It would thus perhaps be natural to call for secular politics, but, as for instance Joan Scott (2007) argues, secular politics, with the purpose of a gender-first protection of Muslim women's autonomy and emancipation, actually hide a monocultural and even racist agenda. In this chapter, the Muslim women that I am referring to are those women who belong to a Shia Muslim religious community.

Earlier research has mainly addressed *the veil* as site of controversy and as the example *par excellence* of how successful or not Muslim integration is, and the veil has also become the symbol for the Muslim woman's deficit of sexual and bodily freedom. I will turn my interest away from the veil as a Muslim practice and instead focus on another practice that has not yet been very much discussed or illuminated. I will, from "a contractual analytical frame," which I soon will return to, examine ideas and conceptions of agency, consent, reciprocity, and self-ownership underpinning the practice of temporal marriage. The practice of temporal marriage is a practice, which, in a similar vein as the veil, has been understood mainly within what can be understood as a "subordination/false consciousness frame," which is a frame in which Muslim women within temporal marriages have been evicted from the realm of agency. As with the veil, Muslim women are depicted and constructed as nonagentic, and the temporal marriage contract is seen as a tool for oppression because it involves a dowry from the man paid directly to the woman, and this enforces asymmetrical power relations between women and men. The dowry is said to restrain the autonomy of women, with the risk of reducing them to sexual commodities and masking a system of legalized prostitution.

Muslim feminists point to another kind of agency that, in earlier research, has been obscured and obliterated. This kind of agency is that of Muslim women's *religious agency,* which is driven by a desire to submit to God rather than the desire to resist social pressure (Bracke, 2008). That is, being religious and following religious traditions, however patriarchal and constraining they may seem, can be understood as an act by a subject constituting one's subjecthood without being altogether determined by the subjectifying and subordinating patriarchal structure. It is crucial, as we can see, to take into account the contingency of the *gender-race-class nexus* and how different social formations or contexts situate, condition, and enable different kinds of transgressive acts. According to the intersectionality framework, gender, race, and class intersect. However, sometimes gender can be of minor importance, or race can be overshadowed by issues of class. Almost always, these three variables interplay in explanations of oppression and agency.

In this chapter, I depart from an assumption that Muslim women are as capable of autonomous choice as any other women in general. However, I believe it is important to distinguish the authenticity of the choice from the moral evaluation of the choice situation. Because of severely restricted choices and valid complaints of the parties entering a contract, I will argue the whole marriage contract situation may be deemed morally unjust and therefore invalid. Following this, I also suggest that the practice of temporal marriage can be interpreted as a site for reformation. I do not wish to depart from a resistance-oriented approach since this risks reducing and impoverishing the analysis to a limited scope of understanding for instance power. I am not affirming the postcolonial hope for oppositional knowledge, even though I do share an aspiration of decolonizing representations of gender relations. I am also convinced that this aspiration is played out through the liberal discourse of social contract and not, as in the postcolonial way, in opposition to it or outside of it. Thus, I am navigating between a postcolonial cultural relativist position and a universalist liberal position. Both of these positions move away from the narrative of Muslim women as oppressed and voiceless. Both approaches allow for a broader scope of analysis that can challenge the ways in which Muslim women are constructed as oppressed, letting Muslim women be depicted in a more nuanced way as struggling and negotiating actors, coping and making choices within particular social contexts, closer to empirical reality. Some Muslim feminists, including Sophie Chamas (2009), claim that it is not Islam that hampers women's rights but how patriarchy has used Islam to oppress women. Hence, we have to be more sensitive to Muslim women's own personal narratives. Liberal democracy and Islam have become depicted as polarized and as almost opposite ideological positions. Islam has mostly been understood as having little to offer but coercion and compulsion. Apart from being deceptive, this view also blurs our analysis of Islam and creates and reinforces racist stereotypes of Muslim women. It is not correct to talk about Islam as if only one homogenic Islamic culture exists (Okin, 1999). In the practice of temporal marriage within Shia communities, I argue that classical liberal issues of consent and choice are fundamental for the marriage to be legitimate. Thus, I am not convinced that conceptions of consent and choice necessarily always have to reveal how liberal contractarian political theory conceals sexist and Islamophobic attitudes. Hence, we need to elaborate fundamental conceptions of consent, autonomy, choice, and reciprocity.

It is important to analyze Muslim sexual contracts with two consenting autonomous adults fused by choice as well as constraint, reciprocity, and the contract as enabling as well as curbing autonomy (Phillips, 2007). The Islamic marriage contract is also interesting as a political phenomenon since it is not regarded as a holy sacrament in the first place but, rather, as a civil contract made legitimate by two consenting parties (Quaraishi & Vogel, 2009). My overall purpose in this inquiry is to examine *Mut'ah* as a general contract situation.

In what way do normative liberal accounts of agency, autonomy, consent, and reciprocity help us comprehend the practice of temporal marriage? Is the conception of a heuristic interactive social contract useful in understanding the nature of temporal marriage as a sexual contract within Islam? These are the two questions that will guide my discussion in this chapter. I argue that it is fruitful to examine *Mut'ah* as a civil contract situation in a way that goes beyond seeing it as solely a patriarchal tool for the oppression of women and that, in turn, raises new and compelling questions of general political interest. There are two kinds of fixed-term marriages and customs practiced within the Islamic community. One is practiced by Shia and is called *Mut'ah*, which means *pleasure* in Arabic. The other, practiced among Sunni, is called *Misyar*. I will here restrict my focus to *Mut'ah* and hopefully be able to return to *Misyar* later on.

Within Islam, despite its diversity, there are shared practices of detailed regulation of sexual relations and also of sexual intimacy between a man and a woman. In what may seem like a paradox, this actually opens up the importance of erotic *desire* in sexual relations in a way different from Judaism and Protestantism, for example. Islamic jurisprudence stipulates sexual rights for both men and women. However, the far-reaching obligations and coercion, along with the practice of *purdah* (gender segregation), for the most part, cannot be understood as other than privileging men as the dominant group and women as the subordinate group. A system of asymmetric power relations between men and women exists, protected and implemented by the Muslim state and its law, and women and men are regarded as morally equal subjects but not politically or socially equal subjects. Women are downright oppressed in various ways. For example, a married woman in a regular Nikha marriage is not permitted to work or leave the house without her husband's approval. And even though Islam and the Islamic jurisprudence are challenged by a thoroughgoing secularization, Shari'ah laws are implemented in varying degrees in Muslim communities. And there are reports of ongoing repression such as open harassment of women in public spaces, to some extent, in many Muslim states (Othman, 2006). Against this backdrop, there are few empirical surveys carried out that address the gap between what is supposed to be inhibiting norm-building effects of Islam and in what ways, and whether international universal norms are sufficiently robust to challenge what must be regarded as oppressive norms against women. You could also downplay the role of religion and instead argue that patriarchal jurisprudence can be found and is practiced in every traditional society, since every traditional society is patriarchal. We can see how the prospects of achieving parity between the genders through reforms are relatively poor in traditional Muslim countries because the laws do not advance women's core rights—for example, basic civil and political rights. We know that these rights are important for the development of democratic institutions (Cherifi, 2010). To be morally valid, I argue that the practice of *Mut'ah* demands core rights for each of the contracting parties, the woman as well as the man, entering the temporal marriage.

The Practice of *Nikah* and *Mut'ah*

Mut'ah might on the one hand be seen as patriarchal, reinforcing men's domination and women's subordination because polygamy is accepted. On the other hand, it might be seen as reformist practice, allowing both men and women to have sexual relations under more relaxed forms than in the demanding forms of "standard marriage." The standard marriage within Islamic jurisprudence is *Nikah*, which literally means *contract*. Islam is also a polygamous religion in which men are allowed up to four wives, but women are not allowed several husbands, about which I soon will elaborate.

   Though the Sunni and Shia diverge on the halaal status of *Mut'ah* today, *Mut'ah* is supported by many different holy sources. Therefore, there is a consensual understanding between Sunni and Shia that Mut'ah was once permitted by the Prophet and is therefore legitimate. However, Sunni has decided to follow the Caliph Umar Ibn-Al-Khattab, who, in one of the Hadiths, has banned the practice of Mut'ah and made it something prohibited (*haraam*). Within the Shia tradition, this interpretation is not agreed upon and, thus, allows for the practice and tradition of fixed-time marriage, *Mut'ah* (Answering Ansar).

Mut'ah is used in the same way as a *Nikah*, a permanent marriage, in order to make men and women *halaal* (clean) for each other and, thus, allows for, among other things, sexual intercourse that otherwise would be *haraam* (prohibited). It also technically allows for a man and a woman to live together as friends. Even though *Mut'ah* is a fixed-term marriage contract, the same restriction of informed legal consent from both parties is required; otherwise, it is considered void and may be annulled. *Mut'ah* lasts as long as the two parties decide to stay together. Therefore, it does not matter if it is for 1 day or for 3 years. It is an agreement between the two contracting parties.

There are many similarities of fundamental importance with the Nikah marriage, including a dowry, called *Mahr*. The dowry is given directly to the bride and not to her father. A married woman is not allowed to be a part of *Mut'ah* and thus cannot be married to more than one man at a time. Here, women are restricted by the same rule in ordinary *Nikah* marriage.

Differences Between *Nikah* and *Mut'ah*

There are some important differences between *Nikah* and *Mut'ah*. One difference is that with *Mut'ah*, the husband and wife, in case of death, do not inherit the property of the deceased. Another difference of fundamental importance is the modified wedding ceremony. The *Mut'ah* must be approved by an *imam* but can be entered without any other witnesses other than the contracting partners. And in the marriage recital ritual, words are added that stipulate the fixed time of the *Mut'ah*. Further, no official *talaq*, or divorce settlement, is necessary, and the marriage is simply void after the time set is passed. Also, in a *Mut'ah* marriage, the woman is allowed to leave the house and spend her money and work as she chooses. Unlike the *Nikah* marriage, if the man and the woman have had sexual intercourse during the *Mut'ah* marriage, a period of *iddah* is required. The woman must wait 4 months until she can remarry again after *Mut'ah*. Further, in *Mut'ah*, it is a common practice—but not an obligation, as in *Nikah*—that the husband provides economically for the wife.

In *Nikah* marriage, the man has an economic obligation to provide economically for any child conceived during the marriage, although he need not pay for his wife's expenses, and there is no restriction in the scriptures against having more than four wives. And since in *Mut'ah*, the husband need not be economically burdened, there are cases in which men have more than four wives. However, in practice, Shia scholars have ruled out the option of having more than four wives, even in a *Mut'ah* marriage, for moral and practical reasons. Moreover, it is permitted for a man to engage in a *Mut'ah* with women of the book, that is, Christian and Jewish women. Since the

Nikah marriage is a unique Islamic practice, with quite far-reaching regulations of women's bodily integrity, a *Mut'ah* marriage is considered within Shia to be an appropriate way of getting to know each other and prepare for the commitment of a *Nikah* marriage. According to the Shia scholar Ayatholla Ali Khamanei, a *Mut'ah* contract is made legitimate through the following oral ritual:

> The temporary marriage contract is as follows: The woman says: "I marry myself to you for the specified dowry (mention the amount) and for the specified time period (mention the time period)." Then the man says: "I accept." (Answering Ansar)

It is clear that the practice of *Mut'ah* presents some limitations, especially for women. Given that with *Mut'ah*, the husband has no economic obligations to cover the woman's expenses, this can in practice make the woman, if she has no income, economically dependent on her husband's good will. And it also makes it economically possible for the man to engage in more than four marriages at the same time. And since the *mahr* is given directly to the woman, and there are no restrictions for how short the fixed time should be, it actually opens up for systematic legal prostitution since there is no technical difference between a *mahr* and a sum of money paid by the man to the woman for having momentary halaal sexual intercourse. However, there are also ways in which *Mut'ah* holds potential for reformist change since it is no doubt a kind of marriage that gives the woman greater freedom of movement and autonomy than Nikah. And, depending on context, a short-term contract under which an exchange of *mahr* and sexual service takes place under the presumed legitimacy of marriage, for pro-sex feminists, *Mut'ah* might be considered a victory for women's autonomy and bodily integrity. In addition, with *Mut'ah*, women have the same opportunities as men to enjoy and embrace their sexual desire. They can have sexual relations with different partners, this time in a legitimate halaal way, without being restrained or confined to one husband, as in the case in a permanent *Nikah* marriage. For instance, it is reported that around the Gulf, young people are now negotiating the marital contracts in new ways, using the Internet and cell phones to consent to fixed-term marriages (Women Living Under Muslim Laws).

Contractualism or Contractarianism?

It interesting to examine *Mut'ah* from a contractualist perspective because it is first and foremost considered a civil contract. A contractualist perspective departs from the basic idea of the social contract between equal parties as fundamental for social integration. The social contract must be understood as an agreement or consented arrangement of individuals who are subjected to collectively enforce social arrangements, and it is the contract that makes those arrangements legitimate, just, and obligating. I find it useful to focus on the moral theory of contractarianism in which moral norms derive their normative force from the idea of a mutual agreement, or a contract. Feminist analysis has shown the moral importance of respecting the intrinsic worth of each person, which is fundamental in contract theory. Also, according to contract theory, it is crucial to recognize the idea of the relational self and of oppression between individuals and between groups.

I do not, however, concur with the contractarian strand in social contract theories, which is based on psychological egoism in which individuals are seen as egoistic and vulnerable and where cooperation is seen as mutually beneficial in that it provides, among other things, protection from each other's selfish greed and violent nature. Rather, I believe the assumption of self-interest, as the primus motor of agency, leads us into a pitfall of a too-far-stretched voluntaristic individuality, which is insufficient in evaluating the moral standard of the practice of strongly norm-based social arrangements (Hampton, 2002). Even though we may appeal to reasonableness, we do not avoid the dilemma of dependency and inequality in resources that affect the ability of self-owning individuals to make autonomous choices (Richardson, 2007). To mitigate the effects of resource inequality, T. M. Scanlon (1998) has argued that we need to further elaborate the Kantian appeal to reasonableness within contractarian theory. Being rational is being respectful of persons and, therefore, moral principles such as the conditions of a contract must be justifiable to each contracting person. Scanlon offers an evaluative tool for assessing on what grounds we could accept or reasonably reject *Mut'ah* as marital principle. I find Scanlon's contractualism useful both in assessing the authority of the internal moral standards underlining *Mut'ah*—are these standards, for instance, mutually recognized by the parties?—as well as from the external surrounding milieu—are these standards equipped to evaluate what might constitute its rightness or wrongness? Here, wrongness is understood as something *that is unjustifiable to others*. Scanlon makes *wrong* the ultimate moral predicate; therefore, *right* is right if it is not defined as wrong.

If I were to *reasonably* reject a principle, I must ask how it impacts others and who might have complaints. If the principle of *Mut'ah* imposes a certain burden on me, but every alternative imposes a greater burden on someone else, then the burden that I experience does not give me a reason to reject the principle. Hence, we can conclude that the principle imposing such a burden on me cannot be *reasonably rejected*. In this way, we can see that contractualism offers a moral theory of contractarianism in which the contracting parties are mutually recognizing each other and mutually empathizing and respectful of the other's needs. *Mut'ah* is a contract, which might be assumed as based on reciprocal love, which in turn makes it highly probable that entering the contract is motivated by mutual affection. The parties are thus motivated not solely by self-interest but also by self-regard and respect for the other. Part of what we owe others is to promote their interests as well as our own. Since one consequential criterion is whose burden and whose complaints should be of moral concern, we should not reject *Mut'ah* just because it imposes a burden, because every other alternative, for instance *Nikah* or no marriage at all, might impose a greater burden. To depart from the conception that we ought to treat persons according to principles they could not reasonably reject requires a strong belief in agency, reason, and the capacity to assess different justifications in an autonomous way (Gauthier, 1986). A contract is thus not simply negotiations for reciprocal utility without further moral deliberation; and it is also something more than assessing the reasonableness in the contract based on whether the contract situation itself is fair (Rawls, 2008).

However, underlying each contractarian theory is the assumption that the contracting parties are equal in power and resources and, thus, change equivalent with equivalent. Carole Pateman (1979), among others, has convincingly problematized this notion from a feminist perspective. The social contract is, no matter its moral form, a contract that historically has excluded women and stipulates men's right to women's bodies. And in the sexual contract, men and women are not equal to start with and can therefore not make an equal exchange. We might also consider what, for instance, Martha Nussbaum (2006) points out as one of the major flaws of the social contract theory. She argues that none of the earlier proponents has included disabilities as part of the unequal distribution of natural resources, or the territorial place where the contracting party has been born and raised. So long as fair contracts between the states do not exist, it is hard to achieve fair contracts between individuals. This objection could be applicable to *Mut'ah*, since the practice presumably originated as a way to enable sexual reproduction in war times when men moved around; when there also is a deficit of men, it allows for both men and women to have temporary sexual relations, thus securing reproduction even in war times and with great social mobility between different territories. We know the consequences of such structural transformations and the effects of migration and mobility on equality and on individuals' capabilities to function on a global scale.

Consent

Another issue of fundamental importance here is that of autonomy and consent. What does it actually mean to say that two informed adults consent to the contract? First, we have to analytically grasp the distinction between legal consent and moral consent. Alan Wertheimer (2003) describes this in the principals for valid consent (PVC), meaning that there are principles of valid consent for the law and principles of valid consent for morality. It is important to underline that both are moral principles. But the moral principles indicative of legal validity are not necessarily the same as those indicative of moral permissibility. Their legal impermissibility is a subset of what is morally impermissible, that is, a subset of the morally unworthy, what is bad and what is wrong. It is clear that consent is the moral glue of any kind of contract, and it is fundamental in marital contracts. The moral and legal force of any economic or physical injuries that a person might suffer is negated or at least weakened by that person's consent to claim, power, immunity, or privilege to another person. If we share the view that autonomy is "responsiveness to reason," that is, a person is autonomous only when she or he has deliberated over the reasons given in the situation, it would also be plausible that the degree of autonomy amplifies the positive or the negative value of a choice. In that case, we can agree that a good autonomous choice is better than a good non-autonomous choice. But a bad autonomous choice is worse than a bad non-autonomous choice (Wertheimer, 2003).

We can also easily see how demands of strong reciprocity, which require equal exchange in amount or in kind, particularly in sexual relations, might lead to disrespect of the agency of the parties. Instead, I find it more fruitful in sexual contract situations to use the notion of *weak reciprocity*, which encompasses the assumption that the parties expect to benefit from a sexual relationship in terms of their own preferences and values but have a weaker view on what is morally permissible sex. Weak reciprocity does not require exchanges that are equal in amount or in kind (Wertheimer, 2003).

Concluding Remarks

Many unsettling issues remain. Perhaps the most disturbing is the issue of why parties—in this chapter, women—consent to arrangements or contracts seemingly detrimental to them. The standard overall feminist critique is that women consent because of patriarchal repressive norms, sanctions, and a naturalized practice of domination and that the women engaging in *Mut'ah* do so in a kind of false consciousness in which they express false or adaptive preferences—that is, not fully autonomous preferences, since false preferences are what we falsely think we prefer, perhaps because we are left with no alternatives or it satisfies momentarily but is not good for us, and adaptive preferences are molded around what others have or prefer. However, false preferences are distorting the view of women as rational autonomous agents, capable of making their own decisions in a *responsiveness to reason*. We risk losing sight of the respect for the person if we attempt to judge when a given consent is so defective that it requires moral or legal intervention.

Every attempt to see past a person's own consent with subjective standards of what is morally good might be considered disrespectfully patronizing. And that is a moral high ground that will not be of any help for the Muslim women who are willing to resist and challenge their Muslim way of living in order to achieve equality, greater autonomy, and sense of worth as persons. On the other hand, we know there are multiple sources of oppression and inequality and also psychological underpinnings of use and abuse, which makes the assumption of valid consent perhaps a bit more problematic than Alan Wertheimer (2003) seems to endorse. His principles of valid consent are not sufficiently elaborated since they do not fully take into account the complexities of the human psyche and the external constraints on the consenting individuals, for instance, the inequality of resources between men and women or the other burdens that women face such as child bearing.

We need more empirical data about the existence and diversity of the practices of *Mut'ah*, and how the contracting parties involved in this process perceive their relationship. We need to find out if and how the practice of *Mut'ah*, on the one hand, enforces sexual oppression and, on the other hand, in what ways it is an emancipatory tool for reformist and political change of sexual contracts. There are inquiries showing how internal critique against neo-patriarchal Islamism in Iran and other Muslim communities might be interpreted as a reformist development of Islamist feminism (Ahmad, 2008). We also know the immense importance of reformist imams for Shia Muslim women. In fact, I believe reformist sexual contracts can pave the way for further emancipation (Chamas, 2009). To understand and evaluate the moral and political conceptions and implications of *Mut'ah* as sexual contract within the Islamic jurisprudence, the *gender-sexuality frame* is too narrow to provide us with sufficient analytical tools for in-depth inquiries of how the practice of Muslim sexual contracts might carry reformist possibilities from deep within the private sphere in Muslim communities.

Therefore, I have, in this chapter, relied on contractarian theory and assumptions of valid consent.

References

Ahmad, I. (2008). Cracks in the "mightiest fortress": Jamaat-e-Islami's changing discourse on women. *Modern Asian Studies, 42*(2–3), 549–575.

Bhimji, F. (2009). Identities, and agency in religious spheres: A study of British Muslim women's experience. *Gender, Place and Culture, 16*(4), 365–380.

Bilge, S. (2010). Beyond subordination vs. resistance: An intersectional approach to the agency of veiled Muslim women. *Journal of Intersectional Studies, 31*(1), 9–28.

Bracke, S. (2008). Conjugating the modern/religious: Conceptualizing female religious agency. *Theory Culture, and Society, 25*(6), 51–67.

Chamas, S. (2009). Sayyid Muhammed Hussein Fadlallah: Muslim cleric and Islamic feminist. *Journal of Alternative Perspectives in the Social Sciences, 1*(2), 246–257.

Cherif, F. M. (2010). Culture, rights, and norms: Women's rights reform in Muslim countries. *Journal of Politics, 72*(4), 1144–1160.

Daly, M. (1973). *Beyond God the father—Toward a philosophy of women's liberation.* Boston: Beacon Press.

Gauthier, D. (1986). *Morals by agreement.* New York: Oxford University Press.

Hampton, J. (2002). Feminist contractarianism. In C. Witt (Ed.), *A mind of one's own: Feminist essays on reason and objectivity* (pp. 337–368). Boulder, CO: Westview Press.

Norris, P., & Inglehart, R. (2002). Islamic culture and democracy: Testing the "clash of civilizations" thesis. *Comparative Sociology, 1*(3/4), 235–264.

Nussbaum, M. (2006). *Frontiers of justice: Disability, nationality, and species membership.* Cambridge, MA: Harvard University Press.

Okin, S. M. (1999). *Is multiculturalism bad for women?* Princeton, NJ: Princeton University Press.

Othman, N. (2006). Muslim women and the challenge of Islamic fundamentalism/extremism: An overview of Southeast Asian Muslim women's struggle for human rights and gender equality. *Women's Studies International Forum, 29,* 339–353.

Pateman, C. (1979). *The problem of political obligation: A critical analysis of liberal theory.* New York: John Wiley & Sons.

Phillips, A. (2007). *Multiculturalism without culture.* Princeton, NJ: Princeton University Press.

Quaraishi, A., & Vogel, F. (2009). *The Islamic marriage contract.* Cambridge, MA: Harvard University Press.

Rawls, J. (2003). *Justice as fairness: A restatement.* Cambridge, MA: Harvard University Press.

Richardson, J. (2007). On not making ourselves the prey of others: Jean Hampton's feminist contractarianism. *Feminist Legal Studies, 15*(1), 33–55.

Scanlon, T. (1998). *What we owe to each other.* Cambridge, MA: Harvard University Press.

Scott, J. W. (2007). *Politics of the veil.* Princeton, NJ: Princeton University Press.

Wertheimer, A. (2003). *Consent to sexual relations.* Cambridge, MA: Cambridge University Press.

Internet sources

Answering Ansar, http://www.answering-ansar.org/.

Women Living Under Muslim Laws, http://www.wluml.org/section/news/results/taxonomy%3A10.

21

The Absence of African American Churches in the Same-Sex Marriage Battle

Why Not at the Front Lines?

Henry Zomerfeld and Kyeonghi Baek

African American churches have played a significant role in mobilizing and socializing their congregants politically, fostering civic skills (Harris, 1999) and, thus, being the epicenter of political activism in the African American community (Brown & Wolford, 1994; McDaniel & McClerking, 2005). Nonetheless, African American churches and leaders are not at the front line in the same-sex marriage battle. In fact, "there are very few mainline black Christian denominations that support marriage equality of lesbian and gay couples" (Moore, 2010, p. 26). Some of these religious communities tend to not be supportive of same-sex marriage, as pointed out by research that shows that 64% of African American Protestants oppose same-sex marriage and 79% of African American Evangelicals oppose same-sex marriage ("Changing faiths: Latinos and the transformation of American religion," 2007). Therefore, the puzzling absence of African American churches is not necessarily due to the lack of political experience or the lack of doctrinal appeal of this issue. Then why are African American churches relatively absent from the same-sex battle? Is it because the same-sex marriage battle has been a highly inflammatory and religiously framed issue and has galvanized conservative religious groups in the United States? In comparison to whites, are African Americans inclined to be more heavily involved with socially conservative church communities? (Griffin, 2000, pp. 93–94).

To answer these questions, in part, we interviewed seven ministers in the greater Buffalo area in-depth on their doctrinal and personal views on same-sex marriage, their ministry, and their congregations' mobilization on the issue of same-sex marriage. Considering the controversial and sensitive nature of the issue, the response rate was low. Despite sending out more than 60 letters over three intervals of mailings directed to ministers in the area and networking to make personal contact with local ministers, the response rate was approximately 11%. We believe that this in-depth method is more suitable for advancing reliability and validity of a complex issue such as African American churches and their leaders' views and mobilization on the same-sex marriage issue (King, Keohane, & Verba, 1994).

Our analysis shows that all the ministers interviewed show a strong opposition toward same-sex marriage. To all the ministers, the issue of same-sex marriage is a doctrinal and religious issue rather than an issue of equal rights. Although there was a strong opposition to same-sex marriage among African American churches based on the biblical teaching of heterosexual marriage, there were no substantial or organized efforts against same-sex marriage. We find that this is due to the following reasons: First, the interviewed ministers lead small congregations and are faced with more pressing issues, such as poverty and crime, than more distant issues like same-sex marriage. Their resources were focused on more immediate community and congregational needs. Second, there is deep-rooted distrust toward conventional media among African American ministers, which may discourage them from engaging in more traditional political or media campaigns.

This chapter proceeds as follows: First, we provide an overview of the battle against same-sex marriage in an effort to explain the background that led up to this furious debate and the apparent lack of African American church involvement with the issue. Given that same-sex marriage has been a national issue across the United States and a highly galvanizing issue across all denominations, we highlight some of the more prominent same-sex marriage battles in an effort to examine whether African American churches mobilized on the issue. Second, we explore why the seeming absence of African American churches is puzzling. We show that many African

American churches, in general, are less supportive of same-sex marriage, and we examine why these churches were relatively absent on the issue. Namely, African American churches have a long and enduring history of political activism, and many African Americans tend to be engaged in more theologically conservative denominations. Third, we conduct a series of interviews with African American ministers in the greater Buffalo area to examine whether African American churches were engaged in political activism on the issue of same-sex marriage and what prevented their active and organized engagement on the issue.

The Battle Against Same-Sex Marriage Among Religiously Conservative Churches

Proposition 22, most commonly known as California's Defense of Marriage Act (DOMA), was voted on in California in 2000 and passed, 61% to 39% (Egan & Sherrill, 2009), but the California Supreme Court later struck it down, allowing for same-sex marriage in the state. The California Supreme Court ruling was highly controversial, and it opened up the door for Proposition 8, the ballot initiative that sought to ban same-sex marriage (Egan & Sherrill, 2009, p. 4). Proposition 8 was one of the most publicized and bitterly contested initiatives on same-sex marriage, as there was a more centralized lesbian, gay, bisexual, and transgender (LGBT) presence in San Francisco and Los Angeles ("California: Same-sex couples," n.d.). Also, many religious organizations coordinated efforts to combat the LGBT movement with the goal to protect traditional heterosexual marriage. Proposition 8 passed, 52% to 48%; opponents of the proposition filed a lawsuit in California Supreme Court, arguing that this legislation was unconstitutional (Egan & Sherrill, 2009, p. 5). The court ultimately upheld the citizens' votes on Proposition 8 and invalidated same-sex marriage while allowing those same-sex couples who had married previously to still hold their married status.

Many Catholics and Mormons knew that Proposition 8 was their last chance to protect traditional heterosexual marriage in California, and they worked diligently to make sure that the proposition was passed. Why was it such a significant issue for Mormons and Catholics? To them, the issue of same-sex marriage is a fundamental doctrinal issue. Conservative Catholics, for example, rely on the belief in procreation, something impossible for same-sex couples outside of adoption or artificial insemination. Both adoption and artificial insemination are unacceptable practices for conservative Catholics (Barron, 2008).

To protect and promote these traditional Christian doctrinal values of heterosexual marriage, religiously conservative organizations such as the Catholic organization the Knights of Columbus, led an active and successful campaign for Proposition 8. "Their efforts, combined with the efforts of the 'Yes on 8 campaign', raised more than $40 million from conservative supporters across the country" (Khan, 2009), making Proposition 8 the most expensive social issue campaign in U.S. history (Sayre et al., 2010, p. 10). Forty percent of the $40 million came from members of the Church of Latter Day Saints, that is, Mormons (Schubert & Flint, 2009). In addition, "the Yes on 8 campaign had more than 100,000 volunteers knocking on doors in every zip code in the state [of California]" (Khan, 2009, p. 23).

With such funding and manpower, "these volunteers and churches were able to penetrate various new media sources" (Schubert & Flint, 2009, p. 47), and this "emotionally charged [media campaign] . . . played out for several months past the November vote" (Sayre et al., 2010, p. 10). The aggressive media campaign reflected the understanding that "passing Proposition 8 would depend on [the] ability to convince voters that same-sex marriage had broader implications for Californians and was not only about the two individuals involved in a committed gay relationship" (Schubert & Flint, 2009, p. 44). "Yes on 8" purchased television ads and broadcast them throughout the state of California. These televisions ads were displayed in several different languages in the hope of reaching a wide range of voters. The timing of the "Yes on 8 campaign" was key in the passage of the proposition in that those involved strategically used volunteers, fundraising, and the power of the churches to put forward a clear and calculated message about Proposition 8 (Schubert & Flint, 2009, p. 45).

Besides conventional media channels and Google ads, more interactive marketing tools such as YouTube were used to clearly explain and promote the positions of people on both sides of this proposition (Thorson et al., 2010). "The greatest proportion of 'Yes on 8' videos . . . were more likely to be scripted and professionally produced than were 'No on 8' videos . . . [which] suggests that the 'Yes on 8' YouTube presence may have been relatively more dominated by powerful, well-funded organizations" (Thorson et al., 2010, p. 342). Given the significant manpower, funding, and motivation, these religious organizations led a successful campaign promoting "Yes on 8" and ultimately seeing that traditional heterosexual marriage was protected.

Both Proposition 22 and Proposition 8 were led heavily by religious organizations; yet African American Christians did not necessarily play a significant role in these efforts to prevent homosexuals from getting married, despite early assertions attributed to voting on Proposition 8 and/or religious culture (Egan and Sherrill, 2009, p. 9; Barnes, 2005, p. 975; Ward, 2005). In California, African American churches were not entirely silent on Proposition 8. Apostle Frederick K. C. Price organized and rallied support from fellow African American Christian leaders and did receive support from more than 50 pastors (Abrajano, 2010, p. 924). However, these pastors never put their objections to same-sex marriage into formalized political activism, while Catholics and Mormons formed strongholds of volunteers and networking across denominational lines to voice a solid and strong opinion against same-sex marriage. Our study addresses this puzzling absence of African American churches from the same-sex marriage battle.

California is often the first state discussed when same-sex marriage is mentioned, for the following reasons. First, there is a large population and presence of the LGBT community in San Francisco and Los Angeles. Additionally, California has legalized and illegalized same-sex marriage over the course of several years through ballot initiatives and court rulings. The length of time that same-sex marriage has been debated back and forth in California and the combination of ballot initiatives and court rulings makes California unique. However, done relatively quietly, states like Massachusetts have legalized same-sex marriage through court rulings.

In *Goodridge v. Department of Public Health* (2003), the Massachusetts Supreme Judicial Court decided that denying same-sex couples the ability to marry was in violation of their equal rights. Unlike California, Massachusetts did not handle this through ballot initiative; it went straight to the court with no citizens' direct input. However, not surprisingly, the Catholic Church played an integral political role in an attempt to prevent destruction of traditional marriage in Massachusetts. In an attempt to replicate Proposition 8 and introduce an amendment similar to California's Defense of Marriage Act (DOMA), the Catholic Citizenship Organization in Massachusetts collected around 170,000 signatures of those approving such an amendment, which was twice as many as they needed (Cunningham, 2009). In an effort to gain support of traditional heterosexual marriage, priests discussed the amendment during their homilies, and volunteers set up tables at churches to discuss the amendment, handing out informative brochures and getting more signatures (Cunningham, 2009). Once the issue entered the court, as the ballot initiative was unsuccessful, the Catholic Church took a stance against same-sex marriage and sent an *amicus curiae* brief to the court under the guidance of the Catholic Action League (CAL). In spite of the efforts of the CAL, Catholics, and other predominately white churches, the Massachusetts Court did not halt same-sex marriage ("*Goodridge v. Department of Public Health* 798 N.E.2d 941 Mass.," 2003). Of all of these briefs, none were from an African American Christian church. The other briefs, which supplement the CAL, were mostly from white Protestant churches. This again shows that African American churches and their relative silence on the issue are not unique in California. Their lack of effective mobilization is apparent in these states. African American churches did not mobilize a more central response.

The Puzzling Absence of African American Churches on the Battle of Same-Sex Marriage

One cannot discuss political mobilization and socialization of African Americans without considering the profound impact of religion and church leaders on African American politics and mobilization. African Americans are firmly rooted in their political activism and remain active in the present day (Barnes, 2005; Ward, 2005, p. 498). The African American church is often considered a "significant element of the social lives and networks [of African-Americans] . . . and is recognized as the central oldest and most influential institution in the black community" (Barnes, 2005, p. 494). Barnes (2005) argues that African American churches have "long been considered a bulwark in the black community" (Barnes, 2005, p. 967). Many other scholars credit "the centrality and importance of African American churches and African American religious culture" as a key to success in the civil rights movement (Calhoun-Brown, 2000, p. 170). African American churches not only are an epicenter of political and community mobilization, but they also play a key role in shaping the political consciousness of African Americans. "Among African-Americans, church attendance has played a significant role in facilitating political mobilization and participation. . . . Blacks who consistently attend church belong to a larger number of politically relevant organizations, harbor more positive political and racial attitudes and vote at higher levels" (Alex-Assensoh & Assensoh, 2001, p. 886). Considering the strong political connections of African Americans and their churches (Calhoun-Brown, 2000, p. 169), it is only plausible to argue that the African American churches were capable of playing a significant role in galvanizing and organizing African Americans on the issue of same-sex marriage.

It is also plausible that African American churches would have been not only capable but also more inclined to mobilize against this issue of same-sex marriage, given that African American churches tend to be more theologically conservative. African Americans, in general, are not only more religiously active but also more active in "theologically conservative Baptist and Pentecostal denominations . . . as 63 percent of African-Americans report

affiliation with Baptist or other sectarian Protestant denominations compared to 30 percent for white Americans" (Sherkat, De Vries, & Creek,
2010, p. 83). For example, the African American votes were crucial to seeing
Proposition 8 pass (Miller, 2009, p. 58), and African American voters were
more supportive of Proposition 8 than whites, 58% to 49%, respectively
(Egan & Sherrill, 2009, p. 26).[1] Thus, it is plausible to argue that African
American churches, considering their more conservative theological stance,
are more likely to mobilize against the legalization of same-sex marriage. Yet
despite their more conservative religious affiliations and active political
mobilization experiences, we did not see visible African American activism
on the issue of same-sex marriage, and they did not respond with the same
efforts that their white counterparts did in California, Massachusetts, and
New York.

Method

In this chapter, we examine whether African American churches mobilize on
the issue of same-sex marriage and what prevents African American
churches from mobilizing effectively and actively. In order to answer these
questions, we used a qualitative interview method, since this in-depth
method is more suitable for advancing reliability and validity of a complex
and controversial issue such as African American churches' views and
mobilization on the same-sex marriage issue (King et al., 1994). We
interviewed seven ministers in the greater Buffalo area in depth on their
doctrinal and personal views on same-sex marriage, their ministry, and their
congregation's mobilization on the issue of same-sex marriage.

The greater Buffalo area, in New York, is the primary focus for our study.
The state of New York is unique in different ways in comparison to
California and Massachusetts, when it comes to the legalization of same-sex
marriage. First, unlike California, New York legalized same-sex marriage
in June 2011 through the state legislature, not ballot initiatives or through
state courts. Given that New York dealt with same-sex marriage through the
state legislature, mobilization took form through protests and letters to state
representatives. We observed hardened opposition from the Roman Catholic
Church. For example, Archbishop Timothy Dolan and the bishops of the
various New York Catholic dioceses sent pastoral letters condemning same-
sex marriage as sinful, unnatural, and against the teachings of the church
(Archdiocese, 2011).[2] However, in all of this, African American churches did
not appear to voice their opinion or at least did not do so as loudly or clearly
as the Roman Catholic Church. Despite these efforts, representatives were

not moved enough by the Roman Catholic Church's argument, as the measure passed. New York is currently the largest state in the union to have legalized same-sex marriage. Thus, preliminary research supports our proposition that African American churches were relatively inactive on the issue of same-sex marriage. Second, while the state of New York is a traditionally liberal northeastern "blue" state as a whole, once you leave New York City, the conservative voice is active, especially upstate and in western New York. Buffalo, the second largest city in the state, is a prime example of such political diversity. Although the inner-city residents have been, in general, ideologically liberal, the residents of suburban and surrounding areas tend to be more politically conservative. Thus, the greater area of Buffalo is composed of rather ideologically and politically diverse residents.

Our study was conducted through two different phases of the same-sex marriage battle of New York State—under Governor Paterson and Governor Cuomo. The period during which we conducted our research coincided with the two battles over the issue of same-sex marriage in the New York state legislature. We initially started conducting interviews in the summer of 2010. At the time, New York was under the guidance of Governor David Paterson, a Democrat who pushed for the rights of same-sex domestic partners. Our second-phase interviews and re-interviews occurred during the second phase of the same-sex marriage battle under Governor Cuomo in 2011.

Governor Paterson introduced legislation that would have legalized same-sex marriage in New York State in April 2009, the same bill as introduced in 2007 by the former governor Eliot Spitzer ("NY governor to propose legalizing same-sex marriage," 2009).[3] However, Governor Paterson suffered from historically low popularity and job approval ratings—only 26% of registered voters considered him excellent or good, and 71% considered him poor or fair in March 2009. His job approval rating fell to 20% in September 2009 (Blain & Lovett, 2009; "Paterson's popularity continues to slide," 2009). The right to share insurance policies was all that Governor Paterson accomplished for same-sex couples.

It was not until his successor, Andrew Cuomo, took the stage in 2011 that the legalization of same-sex marriage came to fruition. Once Governor Cuomo came to power, the issue of same-sex marriage became a key issue in the state's capitol. The legalization of same-sex marriage was one of the key agendas of Governor Cuomo, and during his campaign he pledged that he would legalize same-sex marriage (Healy, 2011, pp. 708–709). The Marriage Equality Act was introduced in May 2011, passed in the state senate in June 2011, and became effective in July 2011 (Kaplan, 2011). Thus, the state of

New York became the sixth state to legalize same-sex marriage and the largest state to do so. Although during our first phase of interviews, the same-sex marriage battle was not at the center of state politics, as we entered into the second phase of interviews it became the key issue of state politics. Thus, we recontacted previously interviewed ministers—initially interviewed in 2010—and gained further insight on this issue during the week of June 20, 2011, the very week that the same-sex marriage vote took place in the New York state legislature.

Findings

Due to the sensitivity of the topic, we only were able to get seven of the ministers we contacted to respond and agree to be interviewed. We compiled a contact list from churches we located through Internet search engines, church listings, and local publications in the greater Buffalo area, such as *ArtVoice* and *Challenger News*, as well as through personal contacts given to us from interviewees and colleagues. In total, we contacted 60 ministers through postal mailing and/or email messages. These mailings were followed up by a second postal mailing, email, or phone call. Despite sending out more than 60 letters directed to ministers in the area, throughout the course of three interval mailings and through networking to make personal contact with local ministers, the response level was very low: Only 11% of ministers contacted responded. However, our seven interviewees represent a diverse demographic and religious spectrum. Of the seven ministers interviewed, six were male and one was female. These ministers were part of non-denominational, Pentecostal, Full Gospel Baptist, and Wesleyan Churches. They all were between the ages of 37 and 66, with an average age of 55. All of the ministers had at least a bachelor's degree, three had their master's degrees, and one had a doctorate degree. All of the ministers led congregations within the City of Buffalo, as many African Americans reside within the city boundary. They all were experienced ministers, having 10 years or more in service. They all ministered to relatively small congregations, serving congregations with fewer than 250 congregants. Six out of the seven ministers were raised in religious households; four out of the seven had a family member who was a church minister or was heavily involved with a Christian church.

Although our interviewees were diverse in demographic, geographic, and denominational aspects, they shared very similar views on key theological issues and issues with regard to same-sex marriage. All the ministers believe that the Bible was the Word of God, and they agreed that same-sex marriage is sinful based on the biblical teachings of their church. The ministers held that marriage, in their view, is both sacred and holy and is something joined by God, not man. Thus, to all of them, same-sex marriage was an unambiguous religious issue based on firm theological opposition toward same-sex marriage. Miller (2009) argues that the issue of same-sex marriage can be perceived either as a civil rights issue or as a religious issue for African Americans, and this potential division on the perception of the same-sex marriage issue might have divided minority voters in California in 2008. For example, the National Association for the Advancement of Colored People (NAACP) supported same-sex marriage and disagreed with Proposition 8. The NAACP supported the nondiscrimination and equality of marriage. This move by the NAACP might make it appear that there is division among African Americans. However, Miller (2009) finds that for African Americans, Proposition 8 was mostly a religious issue rather than a civil rights issue, and religious motivation drove African American support toward Proposition 8 in California (Miller, 2009, p. 58). In addition, African Americans were more supportive of Proposition 8 than whites—58% to 49%, respectively (Egan & Sherrill, 2009, p. 26). Our finding is consistent with Miller's (2009) in that among the interviewees, the issue of same-sex marriage is more of a religious issue than an equal rights issue for African American church leaders. This view remained unchanged, based on our second interviews during the week of July 20, 2011.

None of the churches or leaders mobilized using conventional methods of political mobilization, and none of the ministers saw a substantial push from other local churches on the issue. This is related to the previous finding that all the interviewed ministers considered the issue of same-sex marriage an unequivocal doctrinal issue. It is not to downplay the implications and impact of LGBT issues and same-sex marriage, but their objection to same-sex marriage is firmly grounded on biblical teachings. This, to some degree, explains their seeming inaction or absence of formalized activism against same-sex marriage. There was a sense that ministers would not necessarily dignify the question of same-sex marriage by engaging in the conversation or activism on the issue.

More pressing and immediate community needs discourage activism on the issue of same-sex marriage. Limited resources discourage African American ministers and churches from engaging in the dialogue and activism on same-sex marriage. One minister said that larger churches have more to gain by mobilizing on the issue, but these are the churches that are able to put forth the money, time, and people to make such a mobilization possible. He argued that churches with fewer than 500 congregants could arguably lose people by sending the wrong message. A minister substantiated this claim when he disclosed that his annual income is based on how well he preaches. While making this remark jokingly, there is much truth in this statement, as all of the ministers lead small to intermediate congregations. Another minister said that there are other issues in their churches and neighborhoods that require immediate response. Same-sex marriage is just not as central as these other community needs. In sum, many ministers were heavily involved in addressing other community needs—youth programs, after-school programs, and other community involvements. The issue of same-sex marriage, in spite of its doctrinal significance, is considered a less relevant issue, and ministers tend to focus on more immediate and pressing needs of community and congregators.

Interestingly, some ministers pointed to a concern in media portrayal of African Americans to explain why African American churches do not necessarily mobilize on the issue using more formal channels of political participation. These ministers communicated that they are concerned about the skewed and negative portrayals of African Americans in the media. They were concerned about being misunderstood and portrayed in a wrong light. One minister had a radio program weekly, through which discussed doctrinal issues. The radio show was something he knew would get his message across and not be manipulated by the conventional media or institutions. Another minister pointed out that it is not necessary to approach and use the mainstream media to address the point of the Gospel, since churches move in a spiritual realm. This general mistrust in conventional media and political institutions may explain why African American church leaders decided not to be engaged in activism on the issue of same-sex marriage. Instead of using a conventional method of activism and political mobilization, they chose to engage in a less conventional and more individual form of activism. For example, a couple of ministers encouraged congregators to discuss the doctrinal teaching on the issue of same-sex marriage personally. Mistrust in a conventional media and political institution tends to discourage a more visible form of activism and political participation but encourage a more individual and less conventional activism. This view was again highlighted in the recent interview of Pastor Myrick: "Society has changed . . . the black church has not stepped back . . . the media has played a very bad part as far as the black church is concerned" (Brown, 2011, pp. 2–3). There was the fundamental distrust and suspicion that the media may present unfavorable or unfair portrayal of African American ministers or churches. This may contribute to the seeming absence of African American churches in the same-sex marriage battle.

More importantly, after we conducted our first set of interviews, New York State began preparing for same-sex marriage legislation to pass and thus legalizing same-sex marriage in New York. This was a prime time to examine if African American churches were considering themselves affected by this issue and observe any mobilization on an issue that now was something about to possibly occur in their own state. However, while ministers held that the word *marriage* was sacred, they did not observe any mobilization, nor did they mobilize themselves on the matter, citing a separation of church and state. Interestingly, they held that if the state would consider civil unions versus same-sex marriage, that churches would be more receptive to such. Their key premise, however, was the exemption that allowed churches, clergy, and other religious organizations to avoid performing same-sex marriages if their faith or beliefs were contrary to the soon-to-be state law. The ministers told us that the issue had not changed their opinions or those of their communities regarding same-sex marriage.

Concluding Remarks

The African American church leaders we interviewed demonstrate that these leaders do not support same-sex marriage based on strong and unequivocal doctrinal teaching in their view. Our analysis shows that the African American Christian community is divided on the issue, not on whether it is biblically sound but, rather, on whether it is a pressing issue that compels churches to galvanize. A general consensus was that this is a noteworthy and unequivocal religious issue. The African American Christian community in Buffalo, New York, does have more immediate issues and needs, as pointed out by the ministers we interviewed; the economy, healthcare, childcare, violence, and addiction are just some of those mentioned. Thus, although African American churches considered this a significant religious issue, there was no formalized and organized effort on the part of African American churches in the greater Buffalo area. Even with the churches that did mobilize on a small scale, they never appeared to mobilize using traditional and formal channels of political participation on the issue. Our finding shows that there is still deep-rooted doubt about conventional media and their portrayal of African Americans. This distrust led African Americans to mobilize using more personal and less conventional methods, if they engaged in this issue at all.

Our finding is consistent with the conclusions of the literature that some African American churches and leaders mobilized in a less than visible way. There were some mobilization efforts among African American ministers, such as at a meeting against Proposition 8 (Abrajano, 2010) or in Washington, D.C., at an anti–same-sex-marriage rally (Siker, 2007). However, none of these responses were substantial or substantiated. In addition, our analysis shows that there are a number of factors that limit mobilization of African American churches. Our analysis shows that smaller churches have an issue with media portrayal of the larger community issues that discourage them to act on the issue of same-sex marriage. A lack of substantial financial capabilities and manpower is another factor that discourages such mobilization.[4]

For future study, we hope to expand this study and interview more ministers in the greater Buffalo area to uncover more insights into African American churches and their mobilization on the issue of same-sex marriage. The literature on this issue has not necessarily addressed the minority involvement in the dialogue and activism on the issue of same-sex marriage. By bringing the issue to light through our study, our goal is to close the gap in the literature and attempt to solve the puzzle that exists with African American churches and same-sex marriage.

Appendix: Interview Questions

Personal Questions

1. Name
2. Age
3. Gender
4. Race
5. Education (circle all that apply): Years of education?
   a. High school diploma/GED
   b. Associate's degree
   c. Bachelor's degree
   d. Master's degree
   e. Doctoral/professional degree (Ph.D./Ed.D./D.Div./J.D.)
   f. Seminary/religious degree
6. Public or private institution?
7. Years of religious education?
8. Did you go to religious school at any point prior to college?
   a. If so, when?
9. What is the address and zip code of your residence?
10. Do you:
    a. Own
    b. Rent

c. Church pays for housing
d. Other
11. How long have you lived at your current address?
12. Are you married?
    a. Yes
    b. No
    c. Divorced
    d. Widowed
    e. Never married
    f. Separated
13. Do you have children?
    a. How many?
    b. Ages?
14. What is your annual income?
15. Were you religious growing up?
16. Were you raised in a religious family?
17. Why did you become a minister?
18. What denomination do you minister to?
19. Why did you select this denomination to minister to?
20. What is the doctrine of your ministry?
21. How many years have you been a minister?
22. What is the current address and zip code of your ministry?
23. How long have your served at that location?
24. Have you served at any other ministries?
    a. If so, how many? How long?
25. What is the size of your current congregation?
26. What is the predominant race of your current congregation? With your best estimate:
27. Is your congregation made up of more professional or blue-collar workers?
28. What is the average income of your current congregation?
29. Is community involvement important to your congregation?
30. If so, how is your congregation involved in the community?
31. What social programs does your church have for the community?
    a. After-school program at your church?
    b. Do you have a school at your church?
    c. Bible study program
    d. Summer camp/retreat
    e. Fundraisers for the community
    f. Summer lunch program
    g. Others

Political-Social View Questions **
(cannot ask or discuss party affiliation)

32. Are you a registered voter?
33. Interested in politics?
34. Did you vote in 2008?
   a. Yes
   b. No
35. Do you regularly vote?
   a. Yes
   b. No
36. Your political ideology is:
   a. Strong liberal
   b. Weak liberal
   c. Liberal leaning moderate
   d. Strong moderate
   e. Moderate leaning conservative
   f. Weak conservative
   g. Strong conservative
   h. I do not know
37. Do you follow politics on:
   a. TV?
   b. Radio?
   c. Internet?
   d. Newspaper?
38. Are you a member of any political organizations? (Not party related)
39. Have you attended any political meetings?
40. Are you politically involved in your community?
41. What is the most important issue in politics right now, in your opinion?
42. What is the most important issue in politics right now, in the opinion of your congregation?
43. Should a religious institution support a particular political party?
44. Should a religious institution support any particular political candidates?
45. Does (has) your congregation support(ed) any political candidates?
46. Have any political activities been hosted or sponsored by your church?
47. Do you speak of politics or discuss the current political issues/events in your sermons?

Religious Ideology Questions: Same-Sex Marriage and Homosexuality in Church

48. What is your view on your Holy Book?
    a. Word of God
    b. Translated Word of God
    c. Solely written by man
    d. Is made up of fables
    e. I do not know
49. How important is the issue of homosexuality at your church?
50. How do you address that issue?
51. Homosexuality is:
    a. A psychological problem
    b. A manifestation of evil
    c. Something someone is born with
    d. A lifestyle
    e. None of the above
    f. I do not know
    g. Other
52. Homosexuality is a personal choice?
    a. True
    b. False
    c. I do not know
53. Do you know anyone who is a homosexual?
    a. Yes
    b. No
    c. I do not know
54. If yes, who? (select all that apply)
    a. Self
    b. Family member
    c. Co-worker
    d. Close friend
    e. Acquaintance
    f. Neighbor
    g. Congregant
    h. Other (who)
55. Should homosexuals have all of the same rights as heterosexual couples?
56. Should homosexuals be allowed to adopt?
57. Should homosexuals be allowed to serve in the military?
58. Should homosexuals be allowed to teach in an elementary school?

59. Should homosexuals be allowed to teach in a middle school?
60. Should homosexuals be allowed to teach in a high school?
61. Should homosexuals be allowed to teach in a college?
62. Should homosexuals be allowed to serve as a minister in a Christian church?
63. Should homosexuals be allowed to serve as public officials?
64. The "don't ask, don't tell" policy is a policy that:*
    a. Is crucial to the functionality of the military
    b. Is important simply so that gays are not discriminated against
    c. Is not important
    d. Should be repealed
    e. I do not know
65. How important is the issue of same-sex marriage at your church?
66. How do you address that issue?
67. Is same-sex marriage a religious doctrine issue?
68. Is same-sex marriage an issue that only pertains to homosexuals?
69. Should same-sex marriages be granted on the basis of equal rights?
70. Would you support same-sex marriage in your house of worship?
71. Would you support a secular (non-religious) same-sex marriage?
72. How much does your congregation support or approve of same-sex marriage?
    a. Fully
    b. Somewhat
    c. Neutral
    d. Little
    e. None
    f. I do not know
73. How much do you support or approve of same-sex marriage?
    a. Fully
    b. Somewhat
    c. Neutral
    d. Little
    e. None
    f. I do not know
74. How does your church voice its opinion on same-sex marriage?
75. Are African-Americans homophobic?
76. If yes, how homophobic are African-Americans?
    a. Fully
    b. Somewhat

---

*Note: This question was asked before the "don't ask, don't tell policy" was repealed.

      c. Neutral

      d. Little

      e. Not at all

77. Is same-sex marriage an issue in African-American Churches?

78. What have you observed other African-American churches doing, in relation to expressing their opinions on same-sex marriage?

79. Has the recent New York State bill on same-sex marriage affected your church?

80. Has the bill changed or influenced your opinion on same-sex marriage?

81. Has the bill changed or influenced your congregation's opinion on same-sex marriage?

References

Abrajano, M. (2010). Are blacks and latinos responsible for the passage of Proposition 8? Analyzing voter attitudes on California's proposal to ban same-sex marriage in 2008. *Political Research Quarterly, 63*(4), 922–932.

Alex-Assensoh, Y., & Assensoh, A. B. (2001). Inner-city contexts, church attendance, and African-American political participation. *Journal of Politics, 63*(3), 886–901.

Archdiocese, N. (2011). Statement of the Bishops of New York on SSM. Retrieved from http://www.archny.org/news-events/news-press-releases/index.cfm?i=20810.

Barnes, S. L. (2005). Black church culture and community action. *Social Forces, 84*(2), 968–994.

Barron, M. (2008, November 28). Christian vote key in Prop 8. *National Catholic Reporter.* http://ncronline.org/node/2637.

Blain, G., & Lovett, K. (2009, March 3). Governor Paterson's approval rating plummets 20 points hitting historic low. *Daily News New York.* http://articles.nydailynews.com/2009-03-03/local/17918083_1_governor-patersonapproval-rating-lee-miringoff.

Brown, R. (2011). Baptist Ministerial Alliance wants same sex marriage act repealed. *Minority Reporter.* http://www.minorityreporter.net/fullstory.php?id=545.

Brown, R. E., & Wolford, M. L. (1994). Religious resources and African American political action. *National Political Science Review, 4*, 30–48.

Calhoun-Brown, A. (2000). Upon this rock: The black church, nonviolence, and the Civil Rights movement. *PS: Political Science and Politics, 33*(2), 169–174.

California: Same-sex couples per 1,000 households by census tract (adjusted) (n.d.). *Census snapshot: 2010* Retrieved Feb. 6, 2012, from http://williamsinstitute.law.ucla.edu/census-snapshots/california/.

Changing faiths: Latinos and the transformation of American religion. (2007, April 25). http://www.pewforum.org/Changing-Faiths-Latinos-and-the-Transformation-of-American-Religion.aspx.

Cunningham, M. T. (2009). The Christian coalition for Catholics? The Massachusetts model. *Review of Religious Research, 51*(1), 55–70.

Egan, P., & Sherrill, K. (2009). *California's Proposition 8: Race and voting on same-sex marriage.* Paper presented at the American Political Science Association Conference.

Goodridge v. Department of Public Health 798 N.E.2d 941 Mass. (2003).

Griffin, H. (2000). Their own received them not: African American lesbians and gays in black churches. *Theology and Sexuality, 6*(12), 88–100.

Harris. (1999). *Something within: Religion in African American political activism.* New York: Oxford University Press.

Healy, J. (2011). Band-Aid solutions: New York's piecemeal attempt to address legal issues created by DOMA in conjunction with advances in surrogacy. *Pace Law Review, 31*(2), 691–720.

Kaplan, T. (2011, July 23). After long wait, gay couples marry in New York. *New York Times.* http://www.nytimes.com/2011/07/25/nyregion/after-long-wait-same-sex-couples-marry-in-new-york.html?pagewanted=all.

Khan, S. (2009). Tying the not: How they got Prop 8. *Gay and Lesbian Review Worldwide, 16*(2), 22–24.

King, G., Keohane, R. O., & Verba, S. (1994). *Designing social inquiry: Scientific interference in qualitative research.* Princeton, NJ: Princeton University Press.

McDaniel, E. L., & McClerking, H. K. (2005). Who belongs? Understanding how socioeconomic stratification shapes the characteristics of black political church members. *National Political Science Review, 10*, 15–28.

Miller, K. P. (2009). The Democratic Coalition's religious divide: Why California voters supported Obama but not same-sex marriage. *Revue française d'allergologie,* (1), 46–62.

Moore, M. R. (2010). Black and gay in L.A.: The relationships black lesbians and gay men have with their racial and religious communities. In D. Hunt & A.-C. Ramon (Eds.), *Black Los Angeles: American dreams and racial realities* (pp. 40). New York: New York University Press.

NY governor to propose legalizing same-sex marriage. (2009, April 14). *CNN.* http://articles.cnn.com/2009-04-14/politics/ny.same.sex.marriage_1_same-sex-marriage-david-paterson-full-marriage-equality?_s=PM:POLITICS.

Paterson's popularity continues to slide. (2009, February 24). *Associated Press.* http://www.syracuse.com/news/index.ssf/2009/02/patersons_popularity_continues.html.

Sayre, B., Bode, L., Shah, D., Wilcox, D., & Shah, C. (2010). Agenda setting in a digital age: Tracking attention to California Proposition 8 in social media, online news and conventional news. *Policy & Internet, 2*(2), 7–32.

Schubert, F., & Flint, J. (2009, February). Passing Prop 8: Smart timing and strategic messaging convinced California voters to support traditional marriage. *Politics,* 45–47.

Sherkat, D. E., De Vries, K. M., & Creek, S. (2010). Race, religion, and opposition to same-sex marriage. *Social Science Quarterly, 91*(1), 80–98.

Siker, J. S. (2007). *Homosexuality and religion: An encyclopedia.* Westport, CT: Greenwood Press.

Thorson, K., Ekdale, B., Borah, P., Namkoong, K., & Shah, C. (2010). YouTube and Proposition 8. *Information, Communication & Society, 13*(3), 325–349.

Ward, E. G. (2005). Homophobia, hypermasculinity and the US black church. *Culture, Health & Sexuality, 7*(5), 493–504.

Notes

1. It is important to note that Proposition 8 was on the ballot in 2008 when Barack Obama was running for president. Many scholars have credited Obama's presence for the increase of African Americans at the polls.

2. See the full press release by Archdiocese of New York Against Same-Sex Marriage: http://www.archny.org/news-events/news-press-releases/index.cfm?i=20810.

3. The bill, introduced by the former governor Eliot Spitzer, passed in the Assembly 85 to 61 but did not pass in the state Senate. See the full CNN report: http://articles.cnn.com/2009-04-14/politics/ny.same.sex.marriage_1_same-sex-marriage-david-paterson-full-marriage-equality?_s=PM:POLITICS.

4. Although our analysis did not necessarily delve into the issue, due to the decentralized nature of African American churches, it is possible that they are not unable to come to a unified front. Hierarchical churches, like the Roman Catholic Church or Mormon Church, were able to have a unified voice via the structure of their churches. The various African American churches, by nature, are separate institutions that speak with their own voices—voices that are not always united.

Cultural Diversity

22

Multi Kontra Culti

The Gypsy Punk Counterculture

Alan Ashton-Smith

Introduction

The diversity of the American population means that diverse forms of music can be heard in the United States. Indeed, Ronald Radano and Michael Daley (2001) have stated that "the relationship of race to music is so fundamental to the American experience that it identifies a crucial linkage or even an archetype" (p. 63). This is not a particularly new phenomenon—well-established genres that range from country through zydeco to jazz derive their sounds from the multicultural history of the United States—but Gypsy Punk, the form of music that I discuss in this chapter, has come about very recently. Gypsy Punk emerged in New York in the early 2000s as a self-consciously multicultural form of music and counterculture, and most of the musicians involved in it are migrants to the United States. The best-known Gypsy Punk band, and the group that first began to describe itself as Gypsy Punk, is Gogol Bordello. Gogol Bordello is my focus in this chapter partly because of its prominence in the Gypsy Punk scene but also due to its use of the term *multi kontra culti* to describe its stance on multiculturalism—which can be defined as the endorsement of multiple national or ethnic cultures forming a single society. Despite Gogol Bordello having coined the phrase *multi kontra culti*, it has never fully laid out its position. My aim in this chapter is to determine what that position is.

Gypsy Punk takes elements of its music and visual style from punk and adds melodies, instrumentation, and lyrics that are informed by what is known as "Gypsy" music. This is of course a vague term, as many different styles of music are played by diverse Romani populations, but the main geographical reference point for Gypsy Punk music is Eastern Europe. To this mixture is added other global music styles, including reggae and Latin American music. In many cases, the immigrant musicians who play Gypsy Punk introduce musical elements from their own backgrounds. Gogol Bordello, a Gypsy Punk band, was formed by Ukrainian migrant Eugene Hütz and includes immigrants from Russia, Israel, Ethiopia, and Ecuador. Hütz is a quarter Romani and foregrounds this part of his heritage in the band's music—as is fitting for the frontman of a band that sets out to work with "Gypsy" music traditions. However, he also ensures that his identity as an immigrant remains prominent. A number of Gogol Bordello's songs describe the immigrant experience; the immigrant narrators of these songs often reject assimilation, choosing instead to retain their own identities.

In addition to their engagement with issues facing the Roma and immigrants, Gogol Bordello frequently comments on globalization and multiculturalism. As such, it might seem a particularly political band, but Hütz has rejected this suggestion. During an interview (Kuftinoff, 2011), he declared that he had lost interest in the conversation when the word *politics* was introduced. However, this does not take away from the fact that Gogol Bordello's music often includes clear political messages. In the video for their song "Immigraniada," for example, they comment on immigration policy, declaring that "No human being is illegal"; and in "Break the Spell," they speak out in support of Roma rights. Since Hütz and his colleagues are reluctant to outwardly engage with politics, in assessing Gypsy Punk, one of the tasks of academics is to determine what its politics are. In an attempt to do this, I consider the relationships that Gypsy Punk has with globalization and multiculturalism. For each of these concepts, I consider examples from Gogol Bordello's work in which these issues are raised, and from there I establish what is meant by the concept of *multi kontra culti*.

Globalization

Globalization is not just a process that allows, for example, labor and capital to move between borders with little or no restriction; it also allows for bands to be globally recognized. In 2002, during the Whitney Museum of American Art's biennial exhibition, Gogol Bordello gave a performance and published an artist's statement to accompany their work. This manifesto-like document was highly critical of postmodernity, which was aligned with the notion that "everything is been done [sic]" (Hütz, n.d.a), and declared that the band's task was to "provoke audience out of post-modern aesthetic swamp [sic]" (Hütz, n.d.a). However, it is arguable that Gypsy Punk, in its amalgamation of different forms of music and culture, its appropriation of elements from an array of cultures and languages, and its self-conscious awareness of influences such as punk and traditional "Gypsy" music, might be thought of as being postmodern itself.

Fredric Jameson (1991) described postmodern culture as "global, yet American," adding that it is "the internal and superstructural expression of a whole new wave of American military and economic domination throughout the world" (p. 5). In the context of Gypsy Punk, this is a particularly interesting point. As a band that came together in New York, Gogol Bordello is also "global, yet American" and, as we will see later, the band is arguably postmodern despite its professed opposition toward postmodernity. But if we are able to leave aside the potential contradiction here and consider more of the messages propounded by Gogol Bordello, we may see that it is the state of the global in the postmodern era that concerns Gypsy Punk. This refers to the increasing navigability and accessibility of the world, which is regarded as an important characteristic of the postmodern age. In 1990, David Harvey discussed the idea of "time-space compression," (p. 240) whereby the time it takes to traverse space is diminished; in the intervening 20 years, this has become even more pronounced. It is now possible to travel on a global level with relative ease and speed, and new technologies mean that the movement of information is constantly becoming quicker. One consequence of this is the sense that places are becoming increasingly homogenized. The streets of large cities are now lined with the same shops, and billboards advertise the same products, in almost every country in the developed world. Meanwhile, the more unique aspects of these places are demolished by global brands, and it becomes harder to find cultural differences between places that may be geographically very far removed from one another.

For Gogol Bordello, the distinct identity of specific places is highly important. The multinational composition of the band is one of its defining features, and if there is little difference between different places, then the hybrid identities of the members of the band are lost. The members confront the risk of homogeneity in their song "Through the Roof 'n' Underground," in which they describe how "The local cultures are dying and dying / The programmed robots are buying and buying." In order to escape this situation, they claim that the alternative is to go "through the roof" or "underground," revealing their attitude that globalization is something to be avoided because of its homogenizing effect. Criticisms of globalization often take the form of economic critiques—large corporations that use labor and resources in the developing world are accused of exploitation, and economic inequality on a global level is said to be rising—but in commenting on the demise of localized cultures, Gypsy Punk addresses its impact on culture.

Of course, the cultural effects of globalization are derived from its economics, since a nation's culture is part of its economy, and culture is marketed and sold for profit. In the same way that global fast food chains sell the same burgers around the world, record labels market the same music internationally. As an American band that is known internationally, Gogol Bordello is in fact bound up inextricably with this economic system, yet it rejects the homogeneity that it entails. Hütz has said in an interview (Dansby, 2008) that it is "a big irony to hear my music described as celebrating globalization." Gypsy Punk thus rejects globalization while being caught up in the very system that it allegedly opposes: Although the music is marketed worldwide, the message is one of antiglobalization. As such, it is easy to regard Gogol Bordello as insincere. In a review of its 2002 album, *Multi Kontra Culti Vs. Irony*, on the music website *Pitchfork*, Michael Idov (2003) wrote that the record "feigns rage against fashionable bogeymen of globalization." However, the stance against globalization that Gogol Bordello claim to take seems to be so pronounced and so sustained that, almost a decade further into their career, it is difficult to read it as feigned.

In order to negotiate this debate, it is necessary to introduce the idea that there are two different types of globalization—the homogenizing and the hybrid. As we have seen, one of the consequences of globalization is its homogenizing effect on cultures. In Jameson's words, the world has become "global, yet American"; this suggests that the process of globalization begins in the United States. Anthony Giddens (1999) supports this viewpoint, noting that globalization "bears the strong imprint of American political and economic power" (p. 4). The template for the homogenized world that globalization produces is essentially Western. Critics of globalization argue that the world is becoming increasingly Westernized and that American culture, including fast food, American music, and the English language, is acquiring dominance worldwide. Indeed, Hütz (n.d.b) has vehemently criticized what he describes as the "Favoring of white, English-speaking product." However, it is arguable that this kind of homogenization is in fact limited to the economic aspects of globalization and that cultural globalization is less pronounced, as John Storey (2003) points out:

> Now it is one thing to point to the successful way in which capitalism as a global system has organized the world in terms of the commodity and the

market, but it is quite another to then claim that the result is a homogenized world culture. It is only possible to think this if you already think that commodities equal culture in an obvious and straightforward way. (p. 110)

But even if homogenization is something that impacts commodities rather than cultures, it is certainly the case that culture has changed as a result of globalization. Due to advances in communication and the increased ease of travel, it is now possible for music (and other cultural forms) from any given place to be heard all over the world. In this case, however, we see hybridity rather than homogeneity; it is not the case that a single culture is dominant on a global scale. The reasons for this lie in the increasing value that is placed on localized cultures, as is observed by Giddens (1999), who notes that:

Globalisation is the reason for the revival of local cultural identities in different parts of the world. If one asks, for example, why the Scots want more independence in the UK, or why there is a strong separatist movement in Quebec, the answer is not to be found only in their cultural history. Local nationalisms spring up as a response to globalising tendencies, as the hold of older nation-states weakens. (p. 13)

This is also the case with culture. When the same Western pop songs are replayed around the globe, traditional music is reinvoked as a reaction. In many cases, the reaction occurs on a local level, but the growth of "time-space compression" means that these localized forms of culture are accessible worldwide. The result is a hybridity in which indigenous forms of music are mixed with outside influences and sometimes combined with Western popular forms. We can see examples of this hybridity in genres like Afropop, bhangra and, of course, in Gypsy Punk. Access to global forms of music has come about through two different channels, technology and migration. Technological advances mean that recordings are more readily available on the Internet, and any kind of music can be listened to anywhere in the world. More significantly, immigrants have taken their music with them to the countries in which they have settled; over time, this music has gradually been influenced by the music of the host country and vice versa.

The immigrant experience is an important theme in Gogol Bordello's work. The majority of the band's members are immigrants; they are part of a community of migrants whose music is a manifestation of the hybridity that globalization gives rise to. Gogol Bordello was formed in New York, but its work contains a mixture of musical influences that were brought to that city by its migrant members. Yet, in the band's presentation of the immigrant experience, the idea of a hybrid form is avoided. The immigrants who appear in Gogol Bordello's songs reject assimilation, continuing to use their own languages and traditions. "Avenue B" is a good example of a song in which there is prominent use of languages other than English; in this case Russian is used for several lines, including "*Nesmotrja na SE. SHE. A. ne poterjal azarta / Buhaju strogo kazdoje 8-e marta.*" Translated into English, this means, "In spite of the USA I did not lose the passion / I still drink heavily every 8th of March." March 8 refers to International Woman's Day, a holiday that is observed in many countries, particularly those that were formerly part of the USSR. "Avenue B" therefore presents the figure of an immigrant who has chosen not to assimilate in the way that many new arrivals in the United States have done.

This does not mean, however, that hybridity is rejected or prevented by Gogol Bordello. In fact, the distinctness of the Russian immigrant community described in "Avenue B" means that when it is combined with the extant culture of New York, the effect is all the more striking. Such hybridity can be found throughout Gogol Bordello's music both musically, in the way that traditional Eastern European music is combined with punk, and lyrically, in the use of multiple languages that is characteristic of its work. However, the fact that Gogol Bordello's music is clearly in favor of multiple cultures coming together but at the same time claiming an opposition toward globalization, this kind of contradiction demands unpacking. In some cases, the terms *globalization* and *multiculturalism* are often associated with one another. Both have come about as a result of the time-space compression described by Harvey, and both entail different cultures coming together. Gogol Bordello may claim to be opponents of globalization and the postmodern environment that has contributed to its growth, but another product of postmodernism and the time-space compression is multiculturalism, and this is also an important influence on their work.

Multiculturalism

As a postmodern, multicultural band, Gogol Bordello is in fact impacted by globalization more than the members of the band might be comfortable with. Globalization has come about partly as a result of the increased ease of the movement and communication of people and culture between disparate locations. However, travel and migration between different countries has also become more straightforward and, as a result, many global cities have become home to a wider range of people than ever before. People from different ethnic and cultural backgrounds live alongside each other, and a country like the United States that promotes multiculturalism as an "unofficial" policy recognizes and celebrates the cultural practices of these groups. However, the distinct identities of immigrant groups does persist—as shown in the song "Avenue B," in which a Russian migrant voices his decision not to fully assimilate to the American way of life.

It is hardly surprising that Gogol Bordello should champion multiculturalism, since the band is very much a product of a multicultural society. Its particular style and ethos is a consequence of the band being made up of immigrants from several different countries who came together in one place, New York City. New York is as significant to Gogol Bordello's sound as the origins of the musicians who make up the band and is often used to symbolize the multicultural environment. Gogol Bordello first began to engage with their multicultural element in a self-conscious way in 2002— the same year that the members of the band issued their manifesto as part of their Whitney Museum performance—when they released their second album, *Multi Kontra Culti vs. Irony*. Gogol Bordello claims to oppose irony, which is equated with inauthenticity in the band's manifesto, and the concept of *multi kontra culti* is presented in the title as if it is a weapon against irony. While the album channels styles of global music including East European folk and the guitar music of Russian Roma, it is grounded in New York; there are references to various locations in this city throughout the album. The global sounds are not there to transport listeners away from the USA; they are intended as signifiers of America's multicultural population.

The New York locations that are referenced in the album include East Houston Street in the Lower East Side and Brighton Beach—both areas that have strong associations with immigrant communities. Throughout the 20th century, the Lower East Side served as a settling point for new arrivals, first Russians and Eastern European Jews and, later, Asian and Puerto Rican migrants to the United States. Brighton Beach has a large Russian community, and since Gogol Bordello includes two Russian musicians as well as the Ukrainian Hütz, it is an important part of New York that is described in the band's music. The use of these locations is supplemented by the inclusion of multiple languages—not only Russian, but also Romani and Spanish. The array of languages that can be heard on the album creates the impression of a landscape populated by people with a broad range of backgrounds, and this is exactly what Gogol Bordello represents. Along with the appropriation of styles of music from Eastern Europe, Russia, and Latin America and references to areas of New York that have large immigrant populations, the band ensures that its album has markedly multicultural overtones.

While *Multi Kontra Culti vs. Irony* bears the name of Gogol Bordello's brand of multiculturalism, it is perhaps best exemplified in the song "Think Locally Fuck Globally," which is featured on Gogol Bordello's 2005 album

Gypsy Punks. The essential message of this song is contained entirely within its title, but this can be interpreted in several ways. Firstly, and most obviously, it is a criticism of globalization and a call for the promotion of more localized cultures and products. It is important to note that the local cultures that are referred to need not be indigenous ones, since Gogol Bordello is visibly supportive of migration and the free movement of people between countries. Since 2010, the band has refused to perform in Arizona in response to the state's Senate Bill 1070, which brought into place more stringent measures against illegal immigration. Therefore, this song is not a plea to think primarily of one's local culture but to consider the range of localized cultures that exist globally rather than reducing them to one globalized culture. On another level, there is also the sexual element in the song's title, which can be read as encouraging the engagement with people of other cultures and from other cultures: the exhortation "fuck globally" seems to call on listeners to travel the world and "reproduce" with as wide a range of people as possible.

Gogol Bordello seems far less concerned with ethnic difference than with cultural diversity, and while the multiracial makeup of the band certainly suggests a broad mixture of cultures, they also promote such diversity through other means, for example, their use of multiple languages. David Steigerwald (2004) has observed that "One of the most important indications that the breakdown of physical isolation threatens cultural integrity is the steady erosion of linguistic diversity" (p. 123). He goes on to note that "Ninety-five percent of the world's 6000 languages are spoken by only five percent of its population." He also describes a "concentration of linguistic power" in widely spoken languages such as English, Spanish, Mandarin, and Hindi (p. 123). Gogol Bordello's lyrics are primarily in English: It is unlikely that the band would have achieved any degree of popular success in the United States if its songs were not sung mainly in English. However, many other languages can be heard in the band's work. Of these, Russian and Ukrainian appear most frequently, but significant sections of many songs are sung in Romani. Spanish, Portuguese, Italian, Romanian, and Amharic can also be found in their lyrics. Although English remains dominant, this linguistic diversity serves as a reminder that the use of other languages can have a particular effect when deployed in music. In Gogol Bordello's music, two or more languages can often be heard in the same song. The music reflects the way in which speakers of different languages live side by side in multicultural societies and, in their use of multiple languages, Gogol Bordello represents America's multilingual society.

However, their template for multiculturalism is not solely an American one. Hütz has described how the Carpathian region in Western Ukraine, where he lived as a teenager, was diverse in a way that foreshadowed the society he would later encounter in New York City. In an interview (Kessler, 2006), he described New York City as a "melting pot of Ukrainian, Russian, Hungarian and Romanian cultures." This range of nationalities and cultures may partly explain the use of Eastern European cultural elements in Gogol Bordello's work. Elements of music and culture appear to be taken from several different Eastern European countries. Themes from Romanian folk songs are mixed with vocal stylings that originate with Hungarian Roma and Balkan brass sounds. In addition, Hütz has created a fictional country called Hützovina, which first appeared in their debut album *Voi-La Intruder* in 1999, and which reappears in *Multi Kontra Culti vs. Irony*, specifically in the song "Occurrence on the Border." Hützovina seems, at first, like a generic Balkan state. But in being generic, it has no dominant culture that results in the suppression of nondominant cultures. Combined with the fact that Hützovina is sung about by musicians whose nationalities range from Israeli to Ecuadorian, this means that it is portrayed as a multicultural place.

When Hützovina is injected into New York City, as is the case in *Multi Kontra Culti vs. Irony*, its multiculturalism is compounded. A more pronounced instance of this can be seen in the song "Dogs Were Barking," which appears on the album *Gypsy Punks*. As with *Multi Kontra Culti vs. Irony*, this is an album that is grounded in multicultural New York City, and "Dogs Were Barking" is one of several tracks that directly references a location in the city. The song begins with a description of the chaotic hedonism of a stereotypical Romani wedding celebration, which includes monkeys and dancing bears; a multicultural Eastern European atmosphere is created through the prominence of violin and accordion and the use of Russian lyrics. This atmosphere is then displaced to the Lower East Side in Manhattan when Hütz sings of meeting someone at the intersection of Broadway and Canal Street in a "disco radical transglobal," which refers to a Bulgarian bar called the Mehanata where Hütz used to DJ regularly. The idea of the transglobal is also important to Gogol Bordello. The "Gypsy" figures that are so integral to their work are constantly travelling on a global scale. In this case, the "disco radical transglobal" becomes the epitome of multiculturalism, where many different languages and cultures are seen to converge.

Gogol Bordello's transglobal music might seem to evoke the distances covered and countries visited by migrants, as well as by the Romani people, but in fact they frequently tie their transglobalism to specific places. These sites of multiculturalism may be localized, as with the Mehanata, or they may be cities like New York or Rio de Janeiro, the latter of which is featured prominently throughout the 2010 album *Transcontinental Hustle*. As we have seen, in the example of Hützovina, such sites may even be fictional. In its use of the Gypsy Punk genre, Gogol Bordello seeks to evoke an environment in which immigrant and minority communities are prominent. This is very much the case with their use of "Gypsy" figures. In the song "Sally," a girl from Nebraska starts what is described as a "revolution" after meeting a group of "Gypsies"; in "Underdog World Strike," the "Gypsy part of town" is presented as a conduit to cultural exchange, where punk, hip-hop, and reggae are combined with "Gypsy" music.

While this sounds overwhelmingly positive and suggests a successful multicultural society, multiculturalism is not without its critics. In his critique of multicultural America, Arthur M. Schlesinger, Jr. (1991) writes: "Multiculturalism arises as a reaction against Anglo- or Eurocentrism; but at what point does it pass over into an ethnocentrism of its own? The very word, instead of referring as it should to all cultures, has come to refer only to non–Western, non–White cultures" (p. 74). This argument is not without relevance here, as the cultures engaged with in Gypsy Punk are not exclusively non–Western or non–White; but in the Gypsy Punk version of multiculturalism, we can see that it is possible to have a multicultural society in which the multicultural ethnocentricity described by Schlesinger is avoided. Gogol Bordello has successfully positioned itself outside of non–Western, non–White culture but has not abandoned it completely. In fact, by rejecting the term *world music* and citing as influences the primarily White Western genre of punk alongside the more exotic traditions of "Gypsy" and cabaret, Gogol Bordello ensures that it is thoroughly multicultural without being too detached from the dominant culture. Although the punk underpinnings are almost always apparent, many other voices are at play. Gogol Bordello's brand of multiculturalism is therefore both pervasive and inclusive.

Conclusion: *Multi Kontra Culti*

The name that Gogol Bordello has chosen for its form of multiculturalism is *multi kontra culti*. This designation calls to mind not only multiculturalism but also counterculture, and suggests that a combination of the two is desirable. Hütz has indicated that there is a mainstream of multiculturalism, exemplified in world music compilation CDs, which Gogol Bordello strives to avoid. He has rejected the idea that the band's music might be classified as "world music" and has spoken critically of much of the material that is packaged as such. Hütz (n.d.b) explains, "Even if you are a curious soul and ventured out to get something different, you very well end up with Buddha

Bar or Putamya [sic] record products which promises you something exotic but basically are traps for yuppies who would like to fancy themselves cultured." Such world music compilations are presented as being inauthentic in comparison with the Gypsy Punk that is produced by Gogol Bordello.

As we have seen, the album *Multi Kontra Culti vs. Irony* is grounded in New York City but includes elements that seem to go beyond the perimeters of a multicultural city—such as the use of the fictional Balkan state of Hützovina as the setting for "Occurrence on the Border," the Romani lyrics of "Baro Foro," and "Hats Off to Kolpakoff," which references Russian Roma guitarist Sasha Kolpakov. The album is characterized by a combination of global and American cultures, and the use of multiple languages and diverse musical styles creates an atmosphere that is both global and American. Writing about the specific associations that are created by music, Simon Frith (1987) has written, "Accordions played a certain way mean France, bamboo flutes China, just as steel guitars mean country, drum machines the urban dance" (p. 148). In Gypsy Punk, many such associations mount up to produce a new form of music that is recognizable as a representation of an era in which globalization and multiculturalism are inescapable.

Although globalization and multiculturalism are clearly different, they are unavoidably connected in that both are the products of a globalized era in which the distance between disparate places is diminished. This connection is what Gogol Bordello seeks to express with *multi kontra culti* to describe their expression of multiculturalism. What they oppose is the homogenized state that has burgeoned as a result of globalization and any homogenized culture that is produced within this state. This kind of homogenized culture may appear to have a distinct cultural value, but Gogol Bordello shows that it is in fact motivated by the desires and demands of a globalized society. As we have seen, Gypsy Punk is intended as an authentic response to globalization, and Gogol Bordello purports not to subscribe to the prevailing desires of globalization. Writing on globalization and its effects, David Steigerwald (2004) has pointed out that "Instead of the cozy global village, it is closer to the truth to say that we are falling into lives of ill-defined deracination. We are all becoming rootless" (p. 2). It is this sense of being rootless that Gogol Bordello seeks to overcome: *multi kontra culti* is an alternative set of values for the production of culture and music in a multicultural age.

References

Dansby, A. (2008, March 11). The father of Gypsy punk. *Chron Entertainment.* http://www.chron.com/disp/story.mpl/ent/5610601.html.

Frith, S. (1987). Towards an aesthetic of popular music. In Richard Leppert & Susan McClary (Eds.), *Music and society: The politics of composition, performance and reception* (pp. 133–149). Cambridge, UK: Cambridge University Press.

Giddens, A. (1999). *Runaway world: How globalisation is reshaping our lives.* London: Profile.

Harvey, D. (1990). *The condition of postmodernity.* Cambridge, MA: Blackwell.

Hütz, E. (n.d.a). Gogol Bordello artist's statement. *Gogol Bordello's website.* http://www.gogolbordello.com/the-band/mission/.

Hütz, E. (n.d.b). Intro word. *Gogol Bordello's Myspace page.* http://www.myspace.com/gogolbordello.

Idov, M. (2003, April 1). Album review: Gogol Bordello: Multi kontra culti vs. irony. *Pitchfork.* http://www.pitchfork.com/reviews/albums/3494-multi-kontra-culti-vs-irony/.

Jameson, F. (1991). *Postmodernism or, the cultural logic of late capitalism.* London: Verso.

Kessler, S. (2006, July). Gypsy punk rocker Eugene Hütz. *Passport Moscow.* http://www.passportmagazine.ru/article/477/.

Kuftinoff, N. (2011, January 27). An Interview with Eugene Hütz and Santeri Ahlgren. *sixteentwelve88.* http://sixteentwelve88.livejournal.com/47666.html#cutid1.

Radano, R., & Daley, M. (2001). Race, ethnicity, and nationhood. In Ellen Koskoff (Ed.), *The Garland encyclopedia of world music, vol. 3: The United States and Canada* (pp. 63–75). New York: Garland.

Schlesinger, A. M., Jr. (1991). *The disuniting of America: Reflections on a multicultural society.* New York: W. W. Norton.

Steigerwald, D. (2004). *Culture's vanities: The paradox of cultural diversity in a globalized world.* Lanham, MD: Rowman & Littlefield.

Storey, J. (2003). *Inventing popular culture.* Malden, MA: Blackwell.

Discography

Gogol Bordello. (1999). *Voi-la intruder* [CD]. Brooklyn, NY: Rubric.

Gogol Bordello. (2002). *Multi kontra culti vs. irony* [CD]. Brooklyn, NY: Rubric.

Gogol Bordello. (2005). *Gypsy punks* [CD]. Los Angeles, CA: SideOneDummy.

Gogol Bordello. (2007). *Super taranta* [CD]. Los Angeles, CA: SideOneDummy.

Gogol Bordello. (2010). *Trans-continental hustle* [CD]. New York, NY: Columbia.

23

The Power of Language in the Construction and Representation of Mixed-Race Identities in Nora Okja Keller's *Comfort Woman* and *Fox Girl*

Cynthia Lytle

I touch each part of her body, waiting until I see recognition in her eyes. I wait until I see that she knows all of what I touch is her and hers to name in her own mind, before language dissects her into pieces that can be swallowed and digested by others not herself (Keller, 2000, p. 22).

U ntil the election of President Barack Obama, little attention has been brought to those whose heritage is multiracial. Most discussions about and representations of mixed-race identities[1] have centered on the "problem" of miscegenation. In the United States, the one-drop rule ensured that the race of the subordinate group was marked (Davis, 2002, p. 5), perpetuating the categorization of mixed-race people as the "Other." Moreover, despite claims that the United States is becoming a postracial society after the historic election of Barack Obama as the first "black president," President Obama's race is constantly under scrutiny. For example, in the 2010 U.S. Census, Obama described himself as "Black," leading to criticism directed at him for not identifying himself as mixed race.[2] Thus, in lieu of declaring American society postracial, it is arguably more appropriate to call it hyperracial, as renewed attention is placed on race and particularly on those individuals with multiracial heritages.[3]

The United States is not the only country in which mixed-race identity is scrutinized. In South Korea, for example, having a multiracial heritage is still mostly taboo, especially if the father is White or African American. Multiracialness was not an open topic until NFL player Hines Ward, whose father is African American and mother is Korean, was named MVP of Super Bowl XL in 2006. It was Ward's success that led Koreans to declare him one of their own. However, his mother was quick to point out the societal ostracism she and her son faced for his mixed-race heritage when he was younger (Greenfield, 2006). It was this ostracism, for the most part, that compelled Ward's mother to leave her homeland for the United States, hoping that her son would not face the harsh treatment that most mixed-race people in Korea undergo (Youngmisuk, 2009).

The plight of mixed-race children, particularly Korean and White or Korean and African American, is illustrated in Nora Okja Keller's *Comfort Woman* (2000) and *Fox Girl* (2002), which are set in both Korea and the United States. *Comfort Woman* takes place during and after the Second World War and portrays the exploitation of Korean women in "comfort stations" under Japanese imperial authority and later by American missionaries. *Fox Girl* is set after the Korean War and depicts the racism and struggles of living in "camptowns," or red-light districts that resulted from the cooperation between Korean and American governments in the systematized prostitution of Korean women. As the communities in each novel characterize a coalescence of American and Korean cultures, it is strongly evident that language plays an important role in creating social hierarchies within these communities, particularly affecting the mixed-race children, who are caught between the two worlds, or in what Gloria Anzaldúa calls the "borderlands" (Anzaldúa, 1999, p. 19).

Through the use of Keller's novels, this chapter will explore the role of language in the construction and representation of multiracial identities, particularly of children who have a Korean mother and a White or African American father. These children live in the borderlands of Korean and American societies, as they are not fully accepted by either but are a part of both. This chapter will also demonstrate how historical, political, cultural, and environmental factors have affected and shaped multiracial identities of people with both Korean and American heritages. I argue that the subjugation of mixed-race Korean Americans[4] stems from the strengthening of nationalism in Korea after decades of war and colonization and, later, from neocolonialist ideologies. Language was an effective tool in supporting nationalism while marginalizing the Korean women who were forced to work in sexual milieus, for the most part, to financially support their biracial children. These children were negatively marked with the "moral impurity" of their mothers and their own "impure" multiracial heritage. Hence, the nationalism of the neocolonial United States and patriarchal Korea further stimulated racial and gender hierarchies. In order to understand this marginalizing nationalism, it is important to examine the history of imperialism in Korea during the 20th century.

Colonization and the Construction of the Other

Japan first occupied Korea in 1905, and in 1910 it officially annexed Korea as it sought to expand its empire. Throughout the Second Sino-Japanese War, Koreans were forced to support the Japanese empire, and under the *Yeoja Chongsindae,* or Women's Voluntary Labor Service Corps, women were mobilized for uses such as sexual slavery. The policy of using women to sexually service the Japanese military was created as a way to combat the spread of sexually transmitted diseases from Japanese prostitutes (Soh, 1996, p. 1228). To carry out this plan, the government sought unmarried women who were most likely virgins and thus free of venereal diseases to work in what they called "comfort stations."[5]

While in the "comfort stations," many of the women were assigned Japanese names, marking the replacement of their former selves with a new identity as a colonized subject. This is exemplified in *Comfort Woman,* when the Korean names are removed and the women are essentially prohibited from speaking. By doing so, the Japanese soldiers are able to control the women by decreasing their capability of communication and thus the ability to organize a resistance. Yet through the character of a "comfort woman" named Induk, also called Akiko 40,[6] Keller shows the power language has to not only imprison but also to empower and rebel. Induk, after finding herself unable to withstand the abuse, defies her captors. Keller (2000) writes:

> In Korean and in Japanese, [Induk] denounced the soldiers, yelling at them to stop their invasion of her country and her body. Even as they mounted her, she shouted: I am Korea, I am a woman, I am alive. I am seventeen, I had a family

just like you do, I am a daughter, I am a sister. . . . All through the night she talked, reclaiming her Korean name, reciting her family genealogy, even chanting the recipes her mother had passed on to her. (p. 20)

In the above passage, Induk recovers her voice and repossesses her Korean identity and freedom she had before the invasion of her country and body. She does so through the vocalization of her Korean name in her native tongue.

The removal of an identity served to make the comfort woman an object for military use. According to the documentary *Behind Forgotten Eyes*, the name of the comfort woman was inscribed on the door (Gilmore, 2007). Thus, the woman's identity is even further removed as she is given the name of a room and becomes a part of it. In other words, the comfort woman becomes a piece of furniture, an object. Removing a person's name or identity dehumanizes the already subjugated Other. Moreover, identity removal deems the person and his or her culture irrelevant, as was the case with Japanese imperial policy.[7]

In *Comfort Woman*, women's names are also changed by the American missionaries working at the refugee camps during the war. The missionaries called all female refugees Mary (Keller, 2000, p. 58), implying an insignificance of the refugees' Korean identities. Although Mary is a common Christian name and can refer to the Virgin Mary, it could also be used as an insult or curse. Keller (2000) exemplifies this through the comparison of Akiko to Mary Magdalene whose reputation is historically defamed yet her guilt never proven. Akiko is therefore chastised by her peers and looked down upon by missionaries due to the favoritism given to her by Richard, the minister.

Under the pretense of "saving" Akiko, Richard is the Christian patriarchal savior. He baptizes and marries Akiko but never learns about her personal history or even her real name, as he chooses to call her Akiko. As such, the retention of the colonized name of Akiko and Richard's failure to seek or understand her background marks a continuation of Akiko's identity as a comfort woman, a new form of the colonization of her body and her placement into a new space of silence. Akiko realizes her "body was, and always would be, locked in a cubicle at the camps, trapped under the bodies of innumerable men" (p. 106).

Akiko later moves to the United States, where Richard instructs her on every detail and becomes her voice. Keller (2000) illustrates the common prejudices Akiko encounters from strangers who refer to her as a "poor little orphan Jap" (p. 109) and a neighbor who derides her: "You related to Mrs. Bradley? Never knew she had a son. Never knew he was married to a Chinee [sic]. All them people are so small, see? How adorable! You speakee [sic]

English?" (p. 111). By illustrating the silencing of Akiko and the use of mocking language by strangers, Keller reveals the irony of freedom in the United States and how racialized ethnicity can be assigned. In other words, although life in the United States took Akiko away from the violence of war and forced sexual slavery, it did not free her from subjugation but placed her as the racialized Other, another form of subjugation.

Controlling the Savagery

While living in the United States, Akiko's traumatic past starts to affect her, and she has mental breakdowns. She also begins to communicate with spirits, and this makes her seem crazy. In the novel, Beccah recollects her mother dancing in an alley late at night. Believing Akiko is possessed, Richard tells Akiko to bow before God, but she declines. Instead, she recalls her Korean name Soon Hyo and recounts the violence she faced while at the comfort stations. Yet Richard refuses to listen and accuses Akiko of being a former prostitute. He castigates her and says, "'The sins of the parent shall fall upon their children and their grandchildren.' I ask you to protect our daughter, with your silence, from that shame" (Keller, 2000, p. 196). By asking Akiko to remain silent about her past, Richard ascribes an identity on Akiko and blames her for sins she did not commit. As a way to protect his offspring, he expects to pass his "purity" on to Beccah and filter the "impurities" of Akiko. As such, Richard impedes Beccah's understanding of her own mother just as he refuses to know Akiko. Through this characterization, Keller shows how Richard, a colonizing, American "savior," retains power over Akiko's lesser, non–American voice. Thus, Richard quells the savagery of Akiko to ensure it will not be passed to their biracial daughter.

Korean influence is also seemingly mitigated through Beccah's name. As "Rebecca" is unpronounceable for Akiko, she Koreanizes the name by associating it with the Korean word for lily. Akiko explains, "Bek-hap, the lily, purest white. Blooming in the boundary between Korean and America, between life and death" (Keller, 2000, pp. 116–117). By translating "Rebecca" into her own language, Akiko ensures her daughter is named in both Korean and English and retains both of her heritages. Thus, Beccah is given both a Korean and American identity.

Nonetheless, Akiko's "half-Korean" daughter is unable to understand her. Akiko teaches her daughter Korean words, folklore, and facets of shamanism, but Beccah cannot—or chooses not to—identify with Akiko. Just as her father does, Beccah believes her mother is crazy. In this way,

Beccah Otherizes Akiko just as Richard did. Moreover, Beccah is ashamed of her mother, whose shamanistic rituals and work as a spiritual communicator perpetuate the belief that Akiko is unstable. Beccah hides when she sees her schoolmates call her mother crazy and mock Akiko's foreign accent. Beccah continually fights against the foreignness of her mother and her own guilt by association through embracing her Caucasian Americanness.

Beccah's real guilt, however, comes after Akiko dies. After finding documents collected by her mother, Beccah discovers her mother's silenced past as a comfort woman and the atrocities she experienced under imperial Japan. She also learns her mother's real name is Soon Hyo. As she listens to the tape of her mother giving ritual instructions and prayers for her fellow victims, Beccah calls out the names of the victims and repeats her mother's real name. Through this act of discovery and listening, Beccah gives her mother a voice, which has been speaking for the subaltern but left unheard. In this way, Beccah also faces her mother's past as a comfort woman, which has overpowered Akiko's life and silenced her former Korean identity as Soon Hyo. As Gayatri Spivak (1999) explains:

> It is only in their death that [these elusive figures] enter a narrative *for us*, they become figurable. In the rhythm of their daily living, the elusion is familiarly performed or (un)performed, since to elude constantation in the act is not necessarily a performance . . . they are the figures of justice as the experience of the impossible. (pp. 245–246)

Beccah's act of listening to her mother's voice on tape sets her mother as subaltern Akiko free and reinstates her former name and identity as Soon Hyo. Moreover, by performing the death ritual of preparing her mother's body, Beccah accepts what she has long denied: the language and culture of her mother. She follows the instructions given by her mother and reminisces about watching her mother dance and offer food as part of death rituals. As Beccah performs the cleansing ritual, she faces her shame as she looks at her mother's naked body. Beccah reveals: "[her body] always embarrassed me both in its foreignness and in its similarity to mine. I looked now, fighting my shame, taking her body piece by piece . . . until I could see her in her entirety, without guilt or judgment" (Keller, 2000, p. 209). Beccah's performance of preparing her mother's body demonstrates her acceptance of her mother and Korean heritage, which she long denied. Moreover, by calling her mother both Mommy and *Omoni*,[8] and later placing her mother's ashes in the river, she validates both her American and

Korean heritages while setting her mother's spirit free and allowing her body to rest in nature.

Patriarchy and Camptown "Races"

As the female body was a source of "comfort" under Japanese imperialism, it also played a similar role for American soldiers during and after the Korean War in "camptowns," which are areas of prostitution outside U.S. military bases. Between the 1950s and 1990s, more than one million women from rural areas in Korea worked in camptowns (Cho, 2008). Some of these women made the transition from comfort women to camptown workers, also known as "Yankee whores," "G.I. brides," or *yanggongju,* meaning Western princess (Cho, 2008). Some women resorted to camptowns because they were unable to support themselves or return home since "the act of coming home marked her as a woman whose body had been invaded and contaminated by a foreign nation" (Cho, 2008, p. 95).

Decades under foreign occupation and war led to a stronger sense of Korean nationalism, which deplored any reminder of colonization. After the Korean War, the foreign presence became the United States, which was stationed in the country to protect South Korea from North Korea. Nonetheless, Korean society saw the United States as a foreign body, and with its increasing nationalistic ideologies, shunned camptown workers from society for servicing the U.S. military. In the 1970s, the tides turned after the United States withdrew 20,000 troops. Out of fear for national security and to promote bilateral relations, the Korean government began subsidizing prostitution programs as part of the Camptown Clean-Up Campaign (Lee, 2008). This operation aimed to serve U.S. troops by giving prostitutes etiquette classes and medical check-ups and controlling the spread of sexually transmitted diseases (Lee, 2008). Moreover, as the Korean government urged camptown workers to serve their country by being "sexual ambassadors," a sense of pride was given to the women, placating their shame and ostensibly including them in society. Yet as a focus was placed on rural or poor women, the "better" women were protected (Lee, 2008). Thus, considering them dispensable, the government encouraged poor women to be "ambassadors," while society continued to reject them for their unchaste work for the U.S. military. In this way, the camptown workers, as lower-class targets, were marginalized and made an expendable commodity used to protect the country from an attack by North Korea and prevent an invasion on the "unadulterated" South Korean women by U.S. troops.

Despite the cooperation from the South Korean government, camptowns became a signifier of U.S. neocolonialism as their development exemplified the American influence in postwar Korea. This exchange was a form of what Spivak (1999) calls "internal colonization," where "patterns of exploitation and domination of disenfranchised groups [exist] within a metropolitan country" (p. 172). Because of their displacement from society, camptown workers were easily exploited while contained in the margins of camptown life. Keller (2002) illustrates this dislocation in *Fox Girl*, which is set in a Korean camptown. Protagonist Hyun Jin, who has become a prostitute, wanders outside the limits of the camptown and realizes her place in society:

> When I felt people staring at me, I assumed it was because of my ugliness. . . . Then I noticed. . . . I was dressed like a *kichiton*[9] girl. An America Town whore. But instead of cowering beneath their glares and smirks, I threw back my head and looked each passerby in the eye. I could almost hear the mothers whisper behind their hands: Dirty. No class. Throwaway Korean. (p. 162)

Although Hyun Jin is tenacious, she is still shunned from Korean society and understands she will always be an outcast; camptown life has become a part of her, and her way of life is considered un–Korean.

Taking from Hannah Arendt's argument that nation-states exclude certain national minorities that are considered outside of the assumed national identity, Judith Butler (2007) argues

> The nation . . . is singular and homogeneous, or, at least, it becomes so in order to comply with the requirements of the state . . . [which] derives its legitimacy from the nation, which means that those national minorities who do not qualify for "national belonging" are regarded as "illegitimate" inhabitants. (pp. 30–31)

Considering Butler's argument, although camptown workers like Hyun Jin were Korean citizens, their actions and way of life were not in accordance with the societal requirements of being a Korean woman.[10] Therefore, these women were subjugated, and regardless of how or why the women became camptown workers, the shame inscribed on them revoked them from society.

Not only were camptown workers shunned, their children were also considered illegitimate. Since the children were fathered by non–Koreans, they bore the "adulteration" of their mothers and the "impure blood" of their racial mixture. Moreover, discrimination toward mixed-race children was not only de facto, it became law as the sense of Korean nationalism and patriarchal power grew. For example, Korean citizenship was traced through the paternal line. Therefore, if fathers were unknown or non–Korean, the children were considered noncitizens of the land in which both they and their mothers were born.[11] Thus, these illegitimized children inhabited borderlands that were multiracial, multicultural, and neocolonizer/recolonized spaces in the physical areas of camptowns, where patriarchy from both Korea and America ruled. Since many of these children were multiracial Americans, the dream of going to the United States was a chance for both legal and social acceptance.

This dream is particularly sought by Lobetto, whose mother is a camptown worker and father is an African American soldier named Robert. The name and character of Lobetto signify an unsuccessful attempt of claiming both worlds. Although he is named after his father, his name is difficult to pronounce due to the absence of certain sounds in the Korean language. As he remains Lobetto and never Robert throughout the novel, he is confined to the Korean camptown way of life and his dreams of going to his father and becoming an American remain unrealized. In this sense, since his father is an African American and his mother is a poor Korean, his color, class, and "foreignness" keep him from his desired escape to America. His circumstances and "unfortunate mix," or *tweggi*,[12] ensure that he will remain in the lowest possible caste without the possibility of changing his status.

Keller uses the derogatory Korean term *tweggi* in both novels to portray how the mixed-race children are considered in Korea and *gomshi*,[13] in *Fox Girl*, to describe Black Americans. As non–Korean speakers generally do not understand these terms, they can be alienating and discriminating by marking race and difference without the subject knowing. Yet Keller (2002) also gives an alternate meaning to these words as envisioned by the children who dream about America:

> To me, the country that Lobetto's father described seemed an impossible world, where the fantastical was commonplace. You could slip through a crack in the earth and find on the other side a land without a past, a land of the future where elephants flew and the streets were made of stars. It was a place where leftover *gomshis* were crowned king and girls looked like little boys. *Tweggis* posed in magazines and ugliness was beautiful. (p. 99)

By alluding to Martin Luther King, Jr. and Dumbo, Keller shows the camptown children lack knowledge of not only the world and events such as the civil rights movement but also childhood innocence and imagination. Furthermore, by juxtaposing that which is taboo or shunned with beauty—*tweggi* is contrasted with the model Twiggy—Keller illustrates the children's dreams of opportunity and open doors in America.

To get closer to his fantasy, Lobetto tries to learn English. Yet what he learns and sings is what he repeatedly hears at camptown bars.

I found a whore by the side of the road.

Knew right away she was dead as a toad.

Her skin was all gone from her tummy to her head.

But I fucked her, I fucked her even though she was dead!

I know it's a sin,

But I'd fuck her again.

(Keller, 2002, p. 81)

This song illustrates the brutish thinking of the American soldiers and the disregard for camptown women as humans. Lobetto understands some English words and a vague meaning of what he chants, but he does not understand the implications of imperialism within the lyrics or the explicit, misogynist nature of the song. Instead, he sees his language skills as a way to substantiate his American identity and be better than Sookie, who is also "half American," and Hyun Jin who, although "full Korean," is considered ugly because of the birthmark on her face.

Speaking the nonnative language, or the language of the oppressor, would sometimes be seen as empowering or a road to upward social mobility. In Lobetto's case, his knowledge of English, although limited, enables him to speak with American soldiers, resulting in more opportunities for business. He finds clients for the camptown bars and procures his mother, Sookie, and Hyun Jin. The money Lobetto makes illustrates him as a victim of the circumstances of camptown life but also serves to bring him closer to his goal. This is also true for Sookie and Hyun Jin, who are also sucked into the camptown method of survival and race to get out. The girls learn the phrases necessary to earn a living and smile at what they do not understand. As she was taught by her own mother, Sookie advises a reluctant Hyun Jin to "make the men feel like big shots, but treat them like little babies—laugh, say, 'You are so funny!' Put your hand on their arm, say 'You are so strong!'" (Keller, 2002, p. 130). Sookie then explains that "it's easy because the more you do it, the more you know it's not the real you. The real you flies away, and you can't feel anything anymore" (Keller, 2002, p. 131). In other words, by learning to not express their true feelings, the girls are not only able to numb themselves, but they are also able to create a separate identity as a sex worker and forget their former selves.

Keller demonstrates that using English can be a tool of power. She also utilizes Korean words to trivialize what is culturally taboo to verbalize. For example, the words *jaji* and *boji* are frequently used to name the respective male and female reproductive organs. The words are untranslatable into English, and Korean speakers would normally not use these words, as their utterance is not only taboo but also marks the speaker with lewdness. Also, the vulgarity of these words impedes their usage in a medical setting. Perhaps Keller's frequent usage of these words—which at times seem unnatural—comments on her own lack of understanding of Korean linguistic culture. However, by including these words, Keller calls direct attention to the intense proportions in which Korean women (and in some cases children) were objectified and reduced to their sexual parts in the lecherous environment of both colonial and camptown life and the unmentionable histories of Korea and Korean American communities. These environments were not only consequences of war, they were also created and regulated by the patriarchal governments that, in the name of nation, marked women as objects and made them dispensable; and thus the women and their children become stateless (Butler & Spivak 2007, pp. 90–91).

Mixed-race Identities and Deracination

Under the flag of nationalism, multiracial Korean Americans have been marginalized by the nations of both their Korean mothers and American fathers as a way to reclaim the past and hold power in a position that is "secured by the private conviction of special birth" (Spivak, 2010, pp. 17–19). As a result, the deracination felt by many Korean mothers has also affected their multiracial children, who are living in the borderlands of their Korean and American heritages. As Anzaldúa (1999) explains:

> In a constant state of mental nepantilism, an Aztec word meaning torn between ways, *la mestiza* is a product of the transfer of the cultural and spiritual values of one group to another. Being tricultural, monolingual, bilingual, or multilingual, speaking a patois, and in a state of perpetual transition, the *mestiza* faces the dilemma of the mixed breed: which collectivity does the daughter of a dark skinned mother listen to? (p. 100)

In *Comfort Woman*, this dilemma is represented through the character of Beccah, who chooses to "listen" to her American surroundings. As Akiko was marginalized and made to be a silenced Other, Beccah's rejection of her Korean heritage and mother also contributed to the continued subjugation. Later, the revelation of Akiko's past as a comfort woman deracinates Beccah from her American background that she has long embraced. In turn, Beccah seeks out her Korean heritage.

The situation is different for the biracial characters of *Fox Girl*, who are rejected from Korean society due to their racial mixture and camptown work. Sookie and Lobetto look to their American heritage as an escape from camptown life, but they are unsuccessful and have an unwanted baby.

Although Sookie eventually makes it to Hawaii, she continues her life as a prostitute while Lobetto remains in Korea, as the money he saved to leave is stolen by Hyun Jin, who leaves for Hawaii and takes responsibility for the baby.[14]

As Keller illustrates in both novels, a strong sense of national identity—whether American or Korean—can compel those who are multiracial to subscribe to the very national and racial ideologies that marginalize them. For example, in *Comfort Woman*, following her classmates and father, Beccah believes her mother is crazy due to the shamanistic rituals she performs. In *Fox Girl*, the adoption of self-subjugating racial ideologies is exemplified through the character's regular usage of racially offensive words such as *tweggi,* which has contributed to the construction of their own self-identification. Thus, the power of language, particularly that rooted in nationalism, can lead to both the ousting of a multiracial person from a community and his or her acceptance of this deracination.

The marginalization of multiracial people in Korea is engendered from the language of nationalism that fought to protect the Korean national imaginary after decades of colonial rule. Additionally, the subjugation of multiracial people of Korean heritage in the United States can be tied to neocolonialist views that promoted a racial hierarchy that placed White Americans as the superior "saviors" over the racial "Other." These forms of marginalization result from a sense of attack on the stability of the nation, since a mixed-race population is not clearly classifiable. Thus, as Butler (Butler & Spivak, 2007) argues, people do not become simply abandoned by the homogenous nation but, rather, continue as being a "wanting one" (p. 31). For Keller's multiracial characters, their position of statelessness is from both nations. Butler continues,

> What distinguishes containment from expulsion depends on how the line is drawn between the inside and the outside of the nation-state. On the other hand, both expulsion and containment are mechanisms for the very drawing of that line. The line comes to exist politically at the moment in which someone passes or is refused rights of passage. (p. 34)

For those from a multiracial heritage living in the borderlands, the line is drawn the moment they are asked to classify themselves. This problem is exacerbated with the complexity in terminology that mixed-race individuals are obliged to use.

As the discourse of race is highly complex in both its historical and political backdrops, it is essential to look at the underlying language. Moreover, it is important for the United States, among other increasingly multicultural societies, to acknowledge the histories and identities that contribute to the construction and representation of the national imaginary and how they affect changing attitudes toward race. Through constant questioning and historical recognition can societies begin to accept that histories are neither completely known nor are Black and White. Only once the imagination is able to think beyond these dualisms and embrace diversity without the urge to categorize and/or contain will communities be able to move forward to true equality, where life is precious and not predacious.

References

Anzaldúa, G. (1999/1987). *Borderlands/la frontera: The new mestiza* (2nd ed.). San Francisco: Aunt Lute Books.

Apollon, D. (2011, June 7). Don't call them "post-racial." Millennials say race matters to them. *Colorlines.com.* http://colorlines.com/archives/2011/06/youth_and_race_focus_group_main.html.

Butler, J., & Spivak, G. C. (2007). *Who sings the nation-state? Language, politics, belonging.* London: Seagull.

Cho, G. M. (2008). *Haunting the Korean diaspora: Shame, secrecy, and the forgotten war.* Minneapolis: University of Minnesota.

Danielson, B. (2011, June 12). Defining multiracial citizens. *Articles.boston.com* .http://articles.boston.com/2011-06-12/bostonworks/29650539_1_multiracial-population-race-options-census.

Davis, F. J. (2002/1991). *Who is Black? One nation's definition.* University Park: Pennsylvania State University.

Fishman, J. A. (1999). *Handbook of language & ethnic identity.* New York: Oxford University Press.

Greenfield, K. T. (2006, May 15). The long way home. *SI Vault. sportsillustrated.cnn .com.* http://sportsillustrated.cnn.com/vault/article/magazine/MAG1111192/index.htm.

Keller, N. O. (2000/1997). *Comfort woman.* London: Virago.

Keller, N. O. (2002). *Fox girl.* London: Marion Boyars.

Kim, C. S. (1998). *A Korean nationalist entrepreneur: A life history of Kim Songsu, 1891–1955.* Albany: State University of New York.

Kim-Gibson, D. S. (1997). They are our grandmas. *Positions: East Asia cultures critque, 5,* 255–274.

Lee, M. (2008). Mixed race peoples in the Korean national imaginary and family. *Korean Studies, 32,* 56–85.

Military to introduce measures to help enlisted mixed-race personnel. (2010, October 12). *Yonhap News Online.* http://english.yonhapnews.co.kr/national/2010/10/12/1/0301000000AEN20101012007700315F.HTML.

Protecting the human rights of comfort women. (2007). *Hearing Before the Subcommittee on Asia, the Pacific, and the Global Environment of the Committee on Foreign Affairs House of Representatives*. 110th Congress, First Session. Washington, DC: U.S. Government. foreignaffairs.house.gov/110/33317.pdf.

Root, M. P. P. (1996). *The multiracial experience: Racial borders as the new frontier.* Thousand Oaks, CA: Sage.

Saulny, S., & Steinberg, J. (2011, June 13). On college forms, a question of race, or races, can perplex. *Nytimes.com.* Web. http://www.nytimes.com/2011/06/14/us/14admissions.html?pagewanted=all.

Shin, G.-W. (2006). *Ethnic nationalism in Korea: Genealogy, politics, and legacy.* Stanford, CA: Stanford University Press.

Soh, C. S. (1996). The Korean "comfort women": Movement for redress. *Asian Survey, 36,* 1226–1240.

Spivak, G. C. (1999). *A critique of postcolonial reason: Toward a history of the vanishing present.* Cambridge, MA: Harvard University Press.

Spivak, G. C. (2010). *Nationalism and the imagination.* London: Seagull.

Williams-Leon, T., & Nakashima, C. L. (Eds.). (2001). *The sum of our parts: Mixed-heritage Asian Americans.* Philadelphia: Temple University Press.

Youngmisuk, O. (2009, January 31). Steelers' Hines Ward is making a difference for Korea's bi-racial youth. New York Daily News. http://articles.nydailynews.com/2009-01-31/sports/17916273_1_south-korea-korean-steelers-hines-ward.

Filmography

Gilmore, Anthony (Director). (2007). *Behind forgotten eyes* [motion picture]. USA/South Korea/Japan: The Enigma Factory. Nameless Films.

Notes

1. The words *race, mixed race, multiracial,* and so on have become a basis of description, and my usage is not intended to categorize or ascribe identity. Until new methods of discourse are developed, these superficial descriptions will unfortunately remain.

2. It is this questioning that seeks to categorize and/or contain that which is not clearly staked off; and therefore, it raises the question of whether Obama's racial self-description was a consequence of being disallowed the right to the very act of self-identification. Moreover, as this is the case for many who are multiracial, it illustrates that racial ideologies such as the "one-drop" rule are not as far in the past as once thought.

3. For more information on multiracialness and the contemporary relevancy of race, see Apollon (2011), Danielson (2011), and Saulny and Steinberg (2011).

4. Finding proper terminology is complex, especially in the case of multiracial identities, as terms are continually changing and are usually personal according to the mixed-race individual. *Hapa, Amerasian,* and *multiracial Asian American* are

among the common terms to describe Americans who are multiracial with Asian heritage (Root, 1996, pp. xxiii–xxv). Since Korean antipathy to American troops—regardless of their race—was a factor in the strengthening of Korean nationalism, which perpetuated the marginalization of multiracial peoples, I will use *multiracial Korean American* or *mixed-race Korean American* to generally describe Americans who are racially mixed with one Korean parent (Korean and Caucasian American, Korean and African American, etc.). In Keller's novels, the Korean parent is the mother, who is also discriminated against under the Korean patriarchal system. For more information on multiracial and multiethnic Asian Americans and descriptive terminology, see Williams-León and Nakashima (2001).

5. Women and girls were taken in a variety of ways, and some were lured into volunteering with the guarantee of financial compensation for working in factories. Yet after joining, the girls were taken to comfort stations (Soh, 1996, p. 1228). Some of those taken were women captured on the street and girls taken from their schools. Others included women and girls turned over to the police by parents, neighbors, or even husbands for money. For more information and testimonies, see Kim-Gibson (1997) and "Protecting the Human Rights of Comfort Women" (2007).

6. In *Comfort Woman*, once a "comfort woman" dies, her given Japanese name is reassigned to the new "comfort woman" who will serve as her replacement. The only distinguishing element is the number that follows the name. For example, as Induk has died, her Japanese name is passed to protagonist Akiko 41. It is not until her death that Soon Hyo, her Korean name, is revealed.

7. With a goal of instilling a single imperial identity through the promotion of Shintoism and the Japanese language, the policy of *Naisen Ittai* (Japan and Korea as One) sought to instill Japanese values and culture. Not only did it affect everyday life such as through the control of food and clothing, the policy also prohibited the use of *Hangeul*, or the Korean language, and required Koreans to adopt Japanese names (Kim, 1998, p. 97). However, the prohibition of *Hangeul* actually helped reinforce Korean nationalism by making its use an act of disobedience (Fishman, 1999, p. 410). Korean nationalists responded by working to preserve the language and establish a national literature. Their efforts led to a renaissance in Korean studies including history, art, and geography (Shin, 2006, pp. 51–52).

8. *Omoni* is Korean for "mother" in honorific form.

9. *Kichiton* or *gijichon* is the Korean word for camptown or red-light district surrounding U.S. military bases in Korea (Cho, 2008, p. 8).

10. Since the character of Hyun Jin has two Korean parents, by law she would be a Korean citizen and therefore subject to the moral and cultural standards established by Korean society. However, Sookie and Lobetto, her peers, would be noncitizens, as they have Korean mothers but African American fathers. Thus, as the two are biracial, they are clearly not apart of the homogenous nation and would never be judged by the same standards nor even accepted into Korean society. This lawful rejection is further discussed in the following paragraph.

11. Until as recently as 2005, conscription laws forbade racially mixed males from joining the army, grouping them with criminals and the mentally and physically disabled. Still, "visibly mixed-race men" are banned from serving ("Military to Introduce Measures," 2010).

12. *Tweggi* (*t'oeki*) is an offensive word meaning hybrid.

13. In Korean, *gom, goem, gam,* or *ggam* means black, and *shi* or *ssi* would conventionally be a polite suffix to signify a person, family, or clan, but in this case, it is likely it signifies "breed," as in type of animal. If at all used contemporarily, it is very rare, as other racial slurs are more common.

14. The only seemingly successful one is Hyun Jin, who at the end has escaped the red-light district in Hawaii with Sookie and Lobetto's unwanted baby, who is also biracial black and Korean. With this scenario, Keller unfortunately reinforces negative racial stereotypes and hierarchies by placing Hyun Jin, the "full" Korean, as the savior.

24

Can We?

Visual Rhetoric and Political Reality in American Presidential Campaigns

Jürgen Heinrichs

There are two ways to begin this essay. The first one commences with the receipt of an email from a long-lost friend and former fellow student in the fall of 2008. Featuring "Yes, we can" in its subject line, Monika's message read, "here speaks an old acquaintance of yours.... I want to tell you how much I welcome the election of President Obama for this may signal an end to the global deluge of images of violence and war and that a new age has dawned." I was delighted to hear from my European friend. Unable to share her assessment of the situation, I nevertheless welcomed the fact that the election had put us in touch again with one another. What followed was a series of animated phone conversations on the subject of whether an Obama presidency would signal meaningful political transformation or continuation of the status quo. Our discussion quickly gave way to the sobering realization that Monika was gravely ill as she mentioned her battle with a life-threatening illness. Political debate suddenly seemed less significant. No matter how much our political views may have differed, I deeply respected the meaning that this event held in Monika's life, for she drew promise and hope from it. As she concluded, "I currently happen to battle a severe illness, yet this news gives me new energy and hope to become healthy again in this world" (personal communication, November 2008).

Another way of introducing the subject strikes up a lighter note. Around the time of Barack Obama's election, I observed that the receptionist of a local fitness studio had undergone a noticeable transformation of appearance. The young man, named Michael, had reported to work that day in a hip-hop-style outfit consisting of sweatpants, checkered hoodie, and dress shirt with tie in red paisley design, baseball cap, and a pair of untied canvas shoes. All of his clothes featured variations of a black, red, and gray color scheme. He also wore a button showing a miniaturized replica of Shepard Fairey's well-known portrait of Obama along with the word "HOPE," all rendered in black, red, and blue as well. Struck by the creativity of his attire, I asked Michael whether he would pose for a snapshot. As I told him about my research on the visual rhetoric of the presidential campaign, Michael explained that his choice of apparel indeed served as an outward sign of approval of the new president. Born in Nigeria, Michael had come to the United States as a child. He spoke of his hope to utilize his ongoing college education in business and economics in order to "do good in the world," especially in his country of origin. Aspiring to these goals, he described Obama as a role model and shining ideal. Michael's clothes as well as the creativity and thoughtfulness with which he had crafted each element showed how strongly this young man responded to the promise of the newly elected president.

Monika's email and Michael's attire illuminate how much the Obama presidential campaign had stirred people to imagine a better world. Both narratives register the degree to which people in the United States and around the world experienced the election as a transformative moment in their lives. Responses further reveal the degree to which the political always remains inscribed in the personal, evidenced by the unprecedented number of people around the world who enthusiastically embraced the campaign with its messages of hope and its promise of change. Obama's campaign succeeded in conveying a most favorable image of the candidate that touched people in the United States and around the world as it resonated with their hopes and aspirations.

Image here has a two-fold meaning: first, as an image in the literal sense, a visual representation or the likeness of somebody or something, and, second, as an image in the sense of an idea or a popular conception, reputation, or stance associated with a public figure. Obama's presidential campaign succeeded in mobilizing both. It provided effigies of the candidate while simultaneously communicating the notion of the new president as a conveyor of social and political change. Its success stems from its skillful positioning of images, including works of art, popular imagery, and visually enhanced social media feeds.

Working with a sampling of representations that accompanied the rise of Barack Obama from United States senator to president, this chapter charts how images are utilized, how they draw from historical traditions, and how they engage the day's contemporary social and political realities. I propose to look at these images in their own right, that is, to consider them not as derivative illustrations of political phenomena but as the very arenas in which meaning constitutes itself. The Obama campaign lends itself to this kind of analysis, for it so successfully worked with images to convey its political goals. The stream of images depicting the presidential candidate played a key role in securing political victory while also functioning to popularize the new leader's agenda. Although any campaign engages visual representations in its efforts to sway the electorate in its favor, Obama did so most successfully, for his campaign skillfully positioned images and their embedded meanings.

While the images conjure up goals and ideals that are seemingly within reach under an Obama presidency, the lived realities of people in dismal economic and social conditions tell a different story. A critical analysis of selected images reveals a gap between lofty visual rhetoric and an increasing number of people experiencing harsh economic conditions. This gap between the ambitious visual rhetoric on the one hand, and the plethora of social, economic, and political problems experienced by people at this historical moment, on the other hand, is not meant to be construed as a taking of sides against or in favor of a given political position. Rather, the Obama campaign's sophisticated use of visuals begs examination of the role that these images play in political processes. Visual representations enabled Obama's electoral efforts to convey a set of ideals and goals that are seemingly within reach under an Obama presidency. Featuring a rising sun in its logo and other symbols, Obama imagery frequently references the all-American notion of a capacity for change under adverse conditions. Similar to the idiom of "pulling oneself up by one's bootstraps," this ability describes one's power to recover from severe setbacks through one's own efforts, hard work, and perseverance. Although this recipe for bettering one's own situation through hard work and self-improvement may have functioned in the past, an increasing number of Americans have come to experience that neither labor nor education alone may save them from economic decline or even poverty. A stream of bad news about deteriorating social and economic conditions in the United States and elsewhere, along with the notion of the decline of the middle class, prompts people to question the political rhetoric and the images that communicate it. This gap between representation and reality suggests a continuation of the status quo rather than deep political change. Thus, Obama's path to the presidency, I argue, signals as much a victory in the battle of images as it exposes the difficulty or sheer impossibility of achieving deep, lasting change of the social reality in which we live.

A productive way to launch this analysis is to place contemporary campaign visuals in the historical context of political iconography. This section charts the appropriation and reappropriation of images as vehicles to envision change and transformation. Political iconography, a well-established branch of art historical research, proves most useful here, for it reveals how images have been successfully used to shape abstract concepts and control political processes. Then and now, the struggle for office in elections and broader decision-making processes relies on long-standing visual traditions. Since antiquity, the ruler's portrait, that is, the effigy of a given leader, depicts the highest and most powerful authority of a political community. The equestrian statue of Roman emperor Marcus Aurelius (A.D. 166–80) represents a classical example and prototype of how the visual arts provided strategies for political leaders to define themselves vis-à-vis their constituencies. The sculpture not only conveyed the qualities with which the emperor wanted to be associated, but it also defined the relationship between the ruler and his people as one that was governed by persuasion and reason rather than the exercise of brute force. An idealized representation of political leadership, the equestrian statue of Marcus Aurelius and the myriad works that followed its example, such as Jacques-Louis David's 1800 painting *Napoleon Crossing the Alps*, served to define and to project the notion of good government (Fleckner, Warnke, & Ziegler, 2011).

The use of sculptures and images to shape and to project the notion of an ideal ruler has structured political representational strategies from the Renaissance through the 19th century. More recently, the invention of photography and film and related technological transformations has generated different yet related forms of political imagery. In all instances, images serve as vehicles to define and to disseminate notions of political leadership that acts on behalf of and in the best interest of a people. The equestrian statue is a particularly well-suited example to show how rulers' portraits allow leaders to project their self-image, on the one hand, and to accommodate "the people" to articulate their expectations toward a given ruler, on the other hand.

A look at recent history reveals that these long-standing uses of political imagery have survived in manifold ways. Take, for instance, the 2007 appearance of then-senator Barack Obama in Berlin (Figure 1). The photograph circulated in postcard format. It provides a low-angle shot of the presidential candidate waving and gesturing toward the crowds. The head of the president, in the lower left corner, is seen against the victory column along with the phrase "Greetings from Berlin." Eyeing political victory back home in the United States, the presidential hopeful selected the victory column in Berlin as a backdrop for one of his key European speeches. (This choice of venue is said to have come about because German Chancellor Angela Merkel refused access to the Brandenburg Gate, for this prominent national site is reserved for sitting heads of state only.) To be sure, historical

Greetings from Berlin 2007, postcard.

symbols and monuments of German nationalism such as the victory column are not customarily chosen as stages for foreign officials (Alings, 2000). However, the victory column may be considered an exemption, for its connotations of militarism and nationalism may have been neutralized to a degree through the monument's appropriation by youth culture movements such as the Loveparade, a techno-music dance festival occurring annually between 1989 and 2006 (Borneman & Senders, 2000). As a result, Obama's choice to speak in front of the victory column and to have coverage broadcast around the world for German and European audiences drew from the popularization of this historical monument and its revalorization as a pop culture symbol of the "new" Germany with its reunified capital, Berlin.

The postcard commemorating Obama's Berlin speech is but one of many examples in which Obama and other politicians before him have utilized visual representations to communicate political programs. All American presidents, and other heads of state around the world for that matter, make extensive use of what is commonly known as the "White House photo opportunity," a carefully staged occasion for the production of photographs to represent the president and his office in favorable ways. This practice dates back at least to the 1930s, when Franklin Roosevelt's press secretary advised photographers to avoid taking shots of the president in a wheelchair, ostensibly fearing that such perspectives would depict the leader in a vulnerable pose. The term itself was coined during the Nixon administration, as an aide to the president's press secretary is reported to have instructed journalists that "there will be a photo opportunity in the Oval Office" after the press secretary's prompt to "get 'em in for a picture" (Streitmatter, 1988).

In recent history, the White house photo opportunity regularly extends beyond the confines of the executive mansion, as evidenced on the occasion of President George W. Bush's speech on May 1, 2003, aboard the aircraft carrier USS *Abraham Lincoln*. Planned to mark the end of major combat operations in the Iraq war, the photograph depicts the commander in chief after he himself had copiloted and landed a Viking fighter jet on the deck of the ship. Accompanied by a banner that read "Mission Accomplished," Bush joined a group of a servicemen and servicewomen for a group portrait. Smiling faces, victorious expressions, and colorful military regalia suggest the end of war and the completion of a "job well done." As viewers and commentators knew then and now and as the course of history has since shown, the year 2003 neither concluded military conflict nor did it bring to an end simmering political conflicts (Kellner, 2004).

Bush's speech on the aircraft carrier is a particularly obvious example of the fallacies of the presidential photo opportunity, for this case so glaringly exposes the gap between idealized representation and the sobering reality of ongoing violence and warfare. To be sure, all presidents regardless of political affiliations made extensive use of this form of visual rhetoric. Countless images attest to the ways in which Obama, just like his predecessors of both political parties, casts himself as benign political figure to whom leadership of the nation, if not the world, can be entrusted. A staple of such imagery is the official presidential portrait, in which the effigy of a sitting president is optimized regarding appearance and overall ambiance. For Obama, this photographic effigy has been produced by then newly appointed White House photographer Pete Souza, who released the official presidential portrait in January 2009.

If one set of images of the Obama campaign functions according to the historical legacies of political iconography, another series of representations utilizes different visual strategies to generate meaning. Shepard Fairey's 2006 portrait *Obama* is a good case in point, for it demonstrates how pictorial appropriation functions in the political context. A defining aspect of postmodern art, the appropriation of images is neither new nor restricted to visual arts, as advertising practice, with its ubiquitous borrowing of images, reveals. Fairey's work, a large-scale mixed-media stenciled collage, has become synonymous with Obama's campaign and early presidency. The work features a head shot of the president looking up- and outward, possibly alluding to the fact that his gaze is transfixed in contemplation of his ambitious political goals. The portrait features toned layers of blue and red that accentuate surface and texture at the expense of depth and photographic detail. In concert with the semitransparent word *HOPE* spelled out horizontally in the lower section, Fairey's now iconic work itself utilized a photograph that had originally been taken by Mannie Garcia, a news photographer for the Associated Press. Garcia made the snapshot of then-Senator Obama and actor George Clooney during a National Press Club conference about the crisis in Darfur in April 2006.

The complex legal questions as to whether Fairey's use of Garcia's photograph marks the former's creative acumen or amounts to the latter's copyright infringement have been studied in depth elsewhere (Cartwright & Mandiberg, 2009; Mitchell, 2009). Instead, I am interested in the fact that, regardless of the legal proceedings over ownership of the images, Fairey's reworking and popularization of Garcia's original composition has already shaped the political process. Thus, the Garcia–Fairey case exemplifies the photographer–artist cocreation process of influential political imagery. We recall that Fairey's composition first greeted us in the guise of a button worn by the fitness studio receptionist. Yet Michael's button is only one of many examples in which Fairey's image circulates in the realm of popular culture in the guise of posters, t-shirts, and other political accoutrements.

Fairey's portrait reveals the power of images and their capacity to shape political processes. More than mere visual accessories of political campaigns, images provide the very arenas in which meaning is contested or validated. Fairey's work represents a new brand of popular political imagery that echoes the artistic legacy of Andy Warhol with its frequent appropriation of images from the popular press, the world of commerce, or the celebrity sphere. The American pop artist had long blurred distinctions between fine arts and popular culture through the appropriation of everyday imagery in his works. Warhol also championed the use of press photographs in his iconic silkscreen prints that captured moments in the lives of celebrities such as Hollywood actress Marilyn Monroe or Soviet leader Vladimir Lenin (Stimson, 2001).

Veteran pop artist Robert Indiana also supplied Obama's presidential campaign with artistic inspiration and promotional materials. Between 2006 and 2008, Indiana happened to work on a series of prints titled *HOPE*. Evoking the bold style and the simplicity of his famous 1964 piece *LOVE*, Indiana recently created another iconic image depicting a powerful, short word: HOPE. Indiana's work originally had no political bearings, for the artist had conceptualized it as a "sculpture poem" in reference to the artist's home, an old house called Star of Hope in Vinalhaven, Maine (Ebony, 2008). Indiana had never met Obama at the time, but the artist recalls admiring the candidate's speeches and idealism. As David Ebony reports,

> Indiana was moved by Obama's musings on the American Dream in his book *The Audacity of Hope*, and by his impassioned messages for change in his bid for the White House. Aiming for the design to become a symbol of a new positive initiative, Indiana decided to donate proceeds from the "Hope" series to the Obama campaign. (Ebony, 2008)

At that point, the Obama campaign successfully recruited Indiana, who agreed to the installation of his *Hope* design as a monumental, 6-foot stainless steel sculpture outside the Denver Pepsi Center, site of the 2008 National Democratic Convention. The artist subsequently authorized the production of related postcards and other representations that depict the presidential candidate smiling next to the letters spelling HOPE, all rendered in red, blue, and white (Figure 2). Proceeds of Indiana's work materialized as contributions to the Obama campaign.

In addition to prominent figures such as Shepard and Indiana, many emerging and lesser-known artists put their creative skills to work for the Obama campaign. In 2008, a representative of the popular movement MoveOn.org noted that "Barack Obama's historic candidacy has sparked an unprecedented artistic outpouring" (http://pol.moveon.org/mh/gallery/). The

Robert Indiana, *HOPE* postcard, 2008.

statement accompanied the announcement of a contest for two- and three-dimensional art, the winners of which were exhibited at the Denver National Democratic Convention alongside works from dozens of established and influential artists on the organization's online "Manifest Hope" gallery.

Transcending the political realm, Obama imagery quickly began to proliferate beyond its originally intended context. Noteworthy examples include a presidential parody in a newspaper ad featuring comedian Bill Maher, host of the political talk show *Real Time*. The ad, which ran in the *New York Times*, formally emulates Fairey's composition while replacing Obama's portrait with that of Maher. Another example depicts David Alan Grier, host of Comedy Central's *Chocolate News*, in a pose that closely resembles Obama. Lastly, magazine covers such as *Time Out's* "New York edition" present a close-up, cropped facial portrait of Obama as the cover of an issue that listed venues to celebrate the presidential inauguration. Traces of lipstick on his cheek render the president kissed and kissable, thus evoking the spirit of Obama as an approachable politician, a president of the people. Similarly, the cover of the *Washingtonian* features a casual, full-body portrait of the chest-baring president on the beach as one of 26 reasons to consider setting up residence in the American capital. Here, the most powerful man in the world appears youthful and approachable, as if he lived next door. One may speculate whether there are any precedents in which sitting presidents have been depicted in this casual, seminude fashion. Either way, the practice adds to the insight that Obama's campaign broke uncharted territory in its utilization of popular culture as a political strategy.

The popularity of Obama visuals extends far beyond the United States. The age of instant electronic transmission of news and images enables the global circulation of this kind of imagery. Examples from the German context illustrate geographic reach, formal variation, and creative originality of this phenomenon. There is the Obama-related graffiti on the base of a 19th-century equestrian statue of the Saxon king John in Dresden. A car dealership in Hamlin promotes its line of vehicles with the slogan "Yes, you can," suggesting that, just as Obama achieved the presidency, consumers can attain ownership of prestigious American sport utility vehicles (Figure 3). The popular German news magazine *Stern* features a portrait of Obama on its cover that playfully alludes to the redeemer/seducer theme. Lastly, the flyer of a local nightclub evoking "a world of nocturnal experiences" builds on Obama's "Yes, we can" slogan as a universal motto to provide an assortment of entertainment and diversions (Figure 4). These examples

Jeep Advertisement in Hamlin, Germany, 2009.

GoParc! Nightclub flyer, 2009.

demonstrate the degree to which Obama's campaign resonated with people around the world and how the visual strategies, in turn, have been appropriated in different cultural contexts. The successful use of visual representations as a means to advance political programs is further evidenced in the popularity of the Obama.com campaign website, which had been universally hailed as the new gold standard of "political branding" by professionals across the board.

Lonnie Bunch, scholar of African American history, discussed implications and symbolism of Barack Obama as the first African American president of the United States. The historical election, Bunch proposed at the time, had the potential to free the United States from constricting traditions and paradigms associated with race. Obama's ascent to the presidency, he stated, helped Black America reclaim its "American-ness" and enable millions of Americans to believe that their nation can be made better once again (Bunch, 2009). Though not everybody shared this affirmative view of the new president, Bunch's assessment reflected the overall spirit of a majority of voters and their yearning for change and renewal at that historical moment.

At the same time, critical voices cautioned early on against too much optimism associated with the election of Obama. Instead, some argued, the new leader should not be assessed on the basis of his campaign rhetoric but should be held accountable in light of his policies and deeds. Naomi Klein has most prominently given a voice to this view in her 2009 essay that matches political realities with Obama's campaign promises. In her provocative analysis, Klein reveals the gap between lofty campaign rhetoric on the one hand and the sobering political record on the other hand. Presenting a laundry list of what she perceives to be Obama's political failures, Klein's "Lexicon of Disappointment" condemns some of Obama administration's most problematic deeds (Klein, 2009).

Though Klein's stinging critique targets the Obama presidency in particular, her analysis of the gap between ambitious campaign rhetoric and disappointing political record likely applies to all recently elected leaders in the United States and elsewhere. However, the case of Obama differs from previous efforts of media-driven campaigns, for its unprecedented utilization of images confirms the success and far reach of the campaign. The symbolism of the Obama campaign, accomplished through its successful use of images, stands in glaring opposition to the challenging economic and social realities as experienced by many voters. Cognizant about this gap between representation and reality, between campaign promise and the lived experience of their ever-more-precarious condition, voters of different political convictions register a growing sense of disillusionment with the established political system. Tellingly, neither the iconic images by Fairey and Indiana nor the affirmative "Yes, we can" slogans seem to have had any traction in recent political debate. It appears that many contemporary observers have come to realize the gap between President Obama's once-powerful rhetoric and campaign images on the one hand and what they have come to experience as a disappointing record of political actions and lack of measurable social and economic progress on the other hand.

This chapter explored Barack Obama's political ascent from senator to president of the United States as seen through the lens of selected visual representations. My analysis aimed to chart how such images functioned to advance and augment a discourse of change and renewal at the center of the Obama campaign. This narrative relied on traditions of political iconography and drew inspiration from popular culture. Conjuring up a supposedly postracial, economically just, and otherwise transformed political order, visuals contributed to the success of Obama's campaign. Analysis revealed that change largely remains the function of a visual rhetoric, whereas sameness continues to structure the lives of people in the United States and beyond. Casting itself as an agent of transformation, the campaign presents but a variant of an old strategy of visually packaging political programs. Although one readily registers the success of the Obama campaign's visual rhetoric, the attentive observer questions whether measurable economic, social, and political change is on the way. For a growing number of people whose lives are defined by worsening economic conditions, rising unemployment, and the specter of poverty, the spectacle of hope, justice, and change stands painfully detached from the plethora of problems in which they find themselves mired.

Although it remains questionable whether intellectuals ever have or ever will do more than politicians to bring about meaningful social transformation, we remind ourselves that, at a time of journalism in crisis and relentless information overload, we may still challenge established political discourse. Remembering the heartfelt sincerity with which Monika had rightfully embraced the message of hope and the prospect of change in 2008, we realize that most political work remains to be done. Impelled by the spirit of Monika's yearning for deep, sustainable change, a longing that we all share, we realize that "yes, we can" generate, maintain, and promote societal critique and intervention capable of challenging and counteracting the grand narrative webs that are being spun at this moment in history.

In memoriam Monika
Dommel (1965–2009)

References

Alings, R. (2000). *Die Berliner Siegessäule. Vom Geschichtsbild zum Bild der Geschichte*. Berlin: Parthas.

Borneman, J., & Senders, S. (2000, May). Politics without a head: Is the "love parade" a new form of political identification? *Cultural Anthropology, 15*(2), 294–317.

Bunch, L. (2009). Trapped by tradition. *Museum, 88*(1), 27–30.

Cartwright, L., & Mandiberg, S. (2009, August). Obama and Shepard Fairey: The copy and political iconography in the age of demake. *Journal of Visual Culture, 8*(2), 172–176.

Ebony, D. (2008, November). Art & politics: The perennial optimist. *Art in America, 96*(10), 77–80.

Fleckner, U., Warnke, M., & Ziegler, H. (Eds.). (2011). *Handbuch der politischen Ikonographie*. Munich: Beck.

Kellner, D. (2004, August). Media propaganda and spectacle in the war on Iraq: A critique of U.S. broadcasting networks. *Cultural Studies <=> Critical Methodologies, 4*(3), 329–338.

Klein, N. (2009, April 15). A lexicon of disappointment. *The Nation*. Available at http://www.thenation.com/article/lexicon-disappointment.

Mitchell, W. J. T. (2009, August). Obama as icon. *Journal of Visual Culture, 8*(2), 125–129.

Stimson, B. (2001). Andy Warhol's red beard. *Art Bulletin, 83*(3), 527–547.

Streitmatter, R. (1988). The rise and triumph of the White House photo opportunity. *Journalism Quarterly, 65*(4), 981–985.

25

Chicano Visualities

A Multicultural Rewriting
of Californian Spatialities

Eduardo Barros Grela

Mike Davis' (2001) publication of *Magical Urbanism* problematizes and rewrites Latino urban identities in the United States. As is revealed by the secondary title of his book, "Latinos Reinvent the US City," Davis questions the United States's epistemological rigidity, and discusses how this nation has historically managed its sociopolitical itinerary toward multiculturalism through silencing and invisibilizing ethnic minorities. Hegemonic thinking in the United States, that is, the elitist domination against which minority cultures act (During, 2005, p. 28), protects a traditional identity that provides a certain social homogeneity, but paradoxically it also promotes cultural diversity in urban spaces and border spatialities. This chapter shows how this cultural phenomenon is portrayed through Chicano visualities, which configured both an aesthetic and an epistemological regeneration.

According to urban theory critics such as Henri Lefèbvre or Reyner Banham, the questions of center and centrality are pivotal to the understanding of city space as a 20th-century model site of social growth and development. However, Deleuzian ontological readings of space claim that arborescent conceptions of the urban space are not suitable for fragmented, globalized, or postmodern identities. Together with Guattari, Deleuze argues that both subjectivities and spatialities are constructed on a real yet multidimensional pattern of rhizomatic epistemological devices. The dialectical postures of Lefèbvre and Deleuze will function as theoretical starting points in this chapter, which intends to utilize recent manifestations of Californian visual expressions to articulate the machineries of both centripetal and centrifugal inertias with rhizome-like tendencies of multicultural identification production.

As an example of the confluence of rhizomatic urban development and visual expression of multiculturalism, Asco, a street performance Chicano group whose name means "nausea" or "disgust" in Spanish, attempted, in the 1970s and 1980s, to deconstruct *established* normativities *written for* "Hispanics" by introducing new models of urban landscape configuration, such as *live murals* or *destructive artistic manifestations*. Their aesthetic position questioned the value of Los Angeles *art* per se and focused on murals as political devices to unsettle mainstream ideologies. Today, almost 40 years after their first appearance, a retrospective exhibition of Asco's interventions has been organized at the Los Angeles County Museum of Art, bringing back their proposals into the aesthetic discussions today.

> *(Social) space is a (social) product.* This proposition might appear to border on the tautologous, and hence on the obvious. There is good reason, however, to examine it carefully, to consider its implications and consequences before accepting it. Many people will find it hard to endorse the notion that space has taken on, within the present mode of production, within society as it actually is, a sort of reality of its own, a reality clearly distinct from, yet much like, those assumed in the same global process by commodities, money and capital. (Lefèbvre, 1991, p. 26)

The city of Los Angeles, which is the spatial *subject* in the reflection I propose here, is about the relations between Asco's transgressive art and the reconfiguration of space through discourses of multiculturalism. Los Angeles is well represented by the aforementioned quote from Lefèbvre's *The Production of Space*. According to Reyner Banham (2009), "[a] city seventy miles square but rarely seventy years deep apart from a small downtown not yet two centuries old and a few other pockets of ancientry, Los Angeles is instant architecture in an instant townscape" (p. 21). I am particularly interested in the confluence of Banham's usage of instantaneity to refer to Los Angeles and Lefèbvre's contribution to the critique of territory with his "social space as a social product" (Lefèbvre, 1991, p. 26).

The sight that a visitor to Los Angeles finds most shocking, upon arrival at the largest urban space in California, is probably the shocking ornamented aesthetics of its walls: graffiti, mural art, and colors. Everything has a place on the walls of the Los Angeles River ("The Great Wall of Los Angeles"), in the freeways walls, or in the César Chávez Avenue stores. From the popular street murals that portray different Angelino actors and musicians in Venice's Ocean Front Walk to the canonical Diego Rivera's and José Clemente Orozco's work in the Los Angeles County Museum of Art (LACMA), Los Angeles is a city that could well be defined by the art that gives color to its streets and roads. It is, however, a different type of art that is of interest in this chapter; it is an art that claims a need for immediacy, a demand of transgressive power.

The turn of the century can be defined as a time in which the concept of *nation-state* has been in clear declination in favor of postborder epistemologies (Dear et al., 2003, p. 267). Subject to the emergence of a particular geopolitical restructuring of cultural globalization, the case of Angelino urban spaces and *spatialities* can serve as a reference to analyze how the different artistic manifestations are vehicles for the transformation of border subjectivities. Both in this relaxation of the boundaries of nation-states and in the failure to demarcate the spatial limits between urban and rural, it is necessary to problematize the different transformations to which both spaces and human beings are exposed under their reciprocal influence.

A few questions must be raised in order to configure the plateau—of multiplicities—that allows for a rigorous approach to the study of Chicano visualities in California: What is a city and what do we understand by that? Is an urban conglomeration representable? Is it possible to actually refer to a boundary between an urban environment and the aesthetic representation of the city, or is it precisely that boundary that makes up the identity of such a space? How are identities associated with that space produced, and how do they manifest themselves, organically or inorganically, through the arts?

In order to provide a partial answer to the original question—what is a city and what it means to be urban in our time—we have to explore how late capitalism reconceptualizes the traditionally legitimate center–periphery dichotomy. A provisional answer to this question can be attained by resorting to the example given by Jan Nijman (2000)—quoting the Chicago School—in 2000. He talks about a "paradigmatic city" as a conceptualization of the new type of posturban organization favored by the crisis of the nation-states and claims that this type of city could serve as a starting point to read postmodern urban spaces such as Los Angeles: "The value of the concept of the paradigmatic city lies in exploring and identifying *general directions* of change across the urban system [. . .] rather than about idiosyncratic local outcomes" (p. 135). Nijman's proposal works perfectly in the articulation of Los Angeles as an urban space outlined by the concept of multiplicity, what also applies to the reformulation of the global city as rhizomatic model of 21st-century megalopolis in perennial destruction, reconstruction, and deconstruction.

A city, therefore, that could be considered as paradigmatic would be one that clearly presents the characteristics and trends of the urban system in its broadest sense. Postmodernism has abruptly brought about a paradigm shift in the urban area, giving prominence to global spaces such as the city of Los Angeles. What is it, then, following this pattern, that determines that an area be considered global? Could we talk, licitly, about globalized spaces in cities where there are multiple forms of cultural imperialism? Evidently, the answer to this question cannot be otherwise but affirmative; but coinciding with José Pérez de Lama (2008), it is necessary to advocate a dynamic use of the term *globalization* so that there will be a need to have the paradigmatic city exposed to a continuous flow of deterritorialization and reterritorialization. This type of city should be, necessarily, both apocalyptic and regenerating. According to Edward Soja, what he calls *postmetropolises*, in transverse reference to globalized cities, are characterized by an extreme formal complexity, which simultaneously manages processes of flight and processes of return to create new spatialities in which several binaries converge: urban and nonurban; inherent and extrinsic elements; agglutination of suburbs, farmland, or metropolitan areas; and, finally, urban planning proposals and artistic productions that are committed to the discursive production of the border.

This *heterotopic* discussion of Angeleno urbanities, which introduces the spatial visualities of Chicano cultures, lacks, however, the actantial element that triggers the process of political transformation. The cultural, social, and ideological changes that sprout from the unparalleled magnitude of reterritorialization in Southern California provide a connotation of movement to these urban models, whose emergence had been questioned by the legitimate formality of modern architecture. Los Angeles is thus transformed in a direct flow, in an endless stream of heterogeneous populations on the move, so that *its* space is no longer static but a living being which is endowed with agency by its dis-*organ*-ization.

A clear example of this urban mobility is observed in the gargantuan development of the automotive industry, traditionally, resulting in a decentralization of urban areas through the transformation of the vehicle as a "mode of transportation" into a habitable environment per se. As described by Reyner Banham, in his chapter "Autopia," in *Los Angeles: The Architecture of Four Ecologies* (2009), which offers a new definition of the city based on the special importance of California highways as arteries—or scars—of asphalt—the decentralization of urban space is a result of the proliferation of both the automobile and the uncontrolled construction of highways (pp. 3–6).

Such an augmentation of the road network in Southern California not only gave entrance to the city of Los Angeles but unexpectedly gave also to its inhabitants a possibility of flight from the city. One of the consequences of this series of movements was the geopolitical articulation signed by Mike Davis (2003) about what he has coined as "Dead Cities" (p. 136). These cities are a very extensive space of illusory border between imagined urbanity and idealized rurality—caused by an articulation of the concept of city as "Edge City"—proposed by Joel Garreau in 1991 (Garreau, 1992).

This process of physical urban decentralization is joined by a parallel process in the demographic domain known as *White flight*. This is a process of social and geographical mobility founded on the grounds of segregation, racial and cultural discrimination, and, as Davis (2003) himself claims in *Dead Cities* (p. 157), the classism prevailing from the social capitalism of the American Sun Belt. This demographic movement is read as a Caucasian "escape" toward residential areas in the periphery (suburbs) of the Greater Los Angeles Area. Besides this, from the 1990s on, a social deterritorialization of urban centers is added to these diasporic movements through a process of "Black-out migration." This would be a shift away from urban enclaves that had been traditionally dominated by African American populations and are now displaced by a type of worker who "acts" his American otherness in a reified fashion, conforming what has been coined as a "browning" of labor, as is explained in Rolnik and Guattari's *Micropolítica, cartografías del deseo*. The spatial reoccupation of Chicano subjectivities transcends the boundaries of the *barrio*, thereby reshaping unfinished urban spaces and resulting in a spatial distribution, abject and porous, of the ineffable topography of the city. Geographically, this is translated into a conglomerate of multiple metropolitan centers with highly diverse populations. It is evident that this spatial reconfiguration implies a redistribution of the demographic map of the geography that is affected. As Hanna Arendt (1958), in *The Human Condition*, points out:

> Nothing can remain immense if it can be measured. Prior to the shrinkage of space and the abolition of distance through railroads, steamships, and airplanes, there is the infinitely greater and more effective shrinkage which comes about through the surveying capacity of the human mind, whose use of numbers, symbols and models can condense and scale earthly physical distance down to the size of the human body's natural sense and understanding. (p. 250–251)

Arendt's words not only apply to distances, they also apply to space itself as well as to spatialities. The correlation between space and identity runs

parallel to the human ability to transform our environment, which recipro-
cally transforms the way we understand ourselves.

The explanation for this elastically scattering process, staged by Chicano
communities, can be illustrated through the *imagination* of a posturban
center located in the highly mutable space of Southern California. This
imaginary city-center would be located in a town whose average population
was mainly White. At this city center, its inhabitants enjoy the typical
comforts of an average metropolis and would feature a *modern* aesthetic:
good communications, an emphasis on entertainment, and so forth. Over
time, this center becomes the reception focus of the Mexican immigrant
workforce and transforms its own identity into one that is performed and
articulated by the coalescence of its different cultures. A geographical
settlement of this type would include, inevitably, a cultural settlement as well
as would entail the physical transformation of its ideological and social
norms. The White population would encounter its cultural, social, and
geographic preeminence threatened and would decide to build new barriers,
new borders—real and imagined—and new exclusive identities (they would
gate their communities and would charge to enter public parks in the area).[1]
When these borders are again exceeded, the White population decides to
physically abandon the inner city and settle in the suburbs, constituting to
the aforementioned "edge cities." The inner city becomes, conversely, a
space dominated by a body of low-income, young populations, which
occupy the bottom rung in this strange cultural heteroglossia that makes up
the American social map.

It is evident that the *imagined* space described above applies to a high
percentage of currently existing urban centers throughout Southern
California. This is a process of unstoppable urban abandonment that travels
south to north, suggesting a parody of the "cannibal city," a concept
proposed by Mike Davis (2001, p. 122) to refer to those megacities that
cannibalize surrounding smaller cities in order to exponentially expand their
own growth. To some extent, the process observed here implies that
marginalized minority populations engulf the foundations of the American
dream city, building a new model based on multiculturalism that would be
unthinkable for previous inhabitants. Their proposals concerning alternative
models of radical multiplicity go on about relationality as an anti-identity
performance as well as a possibility rather than as a restriction.

These processes of internal migration discuss the systemically organized
nature that has been traditionally attributed to the modern city as a center
that generates concentric circles of periphery. Such an *organized* yet not
planned *order* is troubled by the subjectified imposition of postmodern
chaos, geographically re-presented as a polycentric and inorganic spatiality.

These proposals question the corporeal character of the city and give continuity to the claims of Slavoj Žižek (2002) to interpret Deleuze's dissertations about the preeminence of the organs without bodies as a form of urban reinterpretation. This permeation of organic spatial boundaries, caused mainly by the relativization of the boundaries between the human and the technological, is projected onto the contemporary conceptualization of urbanity through the rupture of adjacent barriers that are not only geographical but also ontological.

On the aesthetic level, the architecture of Los Angeles shows, explicitly, the transformation of the American urban space through a sort of chromatic *tropicalization* of its buildings. Opposing the monotonous and monotonic condos of suburban Los Angeles, East Los Angeles (Cesar Chávez Avenue, Boyle Heights, or Whittier Avenue) offers a polychromatic architectural mosaic whose bright colors are being integrated in the urban landscape of Los Angeles. Also, this colorful alteration of the urban visual identity is extended to the gray walls and white canals of the city. Mike Davis (2001) explains it extensively in his *Magical Urbanism: Latinos Reinvent the US City*. He notes:

> Inter-cultural skirmishes [. . .] take place on purely audio-visual fronts. Neighborhood aesthetic wars have become common-place as Latino carnivality collides with the psychosexual anxieties of *Truman Show* white residential culture. Thus the glorious sorbet palette of Mexican and Caribbean house paint—*verde-limón, rosa-mexicano, azul-añil, morado*—is perceived as sheer visual terrorism by non–Hispanic homeowners who believe that their equity directly depends upon a neighborhood color order of subdued pastels and white picket fences. (p. 64)

Not only does this quote stress the reactions of those who hold a rather traditional aesthetic idea of Los Angeles, but also the increasing presence of this type of architecture in the heart of the city. American urban reconfiguration is highly affected by Chicano architectural aesthetics and, thus, clearly affects the way America imagines its spatial subjectivities. This urban transformation lacks visibility from dominant populations and arises from a collective consciousness on the part of Chicano aesthetic transgression of legitimate spatialities, resulting in increasingly obvious social achievements that have a definitive impact on the spatial configuration of the Angeleno spatial environment. Davis (2001) continues to explain this shift in the perception of the city:

> Even upwardly mobile Chicanos have joined in the backlash against "un-American" hues, as in the L.A. suburb of South Gate where the City

Council recently weighed an ordinance against tropical house colors, or in San Antonio where writer Sandra Cisneros has long outraged city fathers with her deeply expressive purple home. And the same Puritan spirit that once sent the police to quell all-night "hoolies" in Irish kitchens now calls 911 to complain about lively *quinceañeras* or *fiestas familiars*. In many communities, noise ordinances, like curfews, have become a form of racial profiling. (p. 64)

Having, thus, established a framework that highlights the spatial problematics of border cultures, it is necessary to appoint those foundations as concretized through aesthetic representations. The task of getting into the classical models of representation in Latino/Chicano art and literature is beyond the scope of this chapter, but a minimal approach is necessary to rationalize Chicano aesthetics of protest. Its inherent policy is one that is based, as explained above, on activism and was made visible through the muted demographic presence of Latino art (Pérez-Torres, 2000).

Relevant to this discussion are the artistic contributions made by an ephemeral art group pertaining to the cultural postmodernism of performative kitsch in Los Angeles. Asco, an artistic group whose name in Spanish, as aforementioned, evokes, evidently, the feeling of nausea caused by its aesthetic stance, feeds from both an evolution of the artistic "happening" and a political revision of the performative art.

Asco was an avant-garde movement born directly from the streets of East Los Angeles in the '70s as a collective group of multimedia art whose nature was intrinsically close to political activism and therefore far from the traditional aesthetic canon. Asco is described as a group of artists that repudiated art itself and looked for a *displacement* of legitimate artistic manifestations:

Asco's members were the generation that grew up in the middle of the Vietnam War, and it was about their reaction against many of the things around them. It was also the reaction of many people to what we were doing. For many, "Art? Ugh, this is disgusting [asco]." So we adopted that term Asco, says Gronk, a member of the group, speaking on BBC Mundo. [my translation] (Perasso, 2011, para. 4)

Asco's aesthetic basis laid on parody as a tool to represent *Chicano pop art* through street performances, conceptual art demonstrations, and a proliferation of performances. These "happenings" gave Asco a semantic of extreme distortion from the proposals made by the Chicano movement of the time, implying the necessity of a reconfiguration of the artistic cartographies of Los Angeles. They made an effort to resort to unconventional and subcultural forms of expression, such as comics,[2] photonovels, postal art, or fake media interventions, thus parodying both canonical art forms and counternarratives that did in fact legitimize the former.

One of Asco's most influential legacies is represented by its view of Chicano Mural Art. As an *antiart* group, Asco rejected the classic forms of murals enhanced by the Chicano art movement of the time, representing Aztec mythical figures dramatically camouflaged with the emergent pop culture from *el barrio*. Asco approved of the contesting, antiestablishment attitude present in those murals but also demanded a more powerful artistic action that went beyond a contemplating stance toward a posture of spatial deconstruction, as is expressed in the illustrations "Walking Mural 2" and "Las Estaciones de la Cruz." They wanted to redirect the path of a mural art that was dangerously approaching the canonical aesthetics (approximation precipitated by the system swallowing up any given countersystem), but also they aspired to produce a set of artistic expressions that were colored by the postmodern culture belonging to the marginal periphery of the city.

Supported by a manifest commitment to an aesthetic of displacement, Asco utilized space as a working tool for its artistic interventions in the city based on a *tasteless* creative value and an interest in the parody of exaggeration. Its approach to space was an exercise about the sublimation of artifice; it was an intended mediocrity, an extreme sophistication, and a queer parody. The spatial reconfiguration proposed by Asco as evidence of the necessity to transcend the paralyzing posture of art finds its epitome in the famous "Mural Instantáneo[3] (1972)," in which Patssi Valdez, one of the components of Asco, appears to be literally stuck to a wall.

With their combined use of performance and mural art, Asco parodied to the hyperbole one of the primary qualities of murals: their inherent mutability. Unlike other forms of art, the typically Angeleno murals are products of the street, born with the congenital condition of being susceptible to be reworked over and over again in a sort of infinite palimpsest. Not only are murals integrated in the space of the city, but they also developed the quality of continuously transforming the space they inhabit. Different from pieces of art that are kept away from any kind of interaction with the viewer, in a binary opposition (interior and exterior) set by rationality, murals proposed by Asco are precisely *interaction*. Through performance, they are able to integrate *other* spatialities with the artwork itself and, of course, with the artist.

Such a position integrates the two issues that are being discussed in this chapter: first, a proposal to question the modern two-dimensional space pattern and to favor a multiplicity of spaces that leads to the rhizomatic conception of the work of art; and second, the integration of cultural and artistic multiculturalism in a space that is suitable for such diversity, as opposed to the integration of other cultures in an immutable and pre-established binary space. Asco attempts to provide a framework to deconstruct legitimate spaces in art and society and, thus, open an empty space to be filled by new and horizontal conceptions of culture. A "living mural" that is integrated in the urban space and interacts with urban elements and subjectivities deforms the accepted forms of understanding art, and it does so by resorting to the peripheral and subcultural condition of Chicano culture.[4]

In addition, the titles used for these cultural interventions are indicative of the kind of art they pose: an instant, living, and participative art, one that causes an immediate impact but has an ephemeral life. It is a type of art that will end as soon as the tape is taken off the wall or when the people with whom they interact just go home or the artist gets tired of standing. The exposure of mural art to collective manipulation is today understood as an essential component of the artist's work. In the field of mural art, audience participation—even if it were to function as the obscene nature of censorship—is understood as an inseparable part of the artwork. That ephemeral condition of art is *parodied*[5] *ad infinitum* in an artistic production as Asco's "Instant Mural," in which such a condition appears exaggerated to a considerable extent when put in correlation with the artistically distorted human body. The paradox of this reconfigured *organ*ism, though, lies on the fact that it possesses an active dynamism, yet one that is intrinsically subject to an artistic rooting. Now there are not Aztec mythical figures depicted in these murals but, rather, the exaltation of grotesque distortions of human beings in a diaphanous *camp* interpretation.

Another example of Asco's transgressive art is "Walking Mural 1," in which the muralists themselves are incorporated into the artwork as an essential component of it. This is a street staging that simulates a living mural combining postmodern urban space as art[6] with the moving figures that are part of the mural. The art object, thus, does not distinguish between the living persons and the pictorial and sculptural representations that compose it. Both the guests at the table, the naked doll lying on a towel on the floor, and human figure function as an ornament in the background are but spectra of a city where art has not escaped the global commodification. The Asco group ridicules those decrepit spaces by representing a brutal aesthetic transgression of the city's arteries (the roads) through the performers' *invisible* intervention. They are nothing but ephemeral and translucent ghosts for the undaunted passing cars.

Again, Asco succeeds at exposing the limitations of the "legitimate" mural art of the time by using the core of postmodern urban space, that is, the road, to support its aesthetic proposals. A megalopolis such as Los Angeles can only acquire meaning by resorting to a rhizomatic spatiality based on a cultural multiplicity. Similarly, art discourses must be conceived parallel to these spatial rhizomes that allow for—and require—discourses of multiculturalism. Asco hit the target to add new dimensions to murals (living, walking objects) and also to incorporate elements coming from popular culture of the times into the themes that have been traditional in Chicano mural painting.[7] These two actions helped to reconfigure the aesthetic patterns of the time and created new spaces for underrepresented epistemologies of Los Angeles.

The ultimate expression of the countercultural stance of this group, however, was its celebrated "guerilla performance," with which it covered the Los Angeles County Museum of Art (LACMA) with graffiti and tags that read "Chicano Art" and had its signatures as a parody of traditional conceptions of art.

With these actions (which were in response to the refusal by LACMA executives to accept Chicano art exhibitions), Asco was able to transgress and then reverse the concept of museum. From the "destruction" of the museum as a passive container of art, it was able to transform the building in a work of art per se, one that was made from the outside, signed by *outsiders*, and had popular masses as audiences. The museum was transformed in a walking mural, and its closed space was reverted into a place of multiplicity. That action against the museum in Los Angeles is thus extrapolated to the destruction of urban identity as a way of creating a contradictory spatiality in the metropolis. Asco managed to subvert the invisibility of the Chicano art in the United States through a proposal that not only put in the streets an activation of protest art but also provided a public view of the Chicano *inorganic* body. Through the grotesque parody of the art that was represented as legitimate, Asco covered the streets with moving figures that were alive yet inert, translucent but full of color, muted but empowered. Asco became the natural habitat for a form of protest that used parody as a weapon loaded with artistic power.

In this article, I have offered a view of the different art forms expressed by Asco that affected the spatial transformation in Southern California caused by the cultural concerns of the young Chicano populations. It is important to notice how the Chicano social movement (not just political) was seeking aesthetic tools to reshape urban spatiality that were commensurate to the needs of a postnational identity. In fact, such a multicultural identity would be defined by the reconfiguration of space to shape all the ethnicities involved toward a politics of diversity rather than a politics of difference (Sleeter & McLaren, 1995, p. 107). The social impediments experienced by Chicano populations for being intruders on someone else's spatial property result in art expressions that unavoidably have subversive and transgressive components. Interpreted by their authors through an ephemeral, labile art, mural art reconfiguration transforms the urban spaces of Los Angeles into an open ground of multiplicity that favors the resemantization of the cultural identities of its inhabitants.

References

Arendt, H. (1958). *The human condition.* Chicago: Chicago University Press.

Banham, R. (2009). *Los Angeles: The architecture of four ecologies.* Berkeley: University of California Press.

Davis, M. (2001). *Magical urbanism: Latinos reinvent the US big city.* New York: Verso.

Davis, M. (2003). *Dead Cities: And Other Tales.* New York: The New Press.

Dear, M., Leclerc, G., & Berelowitz, J. (2003). *Postborder city: Cultural spaces of Bajalta California.* New York: Routledge.

Deleuze, G. (1987). *A thousand plateaus: Capitalism and schizophrenia.* Minneapolis: University of Minnesota Press.

During, S. (2005). *Cultural studies: A critical introduction.* New York: Routledge.

Franco, D. (2011, September). Asco en el museo de Los Ángeles. *Ponte al Día.* Retrieved from http://www.pontealdia.com/estados-unidos/asco-en-el-museo-de-los-angeles.html.

Garreau, J. (1992). *Edge city: Life on the new frontier.* New York: Anchor.

Gómez-Peña, G. (2000). *Dangerous border crossers: The artist talks back.* New York: Routledge.

Guattari, F., & Rolnik, S. (2006). *Micropolítica. Cartografías del deseo.* Madrid: Traficantes de Sueños.

Hutcheon, L. (2000). *A theory of parody: The teachings of twentieth-century art forms.* Urbana and Chicago: University of Illinois Press.

Lefèbvre, H. (1991). *The production of space.* London and New York: Wiley-Blackwell.

Nijman, J. (2000). The paradigmatic city. *Annals of the Association of American Geographers, 90*(1), 135–145.

Perasso, V. (2011, September 23). *Asco: Elite of the obscure, a retrospective, 1972–1987.* Retrieved from http://www.bbc.co.uk/mundo/video_fotos/2011/09/110923_galeria_asco_rg.shtml.

Pérez de Lama, J. (2008). *Los Ángeles (California) laboratorio (pos)metropolitano del siglo 20.* In Francisco Jarauta (Ed.), *De la ciudad antigua a la cosmópolis* (pp. 175–205). Santander, Spain: Fundación Marcelino Botín.

Pérez-Torres, R. (2000). Ethnicity, ethics, and Latino aesthetics. *American Literary History, 12*(3), 534–553.

Sleeter, C. E., & McLaren, P. (1995). *Multicultural education, critical pedagogy, and the politics of difference.* Albany: State University of New York Press.

Žižek, S. (2002). *Welcome to the desert of the real.* New York: Verso.

Notes

1. This is explained in depth by Mike Davis (2001) in his *Magical Urbanism*, particularly pp. 67–69.

2. In a recent interview on the occasion of the 2011 LACMA exhibition, Harry Gamboa explicitly referred to the influence of comic books on his aesthetic as a member of Asco (Franco, 2010, para. 3).

3. Photograph property of Harry Gamboa Jr., published in *East of Borneo*, November 16, 2010: Retrieved from http://www.eastofborneo.org/articles/against-the-wall-remembering-the-chicano-moratorium.

4. See illustrations "Walking Mural 2" and "Las Estaciones de la Cruz"

5. I use the term *parody* here following Lynda Hutcheon's discussion of the term (2000).

6. Whittier Boulevard is an important avenue in East Los Angeles that represents the connecting road between the different cultures in Southern California.

7. A more recent and better-known continuity of this practice is represented in the performative work of Guillermo Gómez Peña and Coco Fusco (*The Couple in the Cage*, 1992). Concepts such as "Supernintendo Ranchero," "Cybervato," "Mad Mex," or "Natural Born Matones" all refer to this fusion of elements that belong to the stereotyped Mexican traditions with popular artifacts belonging to the Anglophone American culture. For detailed information on this subject, see Gómez-Peña (2000).

Education

26

Rethinking Speech and Language Impairments Within Fluency-Dominated Cultures

Nicholas D. Hartlep and Antonio L. Ellis

"In a new environment, without the comfort of people who knew me well, I slipped back into my pattern of silence to avoid the shame of stammering and stuttering."

Byron Pitts, 2009, p. 99

Multicultural education textbooks frequently center on issues of race, gender, ethnicity, sexuality, and/or cultural diversity. Rarely, if ever, do readers of these texts have the opportunity to read research conducted on students who suffer from speech and language impairment. William Heward (2009) defines speech and language impairment (SLI) as a communication disorder such as stuttering, impaired articulation, language impairment, or a voice impairment that adversely affects a child's educational performance. The underrepresentation of SLI research in multicultural texts is evident. James Banks and Cherry Banks' (2003) highly referenced edited volume dedicates no pages to SLI issues. Other high-impact literature that inadequately covers SLI student issues is abundant (see, e.g., Banks & Banks, 2005; Gollnick & Chinn, 2009; National Research Council, 2002).

The Merriam-Webster Online Dictionary (2006) defines silence as "absence of mention." We contend that in addition to "an absence of mention" there is a "silence" or "lack of voice" in the research of SLI students and also in what multicultural education textbooks present. "Lack of voice" is caused by many things; misperceptions about people who experience speech or language impairments are one of them.[1] Misperceptions have the ability to cause the non–SLI population to underestimate speech and language disabilities and to not take them seriously. In this chapter, using data from the Data Accountability Center (DAC)—and a critical race theoretical framework—we analyze the distributions of students who are speech or language impaired by race. We focus on the race of students who are speech or language impaired because critical race theory (CRT) is most interested in issues of racial inequity. We believe that the invisibility of SLI students of color[2] is an educational inequity. We introduce and discuss what we are calling the concept of a "cycle of silence, and hope that our chapter motivates readers—be they SLI or not SLI—to further investigate the silencing of SLI students in multicultural texts that many times are devoid of SLI research (Kathard, 2001).

The Byron Pitts epigraph above illustrates what we are labeling the SLI cycle of silence. In his autobiography, Pitts (2009) recounts the pain and anguish he suffered because he stuttered. He acknowledges, "I slipped back into my pattern of silence to avoid the shame of stammering and stuttering" (p. 99). Pitts's experience as a person with a speech or language impairment caused him to become silent in order to avoid personal trauma. Silencing himself was a strategy that he frequently employed in order to avoid the traumatic experiences that accompanied stuttered speech. Pitts mentions, "I rarely spoke in my classes because I didn't have the confidence to express myself" (p. 100). Although self-silencing is completely normal and common for people who are speech or language impaired, it is also dangerous for numerous reasons.

For example, there have been documented cases of students who had speech or language impairments who took their own lives (*Lexington Herald-Leader*, 2008). Children who stutter are at greater risk of victimization and being bullied (Langevin, Bortnick, Hammer, & Wiebe, 1998). By becoming silent, SLI students in effect become invisible to the wider society that is fluency dominant. Mainstream culture is fluency dominant. As Ann Swan (1993) states, "Society values verbal communication

---

*We would like to state explicitly that we are not blaming the victim(s), but merely stating how sometimes SLI students become silent due to stress and in order to protect themselves from being perceived by others as disfluent.

and expects members to speak with ease and fluency. Being a stutterer [or person who is SLI] puts one at a distinct social and economic disadvantage" (p. 139).

Stuttering Stanley is a stereotypical term for speech- and language-impaired individuals. The Urban Online Dictionary (2011) defines a *Stuttering Stanley* as follows: "When a dumb, idiotic person can't speak correctly." Many times students who stutter internalize their disfluency and feel "dumb." Some individuals (both young and old) take drastic measures, including committing suicide. Stephen Patton, a 13-year-old boy, took his own life with a 9-millimeter handgun because he was bullied due to his stuttering; Stephen was only in eighth grade (*Lexington Herald-Leader*, 2008). Dominic Barker, a 26-year-old man, took his own life because he had a stutter (BBC News, 2006). Steven Vickerman, a 6-foot, 200-pound man who was known to stutter, committed suicide by hanging himself (Adely, 2008). Vickerman's suicide challenges the widespread notion that strong people can guard themselves against bullies. Did the stuttering in each of these cases—Barker and Vickermann—lead to suicide, or was there any underlying issue (such as traumatic childhood experience) that led both to the stuttering and suicidal thoughts? This we do not know, but even more alarming, in what has been dubbed the "Ottawa Massacre," Pierre Lebrun, "a tall, lanky 40-year-old bachelor with a stutter, [showed] up at his former workplace with a Remington 760 .30-06 rifle—a slightly modified version of the weapon that James Earl Ray used to kill civil rights crusader Martin Luther King in 1968—and his pockets stuffed with ammunition" (Branswell, 1999, para 2). Lebrun's mother believes that harassment, due to Lebrun's stutter/speech impediment, caused him to kill four people and himself.

We argue that this pattern of shame avoidance (self-silencing), coupled with the mainstream's fluency-dominated culture, contributes to a second form of silencing of SLI student populations. Behaving as if everyone can fluently speak serves to "silence" those who do not, thus rendering SLI students invisible. It is important to note that this second form of silencing is caused not by the student silencing him/herself per se; rather, it is society and schools that help impose the silence.

For example, in many classrooms—be they at the K–12 or college level—students are required to participate in verbal self-introductions in the beginning of each academic year. Normally each student introduces him/herself (i.e., saying his/her name and something fun he/she did during break). This traditional way of beginning a semester or school year is an example of how instructors and teachers assume that every student has the ability to fluently express him/herself. These moments are petrifying for SLI students, who many times find school uninviting. In order to avoid such experiences, SLI students may become self-silencing in order to avoid public ridicule and teasing or even choose to drop out of school (Zhang, Katsiyannis, Barrett, & Wilson, 2007). Research suggests that children who find school uninviting are more likely to become academically disengaged (Alexander, Entwistle, & Horsey, 1997; Anderman, 2003). Studies contend that truancy has a direct impact on dropout rates, delinquency, and poor adult outcomes (Zhang, Katsiyannis, Barrett, & Wilson, 2007).

According to the National Institute on Deafness and Other Communication Disorders (2008), roughly three million Americans stutter. However, we are still unaware of how non–White SLI students are doing when compared to their White counterparts since much of the extant research on SLI student populations does not racially disaggregate or compare race qua race. According to Yairi and Seery (2011), "[I]t is not surprising that a belief has prevailed that stuttering occurs more frequently in African American children than in European American children" (p. 40), although they note that this thinking—that African Americans stutter more than Whites—has recently begun to change. A possible explanation for the common belief that African Americans are more likely to be stutterers is due to media portrayals, feeding the impression that this is a racial reality. For instance, we found several examples of African American men whose own depictions perpetuated this false belief. Insidiously, these comical portrayals in movies[3] and by comedians[4] cause SLI people of color to never be heard. They "suffer in silence," feeling hopeless, constantly reminded that they are not welcome in a fluency-dominant culture.

Given that SLI affects people of all ages and races but occurs most often in children between the ages of 2 and 5 as they are developing their language skills (Dalton & Hardcastle, 1977), it becomes increasingly important for research to study racial group differences. This chapter will shed light on the differences that existed in the SLI student racial groups in 2008. Since approximately 1% or less of adults stutter in the United States (NIDCD, 2010), this chapter will be useful for examining whether SLI students (aged 6–21) *are* or *are not* evenly distributed among races.

Interestingly, when we contacted the National Stuttering Association (NSA; 2010) requesting racial data on SLI students, we were told that data that racially disaggregated student(s) who suffered from SLI (or stuttered) did not exist. Fortunately, the NSA (2010) was misinformed and data *do* exist (see, e.g., DAC, 2011a, 2011b). We believe that our chapter can serve as a beginning point—a "conversation starter," if you will—for such SLI awareness raising. The issues and the investigation that we present here are highly original and noticeably absent in multicultural education texts (see, e.g., Banks & Banks, 2003; National Research Council, 2002). Using critical race theory (Asch, 2001; Delgado, 1995; Delgado & Stefancic, 2001; Dixson & Rousseau, 2006; Hartlep, 2010; Taylor, Gillborn & Ladson-Billings, 2009; among others) as a lens for our study, we examine why there continues to be a lack of SLI research presented in multicultural texts, especially research that racially contextualizes SLI "silence" within racial and/or cultural minorities.

By drawing on critical race theory, we are able to explain the silencing of people of color. This is followed by our statistical analysis of DAC data to show the distributions of students who are speech or language impaired by race. We discuss the results of our analysis and suggest that additional SLI student advocacy is needed to raise awareness by making visible to the wider society those students who suffer from speech and language impairments. We begin our discussion in this chapter by assessing *The King's Speech* as an example of what George Lipsitz (1998) calls "the possessive investment in Whiteness," to show how SLI students of color are absent from such a discussion of who are impacted by speech and language impairments.

Assessing the "Lack of Voice" and Silencing of SLI Students of Color: *The King's Speech*, An Example of the Possessive Investment in Whiteness

George Lipsitz's (1998) theory of "the possessive investment in Whiteness" can be thought of as White Americans' investment in Whiteness, which provides them with resources, power, and opportunity. Lipsitz (1998) says that "[a]ll communities of color suffer from the possessive investment in Whiteness, but not in the same way" (p. 184). No movie illustrates his theory better than *The King's Speech* (2011). *The King's Speech* tells the story of how stuttering impacted Britain's King George VI (actor Colin Firth) from the age of 5 into his adulthood. As an adult, King George felt compelled to overcome his stuttering. He received several forms of therapy, remedies, and advice from multiple SLI experts. Alas, King George's stutter was never entirely cured *per se*. But unsurprisingly, White privilege is evident throughout the king's quest for fluency. In fact, unlike SLI individuals who belong to resource-deprived African American, Native American, Asian American, and other minority groups, King George VI was endowed with institutional resources, power, and opportunities that afforded him a community of "safety nets" and support systems. People of color who are also SLI lack, for the most part, advocacy and support systems.

The King's Speech is representative of what Lipsitz (1997) calls a "romantic narrative." Many times, Lipsitz (1997) says, "the motivations behind romanticism are not necessarily racist" (p. 43); however, romantic myths play an important role in the possessive investment in Whiteness since they "perpetuate rather than mitigate the alienations and injustices that [they seek] to address and redress" (p. 43). While many SLI associations have publicly praised the film for documenting an SLI issue—stuttering—many have not thoroughly examined or critiqued the film for what it truly is. The biopic film gives attention to a White man (a wealthy king) who stutters as opposed to a person of color who stutters. It is important to consider cultural experiences when seeking to understand people who stutter (Cooper & Cooper, 1998; Leith, 1986; Robinson & Crowe, 1987; Shames, 1989). Shames (1989) indicates that little research has examined cultural issues of people who stutter of historically disadvantaged racial and ethnic groups and, according to Daniels, Hagstrom, and Gabel (2006), research needs to be conducted on "how the interaction of race and communication affects the ways in which people who stutter of historically disadvantaged race-ethnic groups" (p. 201) perceive themselves and their SLI status.

The king's story, as captured in the movie—overcoming his speech language impairment, a stutter—is a romantic narrative through and through. Romantic narrative films obscure and/or omit "the social circumstances and the cultural strategies" that surround people with speech and language impairments (Lipsitz, 1997, p. 44). Not only does the film document a romantic narrative, *The King's Speech* reinforces and reifies the widespread misperceptions mentioned earlier in this chapter (Preston, 2011).

According to George Lipsitz (1998), Hollywood creates and invests in Whiteness. This means that Hollywood commodifies King George's struggle and triumph over stuttering in order to invest in Whiteness. This investment and the product (a movie) serve to protect White people's "possessive investment in Whiteness" because speech and language impairment continue to be represented as issues and or concerns that are only of importance to Whites. However, the movie does not illustrate that there are people of color who are speech or language impaired. As Lipsitz (1998, p. 112) comments, "Once these images have been circulated and recirculated, they are extremely difficult to displace." For this reason, *The King's Speech* serves as a mechanism that whitewashes SLI and presents it as an exclusively White problem, one that, with enough hard work and determination, can be overcome.

Linked to the possessive investment in Whiteness are associations and governmental agencies that are equally complicit, as Hollywood, in investing in Whiteness. In fact, Lipsitz (1998) discusses how public policies create a possessive investment in Whiteness. We argue that this investment also marginalizes people of color who suffer with SLI. In contrast, we contend that Whites who benefit from SLI associations receive professional therapeutic assistance, advocates, and even support groups. People of color who are SLI may attempt to receive their own homemade remedies or advice—such as the idea that getting hit in the face with a wet cloth will cure stuttering—from untrained local community and/or family members. According to research, this lack of support primarily results in social stigma, labeling, rejection, exclusion, and discrimination by the nonstigmatized (fluent) population (Boyle, Blood, & Blood, 2009). A cursory examination of SLI associations websites (see, e.g., www.asha.org; www.nsastutter.org; www .nidcd.nih.gov; www.westutter.org) dedicated to speech and language impairment issues reveals that the majority of these websites contain an overwhelming number of pictures of White individuals and relatively few pictures of people of color.[5] *Stuttering: For Kids, By Kids* (2006), a DVD, produced by the Stuttering Foundation of America, embodies this trend of one-sided coverage. Of the more than 15 kids who stuttered and that were interviewed during this 12-minute film, only two were non–White: one Black girl and one Hispanic boy (Scott & Guitar, 2006).

Given that these websites and films, in addressing SLI, choose to focus on Whites and marginalize non–Whites, they illustrate precisely what Lipsitz (1998) refers to "[a]s the unmarked category against which difference is constructed" (p. 2). Whiteness is invisible to most people (Bonilla-Silva, 2010) and has been referred to as "the water fish swim in," providing an analogy for White people's inability to acknowledge they are privileged because they do not see or feel it (Howard, 1999).[6]

Critical Race Theory and the Contexts of Silencing SLI Students of Color

Critical race theory (CRT) has built a reputation as being a fruitful framework for dispelling racial inequities in education and educational research. By using a critical race theoretical framework to support our arguments, we believe we can demonstrate that SLI students of color are "silenced" in numerous ways. One salient way is by demonstrating that they are almost never present in edited multicultural readers, volumes, and textbooks. Another more tacit way that SLI students of color are excluded is by the "whitewashing" of their struggles, meaning the minimization of their struggles as SLI persons. This minimization is primarily hidden through the offering of a plethora of costly therapeutic pathology while not providing advocacy groups to support people of color who suffer with SLI.

CRT has the ability to point out hidden racisms in our society since there can be "racism without racists" (Bonilla-Silva, 2010). It also can competitively challenge ahistorical and acontextual accounts made by society—which are fluency dominant and fluency normative—as well as demonstrate how Lipsitz's (1998) conceptualization of "possessive investment in Whiteness" can be used to show that SLI students of color are rendered invisible and/or silenced.

As we have already mentioned, we believe that there are two contexts for the silence of SLI students of color. First, there is the context in which SLI students of color "choose" to be silent based upon their feelings of embarrassment, humiliation, or desire to blend in. The first context is what we propose as being the SLI cycle of silence. The second context relates to the idea that there is no real advocacy to raise awareness for SLI students of color; thus, society silences SLI students. We believe that this lack of advocacy causes SLI students to silence themselves, simultaneously rendering SLI students of color invisible. Van Riper (1982) provides a lucid account of the self-silencing of SLI students: "A black stutterer said, 'Whenever I stutter, you become whiter and I blacker. Whenever I stutter to a white man, I shame my whole race. If I could only get race off [of] my back, I could handle my mouth'" (p. 231).

Method

Data Source

In order to estimate potential racial differences among students (aged 6–21) identified as SLI, we analyzed Individuals with Disabilities Education Act (IDEA) data procured, in 2011, from the Data Accountability Center (DAC). The DAC provides public access to data about children and youth with disabilities served under IDEA Part B and Part C. DAC was funded in October 2007 by the Office of Special Education Programs (OSEP) and the U.S. Department of Education to provide information and technological assistance to improve the quality of all state-reported data required by the IDEA. Two main strengths of these data are that (1) they are the most current available and (2) they are disaggregated by five race/ethnicity categories and by states.

We sought to test whether there is a difference in the distribution of SLI students by race in the data analyzed using a chi-squared test of independence.

The data consisted of a national sample consisting of N = 6,762,677 students aged 6 to 21 who were served under IDEA Part B. Students were classified by race (American Indian, Asian or Pacific Islander, Black, Hispanic, and White) and whether they had a speech and language impairment (yes/no).

Results

The "% within SLI" percentage refers to the percentage of students calculated by dividing students' SLI status (yes/no) by the total number of SLI students. The "% within race" refers to the percentage of students calculated by dividing students' SLI status (yes/no) by the total number of that racial group. Last, the "% of total" refers to the percentage of students calculated by dividing students' SLI status (yes/no) by the total of all five racial groups.

You can see from the contingency table (Table 26.1) that White students (ages 6–21), nationally, make up the largest percentage of SLI students (60.4%). The remaining 39.6% of SLI students were broken up into the following racial categories: Hispanic (20.7%), Black (14.6%), Asian or Pacific Islander (3.1%), and American Indian (1.2%). Our null hypothesis (χ^2 = 1.986E6, $p < .001$)—that there is no difference between the distributions of SLI for students of different racial backgrounds—was rejected. In other words, speech and language impairment does occur at different rates between races.

The racial distribution of SLI students is presented in Figure 26.1. Of the four non–White racial categories (Native American, Asian or Pacific Islander, Black, and Hispanic) that were aged 6 to 21 and were served under IDEA, Black and Hispanic students comprised the largest number of students who were speech language impaired. A negligible number of Native American and Asian and Pacific Islander students were speech language impaired.

Since we only had data from 2008, and were only looking at a snapshot of what is going on, there was not really a trend we could report on. However, if we compare Figures 26.2 (2008 Census Population Data) to Figure 26.1 (Racial Distribution of Speech Language Impaired students), you can see that even though the largest group of students aged 6 to 21 that were served under IDEA and were speech language impaired were Whites, one must also note that White 6- to 21-year-olds were also most prevalent in the general population among the five racial categories.

Table 26.1 Contingency Table

		Race of Student[a]					Total
		1	2	3	4	5	
Not Speech Language Impaired	Observed	1,343,740	1,290,626	1,156,976	1,085,688	517,269	5,394,299
	Expected	1,085,281	1,063,551	1,082,318	1,091,679	1,071,470	5,394,299
	% within SLI	24.9%	23.9%	21.4%	20.1%	9.6%	100.0%
	% within race	98.8%	96.8%	85.3%	79.3%	38.5%	79.8%
	% of total	19.9%	19.1%	17.1%	16.1%	7.6%	79.8%
Speech Language Impaired	Observed	16,846	42,717	199,895	282,918	826,002	1,368,378
	Expected	275,305	269,792	274,553	276,927	271,801	1,368,378
	% within SLI	1.2%	3.1%	14.6%	20.7%	60.4%	100.0%
	% within race	1.2%	3.2%	14.7%	20.7%	61.5%	20.2%
	% of total	.2%	.6%	3.0%	4.2%	12.2%	20.2%
Total	Observed	1,360,586	1,333,343	1,356,871	1,368,606	1,343,271	6,762,677
	Expected	1,360,586	1,333,343	1,356,871	1,368,606	1,343,271	6,762,677
	% within SLI	20.1%	19.7%	20.1%	20.2%	19.9%	100.0%
	% within race	100.0%	100.0%	100.0%	100.0%	100.0%	100.0%
	% of total	20.1%	19.7%	20.1%	20.2%	19.9%	100.0%

[a](1) American Indian, (2) Asian or Pacific Islander, (3) Black (not Hispanic), (4) Hispanic, (5) White (not Hispanic). Special thanks to Jacqueline Gosz for fielding questions about chi-squared analysis. Adapted from "Data Accountability Center (DAC), Class of 2008," available from www.ideadata.org.

Source: US Department of Education.

Table 26.2   2008 Estimated Population by Race and Age[a]

		Race				
Age	Total[c]	American Indian, Alaska Native	Asian & Native Hawaiian and Pacific Islander[b]	Black or African American	Hispanic Origin[c]	White
6 years old	4,835	50	182	588	934	3,081
7 years old	4,875	50	184	604	919	3,118
8 years old	4,657	48	168	585	848	3,008
9 years old	4,574	47	166	581	804	2,976
10 years old	4,582	47	170	589	798	2,978
11 years old	4,611	47	173	593	796	3,002
12 years old	4,701	48	176	605	802	3,070
13 years old	4,770	49	173	632	802	3,114
14 years old	4,797	50	172	653	792	3,130
15 years old	4,884	52	173	677	790	3,192
16 years old	4,954	55	173	686	785	3,255
17 years old	5,017	55	173	698	776	3,315
18 years old	5,096	56	176	711	771	3,382
19 years old	4,907	55	177	673	728	3,274
20 years old	4,852	54	175	650	725	3,248
21 years old	4,818	53	174	633	720	3,238
Total	76,930	816	2,785	10,158	12,790	50,381

This is as of July 1, 2008, and is presented in thousands (for example 207,007 represents 207,007,000).
Does not include indviduals who identify as "two or more races."

Asian and Native Hawaiin and Other Pacific Islander were combined.

Persons of Hispanic origin may be any race.

Adapted from "Statistical Abstract of the United States: 2008," by the United States Census Bureau, 2008.

Discussion

According to our findings, White students do carry the largest percentage of students who are speech language impaired. Multicultural researchers and texts should not view these results (finding racial differences) as a problem per se. Rather than conducting polemical research that pits Whites versus non–Whites or SLI versus non–SLI, future research based on these results should investigate what can be learned from these racial differences in the distribution of SLI students.

Figure 26.1   Display of Speech Language Impaired Students[a]

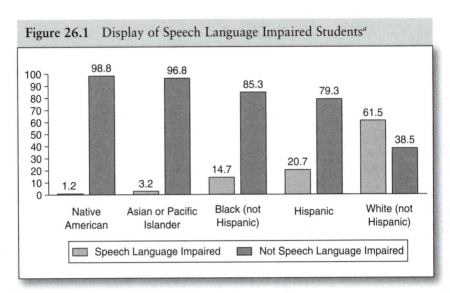

[a]This represents all students aged 6 to 21 who were served under IDEA who were classified SLI in 2008. The racial distribution of speech language impaired students includes five racial groups. Each racial group has two columns: (a) the lighter gray column represents the percentage within that race that is speech language impaired, and (b) the darker gray column represents the percentage within that race that is not speech language impaired.

Note: Due to rounding, percentages within each racial category sum to 100%.

Figure 26.2   Display of 2008 General Population of 6- 21-Year-Olds by Race[a]

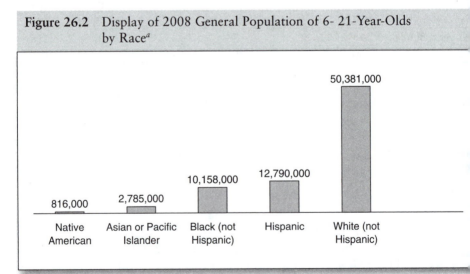

[a]This represents the estimated total number of 6- to 21-year-olds by race in 2008. Each of the five rac group has one column, which represents the total number.

Note: This number was simply the "total" or the last row in Figure 26.1. (tabular form) transformed in graphical form.

Source: US Census Bureau.

Specifically, we feel that future research studies might ask the following: (1) Are SLI differences systematic, institutional, and/or physiological/ psychological in nature? (2) How might schooling and environmental factors impact SLI risk among students of various racial groups? (3) Are certain racial groups more resilient than others in overcoming SLI? If so, how?

One limitation of this study is that the SLI racial population variation we found may be attributable to the states' differential handling of IDEA Part B data. For clarity purposes, the DAC provides information and data notes on the ways in which states collected and reported data differently from the Office of Special Education Programs (OSEP). This information can be found on the DAC website under Part B Data Notes: 2007–08 Reporting Year and Fall 2008 (DAC, 2008).

Lastly, the implications of this study may be pursued by researchers who potentially look at "older" years of data and/or data that were collected "regionally" (as opposed to national data) to ascertain whether our findings are consistent with these aforesaid-collected data. This would be a conceptual difference. Researchers may also entertain the possibility of a different methodological (i.e., qualitative measures) or theoretical (i.e., disciplinary or grounded) approach.

Overall, we feel strongly that one of the myriad goals of multicultural research is to positively effect change in the lives and educational experiences of all SLI students, keeping in mind that many who suffer and are silenced are students of color. This research is highly important given that research indicates that language impairment (such as SLI) is linked with youth suicide (see Figure 26.3). In this chapter, we used George Lipsitz's (1998) theory of "the possessive investment in Whiteness," linking it to *The King's Speech* (2011). We discussed the contexts of the silencing of SLI students of color by drawing on critical race theory to explain this societal- and self-silencing. Our statistical analysis of DAC data followed, showing that speech and language impairment does occur at different rates among races. We discussed the results of our analysis and suggested that additional SLI student advocacy is needed to raise awareness by making visible to the wider society those students who suffer from speech or language impairments.

The King's Speech (2011) is the most recent manifestation of media showcasing the struggle and triumph of a White man who battled SLI. The movie's message and messengers ought to be interrogated for their motivation to produce such a film. This chapter's research is extremely important given that research indicates that language impairment (such as SLI) is linked with youth suicide, as shown in Figure 26.3. Although the data show that more Whites stutter than African Americans, we believe that SLI (including stuttering) is more detrimental for African Americans, especially poor ones. SLI creates a system of institutional, educational, and insular failure, and societal- and self-silencing causes this racial group to go unheard by the fluency dominant society. SLI people of color remain marginalized and misunderstood.

Figure 26.3   Possible Links between Youth Suicide and Speech Language Impairment

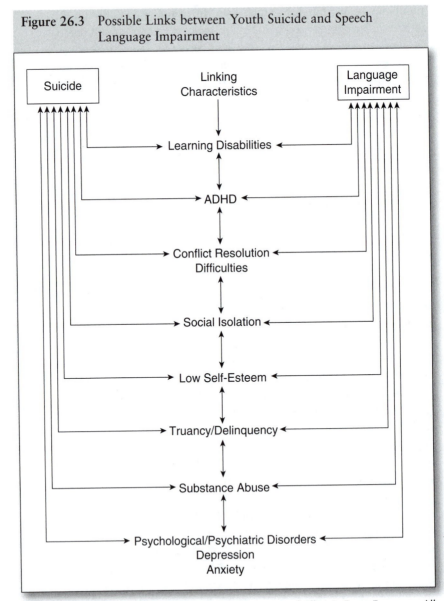

Reed (2011) states that there are possible links between youth suicide and speech language impairment, and we feel that future studies might investigate this linkage.

Conclusion

Rethinking speech and language impairments within fluency-dominated cultures is a difficult task. There is a lack of usable data on the numbers and incidents of SLI students; and SLI students remain an underwritten-about population. However, if multiculturalists are genuinely concerned with equity and equality for all student learners, textbooks must include their stories and struggles. This chapter was our attempt to assess the "lack of voice" and silencing of SLI students of color through the use of critical race theory. Our findings that Whites comprise the largest share of SLI students does not mean that SLI students of color are not silenced, as Pitts' (a Black man) epigraph attests: SLI students may unavoidably slip back into patterns of silence to avoid the shame of stammering and stuttering (Ginsberg, 2000; Ginsberg & Wexler, 2000; Klompass & Ross, 2004; Pitts, 2009). Charles Van Riper's (1982, p. 2) comment, that "Stuttering is not merely a speech impediment; it is an impediment in social living" is correct, given that mainstream American culture is fluency dominant.

Throughout this chapter we have argued that *The King's Speech* and speech language associations are complicit in perpetuating misperceptions of SLI students in that they all attend to a White racial constituency—reinforcing a possessive investment in Whiteness. Whereas comedians make fun of African American stutterers, reifying the belief that African Americans are most likely to be SLI, our analyses revealed otherwise: Whites are more likely to be SLI than African Americans. Past research confirms our study's findings; however, we argue that this knowledge is not enough. This racial distribution discrepancy should cause SLI students of color to receive more equitable attention and more advocacy work in terms of educational researchers' attention. As critical race theoreticians, we feel that SLI is more of an issue for students of color, namely, African Americans, than it is for Whites. This is the urgent issue that we sought to bring to bear and why we are seeking that multicultural texts and future research address SLI students of color.

References

Adely, H. (2008, March 1). Neglected by VA, veteran's war trauma ends in suicide. *The Journal News*. Retrieved on May 14, 2011, from http://archive.truthout.org/ article/neglected-va-veterans-war-trauma-ends-suicide?print.

Alexander, K. L., Entwistle, D. R., & Horsey, C. (1997). From first grade forward: Early foundations of high school dropout. *Sociology of Education, 70*(2), 87–107.

Anderman, L. H. (2003). Academic and social perceptions as predictors of change in middle school students' sense of belonging. *Journal of Experimental Education, 72*(1), 5–22.

Asch, A. (2001). Critical race theory, feminism, and disability: Reflections on social justice and personal identity. *Ohio State Law Journal, 62*(1), 391–423.

Banks, J. A., & Banks, C. A. (2003). *Handbook of research on multicultural education* (2nd ed.). San Francisco, CA: Jossey-Bass/Wiley.

Banks, J. A., & Banks, C. A. (2005). *Multicultural education: Issues and perspectives* (5th ed.). San Francisco, CA: Jossey-Bass/Wiley.

BBC News. (2006, February 2). New research to help stammering. Retrieved on May 14, 2011, from http://news.bbc.co.uk/2/hi/uk_news/england/suffolk/4674080.stm.

Bonilla-Silva, E. (2010). *Racism without racists: Color-blind racism & racial inequality in contemporary America* (3rd ed.). Plymouth, UK: Rowman & Littlefield.

Boyle, M. P., Blood, W. B., & Blood, I. M. (2009). Effects of perceived causality on perceptions of persons who stutter. *Journal of Fluency Disorders, 34*(3), 201–218.

Branswell, B. (1999). Ottawa massacre. *The Canadian Encyclopedia.* Retrieved on March 21, 2011, from http://www.thecanadianencyclopedia.com/index.cfm?Pg Nm=TCE&Params=M1ARTM0011943.

Cooper, E. B., & Cooper, C. S. (1998). Multicultural considerations in the assessment and treatment of stuttering. In D. E. Battle (Ed.), *Communication disorders in multicultural populations* (pp. 247–274). Boston: Butterworth-Heinemann.

Dalton, P., & Hardcastle, W. J. (1977). *Disorders of fluency and their effects on communication.* London, UK: Edward Arnold.

Daniels, D. E., Hagstrom, F., & Gabel, R. (2006). A qualitative study of how African American men who stutter attribute meaning to identity and life choices. *Journal of Fluency Disorders, 31*(3), 200–215.

Data Accountability Center (DAC). (2008). Part B Data Notes: 2007–08 Reporting Year and Fall 2008. Retrieved on March 8, 2011, from https://www.ideadata.org/docs/bdatanotes2008.pdf.

Data Accountability Center (DAC). (2011a). *Children ages 3 through 5 with speech or language impairments served under IDEA, Part B, by the five race/ethnicity categories and state: Fall 2008* [Data files]. Retrieved from https://www.ideadata.org.

Data Accountability Center (DAC). (2011b). *Students ages 6 through 21 with speech or language impairments served under IDEA, by the five race/ethnicity categories and state: Fall 2008* [Data files]. Retrieved from https://www.ideadata.org.

Delgado, R. (Ed.). (1995). *Critical race theory: The cutting edge.* Philadelphia: Temple University Press.

Delgado, R., & Stefancic, J. (2001). *Critical race theory: An introduction.* New York: New York University Press.

Dixson, A. D., & Rousseau, C. K. (Eds.). (2006). *Critical race theory in education.* New York: Routledge.

Ginsberg, A. P. (2000). Shame, self-consciousness, and locus of control in people who stutter. *Journal of Genetic Psychology, 161*(4), 389–399.

Ginsberg, A. P., & Wexler, K. B. (2000). Understanding stuttering and counseling clients who stutter. *Journal of Mental Health Counseling, 22*(3), 228–239.

Gollnick, D. M., & Chinn, P. C. (2009). *Multicultural education in a pluralistic society* (8th ed.). Upper Saddle River, NJ: Merrill-Pearson.

Hartlep, N. D. (2010). *Going public: Critical race theory and issues of social justice.* Mustang, OK: Tate.

Heward, W. L. (2009). *Exceptional children: An introduction to special education* (9th ed.). Columbus, OH: Merrill-Pearson.

Howard, G. R. (1999). *We can't teach what we don't know: White teachers, multiracial schools.* New York: Teachers College Press.

Kathard, H. (2001). Sharing stories: Life history narratives in stuttering research. *International Journal of Language & Communication Disorders, 36*(S1), 52–57.

Klompas, M. & Ross, E. (2004). Life experiences of people who stutter, and the perceived impact of stuttering on quality of life: Personal accounts of South African individuals. *Journal of Fluency Disorders, 29,* 275–305.

Langevin, M., Bortnick, K., Hammer, T., & Wiebe, E. (1998). Teasing/bullying experienced by children who stutter: Toward development of a questionnaire. *Contemporary Issues in Communication Science and Disorders, 25,* 12–24.

Leith, W. R. (1986). Treating the stutterer with atypical cultural influence. In K. St. Louis (Ed.), *The atypical stutterer: Principles and practices of rehabilitation* (pp. 9–35). New York: Academic Press.

Lexington Herald-Leader. (2008). Parents sue school after bullied son commits suicide. Retrieved on February 19, 2011, from http://www.pantagraph.com/news/article_ccd303e9-091c-5c4c-8344-74fa9a78c182.html.

Lipsitz, G. (1997). Remembering Robert Johnson: Romance and reality. *Popular Music & Society, 21*(4), 39–50.

Lipsitz, G. (1998). *The possessive investment in Whiteness: How White people profit from identity politics.* Philadelphia: Temple University Press.

Merriam-Webster Online Dictionary. (2006). Entry for Silence. Retrieved February 22, 2011, from http://www.m-w.com/dictionary/silence.

National Institute on Deafness and Other Communication Disorders (NIDCD). (2010). *Quick stats for voice, speech, and language.* [Online]. Available: www.nidcd.nih.gov/health/statistics/vsl/stats.htm.

National Research Council. (2002). *Minority students in special and gifted education.* Washington, DC: National Academy Press.

National Stuttering Association (NSA). (2010). *What the National Stuttering Association can do for you . . .* [Online]. Available: www.nsastutter.org.

Pitts, B. (2009). *Stepping out on nothing: How faith and family helped me conquer life's challenges.* New York: St. Martin's Press.

Preston, K. (2011, February 21). How *The King's Speech* gets stuttering wrong. Retrieved on March 2, 2011, from http://www.salon.com/entertainment/movies/film_salon/2011/02/21/kings_speech_stuttering/index.html.

Reed, V. A. (2011). *An introduction to children with language disorders* (4th ed.). Upper Saddle River, NJ: Pearson Education.

Robinson, T. L., & Crowe, T. A. (1987). A comparative study of speech disfluencies in nonblack and White college athletes. *Journal of Fluency Disorders, 12*(2), 147–156.

Scott, L. A., & Guitar, C. (Producers). (2006). *Stuttering: For kids, by kids* [DVD]. Memphis, TN: The Stuttering Foundation of America.

Shames, G. H. (1989). Stuttering: An RFP for a cultural perspective. *Journal of Fluency Disorders, 14*(1), 67–77.

Swan, A. M. (1993). Helping children who stutter: What teachers need to know. *Childhood Education, 69*(3), 138–141.

Taylor, E., Gillborn, D., & Ladson-Billings, G. (Eds.). (2009). *Foundations of critical race theory in education.* New York: Routledge.

United States Census Bureau. (2008). Statistical abstract of the United States: 2008. Retrieved on February 24, 2011, from http://www.census.gov/compendia/statab/2010/tables/10s0010.pdf.

Urban Online Dictionary. (2011). Entry for Stuttering Stanley. Retrieved February 24, 2011, from http://www.urbandictionary.com/stuttering+stanley.

Van Riper, C. (1982). *The nature of stuttering* (2nd ed.). Englewood Cliffs, NJ: Prentice-Hall, Inc.

Yairi, E., & Seery, C. H. (2011). *Stuttering: Foundations and clinical applications.* Upper Saddle River, NJ: Pearson Education.

Zhang, D., Katsiyannis, A., Barrett, D., & Wilson, V. L. (2007). Truancy offenders in the juvenile justice system: Examinations of first and second referrals. *Remedial and Special Education, 28*(4), 244–256.

Notes

1. Many authors of multicultural education volumes decidedly or unknowingly do not cover SLI students within their pages. Educational research associations—that is, the American Educational Research Association (AERA)—are also complicit in not reaching the SLI population: Proposal submissions for AERA's 2012 Annual Meeting in Vancouver, BC, Canada, provided only auditory, orthopedic, and visual accommodation options for prospective presenters. The expectation that presenters verbally participate overlooks the diversity of researchers' speaking and articulation abilities, such as those who may not be able to discuss their research findings orally. It seems logical that AERA would offer accommodations for SLI persons given that it is the premier educational research association; however, this is not the case when looking at its proposal submission process. We wonder, is this because the SLI population is silent in the association, or does AERA silence its SLI membership through its practices and policies?

2. We focus on African Americans and use the terms *African American* and *Black* interchangeably.

3. Director Eddie Murphy's (1989) *Harlem Nights* portrays an African American boxer who stutters.

4. The late Bernie Mac, an African American comedian, in director Spike Lee's (2000) *The Original Kings of Comedy*, has a standup routine in which he distastefully mocks a supposed African American stutterer. While the audience clearly cannot contain its laughter, Mac's standup act is very offensive to stutterers and people with SLI. The fact that so many people in the audience find it humorous is indicative of the fluency-dominant culture of the mainstream population. In addition, as a part of his performance, he linked stuttering to mental retardation (in his words).

5. At the time of conducting research for this chapter, all of the National Stuttering Association's Board of Directors and also staff were white men (eight) and/or women (eight).

6. While we have no empirical evidence for these claims, readers of our chapter may want to visit the websites and view the films that we have mentioned above.

27

Color-Blindsided at the Intersection of Multicultural and Integrated Arts Education

Teresa L. Cotner

Introduction

What I have tried to suggest in this short tale is that cultures are like disciplines, in that the boundaries between them are artificial constructs useful only in preliminary stages of dividing and studying. I also want to remind readers that disciplines are like cultures; especially in the way they develop their own lingo, values, and worldviews.

Art educators interested in working across disciplinary boundaries may wish to work across cultural boundaries as well. Both types of boundaries represent once functional, but now less useful, perhaps even outmoded, ways of thinking about the world. Adapting to changing conditions may mean that humans should re-focus on the bigger picture, seeking connections and putting the bits and pieces back together for the common good.

Perhaps it is time for folks to develop a culture of interdisciplinarity and a discipline of interculturality, through which they can re-focus on the end goal, not just the means, of learning about their world.

Melanie Davenport, 2005, p. 3

Education has been, literally and metaphorically, color-blind and blindsided in its attempts to embrace multicultural and integrated arts education. Why would arts teachers and the greater arts community (artists, historians, critics, collectors, enthusiasts) feel disdain for integrated and multicultural arts education practices? Many would say, in response to this question, that they do not feel any aversion to these practices in the classroom or in professional practice. This chapter advances the idea that, indeed, many do and that this inconspicuous disdain is the result of hegemonic cultural norms that has created and sustained a mere marginal role for integrated and multicultural art education in the big curricular picture.

Perspectives and practices in multicultural arts education and integrated arts education share common threads that expose foundational problems that tenaciously shadow these two approaches to both the arts and arts education. These problems have inconspicuously and not so inconspicuously persisted in multicultural arts education and integrated arts education and have compromised the integrity of these educational endeavors. These problems permeate historical contexts, research, and classroom practices. This chapter teases out some misguided ideas that exist at the roots of multicultural arts education and integrated arts education in hopes of elevating them to become the powerful pedagogical practices and proponents of social change that they could and should be.

Multicultural arts education and integrated arts education do not typically share space within any one academic document. As approaches to arts education, they can appear to have existed in separate paradigms; however, another look reveals commonalities between the two, which, when flushed out and examined, may facilitate achieving the intended outcomes of both.

The following provides basic working definitions of multicultural arts education (MAE) and integrated arts education (IAE). MAE is generally known as an approach to teaching art that utilizes art forms and the cultural contexts that produce them, from a wide, inclusive array of cultures, in hopes of shifting away from cultural hegemony and toward an inclusive and culturally egalitarian socio-political future for multicultural nations and in the global context. IAE, often thought of in terms of adding art to the so-called core subjects to make them more fun and engaging, is considered in this chapter as an approach to teaching art by integrating two or more of the five arts (dance, language arts, music, theatre, and visual arts) together in hopes of providing a richer arts experience through the synergy of the creative arts. Both pedagogies enjoy long histories as approaches to arts education, both are popular among some and reviled by some, and there is scant scholarly literature that examines their histories in common.

A discussion of MAE and IAE is not the same as a discussion of multiculturalism or of integrated arts in a broader context of the art world and its practices. Although classroom practices are highly influenced by professional practices, they are also divergent from professional practices. The broader contexts of multiculturalism and of integrated arts outside of the classroom are discussed in this chapter as they can be understood to have direct effects on classroom practices.

Prehistory to Early Modernity

Before consideration of MAE and IAE in the 20th and 21st centuries, a brief view of the historical roots of these two endeavors can help make clear some of the problems that contribute to their marginal place in arts education. Ellen Dissanayake (2007) has written extensively about the origins of human aesthetic responses to the creative arts. She recognizes parent–child interaction as laying the groundwork for aesthetic response, and she also recognizes ritual, which incorporates all five of the creative arts, as the original art. This makes integrated arts the first form of art.

While integrated art appears, like roots rock, to be a roots art form, cultural integration, or cultural diversity, is a relatively new phenomenon in human history that, in addition to tensions and violence, has also led to cultural awareness and classroom practices of multiculturalism in modern times. Dissanayake looks at human history through the lens of evolutionary psychology and recognizes that most of the 250,000 years of *Homo sapiens* evolution prepared modern humans to be successful hunter gatherers who live in small, monocultural groups. Early modern humans began to practice the arts approximately 35,000 years before the present. However, only in the past 10,000 years did the agriculturalist/industrialist modern humans begin to live in super-sized civilizations in which many cultures coexisted. Of course, in such societies, there were always dominant and subordinate cultures, and, often, there were slaves. There was appropriation between cultures, and some aspects of cultures were lost in the process of joining cultures together, one form of multiculturalism. We can extrapolate from recognized tenets of evolution that evolution did not have very much time, relatively speaking, to prepare modern humans for multiculturalism.

Dissanayake does not suggest that integrated arts are the only way to approach arts education just because it is a root form of art, nor does she suggest that due to its relatively short existence among human cultures, culturally diverse human groups cannot coexist. These claims would make multiculturalism in education a losing proposition from the perspective of evolution. Rather, Dissanayake's work can be interpreted to recognize integrated arts as root forms of art and multiculturalism as an evolutionarily determined reality of human civilizations. Approaching MAE and IAE with clearer understandings of how they came to be, we are better equipped to fully understand and successfully and meaningfully enact the MAE and IAE classroom practices that history has set into motion. Thirty-five thousand years of integrated art and 10,000 years of multicultural societies, as further discussed below, have given contemporary humans ample time to develop practices in MAE and IAE that can successfully promote well-rounded individuals who can contribute to a democratic society. However, a re-examination of both must begin first.

Questions to ask at this juncture are: One, if integrated arts is the original form of art, how and when did it fall from grace, if indeed it did? and two, if 240,000 years of evolution prepared humankind for monoculturalism, how did multiculturalism find its way into and change world cultures, world arts, and arts education?

If we continue to follow the path of integrated arts, we see a fall from grace that can be traced directly back to the beginnings of the agricultural revolution 10,000 years ago, the time when humans began to live in large-scale civilizations that also happened to be composed of more than one culture, for example, Mesopotamia (10,000 B.C.E.), predynastic Egypt (5,500 B.C.E.), Mycenae (4000 B.C.E.), and in the Olmec culture (3,500 B.C.E.). (Please note that agriculture and the megacivilizations it produced, like written language, began in different parts of the world at different times.) As the agricultural revolution came to different parts of the world and megacivilizations grew, the arts became more specialized, as did many aspects of culture, such as religious practices. As with language and agriculture, the arts became agents of social control. One's gender and station in life would determine the ways in which one could participate in the arts. By the dawn of the modern era, the 17th and 18th centuries, art and education were utilized for social control, but as postcolonialism took form, the arts were used as a means of reclaiming precolonial culture (Stankiewicz, 2007). Song and dance were common to school curricula in many countries during the 19th century as a form of cultural awareness, that is, awareness of the dominant culture (Buck, 2007; Dils, 2007; Wee, 2007).

Of particular interest to the ideas set forth in this chapter, the arts of the nondominant cultures, including the unofficial art of the dominant culture, often known as folk art, appear to have continued to exercise integration through the centuries. A few examples of this, from throughout time and throughout the world, include the Korean mask dance, the maypole dance, American hoedown, American football half-time entertainment, music videos, hip-hop, breakdancing, and rap. The persistence of integrated forms of art in society, specifically that of marginalized cultures including folk cultures, suggests a centuries-long existence of integrated arts on the fringes of society, after their fall from practice among the dominant cultures.

In the early civilizations, we see evidence of the cultures, including the art forms of many people, being absorbed into a dominant culture's practices. To the degree to which a dominant culture in a multicultural megaculture showed tolerance for the cultural practices of the many peoples who lived within the same walls, it would follow that many cultural practices of the nondominant cultures, including folk cultures, would be more or less marginalized and, in some cases, even clandestine. The African American Underground Railroad and story quilt would be examples of clandestine forms of art practiced outside of the dominant culture—forms practiced in secret or, at the very least, the purpose and interpretation of the art was not known to outsiders. An example of a marginalized art form would be outsider art or the art of the insane.

The 20th Century

Between 1919 and 1930, the New Negro Movement, which promoted the social progress of African Americans, had a profound effect on the American art world. This progressive social movement helped to promote the artists of the Harlem Renaissance, such as painter Jacob Lawrence, poet/writer Langston Hughes, and composer/pianist Duke Ellington, as well as university art professors such as Aaron Douglas and Hale Woodruff. A generation of African American artists found support among black and white patrons. At this time, artists from Europe drew heavily from traditional African and Japanese aesthetics in their art. The African American artists of this period saw tremendous opportunities in comparison to those who came before and, perhaps, after. As educators, Douglas and Woodruff, in particular, were able to push past the "color bar," changing policies for African Americans and African American art at universities, museums, and galleries (Bey, 2011).

If we carry the story of progressivism in America in the 1920s and 1930s back to the American K–12 classroom, we find that integrated forms of art (combining the arts, i.e., dance, language arts, music, theatre, and visual arts) held a dominant place in the elementary classroom, which, in the early 20ths century, happened to be the domain of a significant subculture: women. The journal *School Arts*, which was the preeminent art education journal of the first half of the 20th century, featured articles about elementary school practices with integrated arts in most issues and even had a special issue each year devoted to integrated (also known as correlated) arts. While in the 19th and early 20th centuries, mostly men attended higher-education art academies and practiced nonintegrated forms of art (i.e., just painting, or just violin, etc.), women continued to learn many forms of art at home, such as sewing, which could produce costumes that would become part of dance or theatre. These gender lines in exposure to the arts could contribute to the fact that IAE was very popular in the early days of American children's education.

Often, under the influence of the melting pot view of the United States, many school art projects fulfilled the perceived need to celebrate the many world cultures. These projects might typically include, for example, African masks, Native American totems, European maypole dance, or Indonesian shadow puppets. Notably, African *American*, Asian *American* and Latin *American* cultures were not explored in the arts until after the civil rights movement began. At that time, these cultures gained recognition as *American* cultures, and multiculturalism was recognized and championed by education researchers, notably June King McFee (1998). Unfortunately, authentic art from outside of the white/Western traditions, notably African and Native American cultures, was commonly viewed as savage, primitive, or voodoo (Bey, 2011), which would make it unsuitable for children's education, or it was watered down to fit another stereotype, that of being childlike. The toilet paper totem pole and *papier maché* African mask represent early attempts to bring multiculturalism to the art classroom at a time when well-meaning classroom teachers did not fathom how truly primitive their understanding of the so-called primitive cultures was.

While integrated and multicultural arts forms received much attention in the elementary school classroom, they did not flourish in secondary school or in higher education, which were and remain male-dominated segments of society. This is due largely to the fact that subject matter specialists, unlike the elementary school generalist, are not trained in more than one discipline. Also, secondary school structures are bound to the Carnegie Unit, which, since the late 19th century, has dominated secondary education and segregated the academic disciplines into 120 contact hours with an instructor each. Although higher education is not officially structured around the Carnegie Unit, it operates on the same principles as secondary schools in terms of academic disciplines being offered as discrete subject matter and independent of each other.

Elementary schools were better able to be flexible within the Carnegie structure due to the single-classroom structure, but one cannot help but imagine that the dominant culture in America, the white male culture that produced the Carnegie unit and dominated secondary and higher education, is also culpable for academic subject segregation and lack of attention to any culture but the dominant culture in secondary and higher education. Both MAE and IAE are notably shaped by an American predilection for the segregation of genders, cultures, races, and academic disciplines.

After World War II, nations throughout the world looked to education to help redefine their national identities (Stankiewicz, 2007). Based largely on assumptions and intuition, many launched integrated arts programs of some kind during the 20th century (Kindler, 1987). Many of these assumptions and intuitions have, arguably, yet to be supported by research—for example, that art enhances learning in nonart disciplines (Catteral, 1998; Eisner, 1998). Nevertheless, some intuitions, for example, that the arts share common cognitive processes and that learning is enhanced by creativity, have received support from 21st-century research, as discussed below.

Owatonna in the 1930s and CEMREL in the 1970s were the most large-scale integrated arts reform movements of the 20th century in the United States. Scholars created and distributed integrated arts kits to elementary school. Both projects were organized by education researchers and directly associated with universities. Students showed improvement in creative thinking and risk taking; however, the art kits were costly, and Owatonna and CEMREL could not be sustained (Stokrocki, 2005, p. 5). Both projects noted successful results of integrated arts, and both quietly disappeared as funds and founders felt compelled to move on to other endeavors.

In an address at the InSEA (International Society for Education through Art) Congress in Adelaide, Australia, in 1978, McFee (1998) noted that strict parenting was a likely contributor to closed mindedness and that one's native language dictated, to a great extent, one's ability to readily perceive certain aspects of understanding visual art, such as depth perception and color variation (pp. 33–34). McFee's observations were presented in support of multicultural art education (and by association, one could argue, integrated arts) as a pedagogy that embraces plurality on many levels.

In the last quarter of the 20th century, integrated arts did not have great champions, as multiculturalism in arts education had in McFee (and in many others) and in the civil rights movement. Multiculturalism became somewhat of a household word but lacked uniformity in definition and practice (Boughton & Mason, 1999). By the end of the century, multicultural arts education had a significant body of research and curricula to support it, while integrated arts had virtually none.

Integrated arts education was further marginalized in the face of the growing popularity of standards-based or disciplined-based arts curricula and pedagogy. The Getty Education Institute for the Arts (formerly Getty Institute for Educators on the Visual Arts) was highly instrumental in giving standards-based arts education a secure place in education across the country. Notably, the Getty's version of standards-based art education, discipline-based art education (DBAE), was highly criticized for being Western centric in the examples of art it used in its published art education materials. DBAE and other content-based approaches are still strongly represented today in national, state, and local arts standards. These standards highlight arts disciplines as separate entities that can share some common vocabulary and outcomes concerning creative growth. Both MAE and IAE claim only indirect and, in some cases, perhaps, ancillary mention in the national and in many state and local standards.

As the 20th century drew to a close, MAE and IAE practices existed intermittently in elementary and secondary classrooms as teachers struggled to accommodate the content standards systems that took hold at national, state, and local levels. These systems further separated academic disciplines, including the arts, from each other and included, at best, peripheral lip service to practices in MAE and IAE.

Some education research in the 1960s and 1970s warned against the perils of strict segregation between academic disciplines. In the classic text "Education and the Cult of Efficiency" (Callahan, 1962), Raymond E. Callahan describes how the efficiency of the American auto assembly line became the model for education and resulted in rote learning and segregation of each academic discipline. A related paper by Basil Bernstein (1971), on a theory of classification and framing in curricula, suggests that strong framing, meaning strong boundaries between disciplines, results in a curriculum that entails reduced student opinions, whereas weak framing, when boundaries between disciplines are blurred, results in a range of student opinions. For Bernstein, the stronger the classification and the framing, the more the educational relationship tends to be hierarchical and the student seen as ignorant, with little status and few rights.

Strong lines between disciplines gained momentum. Even though a century of *avant garde* art movements throughout the 20th century, such as Dada and Surrealist stage performances and films and, later, performance art, promoted practices of arts integration, there was virtually no research to back similar practices in the classroom (Kindler, 1987). The end of the 20th century saw heightened attention to the arts as a catalyst for increased test scores in the so-called core subjects (Eisner, 1998), and this only decreased attention to integrating of the arts together, as the arts were seen by many as the handmaiden to the so-called core subjects. (Of course, language arts are considered to be a core subject and, not surprisingly, despite their title of language *arts*, many do not include language arts among the arts.)

Neither the visual and performing arts nor multiculturalism have been a focus of high-stakes testing, and these approaches to education finished out the 20th century as somewhat persistent remnants of the past that lacked the political and research-based backing to secure their place in each child's education. Conversely, in the 21st century, we can begin to see breakthroughs in cognitive studies and in a new generation of culture and gender studies that give new life to multicultural and integrated arts education, two age-old, underappreciated and underutilized endeavors.

The 21st Century

Arts and education research have demonstrated the habit of being the *avant garde* in evolutions of thought and action. For example, in the 20th century, the integrated forms of fine art, generally known as performance art, and progressive education, which opened doors for innovations in education such as multiculturalism, both stood in utter contrast to norms in art and in education that were centuries old. Notably, performance art along with progressive education practices, though today approximately a century old each, continue to encounter resistance in their fields.

Most art educators and art programs in primary, secondary, and higher education continue to teach the various arts media as distinct courses of study; for example, ceramics and printmaking are largely taught separately despite the fact that these two media can be, and often are, integrated together. Also, the other arts—music, theatre, dance, and language arts—are each to be found, in secondary and in higher education, in separate departments and even in separate colleges. Structurally difficult questions arise as a result. Are the language arts included in the arts or as a so-called core subject? Is dance art or physical education? Is theatre an art or a language art? (In California and in many states, in order to earn a teaching credential in theatre, one must have a bachelor's degree in English.)

One result of formal education's segregation of the arts disciplines is that the performance artist, who integrates two or more art disciplines together, can appear to be self-taught because formal education does not teach integrated arts practices—at least, not much. Therefore, performance art, a form of integrated art, often remains questionable and is even reviled by the establishment. It is only natural that this attitude also infiltrates arts education.

In a similar vein, multicultural arts education is not the result of formal teaching practices. There is no degree, no department of MAE. Therefore, MAE is viewed as a self-taught rather than a formally taught endeavor. There is an old (and very tired) adage about teachers in comparison to related professional practice: "those who can't, teach." That is to say, for example, that if you are not a good artist, you can teach art. It could be further extrapolated that there is a population within the fields of art education who feel that "Teachers who can't specialize in one cultural perspective or one arts medium should not be taken seriously as art teachers." There is a firmly entrenched establishment who, due to their own mono- and/or nonintegrated-arts practices, cannot help but to see multicultural and integrated arts education as *other* and see their own practices as formal, authoritative, and superior.

While many progressive curricula and pedagogies are promoted in formal teacher education, our schools continue to value the normative structure of test scores in the so-called core subjects over the healthy mental growth of the whole child. Fortunately, research in the latter half of the 20th and in the first decade of the 21st centuries is beginning to build less-dismissible arguments for integrated arts and multicultural arts education than were available before.

Developments in education research and in cognitive sciences are clearing a path for integrated and multicultural arts education. Building on the work of Dissanayake (2007) and McFee (1998), contemporary art educators Kristen Congdon and Dough Blandy (1999) argue that contemporary movements such as social ecology and ecological democracy promote cultural diversity as essential to human survival. It is generally recognized that genetic diversity is necessary for species survival. Congdon and Blandy (1999) suggest that cultural diversity is equally necessary to survival. This lays the groundwork for an emphasis on, not just recognition of, multicultural arts education, as opposed to peripheral attention or none at all. The argument for cultural diversity and integration further supports disciplinary diversity and integration. Integrated and multicultural arts education—that is, dance, language arts, music, theatre, and visual arts, borrowing from cultural practices from around the globe and integrating them together—can be legitimate art forms and support powerful learning experiences for students.

Current cognitive research (Parsons, 2004) and visual cultures studies (Freedman, 2003) recognize that the human brain is integrative by nature. Thus noted, integrated learning experiences would lend themselves to the natural functions of the brain. Further, recent cognitive research has illustrated the need for educators to "recognize the multiple ways in which students construct knowledge that is not limited to disciplinary boundaries. Disciplines are a construct of the modern world, while an interdisciplinary perspective is a reality of the post-modern educational context" (Boughton, 2005, p. 237).

The abovementioned contemporary views of the integrative nature of the human brain are substantiated by current brain research but were understood, in part (and problematically), by arts educators in the 1970s before the advances of today's research. For example, Betty Edwards's major publication, *Drawing on the Right Side of the Brain* (1979), provided an explanation of the different strengths of the left and right hemispheres of the brain and bolstered the arts in consideration of her idea that half the brain appeared to be dedicated to creative cognition. However, her work lacked supportive research and also remained aligned with the same binary, compartmentalization, and segregation paradigms that set the backdrop for centuries of segregation both of cultures and of disciplines. Today, as stated above, cognitive science recognizes the brain as having areas more or less assigned to different kinds of tasks but overall recognizes the brain as integrative, not binary or segregated.

Plurality is arguably a justifiable approach to education in the 21st century due to what we know about the different aptitudes of different kinds of learners and the different perspectives and paradigms that different cultures and different individuals bring to one table. Nevertheless, the established discipline-based, normative approaches are not easily replaced. In a recent study, Lackey found that elementary teachers who integrated visual art, music, drama, and movement into teaching their entire curriculum found arts integration the "only way they could cope with the increased pressure in their work imposed by the current emphasis on standards and benchmarks" (Lackey, 2005, p. 205).

The teachers in this study also directly connected the sort of rigid curriculum that is imposed by the standards and benchmarks to the same social and political rigidity in the United States that maintains inequalities. In this country, we miserably failed to correct inequalities despite a constitution that seeks to protect the freedom of each American, a civil war that was fought, in part, because some states would not protect these freedoms, and a century of social progressivism and civil rights movements. These teachers also reported that their "appreciation for the integratedness of things and the infusion of the arts, in little ways, is a challenge to dominant ways of knowing what counts as literacy, and to the rigid culture that an emphasis on standardized testing seems to foster and reflect" (p. 208).

Indeed, the same America that produced the educational structures and curricula that resulted in the barely tolerable education setting described above also produced, arguably, the most systemic and wide-ranging racism in modern history, the legacy of which continues to cripple people of color as well as whites who are a part of the dominant culture. For Pinder (2010), an Americanist, who writes on the politics of race and ethnicity, "whiteness" defines the cultural identity of America. "Colorblindsidedness" is embedded throughout American culture. Where can we look for foundations for new approaches to MAE and IAE, where lines between disciplines and between peoples are reconfigured and even deconfigured?

Many issues that may contribute to difficulties with multicultural and integrated art forms can be attributed to their beginnings and to embryonic social and cognitive theories that affected each movement over time. Each arrived early in modern human culture (35,000 to 10,000 years ago). Each was promoted by early-20th-century progressive education movements in the United States. Multicultural arts education was further bolstered by the civil rights and women's movements of the mid 20th century. Both movements resulted from Western, liberal humanist traditions that, today, art educator jan jagodzinsky (1999), among others, argues actually promote hegemony rather than dismantle it. For jagodzinsky (1999), contemporary democratic, liberal humanist theories have only succeeded in promoting a multicultural art education that provides an adding on of "specimens of the Other" (p. 307). He describes a "third space" as an interventionist paradigm in which orthodoxies of a conservative right and liberal humanist theories of a democratic left no longer produce the proliferation of binary (white/nonwhite, the West/the rest) institutionalized racism in education and in which a truly emancipatory and culturally diverse art curriculum allows self-awareness to be the foundation of deep and broad, global understandings (pp. 305–329).

Conclusion: A Fresh Start

The first thing educators and education researchers can do to support a meaningful future for multicultural and integrated arts education is to acknowledge that there are problems. These two education phenomena began unplanned and have existed largely unexamined. Discipline integration and multiculturalism naturally lend themselves to the arts and to education in the arts. Understanding the histories of these education endeavors coupled with understanding contemporary cognitive science and contemporary social, political, and culture studies can reshape multicultural arts education and integrated arts education into meaningful proponents for preparing young people to fully participate in a democratic society in which the rights, practices, and beliefs of each individual are respected and protected.

MAE and IAE have traveled along intersecting paths. MAE and IAE practices have been affected by historical contexts, research, and classroom practices. In the early 20th century, multicultural art education often took the form of Thanksgiving hand turkeys and toilet paper totem poles. This was, in part, a response to the patchwork quilt or melting pot view of the United States as a country that did not celebrate the many distinct cultures of its citizens. Later on, integrated arts education responded to ideas put forth in the progressive education movement such as student-centered activities that sought to make connections between students and the world in which they lived by breaking down barriers between the school and the community and between the different school disciplines themselves. This included breaking down barriers between the arts disciplines and integrating the arts together. The civil rights and women's rights movements, which gained notable momentum and international attention in the late 1950s and through the 1960s and 1970s, directly influenced multicultural arts education. Today, these two curricular paradigms can be seen as continuing to move along intersecting paths from somewhat naïve beginnings to the counterhegemonic influences of civil rights to the continuing evolutions and revolutions of thought, theory, and action in the 21st century.

In the United States, there must be a day of reckoning for the tensions that have endured between deep desires for conformity and mere solutes to individuality and diversity. We must recognize that we have failed, especially in education, to nurture the individual aptitudes and desires of each child who goes through our public school systems. Perhaps then we will be able to clearly see the natural alignment of integrated arts and multicultural arts education with the goals of a truly egalitarian society. It would be irresponsible and reprehensible for education to ignore the faults that exist in current, ill-informed approaches to research and practices in multicultural and integrated arts education. It is even reasonable for artists and educators to feel disdain for these practices in light of their ill-conceived development. If the faults continue to be ignored, potentials for cognitive growth and social evolution presented in multicultural and in integrated arts education will be unrealized. MAE and IAE are worth salvaging. A good friend, who is from Korea, shared a favorite saying of his father's with me, and it seems an appropriate closing to this collection of thoughts. "If you start buttoning your shirt wrong from the bottom, you don't know it till you get to the top" (Kijeong Jeon, personal communication, 2011). With multicultural and integrated arts education, we began buttoning our shirt wrong from the bottom and now, looking back at our work, we know we need to start over.

References

Bernstein, B. (1971). *Class, codes and control: Theoretical studies towards a sociology of language (vol. 1)*. London: Routledge and Kegan Paul, Ltd.

Bey, S. (2011). Aaron Douglas and Hale Woodruff: African America art education, gallery work and expanded pedagogy. *Studies in Art Education, 52*(2), 112–126.

Boughton, D. (2005). Postscript. In Mary Stokrocki, *Interdisciplinary art education: Building bridges to connect disciplines and cultures* (pp. 235–237). Reston, VA: National Art Education Association.

Boughton, D., & Mason, R. (Eds.). (1999). *Beyond multicultural art education: International perspectives*. North Rhine-Westphalia, Germany: Münster.

Buck, R. (2007). International commentaries. On A. Dils, social history and dance education. In Liora Bresler (Ed.), *International handbook of research in arts education (Part 2)* (pp. 117–120). Drodrecht, The Netherlands: Springer.

Callahan, R. E. (1962). *Education and the cult of efficiency*. Chicago: University of Chicago Press.

Catterall, J. S. (1998). Does experience in the arts boost academic achievement? A response to Eisner. *Art Education, 51*(4), 6–11.

Congdon, K., & Blandy, D. (1999). Working with communities and folk traditions: Socially and culturally democratic practice in art education. In Dough Boughton & Rachael Mason (Eds.), *Beyond multicultural art education: International perspectives* (pp. 65–86). New York: Waxmann.

Davenport, M. (2005). Reflecting on interdisciplinarity: A story about bits. In Mary Stokrocki (Ed.), *Interdisciplinary art education: Building bridges to connect disciplines and cultures* (pp. 3–5). Reston, VA: National Art Education Association.

Dils, A. (2007). Social history and dance education. In Liora Bresler (Ed.), *International handbook of research in arts education (Part 2)* (pp. 103–112). Dordrecht, The Netherlands: Springer.

Dissanayake, E. (2007). In the beginning: Pleistocene and infant aesthetics and 21st-century education in the arts. In Liora Bresler, *International handbook of research in arts education (Part 2)* (pp. 783–798). Dordrecht, The Netherlands: Springer.

Edwards. B. (1979). *Drawing on the right side of the brain*. Los Angeles: J. P. Tarcher.

Eisner, E. W. (1998). Does experience in the arts boost academic achievement? *Art Education, 51*(1), 7–15

Freedman, K. (2003). *Teaching visual culture: Curriculum, aesthetics and the social life of art*. New York: Teachers College Press.

jagodzinsky, j. (1999). Thinking through/difference/in art education contexts: Working the third space and beyond. In Doug Boughton and Rachel Mason (Eds.), *Beyond multicultural art education: International perspectives* (pp. 303–330). New York: Münster.

Kindler, A. M. (1987). A review of rationales for integrated arts programs. *Studies in Art Education, 29*(1), 52–60.

Lackey, L. (2005). Elementary classroom teachers, arts integration, and socially progressive curricula. In Mary Stokrocki (Ed.), *Interdisciplinary art education: Building bridges to connect disciplines and cultures* (pp. 199–210). Reston, VA: National Art Education Association.

McFee, J. K. (1998). *Cultural diversity and the structure and practice of art education.* Reston, VA: National Art Education Association.

Parsons, M. (2004). Art and integrated curriculum. In Elliot Eisner & Michael Day (Eds.), *Handbook of research and policy in art education* (pp. 775–794). Reston, VA: National Art Education Association.

Pinder, S. O. (2010). *The politics of race and ethnicity in the United States: Americanization, de-Americanization, and racialized ethnic groups.* New York: Palgrave Macmillan.

Stankiewicz, M. A. (2007). Capitalizing art education: Mapping international histories. In Liora Bresler (Ed.), *International handbook of research in arts education (Part 2)* (pp. 7–30). Dordrecht, The Netherlands: Springer.

Stokrocki, M. (Ed.). (2005). *Interdisciplinary art education: Building bridges to connect disciplines and cultures.* Reston, VA: National Art Education Association.

Wee, S.-J. (2007). International commentaries. On A. Dils, social history and dance education. In Liora Bresler (Ed.), *International handbook of research in arts education (Part 2)* (pp. 113–115). Dordrecht, The Netherlands: Springer.

28

A Comparison of Teacher Perceptions on and Textbook References to Women's Representation in High School Social Studies Textbooks

Christine Dobbins and Mark Malisa

In this chapter, we draw attention to the role that women teachers play in maintaining the masculine hegemony that is prevalent in most United States social studies curricula. Using a feminist critique of texts used in social studies, we examine the extent to which women actively act to transform or reify these existing practices. A feminist critique seemed the most appropriate for this study since, at least in the United States, the teaching profession is overwhelmingly female and White (Milojevic, 2006), and feminism, especially the second wave, is predominantly the preserve of White women (Taylor, 2011) and the focus is always on gender inequality. Race, for the most part, is left out of the debate. As such, it became relatively easier to focus on the ways in which White women can become allies in the struggle for a just and multicultural United States, especially in the field of education.

The general feminization of the teaching profession in K–12 education in the United States has reinvigorated academic interest in the role of gender bias within the school curriculum and some of the ways in which women contribute to the reification of this bias that inhabits the academic world. Research, dating back to the 1970s, indicates many instances of gender bias in the school curriculum. However, only minor improvements on trying to address such a bias have been made since then (Chick, 2006; Trecker, 1971). This chapter presents some of the challenges that exist both in understanding aspects of gender bias within social studies curriculum in the United States and how female educators are addressing such challenges. This is important because schools are generally viewed as one of the few spaces where alternative futures can be constructed in which there is justice for all (McLaren, 2007). And, given that educators are socialized into the norms of masculine hegemony, we sought to investigate the ways women educators perceive gender within the history textbooks they use in their classrooms and whether they are complicit in the material manifestations of that perception. In this chapter, our definition and understanding of hegemony builds on that of Antonio Gramsci (1971) in which the oppressed internalized, in one way or another, their oppression. Our understanding of feminism follows that of Simone De Beauvoir (1973), whose study of "the second sex" was foundational to the academic study of feminism and the role that women could play in enabling their own freedom.

While an argument can be made that gender equality requires the willing cooperation of males, a counterargument can be made that the marginalization of women depends, in part, on the cooperation of women in their own marginalization, especially in light of the concept of hegemony as described in Gramsci's work (1971). This study of female educators' perceptions on women's representation in global history textbooks published in the United States examines the processes through which educators are socialized into the norms of masculine hegemony.

By utilizing a feminist framework, this study shed light on the perspectives female teachers have about the ways women are presented in global studies textbooks. Additionally, the study integrated a brief textbook analysis guided by the methods used by past research designs and the participants' responses. Teachers' perspectives were explored through a feminist theoretical lens and methodology. A feminist perspective allowed for intersubjectivity while utilizing a "view from below" approach that ensured that the research went beyond simply "giving the social sciences better, more authentic and more relevant data" (Bowles & Klein, 1983, p. 123). Data collection methods used open-ended survey questions. This best allowed teachers to express their experiences, beliefs, and perceptions on the subject while integrating the researcher's experiences in a consciously subjective way. This type of feminist methodology may be criticized by some as being too subjective and containing "observer effects" that would inherently make the study itself biased (Bowles & Klein, 1983; Monahan & Fisher, 2010). However, the goal of this study is not to conduct research "on" women, but instead "for" women (Bowles & Klein, 1983). That is, we write as advocates for women to play an active role in their own emancipation as they take control of the curriculum.

Although the feminization of education ideally makes it possible to address issues of institutionalized female oppression, educators are not only ill prepared for this task but are also not part of an environment that fosters important consciousness-raising discourse on such issues. Our view is that educators need to develop a more complex concept of history, which will not only dispel the impression of a gender-neutral curriculum but will also begin to foster a curriculum that is less androcentric.

Mary K. T. Tetreault, (1986) argues that because textbooks place emphasis on political, diplomatic, and military history instead of social history, women's issues, including the politics of gender, are often left out of social studies textbooks. Thus, while women may appear more often in more recent textbooks, they are still stereotyped (Clark, Allard, & Mahoney, 2004). That is, they conform to traditional roles as wives, mothers, or as individuals who take no active role in their constitution. We believe that by highlighting female teacher perceptions on gender bias presented in textbooks, educators might begin to see the inherent need for a reconstruction of women's issues in social studies textbooks used in the United States.

Depiction of Women in Textbooks

While many studies conclude that women are underrepresented in social studies textbooks published in the United States (Clark, Allard, & Mahoney, 2004; Chick, 2006), current research documenting *how* textbooks incorporate or integrate women's issues and women historical figures is not exhaustive. However, some current studies examine gender imbalance in these textbooks by categorizing the material presented in them as well as the visuals in order to analyze how female historical figures and women's issues are incorporated into the textbook content (Campbell, 2010). These studies investigated how women were treated in the text, photographs, and illustrations presented by evaluating the behaviors and roles they were depicted in and how their achievements were discussed within various textbooks. Attention was also paid to the types of history emphasized throughout the textbooks as well as the incorporation of women's issues.

Tetreault (1986) examined 12 United States history textbooks published in the 1970s and 1980s for their treatment of women. She categorized each sentence or visual that referenced women according to different stages of incorporation. These stages were broken up into five different ways of thinking about women's history. These are male history, compensatory history, bifocal history, feminist history, and multifocal, rational history. The first category is the least inclusive while the last is the most inclusive.

Categorizing these textbooks by stages allowed the researcher to make suggestions to textbook authors about what may be included in order to present material in a more gender-balanced manner. Comparisons of the textbooks were then made in order to illustrate areas where textbook authors needed to improve as well as "to identify exemplary instances of inclusion" (Tetreault, 1986, p. 214). Tetreault concluded that women have been incorporated at the second and third levels of compensatory and bifocal history in a majority of the textbooks analyzed. In these textbooks, women were generally depicted as either giving support to male activities or extending their nurturing role within the family. Her study concluded that textbooks placed an emphasis on political, diplomatic, and military history instead of social history and, as a result, women's achievements in the private sphere were left out. Women's achievements in the public sphere were often highlighted in terms of what acceptable women's behavior was (Tetreault, 1986). She also suggested that important aspects of women's history involve changes to social structure. However, "the emphasis of textbooks is on events, a unit too brief to afford a sense of structural change" (Tetreault, 1986, p. 249).

In an earlier study, Tetreault (1984) observed how women were depicted within textbooks that focus on United States history. That study used archival data to illustrate how textbooks often depicted women in traditional roles, often focusing on women's role caring for the poor and unfortunate. Tetreault began by focusing on the traditional roles in which Eleanor Roosevelt was depicted within the textbooks analyzed. Although these textbooks often "present her as a person in her own right" (Tetreault, 1984, p. 546), the roles most often depicted consisted of Roosevelt caring for her husband, concerned for the unfortunate; most did not emphasize her "female-centered activities" (Tetreault, 1984, p. 546). Eleanor Roosevelt's depiction prompted Tetreault to question how other women historical figures were treated in textbooks. Tetreault then dissected the stories of other famous women and suggested that when women were discussed, the event, exploration, or movement they were involved in stood in the foreground and attention was rarely paid to how these women were personally affected by the experience or how their work impacted the lives of other women (Tetreault, 1984). Tetreault also suggested that notable women's accomplishments, such as Eleanor Roosevelt's, were in the areas of childbearing, housework, being a wife. This may reinforce the idea that housework and reproduction are "ahistorical and static" and teach students to diminish the significance of women's concerns and issues (Tetreault, 1984, p. 548).

Julian and Kirby (1984) explored the ways United States history textbooks treated women. These individuals ranged from professional historians to U.S. history graduate students and aided the researchers in coding and reviewing 10 high school United States history textbooks on issues of equality, sex role stereotyping, male supremacy, and the amount of coverage that was given to individual women as well as women's issues. Prior to textbook coding, the researchers made three general assumptions, one of which was that "many students read textbooks and are influenced by them" (Julian & Kirby, 1984, p. 205). Julian and Kirby reached several general conclusions from the results of the textbook analysis. One such conclusion was that although the passages that focused directly on a woman, women, or women's issues were generally *objective and balanced*, passages that focused on another issue or only indirectly on women were frequently misleading about women's concerns or omitted them altogether. They also found that the use of terms that carried masculine connotations, such as *workingmen* and *frontiersmen*, failed to demonstrate women's contributions and obscured women's roles and significance in United States society and history. Another important conclusion made by the same researchers illustrated that although the textbooks included some significant women, the textbooks failed to relate their accomplishments to the "mainstream of American history" (Julian & Kirby, 1984, p. 206). Additionally, the researchers found that, historically, when sexist statements made by men were quoted, their ideas were not "clearly labeled as opinions of men or women of the past and not meant as models of the present" (p. 206). Their conclusion was that efforts needed to be made in order to achieve unbiased and equitable treatment of women in U.S. history textbooks. Nevertheless, this study has both its strengths and weaknesses. This study's primary strength results from the stringent data-collection and -analysis techniques employed by the researchers. The researchers utilized various professionals and thus developed a study with limited bias and high reliability. However, it is important to recognize that this study was conducted three decades ago.

Light, Staton, and Bourne (1989) described a surface-level inclusion within textbooks by stating that women's issues or historical women were generally included as "passing mentions," and "substantive integrated discussions of women" were generally avoided (Light, Staton, & Bourne,

1989, p. 19). When women or women's issues were substantially included, their roles or treatment were marginal and frequently inaccurate. Additionally, the researchers discussed how textbooks often do not substantiate the terms they use to describe women in United States history (Light et al., 1989). The researchers also stated that "focuses or biographies on women commonly appear boxed off outside the main prose, reinforcing their consideration as asides or afterthoughts," only further trivializing and marginalizing women's accomplishments (Light et al., 1989, p. 19). Therefore, this study provides the reader with a more comprehensive example of how textbooks ignore, trivialize, and marginalize women and their accomplishments.

Textbooks in the Social Studies Classroom

Studies have been conducted on how and why teachers use textbooks in their classrooms. Nevertheless, many of these studies have been limited to elementary school classrooms and the subjects of reading and math (Stodolsky, 1989, p. 181). Stodolsky discovered correlations between variables related to instruction—"organization for teaching, access to additional instructional materials, coverage of content, the ability of students to learn from textbooks . . ." and textbook use (Schug, Western, & Enochs, 1997, p. 100). Additionally, they found that social studies teachers use textbooks because they want to, not because they feel forced to do so (Schug et al., 1997).

Research conducted in 1989 by Susan S. Stodolsky studied fifth-grade social studies teachers' use of their textbooks. The researchers determined that "reading the text and answering questions were deemed core activities while group projects and field trips typically were optional" (Stodolsky, 1989, p. 168). Additionally, they found that textbook packages that included interactive materials, such as data cards, teacher's guides, and other suggested procedures, resulted in a stricter following of the content found in the textbook; in comparison to math, the social studies textbook is regularly supplemented by other materials. The point, here, is that gender bias is rampant in textbooks across the curriculum, especially in the selection of textbooks.

Teachers' Perceptions of Women in Social Studies Curricula

Studies examining teacher perceptions of women in history curricula in the United States are generally not limited to women's representation in textbooks but, rather, incorporate other aspects of the curriculum, including women's roles and representation in high-stakes tests, worksheets, the classroom environment, maps, photographs, and web-related materials (Fredrickson, 2004). While all of these additional materials are crucial to the development of a gender-inclusive history curriculum, the textbooks themselves "play an important role in teacher planning and actual classroom instruction" (Stodolsky, 1989, p. 165). Most of the research conducted on this topic is dated. This illustrates why attention should be paid to the way teachers perceive women in the textbooks they use.

Melinda Karnes (2000) looked at methods used by teachers as well as at student interest in women in history. One section of the study focused on teachers' examination of the content of the textbooks. She concluded that, with respect to textbook content, "the absence of women on the 'main stage' is noted, but only in the male-defined context of what determines greatness" (p. 55). They found that their textbooks left out important information on women's contributions; when these contributions were mentioned, they seemed to be tacked onto the main topic of the chapter (Karnes, 2000). Therefore, this study shows that teachers do find instances of gender bias within the pages of the textbooks they use. This also demonstrates a need for additional research into how educators' teaching strategies and methods may be impacted by perceptions of textbook gender bias.

In brief, the studies reviewed here suggest the need for more research on the topic of teachers' perceptions of women's representation in social studies textbooks. Two studies cited above suggest that a gender imbalance in textbook material still exists in recent textbooks (Clark, Allard, & Mahoney, 2004; Chick, 2006). More pertinently, additional studies illustrate that this gender bias manifests itself in the formatting and language used throughout the textbook, the number of women presented, the roles in which women are portrayed, and the descriptions that are given, both in the text and in photographs, maps, and illustrations (Frederickson, 2004; Julian & Kirby, 1984; Karnes, 2000; Light et al., 1989; Tetreault, 1984, 1986). Teachers use their own discretion on integrating the textbook into the curriculum and, therefore, their perceptions on textbook gender bias warrant considerable attention. Furthermore, a review of Bowles and Klein's *Theories of Women's Studies* highlights the importance of looking at the research question through a feminist theoretical lens.

After reviewing past research on the topic, survey questions aimed at uncovering teachers' perceptions on women's representation in high school social studies textbooks were developed. These questions focused on three topics: teachers' textbook usage, thoughts about gender equity, and thoughts about gender issues in the textbooks used in their classes. The first section asked participants to describe the role of the textbook in their classrooms and how they utilized the materials provided by the textbook publisher in their curricula. The second section asked the participants to define the term *gender equity*. The final section explored how the participants felt about women's representation in the textbooks they use in their classrooms. In addition, the final question of the survey allowed the participants to express any concerns that they felt were not addressed by the answers they gave to the previous questions. The survey was piloted by two male graduate students, both of whom were certified to teach social studies by their state departments of education. Although these students were male, they provided insight into the format, wording, and time it would take to complete the survey. After the survey was piloted, suggested corrections were reviewed and selected questions were edited. Once the surveys were returned, they were read and coded in order to identify the various themes presented within the responses.

Data were also collected to more fully develop a description of the visibility of women in high school social studies textbooks. The textbook that some of our participants cited in their survey responses was analyzed. This textbook analysis led to a more complete description of the participants' survey responses. In order to develop an accurate analysis, we drew upon techniques used by past researchers (Chick, 2006; Julian & Kirby, 1984; Tetreault, 1984, 1986) and highlighted in additional literature (Blankenship, 1984).

Data Analysis

The two forms of data collection, open-ended surveys and textbook analysis, were chosen to provide a more holistic picture on the topic of study. A textbook analysis was conducted on the textbook *World History Connections to Today,* which was used by the majority of the participants. Some of the questions were used to determine which sections of the text were to be analyzed. Such questions asked the participants to name some women that the textbook they used "highlights as very important." Some of the participants did not specifically name any women highlighted by the textbook. The index of *World History Connections to Today* was used to find pages that mentioned the women that the two participants named in their responses. This data analysis is organized into three separate subsections: textbook questions, gender equity, and women in the spotlight.

Textbook Questions

Most teachers we talked to stated that they assign students questions from the textbook at least once per week. We analyzed the textbooks to determine if the women whom the participants named as "very important" within the textbook were included in the end-of-section or end-of-chapter questions. Out of the seven women named by the two participants, five of the women had end-of-section questions asked about them. However, all five questions fell under the "identify" section. These section-review questions began with identifications and definitions, respectively, and ended with "critical thinking" and activity-based questions. These questions were arranged from lower-order to higher-order thinking as described in Bloom's Taxonomy. Additionally, end-of-chapter questions explicitly appeared for two of the women mentioned by the participants. One such question required the reader to synthesize the views and ideas of Mary Wollstonecraft. The other question was asked about Catherine the Great and read "Recognizing Points of View: How might each of the following have viewed the reign of Peter the Great: (d) Catherine the Great" (Ellis & Esler, 1999, p. 445). Although this question requires a student to understand perspective and would therefore be considered a higher-order-thinking question as described by Bloom, it frames Catherine the Great's ideas and opinions in relation to Peter the Great's accomplishments, or in other words, the "male experience" (Tetreault, 1986, p. 215). This question did not ask the student to analyze, synthesize, or evaluate Catherine the Great's accomplishments or experiences, thereby trivializing the contributions attributed to her in the pages prior.

Gender Equity

This survey asked one question about the issue of gender equity: "How would you define gender equity?" Two out of the three participants responded to the question. Participant A responded, "Gender equity is the equality of the sexes. . . . Women and men having equal rights, equal pay distribution, equal educational opportunities, etc." Participant B responded, "I would define gender equality as being treated equally and fairly without gender disparity." The textbook itself did not include a definition for *gender equity*, *gender equality*, or *sexism* in its glossary or index.

We began by asking a few female social studies teachers questions related to their textbooks' presentation and integration of gender issues. The first question asked the teachers to name women whom they believed their textbook highlighted as "very important" and discuss the role in which they were depicted within the text. Educators who utilized the same textbook in class responded with a list of women. Among the women named included Indira Gandhi, Catherine the Great, Queen Hatshepsut, Empress Wu Chao, Queen Elizabeth, Mary Wollstonecraft, and Mother Teresa. The teachers stated that the textbook portrayed them as leaders. However, some teachers could not and did not name any specific women and responded, "Few women are highlighted in the book. When they are they are basically rulers of some sort." The responses of "leader" and "ruler" in regard to the roles women were depicted in are consistent with Tetreault's (1986) finding that textbooks emphasize "political, diplomatic, and military history" as opposed to social history.

In response to the question "Do you believe your textbook does a good or bad job of integrating women's issues?" some educators answered, "In the ancient world women did not play a prominent role in the actual [sic] building of dynasties. Therefore, the text recognizes them in an appropriate way." This furthers Tetreault's findings, which suggest that the events, people, experiences, and ideas that students read about in their textbooks are limited to the political, diplomatic, and military spheres. Additionally, others stated that "I believe that women were not allowed the opportunity to make significant contributions in history." Both of these responses also illustrate how women's contributions and roles in the "private sphere" are not only left out of historical narratives but are also deemed to be "ahistorical" by the textbook publisher as well as by these female educators. Although other educators acknowledged a woman's experiences as a "wife or mother," her previous statement, "women were not allowed to make significant contributions in history . . ." suggests that women's domestic roles and contributions were not historically relevant.

The findings from the textbook analysis of the seven women mentioned are consistent with the observations we made when we talked with current teachers in the United States. For example, the sections of the textbook on Catherine the Great discussed her accomplishments, actions, and reforms in the areas of education and the arts and humanities as well as imperialism, but concluded with the statement, "In the end, Catherine's contribution to Russia was not reform but an expanded empire" (Ellis & Esler, 1999, p. 463). This statement illustrates a trivialization of Catherine's accomplishments in the areas of social and cultural reform and an emphasis on her accomplishments in the political sphere.

Women in the Spotlight

Most of the female teachers revealed how women's issues were highlighted in separate sections of the textbooks. For example, some teachers we interviewed stated that women's issues were generally depicted as a "spotlight" with a visual and short blurb about the role they played. A small section stated that "Many of the females are highlighted by quotes or sections of the writing." In general, the responses suggested that although historical women are integrated into the main narrative of the textbook, sections that cluster women's issues or important women are still prevalent. This is true for the sections mentioning Indira Gandhi and Mary Wollstonecraft. Furthermore, the references to Empress Wu Chao appear in a separate subsection that, although it is formatted similarly to the main text, is actually the chapter cover page. Research suggests that separating or clustering topics, issues, or events of women's issues or accomplishments "tends to reinforce the idea that women of note are, after all, optional and supplementary" (Trecker, 1971, p. 134; Zittleman & Sadker, 2003).

The point here is that women educators had, and have, power. And women educators also have power (relatively speaking) to shape the nature and course of the curriculum. To what extent can that power be used to educate for a truly multicultural world using a multicultural curriculum? A general trend in the United States is that of blaming society's ills on schools and educators (Monchinski, 2007). Should the creation of a multicultural curriculum be deemed another chore on the work designed/created for women, in a problem created by patriarchal society? Yet the question also needs to be asked: What can women educators do to transform the conditions that reify masculine domination of society in the United States, even when the appearance of symbolic power gives the illusion of a curriculum in which there is equality?

In this chapter, we have shown some of the ways by which, through their selection of curriculum or textbooks, women educators sometimes participate in forms of education that marginalize women. While there are obvious intersections between gender/sex and race, and while feminism might offer a challenge to sexism, for the most part, feminism tends to leave racism intact. Consequently, it is difficult to envision the birthing and nurturing of a multicultural/multiethnic United States social studies curriculum from a workforce that willingly participates in its own marginalization. Forde argues that women and feminist utopian thinking have the potential to solve the "gendered problem in education" (2006, p. 145). Yet, in their choice of subject matter, most White women teachers remain trapped in Western patriarchal sources of history. Can patriarchal history, in the hands of White women, be a source of emancipation that would make it possible to have a truly multicultural curriculum in the United States? Even though (White) women might constitute the majority of the teaching profession in the United States, they might be simultaneously contributing to their own invisibility in history (Spender, 1982; Stanworth, 1983). It is doubtful whether a cadre of feminist teachers, armed with a patriarchal curriculum, can significantly undo patriarchy and/or racism, in many ways confirming

Audre Lorde's (2007) observation that it would be difficult for the master's tools to undo the master's house.

The school (and the classroom in particular) remains one of the few areas where the birthing of a new and better society might take place. The humanities, especially the social sciences, lend themselves to the utilization of critical, analytic, and interpretive frameworks necessary for critiquing the nature of knowledge and knowledge construction/making. As such, women are ideally positioned to not only critique and decenter patriarchy but also to make genuine multiculturalism institutionally present in the curriculum. Gender and sexism, like multiculturalism, are issues that educators are well placed to address in the ways they teach and the resources they use. The politics of a desired future are reflected not only in what is taught but also in what *is not* taught.

Appendix 1

Survey Instructions

You are being asked to participate in a research project conducted by a graduate student from The College of Saint Rose. If you decide to participate, please read this form in its entirety.

Nature and Purpose of Study

This research project is designed to measure female teachers' attitudes and beliefs on how U.S. history textbooks represent women. The items in the survey ask personal questions about issues of gender. Participation in this process is voluntary. You will not be asked to disclose your identity (name) on any part of the survey. Therefore, you will remain anonymous to the researcher and others reading the results of the survey. You may choose to stop answering questions at any point. There is no penalty for non-participation, or not completing all of the questions on the survey.

Your identity will be kept anonymous. All information you provide will be kept confidential. The assessment should take no more than 45 minutes to complete. Completion is voluntary.

Expectations of Participants

You will be asked to complete a survey consisting of 13 items. It should take you approximately 35-45 minutes. You are encouraged to complete the entire survey. You should answer the questions to the best of your ability and at a length that you feel is appropriate to convey your feelings. Because this survey asks open-ended questions, the length of your answers is up to you. However, you may decline to answer any questions or stop at any time. Your participation is voluntary. There is no penalty for declining to participate.

Potential Discomfort and Risks

Although questions regarding your personal beliefs about issues relating to gender equality will be asked, there is no anticipated emotional discomfort or psychological risk. These questions should not be emotionally upsetting to you.

Potential Benefits

There are no financial payments for participating; however, participants may help the graduate student researcher further her understanding on issues of gender in the classroom and may prompt additional research on this topic.

Alternatives to Participation

None. Participants may choose or decline to participate. There are no potential benefits or costs associated with either.

Appendix 2

Survey Questions

1. How many years of experience do you have teaching Social Studies?

Textbook Use:

2. What textbook do you use in your classroom? (Textbook name; publisher, year)

3. How would you describe the role of the textbook in your classroom?

4. How often do you assign your students questions out of the textbook?

5. How do you use the materials provided by the textbook publisher in your lesson plans?

6. When do you integrate supplemental material into your lessons? Why?

Beliefs About Gender:

7. How would you define gender equity?

Gender Issues In Text:

8. Who are some women your textbook highlights as very important? What roles are they depicted in? Do you believe these interpretations are accurate?

9. Do you think your textbook does a good or bad job of integrating women's issues? Why?

10. How does your textbook format the integration of women and their contributions? Can you describe in-text passages, photographs, and illustrations?

11. Do you believe this formatting strengthens or weakens student understanding of women's contributions to American society? Why?

12. What are some issues of gender equity and/or equality that you have discussed with your class?

Additional Comments:

13. Do you have any additional comments that you feel were not expressed by these survey questions with respect to gender equity in textbooks?

References

Blankenship, G. (1984). How to test a textbook for sexism. *Social Education, 48*(4), 282–283.

Bowles, G., & Klein, R. (1983). *Theories of women's studies*. Boston: Routlege & Kegan Paul.

Campbell, D. (2010). *Choosing democracy: A practical guide to multicultural education*. Boston: Allyn & Bacon.

Chick, K. A. (2006). Gender balance in K–12 American history textbooks. *Social Studies Research and Practice, 1*(3), 284–290.

Clark, R., Allard, J., & T. Mahoney. (2004). How much of the sky? *Social Education, 68*(1), 57–62.

De Beauvoir, S. (1973). *The second sex*. New York: Vintage Books.

Ellis, E., & Esler, A. (1999). *World history: Connections to today*. Boston: Pearson Prentice Hall.

Forde, C. (2006). Feminist utopian thinking: Solutions to the "gender problem" in education. In A. Peters & J. Freeman-Moir (Eds.), *Edutopias: New utopian thinking in education.* Boston: Sense Publishers.

Frederickson, M. (2004). Surveying gender: Another look at the way we teach United States history. *The History Teacher, 27*(4), 476–484.

Gramsci, A. (1971). *Selections from the* Prison Notebooks. New York: International Publishers.

Julian, N., & Kirby, D. (1984). Treatment of women in high school U.S. history textbooks. *Social Studies, 72*(5), 203–206.

Karnes, M. (2000, January/February). Girls can be president. *Social Education,* (7), M5–M8.

Light, B., Staton, P., & Bourne, P. (1989). Sex equity content in history textbooks. *The History and the Social Science Teacher, 25*(1), 18–20.

Lorde, A. (2007). *Sister outsider: Essays and speeches.* New York: Crossing Press.

McLaren, P. (2007). *Life in schools: An introduction to critical pedagogy in the foundations of education.* Boston: Allyn & Bacon.

Milojevic, I. (2006). Hegemonic and marginalized educational utopias in the contemporary Western world. In A. Peters & J. Freeman-Moir (Eds.), *Edutopias: New utopian thinking in education.* Boston: Sense Publishers.

Monahan, T., & Fisher, J. A. (2010). Benefits of "observer effects": Lessons from the field. *Qualitative Research, 10*(3), 357–376.

Monchinski, T. (2007). *The politics of education: An introduction.* Boston: Sense Publishers.

Schug, M. C., Western, R. D., & Enochs, L. G. (1997). Why do social studies teachers use textbooks? The answer may lie in economic theory. *Social Education, 61*(2), 97–101.

Spender, D. (1982). *Invisible women: The schooling scandal.* London: Writers and Readers.

Stanworth, M. (1983). *Gender and schooling: A study of sexual divisions in schools and society.* London: Hutchinson.

Stodolsky, S. (1989). Is teaching really by the book? In P. Jackson & S. Haroutunian-Gordon, *From Socrates to software: The teacher as text and the text as teacher, part 1* (pp. 159–184). Chicago: University of Chicago Press.

Taylor, Y. (2011, May). Intersectional dialogues—a politics of possibility? *Feminism & Psychology, 21,* 211–217.

Tetreault, M. K. (1984). Notable American women: The case of United States history textbooks. *Social Education, 48*(7), 546–550.

Tetreault, M. K. (1986). Integrating women's history: The case of United States history high school textbooks. *The History Teacher, 19*(2), 211–262.

Trecker, J. L. (1971). Women in U.S. history high school textbooks. *Social Education, 35,* 249–260.

Zittleman, K., & Sadker, D. (2003). Teacher education textbooks: The unfinished gender revolution. *Educational Leadership, 60*(4), 59–63.

29

Multicultural Studies and Sexual Diversity

A Postmodern Queer(y) for All

Sean Robinson

The United States is made up of many different racial, religious, sexual, and cultural groups. Yet within our educational systems, all too often scant attention is paid in our curricula to most of these diverse groups of people. A curriculum that centers around the experiences of mainstream Americans largely ignores the experiences, cultures, histories, and knowledge of groups that are not mainstream. A curriculum that is "mainstream-centric" has negative consequences for all. Such a curriculum reinforces dominant power structures, portrays a false sense of superiority, privileges hegemonic knowledge and values, and denies all the ability to benefit from the knowledge, perspectives, and frames of reference that can be gained by studying, experiencing, and working alongside individuals of nondominant or mainstream groups. In addition, such a mainstream-centric view denies those within the mainstream the opportunity to view their own culture and group from the eyes of "the other."

Since the 1960s, educators at all levels have been trying, in various ways, to better integrate diverse, multicultural perspectives and content into the curriculum. Banks (2008) describe four levels of multicultural integration and education—the contributions approach, the additive approach, the transformative approach, and the social action approach. Most educators who do attempt to integrate multicultural content into courses or whole curriculums generally use one of the first two approaches, the contributions approach or the additive approach. The contributions approach is characterized by the insertion of discrete cultural texts and artifacts or the discussion of particular individuals, but only in relation to other individuals. For example, when discussing 19th-century American poets in a course on American literature, Walt Whitman would be among those read, as would Emerson, Holmes, Longfellow, and Thoreau. Given that Whitman's poetry depicts love and sexuality in a more earthy, individualistic way common in American culture before the medicalization of sexuality in the 19th century, it is highly likely that the discussion of his work would include the role that friendship, sexuality, and intimacy played within his poetry (especially within *Leaves of Grass*) and that of others, but no doubt little attention would be played to understanding Whitman's own homoerotic interests and desires and the role his own identity had in shaping his poetry. At best, his own sexuality would be downplayed, or at worst, dismissed entirely as irrelevant.

The additive approach is characterized by the addition of content, themes, or perspectives without changing the overall structure, purposes, or characteristics of the course or curriculum (Banks, 2008). Examples of this approach would be the inclusion of Vito Russo's 1990 documentary film, *The Celluloid Closet: Homosexuality in the Movies*, as one topic of many within a film studies course. Russo's documentary covers nearly a century of films, examining how gays and lesbians have been portrayed in movies. This could be perceived to be framed simply as a discussion of gays and lesbians as "the other" in movies, without a full understanding of the meaning and ways these types of characters came into being or without larger explorations of the power, language, privilege, or culture associated with the dynamics in which nonmainstream Americans have been situated in such movies.

Despite the criticism of the contribution and additive approaches to multicultural education (e.g., Banks, 2008; Edgerton, 1996; Neito, 1999; Rothenberg, 2000), these approaches still seem to be the most pervasive ones used in addressing or attempting to include diversity and multicultural issues within either individual courses or an entire curriculum. Using either of these two approaches is a safe way of teaching about different minority groups in the United States, those who historically might be considered nonmainstream America (e.g. Blacks, Muslims, gays and lesbians, Latinos, immigrants, or the working class), while also ignoring the larger subjective experiences, dynamics, structures, values, beliefs, similarities, or differences found with such groups. The primary pedagogical belief within this strategy is that we, as educators, can make students familiar with "the other" and with other cultures, as if these individuals or groups are static, situated on the margins of a central normative, hegemonic referent point (i.e., White heterosexual, middle class, Anglo-Saxon, Christian), and that once understood, others may be able to sympathize with them or to work on their behalf to raise them up or move them away from the margins.

Scholars and researchers continue to examine dynamic and sociohistorical analyses of various cultural groups, for example, understanding the critical adolescent years of contemporary young men between the ages of 16 and 26 (Kimmel, 2008), uncovering the expressions and perspectives of LGBTQ youth in educational settings (Bertram, Crowley, & Massy, 2010), the ways in which education excludes and silences individuals based on race, class, and gender status (Weis & Fine, 2005), the role of educational policy and politics on Native American assimilation at the turn of the century (Adams, 1995), or the ways in which Black prisoners were used for medical experiments (Hornblum, 2007), all of which are essential to establishing a multicultural awareness of various groups that form the bases of the past, present, and future of the United States. Yet too many educators (and students) still expect a recipe book for what the "other" is, how to approach them, and perhaps how to work with them (cf. Atthill & Jha's [2009] book *The Gender-Responsive School: An Action Guide*). Despite how simplistic the additive and contribution approaches are to multicultural education, they are rooted in the belief that multicultural education and multicultural studies can have a transformative effect within society.

By focusing on representations of race, gender, class, religion, and sexuality and the critique of ideologies that promote various forms of oppression, multicultural studies can lend itself to a program of study that explicitly demonstrates how culture reproduces certain forms of racism, sexism, homophobia, and biases against members of subordinate classes, social groups, or alternative lifestyles. Multicultural studies, ideally, should affirm the worth of different types of cultures and groups as well as the individuals within those groups, claiming, for instance, that Blacks, Latinos, the poor, gays and lesbians, and other oppressed or marginalized voices have their own validity and importance.

As already mentioned, however, it is primarily race/ethnicity, gender, and class that get addressed in learning about the other. Often left out of such critical discussions, and generally absent in most multicultural approaches, are sexual diversity and sexual orientation. Recognition of sexual diversity, when it does occur, is often nothing more than simply adding a "label" (e.g., homosexual, gay, lesbian, bisexual, queer, transgendered) to the ever-growing list of diversity categories that originally only included race and gender and that often includes class and religion. Furthermore, even when addressed in multicultural contexts, sexual diversity is almost never discussed in enough detail for either students or faculty to truly appreciate and interrogate the multiplicity of meanings, identities, contexts, and even subcultures that are represented within the entire spectrum of sexual diversity. Perhaps because sexuality is such a controversial topic to begin with, LGBTQ, queer, or transgender identity issues are generally not part of the curriculum. Perhaps, for the most part, many educators believe that they are not knowledgeable enough to speak to or about LGBTQ issues and perspectives. Why is sexual diversity important to attend to? What gets obscured when it is eventually discussed? Who gets hurt, and how, when this topic is neglected?

Rendered virtually silent by the general discourse and theoretical approaches in contemporary multicultural education and multicultural studies programs, this chapter suggests that we must approach multicultural studies from a critical postmodern perspective (a queery, if you will), that is not simply an addition of a test or the discussion of an individual's contributions. Rather, multicultural studies ought to move beyond LGBTQ as identity politics and categories and, in turn, challenge students and faculty to critically consider all identity categories as both fluid and dynamic; what it means to be male or female, gay or bisexual, or Black or White can be different for every person and should not have to mean the same thing from one instance to the next. In essence, one's identity can shift based on location, understanding, perceptions, and relationships to other people, objects, or texts. Yet it is not enough to simply propose a new way of thinking; one must also have a new way of being. A necessary requirement is the "unlearning" that must occur for new knowledge about the other to take hold. As Neito and Bode (2008) so aptly stated, "Our own re-education means not only learning new things, but also *un*learning some of the old" (p. 425). The heart of this unlearning, or unpacking as I think of it, is laying open our assumptions or perceptions, beliefs, and understandings of ourselves and of those we perceive to be "different." A refusal to unlearn, to unpack, to examine these deeper issues and assumptions comes at a cost. As Sleeter (2000) argues, how can one understand the cultural contexts of others without understanding oneself also as a cultural being? Therefore, this chapter also serves as a starting point for discussion around ways in which we, as educators, can engage in our own re-education and work with our students to create safe spaces for their own unlearning and relearning of issues related to sexual diversity and sexual orientation. By invoking a new paradigm of thinking, speaking, being, and ideally acting, we can move the current practice of multicultural education and the burgeoning field of multicultural studies to include more thought and dialogues related to sexual diversity.

Language

Central to the discussion of critical multicultural studies and sexual diversity is the power and use of language, including such binary terms as heterosexual/homosexual and heterosexism/homophobia. Audre Lorde describes heterosexism as "a belief in the inherent superiority of one pattern of loving over all others and thereby the right to dominance" (p. 3). The dominance of a heterosexist or heteronormative ideology leads to exclusion and homoprejudice. These in turn lead to confrontations and a desire to accentuate differences—socially, politically, culturally, and linguistically. Ultimately, one of the central tensions in discussions about sexual identity and sexual diversity revolves around the notion of difference. Are individuals who identify along the LGBTQ continuum the same as heterosexuals? How do both sameness and difference get played out within groups and between groups? It is the juxtaposition of same-different that is also at the heart of multicultural studies. Do we highlight and celebrate how alike we are? Or do we acknowledge and celebrate our differences? Can we do both, and what does that mean? As we consider the placement of sexual identity, and by extension, sexual diversity, within the realm of multicultural studies, we must grapple with these questions, for within these questions are situated the primary tenets of any identity—language, culture, and power.

While some nonheterosexual individuals easily label themselves as gay, lesbian, bisexual, or transgendered, others embrace the term *queer* as a way to dismantle and then reconstruct their own meanings and notions of what it means to be L, G, B, or T. In all of these instances, LGBTQ individuals have turned a weapon of their adversaries—notably names and labels as derogatory terms—into a set of cultural tools used in the political battle of silencing and "othering." This action might be seen akin to Higginbotham's (1992) discussion of how Black people have traditionally conceptualized the term *race*: "Black people endeavored to dismantle and deconstruct the dominant society's deployment of race. Racial meanings were never internalized by Blacks and Whites in an identical way" (pp. 266–267). In making her argument, Higginbotham builds upon the earlier work of Bakhtin (1981):

> The word in language is half someone else's. It becomes "one's own" only when the speaker populates it with his own intention, his own accent, when

he appropriates the word, adapting it to his own semantic and expressive intention. Prior to this moment of appropriation, the word does not exist in a neutral and impersonal language (it is not after all, out of a dictionary that the speaker gets his words!), but rather it exists in other people's mouths, in other people's contexts, serving other people's intentions. . . . Language is not a neutral medium that passes freely and easily into the private property of the speaker's intentions; it is populated—overpopulated—with the intention of others. Expropriating it, forcing it to submit to one's own intentions and accents, is a difficult and complicated process. (pp. 293–294)

Higginbotham concludes: "Blacks took race and empowered its language with their own meaning and intent" (p. 267). In a similar sense, gay, lesbian, bisexual, transgendered, and queer individuals are in a contemporary battle with their own terms, names, and labels.

Language changes with social and cultural contexts. The same can be said of language identity. "Cultural identity . . . is a matter of becoming as well as being. It belongs to the future as much as to the past" (Hall, 1990, p. 225). At one time, very few people used the term *Black* to identify people of African descent. The same is true of the term *African American*. Still today, many Blacks do not identify themselves as African American. The terms *gay, lesbian, bisexual, transgendered, queer*, and others must also be viewed in the same light. Some may adopt the term *gay* but avoid being labeled *queer*. Others may not refer to themselves as bisexual but instead call themselves polyamorous. The terms *transgendered* and *queer* even have different meanings to different individuals or groups at different times, and understanding the meanings, both implicit and explicit, is a constant challenge, but one that must be addressed when considering to whom we are referring.

Language is clearly circumvented by both individual and collective identity. In the 21st century, LGBTQ individuals are engaged not only in a struggle for individual identity but also a collective identity through social, political, and legislative avenues. For some, the struggle is around what it personally means to "be" gay, lesbian, bisexual, queer, or transgendered. For others, the issue is how we, as the LGBTQ collective, can "be" in the larger social context as current national trends shift in a myriad of ways, from the recent repeal of Don't Ask, Don't Tell to the recent passage of New York State's same-sex marriage bill, which, as of this writing, brings the total to six states and the District of Columbia where same-sex marriage is legal. Ten years ago, LGBTQ individuals were still second-class citizens in the eyes of many, with few to no rights or protections in many parts of the United States. Now, some states and cities allow same-sex marriage, while others allow civil unions, and still other areas allow for registration as domestic partners. These laws or regulations are not the same; the language and definition of each conveys a specific set of rights, protections, privileges, meanings, and even exclusions. Clearly, new legislation and regulation can have and have had deeply profound impacts on those trying to make personal meaning and to find their way as LGBTQ individuals.

As we consider same-sex marriage laws in this country, it is clear that language (*marriage* versus *civil union*, for example) serves as the medium through which power gets enacted, while at the same time language achieves relevancy through the enactment of power. Power circumscribes social interactions, which are shaped by the confines of culture. In turn, social interactions serve to reshape culture. In this light, language, power, and culture form a never-ending web of complex meaning making. It is this web that encircles the LGBTQ community that must be considered in the emerging discourses around and within American multicultural studies.

Culture

It is clear that words and their meanings are never static and are always open to interpretation. This gives rise to an important framework in considering LGBTQ issues: critical postmodernism. Critical postmodernists recognize the power and significant role that language and culture play in shaping individual and group identities. Foucault (1970) notes that

> The fundamental codes of culture—those governing its language, its schemas of perceptions, its exchanges, its techniques, its values, the hierarchy of its practices—establish for every man, from the very first, the empirical orders with which he will be dealing and within which he will be at home. (p. xx)

Foucault (1980) further argues that culture is more than a mere byproduct of social life—culture actually shapes social life. Discourse, as a system of rules and patterns of language, plays an essential role in understanding and shaping the power of a given culture. According to Lamont and Wuthnow (1990), Foucault's work deals with "discourse's role in producing a 'Kafkaesque' system which constrains and frames human potentialities. He analyzes knowledge and truth as bases for the institutionalization of mechanisms of control, and as resources for excluding deviants and framing the context and terrain of social life" (p. 296). One such code and constraint of culture is heterosexuality.

Heterosexuality is both a cultural code and a discourse that has been passed from one generation to the next through various social institutions, including, but not limited to, political, military, healthcare, and religious and educational sites and settings. Historically, heterosexuality is one identity that has become normalized through social surveillance and vigilance (Foucault, 1979). A series of rights and privileges still revolves around compliance and subjugation to such heterocentric and heterosexist norms, attitudes, beliefs, and behaviors. LGBTQ individuals are not supposed to "flaunt" their sexuality by talking about significant others and certainly not by engaging in public displays of affection. Up until the last decade, LGBTQ individuals were not allowed to marry (this is still limited), and 1993 saw the ban on LGBTQ individuals serving in the U.S. armed forces under "Don't Ask, Don't Tell." To step outside of these norms, to "offend" the heterosexuals, is to risk social scrutiny, discrimination, harassment, or ostracism.

Giroux (1983) describes this as social reproduction theory. Social reproduction theory relates to how dominant cultural patterns are continually reconstituted in subsequent generations. Schooling, as one mechanism, has been the principal focus of reproduction theorists. From critical studies of educational institutions, researchers (e.g., Levinson, Foley, & Holland, 1996; Weis & Fine, 2005) have uncovered a powerful force—student resistance against the dominant values and norms. Resistance is a response to cultural forces that attempt to reproduce and, in effect, silence those alienated by the values and norms being taught. Resistance may be thought of as a form of cultural work on the part of a marginalized group such as LGBTQ individuals.

There is an irony in resistance against cultural norms such as heterosexuality. Many LGBTQ individuals want to accentuate the fact that they are not of the norm, not part of the heterosexual community, and demand to be respected and accepted for who they are as LGBTQ individuals. In some ways, LGBTQ people are revolutionaries who want to overthrow the social order, yet, at the same time, be a part of that same order—for example, many in the LGBTQ community do not want to settle for civil union legislation and instead protest and demand legislation providing same-sex marriage equality such as the protests against Proposition 8 in California, which would have banned same-sex marriage in that state. Furthermore, in September 2011, the U.S. Census Bureau (2011) released new revised statistics from the 2010 census on same-sex married-couple and unmarried-partner households, suggesting that there were 131,729 same-sex married-couple households and 514,735 same-sex unmarried-partner households in the United States. The results of the 2010 Census revised estimates are closer to the 2010 American Community Survey (ACS) for same-sex married and unmarried partners, which estimates 152,335 same-sex married couples and 440,989 same-sex unmarried partners. This raises an interesting debate: How do LGBTQ individuals decenter and upset heterosexual social norms while at the same time maintaining viable communities when asking for the right to adopt a subset of heterosexual norms? Indeed, how do we define the LGBTQ community? Is there even one, or are there many? How and where do we place LGBTQ studies within multicultural studies? Is there a single LGBTQ culture, or are there many, just like there may be many LGBTQ communities? Is it one of many, or many of one?

In framing heterosexuality as the norm, culture acts as the source of identity, distributing power in the form of rights, privilege, and status to some while marginalizing others. In conferring the label *deviant* upon LGBTQ individuals, the majority society has created a social identity through which people who exhibit same-sex attraction are, for the most part, categorized and scrutinized as immoral, sinful, sick, perverse, or abnormal. At the same time, the emergence of LGBTQ labels, community, and cultures has made it possible for these same individuals to organize around a common identity. Without such an externally imposed and internally defined identity, one cannot organize around it, nor can there be an effort to legitimize it. As Epstein (1987) notes: "Just as Blacks cannot fight the arbitrariness of racial classification without organizing as Black, so gays could not advocate the overthrow of the sexual order without making their gayness the very basis of their claims" (p. 19). For many in the LGBTQ rights movement, the strategy is fairly simple: Take control of the language and discourse associated with sexual identities. In doing so, those in the LGBTQ community win their struggle over self-representation and the power to name and, by extension, to define and create their own culture.

Power, Knowledge, and Empowerment

Few theorists have done more to unravel the complexities and interrelatedness of power and knowledge in relation to culture than Foucault, who maintains that power must be understood beyond its ability to limit or constrain. For Foucault (1980), power is also the shaper of knowledge:

> Power would be a fragile thing if its only function were to repress, if it worked only through the mode of censorship, exclusion, blockage and repression, in the manner of the great Superego, exercising itself only in a negative way. If, on the contrary, power is strong this is because, as we are beginning to realize, it produces effects at the level of desire—and also at the level of knowledge. Far from preventing knowledge, power produces it. (p. 59)

Foucault, like many critical postmodern theorists, argues that all knowledge is particular; there are no grand narratives that convey a universal truth. If this is the case, then one must necessarily include the stories, narratives, history, and experiences of LGBTQ individuals and the larger LGBTQ community in any discussion of multicultural studies. To do otherwise is to relegate LGBTQ culture and its constituents to a state of powerlessness, further promulgate a second-class citizenship among LGBTQ individuals, and ignore the role that LGBTQ individuals have had within American society as a whole.

For critical postmodernists, there are only localized claims to understanding based on subjectivity and personal experience. Lyotard (1979/1984) poses the following question we must consider in this light: "Who decides the conditions of truth?" (p. 29). As we confront such questions within the realm of multicultural studies, we must ask: Who decides which cultures are relevant, acceptable, and normal? Who decides which sexual identities are normal and acceptable rather than abnormal or perverse? The answer lies in who has the power to define; thus, critical postmodernists seek to uncover knowledge by locating power.

The manner in which LGBTQ individuals challenge traditional views of "being" underscores the relational quality of a critical postmodern view of power. Power is inherent in all social relations; all groups and individuals have at their disposal some degree of power. Burbles (1986), in extending the work of Foucault, elaborates on two key points of a relational conception of power. First, he argues that power is neither chosen nor avoided by social actors; power is the necessary byproduct of circumstances that bring people into a social interaction. Second, he argues that within all power relations, a tension exists between compliance and resistance. Although one individual in a social interaction may be successful in prescribing to another, a certain degree of autonomy is lost by the advantaged/privileged person trying to preserve the relationship. Also, the advantaged/privileged individual is in many ways dependent upon the compliance of the disadvantaged/marginalized and must grant a degree of resistance to this very individual. The idea that the privileged must depend on the involvement of the marginalized is important in understanding social reproduction and resistance theory. As long as multicultural studies continue to passively include, at best, or actively exclude, at worst, LGBTQ individuals in the discourse, sharing in the knowledge and power, heterosexuality will remain front and center as the sole purveyor of power and culture.

Power is revealed by the dominance that certain ideologies have over others, evident in the way advantaged groups shape the lives of disadvantaged groups. Often, one group's power over another is exercised not so much in an organized strategy but is more subtly evident in the way various aspects of their culture—their narrative knowledge, their discourse become legitimized by various institutional mechanisms. Weeks (1988) points out that the prevailing discourse of sexuality "tells us what sex is, what it ought to be, and what it could be" (p. 208). Power has been exercised by the prevailing heterosexual culture to shut out the narratives and knowledge of LGBTQ individuals and to define heterosexuality as the norm and anything outside of that as deviant. Gergen (1991) describes the postmodern condition as "marked by a plurality of voices vying for the right to be reality—to be accepted as legitimate expressions of the true and the good" (p. 7). LGBTQ individuals and communities across the country continue to be engaged in a struggle to have their "culture," their narratives, their knowledge, their experiences, accepted as "legitimate expressions of the true and the good." Once again, the irony of this struggle is clear. By accentuating difference, LGBTQ individuals seek acceptance within society as a whole.

Critical postmodern theorists are concerned not only about power but also about the way that power serves to marginalize a group and the manner in which that group seeks empowerment based on that marginalization. This attempt by postmodern scholars is to help individuals and groups understand how society is organized and how it has structured people's lives in such a way that they themselves must reorganize around personal and community self-determination. Only through such awareness is resistance and emancipation possible. Kellner (1989) points out, in his discussion of society and psyche, that ideology plays a significant role in human oppression. Sexism, for example, has been at the root of much of the feminist critique of women's oppression and heterosexism at the root of oppression for LGBTQ individuals. However, according to hooks (1984):

> Individuals who fight for the eradication of sexism without supporting struggles to end racism or classism undermine their own efforts. Individuals who fight for the eradication of racism or classism while supporting sexist oppression are helping to maintain the cultural bias of all forms of groups oppression. While they may initiate successful reforms, their efforts will not lead to revolutionary change. Their ambivalent relationship to oppression in general is a contradiction that must be resolved or they will daily undermine their own work. (p. 39)

hooks clearly alludes to the intersections of oppression and marginalization within race, gender, class, and sexuality that must be acknowledged and explored within the larger framework of multicultural studies. Furthermore, she sheds light on the major endeavor of critical postmodern theorists—to confront oppression by uncovering cultural and ideological constraints that, in turn, assist groups in the process of self-determination. Finally, hooks maintains that people can become accomplices in their own oppression and demise; for example, hooks would argue that gays and lesbians who stay closeted or only participate in activities with the gay community contribute to their own oppression by limiting their own visibility, by not questioning and fighting against the power and privilege that force them to stay hidden.

Within the mainstream, traditional curricular models of multicultural studies, the term *culture* is often used to refer to a select group of essentialized, normative practices and artifacts abstracted from the socio-historical, economic, and political conditions that, partly, give rise to multicultural studies. At the other end of the spectrum, a critical, postmodern approach to multicultural studies views culture as the terrain of lived experiences and institutional forms organized around diverse forms of language, power, struggle, and domination. Thus, in this perspective, culture embodies the lived experiences, behaviors, and performances that are the result of unequal distribution of power along such dimensions as race, ethnicity, class, gender, religion, and sexual orientation, located within sociohistorical, economic, and political terrains. As people interact with existing institutions and social practices in which the values, beliefs, bodies of knowledge, biases, and discourses are imposed, they are often stripped of their own power to articulate and realize their own goals (Leistyna, Woodrum, & Sherblom, 1996). For example, efforts in the United States to enforce a "common culture" of what marriage and a "traditional" family look like through the Defense of Marriage Act (DOMA) are, in fact, the imposition and reification of a homogenizing and heterocentric social paradigm that serves to grossly limit the rights and privileges of LGBTQ individuals, which, in turn, limits the possibility of a purely democratic society. The important, critical questions then come into being: Whose realities and interests are defining what it means to be an American family and what it means to be married? And from a broader perspective, whose realities are being privileged and whose are being subjugated, how, and by whom? This is but one example; but if institutions and programs are not thoughtful in their approaches, multicultural studies curriculum committees, while generally well intentioned and concerned with the betterment of all, might just neglect the LGBTQ voice and experience completely or relegate such to the fringes as add-on or elective courses, with a single course or two on sexual identity.

If well-intentioned institutions and the multicultural studies departments within them want to create culturally responsive models and curricula, then they should be compelled to engage with the conditions in which people actually live. Furthermore, they should be required to include all voices and experiences in equal measure. Faculty, program developers, and administrators alike need to advocate for a postmodern, critical approach to multicultural studies that exposes students to the issues that they will face in the 21st century—such as the changes in the family structures of same-sex families, the need for social justice policies and practices, the increase in globalization of all sectors, the role of technology both as a means to an end (e.g., cyberbullying) and an end to a means (e.g., new forms of media allow for new identities to emerge). This will not happen just by bringing together a diverse group of faculty from across fields and disciplines and assuming that, just because they have everyone's best interest at heart or know what it feels like to be discriminated against, they will necessarily have a greater understanding of what oppression means, what causes it, and therefore how to redress its injustice. One issue with such an approach and representation of this nature is that experience and understanding are often left at the level of descriptive narratives rather than a truly critical sociohistorical and theoretical analysis of the language, culture, power, and knowledge bases that have served to create those various narratives. Multicultural studies programs should be encouraged to nurture the kinds of critical inquiry and dialogue that work to explain and theorize how everyone involved in a particular experience (e.g., LGBTQ and heterosexual individuals) has played a role, what roles have been played, and what material, political, social, or symbolic conditions operated in concert to produce the experience.

In order to fully understand the ways in which language, power, and knowledge have shaped mainstream practices, policies, and politics in the United States, institutions that focus on education need to help prepare individuals who can think through the complexities of *culture*, recognizing that such a word is loaded with meaning, assumptions, and biases. Furthermore, multicultural studies programs need to build upon the synergy that exists between theory and research but take that to the next level of practice and activism. From a critical postmodern stance, individuals can learn to question the grand and master narratives at play and begin to favor heterogeneity, contingency, intersubjectivity, and indeterminacy. Through recognizing and acknowledging the existence of multiple realities, identities, and voices, including those of LGBTQ individuals, and engaging in a greater degree of reflexivity, individuals may turn toward activism as a means of creating spaces within which the marginalized voices of LGBTQ individuals and their allies can emerge under their own free will. In essence, this stance does not advocate that multicultural studies programs suddenly become queer or sexualized but that they explicate, uncover, analyze, and interpret the manner in which gender and sexuality are both present and silenced through literature, history, politics, or other forms of texts and discourses.

This explicitly marks the desire to move away from seeing LGBTQ individuals as just another category or group of individuals that must be included with and as part of all the other marginalized groups and situates sexuality as an inherent part of every individual regardless of sexual orientation (Pohan & Bailey, 1997).

Although bringing to the foreground sexuality as an important part of multicultural studies does not guarantee that LGBTQ individuals will necessarily be attended to, doing so does serve to bring forth a critical orientation that ensures that issues previously rendered invisible or simply ignored will be addressed. Another advantage to this turn toward active infusion of sexual diversity in multicultural studies is a different epistemological stance, one in which sexual diversity is now part of the foreground and offers the space to move from simply adding marginalized others' lives, experiences, and narratives to the curriculum to a place where one can consciously start from those very lives and experiences to ask the larger critical questions about who, how, when, where, and why. This standpoint also allows sexuality to be viewed as part of a larger identity category that is fluid and shifting and allows individuals to construct, deconstruct, reconstruct, and move more or less freely within the categories. This is not to deny structural impediments that might exist that make movement within or beyond difficult. This is merely to assert that despite such barriers, the existence and fluidity of sexual diversity cannot be denied, nor should it be ignored.

This act of positioning sexuality near the foreground is malleable and encourages thinking from the margins, often by those very ones whose thinking tends toward the hegemonic—White, heterosexual, Anglo-Saxon Protestants. By asking these individuals to interrogate their own assumptions, biases, beliefs, and perceptions about their sexuality and that of others, we can begin to raise new questions. What can be seen from the margins and borderlands? What access to knowledge do LGBTQ individuals and those on the border have? How can such knowledge enhance and alter what ordinarily gets seen from the center? What questions can be asked from the standpoint of the LGBTQ individual? Adopting such an epistemological stance allows one to acknowledge the importance and validity of these ways of knowing, seeing, or interpreting. Multicultural studies programs need to do more interrogating of the discursive vehicles used—the methods, models, course structures, narratives, metaphors, and (re)production of knowledge— from the standpoint of sexuality. Again, it is important to not view such epistemology as essentializing but rather as a powerful means of generating new knowledge.

This shift in multicultural studies/multicultural education toward including the analysis and interpretation of sexual diversity also marks a rethinking of identify politics in which our bodies, gender, and sexuality are continually negotiable and always under construction. Thus, a more critical, postmodern view of sexuality and LGBTQ individuals and their identity construction must start with the notion that "sexuality is a necessary component to all knowing" (Sumara & Davis, 1994, p. 203) and that identity and epistemology are mutually embedded—who we understand ourselves to be intersects with and interacts with what counts as knowledge. Not only does this offer more viable, acceptable, and legitimate narratives for everyone about sex, sexuality, and gender, but it also engenders a more reflective stance on the power of language to name and label by uncovering assumptions about what is natural. Thus, this naming brings to the center of the discussion issues related to power and privilege and what "normal" looks like. In turn, this type of critical engagement and stance would allow the identification, resistance, deconstruction, and reconstruction surrounding the reified power, language, politics, and knowledge that have served to arbitrarily bifurcate groups of people based upon a perceived hetero- or homosexual orientation. This varied repertoire, as it were, can only make for a deeper and greater understanding of what constitutes culture.

Conclusion

There is an interesting Zen story about learning and unlearning. A Japanese master during the Meiji era received a professor who came to inquire about Zen. The professor talked about Zen while the master quietly served tea. He poured the professor's cup full, and then kept on pouring. The visitor watched the master continuing to pour out the tea until he could no longer hold back. "Stop! Stop! It is overflowing, no more tea can go in!" "Like this cup," the Zen master said, "you are full of your own opinions and speculations. How can I show you Zen unless you first empty your cup?" Students and faculty come into the classroom with their own opinions, assumptions, biases, perspectives, and experiences; how can individuals be expected to learn anything without first emptying their minds and letting go of previous knowledge or understandings that may be covered by the "cold mist of bias and ignorance" (Delpit, 2006, p. xxiii)?

It is imperative that educators have students empty their minds and question their own fundamental assumptions, beliefs, biases, and perspectives not just around race, class, and gender but also about sexuality. Like race, class, and gender, everyone has a sexual orientation that is both embodied and performed publicly as well as privately. By learning to think more deeply about language, power, knowledge, and how culture is related to sexuality, one can then begin the process of social transformation. It is not enough to simply critique, analyze, and interpret one's world. As Delpit (2006) contends, we must have a "basic understanding of who we are and how we are all connected to and disconnected from one another" (p. xxv). A superficial, descriptive nodding of the head toward those on the margins and fringes, such as those who are part of the LGBTQ communities, is not adequate to move marginalized groups and individuals from the fringes or to ensure full inclusion in society—socially, economically, politically, and historically. Now, more than ever, is the time to empty the cup and learn to make sense of the world differently.

References

Adams, D. W. (1995). *Education for extinction: American Indians and the boarding school experience, 1875–1928*. Lawrence: University of Kansas Press.

Atthill, C., & Jha, J. (2009). *The gender-responsive school: An action guide*. London: Commonwealth Secretariat.

Banks, J. A. (2008). *Introduction to multicultural education* (4th ed.). Boston: Pearson.

Bertram, C. C., Crowley, M. S., & Massey, S. G. (2010). *Beyond progress and marginalization: LGBTQ youth in educational contexts*. New York: Peter Lang.

Bakhtin, M. (1981). *The dialogic imagination*. Austin: University of Texas Press.

Burbles, N. C. (1986). A theory of power in education. *Educational Theory, 36*(2), 95–114.

Delpit, L. (2006). *Other people's children* (2nd ed.). New York: New Press.

Edgerton, S. H. (1996). *Translating the curriculum*. New York: Routledge.

Epstein, S. (1987). Gay politics, ethnic identity: The limits of social constructivism. *Socialist Review, 17*(3/4), 9–54.

Foucault, M. (1970). *The order of things*. New York: Vintage Books.

Foucault, M. (1979). *Discipline & punish* (A. Sheridan, Trans.). New York: Vintage Books.

Foucault, M. (1980). *Power/knowledge* (C. Gordan, Trans.). New York: Pantheon Books.

Gergen, K. J. (1991). *The saturated self: Dilemmas of identity in contemporary life*. New York: Basic Books.

Giroux, H. (1983). *Theory & resistance in education*. South Hadley, MA: Bergin & Garvey.

Hall, S. (1990). Cultural indentity and diaspora. In J. Rutherford (Ed.), *Identity: Community, culture, difference*. London: Lawrence & Wishart.

Higginbotham, E. B. (1992). African-American women's history and the metalanguage of race. *Signs: Journal of Women in Culture and Society, 17*(2), 251–274.

hooks, b. (1984). *Feminist theory: From margin to center.* Boston: South End Publisher.

Hornblum, A. M. (2007). *Sentenced to science: One Black man's story of imprisonment in America.* University Park: Pennsylvania State Press.

Kellner, D. (1989). *Critical theory, Marxism, and modernity.* Baltimore, MD: Johns Hopkins University Press.

Kimmel, M. (2008). *Guyland: The perilous world where boys become men.* New York: HarperCollins.

Lamont, M., & Wuthnow, R. (1990). Betwixt and between: Recent cultural sociology in Europe and the United States. In G. Ritzer (Ed.), *Frontiers of social theory: The new synthesis* (pp. 287–315). New York: Columbia University Press

Leistyna, P., Woodrum, A., & Sherblom, S. (Eds.). (1996). *Breaking free: The transformative power of critical pedagogy.* Cambridge, MA: Harvard Publishing Group.

Levinson, B. A., Foley, D. E., & Holland, D. C. (Eds.). (1996). *The cultural reproduction of the educated person: Critical ethnographies of schooling and local practice.* Albany: State University of New York Press.

Lyotard, J. F. (1984). *The postmodern condition: A report on knowledge* (G. Bennington & B. Massumi, Trans). Minneapolis: University of Minnesota Press.

Neito, S. (1999). *The light in their eyes.* New York: Teachers College Press.

Neito, S., & Bode, P. (2008). *Affirming diversity.* Boston: Pearson Education.

Pohan, C. A., & Bailey, N. J. (1997). Opening the closet: Multiculturalism that is fully inclusive. *Multicultural Education, Fall,* 12–15.

Sleeter, C. E. (2000). *Culture, difference, and power.* New York: Teachers College Press.

Sumara, D., & Davis, B. (1994). Interrupting heteronormativity: Toward a queer curriculum theory. *Curriculum Inquiry, 29*(2), 191–208.

Rothenberg, P. (2000). *Invisible privilege.* Lawrence: University Press of Kansas.

U.S. Census Bureau. (2011). Census Bureau releases estimates of same-sex married couples. Retrieved from http://2010.census.gov/news/releases/operations/cb11-cn181.html.

Weeks, J. (1988). Against nature. In A. van Kooten Niekerk & T. van der Meer (Eds.), *Homosexuality, which homosexuality?* (pp. 199–214). Amsterdam: Mr. J. A. Schorerstichting.

Weis, L., & Fine, M. (Eds.). (2005). *Beyond silenced voices: Class, race, and gender in United States schools* (2nd ed.). Albany: State University of New York Press.

Index

Contributors

Kulvinder Arora is a visiting assistant professor and cultural critic who teaches courses on transnational film, feminist theory, and gender studies at Beloit College. She is currently working on a book project on positive representations of women of color in feature films that is provisionally titled *Plotting Resistance: Acts of Social Justice in Women of Color Films*. She has also published an article titled "The Mythology of Female Sexuality: Alternative Narratives of Belonging" in *Women: A Cultural Review*.

Jennifer J. Asenas received her Ph.D. in 2007 from the University of Texas at Austin. She is assistant professor of communication studies at California State University, Long Beach. Her primary research interests are narrative, race/ethnicity, and social change. Her most recently published essays include "Political Style for the People: Nonviolence as Political Power" and "Saving Kenneth Foster: Speaking *with* Others in the Belly of the Beast of Capital Punishment."

Alan Ashton-Smith is a Ph.D. candidate in the London Consortium's multidisciplinary program in humanities and cultural studies at Birkbeck, University of London. The subject of his Ph.D. thesis is the increasingly popular musical genre and cultural movement gypsy punk and its relationship with such diverse fields as music, immigration, language, mythology, and Romani studies.

Kyeonghi Baek received her Ph.D. in political science at the University of Mississippi. She currently works for the College at Buffalo, SUNY, and has taught international relations and American politics since 2008. Her research interests are all things political but, in particular, international conflict, international political economy, and public opinion.

Eduardo Barros-Grela has taught English and cultural studies at the University of Coruna (Spain) since 2007. Before that, he was an assistant professor at California State University, Northridge (2003–2007). Academic interests include cultural studies, urban spatialities, posthuman aesthetics, *in*organic bodies and spaces, visual studies, and the different articulations of representation and performance.

Paola Bohórquez holds a Ph.D. in social and political thought from York University in Toronto, Canada. Her dissertation, titled "Living Between Languages: Linguistic Exile and Self-Translation," examines the psychic, textual, and ethical dimensions of the experience of linguistic displacement. Her work has been published in the *Journal of Intercultural Studies, Synthesis,* and in the collection *On and Off the Page: Mapping Place in Text and Culture.* She teaches in the English department and professional writing program at York University.

Cynthia S. Bynoe teaches in the Department of Political Science and Multicultural & Gender Studies Program at California State University, Chico. She also teaches part-time at Butte Community College. She teaches women and politics and has served as the summer codirector for the Butte College and CSU, Chico Safe Place office. At CSU, Chico she serves on the advisory board of the Gender and Sexuality Equity Center.

Teresa L. Cotner earned a B.A. degree in art at California State University, Sonoma, an M.A. degree in art history and teaching credential at CSU Los Angeles, and a Ph.D. in art education at Stanford University. Her research interests include integrated arts, multicultural arts, and classroom discourse. She taught from 2001 to 2006 at CSU San Bernardino and from 2006 to the present at CSU Chico, where she teaches art education and is chair of the Department of Art and Art History.

Christine Dobbins completed her graduate studies at the College of Saint Rose in Albany, New York. Her research interests include gender and social studies. She devotes part of her time to issues of social and environmental justice.

Antonio L. Ellis is an emerging scholar in the urban educational administration and policy doctoral program at Howard University. He holds both a Master's in theological studies and a Master's in educational policy. His research interests include critical race theory in education and disproportionality in special education classrooms, with special attention given to speech and language.

Mariam Esseghaier is currently a student in the joint Ph.D. program in communication studies offered by Concordia University, l'Université de Montréal, and l'Université du Québec à Montréal. Her area of research focuses on representations of Muslim women in Western popular culture with a specific focus on their normalization and commodification.

Nicole Amber Haggard is currently a doctoral candidate in American studies at Saint Louis University completing her dissertation on discourses of Black men and White women in sexual relationships through the lens of American film, literature, and history. Haggard's research and teaching have revolved around the intersection of race, gender, and sexuality in American culture.

Nicholas Daniel Hartlep is an Advanced Opportunity Program fellow at the University of Wisconsin–Milwaukee. He currently is a substitute teacher in the Milwaukee public schools in Milwaukee, WI. Author of *Going Public: Critical Race Theory and Issues of Social Justice,* Hartlep is currently completing his second book, *The Model Minority Stereotype: Demystifying Asian American Success.*

Jürgen Heinrichs is associate professor of art history and museum professions at Seton Hall University. He holds degrees in art history and German from Yale and Hamburg. He is a 2011–12 Fellow of the American Council on Education (ACE) and recently co-edited *From Black to Schwarz: Cultural Crossovers Between African America and Germany.*

Kevin A. Johnson (Ph.D., communication studies, 2007, University of Texas at Austin) is the director of research at the Center for First Amendment Studies at California State University, Long Beach. He also currently serves as the communications director of the Long Beach Branch of the NAACP.

Sarah Kanbar graduated from UC Berkeley with a Bachelor of Arts in history, specializing in the relationship between the United States and the Middle East. She continues to research the experiences of Arab immigrants to the United States.

Cindy LaCom is a professor of English and women's studies at Slippery Rock University. Her areas of research include Victorian studies, disability studies, and women's studies. She has published essays in *Disability Studies Quarterly, NWSA Journal, PMLA, Nineteenth-Century Contexts,* and *Nineteenth-Century Gender Studies,* and in anthologies, including *The Body and Physical Difference* (Ed. Mitchell & Snyder, 1997), *Critical Perspectives on bell hooks* (Eds. Davidson & Yancy, 2009), and *Feminist Disability Studies* (Ed. Kim Hall, 2011).

Helen Lindberg is a senior lecturer in political science at Linköping University, Department of Political Science, Sweden. Dr. Lindberg's research interests are normative and analytical political theory and philosophy of science. She teaches courses in political theory and political philosophy and philosophy of science at all different levels and supervises Ph.D. students.

Cynthia Lytle is a Ph.D. candidate at the Department of English and German Philology at the Universitat de Barcelona in Spain. Her research is on the construction and representation of multiracial identities in postcolonial literature with a current focus on the colored community in South Africa. She is working on her dissertation, titled *DeraciNation: Reading the Borderlands of Coloured Identities in Zoë Wicomb (1945–).*

Babacar M'Baye is associate professor of English and pan-African studies at Kent State University. His work has appeared in *Journal of African Literature and Culture, Journal of Pan-African Studies, New England Journal of History,* and other publications, including the book *The Trickster Comes West: Pan-African Influence in Early Black Diasporan Narratives.*

Mark Malisa teaches at the College of Saint Rose in Albany, New York. He is the author of *Out of These Ashes: The Quest for Utopia in Critical Theory, Critical Pedagogy, and Ubuntu* (2009) and *Anti-capitalisms and Anti-narcissisms: Education and Human Nature in Gandhi, Malcolm X, Nelson Mandela, and Jurgen Habermas* (2010).

Mara Marin is collegiate assistant professor and Harper Schmidt fellow at the University of Chicago. Her first book project develops the idea of commitment, which refers to a relationship that combines two features typically thought to be mutually exclusive: They are voluntary yet not fully under the control of the agent. Her work focuses on issues of authority, political obligation and oppression, feminist theory, and social contract theory.

Mariangela Orabona holds a Ph.D. in cultural and postcolonial studies of the Anglophone world (University of Naples l'Orientale, Italy). Her doctoral thesis, in which she critically examines the works of the artists Renée Green, Lorna Simpson, and Kara Walker in terms of the absence and erasure of the female African American body, represents a synthesis of her studies in the visual arts. This work follows the critical research inaugurated in a Master in "Arts des images et art contemporain" (Université Paris 8). She has written ten articles about the politics of representation of the female body in visual arts. Her main research interests concern visual aesthetics, theories of difference, postrepresentational theory, immaterial and affective labor, precarity, and new media arts practices.

Wendy Peters, Ph.D., is a Native Hawaiian and a cultural development specialist focusing her work on bringing awareness to the existential struggles and challenges of multicultural adaptation, especially among indigenous/native peoples. Her research draws on the areas of transpersonal psychology, indigenous cultures, integral philosophies, and systems/complexity sciences.

Thelma Pinto is the codirector of Africana studies at Hobart and William Smith Colleges. She was the former president of the African Literature Association.

Elizabeth Renfro taught for 35 years in the Department of English and the Center for Multicultural and Gender Studies at California State University, Chico. For the past 15 years, her teaching, research, and publications have focused on feminist and queer theory, multicultural literature, and LGBTQ studies.

Sean Robinson is associate professor of educational leadership at Argosy University in Washington, DC. His teaching interests include leadership theory, higher education administration, organizational behavior, student development theory, and research methodology. His current research centers on the identity formation of underserved and underrepresented individuals within both K–12 and higher education settings.

Nathanael Romero is an activist and writer living in Clinton, Michigan. Based in the Ann Arbor area, he is a radical political organizer and an independent scholar with interests in social and political theory. His recent work with Christopher Zeichmann explores the intersections between political and racial ideology.

Yvonne D. Sims is an assistant professor of English at South Carolina State University. She is the author of several book chapters, peer-reviewed articles, and *Women of Blaxploitation: How the Black Action Heroine Changed American Popular Culture* (McFarland Publishers, 2006). Her book chapter "Florence Griffith Joyner: Sexual Politician in a Unitard" is forthcoming in the anthology tentatively titled *A Locker Room of Her Own: Sport, Gender, and the Construction of Athletic Reputations,* edited by Dr. Joel Nathan Rosen and Dr. David Ogden (University of Mississippi Press), and her article "Blacula and Blade: Tortured Souls/Cultural Outsiders in Vampire Film Narratives" is under review. She is working on a book manuscript that examines Josephine Baker and the construction of stardom.

Karen L. Suyemoto, Ph.D., is an associate professor in psychology and Asian American studies at the University of Massachusetts, Boston. Her research and teaching focus on issues related to social justice and antiracist therapy, research, and education, with a focus on racialized identities, meanings of race and ethnicity, and contributing to social justice from both oppressed and privileged spaces individually and systemically. She has provided consultation and training on antiracist therapy and education both locally and nationally and is the past president of the Asian American Psychological Association.

Jesse J. Tauriac received his Ph.D. in clinical psychology from the University of Massachusetts, Boston and is currently a postdoctoral fellow at the Horizon Center (NIMHD–P20). His research focuses on resources that promote academic success among U.S. Blacks and other underrepresented ethnic minority students, particularly social support, culturally relevant stress-reduction techniques, and cross-racial collaborations.

John Tawa is a doctoral candidate in clinical psychology at the University of Massachusetts, Boston. He is a past recipient of the American Psychological Association's Minority Fellowship Program. Tawa studies relations between Black and Asian individuals and communities with a broader, applied goal of improving relations between marginalized communities. His additional research interests include understanding the effects of racism on mental health and understanding how people conceptualize race and ethnicity.

Jenny Heijun Wills is assistant professor in the English department at the University of Winnipeg, where she teaches American literature and critical race studies. Her current research draws on the narrative representations of transnational transracial Asian adoption. Some of her other interests include Asian American and African American literatures.

Christopher B. Zeichmann is a Ph.D. student at Emmanuel College of the University of Toronto. His research concerns the overlap between ethnicity and political ideology in both the ancient Mediterranean and contemporary North American worlds.

Henry A. Zomerfeld is a J.D. candidate at the University at Buffalo Law School. He holds a B.A. cum laude from College at Buffalo, SUNY, in political science with a minor in legal studies. Zomerfeld is ultimately seeking a career as a prosecutor when he completes law school.

◉SAGE research**methods**

The essential online tool for researchers from the world's leading methods publisher

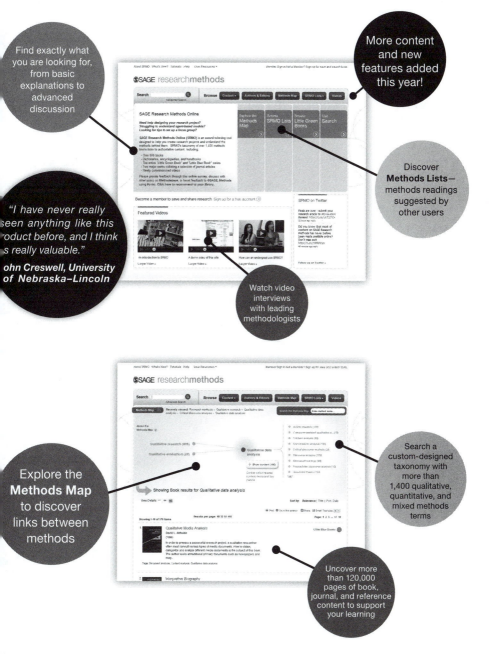

Find exactly what you are looking for, from basic explanations to advanced discussion

More content and new features added this year!

"I have never really seen anything like this product before, and I think is really valuable."

ohn Creswell, University of Nebraska–Lincoln

Discover **Methods Lists**— methods readings suggested by other users

Watch video interviews with leading methodologists

Explore the **Methods Map** to discover links between methods

Search a custom-designed taxonomy with more than 1,400 qualitative, quantitative, and mixed methods terms

Uncover more than 120,000 pages of book, journal, and reference content to support your learning

nd out more at
ww.sageresearchmethods.com

DATE DUE

APR 0 4 2018		
MAY 0 1 2018		